TANKS

TANKS

OVER 250 OF THE WORLD'S TANKS AND ARMORED FIGHTING VEHICLES

CHRIS CHANT

MBI

This edition first published in 2004 by
MBI an imprint of MBI Publishing Company
Galtier Plaza, Suite 200
380 Jackson Street
St. Paul, MN 55101-3885 USA
www.motorbooks.com

The information in this book is true and complete to the best of our knowledge. All recommendations
are made without any guarantee on the part of the author or publisher, who also disclaim any liability
incurred in connection with the use of this data or specific details.

We recognize that some words, model names and designations, for example, mentioned herein are
the property of the trademark holder. We use them for identification purposes only. This is not an
official publication.

MBI titles are also available at discounts in bulk quantity for industrial or sales-promotional use.
For details write to Special Sales Manager at Motorbooks International Wholesalers & Distributors, Galtier
Plaza, Suite 200, 380 Jackson Street, St. Paul, MN 55101-3885 USA.

Library of Congress Cataloging-in-Publication Data available.

ISBN 0-7603-1871-9

Produced by
Amber Books Ltd
Bradley's Close,
74–77 White Lion Street,
London N1 9PF
www.amberbooks.co.uk

Project Editor: Charlotte Judet
Design: Jeremy Williams

Picture credits: photographs cortesy of Abbas-Gamma, Aerospace, Alvis, Associated Press, BAe,
Bundesarchiv, Cadillac Gage, Yves Debay, Finnish Army, Chris Foss, Terry Gander, GDLS, General Dynamics
Land Systems, Hotspur, Howard Gethin, GIAT, GIM Canada, Images Information System, IWM, MoD,
Oerlikon, Orbis, Panhard, Herman Potgeiter, Tim Ripley, Rosvoorouzhenie, Royal Ordnance Factories, Steyr-
Daimler-Punch, Studio Grafico Restani, T.J., TRH Pictures, Tass, Ural Vagon Zavod, US APA, US Army, US
DOD, Xinhua News Agency.

Previously published as part of the reference set *World Weapon*.

Printed in Italy

Contents

Introduction

The tank first lumbered on to the battlefield at Flers-Courcellette in 1916 during the infamous Somme campaign. It single-handedly broke the stalemate that had gripped the Western Front since 1914, and ensured that trench warfare passed into history after the end of World War I. In retrospect we can see that the tank certainly had more impact on combat in the twentieth century than that other debutant of the 1914–18 war, poison gas.

Less than 25 years later after the tank's appearance, German Panzers were dashing across Europe as the spearhead of a new, mobile form of warfare called the Blitzkrieg, or 'lightning war'. Tank terror caused soldiers to flee before the German advance; the tank had demonstrably become a battle-winner, and both sides struggled to develop better-armed and better-armoured tanks. After 1945 the various Arab–Israeli wars saw dramatic and decisive tank battles on a large scale, while the massed tanks of the Red Army stood poised to overwhelm western Europe in the Cold War. Such was the dominance of the tank in combat (and in the planning of the Cold War generals) that it became in effect a symbol of war in the twentieth century.

Although modern armies are now seeking lighter, more mobile, and less expensive armoured vehicles – Canada, for example, has now placed its ageing Leopard I tanks in reserve – the tank once again proved its utility in the recent wars against Saddam Hussein's Iraq. It now seems likely that the main battle tank will remain a key part of most nations' armoury for some time to come, although it is unlikely to ever regain the importance it had during the height of the Cold War.

However it should be said that the tank has rarely fought its battles alone – history has shown that to be successful, an army must support its tanks with armoured personnel carriers and reconnaissance vehicles, for example. Like the tank, these support vehicles have become more sophisticated and deadly over time, so much so that they are beginning to supplant the tank itself.

In this book you will find an introduction to the tank's history, descriptions of how the tank fights and survives in battle, and a directory of key tanks and armoured fighting vehicles over the last 100 years, with full specifications of each vehicle, its armament and protection. From the Mark V 'Male' to the M1A2 Abrams, the 'Queen of the Battlefield' has struck terror in the hearts of all who have encountered her.

A British Army Challenger 2 tanks on manoeuvres. The Challenger 2 served with distinction during the war in Iraq in 2003.

Origins of the tank
A new era in land warfare

The British Tank Mark IV (Female) was armed only with machine guns. The Male version was armed with two six-pounder guns. Over a thousand Mk IVs were produced, making it the most important of British tanks in World War I.

The concept of armoured warfare had been imagined and even practiced to a limited extent over a period of centuries before the first primitive armoured cars appeared in 1914. However, the armoured car was incapable of movement over the shattered terrain of the Western Front from 1915. Then came the marriage of an armed and armoured hull with the type of caterpillar tracks invented for agricultural use to create the tank: a mobile mini-fortress able to defeat machine-gun nests and crush barbed wire.

Right: A British tank moves up in support of Canadian infantry during the Allied advance on the Arras front in the region of Villers-les-Cagnicourt on 2 September 1918. In these final Allied offensives of World War I tanks proved very useful.

A 1918 experiment at Cricklewood, near London, using the exhaust to create a smoke screen. The tank is probably a Mk V. Such smoke screens were intended to provide tanks with a capacity to conceal themselves from enemy gunners, as achieved in action north of Cambrai on 29 September 1918.

British tank development

Written about since the days of Leonardo, the armoured 'landship' did not come to fruition until the development of the internal combustion engine and the invention of the caterpillar track coincided with the needs of armies floundering in the mud of Flanders. Few could know that these early experimental vehicles would lead to the massive armoured forces of World War II and later.

By late 1914 some far-sighted soldiers and others realised that the conditions existing on the Western Front could only be overcome by the use of mobile armoured machines. One of these was Colonel E. D. Swinton, who interested government officials in the concept. A War Office committee was set up to investigate proposals, but its efforts came to nothing. Not deterred, the Royal Navy took a hand as its Royal Naval Air Service armoured car squadrons had at least had some experience of armoured warfare in 1914. From their experience came a number of proposals that involved the use of a 'big wheel' vehicle with massive wheels that could cross trenches. At this point Winston Churchill became more than interested and set up what was to become known as the

Landship Committee to investigate ways of crossing the French battlefields.

The 'big wheel' machine was given the construction go-ahead, and the committee also looked at the Pedrail device, which used a wide central track carrying any load or powerplant above it. This too was ordered for trials, and more machines of the caterpillar track form were ordered for experimental work. The Bullock tractor seemed to offer the greatest promise, and two such vehicles were obtained from the US. Being primarily an agricultural machine, the Bullock could not be classed as intrinsically suitable, but its tracks did offer a way through mud and wire. Accordingly Sir William Tritton of Foster's of Lincoln was asked to redesign the tractor. Tritton used the Bullock track and suspension and built the 'No.

1 Lincoln Machine'. This design was far more promising, but the track was too narrow and gave constant trouble. A new track and some other improvements led to the vehicle later known as 'Little Willie' in December 1915.

'Little Willie' was the first British tank, although at that time the term had not been

coined. Although it appeared to meet the Landship Committee requirements, 'Little Willie' was still too unstable and had virtually no obstacle-crossing capabilities. As a result, Lieutenant W. G. Wilson, who had been working with Tritton at the behest of the Landship Committee, conceived the idea of greatly enlarging the tracks into an 'all-round' form that created the lozenge shape which epitomised the British tanks of World War I. The box body of 'Little Willie' was accordingly altered to accommodate the new track outline and the machine became 'Mother'.

With 'Mother' the War Office once more became interested, and after demonstrations held in Hatfield Park in January 1916, the design was approved. The Landship Committee was then revised to become the Tank Supply Committee, for in an effort to hide the intended role of the new machine the codename 'water carrier' and eventually 'tank' was applied; the latter term was the one that stuck.

'Mother' was used as the prototype for the vehicles that later became the Tank Mk I. An order for 100 such vehicles was placed in February 1916, and with this the era of the tank can be said to have arrived.

Above: 'Little Willie' is seen on completion in its original form with low trackwork and wheeled steering tail. Large 'lozenge' tracks were later added.

'Mother' shows off its paces in trials at Lincoln in January 1916. Other such obstacles were constructed at Hatfield Park for demonstrations in front of the Landship Committee.

Tank Mk V (Male)

The tank was the child of the stalemated fighting along the Western Front in World War I. Mobility for the infantry was denied by barbed wire entanglements covered by carefully sited machine-gun posts, and the cavalry was denied the opportunity to pour through any breach that artillery-supported infantry might make by the ghastly terrain conditions created by massive artillery barrages. What was needed was a means to defeat machine-gun nests, barbed wire and a shell-torn landscape, and this was found in the tank. Mounted on caterpillar tracks based on those of agricultural tractors in combination with a capacious box-like steel hull carrying guns and/or machine-guns as well as the crew, the tank promised to restore mobile warfare by crushing barbed wire and machine-gun positions after advancing inexorably over shattered terrain.

The Tank Mk V was the last British tank to see large-scale use in World War I. There was nothing in this tank that was radically different from its predecessors: the vehicle was little more than a Tank Mk IV revised with a specially designed 112-kW (150-hp) Ricardo petrol engine driving the tracks via the four-speed epicyclic gearbox that Major W. G. Wilson had created to replace the original two-speed gearbox, a rear cupola for the commander, internal access to the unditching beam, and a semaphore arm. Some 400 Mk V tanks had been completed before the Armistice as 200 Male (gun) and 200 Female (machine-gun) vehicles.

The Tank Mk V was powered by a Ricardo engine specially designed for this application in response to an order issued early in 1917. This was a liquid-cooled unit with six cylinders, and developed 112 kW (150 hp) at 1,250 rpm. This engine had an inbuilt radiator with intake and outlet louvres in the sides of the tank, and was supplied with 423 litres (93 Imp gal) of fuel from armoured gravity-feed tanks. Conditions for the eight-man crew inside the tank were still very poor, but not as difficult as those of the Tank Mk I as the Tank Mk V inherited from the Tank Mk IV an engine silencer and long exhaust pipe.

The Tank Mk V was manufactured by the Metropolitan Carriage and Wagon Works of Birmingham from December 1917, and the first vehicles reached the front in May 1918. The armament of the Tank Mk V Male comprised two 6-pdr (57-mm/2.24-in) L/23 guns (one in each lateral sponson) with 332 rounds, and four Hotchkiss machine-guns with 6,272 rounds in ball mountings located in the two sponsons, hull front and hull rear.

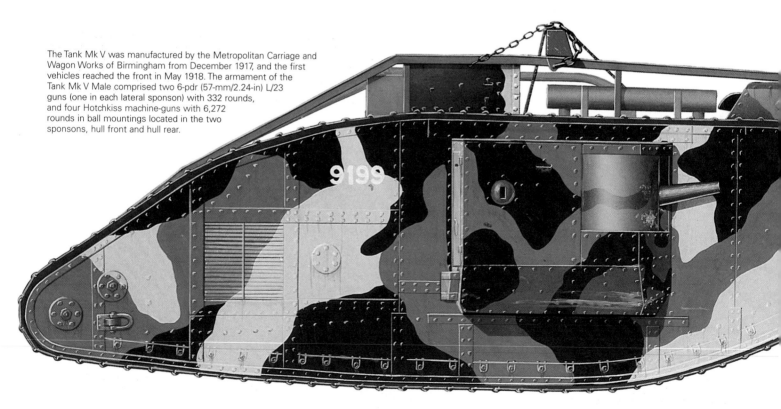

The side view of the Tank Mk V was dominated by its lozenge shape with the tracks running right round this shape. Each track was 52.1 cm (20½ in) wide increased to 67.3 cm (26½ in) on the last 200 vehicles with the idler at the front and the drive sprocket at the rear, and each track's 90 shoes were unsprung and carried on 90 rollers. The upper surface of the tank was characterised by two cupolas (for the driver and commander at the front and rear respectively) and a pair of longitudinal rails that supported the unditching beam and, when this was in use, carried it over the cupolas: the beam was attached to the tracks by chains when needed. The construction of the hull was the same as that of the earlier tanks, soft steel plates being cut and drilled before being hardened and attached to each other via angle irons and girders using rivets and bolts. The front was 16 mm (0.63 in) thick, the sides and back 12 mm (0.47 in), and the belly and roof 8 mm (0.315 in).

The Tank Mk V could cross a trench 3.05 m (10 ft) wide. The main German defence lines encountered in the fighting of 1917 were often as wide as this and to improve the Tank Mk V's trench-crossing ability, Sir William Tritton of Foster's of Lincoln suggested the 'Tadpole Tail' (two longer rear horns) that would be produced as kits shipped to France for installation in the field to add some 2.74 m (9 ft) of length. The horns lacked rigidity, so hulls were instead cut in two to allow the insertion of extra plates adding 1.83 m (6 ft) to the length of the Tank Mk V*, able to cross a 3.96-m (13-ft) trench and carry 25 infantrymen or stores.

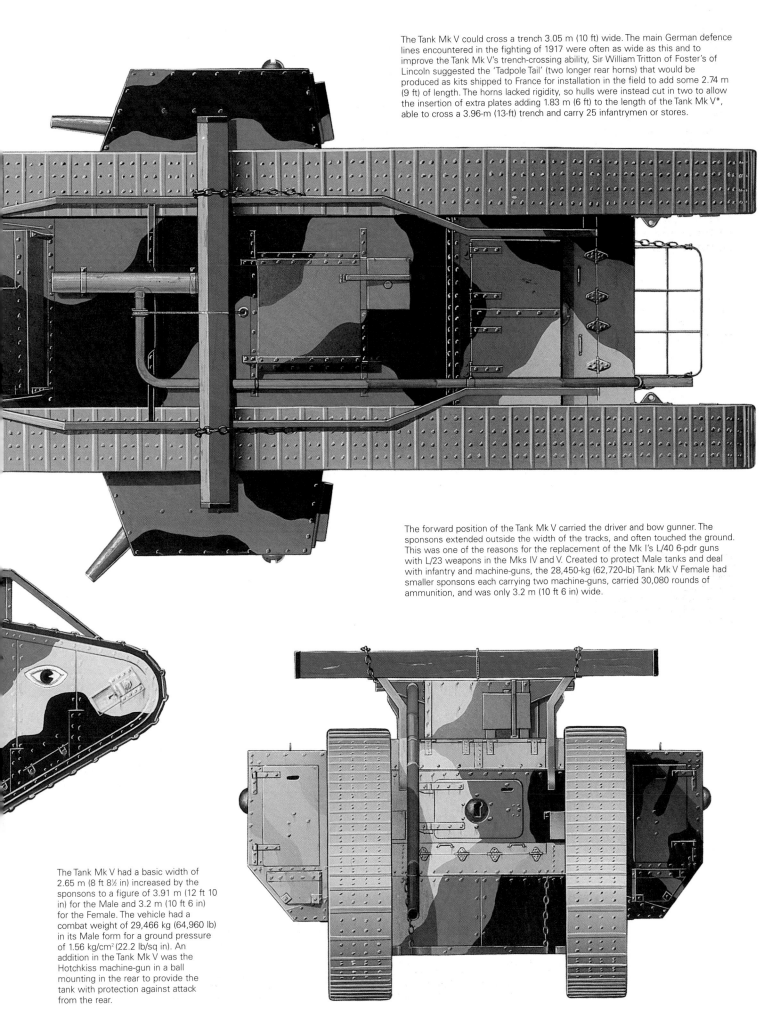

The forward position of the Tank Mk V carried the driver and bow gunner. The sponsons extended outside the width of the tracks, and often touched the ground. This was one of the reasons for the replacement of the Mk I's L/40 6-pdr guns with L/23 weapons in the Mks IV and V. Created to protect Male tanks and deal with infantry and machine-guns, the 28,450-kg (62,720-lb) Tank Mk V Female had smaller sponsons each carrying two machine-guns, carried 30,080 rounds of ammunition, and was only 3.2 m (10 ft 6 in) wide.

The Tank Mk V had a basic width of 2.65 m (8 ft 8½ in) increased by the sponsons to a figure of 3.91 m (12 ft 10 in) for the Male and 3.2 m (10 ft 6 in) for the Female. The vehicle had a combat weight of 29,466 kg (64,960 lb) in its Male form for a ground pressure of 1.56 kg/cm² (22.2 lb/sq in). An addition in the Tank Mk V was the Hotchkiss machine-gun in a ball mounting in the rear to provide the tank with protection against attack from the rear.

Infantry and cavalry tanks
Speed and power

Revolutionising the battlefield by bringing mechanisation and high mobility, infantry and cavalry tanks allowed rapid breakthroughs through enemy lines and the delivery of devastating firepower.

This Vichy tank was captured in Syria in June 1941. Although basic, the hull and turret design featured above would become a standard configuration for all future tank designs up to the present day.

The emergence of the tank in 1916 was to change the face of warfare, although that was not immediately clear to the armies of the time. The first tanks were slow 'moving pill-boxes', fairly lightly armed but heavily armoured. Their primary function was to break through fixed defences ahead of the infantry, going on to provide support at a walking pace as the foot soldiers advanced.

At the end of the war, the first stirrings of a new tank doctrine began to emerge. A number of theorists led by Basil Liddell Hart and J. F. C. Fuller realised that the key characteristic of the tank was not its armour protection or its firepower, but was rather its mobility. In the late 1920s, British tank visionaries experimented with all-mechanised forces, proving the concepts which would eventually become known as Blitzkrieg. But they were ahead of their time. The suc-

cesses at the end of the Great War convinced the General Staff that the proper place for the tank was as an infantry support weapon.

Between the wars, British tank development took widely divergent routes. In the early 1920s, Vickers developed the influential Vickers Medium tank. This established the design characteristics which were to become standard in years to come, with a sprung suspen-

sion that conferred increased mobility and a two-man rotating turret armed with a reasonably powerful 1.9-in (47-mm) gun. A smaller development, the Vickers Six-Ton Tank, was exported widely and licence-built variants of this light machine became the first modern tanks used by armies all over the world.

For a time, tank designers flirted with multi-turreted tanks, the main weapon being supplemented by

smaller machine-gun turrets. These 'land battleships' proved to be a blind alley. The cavalry, who appreciated the virtues of mobility, used much faster vehicles with lighter armour which became known as Cruiser tanks.

Light tanks and armoured cars saw the most extensive use, being deployed throughout the British Empire in Iraq, Persia, Palestine, India and Egypt until 1939, when war clouds once more gathered over Europe.

French Hotchkiss tanks on parade in Paris.

Although its design originated in the 1920s, the French Char B1 series was fitted with a powerful hull gun as well as a turret gun. The B1 was technically a powerful tank, although poor tactics saw it badly employed.

The British experience was reflected in other armies. With the massive reduction in force that came after 1918, the US Army's tank corps had around 800 tanks on strength, but only 154 officers and 2,508 men to man and maintain them. Soon even this force was abolished, since the General Staff saw infantry support as the only role for armour. The heavy tanks were taken out of service, and the War Department limited any vehicles in service to light tanks under 5 tons and medium tanks under 15 tons, stipulating that all such vehicles must be transportable on lorries or trains. The position was made clear in 1922 when the War Department issued a policy statement. The only role for tanks was to 'facilitate the uninterrupted advance of the infantryman in the attack.'

At the end of the war France had more tanks than any other nation, though when responsibility for the tank arm was transferred from the artillery to the infantry in 1920, much research and development was stifled. The far-seeing Colonel Estienne was a strong advocate of mechanised units, and General Aimé Doumenc proposed the concept of the armoured division. But Marshal Philippe Pétain insisted that the proper place for tanks was with the infantry, and other nations quickly surged ahead of France in their ideas for the employment of armour.

The infantry wanted tanks to reinforce assaults. These were called *chars de manoeuvre d'ensemble*, and would use the most powerful infantry tanks. They would be assigned to corps or division commanders as they were needed.

The cavalry persisted in the idea that armour could be a force in its own right. In 1917 each cavalry division was assigned 18 armoured cars, increased in 1923 to become 36. In 1930, a regiment of truck-borne infantry, who were known as Dragons Portés, replaced one of the division's three mounted brigades. In 1932 the armoured elements were formed into a regiment with 80 tanks.

It was only in Germany that the new ideas of tank warfare took firm root. Led by Heinz Guderian, German tank men had learned from experiments by other armies. Germany did not have the artificial division between infantry and cavalry tanks: all tanks were expected to move fast, and rather than slowing panzers down to the speed of an infantryman on foot, the Wehrmacht expected the infantry to keep up with the tanks by mounting them in vehicles. It was the speed of the German advance that contributed to the success of Blitzkrieg in 1939 and 1940.

GUDERIAN: ARCHITECT OF BLITZKRIEG

Possibly the most outstanding Panzer commander of World War II, Generaloberst Heinz Guderian was born in East Prussia. He was commissioned into the light infantry in 1907 and served as a staff officer in World War I. During the 1920s and 1930s he developed Blitzkrieg – the deep penetration armoured tactics that enabled the Wehrmacht to triumph in the first two years of the war.

More than a theoretician, he proved to be an aggressive and capable field commander in Poland, France and in the first months of the invasion of the USSR. However, he was relieved of his command in 1941 when he withdrew his Panzer Group from Moscow as they came under intense Soviet attack. Guderian was brought back from retirement in 1943 and made inspector of Armoured Troops. In July 1944 he was promoted Army Chief of Staff and held this post until 22 March, 1945.

Though Guderian was publicly critical of Hitler's operational leadership – he was one of the few officers who would disagree with the dictator to his face – his reputation was sullied by taking part in the Court of Honour which investigated and convicted the officers suspected of involvement in the 1944 July Plot against Hitler. He had suffered from ill health during the war and died at Schwangau-bei-Füssen in Bavaria on 15 May 1954.

From horse to wheel
The logistics revolution

The industrial revolution which swept through warfare in the 20th century had no place for the horse, which had been used to support combat troops for more than two thousand years.

There is an old military proverb which states that while "Amateurs study tactics, professionals study logistics!" War is not just about fighting battles. You cannot fight a battle without men, and men have to be fed, clothed and provided with weapons and ammunition. Tactics are important of course, and the correct tactics will certainly win battles, but good logistics can win wars.

Modern logistics thinking was largely created by Napoleon. He was one of the first modern generals to organise and develop logistical lines of communications and a modern quartermaster corps. It meant that Napoleon could keep an army fed and supplied for longer than his rivals, allowing him to keep his forces concentrated. Assured supply gave him a mobility and flexibility on the battlefield that was unheard of in its day.

From Napoleon's time into the beginning of the 20th century, logistics meant horses. Horses pulled the artillery. Horses drew the wagons which carried the army's food and ammunition. Horse-drawn vehicles carried tents and bridging equipment, and horse-ambulances took care of the wounded.

Rail mobility

The introduction of the railway greatly changed strategic mobility – the railroads made fighting across vast distances possible during the American Civil War (1861-65), and efficient use of a rail network designed for the purpose enabled the Prussians to concentrate their forces with unbelievable speed against France during the 1870-71 Franco-Prussian War.

But once away from the railhead, supplies still had to be carried to the front, and that still required horses – and horses have to be fed. It was the availability of horse fodder which had dictated the pace of military operations for centuries.

During World War I, horse fodder took up more railway rolling stock than any other single supply item. An average infantry division of the time required about 100 tons of supplies per day, about 60 per cent of which was used to feed the horses.

Motorised transport

The development of motorised transport freed armies from this problem, but created some new difficulties in turn.

With the rapid development of reliable mechanical transport it became obvious to a small number of military thinkers that the motor vehicle could make a significant contribution to the 20th-century battlefield. Mechanisation possessed several distinct advantages over the traditional horse- and mule-drawn transport – you don't need to feed a truck when it is not moving.

Although the armies of the Great War were still reliant on the horse, motor vehicles became increasingly useful. By 1916, the French were using non-stop truck convoys along the 'Voie Sacrée' to support the fortress at Verdun, enabling it to withstand the titanic German offensive.

However, the innate conservatism of the military mind and the natural hostility of influential cavalry circles saw to it that in spite of the experiences of the Great War, it would be decades before the horse would at last be replaced in the armies of the world.

Above: French horse-drawn field artillery on the move in France in 1914. World War I was the last war in which horses played the most important part in the logistics effort of the world's armies.

Right: The mechanisation of warfare in the trenches of World War I signalled the end of the line for the horse. It had no place on a battlefield dominated by artillery and machine-guns.

Left: World War II saw the final replacement of horse-drawn logistics by the internal combustion engine. Here, a British three-ton truck is brought ashore from an LST at Salerno in 1943.

Below: British and US vehicles are landed in Normandy in June 1944. By this time, a typical mechanised or armoured division needed 1,500 tons of supplies a day to keep fighting.

The British were the first to fully mechanise. During the early 1920s the Mechanical Transport Advisory Board began to develop the 6x4 truck, and this became the standard design for the next two decades with a range of light, medium and heavy trucks in 30-cwt, 3-ton and 10-ton capacities. By the outbreak of World War II, the British army no longer used the horse in the front-line.

World War II saw an explosive growth in the use of motor transport. The German Blitzkrieg could only be fought because the Panzers were accompanied by infantry, artillery, engineer and supply units, all mounted in or towed by trucks. However, there were never quite enough trucks for the job and the Wehrmacht was forced to rely on captured vehicles and impressed civil trucks.

Wehrmacht assault

On 22 June 1941, Hitler launched the most titanic invasion in history, aiming to defeat the Soviet Union before autumn. Three German army groups comprised 80 infantry divisions, 18 Panzer divisions and 12 motorised divisions, while behind them waited another 21 infantry, two Panzer and one more motorised divisions in reserve. A total of 500,000 lorries waited in massed parks from East Prussia to Romania to rush millions of tons of supplies forward on demand. To the modern mind the only questionable (indeed alarming) figure to emerge from the tables of statistics among the planning memoranda for Operation Barbarossa is that for 'stabling' – 300,000 horses were to play an essential part in this monumental military exercise.

But the true future of logistics was to come from across the Atlantic. The British army lost much of its equipment at Dunkirk, and turned to America for replacements under Lend-Lease. The US had already begun the development of a series of standard trucks, and the immense power of American industry was gearing up for large scale production, with the 2½-ton GMC six-wheeler being the work horse. Manufactured in huge numbers, the 'Deuce and a half', or 'Jimmy', was the mainstay of all Allied supply operations, from the Pacific Islands and Burma through the Steppes of Russia to Italy and Northwest Europe.

THE 'RED BALL EXPRESS'

The Allied invasion of Normandy marked the beginning of the end for the Third Reich, especially after the breakout from the beachhead. But the headlong pace of the Allied advance out of Normandy left long supply lines to be maintained. Without regular resupply, the vast Allied armies would soon have come to a halt (and on occasion did).

Special supply routes were organised, the most famous being the American 'Red Ball Express'. This organisation ran trucks day and night on selected routes cleared of all civilian and non essential military traffic. Because of the narrow French roads, a one-way system had to be devised. In the Autumn of 1944, supplies were loaded at St Lo, then dumped at an area west of Paris, where they were broken down into divisional packages and ferried onwards by smaller convoys. On the return journey the trucks travelled on a different route, thereby creating a huge loop.

GMC 2½-ton trucks were used in their hundreds on this route to carry fuel, supplies and ammunition. Many trucks towed cargo or fuel trailers. As was to be expected, the long journey took a heavy toll on both drivers and trucks, so maintenance and recovery depots were placed at stages along the route.

Blitzkrieg

The key to the success of Blitzkrieg was in the flexible use of all arms. The tanks were supported by mobile artillery, the Luftwaffe and by mechanised infantry called panzer grenadiers.

In a series of rapid and hard-hitting campaigns from 1939-1941, the German army was able to demonstrate to the whole world that it was master of a new form of warfare. Blitzkrieg overcame the enervating attrition strategies of World War I, using tactics dependent on good reconnaissance and inter-service co-operation.

The roots of Blitzkrieg lay in the German infiltration tactics of 1918. Special assault divisions with heavily armed 'Storm Troopers' broke through weak points in the Allied lines, offering superior firepower at the point of contact.

After the war, some military theorists realised that armoured vehicles would add an extra dimension to the new German tactics, though with varying degrees of success. Nowhere were the new theories embraced more than in Germany.

Guderian's ideas

The main German champion of the Blitzkrieg concept was Heinz Guderian. He proposed that any future armoured force had to be a balance of all arms, with the main striking force being provided by a highly mobile spearhead of tanks, mechanised infantry and artillery.

The first panzers fielded by the Wehrmacht were small, lightly armed and armoured, and had definite tactical limitations. But they were highly mobile.

During the 1930s the Germans developed and refined the tactics of

Blitzkrieg. The first step was to form an overwhelming offensive spearhead at a pre-selected point on a battlefront. This 'Schwerpunkt' was chosen following analysis of all available reconnaissance information. Massed panzers then advanced on this objective under a rain of supporting fire.

Armoured breakout

Exploiting the element of surprise and confusion, the panzers moved forward with mechanised infantry providing flank security. Once the armour was clear of the breakthrough point, further support was provided by the guns of the tanks and pinpoint attacks by dive-bombers.

The intial penetration was then exploited to the utmost. The mobility and firepower of the tanks enabled them to range far and wide in the enemy's rear areas, disrupting communications and interrupting supplies.

With an enemy unable to respond effectively, the panzers were free to advance over hitherto impossible distances and towards distant objectives within periods of days, rather than the months of previous campaigns.

Panzers alone were vulnerable to dug-in infantry. A key to the success of Blitzkrieg was the development of motorised infantry, which could keep pace with the tanks and neutralise opposition.

Below: The Junkers Ju 87 Stuka will forever be associated with Blitzkrieg. The Stuka's role was to provide close support to army units using highly accurate dive-bombing attacks.

COMPONENTS OF BLITZKRIEG

It took a long time for the Allies to understand Blitzkrieg. As late as 1942, the US Army analysis of German offensive doctrine was that its primary aim was to encircle the enemy and destroy him. 'The objective of the combined arms in attack', a staff paper concluded, 'is to bring the armored forces and the infantry into decisive action against the enemy with sufficient firepower and shock. Superiority in force and firepower, the employment of armored forces, as well as the surprise element, play a great part in the offensive.'

The truth was very different. In fact, German tactics did everything possible to avoid such a decisive engagement, relying on speed and flexibility to wreak havoc in enemy rear areas. The fact that the Germans were inevitably the aggressors allowed them to pick the point of attack, and they were helped during the first three years of World War II by the disorganisation of their opponents.

The Germans substituted mobility for power, which meant that all the supporting arms had to move at the same speed as the tanks. Although the bulk of the German army was still largely horse drawn, the panzer divisions which raced through France in 1940 were entirely motorised, the infantry and support units being carried on trucks. The opening phases of any attacks were meticulously planned and executed, while in later stages the high command relied on the excellent training of their troops, good communications, and panic and paralysis on the part of enemy commanders.

Above: A typical panzer division in 1940 had one reconnaissance battalion equipped with 100 armoured cars and 60 motorcycles. *Although the division's motorcycle infantry battalion was classed as motorised infantry, its 500 motorcyclists could also be used in a reconnaissance role.*

Left: Panzer divisions and corps were controlled by fully mobile headquarters units, which enabled senior officers to command on the move. As a result, generals like Heinz Guderian tended to operate much closer to the front than their Allied equivalents.

Right: In 1939 a panzer division operated with two tank regiments each of two battalions. However, in order to bring the light divisions up to full panzer strength, most lost one of their regiments before the invasion of France. This reduced the number of panzers in a division down from 324 in 1939 to around 250 in 1940.

Above: Although the Wehrmacht got many of its parachute techniques from Soviet experiments of the 1930s, the Germans in 1940 were the first to show that unexpected assaults from the air could reap massive tactical dividends, so long as the lightly armed paratroopers were quickly relieved by conventional troops.

Top: Blitzkrieg tactics only worked so long as there was a high degree of co-operation and co-ordination between the different service arms. Although the panzers grabbed the headlines for their deep thrusts and outflanking manoeuvres, the infantry still had to do the hardest fighting as they followed up the fast-moving armour.

The role of the halftrack
Battlefield mobility

Halftracked vehicles were used to enhance the mobility of almost every service arm, from infantry and artillery to engineers and medical staff. Their use as armoured personnel carriers (APCs) heralded the development of modern mechanised infantry tactics.

During World War II the main weapon of every mechanised army was the tank, but this could not operate in isolation. The outside world could be seen only through the narrow confines of periscopes, weapon sights and other limited viewing devices. Tank commanders had to be provided with some form of observation outside the vehicle, and it was not long before this role was undertaken by specialised infantry moving with the tanks to act as the eyes and ears of the tank commander, and warding off enemy tank-killing squads.

The infantry's problem was the need to keep up with the tanks. Early experiments showed that trucks lacked adequate mobility, and also protection against small-arms fire and shell splinters. What was needed was a vehicle that could not only keep up with the tanks, but provide some protection for the occupants, and serve as a weapons platform.

The ideal solution would have been to have the infantry carried in a fully tracked vehicle, but this was initially discarded when it was realised that the vehicles would spend a great deal of their time travelling along paved roads, and that current tracked steering was cumbersome and could not provide adequate manoeuvrability.

Lightweight vehicle

The halftrack, or semitrack, vehicle combined the mobility provided by tracks with the wheeled vehicle's steering. As the vehicle was relatively light, it was not always necessary to make use of heavy steel tracks, so rubber or rubber-based tracks could be used.

Halftracks were generally issued to units known as mechanised infantry, although the name varied from nation to nation: in Germany they were known as *Panzertruppen* and later as *Panzergrenadiere*. The proportion of mechanised infantry to tanks varied somewhat, for some nations decided to go 'tank heavy' and combined two tank battalions with one battalion of mechanised infantry, others had balanced 'one for one' proportions, and some armies even had more mechanised infantry than tanks. The proportions varied not only nationally but according to terrain: open terrain favoured a tank-heavy organisation while close terrain (such as urban areas) demanded an infantry-heavy organisation.

Halftrack artillery

Once mechanised infantry were on the scene it was not long before they were joined by combat engineers in halftracks to help keep up the momentum of the armour. In

Above: This German conversion of a French Somua MCG halftrack was made to accommodate an armoured hull and mount a 7.5-cm (2.95-in) Pak 40 anti-tank gun. These conversions were carried out in France ready for the 1944 Normandy campaign, where this example was knocked out. Probably only 16 such modifications were carried out.

Top: This SdKfz 251/9 was knocked out at Stavelot on 21 December 1944 during the Ardennes fighting. It is armed with a short 7.5-cm (2.95-in) assault gun, and a 7.92-mm (0.312-in) MG 42 is also carried. The unfortunate gunner is still on board next to his gun, killed by a rifle grenade.

Right: This SdKfz 7 8-tonne artillery tractor has a full gun crew on board. A canvas weather protection tilt could be used, but this was usually stowed at the rear to improve all-round vision to guard against air attack. Stores and ammunition could be carried at the rear.

Above: A captured 2-cm (0.79-in) Flakvierling 38 SdKfz 7/1 anti-aircraft vehicle lies by a hedgerow in Normandy. When in action, the sides of this vehicle were folded down to act as a 'working platform' around the gun. This vehicle has an armoured cab to protect the driver; the crew had no such protection.

Right: The USSR supplemented its own range of halftracks with large numbers of American vehicles shipped under the Lend-Lease scheme. Here a Red Army M3 drives into Sofia during the Soviet invasion of Bulgaria in September 1944.

World War II self-propelled artillery was not common, most guns and howitzers being towed. Here the half-track could be used to advantage to keep pace with the tanks, but since the artillery was a supporting arm there was less need for armour. Thus, many half-tracks used as artillery tractors and ammunition carriers were little more than unarmoured halftrack trucks. Armoured artillery tractors were usually used to tow anti-tank guns that operated directly in the face of the enemy. However, some artillery halftracks that also used armour acted as the

mobile forward observation posts that travelled together with the tanks.

With the main combat arms mounted in highly mobile halftracks, it was not long before the rest of the supporting arms travelled in them too. Thus by the end of World War II whole formations moved in halftracks.

Weapons platforms

However, with this move toward protected mobility came an unforeseen shift in combat tactics and capabilities. Many of the halftracks sprouted armament of all kinds, ranging from machine-guns to heavy guns and

howitzers. Halftracks became not just weapons carriers but mobile platforms from which the weapons could be used directly. This was particularly true with infantry vehicles.

Therefore, tactics were introduced that allowed the halftracks to move forward firing as they went to deliver their infantry loads directly onto enemy positions or else move through them to wreak havoc in the rear areas. They

did not do this in isolation, for they still travelled with the tanks, but at times it was not the mechanised infantry who supported the tank but the tank that supported the infantry. By 1945 the half-track had made possible radical alterations in tactics toward today's balanced battle groups and combat teams.

Below: The Krauss-Maffei KM8 halftrack was the forerunner of the mittlerer Zugkraftwagen 8t (SdKfz 7) series. This early model is seen towing a 15-cm (5.9-in) sFH 18 medium field howitzer and full crew. Taken in about 1935, this is a propaganda photograph typical of the period of Germany's early rearmament.

Counter-attack at Arras
Allied armour in action

On 21 May 1940, the British 1st Army Tank Brigade briefly gained superiority over their German counterparts near Arras in northern France, before Rommel forced a devastating counter-attack.

The German invasion of Belgium, Holland and France codenamed *Fall Gelb* – Case Yellow – that began on 10 May 1940 saw futuristic paratroops and conventional foot-slogging infantry begin the war in the West. It began with air attacks on Dutch and Belgian airfields and airborne assaults on the bridges at Moerdijk and Rotterdam and the seat of government at The Hague. With the bridges in German hands the defences of 'fortress Holland' were penetrated and, following a savage air attack on the city of Rotterdam, the Dutch capitulated on 14 May. An elite force, the German 1st Parachute Regiment landed in 10 gliders within the Belgian fort of Eben Emael and neutralised it using revolutionary shaped charges.

Luftwaffe protection
Beginning on 10 May 1940, the German XIX Panzer Corps under General Heinz Guderian had worked their way through Belgium and Luxembourg and, protected by the Luftwaffe, reached the east bank of the Meuse on 12 May.

Though Guderian's tanks were still arriving at the river, supported by the Stukas of General Wolfram von Richthofen's VIII Fliegerkorps, he committed his assault troops and crossed it the following day, seizing the adjoining high ground. By the evening engineers had constructed bridges at Sedan. A door was open for the 1st, 2nd and 10th Panzer Divisions. To the north at Monthermé the XLI Panzer Corps under General Georg-Hans Reinhardt had established a bridgehead by 15 May and the 6th and 8th Panzer Divisions began their drive to the sea. At Dinant and Onhaye the XV Panzer Corps had achieved a lodgement across the Meuse by the 14th. The reconnaissance troops of General Erwin Rommel's 7th Panzer Division

had found an unguarded weir and manoeuvred their motor-cycles carefully across the narrow walkway. The 5th Panzer Division joined the westward dash. To the north the XVI Panzer Corps under General Erich Höpner, actually part of Army Group B, swung left through Belgium and then on into France.

German salient
By 16 May the German salient was between 20 and 40 km (12 and 25 miles) deep. There had been a brief delay at Montcornet on 15 May when an armoured division commanded by General de Gaulle attempted a counter-attack. For the Germans the rivers Aisne and Somme covered their left flank as they pushed westwards. On 20 May the tanks and motor-cyclists of the 2nd Panzer Division reached the sea at Noyelles.

On 21 May 1940, a counter-attack was launched by tanks and infantry of the British Expeditionary Force (BEF) against the advancing German forces. The BEF had

Above: A French Char B knocked out, perhaps by an '88', reveals the fatal damage inflicted to its hull front. This heavy tank was more than a match for contemporary German tanks, but few in number.

Below: By the evening of 20 May, Guderian's panzers had reached Abbeville at the mouth of the Somme. The following day, four British infantry brigades and the 1st Army Tank Brigade were launched southwards from Arras to launch their counter-strike.

A 3.7-cm Pak 35/36 in action during the invasion of France. Such conventional anti-tank artillery failed to make an impression on Allied armour, and Rommel relied on 8.8-cm AA artillery in order to repulse the Anglo-French counter-attack.

CHARLES DE GAULLE: TANK TACTICIAN

One of the few officers to protest against the supine French strategy was Colonel Charles de Gaulle, who launched one of the very few armoured counter-attacks mounted by the French army in 1940. When the Allies declared war on Germany on 3 September 1939, de Gaulle was appointed tank commander of the 5th Army, and is pictured as such (above right), talking to President Reynard. In January 1940, de Gaulle issued a memorandum, *The Advent of a Mechanised Force*, in which he stressed the importance of combined tank and air power. As commander of the 4th armoured division, de Gaulle halted the German advance at Abbeville during 27-30 May 1940.

heavy [Matilda Mk II], had crossed the Arras-Beaumetz railway and shot up our Panzer IIIs. At the same time several enemy tanks were advancing down the road from Bac du Nord and across the railway towards Wailly. It was an extremely tight spot, for there were also several enemy tanks close to Wailly on its northern side...With the enemy tanks so perilously close, only rapid fire from every gun could save the situation.'

8.8-cm tank-killer

The gun that proved the most effective tank-killer at Arras was not the diminutive 3.7-cm (1.46-in) Pak 35/36, a gun that actually failed to make any penetration, but the 8.8-cm (3.46-in) Flak 18/36/37 anti-aircraft gun used in the ground role. Rommel, an energetic commander, had come forward to supervise the siting of the anti-tank guns. He then launched his 25th Panzer Regiment in a counter-attack that at the cost of three PzKpfw IVs, six IIIs and a number of light tanks drove the 1st Tank Brigade back towards Arras.

Though the counter-attack ended in a British defeat, it shocked Hitler who assumed that the Anglo-French Allies were capable of launching further, stronger armoured attacks. It was the beginning of a process that would culminate in the Halt Order that prevented the Panzers destroying the BEF at Dunkirk, and allowed the British troops to be evacuated under Operation Dynamo.

---

310 tanks in France, only 23 of which were the heavily armoured Matilda II the remainder was made up of 174 light tanks and 156 Cruiser tanks.

On the day some 74 tanks of the British 1st Army Tank Brigade composed of the 4th and 7th Royal Tank Regiments were supported by men of the 6th and 8th Durham Light Infantry. These struck Rommel's 7th Panzer Division and elements of the Waffen-SS Division Totenkopf near the French town of Arras. The shock was greater than the effect but the British took nearly 400 prisoners.

Brigadier Douglas Pratt commanding the 1st Army Tank Brigade recalled the fighting: 'We got about four miles forward before any infantry of ours appeared in sight. During this time we played hell with a lot of Boche motor transport and their kindred stuff...His anti-tank gunners, after firing a bit, bolted and left their guns...None of his anti-tank stuff penetrated our Is or IIs [Infantry Tanks Mk I and II Matilda]...The main opposition came from his field guns, some of which fired over open sights. Also the air dive-bombing on the infantry – this of course, did not worry the tanks much.'

Rommel's assault

On the German side Rommel recalled: '...the enemy tank fire had created chaos and confusion among our troops in the village and they were jamming the roads and yards with their vehicles instead of going into action with every available weapon to fight off the oncoming enemy...About [1097 m] 1,200 yards west of our position the leading enemy tanks, among them one

---

Above: Two Panzer 38(t) light tanks and a pair of Panzer IV medium tanks advance at a leisurely pace with their hatches open. After the brisk battle at Arras, Rommel's 7th Panzer Division drove the British forces and a single French light mechanised division back to their original positions and threatened them with encirclement.

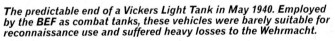
The predictable end of a Vickers Light Tank in May 1940. Employed by the BEF as combat tanks, these vehicles were barely suitable for reconnaissance use and suffered heavy losses to the Wehrmacht.

Soviet motorised attack
Cold War offensive

Had the Cold War ever turned hot, five Soviet armies would have rolled across the East German border and smashed their way across the North German Plain, supported by heliborne assaults by organic Army Aviation forces. In the air, mass formations of bombers and fighters would have poured through sanitised 'corridors' punched through NATO air defences by specialised defence suppression aircraft.

Whatever the underlying philosophy of the Soviet government, its armed forces maintained an overtly offensive posture, especially in Germany. If the Cold War had turned hot, the massive forces in East Germany would have spearheaded the Warsaw Pact's advance. Until the early to mid-1980s, Warsaw Pact military doctrine assumed a major Warsaw Pact strike against NATO in Europe, usually justified as being the Soviet response to the NATO attack which, it was said, would accompany capitalism's inevitable final gasps.

Warsaw Pact armies would then have fought through Germany in their NBC kits and well-sealed tanks and APCs, with Germany occupied within an estimated three days. In theory, the offensive would have then rolled on to the Channel and the Pyrenees.

Motorised rifle units

This kind of attack would have involved an estimated 12,000 tanks and 25,000 APCs. Although the tank was considered the primary Soviet offensive force, tank divisions were outnumbered by motorised rifle units – in October 1990, the Soviet armed forces in East Germany included a declared total of 5,880 tanks and 9,790 armoured vehicles.

The main striking force of the combined-arms army, the motorised rifle units would have been charged with destroying enemy resistance in the battle area, allowing the tank units to make further advances. Furthermore, motorised rifle units, in particular those equipped with BMPs, would have been responsible for small-scale 'thrusting' assaults that would breach the enemy lines. Although conducted by the Red Army towards the end of the Great Patriotic War, such tactics began to return to prominence in the late 1960s and early 1970s. Warsaw Pact forces were maintained at a high degree of readiness, with vehicles

Designed to cross contaminated ground at high speed, the BMP was the first infantry combat vehicle to be armed with cannon and anti-tank missiles. During the Cold War, the BMP was expected to work alongside tanks as well as probing forward independently.

Entering Soviet service in 1963, the BTR-60PA offers complete overhead armoured protection for the troop compartment, unlike its predecessors. This view demonstrates the spartan interior which accommodates up to 16 troops, although 12 is a more usual load. The BTR-60PA has no standard weapons fit – this example is armed with a pintle-mounted 7.62-mm (0.3-in) PKB machine-gun – although the BTR-60PB carries a machine-gun turret. For amphibious operations, the BMP family are fitted with hydrojets, and IR night vision equipment is fitted for both the commander (sitting on the left) and the driver.

SOVIET MOTOR RIFLE REGIMENT: THE ADVANCE

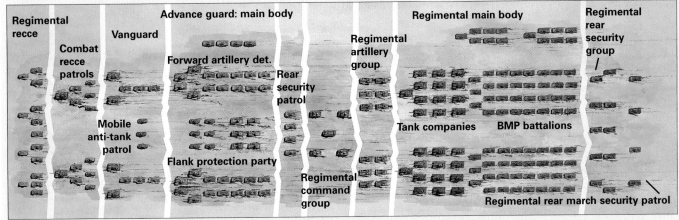

Regimental recce

Vanguard

Combat recce patrols

Advance guard: main body

Forward artillery det.

Rear security patrol

Mobile anti-tank patrol

Flank protection party

Regimental command group

Regimental artillery group

Regimental main body

Regimental rear security group

Tank companies

BMP battalions

Regimental rear march security patrol

A Soviet front would have comprised at least two combined-arms armies in its first echelon. Each army's first echelon usually included two motorised rifle divisions advancing over a 20-80 km (12-50 mile) front. At least one further motorised rifle division, normally equipped only with BTRs, would have been included in the second echelon of the combined-arms army. During defensive operations, the motorised rifle units would have been responsible for holding ground in order that the tank divisions could mount an offensive counter-attack.

armed and ready to go. Some units were ready to move at 45 minutes' notice. Most were ready for war within two hours of being ordered to go.

Motorised rifle unit tactics relied on manoeuvre and surprise, and Soviet APCs and BMPs were designed to undertake high-speed operations under NBC conditions. Any war would have opened with a surprise nuclear attack against NATO installations in Germany. Exercise maps marked the German/Dutch border as being the 'limit of strategic and operational tactical nuclear strikes'. The first wave would have included some 320 warheads, including 60 missiles armed with 200 kiloton yield-warheads – ten times more than the Hiroshima bomb.

Under these conditions, the motorised rifle units were

believed to be capable of sustaining combat for six days. The Soviets demanded a rapid advance of 70-100 km (43-62 miles) per day under NBC conditions, with the average speed of a combined-arms unit being 30-40 km/h (19-25 mph) on the march.

Amphibious vehicles

The first echelon of the standard Soviet Cold War era motorised rifle division comprised two regiments equipped with the amphibious BTR-60PB APC. This was supplemented by the BTR-70 (first identified in 1980) and, from the mid-1980s, by the diesel-powered BTR-80. These vehicles combined excellent cross-country performance with superior NBC protection compared to US equivalents. BTR units would fight mobile battles, or conduct break-

through attacks, prior to exploitation forces being committed. A single regiment equipped with BTRs would join the first echelon if required, but would normally remain in the second echelon.

By 1990, the Soviet army had begun to receive the BMP-3 infantry fighting vehicle, armed with eight 9M117 (AT-10 'Stabber') laser-guided anti-tank missiles. The use of anti-tank weapons would have allowed BMPs to repel

attacks as well as provide fire-support on behalf of the main offensive.

The mobility and firepower of the BMP could be used to hold key positions with tank support, or conduct forward detachments. In the case of particularly rough ground, in close or built-up terrain, or when attacking at night or over water obstacles, APCs or BMPs, rather than tanks, would lead the attack.

Each motorised rifle company would have been preceded by a tank platoon, forming its own combat line 150-200 m (490-660 ft) ahead. Air defence elements would have covered the assault from overwatch positions, with artillery providing fire from behind the combat line.

INVASION EUROPE: WARPAC ATTACK

Soviet plans called for two main axes of advance into Western Europe. One thrust would drive southwest through the Fulda Gap in West Germany, towards Frankfurt am Main, through central France and towards the Iberian Peninsula. The second thrust would drive across the North German Plain, through Belgium, towards the Channel ports in France. These two main attacks would have been flanked in the north by an advance across the Baltic coast to Hamburg and then into Denmark, and in the south by a 'left hook' driving from Czechoslovakia, across Austria and thence into southern West Germany.

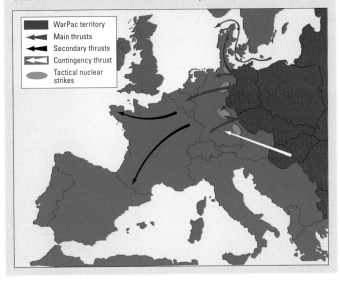

WarPac territory
Main thrusts
Secondary thrusts
Contingency thrust
Tactical nuclear strikes

Soviet wheeled APCs
Post-war development

The BTR-40 4x4 APC was a development of the GAZ-63 truck with an armoured body for use in troop-carrying, command and reconnaissance tasks.

Soviet military doctrine long held the view that the offensive holds the key to success in battle. In order for the Soviet infantry to maintain contact with the armoured spearheads, it was necessary for these troops to be mobile and protected from enemy fire. The solution to the problem was the armoured personnel carrier.

During World War II Soviet infantry went into action on foot or clinging to the sides of tank turrets. Soviet tank losses in the early part of the war meant that there was no production capacity for APCs (armoured personnel carriers). The first wheeled APC to enter service in the post-war period was the BTR-152 in 1951. This was at first based on the 6x6 chassis of the ZIL-151 2.5-tonne truck powered by a ZIL-121 engine developing 68.6 kW (92 hp), but from the BTR-152V1 on that of the ZIL-157 2.5-tonne truck with improvements such as an engine developing 82 kW (110 hp). The engine was in the front, the driver and commander in the centre and the troop compartment at the rear. The BTR-152V1 introduced a front-mounted winch and a central tyre pressure-regulation system, and then came the BTR-152V2 without the winch, and the final open-topped model, the winch-equipped BTR-152V3 with IR driving lights and internal rather than external pressure-regulation lines. In 1961 there appeared the much improved BTR-152K with overhead cover for the troops.

Small APC

The BTR-152 was complemented by the BTR-40 4x4 APC based on a lengthened GAZ-63 2-tonne truck chassis. The BTR-40 entered service in 1951 with a two-man crew and provision for eight infantry. The type was not always used as an APC, however, and was often employed as a reconnaissance or command and control vehicle. The BTR-40 had an open-topped crew compartment, but the later BTR-40B introduced overhead armour. The BTR-40 is not fitted with a tyre pressure-regulation system and, like the BTR-152, lacks an NBC system.

The first model of the BTR-60 series to enter service was the BTR-60P, which had an open-topped troop compartment and was normally armed with one 12.7-mm (0.5-in) and two 7.62-mm (0.3-in) machine-guns on exposed pintle mounts.

Two East German BTR-60P vehicles swim ashore from a landing craft, followed by a BRDM-1 4x4 amphibious scout car. In some East German and Soviet units the BTR-60 series was replaced by the improved BTR-70 8x8 vehicle.

The Soviets realised the shortcomings of the BTR-162 at an early stage and developed the BTR-60P 8x8 vehicle for service from 1961. This has a higher road speed and better cross-country mobility, and is amphibious, being propelled in the water by a waterjet. Its main drawback is its open crew compartment, and an interesting feature is the use of two petrol engines, each driving four wheels on one side of the vehicle.

The BTR-60P was followed by the BTR-60PA with a fully enclosed troop compartment, the BTR-60PB with a manually operated one-man turret carrying single 14.5- and 7.62-mm (0.57- and 0.3-in) machine-guns rather than a single 7.62-mm weapon on an exposed mount. All members of the BTR-60 series have a tyre pressure-regulation system, front-mounted winch and IR night vision equipment.

Steady evolution

The next Soviet wheeled APC was the BTR-70, which is very similar to the BTR-60PB and has the same turret. The BTR-60 is powered by two GAZ-49B petrol engines, each

This Soviet BTR-152 6x6 APC was operated by the US Army for training purposes. The main drawbacks of this vehicle as a first-line 'battle bus' were its lack of cross-country mobility and its open-topped hull, which left the troops very vulnerable to overhead shell bursts. It is still used by several countries.

developing 67.1 kW (90 hp), and though it had been expected that the new vehicle would be powered by diesel engines, the BTR-70 has two ZMZ-4905 petrol engines each developing 86 kW (115 hp). The BTR-60PB has a two-man crew and can carry a maximum of 14 (but typically eight) infantry seated on bench seats down each side and the front and rear of the troop compartment. In the BTR-70 a large bench seat is fitted in the centre of the troop compartment for six men (three outward-facing men on each side), and these can use the three firing ports in each side of the vehicle in a manner impossible for those in the BTR-60. In the BTR-60PB the infantry leave the vehicle via roof hatches and a single hatch in the side of the hull between and well above the second and third axles, but in

the BTR-70 the two roof hatches are supplemented by a door in the lower part of the hull between the second and third axles. The BTR-70 has night vision equipment and an NBC system.

In 1984 the Soviet army started to receive the BTR-80 8x8 wheeled APC. This is basically an improved BTR-70, but its powerplant is based on one KamAZ-7403 turbocharged diesel engine delivering 194 kW (260 hp), replaced from 1993 production by the KamAZ-238M2 delivering 179 kW (240 hp): the diesel improves reliability, speed and range, and runs on less flammable fuel. The turret is an improved version of that used on the BTR-70, and in addition to its

three-man crew the vehicle carries seven infantry who can debus more rapidly via a new door between the second and third axles: the upper and lower parts open forward and downward respectively. The BTR-80A variant has a one-man power-operated turret based on that of the BMP-3 IFV and carrying a 30-mm cannon and 7.62-mm co-axial machine-gun.

The latest wheeled APC is the BTR-90, essentially the BTR-80 scaled up slightly, powered by a 380-kW (510-hp) multi-fuel engine, and carrying the same turret as the BMP-2 tracked ICV with a 30-mm cannon with two-axis stabilisation as well as a 7.62-mm co-axial machine gun. Only small numbers have been produced.

A tough and soldier-proof vehicle, the BTR-60PB continued in production into the early 1980s, despite the introduction of the revolutionary BMP Infantry Fighting Vehicles. This illustration shows a BTR-60PB, as used throughout Africa and the Middle East.

Tank combat
Middle East

Like the aircraft, the tank has become a leading symbol of warfare in the Middle East. Israel, often faced with seemingly overwhelming opposition, has had to evolve an armoured force equal to any threat. As a result of this military prowess, Israel has become the dominant force in the area.

Israeli halftracks pass shattered Egyptian vehicles in the Mitla Pass in Sinai. The essence of Israeli success in the country's many wars has been the classic Blitzkrieg virtues of speed and initiative.

The War of Independence was fought mainly without the benefit of armour. Nevertheless, by the end of 1949 the Israeli state was established and its foes routed, at least for the moment, thanks to fast moving strike columns fighting a deep penetration war behind the enemy lines. However, Israel now had to arm itself for the forthcoming likely hostilities.

Soviet influence

Syria and Egypt gradually fell under the influence of the Soviet Union and began to receive numbers of Soviet tanks. What they did not necessarily receive was the education that went with such weapons, so while their armoured forces looked good

on parade, in battle they were an unknown quantity. In truth, the Arabs lacked the technical background to maintain and use their new weapons and, as time was to show, this was to be a decisive factor.

American tanks

The Israelis had few friends at that time. During the early 1950s they gradually assembled a small nucleus of M4 Sherman tanks of various marks, some armed with old types of gun. With some 50 Shermans, the Israelis were able to form new tank units backed by numbers of old American halftracks that gradually replaced the jeeps as personnel carriers.

The Israeli equipment breakthrough came in 1954

when the French delivered 100 new AMX-13 light tanks armed with high-velocity 75-mm (3-inch) guns. Some of the new guns were immediately switched to M4 Sherman turrets and so by the start of the Suez campaign in 1956 the Israeli army had three armoured brigades. Their opponents had the formidable Soviet T-34/85, but the Syrians still had numbers of old World War II German Panzers.

During the 1956 Suez campaign, the Israelis moved forward into the

Sinai Desert. Using a soon-to-be familiar combination of paratroop actions, air strikes and constant movement the Israelis soon isolated the Egyptian forces in the Gaza Strip and moved forward rapidly into Sinai proper. The Arab armies relied on static and defensive tactical doctrines, which was exactly what the Israelis wanted. Tanks were largely dug-in to 'hedgehog' defensive positions, where they served as little more than armoured pillboxes.

Egyptian tank crews were

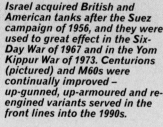

Israel acquired British and American tanks after the Suez campaign of 1956, and they were used to great effect in the Six-Day War of 1967 and in the Yom Kippur War of 1973. Centurions (pictured) and M60s were continually improved – up-gunned, up-armoured and re-engined variants served in the front lines into the 1990s.

FAST STRIKE: ISRAELI HIT AND RUN TACTICS

Following the establishment of the State of Israel, the newly-formed Israeli army obtained a small number of Comet tanks that were stolen or purchased from defecting British soldiers. However, these were too few to deal with the Arab threat to the new nation's existence.

The mobile warfare that took place all around the borders of the new state was primarily the task of jeep-carried infantry armed with little more than small arms. The tactics the Israelis applied would have been familiar to any of Erwin Rommel's tank crews fighting in the Western Desert in 1942. Following the classic Blitzkrieg doctrine which stated that it was not how big your force was, but how effectively you used it, the jeep units acted as independent mobile columns, backed up in some cases by hastily converted armoured cars produced by adding steel plate to truck and bus chassis. The mobile columns produced results totally out of proportion to their numbers. Using deep penetration tactics, they progressively struck deep into the rear areas of their Egyptian, Syrian and Jordanian foes and wrought havoc.

The lessons the Israeli army learned in its first battles were to be applied in an unbroken series of Israeli triumphs over the next 30 years. Speed, flexibility and initiative combined with close air co-operation were to prove decisive against the static, doctrinaire tactics employed by the Arab armies.

at that time suited for little else. They suffered under an autocratic command structure that had little flexibility and allowed few movements to be made without deliberation and delay. The flexible and fast-moving Israelis swept past the defended positions, capturing the essential passes through the western Sinai and rapidly moving south to

One product of Israel's success was captured Soviet weaponry: so much, in fact, that it became worthwhile to set up production plants to convert and upgrade it to Israeli standards.

capture the port of Sharm-el-Sheik on the Red Sea. By the time the Israeli tanks reached the Suez canal, international reaction forced a ceasefire.

Better armour

Re-equipped by the US and the UK after Suez, Israeli tank forces now operated M48 and Centurion tanks. But they faced a resurgent Arab foe. Syria and Egypt received floods of Soviet arms of all kinds and this time Soviet advisers came as well. Vast training schemes at all levels showed the Arab armies not only how to maintain armoured forces but also

how to use them en masse. Within a few years the Egyptians and Syrians were once again carrying out border raids and shelling Israeli territory.

Six-Day War

The 1967 Six-Day War started with a series of pre-emptive strikes by the Israeli air force. While Israeli naval units bombarded the coastal strip three Israeli armoured brigades struck deep into Sinai. They advanced against several Egyptian positions that had been fortified in Soviet style. The Israelis moved with such speed that they were able to attack their foes before they were ready.

This time Jordan became involved in the campaign and the excellent Jordanian armoured units proved to be a tough nut to crack. But a

combination of audacious tactics, good gunnery and co-ordination with the air force resulted in the Israelis entering Jerusalem for the first time since 1949. To the north the battle in the Golan Heights was mainly an infantry one with armoured units, mainly the older M4 Shermans, in support.

The Six-Day War was a remarkable victory for the Israelis. Once again they had shown their tactical supremacy and flair for armoured warfare. They had taken on the whole of the Arab world and won. They won more territory, much weaponry and the respect of the world. At the time they did not realize they had not won the most essential prize of all, and that was peace. That realization came in 1973 with the Yom Kippur War.

Tank warfare in Vietnam
Attack and escort

Vietnam saw armour used in a variety of roles, but rarely in classic tank-versus-tank battles. Tanks instead were used to clear jungle paths, destroy VC bunkers or provide convoy escort.

During World War II Vietnam was occupied by the Japanese, and on their surrender the French moved back in again, so beginning a bitter campaign which finally resulted in the decisive battle at Dien Bien Phu, where the French were defeated in 1954. In Indo-China the French made considerable and often successful use of armour, especially half-tracks, M24 Chaffee light tanks and various armoured amphibious vehicles. Following the withdrawal of French units from Vietnam the country was split into two, North Vietnam and South Vietnam.

US troops arrive

In July 1965 the first American armoured units were deployed to South Vietnam with the arrival of a US Marine Corps tank battalion equipped with the 90-mm gunned M48A3, and in the following year the first

US Army tank battalion arrived with similar vehicles. Initially the tanks were used to defend vital bases such as airfields, but they were soon being used to clear trails through the jungle. When fitted with a dozer blade at the front of the hull they proved to be very successful.

Mine threat

A constant danger to tanks operating in South Vietnam was the threat of mines, or unexploded aircraft bombs rigged as mines. While few tanks were in fact totally destroyed by mines, lengthy repairs often had to be carried out on the vehicle and considerable effort was often required to get the damaged tank back to the main base for repair.

Tanks were also widely used for destroying Viet Cong bunkers with their 90-mm guns firing high explosive or canister rounds with deadly effect; the heavy weight of

Some worn-out M48 main battle tanks were fitted with flamethrowers firing through the gun barrel. A terrifying weapon to unprotected troops, it found its most effective use in clearing possible ambush points on convoy routes.

the tanks also made many of the tunnels cave in, trapping the Viet Cong inside. The helicopter was used on a massive scale in Vietnam but many supplies of fuel, ammunition, water and other essential supplies had to be transported on roads that were wide-open to Viet Cong observation. Tanks were used to escort these convoys and were moderately easy targets for Viet Cong equipped with the Soviet-supplied RPG-7 anti-tank grenade-launcher. This weapon launches an anti-tank rocket fitted with a HEAT warhead capable of

penetrating some 320 mm (12.6 in) of armour. For this reason many M48s were fitted with sandbags and spare track links to their hulls and turrets in the pious hope of detonating the HEAT warhead away from the main armour of the tank. Additional machine-guns were often mounted on the turret roof to provide close protection as the cupola-mounted 0.5-in (12.7-mm) machine-gun was found to be unwieldy when operating in a dense jungle environment.

Although not immediately associated with the Vietnam War, the tank proved to be useful for 'search and destroy' missions. The main armament was especially useful in destroying hardened VC facilities such as command bunkers. Note that this US Army M48 has thrown one of its tracks, rendering it suitable only for the stationary fire support role until it can be repaired.

*Left: **US** power projection: Vietnamese townspeople continue their daily routine alongside the familiar presence of **US** tanks traversing the streets of Cholon, the Chinese quarter of Saigon.*

Below: Tanks used a variety of rounds in Vietnam, from the high-explosive shells seen here to specialised 'Beehive' anti personnel rounds filled with 8,500 razor-sharp 'flechettes'.

Tank-killing role

The Americans first used their M48A3s in the tank-killing role in 1969: in that year they successfully destroyed two PT-76 amphibious light tanks with 90-mm HEAT rounds.

In addition to the basic M48A3 gun tank, the US Army used the M48 scissors bridgelayer in Vietnam, while the US Marine Corps used the M67 series flamethrower tank which was also based on the M48 tank. The M67 was fitted with a flame gun which projected fire to a range of between 90 and 180 m (295 and 591 ft), and carried fuel for 60 seconds of operation. It was normal to fire short bursts rather than one continuous burst.

To operate with the M48 tank the M88 recovery vehicle was also deployed to Vietnam in some numbers, and this proved invaluable in recovering disabled and damaged vehicles.

Australia tanks

It is often forgotten that the Australian army played a major role in Vietnam, and one squadron of the 1st Armoured Regiment, Royal Australian Armoured Corps, was deployed to the country to support Australian infantry. This unit was equipped with the British Centurion tank armed with the 20-pounder gun and supported by the Centurion Mk 2 ARV (armoured recovery vehicle) and Centurion Mk 5 bridgelayer.

By all accounts the Centurion gave a good account of itself, although it was never used to engage enemy tanks, Its superior armour protection over the American M48 enabled it to withstand far better the effect of RPG-7 HEAT projectiles.

Tank combat

Towards the end of the war North Vietnamese armoured units were operating in South Vietnam. Iin 1972 a South Vietnamese tank regiment equipped with the M48A3 successfully engaged PT-76 and T-54 tanks, destroying several with no tank losses to enemy tank fire.

VIETNAMESE ARMOUR SOUTH VIETNAM'S TANKS

After France left Indo-China, South Vietnam was initially equipped with old vehicles such as M3 half-tracks, M24 Chaffee light tanks and M8 and M20 Greyhound armoured cars. With increasing American involvement more modern equipment was supplied, including the M41 light and M48 medium tanks, and the M113 series APC and its countless variants. Artillery supplied included the M107, M109 and M110 self-propelled guns and the 40-mm M42 and the 20-mm M163 self-propelled anti-aircraft guns.

The ARVN tank force played only a minor role in the conduct of the anti-guerrilla operations, though later in the war M113 cavalry vehicles were used extensively. For most of the war, the South Vietnamese tank squadrons were dispersed on security missions in the cities or along the main roads.

The Army of the Republic of Vietnam initially operated US-supplied M24 and M41 light tanks. These later M48 battle tanks are seen on a 'search and clear' operation in downtown Saigon during the 1968 Tet offensive.

M1 Abrams
In the Gulf War

In 1990 the Abrams had already been in service for a decade, but there were doubts about its ability to stand the rough and tumble of combat. Saddam Hussein's invasion of Kuwait meant that it would be battle tested in the harshest terrain and climate of all.

Above: Concerns that the Abrams' complex electronic systems would not cope with the all-pervasive Saudi sand proved to be unfounded, thanks to excellent work by US Army maintenance personnel.

When Iraq invaded Kuwait in August 1990, the US sent the Abrams into battle. Many experts considered that the complex fighting vehicle would not be able to cope with the sand and the heat, and that long months of continuous operation without the luxury of peacetime maintenance facilities would prove to be an Achilles heel. Moreover, it was felt that the advanced turret electronics would be vulnerable.

After President Bush's decision to commit US forces in the defence of Saudi Arabia, and to liberate Kuwait if possible, US Army heavy divisions set in train the largest peacetime movement of military equipment since World War II.

There was no question of moving the armoured divisions by air: the 60-tonne tank could only be carried one at a time by the Lockheed C-5 Galaxy. There were too few of these outsize aircraft available, and they had many other demands on their airlift capability, so that the bulk of the Abrams force deployed to the Gulf were shipped by sea.

Enemies of the Abrams

The clash of old and new in the Gulf War provided military analyst tacticians with an opportunity to evaluate developments in tank design that had not been available since World War II.

The Iraqi Army had a large force of main battle tanks. Most had been supplied by the former Soviet Union, and numbered around 500 T-72s. These modern Soviet tanks were armed with an excellent 125-mm smoothbore cannon, and had many of the same advanced features found on its opponents. But the T-72

was an update of an older design, and the electronics and fire control on the Iraqi examples were not up to the standard of those in Soviet service, let alone when compared with the advanced systems common in NATO vehicles. In action, the T-72 proved to be no match for the American M1s deployed to the Gulf; indeed, they were more on a par with the much older M60A3 tanks used by the US Marine Corps.

But the T-72 was only part of the story; Iraq also fielded over 1,500 T-62s, originally developed in the early 1960s, and about 700 of the

even older T-54. These tanks were clearly inferior to the Abrams or to the British Challenger, but they still carried powerful guns, and their relative simplicity meant that they were expected to be reliable.

M1s deploy in force

A total of 1,848 M1A1s were deployed to the war zone. Most were operated by the Army, but 76 served with the Marines. The American technological advantage was considerable. According to author Norman Friedman:

'The US Army's ability to fire reliably when moving at speed over rough ground, because of the Abrams' stabilised gun, gave it a capability that proved valuable in the Gulf. The Abrams tank also has advanced vision devices that proved effective not only at night, but also in the dust and smoke of Kuwaiti daytime. On average, an Abrams outranged an Iraqi tank by about 1,000 metres.'

Left: Most of Saddam Hussein's tanks were 30- and 40-year-old T-62s and T-54/55s. In battle with the Abrams, they rarely even saw the tank that was killing them.

Below: Equipped with excellent sensors and armed with one of the most powerful guns in the world, the Abrams could kill enemy tanks in all visibility, by day or by night.

For the first months in the desert, the Abrams force spent most of its time working up or in combat exercises. But as Operation Desert Shield turned into Operation Desert Storm, the time for action arrived. After a preparatory bombardment, and behind a screen of attack helicopters and ground attack fighters, the US VII Corps spearheaded the attack on Iraq's border fortifications. Punching through into the enemy rear, its Abrams tanks engaged the Iraqis whenever and wherever possible.

Iraqi tactics

The Iraqis had no experience of true mobile war. During the war with Iran, tanks had been used defensively, dug into fixed positions and used primarily as strongpoints. That is an effective tactic when engaging lightly-armed infantry, but against fast-moving tanks the lack of mobility was to prove fatal.

The Abrams' thermal sights could penetrate the clouds of thick black smoke over the battlefield far better than the optical systems used on the Iraqi tanks. As a result, the Iraqis were being destroyed by tanks they could not even see, but which could see them perfectly well.

The main weapon of the M1A1 is the German-designed M256 120-mm (4.7-in) smoothbore cannon. It is reliable, deadly accurate and has a 'hit/kill ratio' that equals or surpasses any main battle tank armament in the world. Extremely hard-hitting, it can destroy enemy tanks at long range.

FLANKING ATTACKS ON IRAQ AND KUWAIT

About half of Iraq's tank force had already been destroyed from the air before the Coalition forces moved across the border, and General Schwarzkopf's 'left hook' sent the main Allied strike force around the fixed defences. The main strike force was composed of US Army M1A1s, supported by British Challengers and flanked by US Airborne troops and the French light armoured division. Those Iraqi tanks on the front line which did get mobile were quickly destroyed, and in a day the main Allied force was smashing into the Iraqi mobile reserve.

Meanwhile, US Marine tanks, with Saudi armour and troops from other Arab members of the Coalition, were pushing through the Iraqi defences and into Kuwait.

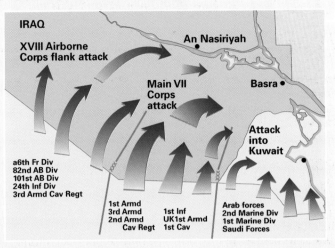

IRAQ

XVIII Airborne Corps flank attack

An Nasiriyah

Main VII Corps attack

Basra

Attack into Kuwait

a6th Fr Div
82nd AB Div
101st AB Div
24th Inf Div
3rd Armd Cav Regt

1st Armd
3rd Armd
2nd Armd
Cav Regt

1st Inf
UK1st Armd
1st Cav

Arab forces
2nd Marine Div
1st Marine Div
Saudi Forces

The strongest Iraqi defences were on the Kuwaiti/Saudi border. The initial Allied attack bypassed those positions, with heavy Coalition armoured units smashing across the border far to the west.

Indeed, successful engagement ranges approaching 4000 m (13,123 ft) were often recorded during Operation Desert Storm.

'Silver Bullets'

The primary armour-defeating ammunition of the Abrams' cannon is the armour-piercing, fin-stabilised, discarding sabot (APDS-FS) round, known to tank crews as 'The Silver Bullet'. This features a depleted uranium penetra-

tor, since depleted uranium has a density two and a half times greater than that of steel and provides high penetration characteristics.

Concerns about the M1A1's high fuel consumption and consequent limited range proved to be unfounded, thanks to a massive resupply operation that was a textbook example of efficiency. Other concerns about the Abrams' reliability and vulnerability to battle damage proved equally

incorrect. There were few reports of mechanical failure – US armoured units maintained an unprecedented 90 per cent operational readiness even at the height of combat.

Only 18 Abrams tanks were taken out of service due to battle damage. Nine of those had suffered repairable damage, mostly from mines, and only nine were complete losses. Not a single Abrams crewman was killed.

Left: An Iraqi T-62 lies wrecked just outside Kuwait, destroyed by a Marine Corps Abrams. Most Marines tank units were equipped with old M60A3s, but they also had 76 M1s on strength in the Gulf.

Below: Abrams tanks carried HEAT ammunition to engage hostile light armour. This Chinese-built YW-531 APC of the Iraqi army graphically shows the effect of being hit by such a round.

Tank versus tank Armour tactics

The tank is the largest and most capable of all battlefield weapons, and as such is a target for all manner of potent weapons. These include other tanks, which combine all the attributes required of a 'tank killer'.

So slow was the pace of German tank development and manufacture in World War I that actions between the tanks of the two sides were singularly infrequent. Although the British had first used the tank in action during September 1916, it was 24 April 1918 before the first engagement between tanks took place. The place was Villers-Bretonneux, and the encounter pitted three German A7V tanks against three British Tank Mk IVs (one Male with guns and machine-guns and two Females with machine-guns). With the crews much incapacitated by having to wear gas masks, the action was fought at close range, the two Female tanks had to retire after being damaged by shell fire, but the sole Male tank managed to hit and knock out one of the A7V tanks.

Slow development

There were other tank versus tank actions in World War I, but most of these involved tanks of mostly Allied manufacture, as the Germans used not inconsiderable numbers of captured Allied vehicles.

There was little real differ-

Above: In the tank versus tank battle there is a constant competition between the firepower and protection that can be worked into the tanks of any generation. These are British Challenger 1 MBTs, seen prior to the 1991 Gulf War.

ence discernible in the tank versus tank actions of World War II, even though the ranges at which the actions were fought were somewhat longer and the speeds of the tanks somewhat greater. There were, of course, a number of 'complications' to the concept of the tank versus tank action. The tanks were increasingly supported by

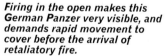

Firing in the open makes this German Panzer very visible, and demands rapid movement to cover before the arrival of retaliatory fire.

infantry riding in armoured personnel carriers (or on the tanks themselves) to protect the tanks from direct-fire engagement by artillery in general and anti-tank guns in particular, and the freedom of tanks to manoeuvre was circumscribed by minefields and the known presence of enemy anti-tank guns and ground-attack aircraft. Nevertheless, open arenas such as North Africa and the open plains of the USSR made possible fast-

moving and wide-ranging campaigns spearheaded by tanks. Here tank versus tank actions were not uncommon, and at times these seemed akin to the naval actions fought in the days of sail.

The fighting that followed the Allied landings of June 1944 in north-west France took place in an altogether closer type of terrain based on a hilly landscape littered with small villages and cut by streams and sunken roads, the latter edged by tall and impenetrable hedgerows. This 'bocage' was ideal country for

A French R-35 knocked out during the Blitzkrieg of 1940. The destruction of a tank can be achieved in many ways, the most decisive being a hull or turret hit that punctures the armour and either detonates the ammunition or ignites the fuel.

When the Allies launched their mainland offensive after D-Day, they were faced with a new type of tank warfare, often conducted under closed terrain. These two German tanks were knocked out in France by Churchill tanks.

to let their enemy's tanks come to them, locating their tanks in hull-down positions that are difficult to spot and attack but allowing accurate long-range fire to be launched. This capability came from Israeli use of British and US tanks offering a gun depression angle of as much as -10° compared with as little as -4° for the Soviet tanks used by their exponents.

Tank tactics

Another tank is still very much the primary target for a tank. The techniques and range of tank-killing have advanced very considerably through the use of more advanced guns firing more capable projectiles with the aid of computer fire-control systems based on capable sights, laser rangefinders and sensors for ambient conditions, but the tactics have changed comparatively little.

Israeli tankers abandon their knocked-out Centurion tank after a clash with Arab forces. Such tanks have to be taken off the battlefield as quickly as possible in order that they can be safely repaired and returned to action.

the armoured ambush, and the Germans proved notably adept at this tactic. A notable exponent was SS-Hauptsturmführer Michael Wittman in a Tiger I heavy tank of the 101st SS Heavy Tank Battalion of the I SS Panzer Corps. On 12 June, Wittmann watched as elements of the British 7th Armoured Division moved toward Villers-Bocage. Using the hedgerows as cover, Wittmann trapped the British, who had to advance in column, and with other tanks during the course of the day destroyed 20 Cromwell and four Sherman Firefly tanks, three light tanks, three scout cars and one halftrack. Wittmann was himself killed on 9 July when his Tiger was attacked by five Canadian Sherman tanks, but by then he had been credited with the destruction of 138 tanks and 132 anti-tank guns.

Israeli tactics

In the years after World War II the Israeli army has emerged as the most battle-experienced force in the world, and has proved its capabilities in five major campaigns against its Arab neighbours. In most of these the tank has been the decisive land weapon, the Israelis having proved themselves masters of tank employment. As they have been outnumbered in their wars, the Israelis have often preferred

Even more than with infantry units, 'fire and move' or 'shoot and scoot' must be the mottoes of tank units, for the position of a firing tank is inevitably betrayed by blast, smoke and muzzle flash, the last being devastatingly evident at dusk or during the hours of darkness, which also offer little concealment in the face of the capabilities offered by modern sensors. Here the main gun of a US Army Abrams MBT is seen in action.

The growth of the gun
Tank armament 1918-45

The armament carried by tanks changed extensively from the end of the Great War. Initially infantry support weapons, armed with conventional artillery pieces, the tank developed a new role as destroyer of other tanks. Armour-piercing capability therefore came to be the prime requirement of the tank gun.

The tanks of World War I were fitted with whatever armament was to hand when they were designed. For the British that meant modified naval 6-pdr guns, for the Germans the very similar 57-mm (2.24-in) gun and for the French the famous '75'. Between the wars relatively little happened in the way of armament development, and the few innovations were introduced at a steady pace.

The first guns designed from the outset for tank use were developed in conjunction with towed anti-tank guns. They used almost identical barrels and fired essentially similar ammunition. Typical of these was the German 37-mm (1.46-in) gun from Rheinmetall. Introduced during the late 1920s, at a time when Germany was supposed to have no tanks, the 37-mm gun had a relatively long barrel and fired a solid shot. The shot was propelled by a comparatively powerful charge and the long barrel gave the propellant gases enough time to build up to a great pressure and so force the projectile out of the muzzle at high velocity. On arrival at the target armour the combination of the dense shot and the energy derived from its mass and velocity punched a hole through the armour into the tank interior, where it was supposed to bang around causing considerable damage.

French tank guns

In 1939 nearly all the tank guns in service relied on this simple principle. The Germans and the Americans both used very similar guns on most of their tanks, while the French relied on a heavier 47-mm (1.85-in) calibre working on the same principle. Some French tanks used short-barrelled guns developed from the trench guns of World War I. These had only limited anti-armour capability, and the same could be said of the short 75-mm (2.95-in) guns fitted to some German and French heavy tanks. Only the Soviet Union had any really heavy tank guns, for even in 1940 they were fitting high-velocity 76.2-mm (3-in) guns to their new designs.

Hollow-charge shells

All these guns relied upon kinetic energy (i.e. force) for their effectiveness. But by 1940 there was available a new form of anti-armour weapon that used chemical energy. This was the hollow-charge shell, which generates a forward-moving jet of high-temperature gas and vaporised metal as it strikes the target's armour. The jet of flame literally burns or melts its way through the armour to set fire to the interior, and for a while this type of round seemed to have definite advantages over the kinetic-energy projectile. This period lasted for some years before it was fully appreciated that hollow-charge warheads were most effective at low terminal velocities and the weapons that produced these velocities generally lacked the range or the horizontal flightpaths that tank gunners required. As a result, designers reverted to the kinetic-energy gun.

The main problem for the gun was that between 1940 and 1945 tank armour increased in leaps and bounds. To give an example from the German stable, the early PzKpfw II had bow armour that was 30 mm (1.18 in) thick, whereas only a few years later the PzKpfw VI Tiger II had massive 100-mm (3.94-in) frontal armour. The small tank guns

The only way for most Allied tanks to guarantee a knock out of the powerful PzKpfw VI Tiger was to get up close, a hazardous operation considering the German tank's 88-mm main gun.

SHERMAN FIREFLY: THE BRITISH SOLUTION

By 1944, the standard 75-mm gun fitted to the ubiquitous M4 Sherman was considerably outclassed by the armour appearing on the German Tiger and Panther tanks. The British solution was to fit the heaviest possible anti-tank gun to the Sherman. The resulting Sherman Firefly was thus armed with a 17-pdr gun that proved capable of knocking out Panzers fom a reasonable distance during the battle for Normandy in 1944.

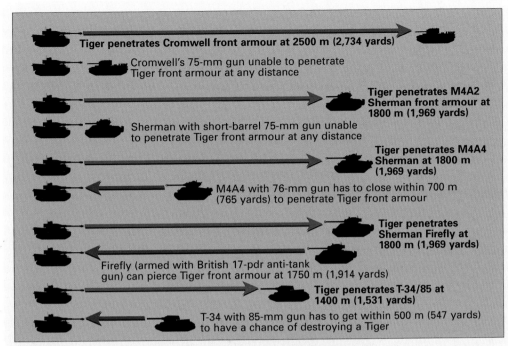

Tiger penetrates Cromwell front armour at 2500 m (2,734 yards)

Cromwell's 75-mm gun unable to penetrate Tiger front armour at any distance

Tiger penetrates M4A2 Sherman front armour at 1800 m (1,969 yards)

Sherman with short-barrel 75-mm gun unable to penetrate Tiger front armour at any distance

Tiger penetrates M4A4 Sherman at 1800 m (1,969 yards)

M4A4 with 76-mm gun has to close within 700 m (765 yards) to penetrate Tiger front armour

Tiger penetrates Sherman Firefly at 1800 m (1,969 yards)

Firefly (armed with British 17-pdr anti-tank gun) can pierce Tiger front armour at 1750 m (1,914 yards)

Tiger penetrates T-34/85 at 1400 m (1,531 yards)

T-34 with 85-mm gun has to get within 500 m (547 yards) to have a chance of destroying a Tiger

TIGER I: TANK-KILLING FROM A DISTANCE

The PzKpfw VI Tiger I was armed with a superb 88-mm gun that could outrange and penetrate more armour than almost any other tank gun of Word War II, with the exception of the Ango-American hybrid Sherman Firefly. Tigers were also heavily protected, the armour plate in the front of the turret and in the front of the hull being over 100mm (3.94in) thick.

Below: The turret gun of the M3 Lee medium tank was typical of tank armament in the years preceding World War II. The 37-mm was soon found to have insufficient power to deal with the new thickness of armour appearing in Europe. As a stopgap the Americans provided their new tank with a sponson-mounted 75-mm gun which proved reasonably effective.

57 mm (1.97 or 2.24 in), but this turned out to be only an interim solution until the 75-mm or 76.2-mm bracket was reached. Even this was not enough for the Germans and the Soviets, who went one better still and built 88-mm (3.46-in) and 85-mm (3.35-in) guns respectively.

Armour penetration

It was around this point that physical laws made themselves felt, and it was soon learned that simply increasing the projectile size did not necessarily produce an increase in armour penetration power; a 75-mm projectile fired at a high velocity could have better penetration characteristics than the equivalent 88-mm projectile, but the 88-mm shot could maintain its power over longer ranges. By 1945 operational ranges for tank combat had increased from the short 200 or 300 m (220 or 330 yards) of 1940 to well over 2000 m (2,185 yards) by 1945. Thus the big gun ruled.

Red Army destroyers

By 1945 the Soviets had placed 100-mm (3.94-in) guns into tank destroyers and a 122-mm (4.8-in) monster into the turret of the IS-2 heavy tank. These were exceptions. The Allies had decided upon 3-in as being the maximum practical limit for their medium tanks and it was left to the M26 heavy tank to carry the 90-mm (3.54-in) gun that was the largest in-service tank gun in the Allied armies. The Germans stuck to the '88', and in the 8.8-cm KwK 43 they were able to field possibly the finest all-round tank gun of the war years.

were unable to make any impression upon such thick carapaces, so the only solution was to produce guns that were larger in calibre to fire a larger shot, and longer in the barrel to increase the muzzle velocity even further. Tungsten was introduced to provide a denser projectile that could impart yet more kinetic energy, and many ballistic ploys were devised to ensure that the projectile metal would not shatter on impact. Ballistic caps for the projectile nose were one solution to this phenomenon.

Thus gun calibres increased from the original 37 mm to around 50 or

British Army soldiers pass a PzKpfw V Panther knocked out during the Normandy campaign. On the Eastern Front the Panther's 75-mm main gun was able to tackle the T-34 and its armour was proof against most of the guns it encountered. However, the massed Panzer forces gathered for the Normandy offensive proved vulnerable to Allied aircraft, whose armour-piercing rockets could knock out any German tank.

Firepower
Battlefield guns

Tank warfare has always been a battle between offence and defence. As armour becomes thicker, guns have become more and more powerful, firing sophisticated ammunition with ever-increasing penetration power.

Above: Typically, muzzle velocity for a projectile leaving a tank gun can be up to 1600 metres per second – which is twice as fast as a rifle bullet.

Being able to destroy opposing tanks has always been a primary task of armoured fighting vehicles. Initially, armour-piercing (AP) shells were full-bore projectiles with hardened tips, which were designed to smash through the relatively thin armour plate protecting enemy tanks. As fighting vehicles grew larger, and armour became thicker, more and more effort was required to smash through into the vehicle's vulnerable interior.

During World War II, guns had to become bigger and longer, and the difference between the 37-mm (1.4-in) and 47-mm (1.8-in) guns that armies used in 1939 and the 88-mm (3.5-in) and 122-mm (4.8-in) guns that dominated the Eastern Front in 1945 was astounding.

Sabot rounds

After the war, a new concept was developed. If you decrease the size of the projectile, while maintaining its density and great speed, then its armour-piercing ability is increased. However, to obtain high projectile speed you need a big gun, and firing small projectiles accurately from a large-calibre weapon is impossible. The solution was the sabot. This involved encasing the small projectile in a discardable 'boot' or 'sabot', which filled the breech of the gun and acted like a normal shell. Once clear of the muzzle, the sabot falls away, leaving the thin, penetrating projectile racing away at high speed.

Armour-piercing rounds are not usually explosive. They are dense projectiles fired at high velocities, using sheer speed and kinetic energy to punch through armour and wreak havoc in the inner spaces of an armoured vehicle.

Penetrators

The harder the projectile, the more effective it is. After the war, tungsten carbide was used in place of the original steel, but while hard and dense, it is also brittle and will shatter, especially when hitting sloped armour. The addition of a more malleable tungsten alloy cap decreased the chances of the round shattering. Early Soviet FSDS (fin-stabilised discarding sabot) rounds were simply made of steel, but since the 1970s most penetrators have been made of tungsten-nickel-copper alloys. In the United States, penetrators are made from

Tanks kill tanks

The primary purpose of tanks is to engage and defeat other tanks. The simplest way of penetrating an enemy's armour is to fire a small, extremely hard projectile at very high speed, its kinetic energy being enough to smash its way through into the target by brute force.

Above: The three main types of anti-tank round all have different ways of penetrating armour: HEAT rounds use an explosively-forged jet of molten metal to punch through into the interior of the tank.

PROJECTILES V ARMOUR

The never-ending battle between tank firepower and tank protection swings first one way and then the other. Currently, the latest laminated armours have given protection the edge, though, as always, gun designers are looking at ways to increase the penetrating powers of their projectiles.

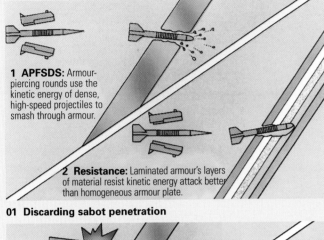

1 APFSDS: Armour-piercing rounds use the kinetic energy of dense, high-speed projectiles to smash through armour.

2 Resistance: Laminated armour's layers of material resist kinetic energy attack better than homogeneous armour plate.

01 Discarding sabot penetration

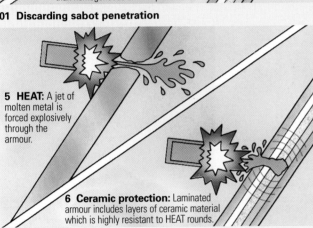

5 HEAT: A jet of molten metal is forced explosively through the armour.

6 Ceramic protection: Laminated armour includes layers of ceramic material which is highly resistant to HEAT rounds.

03 High-explosive shaped-charge

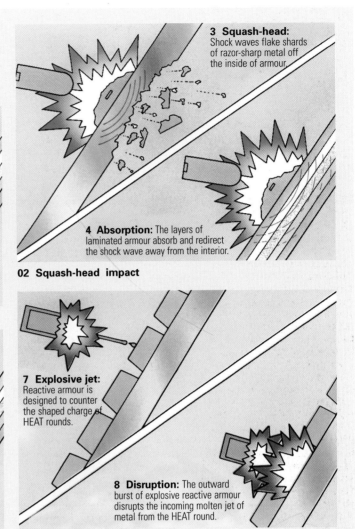

3 Squash-head: Shock waves flake shards of razor-sharp metal off the inside of armour.

4 Absorption: The layers of laminated armour absorb and redirect the shock wave away from the interior.

02 Squash-head impact

7 Explosive jet: Reactive armour is designed to counter the shaped charge of HEAT rounds.

8 Disruption: The outward burst of explosive reactive armour disrupts the incoming molten jet of metal from the HEAT round.

04 Reactive armour protection

depleted uranium, a non-radioactive by-product from the extraction of U-235 for nuclear power-stations. Uranium is the densest naturally-occurring substance, and it also has pyrophoric properties. This means that during armour penetration it will ignite, adding to the destruction within the target. Unfortunately, even non-radioactive uranium is poisonous, and since its use during the Gulf War, serious questions are being asked about its effect on the soldiers exposed to such weaponry.

HESH and HEAT

High explosive plastic (HEP) rounds are used by many armies. Known to the British as HESH, or high-explosive squash-head, these deform on the surface of the target's armour before detonating. The idea is to generate a shock wave in the armour, breaking off razor-sharp scabs of metal on the inner surface to the detriment of anybody inside the vehicle.

Guided weapons do not reach the immense velocities required to penetrate a tank's armour by kinetic energy alone. They instead use high-explosive anti-tank, or HEAT, warheads. These consist of a conical explosive charge. The explosive is shaped so that when detonated it melts a metal plate into a thin jet, which is projected forwards at phenomenally high velocities. This explosively-powered jet has the kinetic energy necessary to smash through normal armour, but laminated armour is less affected.

Tanks also fire HEAT rounds, but because their warheads are limited in size to the calibre of the tank gun, they lack the penetrating power of larger missile warheads. These are most often used against lightly-armoured targets.

Right: These are the principal types of gun and machine-gun ammunition carried by modern main battle tanks, together with some used by lighter armour.

Tank ammunition

1 120-mm APFSDS
2 120-mm HEAT
3 120-mm AP
4 Explosive charge
5 Propellant
6 76-mm
7 30-mm discarding sabot

Whether stationary or on the move, a main battle tank, such as the Cold War-era British Chieftain seen here, depends for its operational effectiveness and survivability on seeing, engaging and hitting an enemy tank before the latter can fire its first round.

Fire-control systems
The aim: first-round hit

Battle tanks are easily detectable when they fire, and the primary objective of the fire-control system is to maximise the chances of a first-round hit and disable if not destroy the enemy tank before it can respond.

For many years tank guns were aimed with the aid of a telescope linked to the main armament, the gunner using manual controls to align the sight (and hence the gun) with the target. This required constant practice and meant that several rounds had to be fired in order to hit the target, even at the relatively short distances involved, usually under 1000 m (1,095 yards). The optical sight did not take into account such vital factors as wind speed and direction, the velocity of the ammunition, and the ambient temperature, all of which affect accuracy. Initially, optical rangefinders of the stadiametric or coincidence type were used to find the exact range of the target, and this information was transferred to a mechanical computer for calculation of the weapon elevation required to hit the target. These rangefinders were difficult to operate and required a considerable amount of training, and armies in the Middle and Far East found these especially difficult to operate.

In the 1950s the UK developed the ranging machine-gun (RMG) concept, in which a 0.5-in (12.7-mm) machine-gun was mounted co-axially with the Centurion's 105-mm (4.13-in) L7 gun. A similar weapon was fitted to the subsequent Chieftain with its 120-mm (4.72-mm) gun, but as the RMG was effective only to 1830 m (2,000 yards) the full potential of the gun, which is effective out to well over 2060 m (2,250 yards), could not be exploited. The RMG was later replaced by a Barr & Stroud Tank Laser Sight with a laser rangefinder accurate to 5 m (16 ft) at all battlefield ranges.

Fire-control systems

There are many types of fire-control system available for MBTs today, but space permits brief descriptions of only two of these, the British Improved Fire Control System and the Belgian SABCA. All British Army Challengers have the IFCS which, coupled with the already installed TLS, allows the tank to engage and hit stationary targets at a range of 3000 m (3,280 yards) and moving targets at a range of 2000 m (2,185 yards) with a high probability of securing a

TARGET ACQUISITION

In a typical anti-tank engagement, the tank commander selects the target which is then acquired by the gunner in his tank laser sight. The gunner lays his muzzle bore sight on the target and selects the main armament (A). The tracking process continues as the laser measures the target's range and the computer calculates the ballistic trajectory needed to destroy the target (B). The computer applies corrections to compensate for wind, temperature, and target movement factors and shifts the ballistic aiming mark (C). The gunner finally retains the target in the aiming ellipse and fires (D).

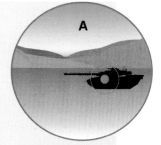
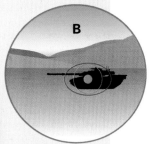
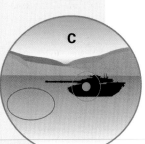
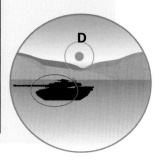

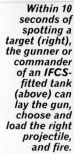

Within 10 seconds of spotting a target (right), the gunner or commander of an IFCS-fitted tank (above) can lay the gun, choose and load the right projectile, and fire.

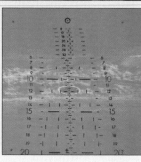

Tanks and other armoured fighting vehicles are capable systems and therefore high-value targets. Tanks are well protected, but their best defence is seeing and destroying the enemy before he can fire. Mountainous terrain is one additional factor that makes fire control all the more important for this Swiss Pz 68 tank (rear).

rangefinder, seven sensors, an analogue computer and an optical sight. The sensors measure ambient and ammunition temperatures, air pressure, gun barrel wear, cross wind, trunnion cant or tilt, and rate of turret traverse. The computer determines the angles between the line of side and the axis of the gun, and the output is transformed into a displacement of cross hairs in the gunner's sight. When the cross hairs are brought back onto the target, the gun is laid correctly onto the target in elevation and azimuth.

Vital training

The widespread introduction of these fire-control systems, taken together with the use of gun-stabilisation systems, has enabled most tanks to hit their targets with the first shot under most operational conditions. But this can only be achieved if the tank crew carries out constant and effective training and is backed up by good workshop facilities in order that any faults in the system can be quickly traced and rectified. For this reason many companies are now offering tank gunnery training systems to enable tank crews to practise tank versus tank engagements without the use of expensive live ammunition and the wear that this causes on even more expensive gun barrels.

first-round hit.

The IFCS has a Marconi 12-12P digital computer which automatically gathers and updates information from a number of sensors for factors such as wind direction, angle of sight, charge temperature, barrel wear, target displacement and ammunition type. It then calculates the ballistic solution and correct laying offsets for each target engagement and controls the automatic laying of the gun in azimuth (line) and elevation (including the tracking of moving targets) in readiness to fire. In the Challenger both the commander and gunner can lay and fire the 120-mm gun, the commander having override control. The IFCS has been fitted to a number of other vehicles for trials purposes and has also been installed in the Khalid MBT for Jordan.

Sweden's Strv 103 is turretless. As a result its traverse is set by pivoting the vehicle on its tracks, its elevation being set by adjusting the hydropneumatic suspension, with the driver acting as the gunner.

It is worth noting that during one trial the crew of a Chieftain fitted with the IFCS obtained nine first round hits within 53 seconds at ranges of between 1600 and 2900 m (1,750 and 3,170 yards) in a 110° arc.

The Belgian SABCA fire-control system has already been fitted to the Leopard 1 tanks of the Australian, Belgian and Canadian armies. It consists of a laser

Below: The French Leclerc MBT is equipped with a roof-mounted SAGEM day/night sight for the commander. The sight incorporates a thermal imager, allowing for passive target engagements.

Above: The interior of the British Army's Challenger 2 MBT showing the commander's and gunner's stations. The Challenger 2's 120-mm L30 main gun is fully stabilised and is provided with 30° of elevation.

Firepower, protection and mobility

Modern MBT design

Firepower, protection and mobility are the three primary factors that must be considered in any tank design: the relationship between these elements ultimately decides whether or not the tank is successful.

Above: Protection for the Leclerc includes advanced modular armour for the turret and hull. Conventional defensive aids include banks of nine smoke/decoy dischargers that can be fitted on each side of the turret.

Left: Tank designers aim to create exactly the right balance of firepower, protection and mobility in a single hard-hitting but survivable vehicle. The AMX-30 is notably fast but relatively lightly armoured.

Firepower allows the tank to undertake its primary offensive role, protection helps to ensure the tank's survivability in the face of the enemy's weapons, and mobility provides the tank with the ability to reach and then move round the battlefield to make use of its own offensive elements and also avoid the enemy's fire through active employment of manoeuvre or passive adoption of a protected position.

Tank designers have on occasion sought to maximise one or two of these features by minimising the third, but without exception these efforts have not yielded a gen-

uinely capable tank. What is required, therefore, is a judicious balance of the features, although within this balance one can detect national preferences: the British, for example, emphasise firepower and protection over mobility, whereas the French and Germans opt for firepower and mobility at the expense of protection. The US and Russian designs have generally sought to equalise the importance attached to the three factors.

Modern firepower generally means a gun of a calibre between 105 and 125 mm (4.13 and 4.92 in), smaller calibres generally being found in

rifled guns and larger calibres in smoothbore weapons optimised for the firing of fin-stabilised sub-calibre projectiles at very high muzzle velocities, maximising the chances of a kinetic-energy 'kill' of an opposing tank. Though the enemy tank remains the primary target of any tank, the need for tactical versatility demands the ability to fire other rounds. These include chemical-energy projectiles that provide a

capability against the full spectrum of battlefield targets including other armoured fighting vehicles.

Fire-control systems

The successful engagement of targets, especially at longer ranges and with a high probability of scoring a first-round hit, depends on the tank's fire-control system. This has to 'know' the position of the firer and the target, as well as a host of ambient conditions, with great precision for an accurate fire solution to be calculated. Thus the tank's

Arguably the best MBT in the world, the Leopard 2 is highly mobile with excellent cross-country mobility and has one of the finest tank guns in the Rheinmetall 120-mm smoothbore. Armour protection may be its only shortfall.

The emphasis in British tanks such as the Chieftain – a Chieftain Mk 5 is seen here in action with the Kuwait Free Brigade during the 1991 Gulf War – and the later Challenger is on first-class firepower and protection. This results in reduced but still adequate mobility.

Russian tanks such as the T-80 aim to combine the requirements of firepower, protection and mobility equally. Defensive features include skirts to protect the upper run of the tracks, and ERA to shield the most threatened frontal parts of the hull and turret.

gun is stabilised in two planes to create a stable firing platform and a number of sensors provide data about weapon and local weather conditions and also the target's position, range and movement.

Active/passive defence

No matter how effective a gun and its fire-control system may be, they cannot be brought to bear on any target if the vehicle carrying them is damaged. This is the province of protection, in which the armour is the single most important element. Tank armour has traditionally been of steel, either cast or rolled. Armour thickness and disposition armour reflects the nature and extent of the threat the designer perceives from any

quarter, and has in general been thickest over the frontal arc. However, the development of specialised mines and anti-armour missiles has demanded the thickening of the lower and upper armour, and the threat of high-velocity projectiles and low-velocity hollow-charge warheads has been reflected in the adoption of spaced, laminate and explosive reactive armour. Further protection is

provided by smoke-grenade launchers, fire- and explosion-suppressing systems and, increasingly, electronic systems to defeat missiles' guidance systems.

The whole package of armament and armour, together with the crew to operate them, has to be as highly mobile as is possible. Despite their great weights, therefore, tanks are provided with powerful engines dri-

ving the tracks though advanced transmission systems. The engine is normally part of a powerpack designed for rapid replacement under field conditions, and is generally a diesel or gas turbine burning low-volatility fuel for greater specific range and improved survivability when hit. Automatic transmissions are becoming increasingly common to ease driver workload.

TANK DEFENCE: ACTIVE PROTECTION

While traditional armour can provide a high degree of passive protection for the tank, more advanced technology has opened the way for the creation of more active defences. These tackle the sighting and guidance systems on which any enemy is reliant for the effective use of their weapons. The oldest and simplest of these outgoing defences is the smoke generator (right), which can create dense and thoroughly opaque clouds of smoke through which the enemy cannot find or track the target as it moves into cover or out of range. This represents one chemical counter to the enemy's optical and optronic sensors, but more advanced by a considerable

degree are the infra-red jammer (above) and the laser sighting jammer (left). These are designed at best to disable, or at worst to confuse, the IR and laser systems on which many of today's rangefinding and missile-guidance systems are reliant, and therefore decoy missiles away from the target tank.

Tank tactics
Rules of engagement

The key to the tank's survival and utility in combat is mutual support: at every tactical level moving tanks are always covered by halted tanks, resulting in a leapfrog movement, using all available natural cover.

Tanks are shock action weapons, but as the Israelis learned during 1973 – in a costly relearning of other nations' experiences in World War II and later – the tank must be supported by infantry. It is the tank that leads the advance, and the advance to contact is a well proven tactic to retake lost ground, to force an enemy to withdraw or to re-establish a border.

In British practice, which is typical of Western concepts, the tactic is practised at brigade level. Three battle groups are spread out with two leading and one in reserve. In each group two 14-tank squadrons lead, with the third in reserve with a company of mechanised infantry. A squadron comprises four troops of three tanks and two HQ tanks. The usual formation is two squadrons up under the squadron leader and two down under the second in command. Within the troop no tank moves unless it is covered, so the best way to advance is to leapfrog by troop: one tank moves as the other two cover it, the other two moving only after this tank has gone 'firm' and can provide cover.

An advance is undertaken in bounds, this being 'a tactical feature that may be held if necessary, and the next tactical feature which enables supporting tanks to give cover'. This translates as a ridge, or a fold in the ground

The modern MBT is large and well protected, but nonetheless vulnerable to missiles and fire from other tanks. Thus the use of any and all methods of concealment is vital to survival. This M1 Abrams is seen in action during Operation Desert Storm.

into which the tank can move and stop so the forward rise provides cover. But the tank must be able to see over the ridge and, if necessary, shoot over the tanks in front of it.

There should not be more than 1000 m (1,095 yards) between bounds. In providing cover for a tank to its front, a

Left: The commander of the tank is seated higher than the gunner and has larger fields of vision from the plenitude of devices in his traversing cupola atop the turret. The gunner has a smaller and lower vision arc, but once cued by the commander can bring higher magnification levels into play as he lays the gun.

Below: A tank on the move is a highly visible object under most conditions, and at the same time is also a poorer gun platform. The object of every commander is therefore to find cover in which he can halt his tank and search for the enemy.

Above: Two tanks on the move are highly visible and therefore vulnerable, but the commander of any enemy tank must be aware that somewhere there is a stationary tank providing cover.

Right: If a tank like this Belgian Leopard 1 does have to move in the open, it is absolutely vital that the members of the crew maintain a watch right around the tank for any sign of a potential attacker.

tank has to cover the 1000 m to its fellow's position and another 1000 m to its front: 2000 m (2,185 yards) is the usual engagement distance.

Movement between bounds must be fast, for a moving tank is an easy target and a poor platform for accurate fire. When a tank on the back of the bound has to move forward, a primary rule is not to drive straight ahead, but to reverse out of the fire position or else an enemy who has spotted the tank will know exactly where it is and will be able to fire as it moves, and it will be going over a skyline and probably silhouetted against the sky.

Reverse out of trouble

When moving into a position, the driver should put the vehicle into reverse so that it can pull back immediately. Thus, when moving, the driver can reverse off the slope and into cover. If he is on a ridge, the driver gets right into the valley and drives along it to its open end, round which he moves keeping to the low ground until reaching the ordained bound.

The driver pulls up the slope slowly, in a low gear to reduce exhaust emission, until the commander can just see over the top of the slope.

Here the commander can use his sight or, if not closed down, binoculars. If the ground is clear, the commander tells the gunner to have the driver move up the slope until the gunner can see the ground in his own sight, making it possible to shoot at anything that pops up. The commander scans his arcs and, when he thinks it clear, reports that he is firm, freeing the tank that was covering him to move.

The mnemonic CRAB-MEAL (Cover, Routes, Arcs, Background, Mutual support, Enemy, Air, Landmarks) encompasses it all: the tank needs a position that gives cover; it must have a good route into and out of the cover; it must be able to cover the entire arc from it; the background should disguise the tank's position; the tank must be able to cover other tanks and be covered by them; the position must face the enemy; the tank should try to get some cover from the air; and it should not choose to stop by the only obvious landmark for some distance as the enemy will watch this.

ENGAGING THE ENEMY: ATTACK AND DEFENCE

Hull-down position: (left) The hull is the single largest component of a tank, and carries the mobility system (engine, fuel, transmission, suspension and tracks) as well as the main bulk of the ammunition. Wherever possible, therefore, the hull must be protected in a hull-down position.

Reduced visual signature: (below) The hull-down position significantly reduces the area of the tank visible to an enemy, especially when only the commander's vision devices are left exposed. However, in this position the main gun can be fired only if it has a good depression angle.

The tank has only a modest ground pressure as a result of the fact that its weight is well spread by the large track area in contact with the ground. This gives the tank better mobility than a man on foot and wheeled vehicles, and opens the possibility for a tank to use many types of terrain for both movement and concealment. The latter is as important in attack as in defence, for a halted tank is a far better gun platform than a moving tank. The worst of all terrains for tank operations, even though it provides for fast movement, is country that is both open and flat, for here there are few opportunities for the crew to find places in which to conceal their tank, either offensively or defensively.

Development
of the APC into the IFV

The mobile battlefield that has been evolving since the end of World War I has required the infantry to match the mobility of other arms. For most of that time, the armoured personnel carrier has delivered the soldier to the front line, but combat has still taken place on foot. Recent developments, however, have concentrated on allowing infantrymen to fight from specially developed vehicles alongside tanks.

Mobility was restored to the battlefield in the later part of World War I, largely as a result of the British introduction of the tank in 1916. Then in 1917 the British used tanks in the supply role to carry up to the front line urgently needed supplies of ammunition and food, and sometimes to carry troops forward. In the following year a Tank Mk V was modified specifically for use as a troop carrier, its side sponsons being removed and the vehicle fitted with sliding doors and seats. Similar conversions were carried out on other marks in France during the same year, and some examples were used in the troop-carrying role in the Battle of Amiens during August 1918. The end of the war halted further development of such troop-carrying armoured vehicles.

In the 1920s and 1930s the major powers experimented with mechanised forces, with perhaps the USSR, UK and Germany taking the lead. These mechanised forces normally comprised tanks,

tankettes, infantry carried in lorries, and towed artillery weapons and anti-aircraft guns. Some countries also started the development of tracked vehicles for towing the artillery, and some self-propelled artillery weapons were also designed.

Fast-moving infantry
The infantry was taken as near to its objective as possible in trucks, whereupon it would dismount and follow the tanks on foot. The Germans, however, understood the requirements of mechanised forces more fully and developed not only tanks and mobile assault guns but also half-track armoured personnel carriers (APCs) to

Left: The AMX-10P MICV typifies modern personnel carriers. With the driver in front, and the gunner and commander in the two-man turret armed with a 20-mm cannon, the vehicle carries eight fully equipped troops as well as MILAN anti-tank missiles. Also typical is the way in which the original vehicle has been adapted for a variety of roles, ranging from ambulance through artillery observation to fire support.

Left: Although the M2 Bradley IFV has been introduced into the US Army, the M113 will remain in service well into the 21st century. At present very large numbers are still in use for a wide variety of roles. The M113 (left) of the 1st Cavalry is here preceded by two M577 command posts during Exercise 'Reforger '83'.

Below: The M2 Bradley allows infantry to fight from within the protection of their vehicle. This retouched photograph indicates the ports for 5.56-mm (0.219-in) rifle fire, together with the 25-mm main weapon and 7.62-mm (0.3-in) co-axial machine-gun. With TOW anti-tank missiles mounted on its turret, the Bradley has the capability to tackle everything from infantry on foot through light armoured vehicles to main battle tanks.

carry the infantry and its equipment. These highly mobile forces outmanoeuvred Allied formations in France during 1940.

The USSR completely neglected APCs during World War II. By the time the US entered the war in 1941 the half-track APC was already in production, over 40,000 of these M2 and M3 vehicles being built in countless configurations including self-propelled anti-aircraft guns and tank destroyers. The main drawbacks of the half-track were that its front axle was unpowered, which limited its cross-country

performance, and that its open-topped troop compartment left the infantry partially vulnerable.

To enable troops to be carried under fire, Canada took the turret off its Ram tanks and converted them into Ram Kangaroo APCs. So successful were these vehicles that similar conversions were carried out on 105-mm (4.13-in) M7 Priest self-propelled howitzers and Sherman tanks to create the Priest Kangaroo and Sherman Kangaroo APCs.

For much of World War II the British army used the Bren Gun Carrier and its rel-

Right: Most modern APCs and their MICV, IFV and ACV relatives are fitted with turreted armament (most generally in a power-operated turret and fitted with stabilisation and fire-control systems) and a power-operated rear ramp/door to facilitate the troops' speedy exit.

Below: The Warrior, which is the UK's primary armoured combat vehicle, carries an infantry squad and is well armed with a 30-mm RARDEN cannon in its power-operated turret. Unusually, the gun is not stabilised.

IFVs such as the M2 Bradley combine high mobility, moderately good protection, light but useful firepower, and the ability to carry a squad of infantry, or otherwise an anti-tank missile team or the like.

atives, mainly to carry the mortars and machine-guns of infantry battalions, although there were also developed numerous specialised versions such as flame-thrower vehicles, command/radio vehicles, and observation post vehicles.

World War II dispelled any remaining doubts that the infantry should be carried only in unarmoured trucks, and most of the major powers soon began developing true APCs.

Most of the APCs developed up to the 1950s were designed mainly to transport infantry across country, where the embarked infantry dismounted to fight on foot. These APCs were normally provided with sufficient armour to protect their crews and the embarked troops from small arms fire and shell splinters, and for armament were provided with a single 7.62-mm (0.3-in) or similar machine-gun in an unprotected mount.

Greater capabilities

By the 1960s and 1970s, the requirement had changed and new vehicles such as the West German Marder and Soviet BMP started to emerge. Not only did these

introduce much superior armour protection, but they also pioneered full provision for the troops to fire their weapons from within the vehicle if required, thereby enabling a rapid rate of advance to be maintained. They are also fitted with more powerful weapons, a 73-mm (2.87-in) low-pressure gun in the case of the BMP

and a 20-mm cannon in the case of the Marder. The provision of more powerful armament has enabled such mechanised infantry combat vehicles (MICVs) or infantry fighting vehicles (IFVs) not only to engage enemy troops but, more importantly, other armoured vehicles on the battlefield, especially the enemy's APCs. The 25-mm cannon of the American M2 Bradley IFV and the 30-mm cannon of the British Warrior armoured combat vehicle (ACV) can defeat the protection of any Russian vehicle of this type, and also penetrate the side armour of some main battle tanks. The anti-

tank missiles carried by the BMP and Bradley allow the vehicles, in theory, to engage enemy tanks before the latter can fire on the missile-firing vehicle.

Vehicles such as the M2 and Warrior are, however, much more expensive than the vehicles they supplemented or replaced (the M113 and the FV432), and cannot replace these types on a one-for-one basis. The new vehicles normally have a system enabling them to operate in an NBC-contaminated area, and also a full range of passive night-vision equipment to enable their crews to see and fight in darkness.

The BMP-1 was a first-generation Soviet IFV, and key features of the type's layout were the one-man turret with a 73-mm (2.87-in) gun and 'Sagger' missile launcher in the centre, the eight troops in the rear, and the commander seated behind the driver.

Rolls-Royce armoured car

When the Royal Naval Air Service went to war in 1914, it sent a variegated squadron of aircraft and vehicles to France and Belgium. Once there, some of the naval officers noted the way in which the Belgians were using armoured cars to harry the advancing Germans and to carry out raiding and other missions, and decided to join in. Within a few days some of the **Rolls-Royce Silver Ghost** touring cars used by the RNAS were converted in Dunkirk to carry armour plating on the sides. A single machine-gun was carried behind the driver. The Admiralty noted the success of the conversion and gave its sanction to the design of proper armoured cars based on the Silver Ghost chassis, and the first of these official designs was in France by the end of 1914.

Great success

The official Rolls-Royce armoured car, sometimes known as the **Armoured Car, Rolls-Royce (1914 Admiralty Turreted Pattern)**, was a straightforward conversion of the

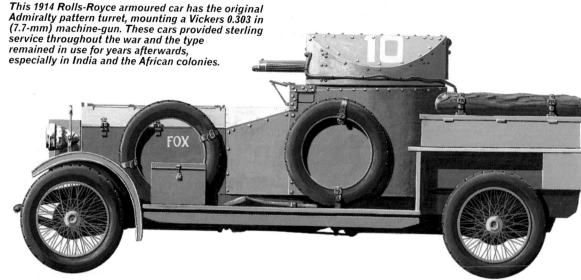

This 1914 Rolls-Royce armoured car has the original Admiralty pattern turret, mounting a Vickers 0.303 in (7.7-mm) machine-gun. These cars provided sterling service throughout the war and the type remained in use for years afterwards, especially in India and the African colonies.

A Rolls-Royce armoured car and its crew are seen at a Guards Division casualty evacuation point near Guillemont during September 1916 when the Somme Offensive was at its height. Note the anti-mud chains around the tyres of the rear wheels and the lack of front mudguards.

civilian Silver Ghost tourer with a turret and armour added. The springs were strengthened to take the extra weight but that was all the modification required on the chassis. The armour extended all around the chassis, and the turret, which mounted a Vickers or

Maxim machine-gun, had peculiar sloping sides rather like the shape of a bishop's mitre. The radiator had an armoured door and the roof armour on the turret could be removed if required. A small area behind the turret was left open to carry stores and a ground-mounted machine-gun. Once in service the Rolls-Royce armoured cars proved very successful, remaining in service until 1922. Maximum armour thickness was 9 mm (0.35 in).

By March 1915 the first RNAS armoured car squadrons were in France, most of them equipped with the Rolls-Royce. Before that the RNAS armoured cars carried out some patrols and reconnaissance work along the French and Belgian coastal areas until the 'Race to the Sea' reached the Channel coast and trench warfare became the norm. Once that was in progress there was little enough for the Rolls-Royces to do and as more squadrons were established they were used for anti-invasion patrols along the east coast of England. When the first formal armoured car squadrons were sent to France they had little to do, so eventually these RNAS armoured car squadrons were disbanded, the cars being handed over to a generally uninterested British army.

Rolls-Royce armoured cars were thereafter used on other fronts and in overseas theatres of war such

as the North West Frontier in India, at Gallipoli (where they could accomplish nothing), German South West Africa (where they accomplished much during a campaign about which little is known) and in Uganda.

It was in the Western Desert and the Arabian peninsula that the Rolls-Royce armoured cars and a number of similar armoured tenders (like the armoured car but without the turret and used for carrying stores or personnel) made their greatest impact. There they proved to be remarkably reliable, fast and capable of crossing some very rough country.

The Rolls-Royce armoured cars soldiered on until 1922 when they began to be replaced by a modernised version, the **Armoured Car, Rolls-Royce (1920 Pattern)**. Even so, some of the old Pattern 1914 cars in service in India lasted until well into World War II.

SPECIFICATION	
Armoured Car, Rolls-Royce (1914 Admiralty Turreted Pattern)	engine
	Dimensions: length 5.03 m (16 ft 6 in); width 1.91 m (6 ft 3 in); height 2.55 m (8 ft 4.5 in)
Crew: 3 or 4	
Weight: 3.5 tons	
Powerplant: 30/37.3-kW (40/50-hp) Rolls-Royce petrol	**Performance:** maximum speed 95 km/h (60 mph); range 240 km (150 miles)

Lanchester armoured car

After the Rolls-Royce armoured car, the **Armoured Car, Lanchester (Admiralty Turreted Pattern)** was the most numerous in service with the Royal Naval Air Service (RNAS) armoured car squadrons that had sprung up by the end of 1914. Originally these armoured cars were supposed to provide support for the air

bases and to retrieve downed airmen, but it was not long before they were used in more offensive roles. By 1915 they were being organised into formal armoured car squadrons as part of a larger Royal Naval Armoured Car Division.

Sloping armour

In layout the Lanchester armoured car was very similar to the Rolls-Royce and also had a turret with sloping sides. However, the Lanchester had sloping armour over the front of the bonnet in place of the more angular bonnet of the Rolls-Royce. It was originally a civilian touring car but by the time the Admiralty designers had been at work, little of the original bodywork remained. However, the

engine was retained for not only did it provide a useful 44.7 kW (60 hp) but it had many advanced design features for its day, along with a very advanced epicyclic gearbox.

Spearhead

When the Royal Navy armoured cars were handed over to the army in August 1915 the latter decided that

the collection of designs it received was too varied for logistic and operational comfort. It therefore decided to standardise the Rolls-Royce design, and the Lanchesters were put to one side. They did not remain neglected for long, however, for in October 1915 they were gathered together in England. The following year they were organised as

No. 1 Squadron of the Royal Naval Armoured Car Division and sent to Russia. Once there, they took part in a number of campaigns about which little has been recorded. For much of the time the Lanchesters had to travel on their own wheels across a country where few roads existed. They were used in Persia, Romania and Galicia, operating in climates that varied from desert heat to near-Arctic conditions. But they kept going.

For much of their operational life the Lanchesters were used in a manner that anticipated what was later to become the norm in armoured warfare. They acted as the spearhead of large motorised columns carrying troops on armoured lorries and personnel trucks that ranged far and wide over the wastes of southern Russia and the Iraq

A Lanchester armoured car in 1914 RNAS markings. These vehicles never gained the fame accorded to the Rolls-Royce armoured cars, but at the time were just as important in service. Many with Royal Navy crews were extensively used in Russia in 1916 and 1917.

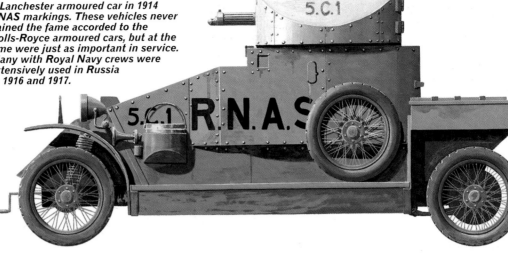

deserts. They acted as scouts, fire-support vehicles and general raiders, roles in which they proved reliable and fast.

The Lanchester remained with the Russians until the final failure of the Brusilov Offensive in mid-1917. Thereafter Russia sank into

the throes of internal disruption and revolution, and there was no part the Lanchester squadron could play in such internal con-

flicts. Thus they were shipped back to the United Kingdom with well over 53,000 miles added to their speedometer clocks.

Royal Navy Lanchester armoured cars in Russia during 1917. These vehicles motored thousands of miles in support of the Russians fighting the Germans and carried out scouting and raiding operations that covered many miles on all parts of the Russian front, including the Brusilov Offensive in mid-1917.

SPECIFICATION	
Armoured Car, Lanchester **(Admiralty Turreted Pattern)** **Crew:** 4 **Weight:** 4.8 tons **Powerplant:** one 45-kW (60-hp) Lanchester petrol engine	**Dimensions:** length 4.88 m (16 ft 0 in); width 1.93 m (6 ft 4 in); height 2.286 m (7 ft 6 in) **Performance:** maximum speed 80 km/h (50 mph); range 290 km (180 miles)

Autoblindo Mitragliatrice Lancia Ansaldo IZ Armoured car

The first **Lancia modello IZ** was not an armoured car but a small truck that had a form of expanding fireman's ladder mounted on the rear, which was used by 102-mm (4-in) artillery units for the observation of fire. While this was certainly a military function it was not long after, in 1915, that the truck was drastically adapted to become an armoured car known as the **Autoblindo Mitragliatrice Lancia Ansaldo IZ**.

For its day the IZ was quite an advanced design. Its layout was conventional, with the engine forward and the main driver's position behind a fully armoured sloping plate. The main fighting compartment was in a box structure at the rear, which mounted a squat round turret with a single machine-gun. On some later versions this turret arrangement was revised to accommodate a second but smaller turret on top of the first, enabling another machine-gun to be carried. A further variation was to place two machine-guns in the lower turret, so the IZ was quite heavily armed for a vehicle of its size

Prominent on the IZ were the twin steel rails that extended from the driver's position to a point below and in front of the wheels. These rails were intended for wire-cutting. Later versions had even more protection against wire by an extension of the armour over the wheels both at the front and rear.

For much of the war the Italian armoured car units could contribute little to the campaigns against Austria-Hungary as most of the fighting took place in mountainous. A small force of 39 IZ armoured cars did a certain amount of reconn-aissance along the Piave during the fighting along that front, and contributed to the

limited period of fluid fighting in the aftermath of the Austro-German break-through of 1917. After that ome were sent to North Africa for policing duties. By 1918 about 120 cars had been produced, remaining in use for some years thereafter. A few were handed over to Albania during the post-war period and long

remained the sole equipment for the small

armoured element of the new nation.

SPECIFICATION	
Autoblindo Mitragliatrice **Lancia Ansaldo IZ** **Crew:** 6 **Weight:** 3.8 tons **Powerplant:** one 26/30-kW (35/40-hp) petrol engine	**Dimensions:** length 5.40 m (17 ft 8⅜ in); width 1.824 m (6 ft 0 in); height with single turret 2.40 m (7 ft 10½ in) **Performance:** maximum speed 60 km/h (37 mph); range 300 km (186 miles)

Minerva Armoured car

The story of the Belgian **Minerva** armoured car is now little known outside Belgium. This is a pity as in many ways the Belgians were the progenitors of armoured car warfare and demonstrated to others how such vehicles could be used, so anticipating a type of mobile combat that was not to realise its full form until World War II.

Improvised armour

Almost as soon as the Germans invaded Belgium in August 1914, cavalry sweeps ahead of the main body of the German army were encountered by the Belgians. Usually the Germans heavily outnumbered the Belgians, who soon took to using the mobility of the motor car as a counter against German numbers.

By the end of the month, two Minerva touring cars were provided with improvised armour at the Cockerill works at Hoboken and sent into action. These early cars were simply commercial models with sheets of 4-mm (0.16-in) armour plating around the engine and sides, and with the top left open for a Hotchkiss machine-gun mounting.

Before very long the first two cars were followed by further examples with a

more formal armoured hull but retaining the same basic layout. With this small force the Belgians showed what armoured cars could do: acting originally as a form of motorised cavalry they carried out long reconnaissance missions, gathered intelligence of the enemy's movements, gave fire and other support to infantry attacks when possible, and also carried out long disruption missions behind the lines of the German advance.

It was perhaps the last type of mission that attracted most attention, for at that stage of the war the Germans were advancing or marching in open order across open country or along roads. The single machine-gun of a Minerva armoured car could create havoc in such conditions, and frequently did just that.

Much-copied

However, this period did not last long. By October 1914 the line of trenches had reached the Yser region, and there the Belgian army remained until 1918. The area was too wet and boggy for armoured cars to achieve anything useful and their period of immediate action passed. However, during the few weeks they had been in

action they had demonstrated to all who cared to learn what the armoured car could achieve. The Belgian example was copied directly by the British Royal Naval Air Service squadrons and the Germans also went ahead with their own designs for armoured cars.

Sterling service

While the Western Front was 'out' as far as Belgian armoured car units were concerned, a special Belgian armoured car unit was formed for service in Russia against the Germans. There the Belgian cars performed sterling service until

A section of Belgian Minerva armoured cars operates near Houthem in September 1917. The cars are all armed with Hotchkiss machine-guns, and the design had by 1917 been sufficiently formalised for spotlights to become standard.

they were eventually shipped home in 1918.

Once back in Belgium the units re-equipped, and in 1919 there appeared yet another version of the basic Minerva armoured car, this

time with an armoured turret. The old 1914 Minervas were retained in service, however, usually for use by the Gendarmerie, with which some were still in use as late as 1933.

SPECIFICATION	
Minerva armoured car	**Dimensions:** length 4.9 m (16 ft
Crew: 3 to 6	1 in); width 1.75 m (5 ft 9 in);
Weight: 4 tons	height 2.3 m (7 ft 6½ in)
Powerplant: one unknown petrol	**Performance:** maximum speed
engine	40 km/h (25 mph); range not known

Austin-Putilov Armoured cars

Although the vehicles known as the **Austin-Putilov** armoured cars had British origins they may be assumed to be Russian, as most of them were produced and used there.

In 1914 the Russian army was so short of equipment that it had to turn to the United Kingdom to supply armoured cars. Various types were involved but one of these was an Austin design, a fairly massive vehicle with twin turrets and solid-tyred wheels. Two types of hull were supplied, one of which had the armour over the driver's position arranged in such a way that it restricted the traverse of both of the gun turrets, each of which mounted a single Maxim machine-gun.

The bulk of the Austin-Putilov is apparent in this side view. Note the riveted armoured plates and the armoured cowls over the heavy machine-gun barrel jackets. These armoured cars were among the best the Russian army had.

Added weight

This early arrangement was soon altered in favour of a lower cab, but on this model the weight was increased by 1.16 tons. This weight increase was brought about mainly by the use of thicker (maximum 8 mm/0.315 in) chrome-steel armour and a revision of the driving arrangements. The original British design could be steered from the front only,

but the Russians wanted steering from the rear as well and the revisions required to accommodate this requirement added to the weight. This was not the only rearrangement demanded by the Russians, who soon found that the harsh Russian conditions were too much for the British vehicles, which broke down often.

Despite such problems, orders were placed for 200

Austin armoured cars, but not many were ever delivered. The main reason was that Austin was already stretched to the limit to supply vehicles for the British army and had few facilities to spare. Instead of complete armoured cars they supplied bare chassis direct to the Putilov works, where the Russians added whatever strengthening they thought necessary and made some of their own modifications to

the hull. This mainly involved staggering the twin turrets so that although each still covered only a 270° traverse they could together cover a slightly wider field of fire. A later innovation was the introduction of tracks in place of the rear wheels, which converted the vehicle into a halftrack; eventually Putilov ceased production of the armoured cars at its St Petersburg plant and concentrated on the halftrack

version. There was even a plan to produce halftracks in place of any more armoured cars but the revolution of 1917 occurred before this could be carried out.

Revolution

From 1914 to 1917 the Russians used many types of armoured car, ranging from direct imports to local improvisations, but the most important type was the Austin-Putilov. It was numeri-

German troops examine a captured Austin-Putilov armoured car, probably in search of loot. Note the prominent Tsarist insignia and the height of these vehicles, which can be assessed by comparison with the nearby soldiers. After 1918 some of the cars were used by Poland and a few ended up in Japan.

cally and mechanically the best the Russians had to hand and eventually proved to be far more suited to the rough conditions under which the Russians had to fight. During 1917 many became involved in the internal fighting that accompanied the events leading to the October Revolution, and the type can frequently be seen in photographs of the period.

SPECIFICATION	
Austin-Putilov	**Dimensions:** length 4.88 m (16 ft);
Crew: 5	width 1.95 m (6 ft 4¾ in); height
Weight: 5.3 tons	2.4 m (7 ft 10½ in)
Powerplant: one 37.3-kW (50-hp)	**Performance:** max. speed 50 km/h
Austin petrol engine	(31 mph); range 200 km (125 miles)

Tank Mk I Heavy tank

The **Tank Mk I** was the production and service model of the prototype vehicle known as **'Mother'**, which was the eventual outcome of a series of development models based on the use of a Holt tractor chassis. Lieutenant W. G. Wilson was, in the main, responsible for the final design of 'Mother' after a great deal of committee and experimental work, and it was he who conceived the idea of using the large and high track outline with its characteristic shape that came to be the classic tank outline of World War I.

The first 'tank'

'Mother' was demonstrated in January and February 1916, and soon after this the first production order was placed. A separate arm was established in March 1916 to use the new vehicle, which was named the 'tank' purely as a cover, though the name stuck. The first production vehicles were issued to the Heavy Section, Machine-Gun Corps in mid-1916, and the first crews were assembled.

The Tank Mk I was a large and heavy vehicle powered by a Daimler 78.3-kW (105-hp) petrol engine carried in an armoured box slung between the two massive lozenge-shaped continuous tracks. Originally it had been intended to mount a turret on the top but this would have made the design unstable so instead the main armament of two 6-pdr (57-mm; 2.24-in) guns was placed in one sponson on each side. The sponsons each had a single Lewis or Hotchkiss machine-gun, and a third such gun was fitted for extra defence. The vehicle was protected by armour plate (ranging in thickness from 6 to 12 mm; 0.24 to 0.47 in) riveted to steel joists, but in action this proved unsatisfactory as bullet 'splash' found its way through the armour seams and caused casualties.

The Tank Mk I could cross trenches up to 2.44 m (8 ft) wide, and steering was at first accomplished by using external twin-wheel 'steering tails' that proved to be unnecessary: in action they were

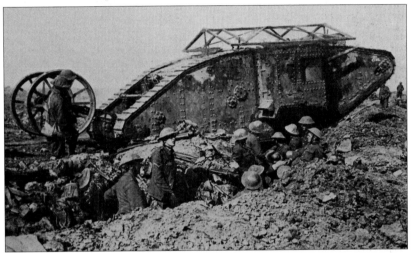

frequently damaged, yet the tanks could still be steered.

Almost as soon as the first tanks appeared in France in mid-1916 they were ordered into action, thus the first Tank Mk Is went into battle on the morning of 15 September 1916 at Flers-Courcelette in a vain attempt to provide some impetus to the flagging Somme Offensive. The tanks did manage to make some local breakthroughs and cre-

ated panic when they appeared, but the sad truth was that too few actually got into action. Many of the 50 that were supposed to make the attack simply broke down or got bogged down in the mud. Individual tanks made impressions into the German line but numbers were too few to have a major impact.

Numerous versions

The Mark I was produced in two versions: the **Tank Mk I (Male)** described above, and intended for the primary offensive mission; and the **Tank Mk I (Female)** with larger sponsons and an armament of four Vickers and two Lewis machine-guns, and intended for the anti-infantry support of the Tank Mk I (Male). Other variants were the **Mk I Tank Tender** with steel boxes in place of the sponsons, and the **Mk I**

A Tank Mk I (Male) moves up into action near Thiepval in September 1916. Items to note are the anti-grenade wire mesh screen over the hull and the clumsy steering 'tail' at the rear; these steering devices were soon discarded as they proved to be of limited value.

Wireless Tank without sponsons but with a tall aerial mast.

Thus the Tank Mk I made history by being the first tank used in combat, but it was something of a fiasco as far as the action was concerned. What the type did achieve in the long term was to impress on the British military hierarchy the fact that the tank did have potential, and the 'Tank Corps' was established in July 1917.

A Tank Mk I (Female) emerges from battle near Flers-Courcelette on 15 September 1916 after the first-ever tank action. Note the armoured machine-gun cowls and the frame for the anti-grenade screen.

SPECIFICATION	
Tank Mk I (Male)	8.05 m (26 ft 5 in); width over
Crew: 8	sponsons 4.19 m (13 ft 9 in);
Weight: 28 tons	height 2.45 m (8 ft ½ in)
Powerplant: one 78.3-kW	**Performance:** maximum speed
(105-hp) Daimler petrol engine	6 km/h (3.7 mph); range 38 km
Dimensions: length with tail	(24 miles)
9.91 m (32 ft 6 in); length of hull	

Medium Tank Mk A 'Whippet' British medium tank

When the first tanks were designed they were intended to be little more than 'machine-gun destroyers' capable of crossing rough country. As a result they were huge lumbering beasts that could cross trenches, but could not move very fast over good ground. By 1916 the idea of using the tank as a form of cavalry began to take root; such a tank would be able to exploit the breakthroughs made in enemy lines. It was proposed that a new design of 'fast' tank with few obstacle-crossing attributes but capable of speed across good ground should be designed and built, and such a product was developed by Sir William Tritton, who had been instrumental in the development of the early landships.

The 'Whippet' arrives

The official name for the new tank was the **Medium Tank Mk A** but it was soon nicknamed '**Whippet**'. Tritton reverted to his early 'Little Willie' layout in which flat, rather than lozenge-shaped, tracks were used. A front-mounted engine bay was slung between the tracks, and this housed two Tylor 34-kW (45-hp) London bus engines, one to drive each track; steering was effected by speeding or slowing individual tracks. Towards the rear was the driver on the left, with the fighting compartment to his right. Originally this latter was to have been a turreted affair, but this was changed to a rigid superstructure mounting one Hotchkiss machine-gun in a special mounting on each face. Armour ranged in thickness from 5 mm (0.2 in) to 14 mm (0.6 in).

The prototype of the 'Whippet' was ready by February 1917, and was

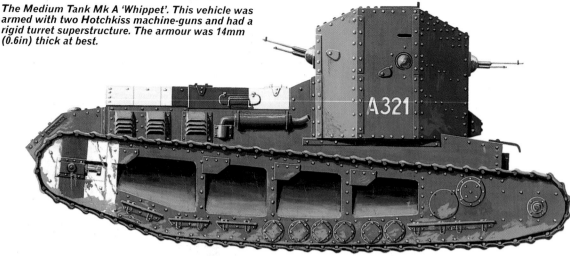

The Medium Tank Mk A 'Whippet'. This vehicle was armed with two Hotchkiss machine-guns and had a rigid turret superstructure. The armour was 14mm (0.6in) thick at best.

ordered into production in June of that year, but production took time and it was not until late 1917 that the first examples appeared. Even then they did not reach France quickly, and it was March 1918 before they saw action. The type proved to be difficult to drive as the driver had to juggle constantly with each engine clutch to control the machine, and in action many were lost when they went out of control. But the 'Whippet' soon proved to be reliable enough, and once on good ground it could notch up speeds greater than that of horsed cavalry.

The 'Musical Box'

At first the 'Whippets' were used to plug gaps in the line during the major German advances, but it was when the time came for counter-attack that they came into their own. Some made deep forays behind enemy lines, creating havoc as they went. One example is the famous 'Muscial Box', which spent nine hours cruising German rear areas and gunning down

This Mk A wears prominent red and white identification stripes at the front of its hull. Note the complex shape of the turret superstructure and the large mud chutes under the track tops, which reflect the muddy Western Front conditions.

unsuspecting rear echelon troops before it was finally knocked out by a field gun.

By the time of the Armistice the 'Whippet' or Mk A was well established, but it did not remain in service long after that date. A few saw service during the Irish 'Troubles' and a batch became the first tanks exported to Japan in 1920. Additionally, prior to the

Armistice the Germans had captured enough examples to take the Medium Mk A

into small-scale service for evaluation, pending the arrival of the similar LK II.

SPECIFICATION	
Medium Tank Mk A	width 2.62 m (8 ft 7 in); height
Crew: 3 or 4	2.74 m (9 ft)
Weight: 14 tons	**Performance:** maximum speed
Powerplant: two 34-kW (45-hp)	13.4 km/h (8.3 mph); range 64.3 km
Tylor four-cylinder petrol engines	(40 miles)
Dimensions: length 6.10 m (20 ft);	

Tank Mk IV Male/Female British heavy tank

The **Tank Mk IV** was the most numerous type used during World War I, and benefited from all the many design and tactical lessons that had been so desperately hard-won since the service debut of the Tank Mk I. Only relatively small numbers of the **Tank Mk II** and **Tank Mk III** had been built (50 of each), and most of these were converted to stores carriers and special duties vehicles. The Mk II featured a wider track shoe at every sixth link, and the Mk III had better armour.

Mk IV appears

When the **Mk IV** appeared in March 1917 it was the forerunner of a batch of

Moving barely faster than a walking soldier, the British Mk IV heavy tank had the archetype 'diamond' shape associated with the machines of this era. Although slow, the Mk IV was a potent adversary for contemporary German tanks.

1,000 that had been ordered in the previous year, the design originating in October 1916.

Operational changes

The Mk IV had several changes over the previous three marks, which differed only in small detail. The main operational change was the introduction of better armour (ranging in thickness from 6 mm/0.24 in to 12 mm/0.47 in), first used on the Mk III, which had to be introduced as the Germans had quickly developed special anti-tank rifles and armour-piercing ammunition. Another change was to armament. The ex-naval 6-pdr (57-mm) guns of earlier marks were 40 calibres long, and were frequently bent or embedded into the ground when the tank was crossing trenches. They were replaced in the Mk IV by much smaller guns only 23 calibres long, and these thereafter remained standard tank guns for several years. Secondary armament was four Lewis machine-guns. The sponsons for the guns were also made smaller and for transport they could be pushed into the vehicle on rails, whereas earlier versions had the sponsons removed altogether for transport. Numerous internal mechanical changes were introduced, and an 'unditching' beam placed ready for use above the hull. This provided the extra traction required to get out of a ditch.

The Mk IV continued a concept that was introduced originally on the Mk I, namely that certain tanks carried four primary machine-guns (two in each sponson) and two secondary guns, the 6-pdr guns being omitted. These were used for direct infantry support and trench-clearing, the variant being known as the **Tank Mk IV (Female)** in differentiation from the heavier-armed **Tank Mk IV (Male)**. There was also a variant with machine-guns in one sponson and a 6-pdr gun in the other; known as the **Tank Mk IV (Hermaphrodite)**.

Combat debut

The first tank 'duel' saw Mk IVs engaging German A7Vs, near Villers-Bretonneux. The Mk IV was also used to good effect at Cambrai and many of the tank battles thereafter, and after 1918 the Mk IV was retained by the Tank Corps for many years. Some were used in Palestine and after the war they were used in Ireland. A few were given to the Italians, but perhaps the greatest users after the British were the Germans; almost inevitably many Mk IVs fell into the hands of the Germans, who then used them against the British, calling them **Beutepanzerwagen IV** (captured armoured vehicle IV). Other Mk IV variants were the **Mk IV Supply Tank**, the **Mk IV Tadpole Tank**, with length increased by 2.74 m (9 ft) at the rear for better trench-crossing, and the **Mk IV Fascine Tank**, fitted to carry trench-filling fascines (chainbound wood bundles some 1.37 m/ 4 ft 6 in in diameter). There was also a crane version for salvage duties.

Keeping one eye on the enemy: the British Mk IV (Male) heavy tank demonstrates its impressive trench-crossing capabilities. Some versions were fitted with fascines to help bridge tank obstacles.

SPECIFICATION	
Tank Mk IV (Male)	(26 ft 5 in); width over sponsons
Crew: 8	3.91 m (12 ft 7 in); height 2.49 m
Weight: 28 tons	(8 ft 2 in)
Powerplant: one 78 or 93-kW (105- or 125-hp) Daimler petrol engine	**Performance:** maximum speed 6 km/h (3.7 mph); range 56 km
Dimensions: length 8.05 m	(35 miles)

Tank Mk V Advanced British heavy tank

The **Tank Mk V** was the last of the classic lozenge-shaped tanks to serve in any numbers, and embodied all the improvements introduced on the Mk IV, together with the Wilson epicyclic gearbox that enabled the tank to be driven by one man, the earlier marks depending on the actions of two men and a great deal of team-work for steering. The Mk V also had a purpose-built engine, the 112-kW (150-hp) Ricardo, which not only gave more power but made life for the engineers inside the confines of the hull a great deal easier.

'Pigeon Post'

Another innovation was the introduction of a cupola for the commander and at long last provision was made for communication with the outside world, by the mounting of semaphore arms on the back of the hull. Until then a tank crew was virtually isolated from other troops not only by the great noise produced by the engine but by poor vision and no method of passing messages in or out. The early tanks could communicate only by sending pigeons to the rear if required. The main armament of the Male version was two 6-pdr (57-mm) guns, supplemented by four Hotchkiss machine-guns, and the armour varied in thickness from 6 mm to 14 mm (0.24 in to 0.55 in).

About 400 Mk Vs had been built in Birmingham by the time of the Armistice, and even by then the mark had begun to sprout variants. The first of these introduced a new 1.83-m (6-ft) section into the hull to improve trench-crossing capabilities and also to provide more internal space for personnel (up to 25 troops) or stores. This was the **Tank Mk V***, which was converted in the field, while the comparable, but much improved, **Tank Mk V**** was introduced on the production lines. As with the Mk IV, this improved vehicle was produced in **Tank Mk V (Male)** and **Tank Mk V (Female)** forms.

The 'American' Tank

The Mk V was also the first American tank. Enough Mk Vs were passed to the newly-arrived US Army to partially equip a battalion, together with some French FT 17s. Post-war the Mk V was used as the standard equipment of the Tank Corps, and although there were several designs based on the Mk V, none was produced or used in any numbers. The Mk V was used for all manner of experiments ranging from bridge-laying to mine-clearing with variations of the **Tank Mk V** (**Tank RE**), but never in any great numbers, as the years after 1918 were not financially conducive to such innovations. Numbers of Mk Vs were also passed to the Canadian army, where they remained in use until the early 1930s.

The Mk V never replaced the earlier Mk IV, although it arrived on the Western Front from about mid-1918 onwards. It proved to be far more reliable and easy to use than the earlier marks, but the war ended before it could take part in the massive armoured operations that had been planned for 1919. These missions called for the massed deployment of Mk Vs, along with some special tanks that never left the drawing board (supply tanks, armoured recovery vehicles and others) along chosen sectors of the front. The infantry would have little part to play as the tanks alone would advance to achieve the big 'break-through' sought so desperately and expensively since 1914. But the Armistice stopped 'Plan 1919' and the world had to wait until 1939 for the envisaged Blitzkrieg.

Using a cable, a Tank Mk V (Male) assists another tank out of difficulties in August 1918. The Mk V carries red and white recognition stripes at the front. The rails over the top are for 'unditching' beams.

SPECIFICATION	
Tank Mk V (Male)	(26 ft 5 in); width over sponsons
Crew: 8	4.11 m (13 ft 6 in); height 2.64 m
Weight: 29 tons	(8 ft 8 in)
Powerplant: one 112-kW (150-hp) Ricardo petrol engine	**Performance:** maximum speed 7.4 km/h (4.6 mph); range 72 km
Dimensions: length 8.05 m	(45 miles)

Char d'Assaut Schneider

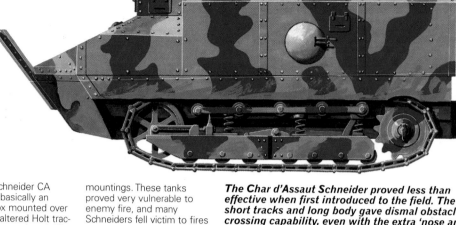

The **Char d'Assaut Schneider** (or **Schneider CA**) was developed at the behest of Colonel J. E. Estienne, who in 1915 envisaged armoured tractors to tow armoured troop-carrying sledges for surprise assaults on German trenches on the Western Front. Estienne proposed a development of the American Holt agricultural tractor's track and chassis, which was then becoming widely used as an artillery tractor. By going direct to the French commander-in-chief, Estienne obtained support for his proposal, and the Schneider armament manufacturer was contracted as developer.

Tardy development

The original proposals called for 200 Schneider CAs by the end of 1916, but progress was so slow that it was the middle of 1917 before useful numbers were

Schneider tanks move up to the front near L'Eglantiers on the Oise. The short 75-mm (2.95-in) gun was on the right of the super-structure, but one machine-gun ball mounting can be seen on this side. The crew are on top to avoid the heat of the engine inside.

ready. The Schneider CA emerged as basically an armoured box mounted over a virtually unaltered Holt tractor suspension and track. The box mounted two machine-guns and a short 75-mm (2.95-in) gun to one side forward. The engine developed 41 kW (55 hp) and was fed from two petrol tanks situated near the machine-gun

mountings. These tanks proved very vulnerable to enemy fire, and many Schneiders fell victim to fires caused by a single armour-piercing bullet. Maximum armour thickness was 11.5 mm (0.45 in), increased to 19.5 mm (0.77 in) on later vehicles. The engine developed 41 kW (55 hp) and was fed from two petrol tanks situated near the machine-gun mountings. The idea of the armoured personnel-carrying sledge had been dropped, and the Schneiders were used mainly for infantry support, proving less than successful as their cross-country capabilities were very limited. By May 1917

The Char d'Assaut Schneider proved less than effective when first introduced to the field. The short tracks and long body gave dismal obstacle-crossing capability, even with the extra 'nose and tail' ramps fitted. The armour was thin and the vehicle burned easily.

some 300 had been produced, but thereafter the gun version was replaced in production by the stores-carrying **Schneider Char de Ravitaillement**, in which the right-hand gun position was replaced by a door opening into the stores-carrying area. Extra 8-mm (0.31-in) armour was added to the sides of most examples as the result of experience in action, and the Schneider CA's greatest contribution lay in teaching the French army how to use and maintain armoured vehicles in the field. The French set up their first armour school at Champlieu in October 1916. They soon learned from actions such as the attack on the Chemin des Dames in April 1917,

when 76 out of a total of 132 Schneider CAs taking part were lost, that lack of maintenance and lack of spares could remove a vehicle from the field as thoroughly as enemy action.

The last Schneider CA was delivered in August 1918, but by then attrition and a move towards the Renault FT 17 had reduced the numbers in service to fewer than 100. Most of these were the unarmed supply version but the gun Schneiders had taken part in several 1918 operations, enjoying some success despite their instability and tendency to catch fire, but also teaching the French the rudiments of armoured warfare.

SPECIFICATION	
Char d'Assaut Schneider **Crew:** 7 **Weight:** 14.6 tonnes **Powerplant:** one Schneider liquid-cooled four-cylinder petrol engine developing 41 kW (55 hp)	**Dimensions:** length 6 m (19 ft 8 in); width 2 m (6 ft 6¾ in); height 2.39 m (7 ft 10 in) **Performance:** maximum speed 6 km/h (3.7 mph); range 48 km (30 miles)

Char d'Assaut St Chamond

The fact that the ordering and development of the Schneider CA had by-passed the normal French army supply channels upset some of the normal supply authorities to a marked degree. These authorities therefore decided to proceed with their own tank design. Using one Colonel Rimailho as the designer, the French army thus set about producing its own original design, and by early 1916 the first prototype had been built at the Saint Chamond factory at Homcourt. As a result, the new vehicle became generally known as the **Char d'Assaut St Chamond**. As with the Schneider CA,

development and production of this other pioneering vehicle were both slow, so it was not until May 1917 that the first service examples were finally ready for operational service.

Long overhangs

Even for a vehicle of the 'first-try' variety, the **St Chamond CA** had several unusual features. Like the Schneider CA it was based on the chassis, suspension and track of the Holt tractor, but on the St Chamond CA the track was lengthened to provide more track length on the ground. The drive to the track was unusual in that a petrol engine was used to

The Char d'Assaut St Chamond's long hull so restricted its use in action that it was often relegated to the supply tank role. It was armed with four machine-guns and a 75-mm (2.95-in) gun, and had an advanced petrol-electric drive.

drive an electric transmission system. While this petrol-electric transmission worked, it was also heavy and bulky, which meant the

projected design weight was exceeded by over 5 tonnes. This overweight feature was not assisted by the configuration of the hull, which extended both forward and to the rear of the track by a considerable degree. This meant that whenever the vehicle had to traverse rough ground or cross even the shortest trench, it became stuck as the front or rear of the hull dug in. In service this proved a considerable drawback, for the Germans soon learned of the St Chamond CA's poor trench-crossing performance and widened their trenches accordingly. The St Chamond CA mounted a conventional 75-mm (2.95-in) Modèle 1897 field gun in the front of the hull, and it was possible to mount as many as four machine-guns around the hull. The maximum armour thickness was 17 mm (0.67 in).

Inadequate mobility
The poor cross-country performance of the St Chamond CA so severely restricted its use in action as 1917 progressed that the type was gradually replaced by the newer Renault FT 17, and many vehicles were converted to **St Chamond Char de Ravitaillement** supply carrier standard. The type was involved in its last major action as a gun tank in July 1918, when 131 took part in a counter-attack near Reims.

By the end of the war there were only 72 out of the production run of 400 left in service. Although the St Chamond CA had many novel features that pointed the way ahead (the forward-mounted 75-mm gun, the petrol-electric drive and the lengthened track), it was basically an unsound design of poor cross-country capability, and in action proved to have limited tactical value.

Char d'Assaut St Chamond tanks move forward near Moyennville on the Oise in 1917. This picture provides a good indication of the great bulk and shape of these tanks compared with the limited length of track run; note also the limited ground clearance under the hull.

SPECIFICATION	
Char d'Assaut St Chamond **Crew:** 9 **Weight:** 23 tonnes **Dimensions:** length (with gun) 8.83 m (28 ft 11¾ in); length (hull) 7.91 m (25 ft 11½ in); width 2.67 m (8 ft 9 in); height 2.34 m (7 ft 5⅔ in)	**Powerplant:** one 67-kW (90-hp) Panhard liquid-cooled four-cylinder petrol engine powering a Crochat-Collardeau electric transmission **Performance:** maximum speed 8.5 km/h (5.3 mph); range 59 km (36.7 miles)

Renault FT 17 Infantry tank

The Renault FT 17 was one of the most successful of the World War I tanks. They were produced in thousands, mainly as infantry support light tanks, but many other uses were found for them. Turret armament was either a machine-gun or a short 37-mm (1.45-in) gun, and a crew of two was carried.

The diminutive **Renault FT 17** was without a doubt one of the most successful of all the World War I tanks. It had its origins in the proposals put forward in 1915 by the far-sighted General Estienne, who saw the need for a light armoured vehicle to support infantry operations directly. It was not until mid-1916 that Renault became involved, and with a potential order for well over 1,000 examples in prospect the Renault company started to produce a design.

Questionable design
By the end of 1916 the design was ready. It emerged as a two-man tank armed with a machine-gun, and did not meet with general approval at the time. The design was considered too cramped and too lightly armed, but an order was pushed through, and it was not long before a further order for 2,500 was placed. By then the armament had been increased to a 37-mm gun, but many examples were produced with only a single machine-gun.

The FT 17 design was the first of what can now be seen as the classic tank design. It had its armament in a small turret with a 360° traverse, and the thin hull had the tracks on each side. There was no chassis as such, the components being built directly onto the armoured hull. The engine was at the rear, the tracks each had a large forward idler wheel that proved ideal for obstacle climbing, and to enhance trench-crossing capability a frame 'tail' was often fitted to the rear.

Renault was unable to produce the numbers required so production batches were farmed out to other concerns. Even the Americans became involved, but as they insisted that their FT 17s would be built to American standards and methods none arrived in France before the Armistice. In France the original cast armoured turret was often replaced on the production lines by an octagonal design using flat armour plates. The 37-mm gun became the virtual norm (**Char-canon FT 17**), although machine-guns could be fitted (**Char-mitrailleuse FT 17**). It was not long before a self-propelled gun version mounting a 75-mm (2.95-in) gun was produced as the **Char-canon Renault BS**, and there was even a special radio version, the **Char Renault TSR**. The maximum armour thickness was 16 mm (0.63 in).

Active service
The first FT 17s were delivered to the French army in March 1917 but it was not until May 1918 that the type was first used in action. By then the French tactics were to use the tanks *en masse*, but this was not always possible in the face of the constant German attacks under way at that time. At first the FT 17s were used in relatively small numbers, but by July things had settled down to the point where 480 could be concentrated for a counterattack near Soissons. Here they were successful, and thereafter the type was used to great effect.

Maintenance was a constant worry, for the FT 17 had been designed with little thought for repairs and long-term spares holdings, so at any one time hundreds were out of action with various faults. But many more were

The FT 17 was a trim little tank, seen here in its form with a cast rather than riveted turret. The type suffered from several reliability problems, and maintenance was a continual concern.

in the line as the sundry manufacturers duly delivered the ordered thousands. Some were passed to American troops. As the war ended there were 1,991 FT 17s fit for combat but another 369 were under repair and another 360 out of use.

Other uses
After 1918 FT 17s remained in large-scale service and was produced or converted to suit a number of new roles such as mobile bridging, self-propelled artillery, radio versions and others. In 1939 large numbers were still in use, and the Germans took over many after the French collapse of 1940. The Germans retained some for their own use until 1944 when they used many in the Paris fighting.

SPECIFICATION	
Renault FT 17 **Crew:** 2 **Weight:** 6.485 tonnes **Dimensions:** length (with tail) 5 m (16 ft 5 in); width 1.71 m (5 ft 7½ in); height 2.13 m (7 ft)	**Powerplant:** one Renault liquid cooled four-cylinder petrol engine developing 26 kW (35 hp) **Performance:** maximum speed 7.7 km/h (4.8 mph); range 35.4 km (22 miles)

Autoblindé Peugeot Armoured car

The first **Peugeot** armoured cars were produced as rather hasty improvisations in 1914, and were typical of their period in that they were based on a commercial model, the 4x2 Peugeot 153. These early conversions used a centrally mounted machine-gun on a pivot in the centre of the open rear body, but once the design had been formalised this armament was increased to a 37-mm (1.45-in) gun. The early slab-sided armour plates (5.5-mm/0.216-in thick) were also revised to provide better all-round protection, but the top was left open.

Heavy armour

By the time the purpose-designed Peugeot armoured cars entered service, the vehicles scarcely resembled the early improvisations. A sloping armour plate now covered the driver's position

and the engine was also armoured. The radiator was protected by steel shutters but the wheels remained as they originally were with their wire spokes, even though the extra weight caused by the armour was partially offset by the use of dual wheels at the rear. Although a machine-gun could be carried on the central pintle, the more usual weapon was a 37-mm gun behind a curved steel shield. This gun was a half-size version of the famous Modèle 1897 field gun, and could fire a useful high explosive shell. This gave the Peugeot armoured car a modest firepower potential that was sometimes used to support infantry attacks. An alternative to the mix of a 37-mm gun and a machine-gun was a pair of machine-guns.

After the end of 1914, there was little enough for

The fully developed form of the Peugeot armoured car used a short-barrel 37-mm (1.45-in) infantry gun as its main armament. Although later replaced in their infantry support role by the FT 17 light tank, the cars remained in use through World War I and were then passed on to the new Polish army.

these armoured cars to do on the Western Front. A few were used for patrols to the rear of the front, but they could do little else until the relatively small number that remained in use in 1918

were able to take their part in containing the large-scale German breakthroughs that occurred on some parts of the line. Thereafter a few were used in the relatively fluid warfare that developed. But most of this fighting was carried out by tanks, particularly the FT 17s, which proved to be of more use over rough country than

the Peugeot armoured cars with their narrow wheels.

Post-war service

When World War I ended, the French army still had 28 Peugeot armoured cars in service, but most of these were later handed over to the Polish army, with which they remained in use for some years.

A French army Peugeot armoured car provides fire support for British infantry during the Battle of the Lys in April 1918. In open country these vehicles were able to provide useful fire support with their gun, but they were often restricted to the available roads.

SPECIFICATION	
Autoblindé Peugeot	height 2.8 m (9 ft 2¼ in)
Crew: 4 or 5	**Armament:** one 37-mm (1.45-in)
Weight: 5 tons	gun and one machine-gun, or two
Powerplant: one 30-kW (40-hp)	machine-guns
Peugeot petrol engine	**Performance:** maximum speed
Dimensions: length 4.8 m	40 km/h (25 mph); maximum range
(15 ft 9 in); width 1.8 m (5 ft 11 in);	140 km (87 miles)

Sturmpanzerwagen A7V Tank

For a nation that was normally well to the fore in the pursuit of military technology, Germany was surprisingly slow to reach a proper appreciation of the potential possessed by the tank and, despite some early and far-sighted proposals put forward by various individuals, no official interest was taken in any form of armoured vehicle other than the armoured car. Thus, it was only after the British had first used the tank in the Battle of Flers-Courcelette in September 1916 that the Germans began to reconsider their position, when they established a committee to undertake the design and production of a German equivalent. Ordered in November 1916, Germany's first tank was planned to meet a requirement for a 30-tonne *Geländespanzer-wagen* (all-terrain armoured vehicle).

Like so many other designs produced by a com-

mittee under time constraints, the result of this venture was not a great success. The vehicle became known as the **Sturmpanzerwagen A7V**, the A7V coming from the committee's departmental abbreviation. The design was based on that of the readily available Holt caterpillar track and suspension, but Joseph Vollmer introduced suspension modifications to the original that improved the possible speed. These efforts were largely negated by the installation on the basic chassis of a large armoured box structure that held a crew of no fewer than 18 men. This box had large slab sides with nose and tail arrangements that extended under the body to such an extent that the ground clearance was only about 40 mm (1.57 in). The length of track on the ground was also rather short, and the overall result was a vehicle that was inherently unstable and

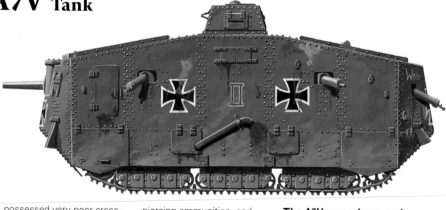

possessed very poor cross-country performance. The main armament was a captured 57-mm (2.24-in) Russian gun (mounted at the front) and six machine-guns, each with a crew of two. The one advantage the A7V had over the British tanks was the thickness of its armour, between 10 and 30 mm (0.39 and 1.18 in). By the time production began, the Germans had developed their own armour-

piercing ammunition, and the A7V's armour was proof against this new projectile.

Limited production

The first A7V was ready by October 1917, and in December that year 100 were ordered. Production of the A7V involved several firms, all of them already pressed to meet existing production needs, with the result that by the end of the war only about 20 A7Vs had

The A7V was a large and bulky vehicle with a crew of 18 and carried six machine-guns. The main armament was a 57-mm (2.24-in) gun in the front hull. The A7V proved to have a poor cross-country performance and its height made it rather unstable, and only about 20 were ever produced. Many of these were pressed into action during 1918.

been produced. In March 1918 the first A7Vs went into action. When used over good going ground as mobile fire support units they proved successful enough, but over rough ground they proved to be less than successful and some of the first examples soon revealed shortcomings in their special armour plate. The A7V's lack of trench-crossing ability often left the tank behind the infantry it was supposed to support, and all too often when opposed by field artillery firing over open sights the type was easily knocked out.

Three A7Vs took part in

Two A7Vs as seen from a sector of the French lines in June 1918. The cloud of smoke came mainly from the twin Daimler-Benz petrol engines, but some was no doubt dust thrown up by the tracks. Some of the machine-guns are visible, but the main 57-mm weapon is obscured by the smoke.

the first tank-versus-tank combat on 24 April 1918 at Villers-Bretonneux. Here three Mk IVs (one Male and two Females) encountered three A7Vs. The two Females were soon damaged and had to retire, but the sole Male

was able to hit and knock out one of the A7Vs. More such combats took place before the Armistice, but the A7Vs rarely shone. In fact the Germans favoured the various British tanks they were able to capture, mainly as a result of the poor cross-country performance of their own machines.

Despite the slow produc-

tion of the A7V, the Germans produced an unarmoured supply version with an open top, the **Uberlandwagen**, and even went so far as to attempt to produce an **A7V/U** version with the 'all-round' tracks and sponsons of the British tanks. This venture came to nothing, as did the **A7V/U2** and **A7V/U3** projects, the former having

smaller sponsons and the latter being a 'female' version armed only with machine-guns. After World War I a few A7V tanks were used in Germany's internal struggles, and a few more examples also remained on the strength of the newly established Polish army for some years.

SPECIFICATION	
Sturmpanzerwagen A7V **Crew:** 18 **Weight:** 33 tons **Powerplant:** two Daimler-Benz petrol engines each developing 74.6 kW (100 hp) **Dimensions:** length 8 m (26 ft	3 in); width 3.06 m (10 ft ½ in); height 3.3 m (10 ft 10 in) **Armament:** one 57-mm (2.24-in) gun, and six machine-guns **Performance:** maximum speed 12.9 km/h (8 mph); range 40 km (25 miles)

Panzerkraftwagen Ehrhardt 1915/1917

Armoured car

The very first German armoured cars were in fact special large car or truck chassis adapted to carry a skyward-looking artillery piece for use against observation balloons. There were several of these weapons, collectively known as *Ballon Abwehr Kanonen* (BAK), but although some were used for army trials none was taken into large-scale use. Thus it was left to the Belgians in 1914 to demonstrate to the German army the potential of the armoured car in mobile warfare. Here, German infantry and cavalry were at times distinctly incommoded by the hit-and-run raiding carried out by the Minerva and other converted touring cars fielded by the outnumbered Belgians. Having suffered somewhat at the hands of the Belgians, the Germany army then decided to produce its own equivalent but, in the absence of any practical experience of its own to fall back upon, approached the problem of designing such a weapon in a typically Germanic fashion.

During 1915, the Germans produced prototypes of three different armoured cars. The manufacturers were Ehrhardt, Daimler and Büssing, which all chose to ignore the fact that the Belgian cars were little more than converted touring cars, and went instead for what they thought were more suitable vehicles. All three turned out to have one feature in common, in that they were all vehicles of massive size. The largest of the three was the Büssing, which used a 'double-ended'

layout that could at least boast a tactically useful high ground clearance. The other two designs were roughly the same, with the engine (surrounded by armour) at the front and a large box-like body at the rear with a turret or cupolas on its top. Both of these other vehicles were tall machines of notably clumsy appearance, and both were also far too heavy for effective fulfilment of the operational tasks demanded of them.

Some indication of this fact is provided by the knowledge that the Daimler and Ehrhardt designs were each reliant on the use of double wheels on each side at the rear, and also flanges on the single wheels at the front of the vehicle, in an effort to reduce the ground pressure and so enhance cross-country mobility to a useful degree. All three cars had a crew of eight or nine men, carried an armament of at least three machine-guns, and possessed a maximum armour thickness of 7 mm (0.28 in).

Internal security role

Along with some improvised conversions, the three prototypes were formed into one unit and sent at first to the Baltic and then to the Western Front. Conditions on both fronts were such that the armoured cars could achieve little, and eventually the vehicles were deployed on the Russian part of the Eastern Front, where they could at least use their mobility to some effect. It was at this stage that there emerged

The Panzerkraftwagen Ehrhardt 1915 was one of the first examples of a type of high and flat-sided armoured car design that the Germans were to use until almost World War II for internal policing duties. It weighed nearly 9 tons, had a crew of eight or nine men and an armament of up to three machine-guns.

the need for more cars, and as Büssing and Daimler were already over-extended on war work, Ehrhardt received the contract, being asked to produce a further 20 armoured cars. These were 1.72 tons lighter than the original **Panzerkraftwagen Ehrhardt 1915** and, completed with the designation **Panzerkraftwagen Ehrhardt 1917**, had revised frontal armour. The vehicles were sent to the Eastern Front until the end of the fighting there late in 1917. Thereafter they appear to have been retained within Germany for internal policing duties, a role in which they were so successful that a further 20 were produced specifically for the purpose in 1919. The Ehrhardt

design was in fact considered just what internal policing required, for its height gave it the capacity to tower over crowds and offer police units better control of riots. Vehicles of the Ehrhardt type were in use almost until World War II.

Such was the requirement for armoured cars, however, that by 1918 the Germans were forced to employ numbers of captured armoured

cars of Rolls-Royce and other makes, and the Ehrhardt armoured cars, clumsy and high though they were, were never around in sufficient numbers. On the Eastern Front the cars were never able to make much of a tactical impression, so the design is now little known and few operational details have survived.

SPECIFICATION	
Panzerkraftwagen Ehrhardt 1915 **Crew:** 8 or 9 **Weight:** 8.86 tons **Powerplant:** one 63.4-kW (85-hp) petrol engine	**Dimensions:** length 5.61 m (18 ft 5 in); width 2 m (6 ft 6½ in) **Armament:** three machine-guns **Performance:** maximum speed 59.5 km/h (37 mph); maximum range 250 km (155 miles)

LT vz 35/PzKpfw 35(t) Light tank

It is a little known fact that Czechoslovakia was a leading exporter of armoured vehicles and artillery prime movers before World War II, with sales made to Austria, Bulgaria, Hungary, Latvia, Peru, Romania, Sweden, Switzerland and Turkey.

In October 1934 the Czech army placed an order for two prototypes of a medium tank called the S-11-a (or T-11), which were completed in the following year. Army trials started in June 1935 and soon uncovered many faults as a result of the tank's rushed development. Without waiting for these faults to be corrected an order was placed for a first batch of 160 vehicles in October 1935, and the first five were delivered in the following year.

So many faults were found that these vehicles were returned to Skoda for modifications. A further batch of 138 was ordered for the Czech army, which called it the LT vz 35, while Romania ordered 126 as the R-2. Gradually most of the faults were overcome and the vehicle gained a good reputation.

The Germans took over the remaining vehicles when they occupied Bohemia and Moravia in 1939, giving them the designation Panzerkampfwagen 35(t). A further 219 were built by Skoda for the Wehrmacht.

Such was the shortage of tanks in the German army at the outbreak of war that the 6th Panzer Division was equipped with the PzKpfw 35(t) for the invasion of France in 1940. These continued in service until 1942 when surviving chassis were converted into other roles such as mortar tractors (German designation *Mörserzugmitel*), artillery tractors (German designation *Zugkraftwagen*) or maintenance vehicles with tank battalions.

Construction

The hull of the LT vz 35 was of riveted construction that varied in thickness from 12 mm to a maximum of 35 mm. The bow machine-gunner was seated at the front of the vehicle on the left and operated the 7.92-mm (0.31-in) ZB vz 35 or 37 machine-gun, with the driver to his right. The commander/gunner and loader/radio operator were seated in the two-man turret in the centre of the hull.

Main armament consisted of a 37.2-mm (1.46-in) Skoda vz 34 gun with a 7.92-mm ZB 35 or 37 machine-gun mounted co-axially to that right. Totals of 72 rounds of 37 mm and 1,800 rounds of machine-gun ammunition were carried. The engine and transmission were at the rear, the transmission having one reverse and six forward gears. The suspension on each side consisted of eight small road wheels, with the drive sprocket at the rear, and a front idler .

An unusual feature of the tank was that the transmission and steering were assisted by compressed air to reduce driver fatigue, so enabling the tank to travel long distances at high speed. Problems were encountered with these systems when the tanks were operated by the Germans on the Eastern Front, because of the very low temperatures encountered.

Czechoslovakia provided many of the tanks used by the Wehrmacht in the battle for France. The PzKpfw 35(t) equipped the 6th Panzer Division in that campaign and continued in service until 1942.

SPECIFICATION	
LT vz 36	developing 89 kW (120 hp)
Crew: 4	**Performance:** maximum road
Weight: 10500 kg (23,148 lb)	speed 40 km/h (25 mph); maximum
Dimensions: length 4.9 m	range 193 km (120 miles); fording
(16 ft 1 in); width 2.159 m	0.8 m (3 ft 4 in); gradient 60 per
(7 ft 1 in); height 2.209 m (7ft 3 in)	cent; vertical obstacle 0.787 m
Powerplant: one Skoda six-	(2 ft 7 in); trench 1.981 m (6 ft 6 in)
cylinder water-cooled petrol engine	

TNH P-S/PzKpfw 38(t) Light tank

The rapidly deteriorating international situation in 1937 led the Czech army to issue a requirement for a new light tank. This time the army was determined that the troubles encountered with the LT vz 35, resulting from a lack of testing, would not be repeated. Skoda entered its S-11-a and S-11-b while CKI entered an LT vz 35 with the engine and transmission of the TNH tank, the LT4, the TNH P-S (already in production as a successful export item) as well as a new medium tank called the V-8-H.

German service

In a series of extensive trials the TNH P-S was found to be the best design and on 1 July 1938 was adopted as the standard light tank of the Czech army under the designation LT vz 38. None had entered service at the time of the German occupation in 1939. The vehicle remained in production for the German army between 1939 and 1942, more than 1,400 being built under the designation Panzerkampfwagen 38(t) Ausf S to PzKpfw 38(t) Ausf G (*Ausführung* is the German word for model or mark). The Germans also exported 69 vehicles to Slovakia, 102 to Hungary, 50 to Romania and 10 to Bulgaria.

During the invasion of France the tank was used by the 7th and 8th Panzer Divisions, the former being commanded with great dash by the ex-commander of Hitler's Army bodyguard, Erwin Rommel. The Panzer 38(t) continued in frontline Wehrmacht service as a light tank until 1942.

The hull and turret of the vehicle were of riveted construction, the top of the superstructure being bolted into position. Minimum armour thickness was 10 mm and maximum thickness 26 mm, although from the Ausf E this was increased to 50 mm.

Armament

The driver was seated at the front of the tank on the right, with the bow machine-gunner operating a 7.92-mm (0.31-in) MG 37(t) machine-gun to his left. The two-man turret in the centre of the hull was armed with a 37.2-mm (1.46-in) Skoda A7 gun, which could fire both armour-piercing and HE rounds. The gun had an elevation of +12° and a depression of -6°. Mounted coaxial with and to the right of the main armament was another 7.92-mm machine-gun. Totals of 90 rounds of 37-mm and 2,550 rounds of machine-gun ammunition were carried.

Powerplant

The engine was at the rear of the hull and coupled to a transmission with one reverse and five forward gears. Suspension on each side consisted of four large rubber-tyred road wheels suspended in pairs on leaf

Used by two Panzer Divisions in 1940, the PzKpfw 38(t) was in production for the German army until 1942. The basic chassis was later used for a number of self-propelled artillery conversions.

springs with the drive sprocket at the front and idler at the rear, and with two track-return rollers.

Outclassed

While the PzKpfw 38(t) was quickly outclassed as a combat vehicle, it continued to be widely used as a reconnaissance vehicle. In that role the Germans fitted some chassis with the turret of the SdKfz 222 light armoured car, complete with its 20-mm cannon.

The chassis of the light tank also proved suitable as the basis for a large number of specialist vehicles, including the effective **Marder** tank destroyer, which was fitted with a new superstructure armed with a 75-mm anti-tank gun. Other conversions included various self-propelled 15-cm (5.9-in) guns, a 20-mm (0.79-in) self-propelled anti-aircraft gun, several types of weapons carriers and the **Hetzer** tank destroyer, to

name just a few.

The Hetzer was armed with a 75-mm gun in a fully enclosed fighting compartment with limited traverse, and was considered by many to be one of the best vehicles of its type during World War II. A total of 2,584 were built between 1944 and 1945, and production continued after the war for the Czech army, a further 158 being sold to Switzerland in 1946-7 under the designation G-13. These were finally withdrawn from service in the late 1960s.

A PzKpfw 38(t) during the invasion of France; the 7th and 8th Panzer Divisions used the tank in this theatre. The commander of the 7th Division became well known later in the war – his name was Rommel.

SPECIFICATION	
TNH P-S **Crew:** 4 **Weight:** 9700 kg (21,385 lb) **Dimensions:** length 4.55 m (14 ft 11 in); width 2.13 m (7 ft); height 2.31 m (7 ft 7 in) **Powerplant:** one Praga EPA six-cylinder water-cooled inline petrol	engine developing 112 kW (150 hp) **Performance:** maximum road speed 42 km/h (26 mph); maximum range 200 km (125 miles); fording 0.9 m (3 ft); gradient 60 per cent; vertical obstacle 0.787 m (2 ft 7 in); trench 1.879 m (6 ft 2 in)

Panzerkampfwagen I Light tank

In 1933 the German Army Weapons Department issued a requirement for a light armoured vehicle weighing about 5000 kg (11,026 lb) that could be used for training purposes, and five companies subsequently

built prototype vehicles. After trials, the Army Weapons Department accepted the Krupp design for further development; the design company being responsible for the chassis and Daimler-Benz for the

vehicles was ordered from Henschel, and production commenced in July 1934 under the designation **PzKpfw I(MG) (SdKfz 101) Ausf A**. The tanks were powered by a Krupp M 305 petrol engine developing

achieved in 1935 when over 800 vehicles were completed.

Lack of fire-power

The Panzerkampfwagen I was first used operationally in the Spanish Civil War, and at the start of the invasion of Poland in 1939 no less than 1,445 such vehicles were on strength. It had already been realised, however, that the vehicle was ill-suited for front-line use because of its lack of firepower and armour protection (7-13 mm), and in the invasion of France in 1940 only 523 were used, although many more were still in service in Germany and Poland.

By the end of 1941 the PzKpfw I had been phased out of front-line service, although the **kleiner Panzerbefehlwagen (SdKfz 265)** command model remained in operational use for a longer period.

Once the light tank was declared obsolete, its chassis underwent conversion to other roles. One of the first of these was the **Munitions-Schlepper**, which was used to carry ammunition and

other valuable cargoes. For the anti-tank role the chassis was fitted with captured Czech 47-mm (1.85-in) anti-tank guns on top of the superstructure with limited traverse. These were used in the East and in North Africa, but became ineffective with the deployment of more heavily armoured Allied tanks on the battlefield.

Infantry gun

The most extreme conversion entailed the installation of a 15-cm (5.9-in) infantry gun in a new superstructure, but this was found to overload the chassis and less than 40 such conversions were made.

The turret was in the centre of the vehicle, offset to the right and was armed with twin 7.92-mm machine-guns, for which a total of 1,525 rounds of ammunition were carried. The driver's seat was positioned to the left of the turret.

The PzKpfw I was heavily involved in the Polish campaign after its operational debut in the Spanish Civil War.

A lightweight PzKpfw I moves through a French town in 1940. Over 500 Panzer Is were used in the campaign in spite of their unsuitability for combat.

superstructure. To conceal the real use of the vehicle, the Army Weapons Department gave the tank the cover name of **Landwirtschäftlicher Schlepper** (industrial tractor). The first batch of 150

only 42 kW (57 hp). There were problems with the engine, however, and the next batch had a more powerful engine, which meant that the hull had to be longer and an additional roadwheel added on each side. This model was a little heavier, but its bigger engine gave it a maximum road speed of 40 km/h (25 mph). This entered service in 1935 under the designation **PzKpfw I(MG) (SdKfz 101) Ausf B**. Most of the vehicles were built by Henschel but Wegmann also became involved in the programme, peak production being

SPECIFICATION	
PzKpfw I Ausf B **Crew:** 2 **Weight:** 6000 kg (13,230 lb) **Dimensions:** length 4.42 m (14 ft 6 in); width 2.06 m (6 ft 9 in); height 1.72 m (5 ft 8 in) **Powerplant:** one Maybach NL 38 TR six-cylinder petrol engine	developing 75kW (100 hp) **Performance:** maximum road speed 40 km/h (25mph); maximum road range 140 km (87 miles); fording 0.58 m (1 ft 11 in); gradient 60 per cent; vertical obstacle 0.36 m (1 ft 2 in); trench 1.4 m (4 ft 7 in)

Panzerkampfwagen II
Light tank

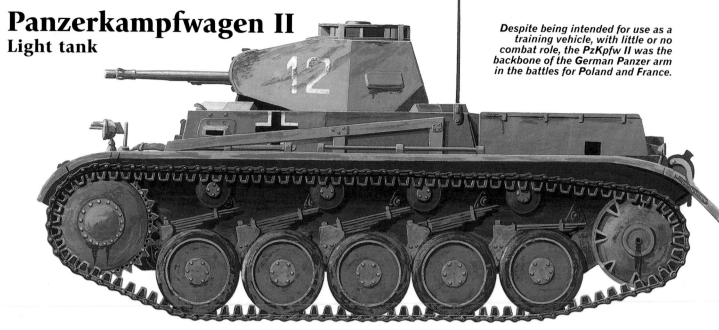

Despite being intended for use as a training vehicle, with little or no combat role, the PzKpfw II was the backbone of the German Panzer arm in the battles for Poland and France.

To bridge the gap until the arrival of the PzKpfw III and PzKpfw IV tanks, a decision was made in 1934 to order an interim model. This became known as the **Panzerkampfwagen II**. Development contracts were awarded to Henschel, Krupp and MAN under the designation **Industrial Tractor 100** or **LaS 100** to conceal its true role.

After evaluation of these prototypes, the MAN model was selected for further development. MAN was responsible for the chassis and Daimler-Benz for the superstructure. Production was eventually undertaken also by Famo, MIAG and Wegmann.

Combat Panzer

The tank formed the backbone of the German armoured divisions during the invasion of France, about 1,000 being in front-line service. The tank was also used in the invasion of the USSR in the following year, although by that time it was obsolete, had inadequate armour protection and lacked firepower.

The Panzer II was in fact never intended for combat, being designed primarily as a training machine. The first production **PzKpfw II Ausf A** vehicles were delivered in 1935, and were armed with a 20-mm cannon and 7.92-mm (0.31-in) co-axial machine-gun. Combat weight was 7.2 tonnes.

Tests with the early production models showed that the vehicle was underpowered with its 97-kW (130-hp) engine, so the **PzKpfw II Ausf B** was introduced with a 104-kW (140-hp) engine and other improvements, notably thicker frontal armour. These pushed up its weight to just under 8 tonnes.

More armour

The **PzKpfw II Ausf C** was introduced in 1937, and had even better armour protection. Additionally, the small bogie wheels were replaced by five independently sprung bogies with leaf springs on each side. This remained as the basic suspension for all remaining production vehicles.

In 1938 the **PzKpfw II Ausf D** and **PzKpfw II Ausf E** were introduced, with new torsion-bar suspension which gave them a much increased road speed of 55 km/h (34 mph), although cross-country speed was reduced. The final production model of the series was the **PzKpfw II Ausf F**. This appeared in 1940-41 and had 35 mm (1.4 in) of armour on the front and 20 mm (0.8 in) on the sides. The total weight of the vehicle was now approaching 10 tonnes. It was felt that the trade-off between reduced speed and greater protection was acceptable.

The hull and turret of the PzKpfw II was of welded steel construction. The driver sat at the front. The two-man turret was in the centre, off-set to the left, and the engine was at the rear.

Right: The Panzer II's armour was found to be inadequate in real combat. Crews often supplemented its protection with additional links of track.

Armament consisted of a 20-mm cannon (for which 180 rounds were provided) on the left side of the turret, and a 7.92-mm machine-gun with 1,425 rounds on the right of the turret.

The PzKpfw II was also used as the basis for a number of fast reconnaissance tanks called the **Luchs** – this name was subsequently adopted by the new West German Army in the 1970s for its 8x8 reconnaissance vehicle. However, these and similar vehicles were not built in large numbers.

Amphibious

One of the more interesting variants was the special amphibious model developed for the invasion of England in 1940. This model was propelled in the water at a speed of 10 km/h (6 mph) by a propeller run off the main engine. A model with two flame-throwers was also produced as the **Flammpanzer II**; 100 were in service by 1942.

When the basic tank was finally declared obsolete, the chassis was quickly adopted for many other roles. One of the first of these was a

highly effective self-propelled anti-tank gun using captured Soviet 76.2-mm (3-in) artillery pieces. It was known as the **Marder I**. This was then followed in production by the **Marder II**, which carried a 75-mm (2.95-in) German anti-tank gun. In all, some 1,200

examples were converted or built from new. The **Wespe**, another effective self-propelled gun using a Panzer II chassis fitted with a 105-mm howitzer, was produced in occupied Poland until 1944.

A Panzer II (right) and Panzer 38(t) in France in May 1940. Superior tactics and radio communications ensured victory of these light tanks over more heavily armoured foes.

SPECIFICATION	
PzKpfw II Ausf F	104 kW (140 hp)
Crew: 3	**Performance:** maximum road
Weight: 10000 kg (22,046 lb)	speed 65 km/h (40 mph); maximum
Dimensions: length 4.64 m (15 ft	road range 200 km (125 miles);
3 in); width 2.30 m (7 ft 6½ in);	fording depth 0.85 m (2 ft 10 in);
height 2.02 m (6 ft 7½ in)	gradient 50 per cent; maximum
Powerplant: one Maybach	vertical obstacle 0.42 m (1 ft 5 in)
6-cylinder petrol engine developing	

Panzerkampfwagen III Medium tank

In the mid-1930s, evolving German army armoured tactics called for each tank battalion to be equipped with three companies of relatively light medium tanks and one company of heavier and more powerful support tanks. The former eventually became the **Panzerkampfwagen III (PzKpfw III)** or **SdKfz 141**, while the latter became the Panzerkampfwagen IV, which was to remain in production throughout World War II.

In 1935 the Weapons Department issued contracts for the construction of prototype vehicles for the lighter concept to Daimler-Benz, Krupp, MAN and Rheinmetall-Borsig. At an early stage it was decided to arm the tank with a 37-mm gun which would fire the same ammunition as that used by the infantry anti-tank gun. The turret ring was made large enough to facilitate up-gunning of the vehicle to 50 mm (1.97 in) if this should be needed.

Early trials

Following trials with the prototype vehicles the Daimler-Benz model was selected, although the first three production models, the **PzKpfw III Ausf A, PzKpfw III Ausf B** and **PzKpfw III Ausf C**, were built only in small numbers, differing from each other mainly in suspension details. In September 1939 the vehicle was formally adopted for service, and mass production was soon underway.

The PzKpfw III was first used in combat during the invasion of Poland. The next model was the **PzKpfw III Ausf D** with thicker armour and a revised cupola.

In 1939 development began on the 50-mm model, which had an uprated engine and only six road wheels.This entered production in 1940 under the designation **PzKpfw III Ausf F**. The **PzKpfw III Ausf G** followed with similar armament but a more powerful engine. A deep-water wading version was developed and used successfully during the invasion of the USSR in 1941. The **PzKpfw III Ausf H** introduced wider tracks and a number of important improvements.

Soviet menace

The 50-mm L/42 gun was inadequate to cope with the Soviet T-34 tank so the longer-barrelled KwK 39 L/60 weapon was installed. This had a higher muzzle velocity. Vehicles fitted with this weapon were designated **PzKpfw III Ausf J**. Many vehicles were retrofitted with the 50-mm gun, and by early 1942 the 37-mm version had almost disappeared from front-line service.

Bigger, heavier

The next model was the **PzKpfw III Ausf L**, which had greater armour protection, pushing its weight up to just over 22 tonnes. This

For operations in North Africa the PzKpfw III was fitted with a tropical kit, which included upgraded filters for the engine and wider tracks to make better passage over sand.

Right: The Panzer III was the backbone of the Afrika Korps armoured force in the first two years of the desert war, though reliability was a problem in the harsh, arid conditions.

was almost 50 per cent more than the weight of the original prototype. The **PzKpfw III Ausf M** and **PzKpfw III Ausf N** fielded the 75-mm (3.0-in) L/24 gun which had been installed in the PzKpfw IV; a total of 64 rounds of ammunition was carried for this gun. Production of the PzKpfw III ceased in August 1943, though its chassis formed the basis for several assault guns and SP howitzers.

All early models (Ausf A–D) were armed with the 37-mm KwK 35/36 L/46.5 gun and three 7.92-mm (0.31-in) MG 34 machine-guns (two in the turret and one in the hull).

SPECIFICATION	
PzKpfw III Ausf M	TRM 12-cylinder petrol engine
Crew: 5	developing 224 kW (300 hp)
Weight: 22300 kg (49,160 lb)	**Performance:** maximum road
Dimensions: length (including	speed 40 km/h (25 mph); maximum
armament) 6.41 m (21 ft); length	road range 175 km (110 miles);
(hull) 5.52 m (18 ft 1½ in); width	maximum fording depth 0.80 m (2 ft
2.95 m (9 ft 8 in); height 2.50 m	8 in); gradient 60 per cent; vertical
(8 ft 2½ in)	obstacle 0.60 m (2 ft); trench
Powerplant: one Maybach HL 120	2.59 m (8 ft 6 in)

Below: A Panzer III engaged in streetfighting in the USSR in 1941. By this time, the type was completely outclassed by Soviet AFVs such as the T-34 and KV-1.

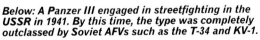

Panzerkampfwagen IV
Medium tank

This late-war Panzer IV has added side armour around the turret and sides to protect against anti-tank weapons.

The **Panzerkampfwagen IV** had the distinction of remaining in production throughout World War II, and formed the backbone of German armoured divisions.

In 1934 the Army Weapons Department drew up a requirement for a vehicle under the cover name of a 'medium tractor', which was to equip the fourth tank company of each German tank battalion. Rheinmetall-Borsig, MAN and Krupp built prototypes designated VK 2001(Rh), VK 2002(MAN) and VK 2001(K) respectively. Krupp eventually took over total responsibility for the vehicle, which was also known as the **Bataillons Führerwagen** (battalion commander's vehicle). This entered production at the Krupp-Grusonwerke plant at Magdeburg as the **PzKpfw IV Ausf A**, or **SdKfz 161**.

Upgradable

When the Panzer IV was designed, the relatively light vehicles of the time were not capable of carrying large high velocity guns. In its original form, the Panzer IV was designed to provide support for these lighter tanks. It was armed with a short L/24 howitzer of 75-mm (3-in) calibre – i.e. the length of the barrel was 24 times the calibre.

The Panzer IV had one co-axial 7.92-mm (0.3-in) machine gun in the turret and another in the hull. The driver sat front left, with the radio operator/ hull machine-gunner on his right. The commander sat in the rear centre of the turret, with the gunner on the left of the howitzer breech and the loader on the right.

The rear-mounted engine was coupled to a manual transmission with six forward and one reverse gears. Turret traverse was powered through 360°, though manual controls were provided for emergency use. The normal ammunition load was 122 rounds of 75-mm and 3,000 rounds of machine gun ammunition. Maximum armour thickness was 20-mm on the turret and 14.5-mm on the hull.

Production totals

None of the early variants were built in large numbers: the 35 'A' models were followed by 42 'B' models, 134 'C' models and 229 'D' types. By 1938 the 'E' type had been authorised. Weight increased from 17 to 21 tons as a larger, 320 hp engine was installed and additional armour fitted. After the fall of France the design was changed again, the 'F' type finishing over a ton heavier with wider tracks to reduce ground pressure.

Throughout the PzKpfw IV's long production life, the basic chassis remained little changed, but as the anti-tank threat increased, so more armour was added and new weapons were fitted. Other

Mid-war Panzer IVs operate on the Eastern Front in mid-1943. These have been up-gunned with a long high-velocity 75-mm weapon, but lack the extra armour added later.

early tanks had to be phased out of production as they were incapable of being upgraded, but the Panzer IV was big enough to be substantially improved.

Late-war Panzer IVs were much more powerfully armed and protected than early versions. The **PzKpfw IV Ausf F2** had a maximum hull armour of 60 mm (2.4 in), with 50 mm (2 in) on the turret. Main armament comprised a long barrelled 75-mm (3 in) KwK L/43 gun fitted with a muzzle brake. This could fire HEAT, smoke, armour-piercing and high explosive rounds. The **PzKpfw Ausf H** had an even longer L/48 gun, which was at least as good as the 76.2-mm guns on Soviet T-34s. The final production model was the **PzKpfw IV Ausf J**, which appeared in March 1944. Total production of the PzKpfw IV amounted to about 9,000 vehicles.

The chassis of the PzKpfw IV was used for a wide variety of specialized vehicles, including tank destroyers, self-propelled anti-aircraft guns, self-propelled artillery, armoured recovery vehicles, and bridgelayers.

Above: A short-barrelled Panzer IV undergoes an engine change in the field. This was not an easy job, since German tanks were more complex than their rivals.

SPECIFICATION	
PzKpfw IV Ausf H	**Powerplant:** one Maybach HL 120
Crew: 5	TRM 12-cylinder petrol engine
Weight: 25000 kg (55,115 lb)	developing 300 hp (224 kW)
Dimensions: overall length	**Performance:** maximum road speed
(including armament) 7.02 m	38 km/h (24 mph); maximum road
(23 ft); hull length 5.89 m	range 200 km (125 miles); fording
(19 ft 4 in); width 3.29 m	depth 1.0 m (3 ft 3 in); gradient
(10 ft 9½ in); height 2.68 m	60 per cent; vertical obstacle 0.6 m
(8 ft 9½ in)	(2 ft); trench 2.20 m (7 ft 3 in)

Panzerkampfwagen V Panther
Medium tank

In 1941 the most powerful tank in service with the German army was the PzKpfw IV. This was rarely a match for the new Soviet T–34 tank which appeared in small numbers on the Eastern Front in that year. Work on a successor to the PzKpfw IV had started as far back as 1937, but progress had been slow because of changing needs. In 1941 Henschel and Porsche had each built prototypes of new tanks in the 30/35-tonne class, designated the VK 3001(H) and VK 3001(P) respectively. These were not placed in production, and further development led to the Tiger (VK 4501).

New armament

Late in 1941 a requirement was issued for a new tank with a long barrelled 75-mm (2.95-in) gun, well-sloped armour for maximum protection within the weight limit of the vehicle, and larger wheels for improved mobility. To meet this requirement Daimler-Benz submitted the VK 3002 (D13) while MAN submitted the VK 3002 (MAN). The former design was a virtual copy of the T-34, but the MAN design

was accepted. The first prototypes of the new tank, the **Panzerkampfwagen V Panther** – given the military designation **SdKfz 171** – were completed in September 1942. The first production models left the MAN factory just two months later. At the same time Daimler-Benz started tooling up for production of the Panther, and in 1943 Henschel and Niedersachsen were also brought into the programme together with hundreds of sub-contractors.

It was planned to produce 600 Panthers per month, but Allied bombing meant that the maximum production

ever achieved was about 330 vehicles per month.

The Panther was rushed into production without proper trials, and numerous faults soon became apparent. Indeed, in the type's early days, more Panthers were lost to mechanical failure than to enemy action. As a result, no matter how much theoretical fighting power it had, crew confidence in the vehicle rapidly dwindled.

The vehicle first saw action on the Eastern Front in July 1943 during the Kursk battles, and from then on it was used on all fronts. Once the mechanical problems

had been overcome confidence in the tank soon built up again, and many consider the Panther to be the best all-round German tank of World War II. In the immediate post-war period the French army was equipped with Panthers until more modern tanks were available.

Panther variants

First production models were the **PzKpfw V Ausf A** which were really pre-production vehicles; the **PzKpfw V Ausf B** and **PzKpfw Ausf C** were never placed in production. Later models were the **PzKpfw V Ausf D**, followed for some reason by another **PzKpfw V Ausf A**. This variant was widely used in Normandy. The final version of the Panther was the **PzKpfw V Ausf G**. Variants of the Panther included the **Jagdpanther** tank destroyer, the **Befehlspanzer Panther** command vehicle, the **Beobachtungspanzer**

Top: The Panther in its late-war form. Skirts have been added to offer some protection to the wheels, and spare track has been used as auxiliary armour. The tank is covered in Zimeritt paste, an anti-magnetic covering protecting against magnetic mines.

Panther armoured observation post, and an armoured recovery vehicle. Some were disguised to resemble M 10 tank destroyers during the Battle of the Bulge.

Main armament was a long barrelled 75-mm (2.95-in) gun for which 79 rounds of ammunition were carried. Mounted co-axial with the main armament was a 7.92-mm (0.31-in) MG 34 machine-gun, while a similar weapon was mounted in the hull front and another on the turret roof for anti-aircraft defence.

The major problem with the Panzer was that it was expensive and difficult to build. As a result, it would be vastly outnumbered by its opponents. Some 4,800 Panthers were built, as compared to tens of thousands of M4 Shermans and T-34s. In fact, the Soviets built more than 11,000 T-34/85s in 1944 alone!

Above: Grossdeutschland troops advance behind a Panther on the Eastern Front in August 1944. The Panther had the measure of most Soviet tanks.

Panthers were heavily committed to Normandy, where they were a formidable threat to Allied armour units.

SPECIFICATION	
PzKpfwV Panther Ausf A **Crew:** 4 **Weight:** 45500 kg (100,310 lb) **Dimensions:** overall length (including armament) 8.86 m (29 ft ¾ in); hull length 6.88 m (22 ft 7 in); width 3.43 m (11 ft 3 in); height 3.10 m (10 ft 2 in) **Powerplant:** one Maybach HL 230	P 30 12-cylinder diesel engine developing 700 hp (522 kW) **Performance:** maximum road speed 46 km/h (29 mph); maximum road range 177 km (110 miles); fording depth 1.70 m (5 ft 7 in); gradient 60 per cent; vertical obstacle 0.91 m (3 ft); trench 1.91 m (6 ft 3 in)

Panzerkampfwagen VI Tiger
Heavy tank

This late-war Panzer VI has added side armour around the turret and sides to provide protection against anti-tank weapons.

As far back as 1938, the German army had realised that the **PzKpfw IV** tank then being designed would have to be replaced by a more capable vehicle some time in the future. Several companies built prototypes, but none was placed in production. In 1941 an order was placed with Henschel for a 36-ton tank, the VK 3601. The specification called for a maximum speed of 40 km/h (25 mph), good armour protection and a powerful gun.

Bigger designs

A prototype of this tank was built, but further work was stopped as an order was placed in May 1941 for a 45-ton tank called the **VK 4501**. This was to be armed with a modified version of the dreaded 8.8-cm (3.4-in) Flak/anti-tank gun, which had by then become the scourge of European armies. It was required that the prototype be ready for testing on Hitler's next birthday, 20 April 1942. As time was short, Henschel incorporated ideas from the VK 3601 and another abortive project, the VK 3001(H).

The end product was the **VK 4501(H)**, the letter suffix standing for Henschel. Porsche also went ahead with its own design and built the **VK 4501(P)** to meet the same requirement. Both prototypes were completed in time to be demonstrated on Hitler's birthday, and the Henschel design was selected for production in August 1942 under the designation **PzKpfw VI Tiger Ausf E, or SdKfz 181**.

Porsche Tiger

In case trials proved the VK 4501(H) a failure, a batch of 90 VK 4501(P) tanks was ordered. These were subse-quently completed as tank destroyers under the designation **Panzerjäger Tiger (P) Ferdinand (SdKfz 184)** – the vehicle was named after its designer, Dr Ferdinand Porsche.

Tiger flaws

For its time, the Tiger was an outstanding design with a powerful gun and good armour, but it was complicated and difficult to produce. One major drawback was its overlapping wheel suspension which became clogged with mud and stones. On the Eastern Front this could be disastrous as during winter nights the mud froze and by the morning the tank had been immobilized, often at the exact time the Soviets would attack. When the vehicle travelled on roads, a 51.5-cm (20.3-in) wide track was fitted. For combat and travel across country a 71.5-cm (28.1-in) wide track was used; this gave a lower ground pressure and so improved traction.

Deadly '88'

The main armament of the Tiger comprised an 8.8-cm (3.46-in) KwK 36 gun, with a 7.92-mm (0.31-in) MG 34 machine-gun coaxial with the main armament, and a similar weapon ball-mounted in the hull front on the right. The tank could carry 84 rounds for the main gun and 5,850 rounds for the machine guns.

The Tiger was first encountered in Tunisia by the British army and from then on appeared on all of the German fronts.

The Tiger was in production from August 1942 to August 1944, a total of 1,350 vehicles being built. There were three main variants. Most production was of the basic gun tank, but a number of **Befehlspanzer Tiger** or Tiger command tanks were built. These had their main armament removed to make more room in the turret for extra communications gear. The Befehlspanzer could also act as a recovery vehicle, being fitted with a winch.

Assault Tiger

The third variant was the heavily-armoured **Sturmtiger**. This had a new superstructure fitted with a huge 38-cm (14.96-in) Type 61 rocket launcher with limited traverse; only 10 were built.

Above: Tigers of the heavy Panzer company of the Das Reich Panzer Regiment were heavily involved in the Kharkhov counter-offensive of March 1943.

Below: It was big, it was slow, and its crews cursed its unreliability. However, in a fight the Tiger's powerful gun and thick armour made it almost unbeatable.

SPECIFICATION	
PzKpfw VI Tiger Ausf E **Crew:** 5 **Weight:** 55000 kg (121,250 lb) **Dimensions:** length (including armament) 8.24 m (27 ft); length (hull) 6.20 m (20 ft 4 in); width 3.73 m (12 ft 3 in); height 2.86 m (9 ft 3¼ in) **Powerplant:** one Maybach HL 230	P 45 12-cylinder petrol engine developing 522 kW (700 hp) **Performance:** maximum road speed 38 km/h (24 mph); maximum road range 100 km (62 miles); fording depth 1.2 m (3 ft 11 in); gradient 60 per cent; maximum vertical obstacle 0.79 m (2 ft 7 in); widest crossable trench 1.8 m (5 ft 11 in)

Panzerkampfwagen VI Tiger II 'King Tiger'
Heavy tank

No sooner was the Tiger in production than the decision was taken to develop an even more heavily armed and armoured version. The primary purpose of the new tank was to counter any heavy tank that the Soviets could introduce in the future. Once again Henschel and Porsche were asked to prepare designs. Porsche first designed a tank based on the earlier VK 4501 design, which was armed with a 15-cm (5.9-in) gun. This was rejected in favour of a new design with a higher-velocity version of the classic 8.8-cm (3.46-in) gun, to be fitted in a completely new turret. This was soon cancelled, as its electric transmission used too much copper, which at that time was in short supply. By this time the turrets were already in production.

'Super' Tiger
The **VK 4503(H)** Henschel design was completed in October 1943, somewhat later than anticipated as a

decision was taken during the manufacturing process to incorporate components of the projected Panther II tank. It was selected for production, and manufacture of the **Panzerkampfwagen VI Tiger II Ausf B (SdKfz 182)** got under way at Kassel in December 1943.

It was built alongside the Tiger, the first 50 production vehicles being completed with the Porsche turret. All subsequent tanks had the Henschel turret, and a total of 485 vehicles was built.

The Tiger II first saw action on the Eastern Front in May 1944 and on the Western Front in Normandy in August of the same year. The Western Allies called the massive new tank the **Royal Tiger**, while the Germans called it the *Königstiger* or **King Tiger**.

Heavy and slow
In many respects the Tiger II was similar in layout to the Panther tank, and was powered by the same engine as later production Panthers. Since the King Tiger was a great deal heavier, it had a lower power-to-weight ratio, and was much slower and less mobile than the PzKpfw V.

The Tiger II had an all-

Left: Later King Tigers were completed with a simpler Henschel turret without the electric drive which made the Porsche turrets so expensive.

Below: King Tigers could dominate the battlefield, but they were heavy and lacked mobility. Many used in the Ardennes battles were abandoned for lack of petrol.

welded hull, with a maximum thickness of 150-mm (5.9-in) in the front of the hull. The driver was seated at the front on the left, with the bow machine gunner/radio operator to his right.

The turret was also of welded construction, with a maximum thickness of 100 mm (3.9 in) at the front, and accommodated the commander and gunner on the left with the loader on the right. The engine was at the hull rear.

'Eighty-Eight'
Main armament comprised a long-barrelled version of the famous 'Eighty-Eight'. This could fire armour-piercing ammunition at a much higher muzzle velocity than the equivalent round fired by the Tiger I. As was standard on German tanks, a 7.92-mm (0.31-in) MG 34 was mounted co-axially with the main armament, with another mounted in the hull

front. Eighty-four rounds of 8.8-cm and 5,850 rounds of 7.92-mm (0.31-in) ammunition were carried.

While its heavy armour was almost impenetrable by the guns carried by most Allied tanks, the Tiger II was not completely reliable. It was very large, and its bulk made it difficult to move about the battlefield and to conceal. Many were abandoned or destroyed by their crews when they ran out of fuel, since by the end of the war no additional supplies were to hand.

Sole Variant
The Tiger II chassis was also used as the basis for the **Jagdtiger B** tank hunter, which was armed with a 128-mm (5.04-in) gun in a new fixed and thickly-armoured superstructure with limited traverse. By the end of the War, only 48 of these powerful tank destroyers had been completed.

Above: One of the first 50 King Tigers, which were completed with the complex Porsche turret. Utilising thick, highly effective sloped armour and carrying a long-barrelled, high-velocity version of the superb 8.8-cm (3.4-in) tank gun, the Tiger II was safe from most Allied tanks at all but the closest of ranges.

SPECIFICATION	
PzKpfw VI Tiger H Ausf B	P 30 12-cylinder petrol engine developing 522 kW (700 hp)
Crew: 5	
Weight: 69700 kg (153,660 lb)	**Performance:** maximum road speed 38 km/h (24 mph); maximum road range 110 km (68 miles); maximum fording depth 1.6 m (5 ft 3 in); gradient 60 per cent; vertical obstacle 0. 85 m (2 ft 10 in); trench 2.50 m (8 ft 2 in)
Dimensions: length (including armament) 10.26 m (33 ft 8 in); length (hull) 7.26 m (23 ft 9¾ in); width 3.75 m (12 ft 3½ in); height 3.09 m (10 ft 1½in)	
Powerplant: one Maybach HL 230	

Inside the Tiger

Pre-war tanks tended to have two-man turrets. The multiple tasks thus inflicted on the commander and gunner had a bad effect on efficiency. The Tiger, however, followed the standard German practice of having a three-man turret. This enabled each man to concentrate on his most important task. The commander directed the tank and found targets, the gunner located the targets in his sight and engaged them, the loader made sure that the correct ammunition – armour-piercing or high-explosive – was loaded for each specific target. At its best, a well-drilled Tiger crew made the Tiger an even more formidable fighting machine.

Seated in the right front of the Tiger's hull, the radio operator also manned the machine-gun mounted in the front plate of the hull. This was primarily used as an anti-infantry weapon.

The gunner's side of the Tiger turret was pierced by two holes for the TZF 9b gun sight. Later tanks were fitted with a shield which could be dropped over the sights, while late-model Tigers had a single sensor hole for the improved TZF 9c gun sight. Other obvious differences between early and late-model Tigers included the two Bosch headlights fitted to the first production tanks as seen here. Late production vehicles carried a single headlight mounted in the centre.

Main armament of the Tiger was the 88-mm KwK 36 L/56, adapted from the anti-tank version of the superb 'eighty-eight' Flak gun. It was the most powerful anti-tank gun then in use by any army, capable of penetrating 123 mm of armour at 1500 m (4,921 ft). The Tiger's turret housed the gun, which was offset to the right and was mounted on a 1.85-m (6-ft) diameter turret ring. The gun was fired electrically by a switch on the gunner's manual traverse wheel. The Tiger carried 92 rounds of main gun ammunition in stowage bins, lockers in the turret floor and anywhere else that was handy. Armour-piercing rounds usually accounted for half of a Tiger's ammunition load. The other half usually comprised high-explosive rounds for use against enemy soft-skinned vehicles and infantry.

Self-defence against infantry was provided by two MG 34 7.92-mm (0.31-in) machine-guns, one mounted co-axially with the main gun which was fired by the gunner, and one in a flexible mount in the front of the hull which was fired by the radio operator. Later a third machine-gun was added to the top of the turret for air defence.

Seated next to the radio operator in the left front of the hull, the driver was tasked with driving the heavy vehicle as smoothly as possible, and was often the oldest, most mature member of the crew.

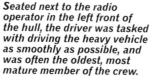

Operational use showed that glowing exhausts could be seen from a long distance away at night. PzAbt 501 was the first unit to fit sheet metal shields around the exhaust stacks in the rear of the hull.

The Commander was the most important member of the crew, directing the vehicle in action and also serving as the primary means of locating targets. Seated at the left rear of the turret, the commander had a rotating cupola equipped with vision blocks, giving limited all-around vision even when the tank was fully 'buttoned up'.

Early Tiger cupolas – a mini-turret on the main turret just for the commander – had simple vision slits like this example: later versions had a rotating hatch and were fitted with periscopes with a greater field of view. Even with those improvements, however, visibility was limited and tank commanders preferred to travel standing in the turret hatch.

Rear protection of the Tiger was not as thick as elsewhere, and the relatively thin armour could be penetrated by the 76-mm gun carried by the Soviet T-34. A large stowage box was fitted to the rear of all Tiger turrets from the 56th built, and was retrofitted to some earlier examples. The MP Klappe or machine pistol port next to the storage bin allowed the commander to fire a sub-machine gun against attacking infantry. This was a feature of earlier tanks only: from the 46th turret this was replaced by an escape hatch.

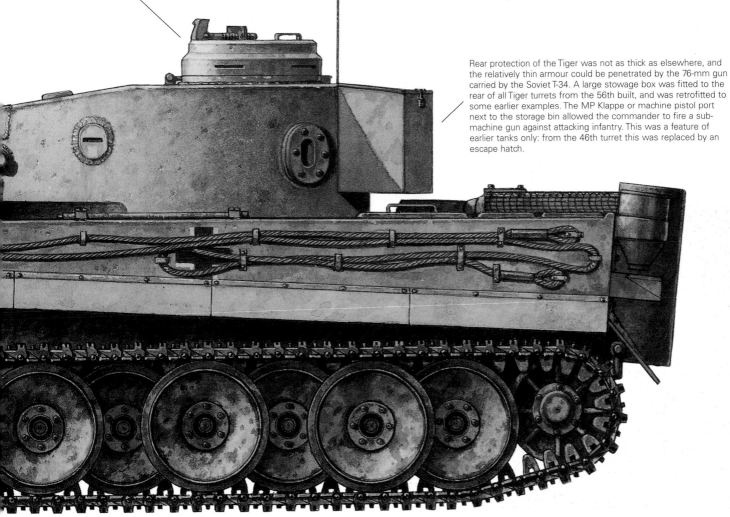

It was big, it was slow, and its crews cursed its unreliability. But when it came to a fight, the Tiger's armour and gun made it almost unbeatable.

PzKpfw VI Tiger
Heavy Tank

When it first appeared in combat at the end of 1942, the massive Tiger was the most powerful tank in the world. Slow, ponderous and none too reliable, it nevertheless dominated the battlefield. Allied tanks could not match its thick armour and powerful 88-mm gun, and no rivals would appear until the very end of the war.

Tiger PzKpfw VI Ausf E

Cutaway key

1 88-mm KwK 36 L/56 gun
2 7.92-mm (0.31-in) MG 34, co-axial machine-gun fired by gunner's foot
3 7.92-mm (0.31-in) MG 34 machine-gun
4 7.92-mm (0.31-in) MG 34 machine-gun ammunition
5 Smoke generator discharge
6 Escape hatch
7 Commander's seat
8 Commander's traverse handwheel
9 Pistol port
10 Traverse gearbox
11 Commander's shield
12 Gunner's traverse handwheel
13 Gunner's elevating handwheel
14 Gunner's seat
15 MG firing pedal
16 Binocular telescope
17 Feifel air-cleaning system
18 Maybach HL 210 P 45 V-12 water-cooled inline petrol engine
19 Gu G5 radio set
20 88-mm ammunition bins
21 Hydraulic traverse foot control
22 Hydraulic traverse unit
23 Disc-brake drum
24 Steering unit
25 Steering wheel
26 Gearbox
27 Driver's seat
28 Handbrake
29 Accelerator
30 Footbrake
31 Clutch
32 Shock absorber
33 Torsion bar suspension
34 Overlapping bogie-wheels
35 Commander's cupola
36 Fan drive clutch lever
37 Air-intake valve control
38 Petrol primer
39 Petrol tap
40 MG ammunition storage

Suspension

Ride comfort in the Tiger was surprisingly good – the interleaving road wheels helped to spread the massive weight evenly, and the torsion bar suspension gave a smooth ride over rough terrain. However, if an inner road wheel was damaged by a mine, field repairs were a major problem. In winter in the the East, mud freezing between the wheels overnight could immobilise the tank.

Tracks

The Tiger needed a track with a width of 72 cm (28½ in) to spread the load. This was too wide for conventional railway flat cars, and so for transport the outer road wheels had to be removed and a narrower 52-cm (20½ in) track fitted. It took considerable effort to refit the outer wheels and wide tracks for combat.

Tigers of the 2nd SS Panzer Division 'Das Reich' move through a Russian wood. The SS heavy tank companies were among the first to be equipped with the Panzer VI. They were particularly effective in combat, combining the tank's fighting power and their own fanatical will to win into a lethal package.

Turret

German tanks introduced the three-man turret layout which became standard on all Main Battle Tanks for four decades after the war. The tank commander sat above and to the left of the gun.   He controlled all aspects of the tank, from selecting targets and controlling the gun through map reading and giving instructions to the driver. The gunner sat in front of the commander, while the loader stood to the right of the turret. His main task was to ensure that the gun was kept loaded and ready to fire.

Powerplant

One of the Tiger's main weaknesses was its engine, which required continuous maintenance. The first 250 Tigers were powered by 12-cylinder Maybach HL 210 P 45 engines delivering 485 kW (650 hp), which was not enough for a 55-tonne tank. All tanks manufactured after May 1943 were fitted with the modified 12-cylinder Maybach HL 230 P 45 engine, with power increased to 522 kW (700 hp), but even with the extra power the big panzer was still under powered. The sound of the Tiger engine starting was distinctive even at a distance – it was a sound which the tank's Allied opponents came to fear and respect.

Armour

The Tiger's great strength was in the protection it offered its crew, and the immense striking power of its gun. The thick, slab-sided armour lacked the good ballistic shape found on contemporary designs like the Panther and the Soviet T-34, but with a thickness which ranged from 25 to 100 mm on the hull and 80 to 100 mm on the turret of the Ausf H, (increased to 110 mm on the Ausf E) it hardly needed to.

SPECIFICATION	
Panzerkampfwagen VI Tiger I	(13 ft 1 in)
Manufacturer: Henschel	**Gradient:** 70°
Type: Heavy Tank	**Vertical obstacle:** 0.80 m (2 ft 7 in)
Crew: 5	**Trench:** 2.50 m (8 ft 2½ in)

Dimensions		**Armament**	
Length (hull): 6.20 m (20 ft 4 in)		**Main armament:** 1 x 88-mm KwK 36 L/56 rifled cannon	
Length (gun forwards): 8.24 m (27 ft)		**Normal effective range:** 2000 m (6,562 ft)	
Width: 3.73 m (12 ft 3 in)		**Maximum range:** 4500 m (14,764 ft)	
Height: 2.86 m (9 ft 3¼ in)		**Muzzle velocity:** 773 m (2,536 ft) per second	
Track width (travelling): 0.52 m (20¼ in)		**Turret traverse:** hydraulic with manual back-up	
Track width (combat): 0.72 m (28¼ in)		**Traverse rate:** 6° per second	

Combat weight	
Early models: 55000 kg (121,250 lb)
Late models: 57000 kg (125,661 lb)

Elevation: +17°/-6.5°

Powerplant
Early: Maybach HL 210 P 45 12-cylinder 485-kW (650-hp) petrol engine
Late: Maybach HL 230 P 45 12-cylinder 522-kW (700-hp) petrol engine
Transmission: Hydraulic pre-selector, 8 forward and 4 reverse gears
Steering: powered hydraulic
Suspension: Transverse torsion bar

Ammunition
Armour-piercing or High-explosive

Secondary armament
Early: 2 x 7.92-mm (0.31-in) MG 34 machine-guns
Late: 3 x 7.92-mm (0.31-in) MG 34/42 machine-guns

Fuel capacity
534 litres (117 Imp gal)

Ammunition load
92 rounds of 88-mm; 5,100 rounds of 7.92 mm (0.31 in) (34 x 150-round belts)

Performance
Maximum road speed: 45.40 km/h (28 mph)
Maximum cross country speed: 20 km/h (12.5 mph)
Maximum road range: 195 km (120 miles)
Maximum cross country range: 110 km (68 miles)
Fording depth without preparation: 1.60 m (5 ft 3 in)
Fording depth with preparation: 4 m

Max armour penetration
171 mm at 100 m (328 ft); 156 mm at 500 m (1,640 ft); 138 mm at 1000 m (3,281 ft); 123 mm at 1500 m (4,921 ft); 110 mm at 2000 m (6,562 ft)

Armour thickness
Gun mantlet: 110 mm
Front hull: 100 mm
Side and rear hull and turret: 80 mm
Top/bottom: 25 mm

Above: Tigers move across the steppe before the Battle of Kursk in 1943, kicking up dust as their turrets nose around looking for Russian tanks.

Below: The crew of a battle-scarred Tiger rests in a pause between the fierce fighting on the Eastern Front. Tigers saw combat in all theatres, becoming a feared opponent to all Allied tank crews.

Light Tank M3

American light tank development can be traced back to the 1920s when several infantry-support light tanks were developed in small numbers. By the early 1930s these designs had evolved into the **Light Tank M2** with a series of designs all using the M2 designation. This series was quite well armed, with a 37-mm (1.46-in) main gun, but by 1940 the type was obsolescent and was used only for training after reaching its apogee with the **M2A4** model.

Thicker armour

The events of 1940 in Europe were followed closely by the US Army, which realised that thicker armour would be required by its light tanks. This involved a better suspension to carry the extra weight. The result was the **Light Tank M3**, based on the M2A4. It was in full-scale production by 1941, and mass production of the **M3A1** got under way once the US had entered the war. Early versions used riveted construction, but welded turrets and eventually welded hulls were introduced, and there were many detail design changes.

By the time M3 production

ceased 5,811 had been built. Basic armament of the M3A1 was one 37-mm gun, co-axial 0.3-in (7.62-mm) machine-gun, and four additional 0.3-in machine-guns (one on the turret roof for anti-aircraft defence, one in the hull front and two in the sponsons for operation by the driver). Armour thickness ranged from 15 mm (0.59 in) to 43 mm (1.69 in).

Reliability

The Light Tank M3 was used wherever the US Army was involved. It proved to be a thoroughly reliable vehicle and was liked by its crews. Large numbers of M3s were passed to America's allies. The largest recipient was the UK, where it was known as the **Stuart**.

To the British, the Stuart was large for a light tank, but crews appreciated the agility and reliability of the vehicle. One thing they did not like was that two main types of engine were fitted to different versions: the normal engine was a Continental 7-cylinder radial petrol engine (**Stuart I**). In order to expedite production at a time of high demand the Guiberson T-1020 diesel engine was substituted (**Stuart II**). This

sometimes caused supply problems but it was a burden the Allies learned to survive.

Variations

Major variants were the **M3A1** (**Stuart III** and **Stuart IV** with petrol and diesel engines) fitted with a gyrostabilised gun, powertraverse turret, and the product-improved **M3A3** (**Stuart V**) with a larger driving compartment and thicker armour. The 37-mm gun was retained throughout the production life of the M3. By 1944 it had little combat value, and many M3s and

Stuarts serving with reconnaissance units had the turret removed to assist concealment. Extra machine-guns were carried instead. Many of these M3s were employed as command vehicles. The M3 and Stuart tanks were used from the North African campaign onwards and others were passed to the Red Army. The **Light Tank M5** was a development powered by twin Cadillac engines, similar to the M3 series and was recognisable by the rear decking accommodating the twin engines. In British ser-

The Light Tank M3A1 was the main combat version of the M2/M3 light tank series in service when the United States entered the war in late 1941. It mounted a 37-mm (1.46-in) main gun, and there was provision for three machine-guns.

vice the M5 was called the **Stuart VI**, the same designation being used for the **M5A1**. The latter had an improved turret with a bulged rear for the radio (as on the M3A3).

The M3 (and the M5) series were used by many Allied armies for reconnaissance. This example is seen negotiating an improvised German roadblock outside Harze in Belgium during the late summer of 1944.

SPECIFICATION	
Light Tank M3A1	main gun; one 0.3-in (7.62-mm)
Crew: 4	coaxial machine-gun; four 0.3-in
Weight: in action 12.9 tonnes	machine-guns
Powerplant: one Continental	**Performance:** maximum road
W-970-9A 7-cylinder radial petrol	speed 58 km/h (36 mph); maximum
engine developing 186.5 kW	road range 112.6 km (70 miles)
(250 hp)	**Fording:** 0.91 m (3 ft)
Dimensions: length 4.54 m (14 ft	**Gradient:** 60 per cent
10¾ in); width 2.24 m (7 ft 4 in);	**Vertical obstacle:** 0.61 m (2ft)
height 2.30 m (7 ft 6½ in)	**Trench:** 1.83 m (6 ft)
Armament: one 37-mm (1.46-in)	

Light Tank M24 Chaffee

By 1942 it was evident that the day of the 37-mm (1.46-in) tank gun had passed, and requests were coming from the field for a light tank with a 75-mm (2.95-in) main gun. Attempts to fit such a gun into the Light Tank M5 were unsuccessful, so a new design was initiated by Cadillac. The first was ready by late 1943 and it carried over several features of the M5, including the twin engines. However, the main change was to the turret and gun.

The new turret mounted the required 75-mm gun, development of which was lengthy. Originally it had been the old 'French 75' field gun altered for use in tanks. Various efforts were made to

lighten the gun, to the extent that it could be mounted in B-25 bomber aircraft for anti-shipping use. The result of this was that the gun could be easily adapted as a light tank weapon and in this form was designated T13E1.

Combat team

The new light tank was initially known as the **T24** but when accepted for service it became the **Light Tank M24** and was later given the name **Chaffee**. The Chaffee did not enter full service until late 1944. As a result, it was able to take only a small part in the fighting in Europe during 1945. Perhaps its biggest contribution was not really felt until the war was over, for the M24 was designed to

Armed with a 75-mm (2.95-in) gun, the M24 was introduced into service in late 1944. Post-war, it formed the basis for a new family of armoured vehicles.

be a single component in what the designers called a 'combat team' of armoured vehicles. The basis of this idea was that a common chassis could be used to provide the basis for a whole family of armoured vehicles that included self-propelled artillery, anti- aircraft tanks and so on. In fact this concept did not make the impression that it might have done as the war ended before the combat team concept could be put into full effect, and indeed the M24 did not make its full combat impact until its apearance during the Korean War of the early 1950s.

Agility

The M24 Chaffee was well armed for its size and weight, but the armour (minimum 12 mm /0.47 in and maximum 38 mm/1.5 in) had to be lighter than in heavier tanks. This was important so as to give the vehicle its agility. The M24 had a surprisingly large crew of five men (commander, gunner, loader, radio operator who sometimes acted as an assistant driver, and the driver himself).

Secondary armament

Apart from the main gun there were two 0.3-in (7.62-mm) machine-guns (one co-axial with the main gun and one in the front hull) and a 0.5-in (12.7-mm) gun on the turret mounted on a pintle. In addition to this weaponry, there was a 2-in (51-mm) smoke mortar. All this was a considerable armament for a vehicle with a tactical responsibility that was limited mainly to reconnaissance missions, but by the time the M24 entered service it had become a luxury that the US could well afford.

Many nations retained the M24 after the war. Several of the countries operating the tank went to the trouble of re-engining the vehicles and updating their fire-control systems.

SPECIFICATION	
Light Tank M24	T13E1 gun; two 0.3-in (7.62-mm)
Crew: 5	machine-guns; one 0.5-in (12.7-mm)
Weight: in action 18.4 tonnes	pintle-mounted machine-gun; one
Powerplant: two Cadillac Model	2-in (51-mm) smoke mortar
44T24 V-8 petrol engines	**Performance:** maximum road
developing 82 kW (110 hp) each	speed 56 km/h (35 mph); maximum
Dimensions: length with gun	road range 161 km (100 miles)
5.49 m (18 ft) and over hull 4.99 m	**Fording:** 1.02 m (3 ft 4 in)
(16 ft 4½ in); width 2.95 m (9 ft	**Gradient:** 60 per cent
8 in); height 2.48 m (8 ft 1½ in)	**Vertical obstacle:** 0.91 m (3 ft)
Armament: one 75-mm (2.95-in)	**Trench:** 2.44 m (8 ft)

Medium Tank M3

When the Germans invaded France in May 1940, the consequent tank tactics and doctrines which were being used were closely observed by various US Army agencies. From their observations the Americans learned that the next generation of medium tanks had to have at least a 75-mm (2.95-in) gun as their main armament. However, this presented the US with problems. This was because their next tank generation, which was already being produced in prototype form, was armed with only a 37-mm (1.46-in). This gun type was already thought to be obsolete.

Revised design

The US answer was swift and drastic: they simply took their existing design and altered it to accommodate the required 75-mm (2.95-in) gun. The turret of the new design (the **Medium Tank M2**, destined never to see active service) could not take the larger gun. The solution was to situate the main gun within the tank's hull. Consequently the revised tank design retained the 37-mm gun turret, while the main armament was located in a sponson on the right-hand side of the hull. The 75-mm gun was a revised version of the famous 'French 75' field piece as manufactured in the US. The major modification to this gun was the new ammunition which converted it into what was for the time a powerful tank weapon. The M3 featured a powerful array of secondary armament. This comprised four 0.3-in (7.62-mm) machine-guns (one in the commander's cupola atop the turret, one co-axial with the 37-mm gun, and two within the hull).

Mass production

The new design became the **Medium Tank M3**. The design was rushed into mass production at a factory which had been earlier earmarked for the M2 model. Almost as soon as production had started for the US Army, a British mission arrived in the United States on a purchasing trip. The British needed to obtain tanks to replace those which the Army had lost in France.

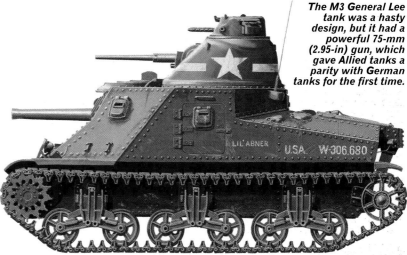

The M3 General Lee tank was a hasty design, but it had a powerful 75-mm (2.95-in) gun, which gave Allied tanks a parity with German tanks for the first time.

The new M3 was high on its shopping list. They requested a few changes to suit their requirements. The most obvious of these modifications was a revised turret rear outline to accommodate radio equipment and the absence of the cupola. This model was produced specifically for the British Army. Once delivered, the British called the M3 the **General Grant I** (or simply **Grant I**). The first of these new tanks went into action at Gazala in May 1942. Their appearance on the battlefield provided the Afrika Korps with a nasty fright as their arrival was entirely unexpected. Their combination of armament and armour (12 mm/0.47 in minimum and 50 mm/1.97 in maximum) proved to be particularly useful.

Popular tank

The Grants were later joined in British Army service by the unmodified M3 which was then labelled the **General Lee I**. Further improvement led to the

The M3 Grant was the 'British' version of the M3 Lee. The main change was to the turret profile, which had a rear overhang to house a radio set, and the silhouette was lowered by omitting the machine-gun cupola of the original turret.

M3A1 (**Lee II**) with welded construction, the up-armoured **M3A3** (**Lee IV**) with two General Motors 6-71 diesels delivering 280 kW (375 hp) and the **M3A4** (**Lee V**) with the Chrysler A-57 multibank engine. This powerplant delivered 276 kW (370 hp). The **M3A5** version was based on the M3A3 but with a riveted hull. By the time production ended in December 1942, the total had reached 6,258 and the M3 was used in virtually every theatre of war in one form or another. Many were passed to the Red Army on a Lend-Lease arrangement.

The M3 turned out to be a reliable and hardwearing vehicle. Despite this, its hull-located main gun was often a cause of tactical difficulties as its traverse was very limited. However, it did provide the punch that Allied 'tankies' required at that time. Another disadvantage was that the tactical silhouette was too high for comfort, but considering that the basic design was improvised and rushed into production, at a time when there were more questions being asked than answers provided, it turned out to be a remarkable effort.

Many of the suspension and automotive features were later incorporated into other designs and continued to provide excellent service, but perhaps the main lesson to be learned from the M3 was the latent power of US industry could design and produce such a vehicle from scratch in a short time.

As soon as the M4 entered service the M3s were usually withdrawn and converted to other roles. These new roles included service as armoured recovery vehicles. However, in the Far East they remained in use until 1945 in both Grant and Lee forms.

SPECIFICATION	
Medium Tank M3A2	main gun and four 0.3-in (7.62-mm)
Crew: 6	machine-guns
Weight: in action 27.2 tonnes	**Performance:** maximum road
Powerplant: one Continental	speed 42 km/h (26 mph); maximum
R-975-EC2 radial petrol engine	road range 193 km (120 miles)
developing 253.5 kW (340 hp)	**Fording:** 1.02 m (3 ft 4 in)
Dimensions: length 5.64 m (18 ft	**Gradient:** 60 per cent
6 in); width 2.72 m (8 ft 11 in);	**Vertical obstacle:** 0.61 m (2 ft)
height 3.12 m (10 ft 3 in)	**Trench:** 1.91 m (6 ft 3 in)
Armament: one 37-mm (1.5-in)	

M4 Sherman Medium tank

The M4A3 was one of the most developed of all the Sherman variants used until 1945, as it had a 76-mm (3-in) gun and HVSS (horizontal volute spring suspension).

While the Medium Tank M3 was being rushed into production, a new design of medium tank with a turret-mounted 75-mm (2.95-in) main gun was being pushed through the drawing board stages. To save time this was to use the same basic hull and suspension as the M3, but the upper hull was revised to accommodate the gun turret. The first example of the new tank was rolled out in September 1941, as the resulting **Medium Tank T6** had proved to be a very good design. The upper hull was cast, and this not only provided added protection but speeded production, which was a definite asset at that time.

Into production

The new weapon was rushed into production as the **Medium Tank M4**, with a 75-mm (2.95-in) main gun and co-axial 0.3-in (7.62-mm) machine-gun, 0.3-in bow gun and 0.5-in (12.7-mm) gun for AA defence. This baseline model had minimum and maximum armour thickness of 15 mm (0.59 in) and 76 mm (3 in), respectively. It proved to be an excellent fighting platform and went on to be one of the war-winning weapons of the Allies, being constructed in thousands. By the time the production lines stopped rolling in 1945 well over 40,000 had been made, and the type was built in a bewildering array of marks, submarks and variants of all kinds. Once in service the M4 series was differently engined; up-gunned to even more powerful 75-mm, 76-mm (3-in) and 105-mm (4.13-in) main weapons; and

developed into numerous 'specials' such as engineer tanks, assault tanks, tank destroyers, flame-throwers, bridging tanks, recovery vehicles, rocket launchers, self-propelled artillery carriages, anti-mine vehicles and so on, which were produced from scratch or improvised in the field. Gradually the M4 series became the T-34 of the Western Allies.

British model

The British Army purchased large numbers of M4s or took them over as part of the Lend-Lease Programme. The first of the tanks went into action with the British at El Alamein in October 1942. Thereafter, the M4 was the most numerous tank in British Army service for the remainder of World War II. To the British the M4 was the **General Sherman** (or simply **Sherman**) and they too added their variations to the long list of M4 specials: one of the best known of these was the 1944 **Sherman Firefly**, which had a 17-pdr main gun. This variant was available for service during the Normandy landings, where it proved to be the only British tank capable of countering the German Tiger and Panther.

The main models of this

seminally important armoured fighting vehicle were as follows: the **M4 (Sherman I)**, engined with the 263-kW (353-hp) Wright Whirlwind or 298-kW (400-hp) Continental R-975 radials; the **M4A1 (Sherman II)** with a fully cast rather than cast/welded hull, and alternatively engined with the 336-kW (450-hp) Caterpillar 9-cylinder diesel; the **M4A2 (Sherman III)** with a welded hull and a 313-kW (420-hp) General Motors 6-71 twin diesel powerplant; the **M4A3 (Sherman IV)** with a 373-kW (500-hp) Ford GAA III engine and horizontal- rather than

Above: Sherman Crab flail tanks were used by the 79th Armoured Division on D-Day and after, and a small number were passed to the US Army during 1944.

Above: By the winter of 1944-45, most US Army M4s had been fitted with 3-in main guns. These examples belonged to the 3rd US Armoured Division, 1st Army.

Left: A US Army M4 provides cover for GIs within an adjacent doorway. Sheer weight of numbers brought the Sherman success during the invasion of Europe.

SPECIFICATION	
Medium Tank M4A3	height 3.43 m (11 ft 2¾ in)
Crew: 5	**Performance:** maximum road
Weight: in action 32.28 tonnes	speed 47 km/h (29 mph); maximum
Powerplant: one Ford GAA V-8	road range 161 km (100 miles)
petrol engine developing 336 or	**Fording:** 0.91 m (3 ft)
373 kW (450 or 500 hp)	**Gradient:** 60 per cent
Dimensions: length, with gun	**Vertical obstacle:** 0.61 m (2 ft)
7.52 m (24 ft 8 in), over hull 6.27 m	**Trench:** 2.26 m (7 ft 5 in)
(20 ft 7 in); width 2.68 m (8 ft 9½ in);	

Several versions of M4, including this USMC M4A3 which was active in the Philippines, were fitted with flame-throwers. Most were mounted in place of the bow machine-gun and utilised the barrel of the old 75-mm M3 gun.

vertical-volute suspension; and the **M4A4 (Sherman V)** with the 317-kW (425-hp) Chrysler five-bank engine. It is also worth noting that in British service the mark numbers were suffixed whenever the Sherman's main armament was not the standard 75-mm gun, **A** indicating a 76-mm gun, **B** a 105-mm howitzer and **C** a 17-pdr anti-tank gun. The suffix **W** in US designations denoted the provision of wet ammunition stowage for reduced fire risk. Armour protection was also devel-oped during the production run, the M4A2 having a minimum and a maximum of 13 and 105 mm (0.51 and 4.13 in), equivalent figures for the M4A3 and M4A4 being 15 and 100 mm (0.59 and 3.94 in), and 20 and 85 mm (0.80 and 3.35 in), respectively.

Strength in numbers

It was the numerical superiority of the M4 that in the end made it a war winner. The M4 had many drawbacks and was far from being the ideal battle tank. It was often left behind in firepower as the German tank guns increased in power and calibre, and the armour thicknesses and arrangement were frequently found wanting. Indeed, many field improvisations had to be used to strengthen the armour. This included the simple expedient of using stacked sandbags. As well as these problems, the tank's silhouette was too high for comfort, and the interior arrangements far from perfect. Another problem frequently encountered was that with so many variants in use, spares were often not available and engine interchangeability was frequently impossible, thus causing considerable logistical troubles.

M26 Pershing US heavy tank

US Army M26 Pershing heavy tanks roll through occupied Germany in 1945. The first 20 T26E3s arrived in Europe in January 1945 and were issued to the 3rd and 9th Armoured Divisions the following month.

The heavy tank did not have an easy time during World War II as far as the Americans were concerned. Early on they realised the operational need for a heavy tank, but initially concentrated their considerable production potential on the medium tank, the M3 and M4 series in particular. A promising design, the Heavy Tank M6 came to nought as the result of this concentration of effort, but low-priority development facilities were thereafter accorded to the heavy tank. This requirement was further emphasised when the German Panther and Tiger arrived on the battlefield, and the heavy tank was then given a greater degree of priority.

Trial model

The first of the new generation of American heavy tanks was a trial model known as the **Medium Tank T20**. It had a 76-mm (3-in) gun and used a suspension very like that of the M4 medium tank but progressive development led to a newer form of suspension of the torsion-bar type. The gun was also replaced by a new 90-mm (3.54-in) main weapon in a revised turret, and after a further series of trials models culminating in the **Heavy Tank T26E3** (via the **Medium Tanks T22, T23, T25** and **T26**), the vehicle was selected for production as the **Heavy Tank M26**. It was given the name **General Pershing** (or simply **Pershing**), but by the time full trials with the new tank had been completed, only a few were ready for action in World War II.

M26s in Europe

It was early 1945 before the first M26s arrived in Europe and of these only a relative handful saw any action there. More were sent to the Pacific theatre where more were used in anger, including during the taking of Okinawa, but by the time they arrived on the scene, there was little a heavy tank could be called upon to perform.

Thus the M26 contributed little to World War II, but its design was the long-term result of the years of combat that had gone before. For perhaps the first time on an American tank, adequate consideration was given to armour protection (a minimum of 12 mm/0.47 in and a maximum of 102 mm/4.02 in) and firepower. With the 90-mm gun, originally intended for use as an anti-aircraft weapon, the M26 had armament that was the equal of and the superior of most contemporary tanks. The secondary armament comprised the standard three machine-guns: one 0.5-in (12.7-mm) and two 0.3-in (7.62-mm) weapons.

Design disadvantages

For all that, the M26 still had a few design drawbacks – the turret shape was criticised for its potential to trap shot rather than deflect it, and the retention of the bow machine-gun was even then seen as something of an anachronism (later developments did away with it). In fact the M26 was only the start of a new generation of US tank design. After 1945 the M26 was progressively developed through various models, including the M47, into the highly successful M48 Patton.

The M26 saw extensive action in Korea and was for a while one of the main types fielded by the US Army in Europe as part of NATO. The M26 also spawned many variants and hybrids as postwar development continued.

SPECIFICATION

Heavy Tank M26	
Crew: 5	(11 ft 6 in); height 2.77 m (9 ft 1 in)
Weight: in action 41.73 tonnes	**Performance:** maximum road speed 48 km/h (30 mph); maximum road range 148 km (92 miles)
Powerplant: one Ford GAF V-8 petrol engine delivering 373 kW (500 hp)	**Fording:** 1.22 m (4 ft)
Dimensions: length with gun 8.79 m (28 ft 10 in) and over hull 6.51 m (21 ft 2 in); width 3.51 m	**Gradient:** 60 per cent
	Vertical obstacle: 1.17 m (3 ft 10 in)
	Trench: 2.59 m (8 ft 6 in)

1st Army Engineers prepare an M26 to cross the Rhine. Almost on a par with the Tiger in a straight shooting match, the Pershing proved more mobile.

Sherman III (M4A2)

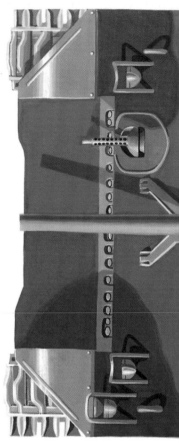

The M4A2 was the third model of the Sherman medium tank series, and by contrast to its predecessor, the M4A1 with a cast hull, it reverted to the type of welded hull first used on the M4 initial production model. The M4A2 was powered by the General Motors 6046 diesel engine, which was in effect two GM 6-71 truck motors located one on each side of the engine compartment and geared to a single propeller shaft. Manufactured to the extent of 11,283 tanks by the Fisher Division of the General Motors Corporation, Pullman Standard Car and Federal Welder after being standardised in December 1941, the M2A2 was actually the second variant to enter production. Production amounted to 8,053 tanks with the 75-mm (2.95-in) gun and 3,230 tanks with the 3-in (76.2-mm) gun, and the M4A2 was delivered mainly to the UK and USSR under Lend-Lease arrangements, being known by the former as the Sherman III or, with the 3-in gun, Sherman IIIA. A 1944 British Army 75-mm Sherman III is illustrated.

The side view of the Sherman III reveals the basic angularity of the tank. The turret and its platform (or basket) could be traversed through 360 degrees either electro-hydraulically or manually, and the main gun and co-axial machine-gun, which were fitted with a gyro-stabilisation system, could be elevated from -10° to +25° by a hydraulic system or, with the stabilisation system deactivated, by hand. Each member of the crew had a periscope for continued vision with the tank 'closed down'; with the exception of that for the co-driver/bow gunner, these periscopes could be rotated and elevated, and the gunner's periscope was mechanically linked to the gun so that the gunner's line of sight followed the alignment of the main gun in elevation and azimuth. The Sherman III's suspension was of the VVSS (Vertical Volute Spring Suspension) type: there were three bogies, each with four road wheels on each side, as well as three track-return rollers. The drive sprockets were at the front and the idlers at the rear, and each track comprised 158 shoes with a width of 0.419 m (16½ in).

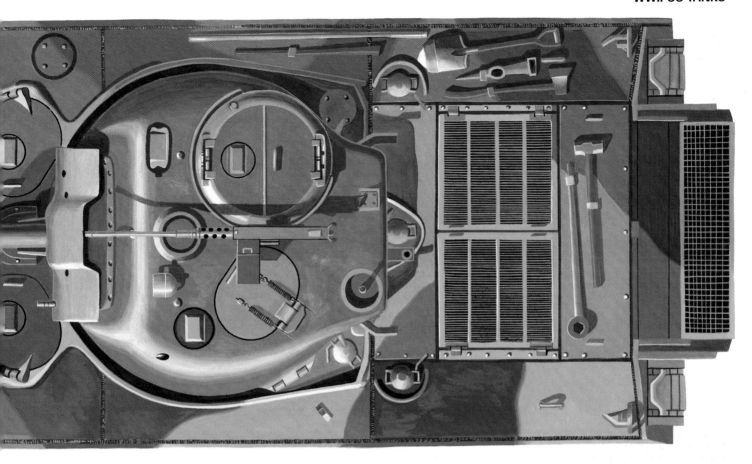

The top view of the Sherman III reveals the planform of the cast turret with its 75-mm (2.95-in) M3 gun emerging through a cast mantlet with a 0.3-in (7.62-mm) M1919A4 machine-gun mounted co-axially to the main gun's right in the M34 combination mount; there was also a 0.5-in (12.7-mm) M2HB machine-gun above the turret for AA and local defence. The turret carried three men (commander and gunner on the right with the commander behind the gunner, and loader on the left) and had two hatches over the loader and commander. There was also a 2-in (51-mm) smoke mortar in the turret roof, and on the left-hand side a pistol port also used for re-ammunitioning and the jettisoning of spent main gun cases.

Evident in the frontal view of the Sherman III are the welded nature of the hull and the single-piece cast turret. The block-like contours of the hull reflected the dictates of mass production requirements more than the operational thinking of the end users, and had three hatches. One of these was located in the belly of the vehicle for emergency use, while the other two were located above the driver and co-driver/bow gunner, located on the left and right respectively of the transmission in the nose. The co-driver/bow gunner was seated behind the ball-mounted bow machine-gun, which was normally a 0.3-in (7.62-mm) Browning M1919A4 weapon.

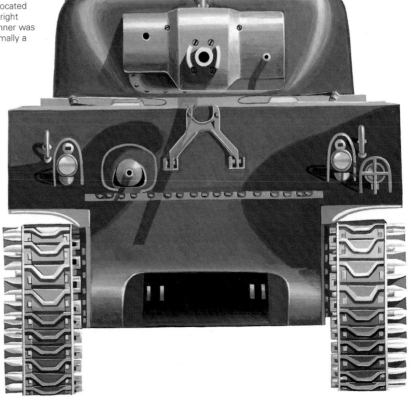

S. Nohara

One of the least-known aspects of World War II was the re-arming of the Free French forces from American sources. These M4s were supplied to the Free French in North Africa, and are seen on parade before a training exercise.

M4 Sherman
In action

What the M4 lacked in overall capabilities, it more than compensated for in its very numbers and great reliability. The original model was the M4 (Sherman I), of which 8,389 were delivered with a welded hull and Continental R-975 radial engine. The M4A1 (Sherman II) was built to the extent of 9,677 vehicles with a cast hull and the Continental engine. The M4A2 (Sherman III) was basically the M4 revised with the General Motors 6046 diesel engine, and these 11,283 tanks were joined by 11,424 examples of the M4A3 (Sherman IV) that differed only in its Ford GAA petrol engine. The M4A4 (Sherman V), of which 7,499 were completed, had a longer hull for the Chrysler multi-bank petrol engine that comprised five 6-cylinder car engines on a common crankshaft. The designation M4A5 was reserved for the Canadian Ram cruiser tank based on the M4 hull. The final production model was the M4A6 (Sherman VII), of which only 75 were completed to a standard that differed from that of the M4A4 in its Ordnance RD-1820 diesel engine.

Above: By the time of the Anzio landings in 1944, M4 crews had already learned the hard way that the tank's armour was vulnerable to most German anti-tank weapons. All manner of improvised armour was often added, one example being the use of spare lengths of track draped over the hull as seen here.

Below: A squadron of US Army M4 medium tanks assembles for the relief of the Bastogne garrison in January 1945 during the period that followed the initial German thrusts of the Ardennes campaign. The lack of any tactical camouflage demonstrates Allied air supremacy following the earlier German surprises and attacks.

Above: Seen in the hands of a British unit, these are Sherman DD (Duplex Drive) amphibious tanks photographed shortly before the D-Day landings on 6 June 1944, when this innovation allowed numbers of Shermans to 'swim' ashore from vessels moored off the Normandy beaches. The flotation screen, seen collapsed against the upper hull, was erected before launch into the water to provide buoyancy, and the propellers provided propulsion until the tracks touched the sea bottom and could take over. The DD tanks provided an answer to the problem of making early delivery of tanks on to the assault beaches before it was safe for tank landing craft to arrive, but offered very little margin for error, and many of the tanks foundered. In practice, the DD system was much more suitable for river crossings and DD Shermans were used during the Rhine crossings of 1945. Although other tanks used the DD system, the Sherman was the standard British army tank for the purpose.

Left: The T34 Calliope rocket launcher mounted on a converted M4 tank created a formidable close-support weapon. The 60 4.5-in (114-mm) rocket tubes mounted on the turret could be fired independently or in a salvo. The rockets were aimed by traversing the turret and elevating the four banks of tubes by raising the gun barrel.

SPECIFICATION	
M4A1 Sherman	**M4A2 Sherman**
Crew: 5	**Crew:** 5
Battle weight: 30164 kg (66,500 lb)	**Battle weight:** 31298 kg (69,000 lb)
Powerplant: one Continental R-975 air-cooled radial piston engine	**Powerplant:** twin General Motors 6-71 diesel piston engines
Dimensions: average length 5.9 m (19 ft 4 in); width 2.6 m (8 ft 7 in); height 2.74 m (9 ft)	**Dimensions:** average length 5.9 m (19 ft 4 in); width 2.6 m (8 ft 7 in); height 2.74 m (9 ft)
Armament: one 75-mm (2.95-in) M3 gun; two 0.3-in (7.62-mm) machine-guns; one 0.5-in (12.7-mm) AA machine-gun	**Armament:** one 75-mm (2.95-in) M3 gun; two 0.3-in (7.62-mm) machine-guns; one 0.5-in (12.7-mm) AA machine-gun
Performance: maximum speed 15-18 km/h (24-29 mph); road radius 160-241 km (100-150 miles) depending on engine type	**Performance:** maximum speed 15-18 km/h (24-29 mph); road radius 160-241 km (100-150 miles) depending on engine type
Fording: 0.91 m (3 ft)	**Fording:** 0.91 m (3 ft)
Vertical obstacle: 0.61 m (2 ft)	**Vertical obstacle:** 0.61 m (2 ft)
Trench: 2.3 m (7 ft 5 in)	**Trench:** 2.3 m (7 ft 5 in)

Seen with an M3 halftrack in the background, this M4 is typical of the US medium tank force that proved so decisive in northwest European operations from the summer of 1944. The M4 may have lacked the outright capabilities of the Germans' Panther battle and Tiger heavy tanks, but were available in far larger numbers and with adequate quantities of fuel.

There were several versions of the M4 tank fitted with flamethrowers, most of which mounted these weapons in place of the bow machine-gun. This 1st Marine Division M4 on Okinawa in May 1945 used the POA-CWS 75-HI, which mounted the flame gun inside the barrel of an old 75-mm (2.95-in) main gun.

War-winning tank

Nobody can doubt that the Medium Tank M4 Sherman was a war winner, serving in such diverse theatres as the North African desert, on the Eastern Front and in the humid heat of the Pacific war. Made in a host of variants, it overcame a definite inferiority to most German designs to spearhead the Allied defeat of the Third Reich.

The Sherman first saw action in the Battle of El Alamein in October 1942. The impact of the Sherman on the Germans was considerable, for they had only just become used to dealing with the M3 Grant and its awkward sponson-mounted 75-mm (2.95-in) gun when the Sherman, with its turret-mounted 75-mm gun and 360° traverse, arrived. This gun was capable of dealing with any of the German tanks then in service, but the Germans soon learned that the Sherman had a definite weak point: it was only relatively lightly armoured. Thus a PzKpfw IV could knock out a Sherman without too much difficulty provided it could avoid the attentions of the 75-mm gun.

This period in the Sherman's career did not last long, for once the chase across the Western Desert was over, Tunisia loomed ahead, and with it the prospect of the arrival of the German Tiger heavy tank. The Tiger was known to have exceptionally thick armour and a powerful 88-mm (3.46-in) gun, and the Sherman would obviously be

no match for this adversary. Thus there started a one-sided race in which attempts were made to add more armour protection to the Sherman, while also trying to upgun the type.

The attempts to provide extra armour were never really achieved. The armament problem could be addressed only in the design centres and in the factories. The early 75-mm guns were soon replaced by longer and more powerful 76-mm (2.99-in) guns, but almost as soon as this increase became commonplace in service it was more than countered by the Germans' introduction of the

Panther, which became the main German opposition to the Sherman as the PzKpfw IV reached the end of its development potential. The Panther had a long 75-mm gun that could easily knock out any Sherman at distances well in excess of the combat range of the 76-mm gun. It was not possible at that time to mount a larger-calibre gun on the Sherman hull. When the original M4 had been conceived, the turret ring had been designed only for a 75-mm gun, and anything heavier would have required a much larger turret ring to accommodate the considerable recoil stresses involved on firing. On the Sherman there was quite simply no room to fit a larger turret ring, so the crews had to make do with what they had, and that was the 76-mm gun. Some Sherman variants were equipped with 105-mm (4.13-in) weapons, but these were

modified howitzers with a low muzzle velocity and only limited anti-tank potential. They were intended for 'bunker-busting' and close support and never as tank-destroyers.

Weapon modification

The answer was found during 1944 in a British development known as the Firefly, which had the British 17-pdr (76-mm) anti-tank gun in a Sherman turret. The turret ring was only just large enough to take the recoil forces, and internal changes had to be introduced. The 17-pdr had considerable recoil length, so the rear of the Sherman turret had to be extended by the addition of an armoured box to accommodate the radio semi-externally. The armoured box helped to counterbalance the long barrel of the 17-pdr, which was a much more powerful weapon than its US equivalent.

In urban combat situations, tanks with rubble- and obstacle-clearing dozer blades are often of greater use than a gun tank. Most dozer tanks retain their main gun, as does this 1st Army M4 busy clearing debris from a street in Kelze, Germany.

Sentinel AC Cruiser tank

In 1939 Australia's armed forces had virtually no modern tanks and the country had virtually none of the heavy engineering capacity to produce them. The Australian government realised that it was unlikely to receive large amounts of heavy war *matériel* from overseas, and thus planned to produce its own. The army issued a specification for the **AC1 (Australian Cruiser 1)** with a 2-pdr (40-mm/1.57-in) gun and two 7.7-mm (0.303-in) machine-guns, and using as many components of the American M3 tank as possible. The powerplant was to

be three Cadillac car engines joined together, and extensive use was to be made of cast armour. A more advanced second model, the AC2, was mooted but not produced. The AC1 had armour ranging from 25 to 65 mm (1 to 2.55 in) in thickness.

Sound design

The first AC1 tanks were ready by January 1942, and were soon named **Sentinel**. The whole project up to the hardware stage had taken only 22 months. But only a few AC1 tanks were produced as by 1942 it had

The outbreak of war found Australia with no modern tank force, little industrial infrastructure and the possibility of Japanese invasion. The Sentinel AC1 was a home-grown tank developed in a very short time.

been realised that the 2-pdr gun was too small, and that the hurried design still had teething problems that had to be modified out of it. Overall, however, the Sentinel turned out to be a remarkably sound design capable of considerable stretch and modification.

This was just as well, for the **Sentinel AC3** mounted a 25-pdr (87.6-mm/3.45-in) gun to overcome the shortcomings of the 2-pdr. The 25-pdr was chosen as it was already in local production as a field gun, but it was realised that this gun would have only limited effect against armour and the prototype of a **Sentinel AC4** with a 17-pdr (76.2-mm/3-in) anti-tank gun was built. This was during mid-1943, and by then there was no longer the

chance that the Japanese might invade Australia. M3 and M4 tanks were pouring off the American production lines in such numbers that there would be more than enough to meet demand. Thus Sentinel production came to an abrupt halt in July 1943 in order to allow the diversion of industrial

potential to other priorities.
The Sentinel series was remarkable also from the design viewpoint. The use of an all-cast hull was advanced, and the acceptance of heavy guns like the 25-pdr and the 17-pdr was also ahead of contemporary thought.

In spite of the speed with which it was produced, the Sentinel AC1 was a remarkably innovative design featuring an all-cast hull and a heavy armament. This is the AC4, which mounted a 17-pdr gun.

SPECIFICATION	
Sentinel AC 1	**Dimensions:** length 6.325 m (20 ft 9 in); width 2.768 m (9 ft 1 in); height 2.56 m (8 ft 4¾ in)
Crew: 5	
Weight: 28450 kg (62,720 lb)	
Powerplant: three Cadillac petrol engines combined to develop 246 kW (330 bhp)	**Performance:** maximum speed 48.2 km/h (30 mph); range 322 km (200 miles); trench 2.438 m (8 ft)

Ram Mks I and II Cruiser tanks

When Canada entered World War II in 1939 it did not have any tank units, and the first Canadian tank training and familiarisation units had to be equipped with old World War I tanks from American sources. It was not long before the Canadian railway industry was asked by the UK if it could manufacture and supply Valentine infantry tanks, and this proved to be a major task. But the Valentines were 'infantry'

Canada had no armoured forces in 1939 but decided to build its own tank to equip the expanding Canadian army. The Ram tank utilised the chassis of the American M3, but mounted its main armament in the turret rather than in a sponson as on the original US vehicle.

tanks and the new Canadian tank units would need 'cruisers' for armoured combat. At that time there was little prospect of obtaining tanks from the UK, and the USA was not involved in the war, so the only solution was tanks of Canadian design and manufacture.

Production decisions

Thought was first given to manufacture of the American M3 (then entering produc-

tion for a British order) but, later known as the Grant/Lee, this had the drawback of a sponson-mounted main gun, whereas a turret-mounted gun was much more efficient. Thus the Canadians decided to combine the main mechanical, hull and transmission components of the M3 with a new turret mounting a 75-mm (2.95-in) gun. But there was no prospect of a 75-mm (2.95-in) gun at the time, so the readily available 2-pdr (40-mm/1.57-in) weapon was chosen for installation, with a larger-calibre gun to be introduced later: this was the 6-pdr (57-mm/2.24-in) weapon.

Building such a tank from

scratch was a major achievement for Canada, and the prototype was rolled out in June 1941 as the **Cruiser Tank Ram Mk I**. This was a remarkably workmanlike design making much use of cast armour. It was not long before the initial 2-pdr gun was replaced by a 6-pdr in the **Ram Mk II**, and production got under way by the end of 1941. The secondary armament was two 7.62-mm (0.3-in) machine-guns (one co-axial and one hull-mounted). The thickness of the armour ranged from 25 to 89 mm (1 to 3.5 in).

Combat role

All the output went to the new Canadian armoured regiments, many of which were sent to the UK. But the Ram was never to see action as a gun tank: by mid-1943 large numbers of M4 Shermans were pouring off American production lines and as this tank already had a 75-mm (2.95-in) gun it was decided

to standardise on the M4 for all Canadian units. Thus the Ram was used only for training, and as they were withdrawn many had their turrets removed to produce the **Ram Kangaroo**, which was a simple yet efficient armoured personnel carrier widely used in the European campaign after June 1944. Some Rams had their guns removed and were used as artillery observation posts (**Ram Command/OP Tank**), while others were more extensively modified to become armoured recovery vehicles. Some were used for various experimental and trial purposes, such as the mounting of a 94-mm (3.7-in) anti-aircraft gun on top of the hull. The Ram's greatest contribution to World War II was as the **Sexton** self-propelled gun with the hull adapted to take a 25-pdr artillery piece in a simple open superstructure on top of the hull. A total of 2,150 was produced for the Allied armies.

SPECIFICATION	
Ram Mk II	width 2.895 m (9 ft 6 in); height 2.667 m (8 ft 9 in)
Crew: 5	
Weight: 29484 kg (65,000 lb)	**Performance:** maximum speed 40.2 km/h (25 mph); range 232 km (144 miles); gradient 60 per cent; vertical obstacle 0.61 m (2 ft); trench 2.26 m (7 ft 5 in)
Powerplant: one Continental R≠975 radial petrol engine developing 298 kW (400 bhp)	
Dimensions: length 5.79 m (19 ft);	

Vickers Light Tanks

The Vickers Light Tanks had their origins in a series of tankettes produced by Carden-Loyd during the 1920s. One of these, the **Carden-Loyd Mk VIII**, acted as the prototype for the **Vickers Light Tank Mk I**. Only a few of these innovative vehicles were made, but they provided a great deal of insight into what would be required for later models. The Light Tank Mk I had a two-man crew and a small turret for a single 0.303-in (7.7-mm) machine-gun.

The Mk I led via the **Light Tank Mk IA** (better armour)

to the **Light Tank Mk II** (improved turret and modified suspension) which appeared in 1930, and this formed the basis for later versions up to the **Light Tank Mk VI**. All these light tanks used a simple hull with riveted armour, which was 10 to 15 mm (0.39 to 0.59 in) thick. From the **Light Tank Mk V** onwards the turret was enlarged to take two men, making a three-man crew in all, and the same mark also saw the introduction of a 0.5-in (12.7-mm) machine-gun alongside the original 0.303-in weapon. Of course there

Mounting a 0.59-in (12.7-mm) and later a 15-mm machine-gun with a 0.312-in (7.92-mm) machine-gun, the Vickers Light Tank was adequate only for armoured scouting.

After suffering heavy losses in France when mistakenly used in close support of the infantry, the Mk VI soldiered on in the Middle East and North Africa.

were other changes: the **Light Tank Mk IV** was the first to use the armour as supporting plates for the chassis, for instance. The series peaked with the **Light Tank Mk VI**, which was agile and fast, and the **Light Tank Mk VIc**, which had a 15-mm (0.59-in) machine-gun in the turret. All manner of changes to items such as engine cooling and vision devices were also introduced on this late mark, and even the machine-gun was changed to the new 0.312-in (7.92-mm) Besa machine-gun.

The tanks were widely used throughout the 1930s and the early war years. Many of the early marks were used in India and for

imperial policing duties, in which they proved ideal, but in action during the early campaigns of World War II they soon revealed themselves as being virtually useless. Their main drawback was their thin armour, which could be penetrated even by

small-calibre armour-piercing projectiles, and their lack of a weapon heavier than a machine-gun. In France in 1940 they were often used incorrectly as combat tanks, but in North Africa they remained useful in the desert campaigns for some time.

SPECIFICATION	
Light Tank Mk V	0.5-in (12.7-mm) machine-gun, supplemented by one 0.303-in (7.7-mm) machine-gun
Crew: 3	
Weight: 4,877 kg (10,572 lb)	
Powerplant: one Meadows ESTL 6-cylinder petrol engine developing 66 kW (88 bhp)	**Performance:** maximum speed 51.5 km/h (32 mph); maximum range 201 km (215 miles)
Dimensions: length 3.96 m (13 ft); width 2.08 m (6 ft 10 in); height 2.24 m (7 ft 6 in)	**Gradient:** 60 per cent
	Vertical obstacle: 0.61 m (2 ft)
Armament: (early models) one	**Trench:** 1.52 m (5 ft)

Light Tank Mk VII Tetrarch

The **Tetrarch** light tank started its life as Vickers' private-venture **Light Tank Mk VII**. The first prototype started its trials in 1938, and these trials demonstrated that the new design, known at that time as the **Purdah**, lacked the attributes that would make it an outstanding weapon. Development of this **A17** continued, though, and the type differed from the earlier light tanks by having four large road wheels on each side. Centrally mounted, the two-man turret was large enough to mount a 2-pdr (40-mm/1.57-in) gun and a 0.312-in (7.92-mm) co-axial machine-gun. The Tetrarch was finally put

into production without any great enthusiasm. By 1941 light tanks were seen as an operational liability so the few that were completed became surplus to all but limited requirements.

However, the fortunes of the Tetrarch changed with the establishment of the airborne forces, and the lightweight vehicle was accepted as the army's first airborne tank. A new glider, the General Aircraft Hamilcar, was produced as the airborne carrier for the Tetrarch, but it was not until April 1944 that the first trial landings were made. For the

tank's new role the turret was revised with a 3-in (76.2-mm) infantry support howitzer to create the **Tetrarch ICS**.

The Tetrarch went into action in the Normandy landings of 6 June 1944 during the second airborne wave. Most of them landed near the River Orne, where their combat life was short. They were next used during the Rhine crossings on 24 March 1945, but only a few were used as their numbers had been supplemented by the American M22 Locust. That marked the limits of the type's airborne operational

Carried in a Hamilcar glider, the Tetrarch was used by the British airborne forces for the Normandy landings. Outclassed by German tanks, this Tetrarch has a Littlejohn adapter fitted to its 2-pdr gun, increasing muzzle velocity and armour penetration.

career, but some were retained after the war until their Hamilcar gliders were withdrawn from service.

The Tetrarch was used for a few developments in the war. One was the **Light Tank**

Mk VIII Harry Hopkins with thicker armour (6-38 mm/ 0.25-1.5 in, as opposed to 4-15 mm/0.15-0.6 in) and another being the **Alecto** light self-propelled 94-mm (3.7-in) howitzer.

Originally a Vickers private venture, the Tetrarch was put into production despite its lack of adequate armour and armament.

SPECIFICATION	
Tetrarch	mm/1.58in) gun; one 3-in (76.2-mm) howitzer; one 0.312-in (7.92-mm) light machine-gun
Crew: 3	
Weight: 7620 kg (16,800 lb)	
Powerplant: one Meadows 12-cylinder petrol engine delivering 123-kW (165-bhp)	**Performance:** maximum road speed 64 km/h (40 mph); range 224 km (140 miles)
Dimensions: length overall 4.31 m (14 ft 1½ in); length of hull 4.12 m (13 ft 6 in); width 2.31 m (7 ft 7 in); height 2.12 m (6 ft 11½ in)	**Fording:** 0.91 m (3 ft)
	Gradient: 60 per cent
	Vertical obstacle: 0.51 in (1 ft 8 in)
Armament: one 2-pdr (40-	**Trench:** 1.53 m (5 ft)

Mks I and II Matilda Infantry tanks

A requirement for a British army 'Infantry' tank was first made in 1934 and the immediate result was the **A11 Infantry Tank Mk I**, later nicknamed **Matilda I**. This was a very simple and small tank with a two-man crew but with armour heavy enough to defeat any contemporary anti-tank gun. The small turret mounted a single 12.7- or 7.7-mm (0.5- or 0.303-in) Vickers machine-gun, and the engine was a commercial Ford V-8 unit. An order for 140 was issued in April 1937, but when the type was tried in combat in France in 1940 it revealed shortcomings: it was too slow and underarmed for any form of armoured warfare, and the small numbers that remained after Dunkirk were used only for training.

Improvements

The Matilda I was intended only as an interim type before the **A12 Infantry Tank Mk II** became available. This project began in 1936 and the first examples were completed in 1938. The Mk II, known later as **Matilda II**, was a much larger vehicle than the Matilda I with a four-man crew, a turret mounting a 2-pdr (40-mm/1.575-in) gun, and cast armour (varying in thickness from 20 to 78 mm/0.8 to 3.1 in) capable of defeating all known anti-tank projectiles. The Matilda II was slow as it was intended for the direct support of infantry units, a role in which speed was not essential. Overall it was a good-looking tank and proved to be far more reliable than many of its contemporaries. And despite the light gun it was found to be a good vehicle in combat.

The main combat period for the Matilda (the term Matilda II was dropped when the little Matilda I was withdrawn in 1940) was the early North African campaign, where the type's armour proved to be effective against all Italian and German anti-tank guns with the exception of the German '88'. The Matilda was one of the armoured mainstays of the British forces until El Alamein, after which its place was taken by better armed and faster designs. But the importance of the Matilda did not diminish, for it then embarked on a career as a special-purpose tank.

Mine clearance

One of the most important of these special purposes was as a flail tank for mine-clearing. Starting with the **Matilda Baron** and then the **Matilda Scorpion**, it was used extensively for this role, but Matildas were also used to push AMRA mine-clearing rollers. Another variant was the **Matilda CDL** (Canal Defence Light), which used a special turret with a powerful light source to create 'artificial moonlight'. Matildas were also fitted with dozer blades as the **Matilda Dozer** for combat engineering, and many were fitted with various flame-throwing devices as the **Matilda Frog**. There were many other special and demolition devices used with the Matilda, not all of them under British auspices for the Matilda also became an important Australian tank. In fact Matilda gun tanks were used extensively by the Australian army in New Guinea and elsewhere until the war's end in 1945, and the Australians devised several flame-throwing variants. The Germans also used several captured Matildas to mount anti-tank weapons.

It is doubtful if a complete listing of all the many Matilda variants will ever be made, for numerous 'field modifications' and other unrecorded changes were made to the basic design. But the Matilda accommodated them all with comparative ease, and many old soldiers look back on this tank with affection for, despite its slow speed and light armament, it was reliable and steady, and above all it had good armour.

Seen in the North African desert as a 'non-runner', this Matilda has its engine covers lifted and its turret traversed right round to the left. The item protruding from the left (in fact the rear) of the turret is the radio antenna in its lowered position.

The Matilda was never fast and was notably undergunned by the standards even of 1940, but had the priceless benefit of offering its crew excellent protection and great mechanical reliability.

SPECIFICATION	
Matilda II	5 in); width 2.59 m (8 ft 6 in);
Crew: 4	height 2.51 m (8 ft 3 in)
Weight: 26926 kg (59,360 lb)	**Performance:** maximum speed
Powerplant: two Leyland 6-cylinder petrol engines each developing 71 kW (95 bhp) or two AEC diesels each developing 65 kW (87 bhp)	24 km/h (15 mph); maximum cross-country speed 12.9 km/h (8 mph); road range 257 km (160 miles); vertical obstacle 0.609 m (2 ft); fording 0.914 m (3 ft); trench
Dimensions: length 5.613 m (18 ft	2.133 m (7 ft)

The Matilda was the only British tank with enough armour to withstand the efforts of German tank guns in the early years of World War II. After a brief moment of French glory in 1940, it won its real reputation in North Africa.

Mk III Valentine Infantry tank

In 1938 Vickers was invited to join in the production programme for the new Matilda II tank, but as the company already had a production line established to produce a heavy 'Cruiser' tank known as the A10, it was invited to produce a new infantry tank based upon the A10. Vickers duly made its plans and its A10-derived infantry tank was ordered into production in July 1939. Up to that date the army planners had some doubts as to the effectiveness of the Vickers submission, largely as a result of its retention of a small two-man turret which would limit possible armament increases, but by mid-1939 war was imminent and tanks were urgently required.

Mass-produced from 1940, the Valentine fought through the North African desert campaigns. Although slow like the Matilda, it was a sturdy vehicle and proved capable of upgunning as the war progressed.

Heavy armour

The new Vickers tank, soon known as the **Infantry Tank Mk III Valentine**, drew heavily on experience gained with the A10, but was much more heavily protected with 8- to 65-mm (0.32- to 2.55-in) armour. As many of the A10's troubles had already been overcome, these solutions were built into the Valentine, which proved to be a relatively trouble-free vehicle. Mass production began rapidly, and the first **Valentine I** examples were ready in late 1940. By 1941 the Valentine

was an established type, and many were used as Cruiser tanks to overcome deficiencies.

The Valentine was one of the most important British tanks, but the main reason for this was quantity rather than quality. By early 1944, when production ceased, 8,275 had been made and during one period in 1943 one quarter of all British tank production was of the Valentine series. Valentines were also produced in Canada and by several British concerns other than Vickers.

Multiple variants

There were numerous vari-

ants on the Valentine. Gun tanks ran to 11 different marks with the main armament increasing from a 2-pdr (**Valentine I-VII**) via the 6-pdr (**Valentine VIII-X**) to a 75-mm (2.95-in) gun (**Valentine XI**), and there was even a self-propelled gun version mounting a 25-pdr field gun and known as the **Bishop**. Special-purpose Valentines ran the whole gamut from mobile bridges (**Valentine Bridgelayer**) to Canal Defence Lights (**Valentine CDL**) and from observation posts (**Valentine OP**) to mine-clearing devices (**Valentine Scorpion** and **Valentine AMRA**). The num-

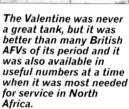

ber of these variants was legion, many of them 'one-offs' for trials or experimental purposes. Typical were the **Duplex Drive Valentine** vehicles used to test the DD system. Actually these tanks were so successful that the Valentine was at one time the standard DD tank. There were also **Valentine Flamethrower** tanks, and one attempt was made to produce a special tank-killer with a 6-pdr anti-tank gun behind a shield. This came to nothing but the Valentine chassis was later used as the basis for the **Archer**, an open-topped vehicle with a 17-pdr gun pointing to the rear. This was used in Europe from 1944 onwards.

An early model Valentine provides the focus of attention as Malta celebrates King George VI's birthday. The Valentine was one of the more successful pre-war designs, and saw service in many theatres.

The Valentine was never a great tank, but it was better than many British AFVs of its period and it was also available in useful numbers at a time when it was most needed for service in North Africa.

The basic Valentine tank was extensively modified throughout its operational career, but it was always reliable and sturdy. The Valentine was one of the British army's most important tanks at one point. It was used by many Allied armies such as that of New Zealand, and many saw action in Burma. The bulk of the Canadian output was sent to the USSR, where the type appears to have given good service. The Valentine did have its drawbacks, but overall its main contribution was that it was available in quantity at a time when it was most needed, and not many British tank designs could claim the same.

SPECIFICATION	
Valentine III/IV	height 2.273 m (7 ft 5½ in)
Crew: 3	**Performance:** maximum speed
Weight: 17690 kg (39,000 lb)	24 km/h (15 mph); maximum cross-
Powerplant: one AEC diesel	country speed 12.9 km/h (8 mph);
developing 98 kW (131 bhp) in	road range 145 km (90 miles);
Mk III or GMC diesel developing	vertical obstacle 0.838 m (2 ft 9 in);
103 kW (138 bhp) in Mk IV	fording 0.914 m (3 ft); trench
Dimensions: length 5.41 m (17 ft	2.286 m (7 ft 6 in)
9 in); width 2.629 m (8 ft 7½ in);	

Mk IV Churchill Infantry tank

Even to provide a list of all the **Churchill** marks and variants would fill many pages, so this entry can provide only a brief outline of what was one of the most important British tanks of World War II. In production terms the Churchill came second to the Valentine, but in the scope of applications and variants it came second to none.

The Churchill was born in a specification known as the A20 which was issued in September 1939 and envisaged a return to the trench fighting of World War I. Hence the A20 tank was a virtual update of the old World War I British 'lozenge' tanks, but experiences with the A20 prototype soon showed that a lighter model would be required. Vauxhall Motors then took over a revised specification known as the **A22** and designed the **Infantry Tank Mk IV**, later named Churchill.

Rushed production

Vauxhall had to work from scratch and yet came up with a well armoured tank with large overall tracks that gave the design an appearance not unlike that of World War I tanks. Unfortunately the early Churchill marks were so rushed into production that about the first 1,000 examples had to be extensively modified before they could even be issued to the troops. But they were produced at a period when invasion seemed imminent and even unreliable tanks were regarded as better than none. Later marks had these early troubles eliminated.

The Churchill was essentially designed for a return to trench warfare conditions. As such it was a classic infantry tank, slow but heavily armoured. Introduced in 1943, its chassis was subsequently used for a host of specialist vehicles.

The Churchill VII introduced an all-cast turret armed with a 75-mm (2.95-in) gun, a high-velocity weapon characterised by a single-baffle muzzle brake to help reduce the recoil forces transmitted to the turret.

The armament of the Churchill followed the usual path from 2-pdr (**Churchill I-II**), via 6-pdr (**Churchill III-IV**) eventually to a 75-mm (2.95-in) gun in the **Churchill IV (NA 75)** and **Churchill VI-VII**. There were also **Churchill CS** (close support) variants with 76.2-mm (3-in) and eventually 95-mm (actually 94-mm/3.7-in) howitzers in the **Churchill V** and **Churchill VIII**. The Churchill I also had a hull-mounted 76.2-mm (3-in) howitzer. The turrets also changed from being cast items to being riveted or composite structures, and such refinements as track covers and

engine cooling improvements were added successively. In all, there were 11 Churchill marks, the last three of them 'reworks' of earlier marks in order to update early models to Mk VII standard with the 75-mm (2.95-in) gun.

Operational use

In action the heavy armour of the Churchill (16-102 mm/0.6-4 in for Mks I-VI and 25-152 mm/1-6 in for Mks VI-VIII) was a major asset despite the fact that the tank's first operational use was in the 1942 Dieppe landings, when many of the Churchills proved unable

Cumbersome and slow on its own tracks, the Churchill was generally moved to its operational area on some type of special transporter whenever possible. This also reduced the wear on the tank's engine, transmission, suspension and tracks.

Churchills move up to the front line in Normandy past a column of US M4 Shermans early in August 1944. Note how the crews have attached large sections of track to the front hull and the turret side as additional armour.

even to reach the beach, let alone cross it. But in Tunisia the type proved it could climb mountains and provide excellent support for armoured as well as infantry units, though it was often too slow to exploit local advantages.

It was as a special-purpose tank that the Churchill excelled. Many of these special variants became established as important vehicles in their own right, and included in this number were the **Churchill AVRE** (Armoured Vehicle Royal Engineers), **Churchill Crocodile** flamethrower tank and various **Churchill Bridgelayer** and **Churchill Ark** vehicles. Then there were the numerous Churchill mine-warfare variants from

the **Churchill Plough** variants to the **Churchill Snake** with Bangalore torpedoes. The Churchill lent itself to modification, and was able to carry a wide assortment of odd gadgets such as wall demolition charges (**Churchill Light Carrot, Churchill Onion** and **Churchill Goat**) mine-clearing wheels (**Churchill AVRE/CIRD**), carpet-laying devices for use on boggy ground (**Churchill AVRE Carpetlayer**), armoured recovery vehicles (**Churchill ARV**), and so on.

The Churchill may have looked archaic, but it gave excellent service and many were still around in the mid-1950s in various guises, the last Churchill AVRE not being retired until 1965.

SPECIFICATION	
Churchill VII	3.454 m (11 ft 4 in)
Crew: 5	**Performance:** maximum speed
Weight: 40642 kg (89,600 lb)	20 km/h (12.5 mph); maximum
Powerplant: one Bedford twin-six	cross-country speed about
petrol engine developing 261 kW	12.8 km/h (8 mph); range 145 km
(350 bhp)	(90 miles); fording 1.016 m (3 ft
Dimensions: length 7.442 m (24 ft	4 in); vertical obstacle 0.76 m (2 ft
5 in); width 2.438 m (8 ft); height	6 in); trench 3.05 m (10 ft)

Below: Fast, but possessing neither the armour nor the firepower of German tanks, the lack of basic balance in the design of the Cruiser Tank Mk VI Crusader had been revealed long before Operation Crusader in 1941. However, the troops in the North African desert had to fight with whatever was available – in this case a Cruiser Mk IV, a type that was fast but also poorly armed and indifferently protected.

SPECIFICATION

A34 Cruiser Tank Comet
Crew: five (comprising commander, gunner, loader/radio operator, driver and hull gunner)
Type: cruiser tank

Dimensions

length: 7.66 m (25 ft 1½ in) with the gun forward; **width:** (overall) 3.07 m (10 ft 1 in) and over tracks 3 m (9 ft 10¼ in); **height:** overall 2.67 m (8 ft 9¼ in)

Combat weight

33225 kg (73,248 lb)

Powerplant

one Rolls-Royce Meteor Mk 3 water-cooled V-12 petrol engine rated at 447.5 kW (600 bhp) at 2,550 rpm
Transmission: Borg & Beck hydraulically operated dry twin-plate clutch and Merritt-Brown Type Z.5 gearbox with five forward and one reverse speeds
Suspension: Christie type with five twin road wheels on each side (hydraulic shock absorbers on the front two and rear two pairs)

Fuel capacity

standard 527.3 litres (116 Imp gal)

Performance

Maximum road speed: 51.5 km/h (32 mph)

Maximum road range: 198 km (123 miles)
Fording: 1.12 m (3 ft 8 in)
Vertical obstacle: 0.91 m (3 ft)
Trench: 2.44 m (8 ft)

Armament

Main armament: one QF 77-mm (3.03-in) main gun with 61 rounds of APCBC and HE ammunition
Secondary armament: two 0.312-in (7.92-mm) Besa machine-guns (one co-axial and one in the bow) with 5,175 rounds of ammunition, one 0.303-in (7.7-mm) Bren machine gun stowed in the rear turret locker with 600 rounds, one 2-in (50.8-mm) bomb thrower on the turret roof with 20 bombs
Smoke dischargers: two on each side of the hull rear

Armour

Welded steel hull: front 76 mm (3 in) vertical; glacis 32 mm (1.26 in) at 32°; nose 63 mm (2.48 in) at 20°; sides and rear 32 mm (1.26 in) vertical; lower sides 29 mm (1.14 in) vertical outer and 14 mm (0.55 in) vertical inner; top 25 mm (0.98 in) horizontal and belly 14 mm (0.55 in) horizontal
Cast/welded steel turret: front and mantlet 101 mm (3.98 in) vertical; sides 63 mm (2.48 in) vertical; rear 57 mm (2.24 in) vertical; top 25 mm (0.98 in) horizontal

Cruiser tanks
In action

The cruiser tank was planned as the successor to the medium tank, and as such was intended to be lighter and cheaper than the infantry tank. The combination of reduced weight and a moderately powerful engine resulted in a tank that was faster and more agile than the infantry tank, and the task of the cruiser tank was therefore determined as longer-range operations to outflank the enemy or exploit any breaches in his line. The fallacy of the concept was brutally exposed in France and North Africa during 1940-42, when the cruisers suffered heavy losses to no good effect.

Above: A Cruiser Tank Mk IV in the Western Desert, probably during July or August 1941. The vehicle has lost one of its tracks, and the process of refitting this vital element of the tank's traction was lengthy and laborious at the best of times, but even more of a challenge under the heat and sand encountered in desert conditions.

In desert operations, natural defensive features are often hard to find. On such occasions, tank units of World War II would cluster into an easily defended laager for the night. The scene, typical of the period of Operation Crusader, includes both of the cruiser tank types that were the mainstays of the 8th Army at time time, namely the Mk IV (left) and Mk VI Crusader (right).

Early cruiser tanks

During the early 1930s the British decided to replace the dual-role medium tank with separate single-role cruiser and infantry tanks optimised for the mobile warfare and infantry support roles respectively. The first cruiser tank was the **A9**, otherwise **Cruiser Tank Mk I** designed by Vickers in 1934 as a simpler and cheaper derivative of the A6 (Medium Tank Mk III). The type entered small-scale production in 1937 as a 12701-kg (28,000-lb) vehicle with a crew of six, armour between 4 and 16 mm (0.16 and 0.63 in) thick, and the armament of one 2-pdr (40-mm/1.57-in) gun and one 0.303-in (7.7-mm) machine-gun in the power-traversed main turret, and one 0.303-in machine-gun in each of two other turrets.

The two types of tank produced by pre-war theory: on the left, the fast but very vulnerable Mk IV Cruiser; on the right, the thickly armoured Matilda, which could only make about 13 km/h (8 mph) cross-country.

Reduced weaponry

The replacement of the previously standard 3-pdr (47-mm/1.85-in) gun by a 2-pdr weapon was a sensible move, despite the reduction in main armament calibre thereby involved, as the smaller calibre weapon had a higher muzzle velocity and thus fired its solid projectile with somewhat greater armour penetrating capability than the earlier weapon. Production of the A9 amounted to only 125 vehicles, and the type remained in service up to 1941, seeing service in France and North Africa.

At much the same time Vickers undertook design of the 13971-kg (30,800-lb) **A10** as an infantry tank based on the A9 but with the armour thickness increased to a maximum of 30 mm (1.18 in). The A9's subsidiary turrets were not retained in the new type, and in 1940 the

Vickers co-axial machine-gun was replaced by a 0.312-in (7.92-mm) Besa, a weapon of the same type sometimes being added in the nose in place of some of the ammunition stowage. By the time the A10 was ready for production it had been reclassified as the **Heavy Cruiser Tank Mk II**. There was also a **Mk IIA** with detail improvements and, as with the A9, an infantry close-support version with a 94-mm (3.7-in) howitzer.

New initiative

There now came a turning point in British tank design with the 1936 decision to develop new cruiser tanks on the basis of the suspension system devised in the US by J. Walter Christie. This led to the **A13** designed by Nuffield. The 14429-kg (31,810-lb) prototype was completed in 1937 and immediately displayed quite excellent performance as a result of the Christie suspension combined with a high power-to-weight ratio. Only moderate armour was provided, to thicknesses of between 6 and 14 mm

Cruiser Mk IVs were armed with the 2-pdr gun, which had weak armour penetration and, worse, no high-explosive round to tackle enemy anti-tank guns and strongpoints.

(0.24 and 0.55 in) as the tank was intended to rely on performance and agility as the main platforms of its protection, and the armament was also modest. This armament comprised a turret-mounted 2-pdr gun and a 0.303-in Vickers co-axial machine-gun. The reduction in the number of machine-guns had the very useful advantage of allowing a reduction in crew number to a mere four men. Deliveries of this **Cruiser Tank Mk III** began in December 1938 and the production programme was completed in 1939. The Cruiser Tank Mk III was used in France during 1940 and in North Africa during 1941, and proved a failure because of its noticeably inadequate armour.

It was this failing that the **Cruiser Tank Mk IV (A13 Mk II)** was designed to over-

come through the thickening of the armour, increasing the protective basis to 20 or 30 mm (0.79 or 1.18 in) in more important areas. Even so, the Mk IV was decidedly under-armoured by contemporary standards. The **Mk IVA** introduced a 0.312-in Besa co-axial machine-gun in place of the original Vickers weapon, and also featured a combined gearchange and steering gearbox. As with the Mk III, range was too limited for effective independent operations, and the angular design of the box-like hull and V-sided turret provided many shot traps.

The **A14** had Horstmann suspension and the **A16** was designed around Christie suspension, but

both were unsuccessful and cancelled in 1939, the A16 even before the prototype had been completed.

Faster model

The next British cruiser tank was therefore the **A13 Mk III** or **Cruiser Tank Mk V Covenanter**. Intended to provide higher speed for enhanced battlefield capability, the A13 was based on the A13 Mk II with a purpose-designed engine, the thickness of the armour was increased to between 7 and 40 mm (0.28 and 1.575 in), and the turret was a low-silhouette unit carrying the same basic armament as its predecessor. The tank did show distinct potential, and total production amounted to 1,771 units.

Cruisers were designed to perform the cavalry roles of reconnaissance and pursuit. These are Mk I A9s, the first Cruiser tanks; they were lightly protected and armed with the feeble 2-pdr. Many were left in France after Dunkirk; survivors served in North Africa until 1941.

SPECIFICATION	
Cruiser Tank Mk V Covenanter	height 2.23 m (7 ft 4 in)
Crew: 4	**Armament:** one 40-mm (1.57-in)
Weight: 18289 kg (40,320 lb)	main gun and one 0.312-in
Powerplant: one Meadows DAV	(7.92-mm) Besa co-axial machine-
petrol engine delivering 224 kW	gun
(300 hp)	**Performance:** maximum road
Dimensions: length overall 5.79 m	speed 50 km/h (31 mph); maximum
(19 ft); width 2.62 m (8 ft 7 in);	road range 161 km (100 miles)

Cruiser Tank Mk VIII Cromwell IV

The A27M Cromwell IV, shown here sporting the 'desert rat' insignia of the 7th Armoured Division, was built to a 1941 General Staff requirement for a 'heavy cruiser' tank. Experience with the earlier cruiser tanks had demonstrated that high speed could not compensate for lack of armour and inadequate firepower, so the Cromwell was nearly 50 per cent heavier than the Crusader it replaced, and proportionally better armoured. The other two main features of this British tank were a 57-mm (2.24-in) gun soon replaced by a capable 75-mm (2.95-in) gun that could fire HE shells as well as AP shot for much enhanced tactical versatility, and a powerful yet compact and trusty Rolls-Royce Meteor engine, which was a development of the classic Merlin aero engine downrated for greater reliability and extended operational life.

Whereas the first three Cromwell marks had been fitted with the 6-pdr (57-mm/2.24-in) anti-tank gun firing only solid shot, the Cromwell Mk IV introduced the 75-mm (2.95-in) QF Gun Mk V. This was a 6-pdr weapon with the barrel bored out, shortened and fitted with a single-baffle muzzle brake. It weighed 692 lb (314 kg), and the L/36.5 barrel fired the 13.75-lb (6.24-kg) projectile with a muzzle velocity of 2,030 ft (619 m) per second. Several types of projectile could be fired, and as well as a capable HE projectile these included an anti-tank type which could penetrate 68 mm (2.68 in) of armour at an angle of 30° from a range of 455 m (500 yards).

The secondary armament of the Cromwell IV comprised two 0.312-in (7.92-mm) Besa machine-guns and one 2-in (50.8-mm) bomb thrower. The machine-guns were installed as one in the front of the hull in a ball mounting providing a traverse arc of 32° (12° left and 20° right of the centreline), and the other co-axial with and to the left of the main armament; 22 boxes of ammunition for these weapons held a total of 4,952 rounds. The bomb thrower was located on the right-hand side of the turret roof, and was provided with 30 bombs. Local defence and anti-aircraft capability was provided initially by two 0.303-in (7.7-mm) Vickers 'K' or one 0.303-in Bren machine-guns, for which 2,000 or 600 rounds respectively were provided. These weapons were later discarded.

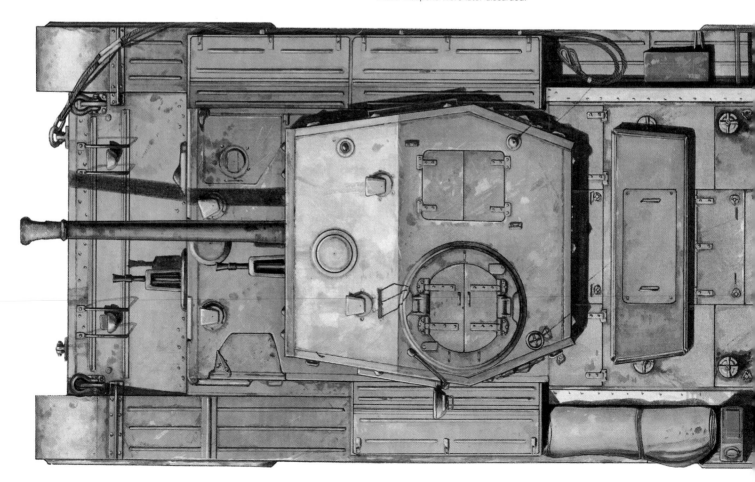

The ammunition for the 75-mm (2.95-in) main gun amounted to 64 rounds carried in the turret and hull. The ammunition types, of which all but the Smoke Emission were American, included the M48 HE, M61 APC, M72 AP, and M64 Smoke White Phosphorus types.

The suspension of the Cromwell series was of the Christie type, with five road wheels on each side. Each of these wheels was independently sprung on pivoting axle arms supported in cross tubes attached to the bottom plate of the hull. Hydraulic shock absorbers were fitted to the first, second, fourth and fifth suspension units. The track, resting on the centres of these road wheels, passed over a rear drive sprocket and front idler, and on each side comprised 125 manganese steel links with a pitch of 100 mm (3.93 in).

The turret of the Cromwell IV was of riveted construction to thicknesses of 76 and 63 mm (3 and 2.38 in) respectively on the front and sides, with 20 mm (0.79 in) on the roof. The turret carried the commander, gunner and loader, and was hydraulically powered for 360° traverse, although a manual system was also provided for emergency use. The gun was manually elevated through 32.5° between -12.5° and +20°.

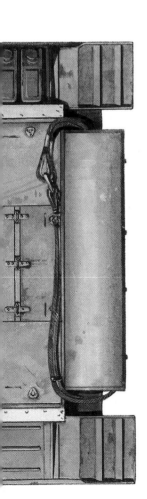

The Meteor petrol engine was a water-cooled V-12 unit with a volume of 27.02 litres (1,649 cu in), and was supplied with fuel from the standard two-tank capacity of 527 litres (116 Imp gal) and then the auxiliary one-tank capacity of 136 litres (30 Imp gal). The engine drove the Merritt-Brown Type Z.5 gearbox (five forward and one reverse speeds) via a hydraulically operated dry twin-plate clutch.

The hull gunner sat in the front left of the hull and the driver on the right with the gear-change lever between his knees and the steering levers on each side. In the turret, the gunner and loader sat on the left and right of the gun, and the commander to the rear of the gunner.

Cruiser Tank Mk VI Crusader

The Crusader III was the first British tank to be armed with an effective gun, the 6-pdr. Its other great strongpoint was its suspension, which was so tough that its theoretical maximum speed could often be exceeded.

The **Cruiser Tank Mk VI**, or **Crusader**, was a Nuffield design and used the Nuffield Liberty Mk III engine and a Nuffield gearbox. In overall terms the Crusader resembled the Covenanter with differences such as the use of five rather than four road wheels on each side. Known as the **A15**, the prototype had the unusual feature of two auxiliary forward turrets, each with a 0.31-in (7.92-mm) machine-gun, one in front of the driver's hood and the other for a gunner seated in the front hull. The driver's gun and turret were eliminated after early trials, which also highlighted inadequate engine cooling and unreliable gearchange arrangements. These and other problems took a long time to remedy and, indeed, many were still present when the Crusader was withdrawn from service.

Early production

The first production model was the **Crusader I**, which had a 2-pdr (40-mm/1.58-in) gun and armour on a 40-mm (1.58-in) basis. When the Crusader I entered service in 1941 it was already inadequate for combat. The new

6-pdr (57-mm/2.24-in) gun was still in short supply, so only the armour was improved, its thickness being increased to a 50-mm (1.97-in) basis to produce the **Crusader II**. It was not until the **Crusader III** that the 6-pdr gun was fitted. This turned out to be the main 'combat' version of the Crusader during the North African campaigns before it was replaced by the Sherman. In action the Crusader was fast, but its armour proved to be too thin, and the tanks armed with the 2-pdr gun were no

match for their German counterparts. Their reliability problems did little for the Crusaders' chances of survival under desert conditions, but gradually improvements were effected. The **Crusader IICS** was fitted with a 3-in (76.2-mm) howitzer.

Other uses

Once they were no longer in use as combat tanks, Crusaders were used for a variety of special purposes. Some were converted as anti-aircraft tanks mounting either a single 40-mm Bofors

gun (**Crusader III AA I**) or twin or triple 20-mm cannon (**Crusader III AA II**). There was a **Crusader ARV** armoured recovery vehicle version without a turret but with an 'A' frame jib, and another turretless version as the **Crusader Dozer** with a dozer blade for combat engineering. Many Crusaders were fitted with an open box superstructure for use as **Crusader Gun Tractor** high-speed artillery tractors, and these were widely used in Europe in 1944-45 to tow

17-pdr (3-in/76.2-mm) anti-tank guns. Many more were used for trials that ranged from engine installations via mine warfare devices to wading trials that led to 'Duplex Drive' tanks.

The Crusader was one of the classic British tanks of World War II, even taking into account its lack of combat efficiency. Despite its low and aggressive silhouette it was outclassed as a battle tank on many occasions, but saw the war out in several special-purpose variants.

Visible on the upper decking of this Crusader's hull is the small auxiliary turret, armed with a Besa 0.31-in (7.92-mm) machine-gun, that was often removed in the field to provide greater stowage volume in the hull.

SPECIFICATION	
Crusader III	or two 0.31-in (7.92-mm) Besa
Crew: 3	machine-guns
Weight: 20067 kg (44,240 lb)	**Performance:** maximum road
Powerplant: one Nuffield Liberty Mk III petrol engine developing 254 kW (340 bhp)	speed 43.4 km/h (27 mph); maximum cross-country speed 24 km/h (15 mph); range with extra fuel tank 204 km (127 miles)
Dimensions: length 5.99 m (19 ft 8 in); width 2.64 m (8 ft 8 in); height 2.24 m (7 ft 4 in)	**Fording:** 0.99 m (3 ft 3 in)
	Vertical obstacle: 0.69 m (2 ft 3 in)
Armament: one 6-pdr (57-mm/ 2.24-in) main gun with 65 rds, one	**Trench:** 2.59 m (8 ft 6 in)

Cruiser Tank Mk VIII Cromwell

In the UK the somewhat spurious distinction between the 'cruiser' and the 'infantry' tank persisted almost to the end of World War II, despite the fact that the unfortunate experiences of the early 'cruiser' designs had highlighted the drawbacks of producing a lightly armed and armoured main battle tank, and continued even when a replacement for the Crusader was being sought. The need for thicker armour protection, a larger-calibre gun and considerably more power was finally realised and in 1941, therefore, a new specification was issued. This requirement was answered by two **A27** variants, the A27L with the Liberty engine (this was to become the Centaur) and the **A27M** with the Rolls-Royce Meteor engine that

became the **Cruiser Tank Mk VIII Cromwell**.

Ready for conflict

The first Cromwell tanks were completed in January 1943. The first three marks were the **Cromwell I** with one main gun and two Besa machine-guns, the **Cromwell II** with wider tracks and only one machine-gun, and the **Cromwell III**, all of them with the 6-pdr (47-mm/ 2.24-in) gun as their main armament. By 1943 it had been decided that something heavier would be required, and for once things moved quickly, allowing the first 75-mm (2.95-in) **Cromwell IV** tanks to be issued in October 1943. Thereafter the 75-mm gun remained the Cromwell's main gun until the **Cromwell VIII** tank, which had a 94-

A Cromwell roars through a village in Normandy, in August 1944. Initially mounting a 6-pdr gun, by D-Day the type was armed with a 75-mm (2.95-in) gun which gave it a reasonable chance against German armour.

mm (3.7-in) howitzer for the close support role.

Perhaps the main value of the Cromwell to British armoured regiments during 1943 was as a training tank, for at last the troops had a tank that was something of

a match for its German counterparts. The Cromwell had thicker armour (8-76 mm; 0.34-3 in) than any early 'cruiser' tank, and the 75-mm gun, which shared many components with the smaller 6-pdr, at last pro-

vided British 'tankies' with an effective weapon. But by the time it was ready for active service, the Cromwell was in the process of being replaced by an American medium tank, the M4 Sherman, for purposes of

Although the majority of British tank units were equipped with the Sherman, the Cromwell was a successful design, doing much to restore the imbalance of quality between British and German armour.

SPECIFICATION	
Cromwell IV	**Armament:** one 75-mm (2.95-in)
Crew: 5	main gun with 64 rds, two 0.31-in
Weight: 27942 kg (61,600 lb)	(7.92-mm) Besa machine-guns
Powerplant: one Rolls-Royce	**Performance:** maximum speed
Meteor V-12 petrol engine	61 km/h (38 mph); road range
developing 425 kW (570 bhp)	278 km (173 miles)
Dimensions: length overall 6.42 m	**Fording:** 1.22 m (4 ft)
(21 ft ¾ in); width 3.05 m (10 ft);	**Vertical obstacle:** 0.91 m (3 ft)
height 2.51 m (8 ft 3 in)	**Trench:** 2.29 m (7 ft 6 in)

standardisation and logistic safety. However, the Cromwell did see useful service. Many of the tanks were used by the 7th Armoured Division in the campaigns that followed from the

Normandy landings. Here the excellent performance provided by the Meteor engine made the Cromwell a well-liked vehicle; it was fast and reliable, and the gun proved easy to lay and fire.

Further development

The Cromwell was but a stepping stone to the later Comet tank, which emerged as perhaps the best all-round British tank of World War II. But the Cromwell was an important vehicle. Some were used as mobile artillery observation posts (**Cromwell OP**) with the main gun removed and extra radios installed. Others had their turrets replaced by the various equipment required for the Cromwell to be used as the **Cromwell ARV** armoured recovery vehicle. The Cromwell was also used as the basis for a heavily armoured assault tank that became known as the **A33**, which was ready by May 1944 but never went into production.

Cruiser Tank Mk VIII Centaur

The **Cruiser Tank Mk VIII Centaur** was a contemporary of the Cromwell and derived from the same specification. Whereas the Cromwell was powered by the Rolls-Royce Meteor engine, the Centaur was a Leyland Motors project and was fitted with the Liberty engine. In many other respects the Centaur and the Cromwell were identical and some Centaurs were fitted with Meteor engines at a later stage and redesignated as Cromwell tanks.

Design problems

Leyland had already produced the **Cruiser Tank Mk VII Cavalier**, which had proved to be a generally unsuccessful design, as a result of poor performance,

mechanical unreliability and short engine life. Leyland reused some features of the Cavalier in the Centaur, but unfortunately carried over some of the earlier design's problems, for the Liberty engine lacked the power to provide the Centaur with the same performance as the Cromwell, and was also less reliable.

Development

The **Centaur I** was produced with the 6-pdr (57-mm/ 2.24-in) gun that was standard for British tanks of the period, and the first examples were ready in June 1942, after which they were used for training purposes. Upgunned with a 75-mm (2.95-in) weapon, the **Centaur III** was produced

only in small numbers with armour varying in thickness from 20-76 mm (0.8-3 in). The **Centaur IV** was the main combat version, specially produced with a 94-mm (3.7-in) close-support howitzer for use by the Royal Marines Armoured Support Group during the D-Day landings in Normandy on 6 June 1944. Eighty of the vehicles were issued, and were intended for use only in the initial stages of the amphibious assault. In fact, most of them performed so well on the beaches and the area immediately inland that many were retained for some weeks for the slow and dangerous combat in the bocage country.

Thereafter the Centaur was withdrawn for conver-

sion to other forms. The simplest conversion was as an artillery observation post (**Centaur OP**), while others simply had their turrets removed to become **Centaur Kangaroo** armoured personnel carriers. The usual armoured recovery conversion was the **Centaur ARV**, and the **Centaur Dozer** turretless version carried a dozer blade for the combat engineer role. Two Centaur

conversions that did mount guns were the **Centaur III/IV AA I** and **Centaur III/IV AA II** with the same 20-mm anti-aircraft turret as the earlier Crusader AA, but revised with 20-mm Polsten cannon in place of the earlier Oerlikon cannon. Both these variants took part in the early stages of the Normandy campaign, but were withdrawn once the anticipated air attack did not materialise.

SPECIFICATION	
Centaur III	(3.7-in) howitzer with 51 rds, one or
Crew: 5	two 0.31-in (7.92-mm) Besa
Weight: 28849 kg (63,600 lb)	machine-guns
Powerplant: one Nuffield Liberty	**Performance:** maximum road speed
Mk V V-12 petrol engine developing	43.4 km/h (27 mph); maximum cross-
295 kW (395 bhp)	country speed about 25.7 km/h
Dimensions: length 6.35 m (20 ft	(16 mph); range 265 km (165 miles)
10 in); width 2.9 m (9 ft 6 in); height	**Fording:** 0.91 m (3 ft)
2.49 m (8 ft 2 in)	**Vertical obstacle:** 0.91 m (3 ft)
Armament: (Mk IV) one 94-mm	**Trench:** 2.29 m (7 ft 6 in)

Cruiser Tank Challenger

The **Cruiser Tank Challenger** was one of the British tank industry's least successful efforts. It was the result of a 1941 request for a tank carrying a gun capable of tackling even the heaviest German tanks, and it was decided to mount the 17-pdr (3-in/ 76.2-mm) gun on a development of the A27 Cromwell/Centaur chassis. The new gun required a much larger chassis to accommodate the weights involved, and a larger turret ring to cope with the greater recoil forces. The Cromwell

chassis was lengthened and another road wheel was added on each side, which permitted the turret ring section to be widened to make feasible the installation of a larger ring. This formed the basis of the **A30**, later named Challenger.

Early trials

The first pilot model was ready in March 1942 and performed badly during trials. The extra weight of the high and awkward turret was not balanced by the lengthened suspension, which proved to

be a source of many troubles, and the mounting of the heavy gun made the traverse of the turret so slow that the original mechanism had to be redesigned. The large size of the fixed ammunition meant that only a restricted number of rounds could be carried, requiring the hull machine-gun to be removed to make more room, leaving only the co-axial 0.3-in (7.62-mm) gun. Perhaps the biggest problem was that weight considerations demanded a reduction in the armour protection to between 20-102 mm (0.8-4 in).

The first examples were not ready until March 1944, and by then it was too late for the Challenger to have the extensive waterproofing required for the Normandy landings. Another blow was that the M4 Sherman had been adapted to take the 17-pdr, and as the Firefly this conversion assumed many of the responsibilities

The Challenger was a stretched Cromwell armed with a 17-pdr gun, armour being reduced to keep weight down. The Sherman Firefly was adopted in its stead.

intended for the Challenger during the early stages of the campaign in France after the Normandy landings.

Some Challenger tanks did see active service from late 1944. Numbers were issued to the reconnaissance regiments of British armoured divisions to provide extra fire support to the

75-mm (2.95-in) Cromwell tanks which were by then the main equipment of these units. As soon as the war ended most Challengers were withdrawn. Some were sold overseas, but the type rapidly vanished. The **Challenger II**, with a lower turret, was produced only in prototype form.

SPECIFICATION	
Challenger	76.2-mm) main gun with 42 rds,
Crew: 5	one co-axial 0.3-in (7.62-mm)
Weight: 33022 kg (72,800 lb)	Browning machine-gun
Powerplant: one Rolls-Royce	**Performance:** maximum speed
Meteor V-12 petrol engine	51.5 km/h (32 mph); range 193 km
developing 447 kW (600 bhp)	(120 miles)
Dimensions: length overall 8.15 m	**Fording:** 1.37 m (4 ft 6 in) after
(26 ft 8¾ in); width 2.9 m (9 ft	preparation
6½ in); height 2.78 m (9 ft 1¼ in)	**Vertical obstacle:** 0.91 m (3 ft)
Armament: one 17-pdr (3-in/	**Trench:** 2.59 m (8 ft 6 in)

T-40, T-60 and T-70 Light tanks

The T-70 light tank was a useful reconnaissance vehicle, but it had only a 45-mm main gun and was thus of little use in combat against heavier German tanks. In action, the T-70 proved itself to be adequate but wholly unexceptional.

During the 1920s and 1930s the tankette was a continuing attraction for the military mind and the tank designer, and the USSR was no exception to this trend. By the late 1930s the Red Army had progressed through the stages in which the one-man tankette had been tested and dropped, and was at the usual stage where the tankette had been developed into the two-man light tank. By the time the Germans attacked in 1941 the Red Army had invested fairly heavily in the light tank, and the models in service came from years of development.

One of the main types in 1940 was the **T-40** amphibious light tank. This was the latest in a long line of models that could be traced back to the T-27 of the early 1930s and had progressed through the T-33, the T-34 (not to be confused with the T-34 medium tank), the T-36, the T-37 and finally the T-38. Most of these lacked the amphibious capabilities of the T-40, which was placed in production in about 1940, so that by the time of the invasion of June 1941, only a few (about 230) had been completed. Many of the later T-40 models (with streamlined nose and foldable trim vane) were converted into rocket-launcher carriers and were never used as turreted tanks, whose normal armament was one 12.7-mm (0.5-in) and one 7.62-mm (0.3-in) machine-gun. Armour ranged from 6 to 13 mm (0.25 to 0.5 in) in thickness.

Rapid production

While the amphibious T-40 was being developed, a non-amphibious version, the **T-40S**, was proposed. When Germany invaded, the call was for many more tanks delivered as rapidly as possible, so the simpler T-40S was rushed into production and redesignated the **T-60** light tank. Unfortunately this proved problenmatic in service and carried over the primary bad points of the T-40: it was too lightly armoured and, having only a 20-mm cannon and a co-axial 7.62-mm (0.3-in) machine-gun as armament, was useless against other tanks. Also it was so underpowered that it could not keep up with the heavier T-34 tanks across country. T-60s were kept in production simply because they could be produced quickly from relatively basic factories. They were powered by truck engines, many components being taken from the same source, and the improved **T-60A** appeared in 1942 with slightly thicker frontal armour (35 mm/1.37 in instead of 25 mm/1 in) and solid instead of spoked wheels.

By late 1941 work was underway on the T-60's successor. This was the **T-70**, whose first version used a twin-engined power train that could never have worked successfully in action and which was soon replaced by a revised arrangement. The T-70 was otherwise a considerable improvement over the T-40 and T-60. It had heavier armour (proof against 37-mm/1.46-in anti-tank gun rounds) and the turret mounted a 45-mm (1.77-in) gun and 7.62-mm machine-gun. This was still only of limited use against heavier tanks but was better than a mere machine-gun. The crew remained at two men, the commander acting as gunner and loader in a fashion hardly conducive to effective operation of the tank or tank units.

Production of the T-70 and **T-70A** ended in October 1943, by which time 8,226 had been produced. In service the type proved wholly unremarkable, and the vehicles appear to have been confined to the close support of infantry units and some limited recce tasks. By 1943 the light tank was an anachronism, but the Soviets nonetheless went ahead with a replacement, the **T-80**. Almost as soon as it went into production its lack of value was realised and the production line was switched to manufacturing components for the SU-76 self-propelled gun.

The 20-mm gun-armed T-60 light tank was not a great success in action, for it was too lightly armed and armoured, and also lacked power and mobility. It was kept in production simply to get some sort of vehicle to the Red Army following the disasters of the 1941 campaigns.

SPECIFICATION

T-40
Crew: 2
Weight: 5.9 tonnes
Powerplant: one 52-kW (70-hp) GAZ-202 petrol engine
Dimensions: length 4.11 m (13 ft 5⅞ in; width 2.33 m (7 ft 7⅝ in); height 1.95 m (6 ft 4¾ in)
Armament: one 12.7-mm (0.5-in) machine-gun, one 7.62-mm (0.3-in) machine-gun
Performance: maximum road speed 44 km/h (27.3 mph); road range 360 km (223.7 miles)
Fording: amphibious
Gradient: 34°
Vertical obstacle: 0.7 m (2 ft 3¾ in)
Trench: 1.85 m (6 ft 1 in)

T-60
Crew: 2
Weight: 6.4 tonnes
Powerplant: one 63-kW (85-hp) GAZ-203 petrol engine
Dimensions: length 4.11 m (13 ft 5⅞ in) width 2.3 m (7 ft 6½ in), height 1.74 m (5 ft 8½ in)
Armament: one 20-mm cannon, one 7.62-mm (0.3-in) machine-gun
Performance: maximum road speed 45 km/h (28 mph); road range 450 km (280 miles)
Gradient: 29°
Vertical obstacle: 0.54 m (1 ft 9¼ in)
Trench: 1.85 m (6 ft 1 in)

T-70
Crew: 2
Weight: 9.2 tonnes
Powerplant: two GAZ-202 petrol engines delivering 104 kW (140 hp)
Dimensions: length 4.29 m (14 ft 1 in); width 2.32 m (7 ft 7⅛ in); height 2.04 m (6 ft 8½ in)
Armament: one 45-mm (1.77-in) gun, one 7.62-mm (0.3-in) machine-gun
Performance: maximum road speed 45 km/h (28 mph); road range 360 km (223.7 miles)
Gradient: 34°
Vertical obstacle: 0.7 m (2 ft 3⅜ in)
Trench: 3.12 m (10 ft 2¾ in)

T-26 Light infantry tank

In the late 1920s Red Army planners launched a programme to re-equip the USSR's tank arm. In common with many other nations, the USSR decided upon an infantry support tank for its non-cavalry units and, after attempting without success to develop a new design, decided on the mass production of a British commercial model, the Vickers 6-ton Type E light tank. This was named the **T-26**, and the first examples of the British model arrived during 1930, receiving the designation **T-26A-1**.

Soviet production of the T-26 started during 1931. Early models had two turrets mounting machine-guns (two 7.62-mm/0.3-in weapons in the **T-26A-2**, and one 12.7-mm/0.5-in and one 7.62-mm gun in the **T-26A-3**), but some models had a machine-gun in one turret and a gun (27-mm/1.06-in in the **T-26A-4** and 37-mm/1.46-in in the **T-26A-5**) in the other. This arrangement did not survive for long, and later **T-26B** models had a single turret mounting only a gun (37-mm in the **T-26B-1**, although a 45-mm/1.85-in weapon was used later).

Soviet developments

The early T-26 tanks were straightforward copies of the British original, and were simple, robust vehicles of largely riveted construction. The first model was the **T-26 Model 1931** (**T-26A**), but this was superseded in production by the **T-26 Model 1933** (T-26B), which introduced a number of design improvements. The Model 1933 was the most widely produced of all Soviet tanks before 1941, about 5,500 being built by the time production ceased in 1936. A new model, the **T-26S Model 1937**, was then placed in production. This series was characterised by several changes from the standards of the preceding versions. The T-26S carried the 45-mm main gun fitted to later versions of the Model 1933, but this was installed in a turret of improved design and all-welded construction as introduced on the **T-26B-2**.

The use of welding in place of riveting was introduced as a result of the Red Army's operational experiences in its border clashes with the Japanese army that took place along the Mongolian and Manchurian boundaries in 1934 and 1935. Here combat showed that a T-26 that was hit by hostile fire was likely to have its rivets knocked out to fly around the interior, to the severe detriment of the occupants. Welding was introduced with the later Model 1933 tanks but was standard on the T-26S.

Throughout their lives the T-26 tanks underwent many production and in-service changes, most of them aimed at improving the armament and the protection (minimum and maximum of 6 and 25 mm/0.24 and 1 in

of armour respectively). There were also many special versions. Perhaps the most numerous of these were the flame-throwing tanks prefixed by the designation OT. Again there were several of these variants, the earliest being the **OT-26** and the last the **OT-133**. Most of these had the flame-throwing projector in the turret in place of the main gun, but later models retained a gun in addition to the projector. There were also bridge-carrying versions (**ST-26**) and attempts were made to mount 76.2-mm (3-in) guns

for increased infantry fire support. The type was also developed as a command vehicle, variants being the **T-26A-4(U)** and **T-26B-2(U)**.

End of the road

Production of the T-26 series ceased in 1941 as the invading German forces overran most of the tank's production facilities. New production centres in the Soviet hinterlands launched the production of later tank designs, but by 1941 well over 12,000 T-26 tanks of all kinds had been made. Consequently they were among the most numerous of the armoured fighting vehicles used by the Red Army in the early stages of the 'Great Patriotic War', and were also used in the 1939-40 campaign in Finland. Some had been earlier used during the Spanish Civil War.

After 1941 huge numbers of T-26 tanks were destroyed or passed into German

One of the many variants of the T-26 light infantry tank was the Model 1931, which had dual turrets, usually mounting two 7.62-mm machine-guns, but sometimes one of these was replaced by a 37-mm short infantry support gun. The later T-26 Model 1933 had a single turret.

hands. Many were later converted to artillery tractors or self-propelled gun carriers, usually by the Germans who always had a need for such vehicles.

Overall the T-26 was an unremarkable tank that was

unable to stand up to the demands of 1941, but it enabled the USSR to establish its own mass production facilities and build up its armour know-how, and these factors stood them in good stead after 1941.

SPECIFICATION	
T-26B	**Armament:** one 37-mm (1.46-in) or 47-mm (1.85-in) gun
Crew: 3	**Performance:** maximum road speed 28 km/h (17.4 mph); maximum road range 175 km (109 miles)
Weight: 9.4 tonnes	
Powerplant: one 68-kW (91-hp) GAZ T-26 8-cylinder petrol engine	
Dimensions: length 4.88 m (16 ft); width 3.41 m (11 ft 2¼ in); height 2.41 m (7 ft 11 in)	**Gradient:** 40°
	Vertical obstacle: 0.79 m (2 ft 7 in)
	Trench: 1.9 m (6 ft 2¾ in)

T-28 Medium tank

The Soviet **T-28** medium tank was an indigenous design that entered production in Leningrad during 1933. It was greatly influenced by trends revealed in German and British (Vickers) experimental designs in features such as the multi-turret armament layout fashionable at that time. The T-28 had three turrets, that for the main gun being partially flanked by two smaller turrets armed with machine-guns, with the driver's position located between the two auxiliary gun turrets.

Slab-sided tank

The prototype of the T-28 series had a 45-mm (1.77-in) main gun, but on the T-28 and T-28A production models (the latter with thicker front armour) this was replaced by a short-barrel 76.2-mm (3-in) gun, while **T-28B** production models after 1938 had a newer and longer-barrel 76.2-mm gun of

improved performance. The secondary armament was three 7.62-mm (0.3-in) machine-guns. Overall the T-28 was large and slab-sided, but Soviet tank design teams were still learning their trade, and experience gained with the T-28 was greatly important.

Construction of the original **T-28 Model 1934** lasted until 1938, when there appeared the improved **T-28B Model 1938** with the new gun, rudimentary gun stabilisation and a number of engine modifications. Manufacture of this version lasted until 1940, when production ceased in favour of later models. Armour thickness of the different versions ranged from a minimum of 20 mm (0.79 in) to a maximum of 80 mm (3.15 in).

Useful experiments

There were several experimental versions of the T-28, including some self-propelled guns and 'specials' such as

bridging and assault engineering tanks. None of these experimental variants proceeded past the prototype stage, but experience with them was of great importance when later variations on production tanks were contemplated. In fact the T-28 was of more value as an educational tank than as a combat tank. Its service life was short, spanning only the years from 1939-41. In 1939 the T-28 was first used in action against the Finns during the 'Winter War'. In that short conflict the T-28 fared badly as its crews found out, in the hardest way possible, that the vehicle's armour was too thin for safety. The tanks that survived the war then underwent a hasty course of modification to add extra armour (up to 80 mm),

The Soviet T-28 heavy tank weighed 28 tonnes but was termed a medium tank. It had a crew of six and had a short 76.2-mm (3-in) gun as its main armament, plus machine-guns in the two auxiliary turrets mounted in front of the main turret. They were clumsy vehicles with armour that proved to be too thin once in action.

The T-28 medium tank was one of the least successful pre-World War II Soviet tank designs. In action in 1940 and 1941 it proved to be cumbersome, inadequately armoured and undergunned. The main gun was a short 76.2-mm (3-in) weapon that was replaced in some cases by a longer gun of the same calibre.

resulting in the revised designation **T-28E** (*Ekanirovki,* or screened, i.e. up-armoured). However, the continued indifferent performance of the T-28 in its T-28E form after the German invasion of June 1941 suggests that this crash improvement programme was of doubtful effectiveness. The T-28E was also known as the **T-28M** or **T-28 Model 1940.**

Great vulnerability

Thus in 1941 the surviving T-28 tanks demonstrated themselves to be of only limited combat value. Their large slab sides and stately perfor-

mance made them notably easy prey for the German anti-tank artillery arm. The tanks also proved themselves to be vulnerable to mines, and in an effort to obviate this threat during the 'Winter War' of 1939-1940 some T-28 tanks had been modified to carry anti-mine rollers in front of their hulls' nose sections. These rollers were not a success but, once again, the experience gained with them proved to be of great value later. Thus the T-28 medium tank passed from the scene, proving it to belong to an earlier era of tank design.

SPECIFICATION	
T-28	and three 7.62-mm (0.3-in) machine-guns
Crew: 6	
Weight: 28 tonnes	**Performance:** maximum road speed 37 km/h (23 mph); maximum road range 220 km (136.7 miles)
Powerplant: one M-17 V-12 petrol engine developing 373 kW (500 hp)	
Dimensions: length 7.44 m (24 ft 4¼ in); width 2.81 m (9 ft 2¾ in); height 2.82 m (9 ft 3 in)	**Gradient:** 43°
	Vertical obstacle: 1.04 m (3 ft 5 in)
Armament: one 76.2-mm (3-in),	**Trench:** 2.9 m (9 ft 6 in)

BT-7 Fast tank

When the Red Army tank staff decided to modernise its tank fleet during the late 1920s, it authorised the design bureaux to use whatever sources they liked to obtain the best ideas available. Accordingly, many promising design concepts from all over the world were embraced, and among these were ideas of the US mechanical engineer J. Walter Christie. His advanced suspension designs had little impact in his own country at that time, but the Soviets embraced his concepts willingly and took them over for their own further development. The Christie suspension was integrated into the BT series (bystro-chodya tank, or 'fast tank').

The first Soviet BTs were copied exactly from a Christie prototype delivered to the Soviet Union in 1930 and designated **BT-1**. The first Soviet model was the **BT-2**, and from 1931 onwards the BT series progressed through a number of design developments and improvements until the **BT-7** was produced in 1935. Like the earlier BT tanks the BT-7 was a fast and agile vehicle intended for Red Army cavalry units, and was powered by a converted aircraft engine.

Suspension

The suspension used the Christie torsion bars that allowed a high degree of flexibility at high speeds. The hull was all-welded and well-shaped, but the main gun was only a 45-mm (1.77-in) weapon, although this was still larger than that fitted on many contemporary equivalents. The secondary armament was two 7.62-mm (0.3-in) machine-guns, and armour varied from 10 to 22 mm (0.39 to 0.87 in).

The BT-7 proved to be very popular with its users. By the time it entered service (in its original **BT-7-1** form with the cylindrical turret, replaced by a conical turret in the **BT-7-2**) many

The BT-7 was introduced into service in 1935 and was made in two main versions, both armed with a 45-mm (1.77-in) gun. Although fast and mobile in action, the BT-7 proved to be too lightly armoured, but it led in time to the development of the successful T-34 series.

of the automotive snags that had troubled some of the earlier BT models had been eliminated, and the BT-7 thus proved to be fairly reliable. Also, by the time it appeared there were many BT variants: some were produced as flamethrower tanks, and there was a special **BT-7A** close-support version carrying a short 76.2-mm (3-in) main gun. Other experimental models included amphibious and bridging tanks, and variants with different tracks to improve terrain-crossing capabilities.

The BT-7 did have one major tactical disadvantage in that it was only lightly armoured. On the entire BT series armour protection had been sacrificed for speed and mobility, and once in action during 1939 the BTs, including the BT-7, proved to be unsurprisingly vulnerable to anti-tank weapons such as anti-tank rifles. BT-5s had demonstrated this fact when small numbers were used during the Spanish Civil War, but even though the BT-7 had some armour increases it was still not enough, as revealed in Finland during 1939 and 1940. As a result the design of a successor to the BT series was undertaken and this led ultimately to the adoption of the T-34. Further variants of the BT-7 included the **BT-7-I(U)** command tank and **BT-7M** (or **BT-8**) improved model with full-width and a well-sloped glacis plate plus a V-2 diesel engine.

Thus the BT-7 played its major part in World War II well before the Germans invaded the Soviet Union in 1941. Large numbers were still in service in 1941, but they fared badly against the advancing Panzers. Despite their mobility the Soviet tank formations were poorly handled and many tanks, including BT-7s, were lost simply because they broke down as the result of poor maintenance or poor training of their crews. It was an inauspicious beginning for the Red Army, but worse was soon to follow and the large fleet of BT-7s had been virtually eliminated by the end of 1941.

SPECIFICATION	
BT-7	main gun and two 7.62-mm (0.3-in) machine-guns
Crew: 3	**Performance:** maximum road speed 86 km/h (53.4 mph); maximum road range 250 km (155 miles)
Weight: 14 tonnes	
Powerplant: one 373-kW (500-hp) M-17T V-12 petrol engine	
Dimensions: length 5.66 m (18 ft 7 in); width 2.29 m (7 ft 6 in); height 2.42 m (7 ft 11 in)	**Fording:** 1.22 m (4 ft)
	Gradient: 32°
	Vertical obstacle: 0.76 m (2 ft 6 in)
Armament: one 45-mm (1.77-in)	**Trench:** 1.83 m (6 ft)

T-34 Medium tank

It is difficult to write about the **T-34** medium tank without using too many superlatives, as the T-34 has passed into the realms of legend. It was one of the decisive weapons of World War II, and was produced in such vast numbers and in so many versions that entire books have been written on the subject without exhausting the stories of the vehicle and its exploits.

BT-7 successor

In simple terms the T-34 had its origins in the shortcomings of the BT-7 and its forebears. The first result of the BT series' improvements were the designs known as the **A-20** and **A-30**, produced in 1938 as developments of the **BT-IS**, but passed over in favour of a heavier-gunned tank with increased armour and known as the **T-32**. In the T-32 can be seen most of the features of the later T-34. It had a well-shaped hull with sloped armour, and a cast and sloped turret which mounted a 76.2-mm (3-in) high velocity gun. The Christie suspension, suitably strengthened, was carried over from

The T-34 tank was a very advanced design for its time. This is a late production T-34/76 armed with a 76.2-mm (3-in) main gun, and well provided with sloping armour for added protection. The tank was produced in thousands and proved durable, mobile and highly effective in service.

the BT series, but the ability to run on wheels without tracks was abandoned.

Good as the T-32 was, a selection panel requested more armour and so the T-34 was born. It went into production in 1940 and mass production of the **T-34/76A** soon followed. When Germany attacked the Soviet Union in 1941 the type was already well established, but its appearance came as a nasty shock to the Germans.

The T-34's well-sloped and thick armour (minimum of 18 mm/0.71 in and maximum of 60 mm/2.36 in) protected the tank against most German anti-tank weapons and the L/30 76.2-mm gun, soon replaced in service by an even more powerful L/40 gun of the same calibre, was effective against most Panzers. The secondary armament was two 7.62-mm (0.3-in) machine-guns.

From 1941 onwards the

T-34 was developed into a long string of models, many of them with few external differences. Production demands resulted in many expediences, the finish of

SPECIFICATION	
T-34/76A	machine-guns
Crew: 4	**Powerplant:** one V-2-34 V-12 diesel developing 373 kW (500 hp)
Weight: 26 tonnes	
Dimensions: length 5.92 m (19 ft 5 in); width 3 m (9 ft 10 in); height 2.44 m (8 ft)	**Performance:** road speed 55 km/h (34 mph); range 186 km (115 miles)
	Gradient: 40°
Armament: one L/40 76.2-mm (3-in) main gun and two 7.62-mm (0.3-in)	**Vertical obstacle:** 0.71 m (2 ft 4 in)
	Trench: 2.95 m (9 ft 8 in)

Below: The 85-mm (3.34-in) main armament of the later T-34 is clearly visible on the turret, together with one of the pair of 7.62-mm (0.3-in) machine-guns.

most T-34s being rough to an extreme, but the vehicles were still very effective fighting machines. Despite the disruption of the production lines during 1941, ever-increasing numbers poured off the extemporised lines, and all manner of time-saving production methods (ranging from automatic welding to leaving whole sections of surface unpainted) were used. The second major production model was the **T34/76B** with a rolled-plate turret.

T-34 variants

In service, the T-34 was used for every role, ranging from main battle tank to reconnaissance vehicle, and from engineering tank to recovery vehicle. It was converted into the most basic of armoured personnel carriers by simply carrying infantry on the hull over long distances. These 'tank descent' troops became the scourge of the Germans as they advanced westwards

through the liberated Soviet Union and subsequently Eastern Europe.

Successively improved models of the T-34/76 were the **T-34/76C** with a larger turret containing twin roof hatches in place of the original single hatch; the **T-34/76D** with a hexagonal turret and wider mantlet, plus provision for jettisonable exterior fuel tanks. The **T-34/76E** was fitted with a cupola on the turret and was of an all-welded construction. The **T-34/76F** was identical to the T-34/76E apart from its cast rather than welded turret. (It should be noted that the designations are Western, and were designed to provide a means of identification in the absence of Soviet information).

In time, the 76.2-mm gun was replaced by an 85-mm (3.34-in) gun using the turret taken from the KV-85 heavy tank. This variant became the **T-34/85**, which remains in

service today in some parts of the world, including Afghanistan, where they have been used by the Taliban militia. They are also used by China which deploys over 500; Croatia, Congo and Mali which deploy 20 each; and Angola and Laos which deploy between 10 and 15 each. Special assault gun versions using the 85-mm gun and later the 100-mm (3.94-in) or 122-mm (4.8-in) artillery pieces were developed and flamethrowing, tractor, engineer and mine-clearing versions also rolled off the production lines.

However, it was as a battle tank that the T-34 has its main claim to fame. High production ensured that the T-34 was available in thousands and the T-34 assumed mastery of the battlefield. This forced the Germans on to the defensive and also took from them both the tactical and the strategic initiative, thus helping win the Great Patriotic War for the Soviet Union.

Above: The appearance of the T-34 spurred the Germans to up-gun their existing Panzers and pursue the development of powerful tank-killers.

Below: The T-34 was manufactured in very large numbers, although production was basic and hulls were sometimes left unpainted. However, such labour-saving measures accelerated the production.

T-35 Heavy tank

The **T-35** was one of the major disappointments for the Soviet tank designers before World War II. It had its origins in design studies that began in 1930, and the first prototype was rolled out in 1932. In appearance and in many other ways the T-35, via the T-28, was greatly influenced by the design of the British Vickers Independent, a tank that was produced as a one-off only and which featured in a

notorious espionage court case of the period. The T-28 carried over from the Vickers design one major feature, namely the multi-turret concept.

Although there were changes between the various production batches, the tanks of the main batch (produced between 1935 and 1938) were longer than the originals. This increase in length made the T-35 an unwieldly machine to steer,

and its ponderous weight did little to improve matters. The multi-turret approach to tank weaponry also proved to be of limited value.

Multi-turret trouble

Aiming and co-ordinating the fire of the five turrets proved very difficult, and the overall effectiveness of the armament was further limited by the relatively small calibre of the main gun. In fact the main gun and turret were exactly the same as those used on the lighter T-28 medium tank. Armour varied from 10 to 30 mm (0.39 in to 1.18 in) in thickness.

The T-35 heavy tank made an impressive showing on parade, but made little impact in action. Control of the five turrets proved very difficult and their bulk and length of hull made these awkward vehicles to manoeuvre.

Production of the T-35 was slow and limited compared with that of other Soviet tank programmes of the time.

Only 61 were produced between 1933 and 1939, and all of these vehicles served with just one tank brigade stationed near Moscow. This was politically useful, for the T-35s featured regularly in the Red Square parades of the time and thus provided a false impression of Soviet tank strengths. The massive vehicles made a great

impression as they rumbled past, but the service reality was considerably different.

When they had to go to war in 1941 only a handful actually saw action, for many were retained in Moscow for internal duties and for purely local defence. There appears to be no record of any T-35s going into action around Moscow, but the few used elsewhere to try to halt the German advances did not fare well. They were too lightly armed and their weight made them easy prey for the Panzers.

SPECIFICATION	
T-35	
Crew: 11	on main turret, one 37-mm (1.45-in) or 45-mm (1.77-in) gun on each of two secondary turrets, plus up to six 7.62-mm (0.3-in) machine-guns
Weight: 45 tonnes	
Powerplant: one M-17M V-12 petrol engine developing 373 kW (500 hp)	**Performance:** maximum road speed 30 km/h (18.6 mph); maximum road range 150 km (93.2 miles)
Dimensions: length 9.72 m (31 ft 11 in); width 3.2 m (10 ft 6 in); height 3.43 m (11 ft 3 in)	**Gradient:** 20°
	Vertical obstacle: 1.20 m (4 ft);
Armament: one 76.2-mm (3-in) gun	**Trench:** 3.5 m (11 ft 6 in)

KV-1 Heavy tank

By 1938 the Soviets appreciated the need for a T-35 heavy tank successor, and several design bureaux became involved. Many proposed multi-turret designs, but most prototypes had just two turrets. However, one team designed a single-turret heavy tank named after Klimenti Voroshilov, defence commissar at the time. This **KV-1** was far more mobile than the other submissions, and was field-tested during the campaign against Finland in 1940 in a form with a 76.2-mm (3-in) short-barrel gun, three or four 7.62-mm (0.3-in) machine-guns, and armour up to 100 mm (3.94 in) thick.

The KV-1 was ordered into production as the **KV-1A** with a 76.2-mm long-barrel gun and the KV-2 with a large slab-sided turret mounting initially a 122-mm (4.8-in) but later a 152-mm (5.98-in) howitzer. The high turret was a ponderous load for the vehicle, though, and the KV-2 (and improved KV-2B) did not shine in action. With the KV-1 the immediate future for Soviet tank design was established, and the KV-1 was a formidable vehicle that served the Red Army for years. It was often used as an assault (breakthrough) tank, spearheading many attacks. The **KV-1B** had an extra 25-35 mm (0.98-1.38 in) of armour on the hull front and sides. The turret progressed from being a mainly plated affair to a cast component, which on the **KV-1C** also gave increased protection. Much of the extra armour was simply bolted onto the existing armour.

Gun modifications

For its size, the KV-1 was undergunned, but a scheme to increase the armament to a 107-mm (4.21-in) weapon proceeded no further than trials. Instead the 76.2-mm gun was lengthened and the clumsy 152-mm gun turret was withdrawn. After 1943 the introduction of an 85-mm (3.34-in) gun created the **KV-85**.

The KV-1 did at first have serious automotive problems, but many were eventually eliminated. The numerous increases in armour protection were usually unmatched by increases in engine power,

though the KV-1C had an extra 74.6 kW (100 hp). Thus many examples could not reach their expected speed, and on a small number of **KV-1S** (*Skorostnoy*, or fast) tanks all appliqué armour was omitted to reduce weight and raise speed. One problem was the fact that the commander had to double as gun loader, which often put him out of touch with the tactical situation outside the tank.

The KV-1 heavy tank originally mounted a 76.2-mm (3-in) main gun on a chassis that was to be adapted for later models of Soviet heavy tanks. Several versions existed as progressive production changes were introduced to speed manufacture and improve protection for the crew of five.

A KV-1 rolls through Moscow streets to the front in December 1941. The tank had a 76.2-mm main gun and was used by the Red Army for the breakthrough role in which its lack of speed was not a handicap.

SPECIFICATION	
KV-85	7.62-mm (0.3-in) machine-guns
Crew: 5	**Performance:** maximum road
Weight: 43 tonnes	speed 35 km/h (21.75 mph);
Powerplant: one V-2K V-12 diesel	maximum road range 150 km
developing 448 kW (600 hp)	(93.2 miles)
Dimensions: length 6.68 m (21 ft	**Gradient:** 36°
11 in); width 3.32 m (10 ft 10¾ in);	**Vertical obstacle:** 1.2 m (3 ft
height 2.71 m (8 ft 10¾ in)	11¼ in)
Armament: one 85-mm (3.34-in)	**Trench:** 2.59 m (8 ft 6 in)
main gun, and three or four	

KV-2 Heavy tank

The Soviets appreciated that the KV-1 had the makings of an effective heavy tank offering good protection and adequate mobility after the type's automotive problems had been eradicated, but only indifferent firepower. This fact stemmed from the use of the same 76.2-mm (3-in) gun as used in the T-34/76 medium tank: this was an L/30.5 weapon that was soon replaced by an L/41.2 weapon. Further improvements in firepower were considered and trialled, but the Red Army also appreciated the need for a considerably more powerfully armed artillery fire-support variant to aid breakthrough operations. The hull and running gear of the KV-1 were adequate to the task, and to make the **KV-2A** the designers added a large

and totally unwieldy turret carrying a 122-mm (4.8-in) M1938 L/22.7 howitzer. The turret was high and slab-sided, and although constructed of thick armour, up to a maximum thickness of 76.2 mm (3 in) on the front and sides, offered a very tempting target.

Large calibre weapon

The 122-mm weapon had been installed in only a few vehicles before it was superseded by the 152-mm (6-in) M1938 L/24.3 howitzer, the largest-calibre weapon ever installed in a mass-production tank. The 152-mm weapon was provided with 36 rounds of ammunition fired at a muzzle velocity of 508 m (1,667 ft) per second for the AP projectile and 432 m (952 ft) per second for the HE projectile, which

The tall, slab-sided turret of the KV-2 was vulnerable to attack as it presented a large and tempting target. In addition, it was virtually unmovable except when the tank was on level ground.

had a maximum range of 12400 m (13,565 yards). The standard defensive armament was two or three 7.62-mm (0.3-in) machine guns (bow, co-axial and turret rear) with 3,087 rounds. The turret was power-operated through 360°, but one of the KV-2A's most limiting tactical failings was the fact that the turret was virtually immovable except when the tank was level. To this was added very poor cross-country mobility: the KV-2 was more than 6 tonnes

heavier than the KV-1 but had no more power.

Improved standard

Later production vehicles were completed to the **KV-2B** improved standard based on the chassis of the KV-1B, with the main gun emerging from an asymmetric mantlet on the front of a turret provided with greater

protection by the addition of 35 mm (1.38 in) of appliqué armour on its front. A few of the KV-2B vehicles were later adapted as flamethrower tanks. Battlefield experience quickly revealed that the KV-2 series was of only limited operational use, and most surviving vehicles were soon removed from first-line service.

SPECIFICATION	
KV-2B	M1938 howitzer and two or three
Crew: 6	7.62-mm (0.3-in) machine-guns
Weight: 57 tonnes	**Performance:** maximum speed
Powerplant: one V-2K V-12 diesel	26 km/h (16 mph); maximum road
developing 410 kW (550 hp)	range 160 km (100 miles);
Dimensions: length 6.8 m (22 ft	**Fording:** 1.45 m (4 ft 9 in)
4 in) overall; width 3.33 m (10 ft	**Gradient:** 34°
11 in); height 4.18 m (13 ft 8 in)	**Vertical obstacle:** 0.9 m (3 ft);
Armament: one 152-mm (6-in)	**Trench:** 2.8 m (9 ft 2 in)

IS-2 Heavy tank

The ultimate development of the Soviets' enthusiasm for the heavy tank was the Iosef Stalin (IS, sometimes rendered JS) series, planned from a time early in 1943. Weight no greater than that of the KV was demanded, and as initial plans called for an 85-mm (3.35-in) main gun the designation **IS-85** was allocated.

The first of three prototypes appeared in the autumn of 1943 and, although clearly derived from the KV series in its hull and running gear, was a much more formidable machine with highly sloped armour: the hull armour was welded and varied in thickness from 19 to 120 mm (0.75 to 4.72 in), while the turret was the same cast unit as fitted

on the KV-85 with thickness between 30 and 100 mm (1.18 and 3.94 in). The care taken in design was indicated by the fact that the IS-85 emerged with 50 mm (1.98 in) more armour than the KV-85 but weighed some 2000 kg (4,409 lb) less, allowing a slightly higher maximum speed on a slightly less powerful engine. It is thought likely that the IS-85 saw limited operational service as the **IS-1**.

Weaponry

To provide armament heavier than that of current medium tanks, the **IS-100** was developed with a 100-mm (3.94-in) main gun.

A small number of IS-100 tanks was built for evaluation purposes, but the type proceeded no further. The reason behind this was that General F. Petrov, designer of the turret used in the KV-85, T-34/85 and IS-1, proposed an altogether more formidable machine with a new turret of superior ballistic shape and fitted with the 122-mm (4.8-in) D-25 L/43 gun firing a 24.95-kg (55-lb) armour-piercing shot at 780 m (2,559 m) per second.

When the Red Army reached Berlin in 1945, it was IS-2 tanks that led the way; this example is seen near the Reichstag. Note the great length of the 122-mm (4.8-in) gun and the shaping of the turret and glacis plate to deflect armour-piercing projectiles.

The IS-2 was introduced into service with the Red Army during 1944. It mounted a long 122-mm (4.8-in) gun in a well-protected cast turret, and carried a crew of four. Ammunition stowage was limited to 28 rounds.

After development as the **IS-122**, the type was placed in production as the **IS-2**, and the considerably more potent turret/armament combination was also retrofitted to the small number of IS-100s that had been built to create the variant known

in the West as the **IS-1B**, the original IS-1 being redesignated **IS-1A** to avoid confusion. The IS-2 was accepted for production in October 1943 after an extremely rapid development programme, and proved excellent in combat.

SPECIFICATION	
IS-2	main gun, one 12.7-mm (0.5-in)
Crew: 4	machine-gun, and one 7.62-mm
Weight: 46 tonnes	(0.3-in) machine-gun
Powerplant: one V-2-IS (V-2K)	**Performance:** maximum road
V-12 diesel developing 447 kW	speed 37 km/h (23 mph); maximum
(600 hp)	road range 240 km (149 miles)
Dimensions: length 9.9 m (32 ft	**Gradient:** 36°
5½ in); width 3.09 m (10 ft 1½ in);	**Vertical obstacle:** 1 m (3 ft 3 in)
height 2.73 m (8 ft 11½ in)	**Trench:** 2.49 m (8 ft 2 in)
Armament: one 122-mm (4.8-in)	

IS-3 Heavy tank

The IS-2 entered combat for the first time during February 1944 at Korsun Shevkenskovsky, and General Zh. Kotin, one of the USSR's most capable tank designers, was present in the battle to gain first-hand information about the IS-2's operational capabilities, both positive and negative. This paved the way for the design and prototype evaluation of several experimental tanks, an evolutionary process which facilitated more advanced thinking about armour layout enhancements. Toward the end of 1944, therefore, the Soviets were in the position to start the introduction of their definitive heavy tank of World War II, the **IS-3**, designed by a team under the supervision of N. Dukhov, that may also be seen as the first of the classic tank designs that formed the core of the Soviet armoured force's equipment in the period after the war.

Increased protection

The IS-3's major improvement over the IS-2 was its protection, for the Soviets were satisfied that the mobility and firepower of the IS-2 were more than adequate. The better protection may be regarded as a direct evolutionary step in

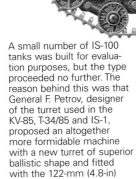

The IS-3 was the definitive Soviet heavy tank of World War II, with excellent armour protection, and a formidable 122-mm (4.8-in) rifled gun plus three machine-guns. The tank was in service until the late 1970s.

the process that had given birth to the T-34 series, with the armour both increased in thickness and made more capable by effective angling. Thus the hull of the IS-3 was basically that of the IS-2 revised in thicker rolled plate for better ballistic protection, while the totally new cast turret introduced the smooth inverted-saucer or carapace shape that has remained standard with the Soviets and their successors ever since. The hull armour varied from a minimum of 20 mm (0.79 in) on the belly to a maximum of 120 mm (4.72 in) on the front, while the turret was still better protected with minimum and maximum thicknesses of 25 and 230 mm (1 and 9.06 in) respectively.

Yet despite the thickness of the armour, its excellent shaping and disposition meant that the weight of the IS-3 was no greater than that of German tanks with notably less potent armament: the mass was still only 46500 kg (102,513 lb), a figure somewhat lower than that of the Germans' Tiger with an 88-mm (3.46-in) gun, yet the firepower and protection of the Soviet tank were immeasurably superior to those of the Tiger without any adverse effect on mobility.

Weaponry

The armament of the IS-3 comprised one 122-mm (4.8-in) rifled gun. This was the D-25 (M1943) L/43 rifled weapon, for which 28 rounds of ammunition were carried.

The gun was carried in the front of the turret, which was electrically operated for traverse through 360°, and could be elevated through an arc of 23° (-3° to +20°). The secondary armament comprised three machine-guns in the form of two 7.62-mm (0.3-in) DT weapons (one coaxial and one bow) with

1,000 rounds and one 12.7-mm (0.5-in) DShK weapon with 945 rounds on the turret roof for AA defence.

The IS-3 saw limited service in the last months of World War II, but remained in service with the Red Army into the late 1970s, latterly only as a reserve weapon.

SPECIFICATION	
IS-3	(0.5-in) DShK machine-gun, and
Crew: 4	two 7.62-mm (0.3-in) DT machine-
Weight: 46.5 tonnes	guns
Powerplant: one 387-kW (519-hp)	**Performance:** maximum road
V-2-IS V-12 diesel engine	speed 37 km/h (23 mph); maximum
Dimensions: length 10 m (32 ft	road range 210 km (130.5 miles)
10 in) overall and 6.66 m (21 ft	**Gradient:** 70 per cent
10 in) hull; width 3.2 m (10 ft 6 in);	**Fording:** 1.3 m (4 ft 6 in)
height 2.71 m (8 ft 11 in)	**Vertical obstacle:** 1 m (3 ft 3 in)
Armament: one 122-mm (4.8-in)	**Trench:** 2.5 m (8 ft 2 in)
D-25 main gun, one 12.7-mm	

Fiat L.6/40 Light tank

Based on the Carden-Loyd series of British tankettes, the L.6/40 was armed with a 20-mm cannon together with an 8-mm (0.315-in) co-axial machine-gun in the small manually-operated turret.

In the 1930s Fiat Ansaldo built an export tank based on the chassis of the L.3 tankette, itself a development of the British Carden Loyd Mark VI tankette. The first prototype was armed with twin machine-guns in the turret and a 37-mm (1.46-in) gun in a sponson. This was followed by models with a turret-mounted 37-mm (1.46-in) gun and a co-axial machine-gun, and another with twin turret-mounted 8-mm (0.315-in) machine-guns. The production version, designated **Carro Armato L.6/40**, was built from 1939 and armed with a 20-mm Breda Modello 35 cannon with an 8-mm (0.315-in) Breda Modello 38 co-axial machine-gun. Totals of 296 rounds of 20-mm and 1,560 rounds of 8-mm (0.315-in) ammunition were carried. At the time of its introduction the L.6/40 was roughly equivalent to the German PzKpfw II, and was used by reconnaissance units and cavalry divisions. A total of 283 vehicles was built, and in addition to being used in Italy itself the type was also used in North Africa and on the Russian front. The L.6/40 continued in service with the militia in post-war Italy, finally being phased out of service in the early 1950s.

Construction

The hull of the L.6/40 was of all-riveted construction varying in thickness from 6 mm (0.24 in) to 30 mm (1.26 in). The driver was seated at the front right, the turret was in the centre, and the engine at the rear. The turret was manually operated and could be traversed through 360°; its weapons could be elevated from -12° to +20°. The commander also acted as gunner and loader, and could enter the vehicle via the hatch in the turret roof or via a door in the right side of the hull. The suspension on each side consisted of two bogies each with two road wheels, with the drive sprocket at the front and idler at the rear; there were three track-return rollers.

A knocked-out L.6/40 light tank is inspected by Australians in the desert. In spite of being unsuitable for front-line service, the L.6/40 saw action in North Africa and the USSR as well as in Italy.

There was also a flamethrower version of the L.6/40 in which the 20-mm cannon was replaced by a flamethrower for which 200 litres (44 Imp gal) of flame liquid were carried. The command model had additional communications equipment and an open-topped turret. Some of the L.6/40s were completed as **Semovente L.40 da 47/32** self-propelled anti-tank guns, which were essentially L.6/40 with the turret removed and a 47-mm anti-tank gun mounted in the hull front to the left of the driver. This had an elevation from -12° to +20°, with a total traverse of 27°; 70 rounds of ammunition were carried. In addition to conversions from L.6/40 standard about 300 vehicles were built as such, and the type saw service in Italy, North Africa and the USSR from 1941. A command version was also built on the same chassis and this had its armament replaced by an 8-mm Breda machine-gun, which was made to look like the larger-calibre gun to make detection of the vehicle more difficult.

SPECIFICATION	
Carro Armato L.6/40	52 kW (70 hp)
Crew: 2	**Performance:** maximum road speed 42 km/h (26 mph): maximum range 200 km (124 miles); fording 0.80 m (2 ft 8 in); gradient 60 per cent; vertical obstacle 0.70 m (2 ft 4 in); trench 1.70 m (5 ft 7 in)
Weight: 6800 kg (14,991 lb)	
Dimensions: length 3.78 m (12 ft 5 in); width 1.92 m (6 ft 4 in); height 2.03 m (6 ft 8 in)	
Powerplant: one SPA 18D four-cylinder petrol engine developing	

Fiat M.11/39 and M.13/40 Medium tanks

In 1937 the prototype of the **Carro Armato M.11/39** tank was built, with the suspension system of the L.3 tankette but with six road wheels on each side. In layout this was similar to the American M3 Lee tank, but with a 37-mm (1.46-in) rather than 75-mm (2.95-in) gun in the right sponson, driver on the left, and in the centre of the hull a one-man turret armed with twin 8-mm (0.315-in) machine-guns. Further development resulted in a model with eight road wheels and this basic chassis was used for all subsequent Italian medium tanks. Only 100 M.11/39s were built as the design was already considered obsolete, and in 1940 70 of these tanks were sent to North Africa, where many were captured or destroyed during the first battles with the British army.

Further development resulted in the **M.13/40**, which had a similar chassis but a redesigned hull of riveted construction varying in thickness from 6 mm (0.24 in) to 42 mm (1.65 in). The

With a 47-mm sponson-mounted main gun and twin 8-mm (0.315-in) machine-guns in the two-man turret, the M.11/39 was soon outclassed with the introduction of improved Allied tanks.

driver was seated at the front of the hull on the left with the machine-gunner to his right; the latter operated the two 8-mm (0.315-in) Modello 38 machine-guns as well as the radios. The two-man turret was in the centre of the hull, with the commander/gunner on the right and the loader on the left,

and with a two-piece hatch cover in the turret roof. Main armament comprised a 47-mm (1.85-in) L/32 gun with an elevation of +20° and a depression of -10°; turret traverse was 360°. An 8-mm Modello 38 machine-gun was mounted co-axial with the main armament, and a similar weapon was

mounted on the turret roof for anti-aircraft defence. Totals of 104 rounds of 47-mm and 3,048 rounds of 8-mm ammunition were carried. The engine was at the rear of the hull, its power being transmitted to the gearbox at the front of the hull via a propeller shaft. Suspension on each side consisted of four double-wheel articulated bogies mounted on two assemblies each carried on semi-elliptic leaf springs, with the idler at the rear; there were three track-return rollers.

The M.13/40 was built by Ansaldo-Fossati at the rate of about 60 to 70 vehicles per month, a total of 779 being

M.13/40 tanks in the desert, 1941. These are of the Semovente Comando version, without turrets and with additional radio gear. Many were abandoned by the Italians and taken over by the British.

produced. The tank was widely used in North Africa by the Italian army, but was cramped, proved to be very unreliable in service, and was prone to catching fire when hit by anti-tank projectiles.

Captured vehicles

Many such vehicles were captured by the British army after being abandoned by their crews and subsequently issued to the British 6th Royal Tank Regiment (RTR) and the Australian 6th Cavalry Regiment early in 1941 when tanks were in very short supply on the Allied side. The Australian

regiment had three squadrons of captured vehicles which they called Dingo, Rabbit and Wombat. So that they were not engaged by Allied units, white kangaroos were painted on the sides, glacis and turret rear.

The **Semovente Comando M.40** command vehicle was basically the M.13/40 tank with its turret removed and fitted with additional communications equipment for use in the command role. Further development of the M.13/40 resulted in the M.14/41 and M.15/42, for which there is a separate entry.

SPECIFICATION	
Carro Armato M.13/40	93 kW (125 hp)
Crew: 4	**Performance:** maximum road
Weight: 14000 kg (30,865 lb)	speed 32 km/h (20 mph); maximum
Dimensions: length 4.92 m (16 ft	range 200 km (125 miles); fording
2 in); width 2.20 m (7 ft 3 in);	1.0 m (3 ft 3 in); gradient 70 per
height 2.38 m (7 ft 10 in)	cent; vertical obstacle 0.80 m (2 ft
Powerplant: one SPA TM40 eight-	8 in); trench 2.10 m (6 ft 11 in)
cylinder diesel engine developing	

Fiat M.15/42 Medium tank

The **Carro Armato M.14/41** was essentially the M.13/40 fitted with a more powerful diesel engine, which was equipped with air filters designed to cope with the harsh conditions of the desert. Production amounted to just over 1,100 of these vehicles, which had a similar specification to the M.13/40 except for an increase in speed to 33 km/h (20 mph) and in weight to 14.5 tonnes. Further development resulted in the **Carro Armato M.15/42**, which entered service in early 1943. A total of 82 of these was built, most being issued to the Ariete Division which took part in the Italian attempt to deny Rome to the Germans in September 1943. Some of these vehicles were captured by the Germans and then used against the Allies.

The M.15/42 was slightly longer than the M.14/41 and distinguishable from it by the lack of a crew access

door in the left side of the hull. It was driven by a more powerful engine, which made it slightly faster, and had improved armour protection and other more minor modifications as a result of operator comments.

The hull of the M.15/42 was of all-riveted construction that varied in thickness from 14 mm (0.55 in) to 42 mm (1.65 in), with a maximum of 45 mm (1.77 in) on the turret front. The driver was seated at the front of the hull on the left, with the bow machine-gunner to his right, the latter operating the twin 8-mm (0.315-in) Breda Modello 38 machine-guns as well as the radios. The turret was in the centre of the hull and carried a 47-mm (1.85-in) L/40 gun with an elevation of +20° and a depression of -10°; turret traverse, which was electric, was 360°. An 8-mm Modello 38 machine-gun was mounted co-axial with the main armament,

and a similar weapon was mounted on the turret roof for anti-aircraft defence. Totals of 111 rounds of 47-mm and 2.640 rounds of 8-mm ammunition were carried. The suspension on each side consisted of four double-wheel articulated bogies mounted in two assemblies each carried on semi-elliptical springs, with the drive sprocket at the front and the idler at the rear; there were three track-return rollers. The engine was at the rear of the hull and coupled to a manual gearbox with eight forward and two reverse gears.

By the time the M.15/42 had been introduced into service it was already obsolete, and design of another tank had been under way for several years. In 1942 the first prototypes of the **Carro Armato P.40** heavy tank were built. This was a major advance on the earlier Italian tanks and used a similar type of suspension to the

A squadron of M.14/41 tanks in Cyrenaica in 1942. More than 1,100 of these tanks, in effect tropicalised M.13/40s, were produced.

M.15/42. The layout was also similar with the driver at the front, turret in the centre and engine at the rear. Armour protection was much improved and the hull and turret sides sloped to give maximum possible protection within the weight limit of 26 tonnes. The P.40 was powered by a V-12 petrol engine that developed 420 hp (313 kW) to give it a maximum road speed of 40 km/h (25 mph). The main armament comprised a 75-mm (2.95-in) L/34 gun

Another M.14/41, abandoned after the 1st Battle of El Alamein. The M.15/42 looked similar but had no side hatch. Only 82 were built.

with an 8-mm Modello 38 co-axial machine-gun, and totals of 75 rounds of 75-mm and 600 rounds of machine-gun ammunition were carried. The P.40 was produced by Fiat in northern Italy, but none of these tanks entered service with the Italian army and most were subsequently taken over by the German army, which ensured continued production for itself. Some reports state that over 50 vehicles were built specifically for German use.

SPECIFICATION	
Carro Armato M 15/42	developing 143 kW (192 hp)
Crew: 4	**Performance:** maximum road
Weight: 15500 kg (34,800 lb)	speed 40 km/h (25 mph); maximum
Dimensions: length 5.04 m (16 ft	range 220 km (136 miles); fording
7 in); width 2.23 m (7 ft 4 in);	1.0 m (3 ft 3 in); gradient 60 per
height 2.39 m (7 ft 11 in)	cent; vertical obstacle 0.80 m (2 ft
Powerplant: one SPA 15 TB M42	8 in); trench 2.10 m (6 ft 11 in)
eight-cylinder petrol engine	

Japanese Light tanks

Japan's first light tank was the four-man **Light Tank Type 89 Experimental Tank No. 2**. The 9800-kg (21,605-lb) Type 89's turret was mounted over the front of the hull and carried a 37-mm or, according to some sources, 57-mm (2.24-in) gun and a rearward-firing 6.5-mm (0.256-in) machine-gun, a second machine-gun of the same type being located in the bow. The prototype appeared in 1929, but it

soon became clear that the vehicle was better suited to the medium tank role.

First production

First into production was the **Light Tank Type 95**. An improved version was the **Light Tank Type 98 (KE-NI)**, which entered service in 1942. By this time the day of the light tank was over except for Japanese operations in China, to which the Type 98 was admirably suited. The **Light Tank Type**

2 **(KE-TO)** was essentially similar but for its 37-mm gun, secondary armament limited to one 7.7-mm (0.303-in) machine-gun, and armour varying in thickness between 6 and 16 mm (0.24 and 0.63 in). Only a few were built from 1944. Closer to the Type 95 were the **Light Tanks Type 3 (KE-RI)** and **Type 4 (KE-NU)**, both based on the Type 95 hull but the Type 3 having the standard turret reworked to accommodate a 57-mm gun, and the Type 4 being fitted with the complete turret/gun assembly of the Medium Tank Type 97. The Type 3 weighed 7400 kg (16,314 lb)

The Light Tank Type 95 was one of the best tanks developed by Japan before World War II. Though most of the rolled plate armour was riveted and bolted, some of the plates were welded.

One of the first Japanese tanks to enter production was the Type 89. This was derived from the thinking behind a British type, the Vickers Mk C, of which the Japanese had imported a single example in 1927.

and proved impractical because of its extremely cramped turret, and the Type 4 was too unwieldy at a weight of 8400 kg (18,519 lb).

Only for evaluation

The **Light Tank Type 5 (KE-HO)** was designed in 1942 and evaluated in prototype

form with first-class results, but was not considered for production until too late. It was a four-man machine turning the scales at 10000 kg (22,046 lb) with armour from 8 to 20 mm (0.315 to 0.79 in). The tank was armed with one 47-mm gun and just one 7.7-mm machine-gun.

SPECIFICATION

Light Tank Type 98 KE-NI	
Crew: 3	**Powerplant:** one air-cooled 6-cylinder diesel engine developing 112 kW (150 hp)
Weight: 7300 kg (16,093 lb)	
Dimensions: length overall 4.10 m (13 ft 5 in); width 2.12 m (6 ft 11 in); height 1.80 m (5 ft 11 in)	**Performance:** maximum road speed 50 km/h (31 mph)

Type 95 Light tank

The **Light Tank Type 95** was developed to meet the requirements of the Imperial Japanese army in the early 1930s, the first two prototypes being completed in 1934 by Mitsubishi Heavy Industries. These were tested in China and Japan, and the type was then standardised, the company calling the vehicle the **HA-GO** while the army called it the **KE-GO**. Over 1,100 were built before production was completed in 1943, although some sources have stated that production continued until 1945.

The Light Tank Type 95 had a 37-mm main gun and a hull-mounted 7.7-mm (0.303-in) machine-gun together with another 7.7-mm gun at the rear of the turret.

Construction details

The hull and turret of the Type 95 were of riveted construction and varied in thickness between minimum and maximum figures of 6 and 14 mm (0.25 and 0.55 in) respectively. The driver was seated at the front of the vehicle on the right-hand with the bow machine-gunner to his left. The latter operated the 6.5-mm (0.255-in) Type 91 weapon (with a traverse of 35° left and right), which was later replaced by a 7.7-mm (0.303-in) Type 97 machine-gun. The turret was in the centre of the hull, off-

set slightly to the left, and carried the vehicle's primary armament of one 37-mm Type 94 tank gun firing armour-piercing and HE ammunition. This gun was later replaced by a Type 98 weapon of a similar calibre but with a higher muzzle velocity. There was no co-axial machine-gun, but another machine-gun was mounted in the turret rear on the right-hand side. The ammunition totals were

2,970 rounds for the two machine-guns, and 119 rounds for the main armament. A major drawback of this tank, as it was for many tanks of the period, was the fact that the tank commander also had to aim, load and fire the main armament in addition to carrying out his primary role of commanding the tank.

The Mitsubishi air-cooled six-cylinder diesel engine was mounted in a compart-

ment at the rear of the hull, and was coupled to a manual transmission with one reverse and four forward gears. The steering was of the clutch and brake type, and the tank's suspension was of the bell-crank type consisting of each side of four rubber-tyred road wheels, with the drive sprocket at the front and idler at the rear; there were two track-return rollers. In the absence of any type of

air-conditioning system to keep the interior of the tank at a bearable temperature in semi-tropical and even tropical conditions, the walls of the crew compartment were lined with asbestos padding, which in addition gave some protection to the crew during cross-country movement.

In 1943 a few Type 95 light tanks were modified to carry a 57-mm gun under the name **KE-RI**, but the variant was not useful as the turret was too cramped. The **KE-NU** was another Type 95 subvariant with the turret of the Type 97 CHI-HA medium tank. The Type 95 was succeeded in production by the **Type 98 KE-NI** light tank, but only about 200 of these were built before production was completed in 1943. The **Type 2 KA-MI** amphibious tank used automotive components of the Type 95 light tank, and was widely used in the early Pacific campaigns of World War II. Japan also used tankettes on a large scale, these including the Types 92, 94 and 97, the last being the most common model.

When used in China and in the early World War II campaigns against the Allies, the Type 95 proved useful, but after it had been confronted by American tanks and anti-tank guns, it was wholly outclassed.

Right: Type 95 tanks cross paddy fields while on exercise. The Type 95 suffced in its anti-infantry role, as the Japanese army did not come up against any armour of consequence until meeting the US Army and US Marine Corps in 1943.

Below: A Type 95 at speed, probably in Manchuria. Japan's conquests were aided considerably by the fact that none of its opponents possessed any significant amount of armour, or even any useful anti-tank capability.

Type 97 Medium tank

In the mid-1930s a requirement was issued for a new medium tank to replace the Type 89B medium tank, which by then was rapidly becoming obsolete. As the Engineering Department and the General Staff could not agree on the better design, two prototypes were built. Mitsubishi built the design of the Engineering Department while Osaka Arsenal built the design of the General Staff. There was little to choose between the two designs, although the Mitsubishi tank was heavier and driven by a more powerful engine. The Mitsubishi prototype was standardised as the **Medium Tank Type 97 (CHI-HA)**, of which 3,000 were built before production was completed during the middle of World War II.

The hull and turret were of riveted construction that varied in thickness from 8 mm (0.315 in) to 25 mm

(0.98 in). The driver was seated at the front on the right, with the 7.7-mm (0.303-in) Type 97 machine-gunner to his left. The two-man turret was in the centre of the hull, offset to the right, and could be traversed manually through 360°. The main armament consisted of a 57-mm (2.24-in) Type 97 gun with an elevation of +11° and depression of -9°, and another 7.7-mm machine-gun was located in the turret rear. Totals of 120 rounds of 57-mm (80 high-explosive and 40 of armour-piercing) and 2,350 rounds of 7.7-mm ammunition were carried.

Simple propulsion
The air-cooled 12-cylinder diesel was mounted at the rear of the hull and transmitted its power via a propeller shaft to the gearbox in the nose of the tank; the gearbox had four forward and

one reverse gears. Steering was of the clutch and brake type, and the suspension on each side consisted of six dual rubber-tyred road wheels, with the drive sprocket at the front and idler at the rear; there were three track-return rollers. The four central road wheels were paired and mounted on bell-cranks resisted by armoured compression springs, while each end bogie was independently bell crank-mounted to the hull in a similar manner.

Service introduction
When first introduced into service, the Type 97 was quite an advanced design apart from its main armament, which had a low muzzle velocity. A feature of most Japanese tanks of this period was that they were powered by diesel rather than petrol engines, which

Japanese light and medium tanks were adequate for operations in Asia and the Pacific until they met the better protected and more powerfully armed tanks deployed by the Allies from 1942 onward.

gave them a much increased operational range as well as reducing the ever-present risk of fire, the dread of any tank crew.

In 1942 the **Medium Tank Type 97 (SHINHOTO CHI-HA)** appeared, with a new turret armed with a 47-mm Type 97 gun that fired ammunition with a higher muzzle velocity and so improved penetration characteristics. This weapon used the same ammunition as Japanese anti-tank guns and therefore helped ammunition commonality.

The chassis of the Type 97 was also used as the basis for a number of other vehicles including a flail-equipped mine-clearing tank, self-propelled guns (including the 150-mm/5.9-in **Type 38 HO-RO**), self-propelled anti-aircraft guns

Probably the best Japanese armoured vehicle to see any great amount of service, the Type 97 was a fairly advanced design that was handicapped by an inadequate gun.

(including 20-mm and 75-mm/2.95-in), an engineer tank, a recovery vehicle and an armoured bridgelayer. Most of these were built in such small numbers that they played little part in actual operations. The Type 97 was replaced in production by the **Type 1 CHI-HE** medium tank, followed by the **Type 3 CHI-NU**, of which only 60 were built by the end of the war. The last Japanese medium tanks were the Type 4 and Type 5, but neither of these well-armed vehicles saw combat.

Renault R-35 Light tank

The **Renault R-35** light tank had its origins in a design known originally as the **ZM**, produced late in 1934 in answer to a French army request for a new infantry support tank to supplement and eventually replace the ageing Renault FT-17 which dated back to World War I. Trials of the new tank started in early 1935, and in that same year the design was ordered into production before its evaluation had been completed as Germany appeared to be in a mood for conflict. Before production got under way, the French army decided to increase the armour basis of the new **Char Léger Renault R-35** from 30 to 40 mm (1.18 to 1.575 in).

The R-35 never entirely replaced the FT-17 in ser-

A two-man infantry support tank in the 'Great War' tradition, the R-35 was built in the erroneous belief that tank warfare had changed little in the years since 1918.

vice, but by 1940 over 1,600 and possibly as many as 1,900 had been built, and the type was the most numerous French infantry tank in use. Its overall appearance was not unlike that of the FT-17, for it was a small tank with a crew of only two. The design made much use of cast armour, and the suspension followed the Renault practice of the day, being of the scissors-type horizontal coil-spring type used on the company's cavalry tank designs.

The driver's position was forward, while the comman-

The R-35 reflected obsolescent tactical thinking in its conception, and therefore provided an inadequate battlefield tank. The commander is seated on the opened back of the turret.

der in the cast turret had to act as his own loader and gunner firing the 37-mm (1.46-in) L/21 gun (later replaced by a longer L/33 weapon of the same calibre) and the co-axial 7.5-mm (0.295-in) machine-gun: the ammunition totals were 100 37-mm and 2,400 7.5-mm rounds. This turret was poorly equipped with vision devices, and its internal disposition was such that the commander had to spend much of his time in action standing on the hull floor. With the vehicle out of action, the rear of the turret opened as a flap on which the commander could sit.

Limited use

For its day the R-35 was a sound enough vehicle, and was typical of contemporary French design. The **AMX R-40** version appeared in 1940 with revised suspension, and a few of this variant were produced before the Germans invaded in May 1940. The little R-35 soon proved to be no match for the German Panzers. For a start it was usually allocated in small numbers in direct support of infantry formations, and could thus be

The cast turret of the R-35 was hand operated for traverse through 360 degrees, and the 37-mm (1.46-in) gun could be elevated in the arc between -18 and +18 degrees. The armour was generally adequate.

picked off piecemeal by the massed German tanks. Its gun proved virtually ineffective against even the lightest German tanks, though in return its 40-mm (1.575-in) armour was fairly effective against most of the German anti-tank guns. Thus the R-35 was able to contribute little to the campaign, and many were destroyed or abandoned by their crews in the disasters that overtook the French army as the Germans swept through France.

Large numbers of R-35s fell into German hands virtually intact. These were put to use by garrison units in France with the designation **PzKpfw 35-R(f)**, many later passing to driver and other tank training schools. With the invasion of the USSR many R-35 tanks were stripped of their turrets for service as artillery tractors or **Munitionpanzer 35-R(f)** ammunition carriers. At a later date many of the R-35 tanks still in France had their turrets removed so that their hulls could be converted as the basis of several types of self-propelled artillery or an anti-tank gun known as the **4.7-cm Pak(t) auf GW 35-R(f)**. The turrets were emplaced in concrete along the 'Atlantic Wall' coastal defences.

Thus the R-35 passed into history, and despite its numbers its combat record was such that it proved to be of more use to the Germans than to the French.

SPECIFICATION	
Renault R-35	cylinder petrol engine delivering 61 kW (82 bhp)
Crew: 2	
Weight: 10000 kg (22,046 lb)	**Performance:** maximum road speed 20 km/h (12.4 mph); range 140 km (87 miles); fording 0.8 m (2 ft 7 in); vertical obstacle 0.5 m (1 ft 7.7 in); trench 1.6 m (5 ft 3 in)
Dimensions: length 4.20 m (13 ft 9.25 in); width 1.85 m (6 ft 0.75 in); height 2.37 m (7 ft 9.25 in)	
Powerplant: one Renault 4-	

SOMUA S-35 Medium tank

When the re-equipment of the French cavalry arm with tanks started during the mid-1930s, among the several concerns that became involved was a Schneider subsidiary known as SOMUA (Société d'Outillage Mécanique et d'Usinage d'Artillerie). In 1935 this revealed a tank prototype that attracted immediate attention, and its very advanced design was soon recognised by the award of a production order. One of the best armoured fighting vehicles of its day, the **SOMUA S-35** was more formally known as the **Auto-Mitrailleuse de Combat (AMC) modèle 1935 SOMUA**.

The S-35 had many features that were later to become commonplace. The hull and turret were both cast components at a time when most vehicles were based on structures of riveted steel plate. The cast armour was not only well shaped for extra protection, but also much thicker than the norms of the time: the minimum was 20 mm (0.79 in) and the maximum 55 mm (2.16 in). For all that, the tank still had a good reserve of power for lively battlefield performance, and a good operational radius of action was ensured by large internal fuel tanks. Radio was standard at a time when hand signals between tanks were still common. To add to all these advantages the S-35 was armed with a capable main gun: the 47-mm (1.85-in) SA 35 was one of the most powerful

In 1940 many S-35 tanks were damaged and abandoned, such as the vehicle seen here, but the vehicle was good enough for the Germans to use against the Allies four years later.

weapons of the day and a gun that could still be regarded as a useful weapon in 1944. The secondary armament was a single 7.5-mm (0.295-in) coaxial machine-gun.

Labour problems

The S-35 was ordered into production but, as in nearly all other sectors of the French defence industry before 1939, this production was slow and beset by labour and other troubles. Only about 400 S-35 tanks had been produced by the time the Germans invaded in May 1940, and only about 250 of these were in front-line service. In action the S-35 gave a good account of itself though revealing a serious design defect when under fire: the upper and lower hull halves were joined by a ring of bolts along a horizontal join, and if an anti-tank projectile hit this join line the two halves split apart with obvious dire results. But at the time this mattered less than the way

Despite the weakness of having the commander operate the main armament, the S-35 was a fine tank.

in which the tanks had to be handled: the S-35 had a crew of three (driver, commander and radio operator), and it was the location of the commander alone in the small turret that caused the problems, for this unfortunate had not only to keep an eye on the local tactical scene, but also to assimilate orders from the radio while loading and firing the gun. The tasks were too much for one man, so the S-35's potential was rarely attained.

As with other French tanks of the day, the S-35s were split into small groups scattered long the French line, and were grouped on only a few occasions for worthwhile counterstrokes against the Panzer columns.

After the occupation of France the Germans took over as many S-35 tanks as they could find for issue to

SPECIFICATION	
SOMUA S-35	(190 hp)
Crew: 3	**Performance:** maximum road
Weight: 19500 kg (42,989 lb)	speed 40 km/h (24.85 mph);
Dimensions: length 5.38 m (17 ft	maximum road range 230 km
7.8 in); width 2.12 m (6 ft 11.5 in);	(143 miles); fording 1 m (3 ft 3 in);
height 2.62 m (8 ft 7 in)	vertical obstacle 0.76 m (2 ft 6 in);
Powerplant: one SOMUA V-8	trench 2.13 m (7 ft)
petrol engine delivering 141.7 kW	

occupation and training units under the designation **PzKpfw 35-S 739(f)**. Some were handed over to the Italian army, but many were still based in France when the Allies invaded in 1944 and the S-35 tank was once more in action, this time in

German hands. Any S-35s taken by the Allies were passed over to the Free French, who in their turn used them in the reduction of the beleaguered German garrisons locked up in their Atlantic sea-port strongholds.

Well protected and manoeuvrable, the SOMUA S-35 was undoubtedly the best Allied tank in 1940. It had a radio and its 47-mm (1.85-in) gun could fire both armour-piercing shot and HE shell, an obvious requirement which had escaped British designers.

Hotchkiss H-35, H-38 & H-39
Light tanks

During the early 1930s the French army, in common with the armies of many other European countries, decided that the worsening political situation in the continent made it sensible to embark on a programme to re-equip its ageing tank parks with modern equipment. At that time the French army followed the current practice of dividing tank functions into faster-moving 'cavalry' and slower-moving 'infantry' elements, and one of the tanks intended for cavalry use was a design known as the **Char Léger Hotchkiss H-35**.

The origins of this tank can be found in 1933 with a requirement for a light infantry tank to partner the SOMUA S-35. The Hotchkiss prototype of 1934 was then rejected by the infantry in favour of the Renault R-35, but was then accepted by the cavalry as the **Char de Cavalerie 35H** before finally being accepted by the infantry as the Char H-35. The type thereby became one of the most important French tanks of the day.

The H-35 was a small vehicle with a crew of two, and it was lightly armed with only a 37-mm (1.46-in) short-barrel gun and a 7.5-mm (0.295-in) machine-gun. The armour was also light, ranging in thickness from 12 to 34 mm (0.47 to 1.34 in). The tank was also underpowered by a Hotchkiss petrol engine delivering only 55.9 kW (75 hp) in a vehicle turning the scales at 11400 kg (25,132 lb) for a maximum speed of just 28 km/h (17.4 mph). After 400 had been produced from 1936 onward,

the basic model was supplemented by the **H-38** and then the **H-39**. The H-38 had thickened armour, up to a maximum of 40 mm (1.57 in), and an engine delivering 89.5 kW (120 hp) for a speed increased to 36 km/h (22.4 mph) despite an increase in weight to 12000 kg (26,455 lb). The H-39 was a further development of the H-38 with armour up to 45 mm (1.77 in) thick and, in place of the earlier variants' 37-mm SA 18 L/21 gun, a longer SA 33 L/33 weapon firing exactly the same round with a muzzle velocity of 701 m (2,300 ft) rather than 388 m (1,273 ft) per second for greater armour penetration.

The production total for the H-38 and H-39 eventually reached some 890 units. It is worth noting that in

general French tank production was slow, being severely limited by a lack of mass production facilities, and was also beset constantly by labour troubles, even after the outbreak of World War II in September 1939.

Detail differences

The H-38 and H-39 thus differed from the H-35 in their thicker armour, more powerful engine and, in the H-39, more capable gun, and were visually distinguishable from the first model by their raised rear decking, which was almost flat compared with the pronounced slope of that on the H-35. Despite the improved performance of the SA 38 gun over the SA 18, the French were soon to learn that even the better gun was virtually

Fitted with the 37-mm (1.46-in) SA 38 L/33 gun, the H-39 had a respectable performance by the standards of the 1930s. Its only major disadvantage was that the commander had to work the gun.

useless against the more capable of the German armour, most notably the PzKpfw III medium and PzKpfw IV battle tanks.

Wrong tactics

The H-35, H-38 and H-39 were all used in action in France after the German invasion of May 1940, and in general gave a moderately good account of themselves despite their indifferent armament. However, the tanks suffered from dismal tactical use. Instead of being used en masse in the German fashion, the French tanks were scattered along the line in penny packets for infantry support rather than being grouped as an effective anti-armour force. On occasion they were able to surprise the Germans, but only in purely local actions, so many were either destroyed or captured by the advancing Germans. Always

The H-35, seen here on parade, equipped many French mechanised cavalry units. Although armed with the ineffectual 37-mm (1.46-in) SA 18 L/21 gun, the type could still have performed effectively in the reconnaissance role but was instead used to bolster the infantry.

short of matériel, the Germans took many Hotchkiss tanks into their own service as the **PzKpfw 35-H 734(f)** and **PzKpfw 39-H 735(f)**, and these were used for some years by second-line and occupation units. At a later date many of the tanks had their turrets removed and replaced by German anti-tank guns for use as mobile tank destroyers, the turret being used in the 'Atlantic Wall' coastal defences.

Not all the French tanks fell into German hands. Many were located in the French Middle East possessions and some were either taken over by the Free French or were used in action by the Vichy French during the campaign in Syria in 1941. Perhaps the Hotchkiss tanks with the most unusual travel tales were those taken to the USSR in 1941 by the Germans when they were so short of tanks that even the captured French vehicles were found useful.

By 1945 there were few H-35 and H-39 tanks left anywhere: the Middle East examples survived in small numbers, and some were used to form part of the Israeli army tank arm to a time as late as 1956.

SPECIFICATION	
Hotchkiss H-35 **Crew:** 2 **Weight:** 12100 kg (26,675 lb) **Dimensions:** length 4.22 m (13 ft 10 in); width 1.95 m (6 ft 4.8 in); height 2.15 m (7 ft 0.6 in) **Powerplant:** one Hotchkiss 6-cylinder petrol engine delivering	89.5 kW (120 hp) **Performance:** maximum road speed 36 km/h (22.3 mph); maximum road range 120 km (74.5 miles); fording 0.85 m (2 ft 10 in); vertical obstacle 0.5 m (1 ft 8 in); trench 1.8 m (5 ft 11 in)

Char B1 Heavy tank

The series of tanks known as the **Char B** had a definite look of the 'Great War' era about them, and this is not surprising for their development can be traced back as far as 1921 and the immediate aftermath of World War I. What was demanded at that time was a tank with a 75-mm (2.95-in) gun set in a hull-mounted embrasure, but it was not until about 1930 that the result of this request was finally built. This was the Char B heavy tank with a weight of about 25 tonnes, and prolonged development led in 1935 to the full production version, the **Char B1**.

Advanced design

The Char B1 was a powerful tank for the period as it had a turret-mounted 47-mm (1.85-in) gun with 50 rounds of ammunition and a 75-mm (2.95-in) gun with 74 rounds of ammunition set in the front of the hull; the secondary armament was two 7.5-mm (0.295-in) machine-guns with 5,100 rounds of ammunition. The limited traverse of this hull gun was partially offset by a complex steering system that allowed the vehicle to be aligned rapidly on to the correct target sector. Although its archaic appearance belied the fact, the Char B was full of very advanced design features that ranged from self-sealing fuel tanks to grouped lubrication for the many bearings; an electric starter was also provided and attention was given to internal fire protection. The crew of four men was scattered about the interior in a way that made internal communication difficult, however, and this led to many operational problems. The crew of the Char B1 had to be a highly trained group of specialists to make the best of the tank's potential as a fighting vehicle, and in 1940 these teams were few

and far between.

The final production variant was the **Char B1-bis**, which had thicker armour (minimum of 14 mm/0.55 in and maximum of 65 mm/2.56 in) by comparison with the Char B1's figures (14 and 40 mm/0.55 and 1.57 in), a revised turret design and a more powerful engine. Later production models had an even more powerful engine of aircraft origins and still more fuel capacity.

Slow manufacture

Production of the Char B1-bis started in 1937, and by 1940 there were about 400 Char B tanks of all types in service. By then the Char B1 and Char B1-bis were the most numerous and powerful of all the French heavy tanks, and the basic type was the main battle tank of the few dedicated armoured formations fielded by the French army.

The Germans had a great respect for the Char B1, for the 75-mm gun was quite capable of knocking out even the PzKpfw IV battle tank, but the Germans were considerably assisted during the fighting of May and June 1940 by several factors. One of these was that the Char B1 was a complex beast and

required a great deal of careful maintenance: many simply broke down *en route* to battle and were left for the Germans to take over undamaged. Another drawback for the French was that, as was the case with other tank units, those operating the Char B1 were frequently broken up into small local-defence groups instead of being grouped to provide a cohesive mass that could meet and perhaps

even halt the advances of Germany's fast-moving armoured divisions.

German service

The Germans took over the Char B1-bis as the **PzKpfw B1-bis 740(f)** and used it for a variety of purposes. Some of the vehicles were passed intact to occupation units such as those in the Channel Islands, while others were converted for driver training or were

Above: The 400 or so Char B1 tanks possessed by the French army in 1940 were potentially a devastating strike force.

altered to become self-propelled artillery carriages. Some were fitted with flamethrowers as the **PzKpfw Flamm(f)**. In 1944 a few were still around to pass once more into French army use, but by 1945 only a handful were left.

Left: The Char B1 could cope easily with any German tank in existence, but abysmal tactical handling rendered the type useless as the weapon that might have checked Germany's advances.

Above: The tanks of the Char B series were well armoured and possessed good performance, but the whole of the vehicle's mass had to be manoeuvred in order to train the hull-mounted main gun on its target.

SPECIFICATION	
Char B1-bis	229 kW (307 hp)
Crew: 4	**Performance:** maximum road
Weight: 31500 kg (69,444 lb)	speed 28 km/h (17.4 mph);
Dimensions: length 6.37 m (20 ft	maximum road range 180 km
10.8 in); width 2.5 m (8 ft 2.4 in);	(112 miles); fording not known;
height 2.79 m (9 ft 1.8 in)	vertical obstacle 0.93 m (3 ft 1 in);
Powerplant: one Renault 6-	trench 2.74 m (9 ft)
cylinder petrol engine delivering	

Panzerjäger I Tank destroyer

When the first PzKpfw I (Panzerkampfwagen I) light tanks were produced in 1934, it was intended that they would be used only as training vehicles. In the event they had to be used as combat tanks during the early years of World War II for the simple reason that larger and heavier tanks were not yet available in sufficient numbers. However, the PzKpfw I had a crew of a mere two men, carried only a machine-gun armament and was poorly protected. By no stretch of the imagination was it a viable battle tank and most were phased out of operational service in 1941 but retained for the original training role. This left a number of spare tank chassis with no operational role, so the opportunity was taken to convert these vehicles into the first German self-propelled anti-tank guns.

It had already been decided that some form of mobile anti-tank gun would be a great asset to the anti-tank units, which otherwise had to use towed guns. Thus the first example of this requirement was met by mounting a 3.7-cm (1.46-in) Pak 35/36 onto a turretless PzKpfw I. While this conversion showed promise, it was not adopted because even by mid-1940 it was appreciated that the 3.7-cm gun lacked the power to deal with future armour. Thus a Czech 4.7-cm (1.85-in) anti-tank gun was mounted instead, and this combination was adopted for service as the **Panzerjäger I für 4.7-cm Pak(t)**.

The Czechoslovakian gun was a powerful, hard-hitting weapon that was well capable of penetrating most armour it was likely to encounter during the early 1940s, and Alkett AG produced a total of 132 conversions. The result was

This photograph of a Panzerjäger I reveals the extemporised nature of this early German conversion, made in an attempt to prolong the service life of the PzKpfw I light tank. The gun was powerful enough but the mounting provided virtually no protection.

very much a first attempt, for all that was required was the removal of the tank turret, plating over the front of the turret ring and arranging a small working platform over the engine covers. The gun itself was mounted behind a lightly armoured shield that was left open at the top and rear.

The crew consisted of the driver, still seated in his original PzKpfw I position, and two soldiers serving the gun. A total of 74 rounds could be carried as standard, although more could be added to this figure. The chassis mainly used for the conversion was that of the PzKpfw I Ausf B. Similar conversions mounting either the German 3.7-cm or Czechoslovakian 4.7-cm gun were created on all manner of captured tracked, half-tracked and even wheeled chassis. The majority of these conversions were carried out at unit level rather than being officially sanctioned, usually in order to provide extra local mobility for what would otherwise be towed guns.

Vulnerable target

The Panzerjäger I served in North Africa and during the early stages of the campaigns in the USSR. It proved to possess sufficient firepower to defeat opposing tanks, but its overall lack of protection for the crew made the type a very vulnerable target. As soon as better equipment became available the type was withdrawn from front-line use and assigned to theatres where it could be used for policing rather than for combat

duties. Among the locations so honoured were the Balkans, where the vehicles were used on anti-partisan operations. Units operating on the Eastern Front after about the end of 1942 frequently removed the guns and used the chassis for supply carrying, and some units replaced their Czech guns with captured French 4.7-cm guns. Few Panzerjäger Is remained in service after mid-1944.

This SdKfz 101 Panzerjäger I was the first example captured by the Allies in North Africa, and was then subjected to a great deal of technical scrutiny. It mounted an ex-Czechoslovak 4.7-cm (1.85-in) anti-tank gun in an open mounting that provided only a frontal shield for crew protection.

SPECIFICATION	
Panzerjäger I	6 cylinder petrol engine
Crew: 3	**Performance:** maximum road speed
Weight: 6000 kg (13,228 lb)	40 km/h (24.9 mph); maximum road
Dimensions: length (overall) 4.14 m	range 140 km (87 miles)
(13 ft 7 in); width 2.01 m (6 ft 7¼ in);	**Fording:** 0.6 m (2 ft)
height 2.1 m (6 ft 10¾ in)	**Gradient:** 57 per cent
Powerplant: one 74.6-kW (100-hp)	**Vertical obstacle:** 0.37 m (14½ in)
Maybach NL 38 liquid-cooled	**Trench:** 1.4 m (4 ft 7¼ in)

Marder II Tank destroyer

As with the PzKpfw I, when it entered service in 1935 the PzKpfw II was meant to be used only as a training and development tank. In the event it had to be used as a combat tank from 1939 to 1942 simply because there were not enough combat tanks to replace the type, which acquitted itself well enough despite the fact that its main armament was limited to a 20-mm cannon. By 1941 the PzKpfw II was overdue for replacement as its armament was able to penetrate only soft-skinned targets and the small turret ring could not accommodate a heavier weapon. The production line for the chassis was still in operation, however, and at the time this seemed to be too valuable to waste so the opportunity was

This Marder II profile shows the rather high mounting of the 7.5-cm (2.95-in) Pak 40/2, a special version of the standard German anti-tank gun of the period late in World War II.

The SdKfz 131 Marder II mounted a 7.5-cm (2.95-in) Pak 40/2, and was one of the more important of the Panzerjäger conversions. Based on the PzKpfw II Ausf A, C or F, 1,217 were produced for service on all fronts. There was a crew of four including the driver.

was taken to convert the PzKpfw II to a Panzerjäger.

The prototype of this new Panzerjäger was fitted with a 5-cm (1.97-in) anti-tank gun, but the full production version was fitted with the special Pak 40/2 version of the 7.5-cm (2.95-in) Pak 40

anti-tank gun. This powerful gun was the German army's standard anti-tank weapon, and the incorporation of greater mobility added considerably to the gun's anti-armour potential. The gun was placed behind a 10-mm (0.39-in) thick armoured shield that sloped to the rear to provide the gun crew with adequate protection. To balance the weight of the gun, the engine was moved to the rear of the hull and the engine covers were used as a working platform to serve the gun. The vehicle was known as the **Marder II** (Marder meaning marten), although other and more cumbersome designations (such as **7.5-cm Pak 40/2 auf Slf II** and **SdKfz 131**) were used in official documents.

Widespread service

The Marder II remained in production until 1944 and became one of the most widely used of all the many German self-propelled gun conversions. In production terms it was manufactured in greater numbers than any other weapon of its type – 1,217 were made. The Marder II was certainly a useful and efficient weapon in combat, for it was relatively small, had a good cross-country performance, and possessed a gun able to knock out virtually any Allied tank other than super-heavy Soviet tanks such as the IS-2. Racks for 37 rounds of main armament ammunition were provided over the engine covers, and there was also space for stowing 600 rounds for the machine-gun; this was usually a 7.92-mm (0.312-in) MG 34 or MG 42 weapon.

Most Marder II production was sent to the Eastern Front, but the Marder II was found wherever German troops were in action. By 1944 the type was out of production and the crew was often reduced by one man to conserve manpower, but development did not cease. During the latter stages of the war some Marder IIs were equipped with infra-red (IR) searchlights to provide a night engagement capability, and some of these were used in action on the Eastern Front during the last stages of the war. By then such novel equipment could have but little impact on the outcome of the war.

SPECIFICATION	
Marder II	**Performance:** maximum road speed
Crew: 3 or 4	40 km/h (24.8 mph); maximum road
Weight: 11000 kg (24,251 lb)	range 190 km (118 miles)
Dimensions: length 6.36 m (20 ft	**Fording:** 0.9 m (2 ft 11 in)
10¾ in); width 2.28 m (7 ft 5¾ in);	**Gradient:** 57 per cent
height 2.2 m (7 ft 2½ in)	**Vertical obstacle:** 0.42 m (1 ft
Powerplant: one 104.4-kW (140-hp)	4½ in)
Maybach HL 62 liquid-cooled	**Trench:** 1.8 m (5 ft 11 in)
6-cylinder petrol engine	

Marder III Tank destroyer

There were two self-propelled guns known as the Marder III, both using the same chassis derived from that of the Skoda TNHP-S tank. This tank was originally produced by Skoda at Pilsen for the Czechoslovak army, but with the seizure of the rump of the Czechoslovak state by Germany in 1939, Skoda continued production under the designation PzKpfw 38(t) for the German army. The Germans introduced so many production and in-service changes to the original Skoda design that by 1941 the PzKpfw 38(t) could be regarded as a German tank, but the original turret was too small to carry weapons powerful enough to defeat Allied armour after 1941. The chassis was kept in production for other purposes.

By 1941 the appearance of more modern Allied tanks meant the German army

lacked a tank powerfully enough armed to knock out types such as the Soviet T-34, so hasty improvisations were made to remedy this problem. One was the installation of a captured Soviet field gun, the 76.2-mm (3-in) Model 1936, on the chassis of the PzKpfw 38(t). The gun was a dual-purpose weapon with anti-tank capability, and in addition the Germans also adapted many as dedicated towed anti-tank guns.

Potent capability

On the PzKpfw 38(t) the gun was mounted behind a fixed shield and the conversion went into production in early 1942 as the **Marder III**, otherwise the **Panzerjäger 38(t) für 7.62-cm Pak 36(r)**. Some 344 of these conversions were made for deployment on the Eastern Front, North Africa and elsewhere. However, this type

This Marder III was captured in North Africa in April 1943 and mounted its 7.5-cm (2.95-in) Pak 40/3 in a central position. It was a very simple conversion of a Czechoslovakian tank chassis but proved effective.

was regarded only as a stop-gap until sufficient numbers of the German 7.5-cm (2.95-in) Pak 40 became available during 1942. Production of the Soviet-gunned Marder III was then replaced by that of the German-gunned version. The gun/chassis combination was still the Marder III, but had the designation **Panzerjäger 38(t) Ausf H für 7.5-cm Pak 40/3**, otherwise **SdKfz 138**, using a slightly different gun shield and mounting from the earlier model.

Pak 40-armed Marder IIIs were rushed into action during the last stages of the Tunisian campaign. Up to 1943 the various German self-propelled guns using the Skoda PzKpfw 38(t) tank as a basis. Early conversions (including the original Marder III) were

nose-heavy, which limited mobility and so German engineers relocated the engine to the front of the chassis and moved the combat platform to the rear. Marder III production then changed once more to the new **Panzerjäger 38(t) Ausf M für 7.5-cm Pak 40/3** with

the gun and its protection at the rear. This provided a vehicle of better balance, and the new chassis was used to mount a variety of other weapons. The late Marder III was manufactured by BMM of Prague. Production ended in May 1944, after 799 vehicles.

The later Marder IIIs had the main gun position moved to the rear of the chassis and the engine to the front. This provided a better balanced and more useful vehicle, and nearly 800 were produced, still using the basic components of the PzKpfw 38(t) tank.

SPECIFICATION	
Panzerjäger 38(t) Ausf M	**Performance:** maximum road
Crew: 4	speed 42 km/h (26 mph); maximum
Weight: 11000 kg (24,251 lb)	road range 140 km (87 miles);
Dimensions: length (overall) 4.65 m	**Fording:** 0.9 m (2 ft 11 in)
(15 ft 3 in); width 2.35 m (7 ft 8½ in);	**Gradient:** 57 per cent
height 2.48 m (8 ft 1½ in)	**Vertical obstacle:** 0.84 m (2 ft
Powerplant: one 112-kW (150-hp)	9 in)
Praga AC liquid-cooled petrol engine	**Trench:** 1.3 m (4 ft 3 in)

Hetzer Light tank destroyer

Tank-destroyer conversions of existing tank chassis to produce weapons such as the Marder III were moderately successful. In overall terms, though, the results were high, clumsy, lacked finesse and showed every sign of the haste in which they had been produced. In contrast, the various Sturmgeschütz close-support artillery vehicles showed that they too could be used as tank destroyers. Thus in 1943 it was decided to produce a light tank destroyer along assault gun lines, the chassis of the PzKpfw 38(t) being taken as the basis.

Small but potent

The result was one of the best of all German tank destroyers: the **Jagdpanzer 38(t) für 7.5-cm Pak 39**, or

This Jagdpanzer 38(t) Hetzer has a roof-mounted machine-gun for local defence. The small stand-off armour side plates are fitted over the upper part of the tracks to provide more side-on protection. Well over 1,500 of these vehicles were produced.

The low height of the Hetzer can be clearly appreciated. Note the well-shaped 'Saukopf' (pig's head) gun mantlet that provided extra head-on protection and the lack of a muzzle brake, usually fitted to other German vehicles of this type.

Hetzer (baiter, as in bull-baiting), otherwise the **SdKfz 138/2**. The Hetzer used the basic engine, suspension and running gear of the PzKpfw 38(t) allied to an armoured hull that sloped inward to provide extra protection for the crew of four.

The armament was a modified 7.5-cm (2.95-in) tank gun and a roof-mounted machine-gun. Production began in Prague at the end of 1943. In action the Hetzer proved to be a very successful gun/chassis combination. It was small and low, yet well protected and with a good cross-country performance. The gun could knock out all but the heaviest Allied tanks, yet the Hetzer itself was difficult to knock out. In

combat it was so small as to be virtually invisible to enemy gunners. Calls for more and more came from the front line, to the extent that by late 1944 all available PzKpfw 38(t) production was diverted to the Hetzer programme. Manufacture continued until the factories were overrun in May 1945, by which time 1,577 had been built.

Normal variants

Several versions of the Hetzer were produced. One was the **Flammpanzer 38(t)** flamethrower, and another the **Bergepanzer 38(t)** light recovery version. The Hetzer story did not cease in 1945, moreover, for the type was soon restored to production for the Czechoslovakian army and exports to Switzerland in 1947-52. The Swiss continued to use the type into the

1970s.

Wartime Hetzers were used for a series of trials and various weapon mountings, including guns with no recoil mechanism connected directly to the front hull armour for successful evaluation of the concept. One trial model was an assault howitzer mounting a 15-cm (5.91-in) infantry howitzer, and there were several similar projects. None reached the production stage, for the assembly lines concentrated on the basic Hetzer.

The Hetzer was regarded as one of the best of all the Panzerjäger. It was a small but powerful vehicle that was much more economical to produce and use than many of the larger vehicles. It could knock out nearly every tank it was likely to encounter yet it was little higher than a standing man.

SPECIFICATION	
Hetzer	**Performance:** maximum road speed
Crew: 4	39 km/h (24 mph); road maximum
Weight: 14500 kg (31,967 lb)	range 250 km (155 miles)
Dimensions: length (overall) 6.2 m	**Fording:** 0.9 m (2 ft 11 in)
(20 ft 4 in); width 2.5 m (8 ft 2½ in);	**Gradient:** 75 per cent
height 2.1 m (6 ft 11 in)	**Vertical obstacle:** 0.65 m (2 ft
Powerplant: one 112-119 kW (150-	1½ in)
160 hp) Praga AC/2800 petrol engine	**Trench:** 1.3 m (4 ft 3 in)

Jagdpanzer IV Tank destroyer

Combat experience gained during the 1942 campaigns showed the German staff that its Sturmgeschütz close-support artillery vehicles would have to be upgunned if they were to remain viable as tank-destroyers. The future standard weapon selected was the long version of the 7.5-cm (2.95-in) tank gun fitted to the Panther tank.

L/70 gun

This gun was an L/70 weapon, whereas the tank and anti-tank versions of the Pak 40 family were L/48 weapons, and the accommodation of this gun would entail considerable modification of vehicles such as the Sturmgeschütz III. These modifications would take time, so it was decided to adapt the larger PzKpfw IV

The Jagdpanzer IV (SdKfz 162) was a Panzerjäger version of the PzKpfw IV tank and housed its 7.5-cm (2.95-in) main gun in a superstructure formed from well-sloped armoured plates. This is an early example with the gun still retaining the muzzle brake, an item later omitted.

tank chassis to act as a 'fail safe' model. Design work was soon under way on this new model, which emerged in 1943 as the **Jagdpanzer IV Ausf F für 7.5-cm Pak 39**

or **Panzerjäger 39**, otherwise the **SdKfz 162**.

However, by the time the first examples were ready, the long 7.5-cm guns were earmarked for Panther tanks

and so the first examples had to be content with model L/48 guns.

The first Jagdpanzer IVs appeared in October 1943 as the well-tried suspension

and propulsion layout of the PzKpfw IV allied to a new armoured carapace with well-sloped sides. The resultant silhouette was much lower than the hull/turret combination of the tank, and mounted the gun in a well-protected mantlet on the front hull. The result was well-liked by the Panzerjäger crews, who appreciated the low silhouette and the well-protected hull, so the Jagdpanzer IV was soon in great demand. The gun was powerful enough to tackle virtually any Allied tank, and in action the Jagdpanzer IV was soon knocking up appreciable 'kill' totals, especially on the Eastern Front, to which most were sent. The secondary armament of two 7.92-mm (0.312-in) MG 34 or MG 42 machine-guns also proved highly effective.

Many Panzer commanders considered that the Jagdpanzer IV was good enough in its original form to require no upgunning, but Hitler insisted that the change to the long gun had to be made. Thus during 1944 there appeared some **Jagdpanzer IV mit 7.5-cm StuK 42** equipments with the longer L/70 gun. However, the changeover on the production line took time, too much time for Hitler, who insisted that the switch to the new gun had to be made even if it meant diverting all PzKpfw IV tank production to that end.

Interim model

Thus a third Jagdpanzer IV appeared, this time a hasty conversion of a basic PzKpfw IV hull to take a form of Jagdpanzer IV sloping carapace and again mounting the 70-calibre gun. This conversion was known as the **Panzer IV/70 Zwischenlösung** (interim) and was in production by late 1944. Not many were produced as by then many of the main PzKpfw IV production centres, along with the industrial transport infrastructure, were in ruins as a result of Allied bombing.

In service the Jagdpanzer IV vehicles with the L/70 gun proved to be powerful tank killers, but the extra weight of the long gun made the vehicles nose-heavy to the extent that the front road wheels had to be ringed with steel instead of rubber to cope with the extra weight. The gun weight also unbalanced and reduced the overall performance of the vehicle, especially across

This early production Jagdpanzer IV has the muzzle brake still fitted. Later versions used a much longer 7.5-cm (2.95-in) main gun, but this longer gun rather overloaded the chassis, and later versions also used side armour plates. This Panzerjäger was later considered to be one of the best of its type.

rough terrain. By late 1944 and early 1945 such drawbacks simply had to be overlooked, for the Allies were at the gates of the Reich and anything that could be put into the field was used.

The Jagdpanzer IV proved to be a sound Panzerjäger that enabled the Germans to utilise existing production capacity and maintain the PzKpfw IV line in being

when it would otherwise have been phased out. In service the Jagdpanzer IV was a popular vehicle and a powerful tank-killer. It was a good example of how a sound basic armoured vehicle design, that of the PzKpfw IV tank, could be adapted to assume a combat role that had not even been imagined when the tank design was first mooted in the early 1930s.

SPECIFICATION	
Jagdpanzer IV mit 7.5-cm Stuk 42	engine
Crew: 4	**Performance:** maximum road speed 35 km/h (22 mph); maximum road range 214 km (133 miles)
Weight: 25800 kg (56,879 lb)	
Dimensions: length (overall) 8.58 m (28 ft 2 in); width 2.93 m (9 ft 7½ in); height (overall) 1.96 m (6 ft 5 in)	**Fording:** 1.2 m (3 ft 11 in)
	Gradient: 57 per cent
	Vertical obstacle: 0.6 m (23½ in)
Powerplant: one 198-kW (265-hp) Maybach HL 120 petrol	**Trench:** 2.3 m (7 ft 6½ in)

Nashorn Tank destroyer

In the middle of World War II the German army adopted a large number of hurried improvisations in order to get useful numbers of Panzerjäger into the field, and some of these improvisations fared better than others. One of these hasty measures was the adoption of the special weapon-carrier vehicle that had originally been produced to carry the large 15-cm (5.91-in) sFH 18 field howitzer. It was known as the Geschützwagen III/IV as it was based on the chassis of the PzKpfw IV but used some of the drive components of the PzKpfw III.

Design modifications

Despite the great demand for the artillery version of this weapon carrier it was decided to adapt it to carry the large 8.8-cm (3.46-in) Pak 43 anti-tank gun as the **8.8-cm Pak 43/1 auf GW**

The SdKfz 164 Hornisse was the first Panzerjäger to mount the famous 8.8-cm Pak 43/1, and used the same chassis as the Hummel self-propelled artillery vehicle.

III/IV, or **SdKfz 164.** The first of these new Panzerjäger were issued during 1943, and the type went under two names: the official name was **Nashorn** (rhinoceros) but **Hornisse** (hornet) was also widely applied in service.

The Nashorn was very much one of the interim Panzerjäger designs, for although the gun was mounted behind armour at the front and sides this armour was relatively thin, and the top and rear were open. The gun mounting itself was rather high, so the Nashorn had definite

combat deficiencies, not the least of which was the problem of battlefield concealment of the vehicle's height and bulk. As the chassis had been intended as an artillery carrier, the bulk problem was originally of little significance, but for a tank destroyer it was of considerable importance, making the stalking of tank targets very difficult. Thus the Nashorn was often used as a 'stand-off' weapon that was able to use the considerable power and long-range accuracy of its gun to pick off targets at ranges of 2000 m (2,185 yards) and more; most of the other Panzerjäger types fought at much closer combat ranges.

The Nashorn carried a crew of five, with only the driver under complete armour protection. The rest of the crew was carried in the open fighting compartment with only a canvas cover to protect it from the elements. Most of the 40 rounds carried were located in lockers along the sides of the open compartment. The

gunner was equipped not only with the usual direct-vision sighting devices but also with artillery dial sights for the occasions when the Pak 43 could be used as a long-range artillery weapon. During the later stages of production the Pak 43 gun was replaced by the similar 8.8-cm Pak 43/41, a weapon introduced to speed production of the Pak 43; although it was manufactured differently from the original it was identical as far as ballistics were concerned. The Nashorn also carried a machine-gun for local defence and the crew was supposed to be issued with at least two sub-machine

guns for self-defence.

Powerful weapon

Most Nashorn production was centred at the Deutsche Eisenwerke at Teplitz-Schönau and Duisburg, and 473 had been made by the end of production in 1944. In combat the powerful gun made the Nashorn a potent vehicle/weapon combination, but it was really too high and bulky for the Panzerjäger role and only a shortage of anything better at the time maintained the type in production. The type was eventually succeeded in service by the Jagdpanther model.

On this captured example of a rather battered Nashorn, the soldier provides an indication of the weight and size of the powerful 8.8 cm (3.46 in) Pak 43/1 anti-tank gun. The rear decking and side armour appear to have been removed.

SPECIFICATION	
Nashorn	cooled petrol engine
Crew: 5	**Performance:** maximum road speed 40 km/h (25 mph); maximum road range 210 km (131 miles)
Weight: 24400 kg (53,793 lb)	
Dimensions: length (overall) 8.44 m (27 ft 8 in) and (hull) 5.8 m (19 ft); width 2.86 m (9 ft 4½ in); height 2.65 m (8 ft 8 in)	**Fording:** 0.8 m (2 ft 7½ in)
	Gradient: 57 per cent
	Vertical obstacle: 0.6 m (1 ft 11½ in)
Powerplant: one 197.5-kW (265-hp) Maybach HL 120 liquid-	**Trench:** 2.3 m (7 ft 6½ in)

German tank destroyers
In action

Germany made great use of tracked tank destroyers throughout World War II. The earliest such vehicles were Panzerjäger (literally 'tank hunter') types, which were little more than older chassis adapted to carry a standard anti-tank gun mounting. These types paved the way for the Jagdpanzer (hunter tank) based on the hull of a more advanced tank built up with a well-protected barbette in whose front was fitted a larger-calibre anti-tank gun. These varied from the 7.5-cm (2.95-in) Pak 39, via the 8.8-cm (3.46-in) Pak 43, to the 12.8-cm (5.04-in) Pak 44 carried only by Tiger heavy tank adaptations.

Below: Based on the hull and propulsion arrangements of the Panther battle tank, what began life as the 8.8-cm Pak 43/3 auf Panzerjäger Panther was renamed as the Jagdpanther at Hitler's suggestion in February 1944. The basic lines of the hull were continued upward and inward to create a large superstructure containing the fighting compartment with its exceptional 8.8-cm (3.46-in) anti-tank gun.

Left: Allied soldiers examine a knocked-out Jagdpanther. This is an early version lacking the later bolt-on mantlet around the gun barrel. Note the size of the spent propellant case in front of the vehicle and the distinctive appearance given to this excellent tank destroyer by its well-sloped superstructure.

A Sturmgeschütz IIIF with a short 75-mm (2.95-in) gun and armoured skirts resists the Allied landings at Salerno. The StuG was based on the chassis of the Panzer III. The driver's station was unaltered from that of the tank, but behind him was now a very cramped compartment, which made fighting with hatches down an extremely arduous experience.

SdKfz 173 Jagdpanther

Despite the limitations imposed by its turretless design, the Jagdpanther proved to be the most outstanding tank destroyer of World War II. Well armoured and therefore heavy, its Maybach engine still provided enough power to give the Jagdpanther vital mobility, and the projectiles fired by the vehicle's formidable 8.8-cm (3.46-in) Pak 43/3 L/71 gun could defeat any Allied tank. Taking every advantage of terrain, the Jagdpanther had to defend Germany's positions against vastly superior numbers of Allied tanks advancing from the east, west and south.

The rear of the Jagdpanther's hull and superstructure was fabricated of steel armour 40 mm (1.575 in) thick and angled at 60 degrees, and the other major element of the vehicle as viewed from the rear was the pair of exhausts for the Maybach HL 230 P30 petrol engine, upswept to keep their ends above the water as the Jagdpanther waded across small rivers and streams.

The front view of the Jagdpanther was dominated by the mantlet of 120-mm (4.72-in) armour for the Pak 43/3 gun. This was located centrally in the vehicle's front plate, itself 80 mm (3.15 in) thick and angled at 35 degrees, with the 7.92-mm (0.312-in) MG 34 or MG 42 ball-mounted defensive machine gun to its right.

The rear decking of the Jagdpanther was dominated by the central engine hatch and the large circular fan units required to cool the water for the large 23.88-litre Maybach engine. Rated at a nominal 522 kW (700 hp) at 3000 rpm, but actually delivering 485 kW (650 hp) at a governed 2,500 rpm, this engine powered the vehicle via a ZF AK 7-400 gearbox with seven forward and one reverse gears. The fuel capacity amounted to 720 litres (158.4 Imp gal).

Although the Jagdpanther was best protected against frontal fire, the likelihood of attack from the side was not ignored and good protection was therefore provided on the sides of the vehicle. The upper sides were 50 mm (1.98 in) thick and angled at 60 degrees, while the lower sides were 40 mm (1.575 in) thick and angled at 90 degrees. Also evident are some of the tools that were carried on the outside of the vehicle. The Schuerzen plates (skirt armour) attached to the sides of the hull protected the upper part of the tracks from the worst effects of shaped-charge warheads.

The running gear of the Jagdpanther comprised eight interleaved road wheels with torsion-bar suspension (swing arms acting forward and rearward on the left- and right-hand sides), a front-mounted idler, and a rear-mounted drive sprocket; there were no track-return rollers.

Jagdpanther Tank destroyer

When the **Jagdpanther** was first produced in February 1944, it marked a definite shift away from a period when Panzerjäger were hasty conversions or improvisations to the point where the tank destroyer became a purpose-built combat vehicle. The Jagdpanther was first mooted in early 1943 at a time when tank destroyers were required in ever-increasing quantities. By taking the best readily available tank chassis as the basis for the new vehicle, it was hoped that production totals would finally meet demand. The Panther chassis was thus used virtually unaltered as the basis for the new vehicle and an 8.8-cm (3.46-in) Pak 43 anti-tank gun was mounted on a well-sloped armoured superstructure, with a 7.92-mm (0.31-in) MG34 or MG42 machine-gun for local defence.

The prototype, then known as the **Panzerjäger Panther**, was demonstrated to Hitler in October 1943. He decreed that the name should be changed to Jagdpanther and then took a personal interest in further developments, providing the programme with his own personal priority rating.

Fearsome reputation

The Jagdpanther was one of those vehicles where superlatives could be justifiably lavished, for it was a superb combat vehicle and destined to be one of the most famous of all World War II armoured fighting vehicles. It was fast, well protected and it mounted a potent gun. Not content with all that, it had about it a definite aura that distinguished it from its contemporaries. So

This Jagdpanther, straight off the production line, has its tool and other stowage intact. The superstructure is coated with Zimmerit, a substance intended to prevent magnetic charges being applied; the overlapping road wheels added extra side protection against incoming projectiles.

well balanced was the design that it would not be too out of place in any tank park today, 60 years after it first appeared.

The Jagdpanther could knock out virtually any enemy tank it was likely to encounter, including the heavy Soviet IS-2s (although for them a side shot was required for a certain kill). For an indication of its power, the 7.3-kg (16.1-lb) armour-piercing projectile could penetrate 226 mm (8.9 in) of sloped steel armour at a range of 457 m (500 yards) and it could knock out or severely damage most Allied tanks at 1,000 m (1,093 yards). At times, single Jagdpanthers or small groups of them could hold up Allied armoured advances for considerable periods. Fortunately for the Allies, production of the Jagdpanther never reached

anywhere near the planned rate of 150 per month. By the time the production facilities were overrun during April 1945, only 382 had been completed and not all those had been delivered – a fact for which Allied tank crews must have been very grateful. The main cause of these low and slow production totals was the disruption and damage caused by Allied bomber raids on the two main centres of production, the MIAG plant at Braunschweig and the Brandenburg Eisenwerk Kirchmöser at Brandenburg, and the German transport infrastructure. These disruptions led to several variations of Jagdpanther. Some early models had large bolted-on gun mantlets while others had much smaller mantlet collars. Late-production versions used guns built with the barrels in two parts to

ease barrel changing when the bores became worn, and the stowage of tools and other equipment on the outside also varied considerably.

Weaponry

The Jagdpanther had a crew of five and there was space inside the well-sloped and heavily-armoured superstructure for 60 rounds of ammunition. When the war ended, plans had been made to produce a new version mounting a 12.8-cm (5.04-in) anti-tank gun, though in the event only a wooden mock-up had been built. But even with the usual 8.8-cm gun the

Jagdpanther was truly a formidable tank destroyer that was much feared and respected by Allied tank crews. Few other armoured fighting vehicles of World War II achieved its unique combination of power, lethality, mobility and protection. If the war had continued as the Germans planned (and the factories had been producing at the planned rate) the prospect of Panzer divisions equipped with a combination of Tiger II and Panther tanks – along with ever-growing numbers of Jagdpanthers – was enough to make any Allied tank commander shiver.

SPECIFICATION	
Jagdpanther	Pak 43 main gun, one 7.92-mm
Crew: 5	(0.31-in) MG34 or MG42 machine-gun
Weight: 46000 kg (101,411 lb)	
Powerplant: one Maybach HL 230 petrol engine developing 447.4-522 kW (600-700 hp)	**Performance:** maximum road speed 55 km/h (34.2 mph); road range 160 km (99 miles)
Dimensions: length overall 9.9 m (32 ft 6 in) and hull 6.87 m (22 ft 6½ in); width 3.27 m (10 ft 9 in); height 2.7 m (8 ft 11 in)	**Gradient:** 70 per cent **Vertical obstacle:** 0.9 m (35 in) **Trench:** 1.9 m (6 ft 3 in) **Fording:** 1.7 m (5 ft 7 in)
Armament: one 8.8-cm (3.46-in)	

Panzerjäger Tiger (P) Elefant Tank destroyer

When the tank that was to become the Tiger was still in its planning stage, two concerns, Henschel and Porsche, competed for the production contract. The Porsche entry was at one time the more favoured as the design employed a petrol-electric drive with electric motors propelling the vehicle. However, this approach proved to be technically over-complicated so the Henschel entry became the PzKpfw VI Tiger.

Early development

By the time the Henschel design was in production, Porsche drives and the hulls to put in them were also ready for production. It was decided to produce the Porsche design as a heavy tank-destroyer mounting the 8.8-cm (3.46-in) Pak 43/2 anti-tank gun. The gun was

installed in a large armoured superstructure with limited traverse, and 90 examples were produced to become the **Panzerjäger Tiger (P)**, later known as either **Ferdinand** or **Elefant**. The (P)

denoted Porsche. The Elefants were produced at the Nibelungwerke in a great rush during early 1943, the urgency being occasioned by the fact that Hitler demanded them to be ready for the

The Panzerjäger Tiger (P) Elefant used a complex twin-engine power pack driving an electric transmission that did not work very effectively in service. The vehicle was heavy, slow and ponderous, making it more of a heavy assault gun than a Panzerjäger. Most were used in Russia but a few ended up in Italy in 1944.

opening of the main campaign of 1943 against the Kursk salient on the Eastern Front. Production delays and training the Panzertruppen to use their new charges delayed the start of the offensive until 5 July 1943.

Inauspicious start

By the time the tanks were ready for battle, the Red Army was prepared for them. The defences of the Kursk salient were formidable and the delays had enabled the Red Army to add to their effectiveness. When the Germans finally attacked, their efforts were of little avail. For the Elefants the Kursk battles were a dreadful baptism of fire. The Elefants were organised in two battalions (*Abteilungen*) of Panzerregiment 654, and even before going into action their troubles began. The Elefants had been rushed into service before

their many technical bugs had been eliminated, and many broke down as soon as they started to move forward. Those that did make it to the Soviet lines were soon in trouble, for although the vehicles were fitted with the most powerful anti-tank guns then available, they lacked any form of secondary armament for self-defence. Soviet infantry tank-killer squads swarmed all over them and placed charges that either blew off

The Elefant was one of the failures of the German Panzerjäger designers, for despite its main 8.8-cm (3.46-in) gun it was too cumbersome. More importantly, the first examples lacked any kind of self-defence armament. It was also too complicated and was generally unreliable.

their tracks or otherwise disabled them. The Elefant crews had no way of defending themselves. Those that could either withdrew or abandoned their vehicles.

Some Elefants did survive Kursk and were later fitted with machine-guns to defend themselves, but the Elefant never recovered from its inauspicious debut. The few left were withdrawn to other fronts such as Italy but even there their unreliability and lack of spares soon rendered them useless.

SPECIFICATION	
Elefant	height 2.9 m (9 ft 10 in)
Crew: 6	**Armament:** one 8.8-cm (3.46-in)
Weight: 65000 kg (143,300 lb)	Pak 43/2 main gun
Powerplant: two Maybach HL 120	**Performance:** maximum road
TRM V-12 petrol engines, each	speed 20.1 km/h (12.5 mph); road
developing 395.2 kW (530 hp) and	range 153 km (95 miles)
driving a Porsche/Siemens-	**Gradient:** 40 per cent
Schuckert petrol-electric drive	**Vertical obstacle:** 0.8 m (31.5 in)
Dimensions: length overall 8.1 m	**Trench:** 2.65 m (8 ft 8 in)
(26 ft 8 in); width 3.4 m (11 ft 1 in);	**Fording:** 1 m (3 ft 3 in)

Jagdtiger Tank destroyer

By 1943 it was an established German policy that when any new tank design became available, a fixed-superstructure version mounting a limited-traverse gun would be produced. Thus when the massive Tiger II appeared, a corresponding Panzerjäger was developed. A mock-up of this super-heavy tank destroyer appeared in October 1943, with production commencing during 1944 under the designation **Panzerjäger Tiger Ausf B**, or **Jagdtiger**.

Heavy armour

With the Jagdtiger the Germans produced the most powerful armoured vehicle of World War II. It had an official weight of 70,000 kg (154,324 lb) but

by the time combat equipment, ammunition and the crew of six had been added the weight rose to around 76,000 kg (167,551 lb). The main armament was originally a 12.8-cm (5.04-in) Pak 44 anti-tank gun, later changed to the similar Pak 80. At one time a shortage of these guns meant that the smaller 8.8-cm (3.46-in) Pak 43/3 had to be used. The 12.8-cm guns were the most powerful anti-tank weapons used by any side during World War II, although the bulk of the ammunition meant each Jagdtiger could carry only 38 or 40 rounds. The defensive armament was two 7.92-mm (0.31-in) machine-guns. Armour thickness was 250 mm (9.84 in) on the superstructure front.

The massive Jagdtiger with its 12.8-cm (5.04-in) gun was a powerful weapon, but it was underpowered and too heavy to be anything other than a purely defensive weapon. Not many were made before the war ended, but the 250-mm (9.84-in) frontal armour made it a difficult vehicle to knock out.

The Jagdtiger was a massive, powerful vehicle as far as weaponry and protection were concerned, but in mobility terms it had to be regarded as extremely ponderous. It was driven by the same engine used in the Jagdpanther, but this engine had to drive the much

Two types of suspension were used on the Jagdtiger. This example has the Henschel suspension; the other type used larger road wheels from Porsche. Based on the Tiger II tank chassis, only about 70 were produced, and it was the heaviest armoured fighting vehicle (AFV) to see service during World War II.

greater weight of the Jagdtiger. This considerably increased the fuel consumption and reduced range across country. The Jagdtiger had a speed of only 14.5 km/h (9 mph), often less, and the maximum possible cross-country range was 120 km (74.5 miles).

The Jagdtiger production centre was the Nibelungwerk at St Valentin where total production ran

to only 70 vehicles. By the time the war ended two types of Jagdtiger could be encountered, one with Henschel suspension. Later versions had an extra road axle and Porsche suspension. In both forms the Jagdtigers were ponderous to an extreme and they remained underpowered, reducing them to little more than mobile weapon platforms.

SPECIFICATION	
Jagdtiger	**Armament:** one 12.8-cm (5.04-in)
Crew: 6	Pak 44 or Pak 80 main gun, two
Weight: 76000 kg (167,551 lb)	7.92-mm (0.31-in) machine-guns
Powerplant: one Maybach HL 230	**Performance:** maximum speed
petrol engine developing 447.4-	34.6 km/h (21.5 mph); road range
522 kW (600-700 hp)	170 km (105 miles)
Dimensions: length overall	**Gradient:** 70 per cent
10.65 m (34 ft 11½ in); width	**Vertical obstacle:** 0.85 m (33½ in)
3.63 m (11 ft 11 in) ; height 2.95 m	**Trench:** 3 m (9 ft 10 in)
(9 ft 8 in)	**Fording:** 1.65 m (5 ft 5 in)

Semovente L.40 da 47/32 Light tank destroyer

During World War II Italy was not noted for dramatic innovations in armoured vehicle design. In one field, however, Italy was abreast of tactical thinking as it became interested in the tank destroyer concept during the late 1930s. At that time Italy produced an intriguing design known as the **Semovente L.3 da 47/32** mounting a 47-mm (1.85-in) anti-tank gun with a barrel 32 calibres long (hence 47/32). The L.3 had the gun on an open mounting at the front of a small and low chassis based on that of the L.3 tankette; a two-man crew was carried. This early project did not get far for there was virtually no protection for the crew.

When Italy entered the war in 1940 it soon realised that their much-vaunted tank arm was seriously undergunned and lacked protection. This was particularly true of lighter tanks, in which the Italian treasury had

The Italian Semovente L.3 da 47/32 was an early attempt to mount an anti-tank gun on a light tank chassis, and was much used for trials and various gunnery tests. It lacked adequate protection and was later replaced by better designs.

invested to a considerable degree, especially the L.6 series that generally lacked protection and were armed only with a short 37-mm (1.46-in) gun of limited anti-armour capability. The main

The Semovente L.40 da 47/32 was used in some numbers by the Italian and later the German armies, and was a conversion of the L.6/40 light tank to take the powerful Italian 47-mm (1.85-in) anti-tank gun. Its box-like superstructure was later widely used to act as a mobile command post or ammunition carrier.

combat version, the L.6/40, soon proved to be of little combat value against the British armour in North Africa and was obviously ripe for the usual limited-traverse anti-tank gun treatment. It was not long in coming when Fiat-SPA and Ansaldo combined to use the chassis for the basis of a tank destroyer.

Small tank destroyer

The gun used for the new vehicle was a licensed version of a powerful Austrian weapon, the Böhler 47-mm dual-role anti-tank/infantry support gun, one of the hardest-hitting of all anti-armour weapons in its day. On the new **Semovente L.40 da 47/32** the gun was mounted in a simple box-like superstructure built directly onto the light tank chassis, and while this arrangement worked well enough, the slab sides of the superstructure lacked the added protection that sloping sides would have provided. However it was better than nothing and went

straight into service in 1942. About 280 were produced, and in action the type proved to be capable of dealing with the lighter British and other armour on the battlefields of North Africa. Ammunition stowage was 70 rounds.

When the Italians surrendered to the Allies in 1943 the Germans seized as much Italian equipment as they could. The Semovente L.40 da 47/32 was among this booty, and was quickly impressed as part of the equipment of German units fighting in Italy. However, the terrain of many of the Italian battlefields in 1944-45 was

such that armour could seldom be used, and the Semovente L.40s often had their anti-tank armament removed for service as mobile command posts for senior commanders, with an armament of one 8-mm (0.315-in) machine-gun.

The Semovente L.40 da 47/32 was a simple conversion that had little impact on enemy armour, but demonstrated that the Italians had absorbed the tank destroyer concept at an early stage of the war and used it as well as their limited production basis allowed.

SPECIFICATION	
Semovente L.40 da 47/32	1.63 m (5 ft 4 in)
Crew: 2	**Performance:** maximum road
Weight: 6500 kg (14,330 lb)	speed 42.3 km/h (26.3 mph); road
Powerplant: one SPA 18D	range 200 km (124 miles)
4-cylinder petrol engine developing	**Gradient:** 84 per cent
50.7 kW (68 hp)	**Vertical obstacle:** 0.8 m (31½ in)
Dimensions: length 4 m (13 ft	**Trench:** 1.7 m (5 ft 7 in)
1½ in) and hull 3.78 m (12 ft 5 in);	**Fording:** 0.8 m (31½ in)
width 1.92 m (6 ft 3½ in); height	

Semovente M.41M da 90/53 Heavy tank destroyer

Italy used the M.13 tank chassis for several self-propelled guns, but most of them were built along the lines of the German Sturmgeschütz types and were intended for use as close-support assault artillery. At times they could be used against tanks with some degree of success, but that was not their primary function and the Italians produced only one really heavy type of tank destroyer. This was the **Semovente M.41M da 90/53**, which used the chassis of the M.14/41 or later the M/15/42 tank.

The Semovente M.41M da 90/53 carried a powerful anti-armour weapon in the form of the cannone da 90/53 anti-aircraft gun, a long and very powerful weapon with performance very similar to that of the famous

The Semovente M.41M da 90/53 was the most powerful Italian tank destroyer, and combined the 90-mm (3.54-in) anti-aircraft gun with the chassis of the M.14/41 or M.15/42 tank.

A Semovente M.41M da 90/53 is examined by American troops after being knocked out in Sicily during 1943. To serve the gun, the crew had to stand behind the breech and only the driver had all-round armour. These guns were first used in North Africa in late 1943 and were much respected.

German 8.8-cm (3.46-in) Flak series. The gun's primary characteristics were denoted by the 90/53 designation, for it was a 90-mm (3.54-in) gun with a barrel 53 calibres long. To accommodate the gun mounting at the rear, the engine was moved to the front of the chassis.

In action two men sat on the gun mounting behind the only protection, a gun shield. No ammunition was carried on the vehicle, but 26 were carried in a special conversion of the L.6 light tank that had a box-like superstructure very similar to that of the Semovente L.40 da 47/32, and another 40 rounds were carried in a trailer towed by the ammunition carrier. In action the long rounds were loaded into the gun breech by ammunition numbers standing on the ground behind the Semovente M.41.

German impetus

After noting the power of the German 8.8-cm Flak series the Italians were quick to get their Semovente M.41M into production. The first examples came off the Fiat, SPA and Ansaldo lines during 1941, but in the end only 48 were produced. The main reason for this small total was the lack of production potential within Italian industry and the ever-pressing requirements for the cannone da 90/53 in its original role as an anti-aircraft gun.

In the field the M.41M proved to be a powerful weapon, especially across the flat wastes of the North African deserts, but once that campaign ended, so did the gun's career with the Italian army. Soon after the fall of Sicily and the invasion of the Italian mainland the Italians surrendered. The Germans had been expecting such a move and promptly took control of as much Italian *matériel* as they could, and among the loot were several Semovente M.41Ms. The Germans soon had control of the gun's ammunition production facilities and thus the weapon ended in the German army's inventory, and was still in full service in northern Italy when the war ended. By then there was little call for their tank-killing capabilities, for much of the Italian campaign took place over mountainous country where few tanks could move, so the Semovente M.41M equipments were used mainly as long-range artillery.

SPECIFICATION	
Semovente M.41M da 90/53	height 2.15 m (7 ft)
Crew: (on gun) 2	**Performance:** maximum road
Weight: 17000 kg (37,479 lb)	speed 35.5 km/h (22 mph); road
Powerplant: one SPA 15-TM-41	range 200 km (124 miles)
8 cylinder petrol engine developing	**Vertical obstacle:** 0.9 m (35.4 in)
108.1 kW (145 hp)	**Trench:** 2.1 m (6 ft 11 in)
Dimensions: length 5.21 m (17 ft	**Fording:** 1 m (3 ft 3 in)
1 in); width 2.2 m (7 ft 2½ in);	

Archer Tank destroyer

Although the British Army tended to lag behind the Germans in upgunning its tanks as World War II progressed, an early decision by British planners to make a quantum leap in anti-tank gun calibre, from 57 mm (2.244 in) in the 6-pdr to 76.2 mm (3 in), was bold as it was made at a time when the 6-pdr was only just getting into production.

Long and heavy

It was realised that the new 3-in gun, soon to be known as the 17-pdr, would be a very large and heavy weapon on its towed carriage, so it was decided to find some means of making it mobile. Ideally the 17-pdr was to be used as a tank gun, but the tanks large enough to carry such a large weapon were still a long way off (indeed had not even left the drawing boards) so a short-term alternative had to be found.

After in-production chassis such as the Crusader tank had been considered, it was decided to mount the 17-pdr on the Valentine infantry tank chassis. The Valentine was in production and could be rapidly adapted for its new gun-carrying role by adding a sloping super-structure, open at the top, on the forward part of the hull. To ensure the gun/chassis combination would not be nose-heavy and unwieldy, it was decided to place the gun in a limited-traverse-mounting facing over the rear of the chassis. This vehicle was obviously meant to be a tank destroyer and it was placed in production in late 1943.

Supreme ambusher

It was March 1943 before the first **Self-Propelled 17-pdr Valentine** rolled off the production lines. The troops looked at the new vehicle with some trepidation, for the idea of having a gun that faced only to the rear was against established practice. Drivers were also less than enchanted, for they were positioned at the centre front of the fighting compartment and the gun breech was directly behind their heads: on firing, the breech block came to within a short distance of the back of the driver's head. The rest of the crew was made up of the gun layer, the commander and the loader. Protective fire could be supplied by one 0.303-in (7.7-mm) Bren gun.

It was October 1944 before the first of these Valentine/17-pdr combinations reached the fighting in Europe. By then the type had become known as the **Archer**, and in action the Archer's tank-killing capabilities were soon revealed. The rear-facing gun was soon seen to be a virtue. The Archer was soon in use as an ambush weapon where its low silhouette made it easy to conceal in a hide. As enemy tanks approached a few shots could be fired to kill a tank, and then the

The British Archer was a conversion of the Valentine infantry tank to mount a 17-pdr (3-in/76.2-mm) anti-tank gun that fired over the rear of the hull. The first of the weapons were used in action late in 1944, and proved to be very useful weapons with a low silhouette. They were used by the Royal Artillery.

Archer was facing the right way to make a quick get-away before enemy retaliation arrived. The Archers were used by the anti-tank companies of the Royal Artillery, and they were definitely preferred to the weight and bulk of the towed 17-pdr guns used by the same companies.

The end of the war brought a halt in Archer production at a point where 655 of the original order for 800 had been produced. The Archers went on to equip British army anti-tank units until the mid-1950s.

Although the rear-facing main gun of the Archer could have been a tactical liability, crews used the layout to advantage by placing their Archers in ambush positions and then driving away after the action with the gun barrel still pointing to the rear.

SPECIFICATION	
Archer	2.25 m (7 ft 4½ in)
Crew: 4	**Performance:** maximum road
Weight: 16257 kg (35,840 lb)	speed 32.2 km/h (20 mph); road
Powerplant: one General Motors	range 225 km (140 miles)
6-71 6-cylinder diesel developing	**Gradient:** 32°
143.2 kW (192 hp)	**Vertical obstacle:** 0.84 m (33 in)
Dimensions: length overall 6.68 m	**Trench:** 2.36 m (7 ft 9 in)
(21 ft 11 in) and hull 5.54 m (18 ft	**Fording:** 0.91 m (3 ft)
6 in); width 2.76 m (9 ft); height	

M10 3-in gun motor carriage

During the late 1930s and early 1940s the US Army formulated a novel tactical doctrine in which fast-moving armoured formations were to be countered by a new tank destroyer force comprising towed and self-propelled high-velocity anti-tank guns. This tank destroyer force was to be used en masse and armed with powerful guns. One of the first operational results of this doctrine was the **Gun Motor Carriage M10** self-propelled mounting armed with a 76.2-mm (3-in) M7 gun, a development of an anti-aircraft weapon. The secondary armament was one 12.7-mm (0.5-in) Browning machine-gun.

Sherman chassis

The M10 used the chassis of the M4A2 medium tank allied to a thinly armoured upper hull and an open-topped turret. The relatively thin armour of the hull was improved by the use of sloping armour plates to increase protection, and sloped armour was also used on the turret. The M10 had a turret with 360-degree traverse, for although the M10 was intended for use as a tank destroyer it was seen by the US Army as a

gun carrier and a close-combat vehicle, hence the relatively thin armour.

Production commenced during September 1942, and such was the capability of American industry, 4,993 had been manufactured by the end of production in December 1942.

The bulk of this total went to US Army's 106 active tank

Above: The American M10 was designed to be the main weapon of the Tank Destroyer Command's mobile units, and mounted a 76.2-mm (3-in) gun in an open-topped turret. The armour protection was relatively thin, as the weight of better armour was sacrificed for all-round performance and speed in action.

destroyer battalions. As World War II continued, their number gradually decreased as it became clear that the best counter to a tank was another tank. But the tank destroyer force remained in being until the war ended, most of the battalions being used in Europe.

Assault gun service

By the end of the war many of the M10s were being used more as assault guns than as tank destroyers, by then distributed among the more conventional armoured formations. The M10 was the primary equipment of these battalions and was used not only by the US Army but, via Lend-Lease, by the British (who knew

Late in World War II the M10 (left) was supplemented by the M36 (right) which used a 90-mm (3.54-in) gun, though still in an open-topped turret. The M36 was designed as early as 1942 but took a long time to get into production, so that it was late 1944 before the first of the type reached units fighting in Europe. By then they were used mainly as assault guns.

the M10 as the **Wolverine**) and later by the French and Italians. The M10 was a large and bulky vehicle and, as time went on, the gun lost much of its anti-armour effectiveness against German tanks.

When the war ended the British had re-gunned many of their M10s with 17-pdr

guns and re-named the type **Achilles**. The M10 was joined by the **M10A1**, the same vehicle as before but using the chassis of the M4A3 medium tank with its different engine installation and some other changes. By 1945 turretless examples of both were used as artillery tractors.

SPECIFICATION	
M10	engines each developing 276.5 kW
Crew: 5	(375 hp)
Weight: 29937 kg (66,000 lb)	**Performance:** maximum road
Dimensions: length (overall) 6.83 m	speed 51 km/h (32 mph); maximum
(22 ft 5 in); width 3.05 m (10 ft);	road range 322 km (200 miles);
height 2.57 m (8 ft 5 in)	fording 0.91 m (3 ft 0 in); gradient 25
Powerplant: two General Motors	per cent; vertical obstacle 0.46 m
liquid-cooled 6-cylinder diesel	(1 ft 6 in); trench 2.26 m (7 ft 5 in)

M18 Hellcat 3-in gun motor carriage

Whereas the M10 was produced for the tank destroyer battalions by converting an existing tank chassis (the M4A2), the **Gun Motor Carriage M18** was designed from the outset for the tank destroyer role. Development as the **Gun Motor Carriage T70** began during 1942, and the first examples were ready during 1943.

In service the M18 proved to be one of the best and most successful examples of the American tank destroyer concept. It was much smaller and more compact than the M10, making it difficult to spot, and weighed only about half as much, but it carried a more powerful gun and was much faster. Indeed, the M18 was the fastest tracked vehicle used in action during World War II.

The gun was the 76.2-mm (3-in) M1A1 or M1A2, the latter having a muzzle brake. The M1A1 gun was a devel-

The M18 Hellcat had the distinction of being the fastest of all AFVs used during World War II. Armed with a long 76-mm (3-in) gun, it was an ideal tank-hunting vehicle, but as with other vehicles of its type it generally lacked armour and was fitted with an open-topped turret.

opment of the gun used in the M10, but had a better all round performance and it was mounted in an open-topped turret. The gun could penetrate 100 mm (3.94 in) of armour at 915 m (1,000 yards).

In appearance the M18 resembled a tank, and it did indeed have a 360-degree

traverse turret, but its armour protection was much less than would be expected in a tank, to a maximum of 12.7 mm (0.5 in). In addition, the top of the turret was left open (apart from canvas weather protection), exposing the turret occupants to the effects of overhead fire. The M18 therefore had to

rely on its agility, low silhouette and striking power to survive in combat.

Power to weight ratio

The engine was positioned at the rear of the hull and was an air-cooled radial petrol engine with aviation origins and the rating to give the M18 a good

power/weight ratio and thus excellent acceleration and agility. Internal stowage was such that as well as carrying the crew of five men there was space for 45 76.2-mm rounds and a 12.7-mm (0.5-in) heavy machine-gun for local and anti-aircraft defence. The rear of the turret was provided with a

The M18 Hellcat went out of production in October 1944 after 2,507 had been built. The M18 was the only vehicle specifically designed for the US Army's tank destroyer role, and was a most successful combat vehicle capable of tackling all but the very heaviest German tanks.

bustle acting as a stowage box for extra equipment and the crew's personal kit.

In service with tank destroyer battalions, the M18 was given the name Hellcat. Despite its success in action the M18 was gradually switched from the tank destroyer battalions as the enthusiasm for the exclusive tank destroyer concept dwindled, and by 1945 many M18s had been reassigned to conventional armoured formations within the US Army. By then they were being used more and more as assault guns or conventional self-propelled artillery.

Numerous variants

The production run of the M18 lasted from July 1943 to October 1944, when it was obvious that the war was not going to last much longer. Between those dates 2,507 M18s were produced, some being completed without turrets to the **M39** standard for use as high-speed troop or supply carriers. They were also used as heavy artillery tractors, a mobile command and communications post, and as a front-line utility carrier. There was also a **Flame Tank T65** based on the M18 with a much revised upper hull mounting a flame gun in front. The **Howitzer Motor Carriage T88** was an attempt to mount a 105-mm (4.13-in) howitzer on the basic M18, and there were also attempts to mount a 90-mm (3.54-in) gun and turret on the chassis. None of these versions got past the experimental stage – a fate shared by many other trial versions of the basic M18, including an amphibious variant. Numbers of M18s were distributed on Lend-Lease terms to various Allied nations before 1945, one recipient being the USSR.

SPECIFICATION	
M18	R-975 C1 radial petrol engine developing 253.5 kW (340 hp)
Crew: 5	**Performance:** maximum road
Weight: 17036 kg (37,557 lb)	speed 88.5 km/h (55 mph); road
Dimensions: length (overall) 6.65 m (21 ft 10 in) and (hull) 5.44 m (17 ft 10 in); width 2.87 m (9 ft 5 in); height 2.58 m (8 ft 5½ in)	range 169 km (105 miles); fording 1.22 m (4 ft 0 in); gradient 60 per cent; vertical obstacle 0.91 m (3 ft 0 in); trench 1.88 m (6 ft 2 in)
Powerplant: one Continental	

M36 90-mm gun motor carriage

The 90 mm (3.54-in) **Gun Motor Carriage M36**, originally the **T71** during its development period, can be regarded as an enhanced M10 tank destroyer, the main change coming with the larger-calibre gun, namely the 90-mm M3. This was a powerful high-velocity weapon that became a maid-of-all work for the US Army as it had close anti-aircraft, towed anti-tank and tank gun variants. Before type classification in June 1944, M10A1 chassis were used for development of the new type. Production was not entirely carried out from new as 2,324 examples were converted (in the USA and Canada) to the up-gunned state using existing M10A1 hulls as the basis, although an undefined number of pilot vehicles were also manufactured by the Chevrolet Division of General Motors. A further 187 examples of the **M36B1** variant were built based on the M4A3 tank hull. A further variant was the **M36B2** based on the M10; 237 examples of this model were produced.

Larger turret

Apart from the gun (with or without a muzzle brake), the engine was brought up to M10A1 standard by installing a Ford GAA V-8 petrol engine, and a larger turret with a revised outline was introduced, though this remained open-topped. Some modifications were introduced to cater for the stowage of the heavier 90-mm ammunition, the number of rounds carried being reduced to 47 from the M10A1's figure of 54. One detail was the addition of an auxiliary generator in the engine compartment to save fuel, conserve main engine life and provide power for routine services when the vehicle was in a stand-by state for extended periods. Despite all the changes, the M36 emerged as slightly lighter than the M10, although overall performance remained much the same.

Potent but flawed

The M36 inherited many of the M10's shortcomings in that the armoured protection remained as before and the overall height made the vehicle conspicuous and bulky. Even so, the gun and vehicle combination created a successful and potent tank destroyer. The gun possessed the power to knock

The 90-mm Gun Motor Carriage M36 was a highly successful and potent tank destroyer, able to knock out any tank it encountered. Based on the M10A1 hull, it had a larger turret to accommodate the 90-mm gun.

out any German tank – including the Tiger II – that was likely to be encountered. The gun's armour-penetrating projectiles were able to defeat 76 mm (3 in) of armour at a range of 4300 m (4,700 yards), assuming that a target could be detected at that extreme range. As tank targets dwindled during 1945 the M36 became a specialist bunker-buster and was gradually integrated into armoured divisions rather than operating within the context of specialised tank destroyer battalions.

After 1945 the M36 was handed out in substantial numbers to several nations friendly to the US cause. They served on for many years, the last of them emerging (to the surprise of many) during the early stages of the Balkan troubles of the late 1990s, when the type appeared in both Bosnian and Serbian hands. That appearance marked the M36 as the last of the US tank destroyers of World War II to remain in combat service.

SPECIFICATION	
M36	engine developing 335 kW (450 hp)
Crew: 5	**Performance:** maximum road speed 48 km/h (30 mph); maximum range 241 km (150 miles); fording 0.91 m (3 ft 0 in); gradient 60 per cent; vertical obstacle 0.61 m (2 ft 0 in); trench 2.29 m (7 ft 6 in)
Weight: 28554 kg (62,950 lb)	
Dimensions: length 6.15 m (20 ft 2 in); width 3.05 m (10 ft); height 2.72 m (8 ft 11in)	
Powerplant: one Ford GAA V-8	

Demolition charges

The demolition charges used by the British 'funnies' of World War II were mainly carried by Churchill AVREs, for the emplacing of these powerful charges was one of the tasks for which the AVRE was created. The charges themselves were special obstacle-demolishing packs of high explosive that had to be placed against the target, which could be anything from a sea or anti-tank wall to a blockhouse or an offending building.

Various charges

Sometimes the charges were large single chunks of explosive, and in others they were small charges set in a pattern and held in a steel frame. One thing all the various charges did have in common was odd and even bizarre names. One of the more straightforward of these charge devices was the **Bangalore Torpedo**.

These pipe charges were intended for clearing mines and barbed wire entanglements, but could be used for other purposes.

Jones Onion

On the AVRE they were held in front-mounted frames, also used for the **Jones Onion**. The Jones Onion first appeared in 1942 and was the codename given to a frame on to which various charges could be attached. The frame was carried on two arms, one on each side of the AVRE, and held upright as the target was approached. Once in position the frame was released by pulling on a cable, and two legs on the bottom of the frame were so arranged that the frame always fell against the target obstacle. The charges could then be fired electrically by a trailing cable after the AVRE had reversed away.

Another device that appeared in 1942 was the **Carrot**. This was a much simpler device than the large Onion and consisted of a charge held in front of the AVRE on a simple steel arm. The idea was that the AVRE simply moved up to the target and the charge was then ignited. The charges involved ranged in weight from 12 lb (5.44 kg) up to 25 lb (11.34 kg), the smaller charge rejoicing in the name of **Light Carrot**. The Carrot was used extensively for trials but was abandoned during late 1943 and not used in action. The **Goat** was used in action, and may be considered as a development of the Onion although it was much larger and involved the use of a frame 3.2 m (10 ft 6 in) wide and 1.98 m (6 ft 6 in) long. On to this frame could be arranged up to 816 kg (1,800 lb) of explosives, and the whole

The Jones Onion, seen here carried by a Churchill tank, was a demolition device carried on a steel frame that could be placed against an obstacle such as an anti-tank wall. The frame was then released to allow the tank to retire to safety and detonate the charge.

device was carried on the AVRE by side arms.

Goat variants

The Goat was so arranged that it could be pushed against the structure to be demolished and the frame would automatically release in a vertical position. The AVRE would then reverse, leaving the charges in position to be fired either electrically or by means of a pull igniter. A close cousin of the Goat was the **Elevatable Goat**. This was intended for use against high obstacles such as anti-tank walls, and when fitted on the AVRE was carried on the nose of the hull rather like an assault bridge.

Linked charges

The 'bridge' was in fact a frame on which linked charges were slung. The frame was placed against the wall to be demolished and then released from the AVRE. Once in position, another release cable allowed the linked charges to fall away from the frame. The top section of the frame was above the top of the wall, and this allowed the charges to fall onto each side of the wall, which could then be destroyed once the

An alternative view of the Jones Onion charge-carrying frame being lifted into position on its Churchill AVRE carrier. No charges have yet been installed.

AVRE had moved away. Although some of these devices were used in action, they were somewhat clumsy contraptions that relied upon the carrier getting very close to the target and becoming exposed to retaliatory fire. Any wrong emplacement resulted in less than optimum results.

Spigot mortar

The obstacle demolition solution for the AVRE turned out to be the **'Flying Dustbin'**, a spigot mortar that fired a 290-mm (11.4-in) demolition charge with reasonable accuracy from a safer stand-off position.

In combat, the demolition charges laid by the AVREs amply fulfilled the expectations of the engineers who designed them. In 1944-45, the Western Allied armies broke through the strongest defences ever created, from the Normandy defences to the Siegfried line of fortifications that shielded the German border. These concrete and steel emplacements, surrounded by mines and barbed wire, were a tougher proposition than anything tackled by either the Germans themselves, when they were on the offensive, or the Russian armies closing in from the East. The use of specially converted armoured vehicles to lay demolition charges paved the way for today's AEVs (Armoured Engineer Vehicles) used by most major armies.

Churchill AVRE
Combat engineer vehicle

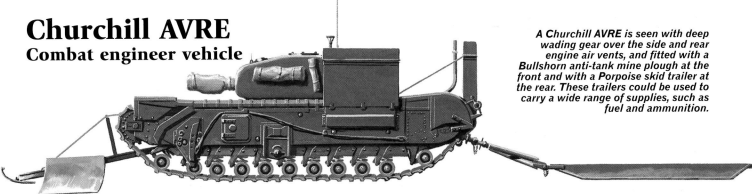

A Churchill AVRE is seen with deep wading gear over the side and rear engine air vents, and fitted with a Bullshorn anti-tank mine plough at the front and with a Porpoise skid trailer at the rear. These trailers could be used to carry a wide range of supplies, such as fuel and ammunition.

One of the lessons learned during the Dieppe raid of 1942 was that the Canadian engineers were unable to proceed with their obstacle demolitions and general beach-clearing because of a complete lack of cover against enemy fire. In the period after the raid, a Canadian engineer officer put forward the idea of using a tank converted to the combat engineer role so that it could carry engineers to the point at which they had to operate, and be capable of carrying a heavy demolition weapon. This would enable the combat engineers to operate from under armoured cover and would also enable them to operate in close co-operation with armoured formations.

'Flying Dustbin'
The idea was accepted, and after some deliberation the Churchill tank was selected as the basic vehicle for conversion. The task consisted mainly of completely stripping out the tank's interior and removing the main armament, the interior then being completely rearranged to provide stowage for the

Right: The Churchill AVRE Mk II featured a fixed turret mounting a dummy gun. It could carry a front-mounted dismountable jib crane or a rear jib with a greater lift capacity. There was also a powerful front-mounted winch that could be used in conjunction with the jibs, and an earth anchor was mounted at the rear to stabilise the vehicle in winching mode.

various items combat engineers have to use, such as demolition explosives, special tools and mines. The main turret was retained but in place of the normal gun a special device known as a Petard was fitted. This was a spigot mortar that fired a 290-mm (11.4-in) demolition charge known to the troops from its general shape as the 'Flying Dustbin'. The Petard projectile weighed 40 lb (18.14 kg) and could be fired to a range of 73 m (80 yards) to demolish structures such as pillboxes, bunkers and buildings. The Petard could be reloaded from within the vehicle.

Chuchill version
The Churchill version was known as the **Churchill AVRE (Armoured Vehicle Royal Engineers)** and quickly became standard equipment for armoured engineers attached to formations such as the 79th

Armoured Division and the assault brigades, RE. As well as providing protection, the AVRE was soon tasked to carry many types of special equipment.

Mk III and IV
The Churchill versions used for the AVRE were the **Mks III** and **IV**. Many of the conversions were effected with kits, some by industry and some by REME workshops. The conversions included brackets and other attachment points around the hull to which specialised equipment items could be fixed. A hook at the rear was used to tow a special AVRE sledge for carrying combat stores.

New gun
The AVREs were first used on a large scale during the Normandy landings of June 1944, where they excelled themselves to such an extent that AVRE vehicles are still in service. The Churchill AVRE remained in service until the mid-1950s, and even later with some units. They were used to lay fascines, place mats across

A Churchill AVRE special-purpose armoured vehicle climbs a ramp-type bridge toward the crest of an obstacle. Held at the front of the AVRE is a large fascine, which was a bundle of wooden stakes, about 3.66-4.26 m (12-14 ft) long and bound into a bundle some 2.44 m (8 ft) in diameter, used to fill gaps.

soft ground, demolish strongpoints with their Petard mortars, bring forward combat engineering stores, place heavy demolition charges and generally make themselves useful. Perhaps the most important long term function of the Churchill AVRE was to emphasise that specialised combat engineer tanks were an essential adjunct to armoured formation operations. One important post-war Churchill AVRE development was the replacement of the 'Flying Dustbin' spigot mortar by a specially developed 165-mm

(6.5-in) demolition gun firing a 60-lb (27.2-kg) projectile with a HESH payload that could shatter even the strongest concrete obstacle. This gun was not only more accurate than the 'Flying Dustbin' but it could be breech loaded from within the protection of an AVRE turret. During the early 1950s about 13 Churchill AVREs were provided with the new gun. They served until 1962, when the last of them was replaced by the updated Centurion AVRE, still using the 165-mm demolition gun.

Having dropped its fascine, a Churchill AVRE teeters on the forward edge of an obstacle before nosing down onto the fascine and, if all goes well, moving forward away from the obstacle that had to be crossed. This was a training exercise.

SPECIFICATION	
Churchill AVRE	height 2.79 m (9 ft 2 in)
Crew: 6	**Performance:** maximum road
Weight: 38 tons	speed 24.9 km/h (15.5 mph);
Powerplant: one Bedford Twin-Six	maximum road range 193 km
liquid-cooled petrol engine	(120 miles)
developing 261 kW (350 hp)	**Fording:** 1.02 m (3 ft 4 in)
Dimensions: length 7.67 m (25 ft	**Vertical obstacle:** 0.76 m (2 ft 6 in)
2 in); width 3.25 m (10 ft 8 in);	**Trench:** 3.05 m (10 ft)

Mine-clearing rollers

The mine-clearing roller was one of the very first anti-mine devices used with tanks, and in theory rollers are among the simplest to use. They consist of a set of heavy rollers pushed ahead of the tank, their weight and pressure alone being sufficient to destroy the mines by setting them off in front of the tank. Translating this theory into practice should also have been simple, but was not. The main problem was the weight and bulk of the rollers that had to be used: in order to make the rollers heavy enough they had also to be large, and this made them very difficult loads to handle using the average tank of the period. In fact some of them were so large and awkward to push that it sometimes took two tanks (the carrier tank plus another behind it to provide extra 'push') to move them forward. This two-tank arrangement was often necessary when rollers had to be pushed over soft or rough ground.

The Lulu roller device did not detonate mines by pressure, as the front rollers were only light wooden containers carrying electrical sensor devices to denote the presence of buried metal objects such as mines. Although it worked in practice, the Lulu was considered too fragile for operational use.

Early experimentation

The British were probably the first to develop anti-mine rollers, and experimented with them in the years before World War II fitted to vehicles such as the Covenanter. They knew their first models as the **Fowler Roller** or the **Anti-Mine Roller Attachment (AMRA)**. From these were developed the **Anti-Mine Reconnaissance Castor Roller (AMRCR)** system that was fitted to Churchills and British Shermans. These rollers used leaf springs to keep the rollers in contact with the ground, but they were so cumbersome that they were not used operationally. A more successful design appeared in 1943 as

the **Canadian Indestructible Roller Device (CIRD)**. This used two heavy armoured rollers mounted on side arms, and was so arranged that if a roller detonated a mine the resulting blast lifted the roller, and a lever came into contact with the ground. The subsequent movement of the tank then operated the lever so that the roller returned to the ground for further use. CIRD was fitted to both Churchills and Shermans, but the system was not used in action.

Rollers were an apparently obvious solution to a minefield, but it proved exceedingly difficult to detonate enough mines by the rollers' weight alone. Solutions included rollers so heavy that it took several vehicles to move them, and various plough and roller combinations.

The Americans also became involved with mine rollers and produced three main models. The first version was the **Mine Exploder T1** and was intended for use with M3 Lee tanks, but not many were made as these tanks had passed from front-line service by the time the rollers had been developed. From this evolved the **Mine Exploder T1E1** or **Earthworm**, but again this was devised for use by one vehicle only, in this case the M32 Tank Recovery Vehicle. For use with the M4 Sherman there came the **Mine Exploder T1E3** (later the **Mine Exploder M1**), generally known as the **'Aunt Jemima'**. This used two very large sets of roller

An M4 Sherman medium tank with one of the prototypes of the Mine Exploder T1E3 (later the Mine Exploder M1), generally known as the 'Aunt Jemima'. The size and bulk of this device are clearly shown.

discs mounted on side arms in front of the carrier, and the system was used in action despite its great bulk and awkwardness. It proved to be successful enough, and was developed into an even heavier **M1A1**.

US developments

The Americans developed a whole string of other types of mine roller, few of which got past the experimental stage. Perhaps the oddest of them was the **Mine Exploder T10** on which the rollers became the road wheels for an M4 tank body, complete with gun turret. Two rollers were mounted forward and another set of roller discs was at the rear with the tank body slung between them. This device got no further than trials, and neither did the series of vehicles known as the **Mine**

Resistant Vehicle T15. This was an M4 tank fitted with extra body and belly armour and intended to set off mines by simply driving over them, relying on its extra protection for survival. None of these vehicles was ready for use by the time the war ended, and work on the type then ceased.

Mine rollers are still employed, especially by former Warsaw Pact armed forces, but other mine-clearing methods such as ploughs or flails are now more favoured. Apart from their awkwardness, mine rollers can be easily overcome by special land mine fuses that do not react to the first pressure so may detonate under the carrier tank. In addition, no matter how solid they may appear rollers have only a finite life before replacement.

Mine-clearing flails

The notion of using chain flails to detonate mines in the path of a tank came from a South African engineer, Major A. S. J. du Toit. The idea was that a horizontally mounted drum carried on arms in front of a tank would be rotated under power and, as it turned, would beat the ground in front with chains weighted at their ends: this beating would provide enough pressure to set off any mines under the flails. Early trials proved the effectiveness of the idea, and the first sets of mine flails were fitted to Matilda tanks in North Africa during 1942.

First models

These first flails had the name **Scorpion**, and on the **Matilda Scorpion** the flail drum was powered by an auxiliary engine mounted on the right-hand side of the tank. These Scorpions were used during the El Alamein battle in October 1942 and also during some later North African actions. They proved to be so effective that a more specialised version, known as the **Matilda Baron**, was developed. On the Baron the turret was removed and the flail drum was powered by two auxiliary engines, one on each side. However, the Scorpion concept offered more long-term promise as it could be fitted to several types of tank to produce, for example, the **Grant Scorpion** and the **Valentine Scorpion**. However, before that could happen a great deal of further development work had to be carried out, for the early flails had demonstrated some unwelcome traits. Among these were uneven beating patterns that left unbeaten patches, and flail chains that either became tangled and useless or simply beat themselves to pieces. Another problem became apparent on uneven ground, where the flails were unable to beat into sudden dips.

The development work carried out in the UK resulted in a device known as the **Crab** which was usually fitted to Sherman tanks to produce the **Sherman Crab**. The Crab had 43 chains mounted on a drum powered by a take-off from the main engine and had such features as side-

Above: The Sherman Crab was the most widely used mine flail tank of World War II. Although the Crab was fitted to other tank types, the Sherman was the preferred carrier. The odd-looking device at the hull rear is a station keeping marker to guide other flail tanks.

mounted wire cutting discs to hack through barbed wire entanglements, screens to shield the front of the tank from flying dust and debris and, later in the Crab's development, a device to follow ground contours and enable the flail drum to rise and fall accordingly. Crabs were used by the 79th Armoured Division and later a number were handed over to the US Army for use in North West Europe The main advantages of the Crab system were that it was very effective in its own right, and also permitted the carrier to retain its turret and main gun, enabling it to be used as a gun tank if the occasion arose.

Needless to say there were many other experimental models of mine flails. One was the **Lobster**, a device that came chronologically before the Crab but was not accepted for service. The **Pram Scorpion** was an offshoot of the Scorpion with the drum drive coming from

gears on the front sprockets of the carrier tank. Again, it was passed over in favour of the Crab.

The US did not spend much development time on mine flails. Instead they concentrated on anti-mine rollers and when they did require flails, as they did when they encountered the large defensive mine belts along the German borders in the winter of 1944-45, they used numbers of British Crabs which they redesignated the **Mine Exploder T4**.

Right: The Matilda Scorpion prototype shown here was an early attempt to produce a mine flail tank. The main flail drum was driven by two 22.4-kW (30-hp) Bedford auxiliary engines, one mounted each side of the hull, and the device was later fitted to Valentine and Grant tanks as well as the Matilda.

Above: Soft sand was one of the specialist tanks' most feared terrain, and its hazards are clearly shown by this bogged-down Sherman Crab. Note the deep wading gear fitted to the engine intakes at the rear.

Top: This Sherman Crab has its flail drum and chains in the lowered position ready to start. The Crab was the standard British mine-clearing vehicle; not only were its flails efficient, but they were so arranged that the carrier tank could retain its 75-mm (2.95-in) gun.

ARK

The **ARK** bridging tanks were only one type of armoured bridging vehicles used by the Allies during World War II. The British army had for long had an interest in producing bridging tanks, producing its first such equipment during the latter stages of World War I. In the years just before World War II, the British army carried out a great deal more experimental work, and one of its main achievements was a scissors-type bridge carried and laid by a Covenanter tank. During the early war years this work had to be put aside for more pressing things until the 1942 Dieppe landing emphasised the need for armoured bridging vehicles, not only to cross wet or dry gaps, but to enable other vehicles to cross obstacles such as sea walls.

It was the 79th Armoured Division that produced the first ARK (Armoured Ramp Carrier) late in 1943. This **ARK Mk I** was a Churchill tank conversion with the turret removed and a blanking plate (with an access hatch in the centre) welded over the turret aperture. Over the tracks were placed two timbered trackways carried on a new superstructure, and in front, in line with the trackways, were two ramps, each 1.05 m (3 ft 5.25 in) long. At the rear were two more ramps, each 1.72 m (5 ft 8 in) long.

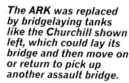

A Churchill ARK Mk I is shown with its approach ramp raised. These vehicles were supposed to be driven up against anti-tank walls as far as possible, to enable other vehicles to be driven up and over the roadway carried above their tracks.

In use the ARK Mk I was driven up to an obstacle such as a sea wall and pushed up the obstacle as far as possible. The front and rear ramps were then lowered from their travelling positions and other vehicles could then use the ARK to cross the obstacle. The ARK could also be driven into a wet or dry obstacle to act as a bridge.

Improved ARK

The ARK Mk I was soon supplemented by the **ARK Mk II**. Again this used a Churchill tank as the basis, and the same superstructure/ramp layout was used. But the ARK Mk II used much longer ramps (3.8 m/12 ft 6 in) at each end, and the right-hand set

of trackways and ramps was half the width of the other (0.61 m/2 ft) as opposed to 1.213 m (4 ft). This enabled a much wider range of vehicles to use the ARK. In use the ramps were set up front and rear and held in the travelling position by cables and chains connected to front and rear kingposts. When the ARK came to a gap it drove into it and then released the cables to allow the ramps to drop. Other vehicles could then cross the ARK bridge. The 8th Army in Italy produced its own ARK Mk IIs, but made them much simpler by omitting the trackways over the Churchill tank, the tank tracks and the top of the body being used as the

The ARK was replaced by bridgelaying tanks like the Churchill shown left, which could lay its bridge and then move on or return to pick up another assault bridge.

roadway instead. This version was known as the **ARK Mk II (Italian Pattern)**.

There were numerous variations on the basic ARK design. One was a raised ramp system carried on a Churchill and known as the

Churchill Great Eastern, but that project was discontinued. Some Shermans were converted in Italy to what was roughly the equivalent of the ARK Mk II, but the numbers involved were not large.

Rocket bridge

Another system, known as the **Churchill Woodlark**, was generally similar to the ARK Mk II but went into action with the ramps closed down: they were meant to be opened up into position by the use of rockets on the end of each ramp, and more rockets were used to soften the shock of the ramps hitting the ground. The type did not pass the trials stage.

No data can be provided regarding these Churchill conversions but a Churchill ARK Mk II had a crew of four men and weighed 38.5 tons. Most conversions were made using Churchill Mks III and IV.

The ARK 'drive over' concept was replaced by front-mounted assault bridges lowered across an obstacle. The original concept meant that once in place an ARK had to remain there to be used. An assault bridge allowed the carrier to deploy its bridge and then move off for use in other purposes.

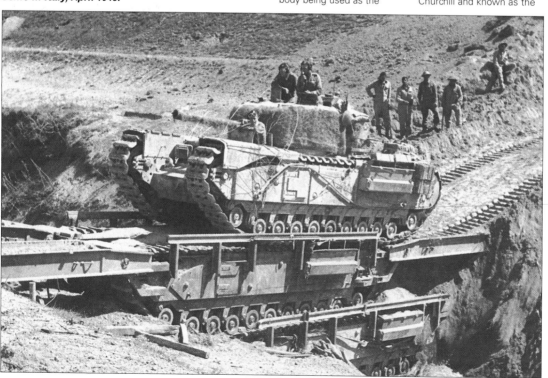

Two Churchill ARK Mk IIs are used to allow other vehicles to cross a deep ravine. The first ARK was driven into the ravine and the second ARK was then driven onto it, after which its ramps were lowered to form a bridge. The ravine was formed by the River Senio in Italy, April 1945.

Fascine and mat-laying devices

The **fascine** is an item of combat engineering equipment that dates back to ancient times, and for armoured warfare the type was resurrected during World War I to be dropped by tanks taking part in the Battle of Cambrai. At that time they were used traditionally, being dropped into trenches to allow other tanks to cross, and they were used for the same purpose during World War II. The advantage of the fascine for the combat engineer is that he can make them on the spot when they are required. The usual method was to cut brushwood and tie it into large bundles 3.35 m (11 ft) or more long. The bundles were tied into rolls between 1.83 m (6 ft) and 2.44 m (8 ft) in diameter and pulled on to wooden or steel cradles on the front of the tank. They were then held in place by cables that could be released from within the carrier tank. The main disadvantage was that the fascines usually restricted the driver's vision so that a crew member had to position himself to give driving instructions. Attempts were made to use periscopes to overcome this drawback but in the end the solution was found by redesigning the form of fascine cradle.

Assault roadway

A type of fascine could also be used to make an assault roadway over soft or rough ground. This was formed by rolling up lengths of chespaling joined together by wire, rather like a length of fencing. A Churchill AVRE would carry this roll into position, where one end of the roll could be placed under the front tracks. As the AVRE moved forward it unrolled the mat and rolled over it to allow other vehicles to use the rough roadway so formed. Rolls of up to 30.5 m (100 ft) could be laid using this method, and more durable roadways could be

produced by using a similar arrangement involving logs tied together (**Log Carpet**). These chespaling or log roadways were intended for heavy use, but for assault purposes hessian mats were also employed. These mats were carried in front of a Churchill AVRE on bobbins held by side arms or, on one model, above a **Churchill AVRE Carpetlayer** turret. There were two main types: the **Bobbin Carpet** unrolled a hessian mat reinforced by chespaling at intervals that was wide enough to cover the full width of a tank; the other was wide enough to cover only a track width. Both were intended to cover wire obstacles, so allowing troops or wheeled vehicles to cross. The first of them was used during the Dieppe raid of 1942. The bobbin could be dropped when empty or in an emergency.

Sherman variant

Most of these fascine- or mat-laying devices were carried on Churchill AVREs, but Shermans were also used. In fact a special fascine carrier, known as the **Crib**, was

This Churchill AVRE is equipped with deep wading engine intakes at the side and rear and is fitted with a Carpet-Layer Type C, which laid a hessian carpet to allow following vehicles to cross areas of sand or other soft terrain.

Right: This post-war Churchill AVRE has an early Centurion-style turret equipped with smoke dischargers. The cargo remains much as it would have looked in 1944 – or 1917 for that matter – and the restrictions the fascine placed on the driver's field of vision are obvious.

developed for the Sherman. This was a frame that could be tilted forward to drop a fascine or a log mat. Some 'war weary' Shermans even had their turrets removed to allow them to be used as full-time fascine carriers.

It should be stressed that the mat-laying devices were meant only for short-term use. Prolonged use by heavy or tracked vehicles soon broke them up or simply tore them to pieces, so they were used only for assault purposes or during amphibious landings. It was not until well after World War II that flexible metal roadways were developed to replace the earlier devices.

Above: A Churchill AVRE operates a Carpet-Layer Type C, used to lay a continuous hessian mat over rough or soft ground to enable other wheeled or tracked vehicles to follow. These devices were used to cross the sand on some of the Normandy beaches on 6 June 1944.

Left: A Churchill AVRE carries a brushwood fascine at the front and tows another fascine on an AVRE skid trailer. The fascines were released from their carrier frame by a quick-release device, and once in position could enable most tanks or tracked vehicles to cross with relative ease.

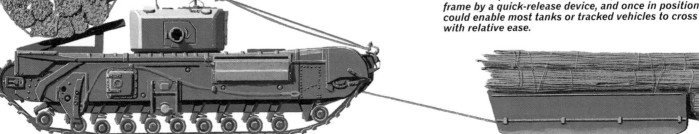

ARV Armoured recovery vehicles

To the front-line soldier every tank is a valuable asset, so any damaged or disabled tank that can be got back into action is a useful item. As a result, the recovery from the battlefield of damaged or broken-down tanks is a very important aspect of armoured warfare. Very often these recovery operations have to be undertaken under enemy fire, however, so it makes sense to provide the recovery crews with their own armoured vehicles and even more sense to provide these vehicles with mechanical handling devices, winches and other special recovery tools. Thus World War II saw the first large-scale use of recovery vehicles, and on the Allied side there were many different types of varying capabilities.

Enter the ARV

Virtually all types of **ARV** (armoured recovery vehicle) were conversions of existing tanks, usually models that were obsolescent and could therefore be spared for the role. Nearly every type of Allied tank was used for the ARV role at some time or another, but the main types involved on the British side were Crusader, Covenanter, Centaur, Cavalier, Cromwell, Ram and inevitably the Churchill. Most of the early ARV conversions to the so-called **ARV Mk I** standard involved the removal of the turret (along with the main armament) and its replace-

ment by an open compartment for the crew. Winches were installed and various forms of jib crane or sheerlegs were added. Many types also had the assistance of an earth spade to provide the winch with better purchase and thus extra pull. The British also made extensive use of turretless Shermans for the ARV role.

The **ARV Mk II** conversion, which was effected on Churchill III and IV, and also on the Sherman V, resulted in a similar overall capability but with a number of operational improvements. The most obvious improvement was the adoption of a fixed turret (complete with a dummy gun) in place of the ARV Mk I's open compartment. This fixed turret accommodated the 60-ton winch's operator, who therefore had both a higher field of vision and a good measure of protection. The ARV Mk II also had the 3.5-ton jib crane relocated to the back of the hull, which also featured an earth anchor, to free the forward position for

A Cromwell ARV is caught by the camera as it tows a captured German PzKpfw IV tank out of the way of other vehicles. The Cromwell ARV was a turretless conversion of an early mark of Cromwell tank that could be fitted with a jib crane and other gear.

a 6-ton jib crane.

American ARVs

The American ARVs were generally more complex vehicles. They too were based on existing tank chassis, but the conversions were often carried out in factories rather than the base workshops of the other Allied armies (including the British) and thus more detail design care could be lavished upon the final product. A typical American product was the **Tank Recovery Vehicle M32**. On this the turret was fixed and a

smoke-firing 81-mm (3.2-in) mortar was fitted. In the volume normally reserved for the fighting compartment was placed a powerful 27216-kg (60,000-lb) capacity winch, and an A-frame jib was mounted on the forward hull. Extra stowage points for special equipment were added all over the hull. Several sub-variants of the M32 were produced. The M3 medium tank series was also used to produce the **Tank Recovery Vehicle M31** with a jib crane over the rear of the hull. The British also made their own conversion

of the M3 Grant by removing all the armament and installing a powerful winch in the main compartment.

The American ARVs were produced in large numbers, so large in fact that some of the M32 vehicles could be made available for conversion to an allied but somewhat different role, namely that of the artillery tractor.

But there was one factor that both British and US ARVs had in common, and that was that none of them could match the power of the German Bergepanther

armoured recovery vehicle based on the Panther battle tank. The Bergepanther was unassailed in its position as the most powerful ARV of the World War II period as far as operational models were concerned. Even so, the Allied ARVs were adequate for the workaday task of recovering armoured fighting vehicles without undue difficulty, for they did not have to cope with seeking to recover the altogether larger and heavier Tiger heavy tanks and Panther battle tanks used by the German army.

Beach ARV

Included in the planning for the D-Day invasion of North-West Europe was the provision of vehicles able to recover 'drowned' or otherwise disabled armour and vehicles from positions both above and below the high water mark on the invasion beaches. For this work the REME Experimental Beach Recovery Section created for trials purposes in 1943 **BARV (Beach Armoured Recovery Vehicle)** prototypes based on the Churchill and Sherman tanks.

These early BARVs were ordinary Sherman and Churchill tanks with the gun turrets replaced by a fixed rectangular structure and the engine air inlets and exhaust revised with tall metal cowls. The hulls were also waterproofed so that the vehicles could wade in water up to a depth of some 2.1 m (7 ft). The BARV crews were trained to use shallow diving apparatus so that they could operate under the water level to attach tow ropes to vehicles awaiting recovery.

The Churchill BARV was abandoned at the prototype stage since the hull with its side entry doors needed more waterproofing atten-

tion than the Sherman, and the Churchill needed three cowls to the Sherman's one. Further development of the BARV was therefore based on the Sherman in the forms first of the Ford petrol-engined model and later of the diesel-engined Sherman III. A multi-sided superstructure was created to allow the tank to operate in water up to 3.05 m (10 ft) deep according to weather conditions. Other additions included towing equipment, and a pair of wooden railway sleepers was attached to the BARV's front to reduce the chances of damage when vehicles were being pushed or landing craft were being nudged off the beach. A trackway was added round the top of the hull for the crew, and hanging ropes (as on lifeboats) were attached to the sides.

As with other ARVs, 'production' conversions to Sherman BARV standard were performed under REME supervision at two Ministry of Supply workshops.

The vehicles were very successful in helping to keep the D-Day beaches clear and one BARV even caused the Germans a measure of worry as being an Allied 'secret weapon' as the crew of the landing craft carrying this Sherman BARV made a mistake and brought their craft in to the beach at a stage far earlier than had been planned.

It is worth noting that the REME was also responsible for the creation and production of an armoured amphibian tractor based on the Caterpillar D8. This too was generally successful, operating in much the same way as the BARV on the Normandy beaches, though it was a more limited type, lacking the Sherman BARV's submersible capability.

Top: A Churchill ARV Mk I has its front jib erected and twin 7.7-mm (0.303-in) Bren machine-guns mounted in the hull. This vehicle had a crew of three and carried special tools and welding equipment for the recovery role. The vehicle was basically a turretless Churchill Mk IV.

Above: A Sherman ARV Mk I tows a Sherman gun tank during the campaign in Normandy during June/July 1944. This ARV was a British conversion of a Sherman tank with the turret removed, and a front-mounted jib crane and other equipment added.

Right: A Tank Recovery Vehicle M32 rolls through a village in north-west Europe, 1945. Based on the M4 tank hull, these vehicles were used from 1943 onwards and used a fixed superstructure in place of the M4 turret. A large winch was fitted along with other special recovery gear and tools.

SPECIFICATION	
Churchill ARV Mk II	liquid-cooled petrol engine
Crew: 5 or 6	developing 261 kW (350 hp)
Weight: 40 tons	**Performance:** maximum road speed
Dimensions: length 8.28 m (27 ft	24.9 km/h (15.5 mph); maximum road
2 in); width 3.35 m (11 ft); height	range 193 km (120 miles)
3.02 m (9 ft 11 in)	**Armament:** one or two 7.7-mm
Powerplant: one Bedford Twin-Six	(0.303-in) machine-guns

Munitionpanzer IV Ausf F Karl ammunition carrier

When the design teams that produced the massive Karl siege howitzer were drawing up their plans they at first overlooked one item: the massive short-barrelled howitzers they were producing were mounted on large tracked chassis to provide some measure of mobility (even though this mobility was strictly limited by the sizes and weights involved), but they forgot the matter of ammunition supply. This oversight was soon realised and plans were made to provide special ammunition carriers that could move to wherever the Karls might be emplaced, and these carriers had to be tracked as well. They also had to be large, for the Karls fired a huge concrete-busting projectile that weighed no less than 2170 kg (4,784 lb) and with a diameter of 60 cm (23.62 in). Later versions of the weapon had a 54-cm (21.26-in) calibre and fired a projectile weighing 1250 kg (2,756 lb).

Construction

The vehicle selected as the basis of the ammunition carrier for the Karls was the PzKpfw IV Ausf F. The type was not produced as a conversion, but was built from new using the basic tank hull, suspension and other components but with the usual turret replaced by a platform that covered the entire top of the hull. At the front of the platform was a crane with a capacity of 3000 kg (6,614 lb), offset to the left and with the swivelling jib normally stowed facing to the rear. The main platform was used as a carrying area for the projectiles, with space for two or three shells. Small metal side walls were fitted, but these were often removed in the field.

Much of the movement of the Karl equipments had to be carried out on railways, and the train that carried the Karl components also had a couple of flat-cars to carry the standard complement of two **Munitionpanzer** (or **Munitionschlepper**) ammunition carriers.

Close to the intended firing position the Karls were assembled and moved off to the exact firing position. Projectiles for the weapons were taken from the train box-cars either by overhead gantry or the crane mounted on the carriers. The carriers then moved to the firing posi-

tion and unloaded their projectiles by parking next to the Karl's breech and lifting the ammunition directly to the breech loading tray with its crane. Special ammunition handling grabs were used on the crane itself. Once their load had been fired, the carriers trundled off for more.

Not all Karl moves were made by rail. There was an arrangement whereby a Karl could be broken down into relatively small loads for road traction, but it was a long and arduous process to assemble the weapon on site. When this occurred the carriers were towed on wheeled trailers towed by large halftracks.

Also included in each Karl 'train' were two trucks, two light staff cars and at least one 12-tonne halftrack to carry the Karl's crew.

The Karl howitzers were among the most specialised of all German artillery weapons. They were designed as fortification smashers, and during World War II were not much in demand. However, they and their ammunition carriers did see use during the siege of Sevastopol, and in 1944 saw more action during the Battle of Warsaw against the unfortunate Polish home army.

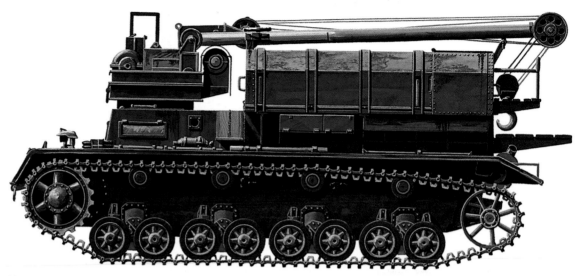

Above: Munitionpanzer IV Ausf F carried shells for the Karl self-propelled mortar on a platform over the hull. The shells were lifted on to the Karl loading tray by a front-mounted jib crane, seen here folded over the shell platform.

Above: The Munitionpanzer IV Ausf F is shown in its travelling configuration with the jib folded and with the shell lifting grab stowed on the front of the hull. Each of these ammunition carriers could carry three 60-cm (23.62-in) projectiles for the Karl siege howitzer.

Left: The unarmed Munitionpanzer IV Ausf F was used to carry the heavy projectiles for the 60-cm Karl self-propelled mortar, and is seen here with its lifting jib raised ready for use. The jib could be traversed through 360 degrees.

Below: The acute nature of the weightlifting task allocated to the Munitionpanzer IV Ausf F is attested by the fact that the tank chassis used as the basis of the shell carrier was the PzKpfw IV battle tank.

SPECIFICATION	
Munitionpanzer IV Ausf F	**Dimensions:** length 5.41 m (17 ft 9 in); width 2.88 m (9 ft 5½ in)
Crew: 4	
Weight: 25 tonnes	**Performance:** maximum road speed 39.9 km/h (24.8 mph); maximum road range 209 km (130 miles)
Powerplant: one Maybach HL 120 TRM liquid-cooled petrol engine developing 223.7 kW (300 hp)	

SdKfz 265 kleiner Panzerbefehlswagen
Armoured command vehicle

Once the German army had accepted the concept of the Panzer division with its large tank component, it also appreciated that the large mass of tanks would entail considerable command and control problems. Tank formation commanders would have to move forward with the tanks and maintain contact with them at all times, and at first it seemed that the best way of doing this was to have the commanders travelling in tanks. However, it was also appreciated that commanders would have to have available to them all manner of special equipment and extra personnel to transmit orders and generally assist the commander in his task. Thus some form of dedicated command tank was needed.

In typically thorough style, the German designers came up with an answer as early as 1938. They decided to convert the PzKpfw I training

Above: Kleiner Panzerbefehlswagen was a command version of the PzKpfw I light tank. It had a crew of three, and the fixed superstructure contained two radios, a map table and extra electrical equipment. The vehicles were widely used, as they allowed commanders to keep up with the armoured formations they were supervising.

Right: Just how cramped the PzKpfw I command tank was can be gauged from this photograph of the basic model PzKpfw I. About 200 conversions were made but they proved too small for the task, and they were replaced by modified versions of later tanks.

tank for the command role, and the result was the **SdKfz 265 kleiner Panzerbefehlswagen** (small armoured command vehicle). The command vehicle was a relatively straightforward conversion of the basic tank in which the rotating tank turret was replaced by a box-like superstructure to provide extra internal space. The crew was increased from the two of the tank to three, in the form of the driver, the commander and a signaller/general assistant.

The extra internal space was taken up with items such as a small table on which the commander could work, map display boards, stowage for more maps and other paperwork, and two radios – one for communicating with the tanks and the other to provide a link to higher command levels. These radios required the provision of extra dynamo capacity to power them and keep their associated batteries fully charged. For armament, a single 7.92-mm (0.312-in) MG 34 machine-gun was mounted in the front plate.

Three variants

There were three variants of this command vehicle, one of them with a small rotating turret set onto the superstructure. This feature was soon discontinued as it took up too much of the limited internal space and was found to be unnecessary. The other two variants differed only in detail. In all of them the small size of the vehicle inflicted space limitations, and with two men attempting to work within the close confines of the body things could get very cramped.

However, the concept worked very well and about 200 such conversions from PzKpfw I tank standard were made. The first of them saw

action during the Polish campaign of 1939 and more were used in France during May and June 1940. Later these command vehicles equipped the Afrika Korps. One of these North African campaign examples was captured by the British Army and taken back to the UK where it was closely examined by tank experts who produced a large report on the vehicle's capabilities.

Despite its relative success in the command role, the diminutive PzKpfw I tank conversion was really too small and cramped for efficiency, and in time the type was replaced by conversions of larger tank models.

The PzKpfw I was intended mainly as a training tank for the creation of the crews who would operate the larger and more capable tanks that followed the PzKpfw into service, but formed the basis of a useful though small and therefore interim light command tank vital to German successes in 1939 and 1940.

SPECIFICATION	
kleiner Panzerbefehlswagen I	7 in); width 2.08 m (6 ft 10 in);
Crew: 3	height 1.72 m (5 ft 7¾ in)
Weight: 5.8 tonnes	**Armament:** one 7.92-mm (0.312-in)
Powerplant: one Maybach NL 38	MG 34 machine-gun
TR liquid-cooled petrol engine	**Performance:** maximum road
developing 74.6 kW (100 hp)	speed 40 km/h (25 mph); maximum
Dimensions: length 4.45 m (14 ft	road range 290 km (180 miles)

Panhard 178 French armoured car

The **Automitrailleuse Panhard et Levassor Type 178** armoured car was first produced in 1935, and was developed from a design known as the TOE-M-32, which was intended for use in the French North African colonies and mounted a short 37-mm turret gun. Panhard used this design as a basis for a new French army requirement but gave the new vehicle a 4x4 drive configuration and moved the engine to the rear of the vehicle. The result was the Panhard 178 and the armament varied from a single 25-mm cannon on some vehicles to two 7.5-mm (0.30-in) machine-guns on others, while some command vehicles had extra radios but no armament. The Panhard 178 was known also as the **Panhard Model 1935**.

The Panhard 178 was put into production for the French infantry and cavalry formation reconnaissance groups. Production was slow, but by 1940 there were appreciable numbers available for the fighting which followed the German invasion in May.

Into service

Many of the Panhard 178s were in widely scattered units and were unable to take much part in the fighting that ensued, so many were seized intact by the victorious Germans. The Germans liked the sound design of the Panhard 178 and decided to adopt it for their own service as the **Panzerspähwagen P 204(f)**, some of them being rearmed with 37-mm anti-tank guns and/or German machine-guns. Some of these were retained for garrison use in France, but others were later sent to the USSR, where the type was used for behind-the-lines patrol duties against Soviet partisans. Some were even converted for railway use,

Two Automitrailleuse Panhard et Levassor Type 178s are seen here in German service following the fall of France in 1940. The Germans found these vehicles good enough to take into their own service, and many were used for anti-partisan operations in the USSR.

having their conventional wheels changed to railway wheels, and many of these 'railway' conversions were fitted with extra radios and prominent frame aerials.

Perhaps the most unusual use of the Panhard 178s took place in 1941 and 1942, when 45 vehicles, hidden from German forces by French cavalry units following the defeat of 1940, were prepared by Resistance personnel for possible use against the enemy. These vehicles had no turrets, but were manufactured under the nose of the Germans and fitted with 25-mm or 47-mm guns and/or

machine-guns. The armoured cars were then secretly distributed throughout centres of resistance mainly in unoccupied France, where many were subsequently taken over by the German forces when they took over the unoccupied areas of France in November 1942.

Further production

After the Liberation, the Panhard 178 was once more put into production during

August 1944 at the Renault factory outside Paris. These new vehicles had a larger turret with a 47-mm gun, and were later known as the **Panhard 178B**. The new vehicles were issued to the new French cavalry units and were used for many years after 1945. Some saw action in Indo-China, and it was not until 1960 that the last of them was taken out of service.

SPECIFICATION	
Panhard 178	78 kW (105 bhp)
Crew: 4	**Performance:** maximum road
Weight: (in action) 8.5 tonnes	speed 72 km/h (45 mph); road
Dimensions: length overall 4.79 m	range 300 km (186 miles)
(15 ft 8½ in); width 2 m (6 ft 7¼ in);	**Fording:** 0.6 m (1 ft 11½ in)
height 2.31 m (7 ft 7 in)	**Gradient:** 40°
Powerplant: one 6.3-litre water-	**Vertical obstacle:** 0.3 m (11¾ in)
cooled petrol engine developing	**Trench:** 0.6 m (1 ft 11½ in)

leichter Panzerspähwagen SdKfz 222 Light armoured car

When the Nazis came to power in Germany, the army was given a virtually free hand in selecting new equipment for the expanding German armed forces, and among the equipment requested was a new series of light armoured cars to be built on a standard chassis.

New design

The requirements laid down by the army were so demanding that commercial models could not be adapted to meet them, so an entirely new design was produced and in 1935 this was used as the basis for the **leichter Panzerspäh-wagen SdKfz 221** 4x4, a light three-man vehicle with a small turret mounting a single 7.92-mm (0.31-in) machine-gun. From this evolved the **SdKfz 222** armoured car with a slightly larger armoured turret with an open top and the potential to mount a slightly heavier armament. The first SdKfz 222 appeared in 1938 and thereafter was adopted as the standard German army armoured car for use by the new divisional reconnaissance units.

The SdKfz 222 was initially referred to as a Waffenwagen, or weapons vehicle, as it mounted a 20-mm KwK 30 cannon, a version of the standard anti-aircraft cannon adapted for use in armoured vehicles.

A leichter Panzerspähwagen SdKfz 222 is seen here in the type's usual form, armed with a 20-mm cannon and MG 34 machine-gun. The wire mesh anti-grenade screen roof is in position. Note the tool and fuel can stowage and the number of stowage boxes on the exterior, the result of a rather cramped interior.

Later the 20-mm KwK 38 was also used. Mounted alongside this cannon was a 7.92-mm MG 34 machine-gun, and this combination left little room inside the turret for the commander/

gunner and the radio operator, who were further restricted in action by the use of a wire screen over the top of the open turret to prevent hand grenades from being lobbed into

the vehicle. The driver was situated centrally in the front of the hull, and the superstructure was made up from well-sloped armoured plates to provide extra protection. During the war the thickness of the front hull plates was increased from 14.5 mm (0.57 in) to 30 mm (1.2 in) and the 20-mm cannon mounting was adapted to provide more elevation for use against aircraft targets.

Once in widespread service the SdKfz 222 proved to be a reliable and popular little vehicle. It served well in France during 1940, often racing far ahead of the fol-

lowing Panzer columns, and in North Africa the type proved itself to be a very useful reconnaissance vehicle, although somewhat restricted in its operational range by the amount of fuel that could be carried in the internal tanks. This restriction proved to be a problem during the invasion of the Soviet Union after 1941, to the extent that the SdKfz 222 was replaced by the SdKfz 250/9 halftrack mounting the same turret and used for the same role. In the west the SdKfz 222 continued in service until the end of the war, and in the Soviet Union the type was used for patrol duties in rear areas.

The SdKfz 221 and SdKfz 222 were not the only

armoured cars of their line. There was also the SdKfz 223, which could be recognised by a large frame aerial over the rear of its hull; as the vehicle was used as a command and communications centre it carried only a single machine-gun. The SdKfz 260 was a long-range radio vehicle used at higher command levels only, and the

SdKfz 261 was similar. The SdKfz 247 was a personnel and stores carrier.

The SdKfz 222 was exported in some numbers to China before 1939, and once there, was adapted to take a wide range of armament that ranged from heavy machine-guns to light anti-tank guns. Numbers of SdKfz 221s were also sent to China.

On the left is an SdKfz 223 light communications vehicle with its large and distinctive frame aerial; on the right is an SdKfz 250/3 halftrack, a type of vehicle that proved more suited to service in the USSR.

SPECIFICATION

SdKfz 222
Crew: 3
Weight: (in action) 4.8 tonnes
Dimensions: length overall 4.80 m (14 ft 8½ in); width 1.95 m (6 ft 4¾ in); height 2 m (6 ft 6¾ in) with grenade screen
Powerplant: one Horch/Auto-Union V8-108 water-cooled petrol

engine developing 60 kW (81 hp)
Performance: maximum road speed 80 km/h (50 mph); maximum cross country speed 40 km/h (25 mph); road radius of action 300 km (187 miles); cross-country radius of action 180 km (110 miles)
Gradient: 20°
Fording: 0.6 m (1 ft 11½ in)

schwerer Panzerspähwagen SdKfz 231
Heavy armoured car

The **schwerer Panzerspähwagen SdKfz 231** 6x4 heavy armoured car had its origins at the Kazan test centre established in the Soviet Union during the 1920s. At the centre the German automobile industry developed an 8x8 armoured car chassis that proved to be too expensive for further development, so a 6x4 chassis was tried instead. This model used a truck chassis as its basis, and originally this was a Daimler-Benz product, but later Büssing-NAG and Magirus chassis and engines were employed. These chassis were fitted with suitable armoured hulls and turrets, and modifications were made to allow steering from either end of the hull.

Trial phase

Early trials demonstrated the need for stronger front axles and revised radiators, and the resulting vehicle was issued to German army units during 1932. Production continued until 1935, by which

The SdKfz 231 was really too heavy for the lorry chassis on which it was based. Nevertheless, where the going was good, it proved an effective fighting vehicle.

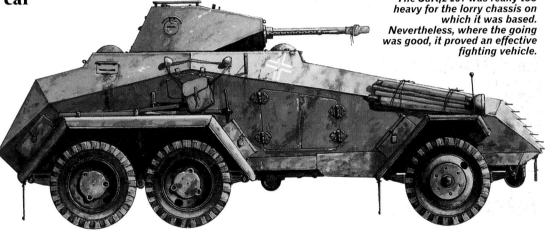

Schwerer Panzerspähwagen SdKfz 232s seen during a pre-war parade in Berlin. These vehicles were equipped with a large and cumbersome radio antenna mounted over the turret, which remained static while the turret rotated.

time about 1,000 had been produced.

The 6x4 armoured cars were not a great success, but they were produced at a time when the German army lacked experience in the use of armoured vehicles, and were thus invaluable as training and preparation equipments. Using lorry chassis carrying armoured hulls that were really too heavy for

their supporting structures, the six-wheeled armoured cars were underpowered and had only limited cross country capabilities. But when used on roads they were as good as anything else available, and were used to good effect during the occupations of Austria and Czechoslovakia during 1938 and 1939. They were also used in combat in Poland and France. Their very appearance had great propaganda impact, and they were accordingly given great media coverage at the time. After 1940 they gradually faded from front-line use and were

relegated mainly to training second-line roles.

Early examples of the six-wheeled heavy armoured cars had provision for only one 7.92-mm (0.31-in) MG 34 machine-gun in the turret, but the version used mainly by the heavy platoons of the German army motorised units was the SdKfz 231. This had a turret mounting a 20-mm cannon, originally the KwK 30 but later the KwK 38 with a higher rate of fire. Mounted co-axially with this cannon was a 7.92-mm MG 34, and there was provision for an anti-aircraft machine-gun on the turret roof.

Tactical vehicle

The SdKfz 231 was used as a tactical vehicle (undertak-

ing a combat role in direct fire support of motorised infantry units mounted on trucks or later on halftracks), and also in support of light reconnaissance units for Panzer formations. Another vehicle that was very similar to the SdKfz 231 was the SdKfz 232. This was essentially an SdKfz 231 fitted with a long-range radio set that required the fitting of a large and prominent frame aerial above the turret and over the hull rear, the turret acting as a support for the forward part of the aerial. Another similar vehicle was the SdKfz 263, which also had a large frame aerial, though on this the turret was fixed and had provision for a single machine-gun only. The SdKfz 263 was used as a command vehicle.

SPECIFICATION

SdKfz 231
Crew: 4
Weight: (in action) 5.7 tonnes
Dimensions: length overall 5.57 m (18 ft 6¾ in); width 1.82 m (5 ft 11½ in); height 2.25 m (7 ft 4½ in)
Powerplant: one Daimler-Benz, Büssing-NAG or Magirus water-cooled petrol engine developing

between 45 and 60 kW (60 and 80 bhp)
Performance: maximum road speed 65 km/h (40 mph); maximum road range 250 km (150 miles); maximum cross-country range 200 km (125 miles)
Gradient: 20°
Fording: 0.6 m (24 in)

schwerer Panzerspähwagen SdKfz 231 (8-Rad)

Heavy reconnaissance car

The wide-ranging war in North Africa provided German reconnaissance units with the ideal terrain to test the abilities of their armoured cars. The Achtrad ranged ahead of the armoured columns of the Afrika Korps, seeking out the information which would allow Rommel, the Desert Fox, to make his tactical decisions.

Almost as soon as the first six-wheeled armoured cars were issued to the expanding German army during the mid-1930s, the German staff planners realised that they were not the vehicles that would be required in the long term as they were underpowered and lacked cross-country mobility.

They requested an eight-wheeled armoured car with an engine to match, and decided to develop a Büssing-NAG 8 x 8 chassis for use as an armoured car. Development began in full during 1935 and the first production examples were issued to the army in 1937.

This 8 x 8 heavy armoured car was the **schwerer Panzerspähwagen SdKfz 231**, and to avoid confusion with the six-wheeled armoured cars with the same designation, the new series was always suffixed **(8-Rad)**. The troops knew the type as the *Achtrad*.

When the new eight-wheelers appeared in service they were among the most advanced cross-country vehi-

cles yet produced, but their high road-speeds and mobility had been purchased at an equally high price in chassis complexity. The vehicles were highly complicated, expensive and very slow to produce.

The chassis had all-wheel drive and steering, and fully independent suspension – the vehicle was even able to travel across the thick mud of the Eastern Front. If the vehicle had one major fault other than its complexity, it was that it had rather a high profile and was difficult to hide in combat.

Early war production

The SdKfz 231 series remained in production until 1942, when it was phased out in favour of the improved SdKfz 234 series. By then 1,235 had been produced, and the type remained in widespread use throughout the war on all fronts. The type was particularly prominent in the North African campaigns.

The SdKfz 231 (8-Rad) had a turret with a 20-mm KwK

Right: An SdKfz 231 Achtrad crew mounts up. The distinctive tank berets, which covered a leather protective helmet, indicate that this photograph was taken prewar or in Poland, since they had mostly fallen out of use by 1940.

30 or KwK 38 cannon with a co-axial 7.92-mm (0.31-in) MG 34 machine-gun. The **SdKfz 232(8-Rad)** was the radio version with a prominent frame aerial, and the **SdKfz 263(8-Rad)** was a command version with a fixed superstructure in place of the rotating turret, and featuring a large frame aerial for the long-range radio equipment carried.

Fire support

The **SdKfz 233** had no direct six-wheeler equivalent, for it mounted a short 75-mm (2.95-in) tank gun (*Stummelkanone*) as used on early PzKpfw IV tanks. This gun was mounted in an open compartment formed by the removal of the normal

turret and there was only a limited traverse. This vehicle had a crew of only three men, and was used to provide armoured reconnaissance units with improved offensive power and to give them fire support.

The first SdKfz 233 was issued during late 1942 and proved to be highly effective,

but there were times when the gun's limited traverse and lack of armour-piercing performance proved to be a liability. However, when pitted against the usual run-of-the-mill reconnaissance vehicles it was likely to encounter, the SdKfz 233 was very effective and often provided covering fire for other *Achtrads*.

SPECIFICATION	
SdKfz 231(8-Rad)	**Performance:** maximum road speed 85 km/h (53 mph); maximum cross-country speed 30 km/h (19 mph); road radius of action 270 km (170 miles); cross-country radius of action 150 km (95 miles); fording 1 m (3 ft 3½ in); gradient 30 per cent; vertical obstacle 0.5 m (1 ft 7¾ in); trench 1.25 m (4 ft 3 in)
Crew: 4	
Weight: (in action) 8.3 tonnes	
Dimensions: length overall 5.85 m (19 ft 2 in); width 2.20 m (7 ft 2½ in); height 2.34 m (7 ft 8 in)	
Powerplant: one Büssing-NAG L8V-Gs water-cooled petrol engine developing 112 kW (150 hp)	

This early example of an SdKfz 231(8-Rad) is armed with a 20-mm cannon and shows the distinctive spaced armoured stowage bin mounted on the front hull. The size and bulk of this vehicle in relation to the armament carried is obvious; its internal complexity is less so.

SdKfz 234(8-Rad)
Heavy reconnaissance car

In 1940 German army planners issued a requirement for a new 8 x 8 armoured car series to be based on the SdKfz 231(8-Rad) series, but having a monocoque hull (one in which the basic hull structure was made up of the plates themselves rather than a framework on which the body was fixed) and an engine more suited to operations in hot climates.

The resultant vehicle was built by Büssing-NAG with other firms under its control, and the basic hull and chassis was known as the **ARK**. It was delivered in July 1941, but the original engine installation proved troublesome and was replaced by another. A different engine installation was intended for vehicles used in North Africa, but with the end of that campaign early in 1943, the project proceeded slowly and it was not until 1944 that the first 'tropical' version was delivered.

New variants

The new series of vehicles was designated **schwerer Panzerspähwagen SdKfz 234** and was much lower and more streamlined than the earlier SdKfz 231(8-Rad) series. The vehicles had thicker armour, increased internal fuel capacity and a more powerful engine bestowing a better all-round performance. It is now generally acknowledged that the variants of the SdKfz 234 series were probably the best all-round vehicles in their class used during World War II.

Most of the mechanical attributes of the SdKfz 231(8-Rad) vehicles were carried over, and there were four basic versions of the SdKfz 234. By the end of the war about 2,300 had been produced after the type had entered full production during 1943.

Designations

In designation order, the first version was the **SdKfz 234/1**, a commander's vehicle with a 20-mm KwK 30 or KwK 38 cannon in a small open-topped turret along with a co-axial 7.92-mm (0.31-in) MG 42 machine-gun. Normally, the turret was covered by a wire screen to prevent the ingress of hand grenades.

The most famous of the range was the **SdKfz 234/2 Puma**, a superb armoured car with a turret enclosing a 50-mm (1.96-in) KwK 39/1 gun. The turret had originally

Above: A captured SdKfz 234/1 has its third axle welded into place for the camera. This damaged example has the turret with its 20-mm cannon traversed to the rear, and the anti-grenade mesh screen can be seen over the open turret top. Note the stowage bins, one with the cover missing.

Below: A wrecked SdKfz 234/1 Puma. Well able to take care of itself against other armoured cars and light tanks, the Puma was still vunerable to heavier tanks.

been intended for the Leopard light tank, which was cancelled, and when reworked for the Puma the result was powerful enough for the vehicle to counter the increasing use of light and other tanks in Soviet army reconnaissance units. The turret had an excellent ballistic shape and also mounted a co-axial MG42.

So good was the vehicle that by 1945, when German industry was being drastically reorganised to maintain war production outputs, the Puma was the only reconnaissance vehicle to be kept in production (along with a Skoda light tank).

Tank-killer

There were times when the 50-mm gun of the Puma was unable to cope with enemy tanks, and so the **SdKfz 234/3** was produced to replace the earlier SdKfz 233. It, too, mounted the short 75-mm (2.95-in) tank gun of the SdKfz 233, and was placed in production at the direct order of Hitler, who by 1944 was concerning himself directly with such matters as fighting vehicle armament. The last variant of the SdKfz 234 series was another placed in production as the result of a direct order from Hitler. The **SdKfz 234/4** mounted a 75-mm PaK 40 anti-tank gun in an open compartment in place of the turret. Only a few trial models were produced, but by the time they appeared things were becoming so desperate that they were rushed into operational use, and some were subsequently captured by the Allies.

Probably the best balanced armoured car of World War II in terms of speed, firepower and protection, the Puma was complex and expensive to manufacture. Even so, it remained in production until 1945.

SPECIFICATION	
SdKfz 234/2 Puma **Crew:** 4 **Weight:** (in action) 11.74 tonnes **Dimensions:** length (gun forward) 6.80 m (22 ft 3⅖ in); length (hull) 6.00 m (19 ft 8¼ in); width 2.33 m (7 ft 6½ in); height 2.38 m (7 ft 9½ in) **Powerplant:** one Tatra Model 103 air-cooled diesel engine developing 157 kW (210 hp)	**Performance:** maximum road speed 85 km/h (53 mph); maximum cross-country speed 30 km/h (19 mph); road radius of action 1000 km (625 miles); cross-country radius of action 550 km (350 miles) **Obstacle handling:** fording 1.2 m (3 ft 10¾ in); gradient 30 per cent; vertical obstacle 0.5 m (1 ft 7¾ in); trench 1.35 m (4 ft 5 in)

SdKfz 234/2

The schwerer Panzerspähwagen SdKfz 234 was one of the finest armoured cars produced in World War II. The SdKfz 234/2 definitive version had the enclosed turret and 50-mm (1.97-in) gun with which the cancelled Leopard reconnaissance tank was to have been armed. With its powerful armament in a turret of excellent ballistic shape, the Puma, as the SdKfz 234/2 became known, was a match for many of the light tanks used by the reconnaissance units of other armies.

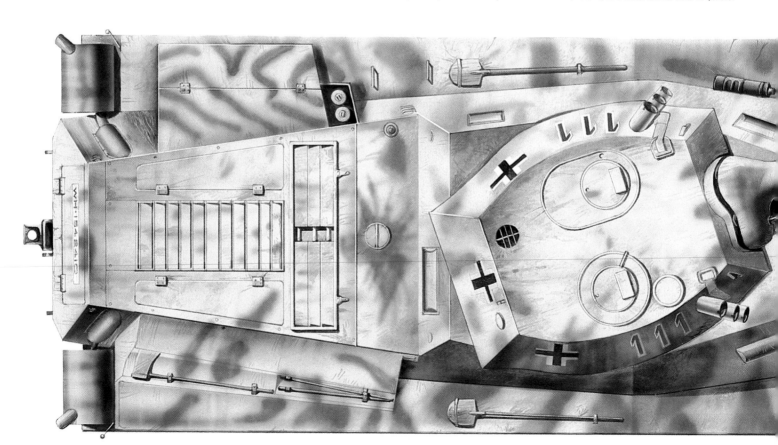

The process that led to the schwerer Panzerspähwagen(8-Rad), a designation meaning eight-wheeled heavy armoured reconnaissance vehicle, began in 1937 with the sPzSpw(8-Rad) that had the inventory designation SdKfz 231. Unlike earlier German armoured cars, which were based on chassis developed for commercial purposes, this was developed and manufactured by Büssing-NAG as an armoured car specifically for German army service. This four-man type had an 8x8 wheel layout with front and rear driving positions, a Büssing water-cooled V-8 petrol engine at the rear, a central turret with a 20-mm cannon and 7.92-mm (0.312-in) co-axial machine-gun, and a structure in which a light chassis was given rigidity by the armoured hull. The sPzSpw(8-Rad) SdKfz 232 and 263 differed only in their radio equipment, while the sPzSpw(8-Rad) SdKfz 233 was intended to support its brethren and had an open top carrying the same 7.5-cm (2.95-in) StuK L/24 short gun as the early versions of the PzKpfw IV battle tank. From 1943 the 1,200 of so of these models were followed by 200 of the the SdKfz 234/1 with a strengthened hull, a diesel engine of Czech origin, and the armament of one 20-mm cannon and one 7.92-mm machine-gun in an open turret.

The two variants of the sPzSpw(8-Rad) SdKfz 234 had radically different armament. The original SdKfz 234/1 was lightly armed, with a turret that resembled that of the SdKfz 231(6-Rad) but with the front plate coming down to the roof of the hull to remove the dangerous re-entrant that had proved something of a shot trap. In the SdKfz 234/1 this turret carried one 2-cm KwK cannon with 180 rounds and one 7.92-mm (0.312-in) machine-gun with 1,000 rounds, but in the SdKfz 234/2 the machine-gun was partnered by a 5-cm (1.97-in) KwK 39 gun with 55 rounds.

The turret of the SdKfz 234/2 was manually operated for 360° traverse, and provided the 5-cm (1.97-mm) gun with an elevation arc of 32° between -7° and +25°. There was also a bank of three dischargers for smoke grenades on each side of the turret. The turret was comparatively well protected by armoured car standards, the front being 30 mm (1.18 in) thick. The other armoured surfaces were the sides and rear, which were each 10 mm (0.39 in) thick. The KwK 39 was an L/60 weapon that fired its 2.05-kg (4.52-lb) shot at a muzzle velocity of 825 m (2,707 ft) per second to penetrate 60 mm (2.36 in) of armour at 500 m (545 yards).

The sPzSpw(8-Rad) SdKfz 234 series introduced a revised powerplant. Like that of the preceding SdKfz 231, 232 and 233, this was based on a rear-mounted engine, but this was a Tatra 103 air-cooled V-12 diesel engine of Czech origins rather than the Büssing-NAG L8V-GS water-cooled V-8 petrol engine of the earlier armoured cars. While the petrol engine was rated at 112 kW (150 hp) at 3,000 rpm, the diesel engine delivered 164 kW (220 hp) at 2,250 rpm. The greater power gave the SdKfz 234 series a higher power/weight ratio, and although the maximum speed was reduced from 100 to 85 km/h (62 to 53 mph), the range was boosted from 300 to 600 km (186 to 373 miles), and safety was much enhanced by the use of low-volatility fuel.

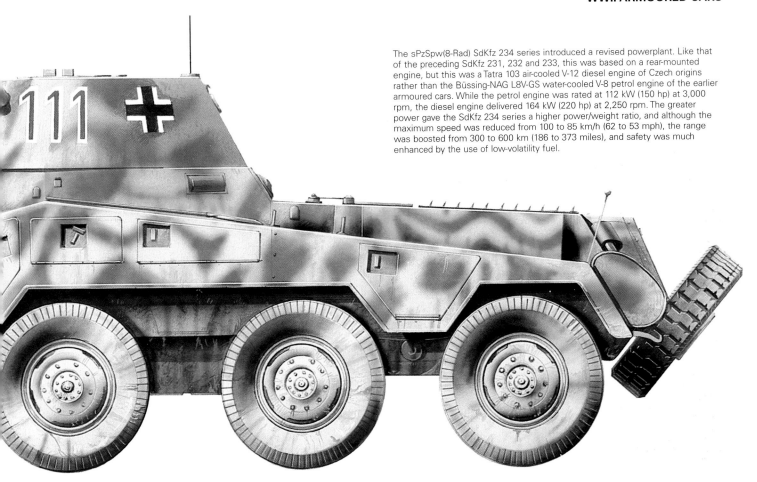

As with all other armoured fighting vehicles, the sPzSpw(8-Rad) was most heavily protected over its front, rightly seen in general as the direction from which most threats would come, and particularly true of reconnaissance vehicles such as this which were designed to investigate enemy positions. The hull front of the SdKfz 234 series was 25 mm (0.98 in) thick, and the figures for the sides and rear were 8 and 15 mm (0.315 and 0.59 in) respectively. The fact that the rear was better protected than the sides reflects the likelihood of the armoured car having to beat a hasty retreat if and when it met tanks or other armoured fighting vehicles with heavier armament.

The 5-cm (1.97-in) KwK 39 main gun and the 7.92-mm (0.312-in) co-axial machine-gun emerged from the front of the SdKfz 234/2's turret via a mantlet, which was a well-shaped unit of cast armour that protected the otherwise vulnerable opening in the armour of the turret's front.

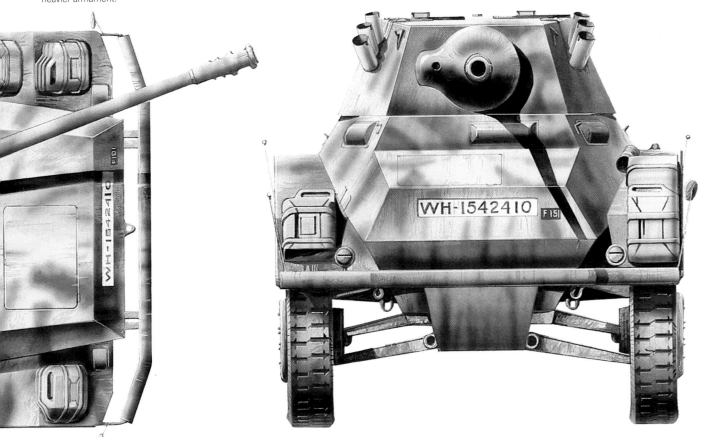

Autoblinda 40 & 41 Armoured cars

The **Autoblinda 40** and **Autoblinda 41** armoured cars had their origins in a requirement for a high-performance car for use by the Italian colonial police in the new Italian colonies in Africa. The Italian cavalry branch had a requirement for a new armoured car at about the same time, so the two projects were merged to produce a new vehicle design that appeared in 1939. This new design had the engine at the rear and a turret (mounting a machine-gun) towards the front. There was another machine-gun in the hull rear and the vehicle could be driven from either the normal front position or another position in the hull rear. From this design evolved the Autoblinda 40, of which production began by the middle of 1940.

Cannon armament

When the original production order was placed it was specified that a small number of Autoblinda 40s would be produced with a 20-mm cannon in place of the two

This Autoblinda 41, one of the most numerous Italian armoured cars, carried one 20-mm cannon and one co-axial machine-gun in the turret, and one machine-gun at the rear of the fighting compartment.

8-mm (0.315-in) machine-guns in the turret. This was achieved by using the turret of the L 6/40 light tank in place of the original turret. With the appearance of this version known as the Autoblinda 41, it was realised that this vehicle/weapon combination was far more effective than the machine-gun version, and thereafter production cen-

An Autoblinda 41 in North Africa in 1941 where both variants were used extensively by reconnaissance units. In German hands, the armoured cars were known as the Panzerspähwagen AB 40 and 41.

tred on the Autoblinda 41. Relatively few Autoblinda 40s were produced, and many of these were later converted to the Autoblinda 41 configuration.

For its time the Autoblinda 41 was an advanced design and possessed good performance marred only by recurrent steering troubles that were never entirely eliminated. The main armament was a converted 20-mm Breda Modello 35 anti-aircraft cannon, and this weapon was mounted co-axially with an 8-mm Breda Modello 38 air-cooled machine-gun, which was a type specially designed for use in armoured vehicles. Another of these machine-guns was mounted at the hull rear. One vehicle in four had provision for an anti-aircraft machine-gun mounting on top of the turret. Special sand or normal road tyres could be fitted and there was a kit available to convert the vehicle for use on railway tracks. This kit included

railway wheels and extra lighting and signalling devices, along with a searchlight to be mounted on the turret. Autoblinda 41s fitted with these kits were used extensively for anti-partisan patrols in the Balkans.

The Autoblinda 40 and Autoblinda 41 were widely used by Italian reconnaissance units in the Western Desert and Tunisia. At the end of September 1942 there were 298 Autoblinda 41s in use, and more were employed by the colonial

police. Some development work was carried out on the basic design, which later led to the mounting of a 47-mm (1.85-in) gun in the turret to create the **Autoblinda 43**, while an open-hulled variant had a German 50-mm (1.97-in) tank gun. However, neither of these vehicles was placed in production. There was also an open-hulled variant that was produced in small numbers as a command vehicle or as a mobile observation post for artillery units.

SPECIFICATION	
Autoblinda 41	**Performance:** maximum road speed 78 km/h (49 mph); maximum cross-country speed 38 km/h (24 mph); maximum road range 400 km (248 miles)
Crew: 4	
Weight: 7.5 tonnes	
Dimensions: length (overall) 5.2 m (17 ft 1½ in); width 1.92 m (6 ft 4¼ in); height 2.48 m (7 ft 11½ in)	
Powerplant: one SAP Abm 1 water-cooled 16-cylinder petrol engine developing 60 kW (80 bhp)	**Fording:** 0.7 m (28 in) **Gradient:** 40 per cent **Vertical obstacle:** 0.3 m (12 in)

Marmon Herrington armoured cars

Despite the fact that the vehicle construction industry in South Africa had never before produced any armoured vehicles, in 1938 the government of the day ordered the development of two types of armoured car. Work on these was slow until the outbreak of war in 1939 when, after a quick survey of possible alternatives, the experimental vehicles were ordered into production. Orders soon swelled to 1,000 and, despite the fact that no facilities existed for the large-scale production of such vehicles, within only a few months the first examples were appearing.

The South Africans produced their armoured cars by importing Ford truck chassis from Canada, four-wheel drive transmissions

from Marmon Herrington in the US, and the armament from the United Kingdom. Local assembly and production were undertaken in vehicle assembly plants and railway workshops, and the armour plate was produced at South African steel mills. The first vehicles were known under the designation **South African Reconnaissance Vehicle Mk I**, and these had a long wheelbase and a 4x2 drive configuration. The **South African Reconnaissance Vehicle Mk II** had a shorter wheelbase and a full 4x4 drive. After early experience with the Mk I vehicles against the Italians in East Africa, the South Africans thereafter confined the vehicles mainly to training purposes, but the Mk IIs went on to better things.

This Marmon Herrington Mk II in desert guise is armed in typical fashion with a Vickers water-cooled machine-gun, a Bren air-cooled machine-gun and a Boys 0.55-in (13.97-mm) turret-mounted anti-tank rifle.

This official photograph shows a Marmon Herrington Mk II armoured car in its original form with a Vickers 0.303-in (7.7-mm) machine-gun in the turret and another in a side-mounted mantlet. This latter weapon position was soon discarded and extra weapon positions were provided around the open turret.

The Mk II, known to the British as the **Armoured Car, Marmon Herrington, Mk II**, was a fairly simple but effective conversion of the original truck chassis to take the new 4x4 transmission and a well-shaped armoured hull. The early versions had a turret on the roof mounting a Vickers 0.303-in (7.7-mm) machine-gun, another light machine-gun being located in the hull front, but once this combination had been tried in action it was changed to a Boys 0.55-in (13.97-mm) anti-tank rifle mounted alongside a 0.303-in machine-gun in the turret. The vehicle had a crew of four housed in the roomy hull, and the engine was a Ford V-8.

When they were first produced and issued to South African and British units in North Africa, the Marmon Herringtons were the only armoured cars available in any numbers, and thus they formed the main equipment of reconnaissance units operating during the early Western Desert campaigns. They proved to be surprisingly effective vehicles, but their 12-mm (0.47-in) armour was often too thin to be of much use, and the armament was really too light. The troops in the field made their own changes to the armament and all manner of weapons sprouted from the turrets or from the open hulls once the turrets had been removed. One of the more common weapon fits was a captured Italian 20-mm Breda cannon, but Italian and German 37-mm (1.45-in) and 45-mm (1.77-in) tank or anti-tank guns were also used. One vehicle mounted a British 2-pdr (40-mm; 1.57-in) tank gun, and this became the preferred armament for later marks. The **Armoured Car, Marmon Herrington**

Mk III was basically similar to the Mk II though based on slightly shorter chassis, and lacked the double rear doors of the Mk II.

The Mk IIs had a hard time during the desert campaigns, but they kept going and were well-liked and sturdy vehicles. Local modifications were many and varied, and ranged from command and repair vehicles to versions with as many as four Bren guns in a turret. Gradually they were supplemented and eventually replaced by more formal armoured car designs such as the Humber. Later marks of Marmon Herrington served in other theatres, some even falling into Japanese hands in the Far East, and the number of formal versions was later

extended to eight, including the Mk IV inspired by the German eight-wheeler armoured cars, but after the Mk IV most remained as prototype vehicles only. The **Armoured Car, Marmon Herrington Mk IV** was a markedly different vehicle, being a monocoque design with rear engine. Weighing 6.4 tons, the Mk IV was armed with a 2-pdr gun and co-axial 0.3-in (7.62-mm) Browning machine-gun. A variant was the **Mk IVF** with Canadian Ford rather than Marmon Herrington automotive components.

For a nation with limited production and development potential the Marmon Herrington armoured cars were an outstanding South African military and industrial achievement.

SPECIFICATION

Marmon Herrington Mk IV	**Powerplant:** one 63-kW (85 hp)
Crew: 4	Ford V-8 petrol engine
Weight: 6.4 tonnes	**Performance:** maximum speed
Dimensions: length 4.57 m (15 ft)	80.5 km/h (50 mph); maximum
without gun; height 2.13 m (7 ft);	range 322 km (200 miles)
width 1.83 m (6 ft)	

BA-10 Armoured car

The first **BA-10** six-wheeled armoured car appeared in 1932. It was produced at the Gorki automobile plant, and was the logical outcome of a series of six-wheeled armoured cars that could be traced back to World War I, even though the configuration had been in abeyance for some years. The BA-10 was built on the chassis of the GAZ-AAA six-wheeled civilian truck, although the suspension was modified to assume the loads involved, and some reinforcements were made to the chassis members. The layout of the BA-10 was orthodox, with the engine under an armoured cover at the front and the turret mounted at the rear over the twin rear axles. There were several variations in the armament carried, but the main armament was either a 37-mm tank gun or a 12.7-mm (0.5-in) DShK heavy machine-gun. Later versions mounted a 45-mm (1.77-in) main gun.

All-terrain equipment

Like other Soviet armoured fighting vehicles, the BA-10 was a functional and hefty item of equipment. It had several typically Soviet design sub-features such as the ability to wear tracks or chains on the rear wheels to assist traction in mud and snow, and the spare wheels were located so that they could turn when obstacles under the chassis were encountered, and thus take some of the load. There was a crew of four, one of whom attended to the 7.62-mm (0.3-

The Soviet BA-10 armoured car looked as though it belonged to a previous era, but despite its weight and bulk it proved to be well suited to the distances and terrain of the USSR. The large turret mounted a 37-mm (1.46-in) or 45-mm (1.77-in) main gun.

in) machine-gun fitted into a mounting on the front superstructure to the right of the driver.

Later versions of the BA-10 are sometimes known as the **BA-32**, and to confuse matters further one of these latter variants is sometimes known as the **BA-10M**. This first appeared in 1937 and used the turret of the T-26B light tank with its 45-mm gun. This was not the only tank turret so used, others known to have been fitted were the turret of the experimental T-30 light tank and

that of the BT-3 tank. One odd variation of the BA-10 that appeared in 1932 was the **BAZ** amphibious vehicle, which used the basic BA-10 hull allied to a flotation body derived from contemporary German experimental vehicles. Only a few were produced.

When the Germans invaded the USSR in 1941, the BA-10 and its later derivatives were in service in some numbers with the Red Army, the number 1,200 often being quoted. However, the events of 1941-42 decimated

the numbers of BA-10s, and large quantities fell into the hands of the Germans, who found these Soviet types to be serviceable vehicles, although they considered them not really modern or mobile enough for use with their Panzer units, and kept them for use with anti-partisan units both in the USSR and in the Balkans. The Germans knew the BA-10 as the **Panzerspähwagen BAF**

203(r); some of their reports mention the vehicle as a Ford product.

After 1942 the Soviets started to phase out the use of heavy armoured cars such as the BA-10. Those that remained were often relegated to the armoured personnel carrier role, having their turrets removed and the interiors stripped of all equipment other than the driver's seat and controls.

SPECIFICATION

BA-10M	cooled 4-cylinder petrol engine
Crew: 4	developing 63 kW (86 hp)
Dimensions: length 4.7 m (15 ft 5 in); width 2.09 m (6 ft 10 ½ in); height 2.42 m (7 ft 11¼ in)	**Performance:** maximum speed 87 km/h (54 mph); maximum range 320 km (199 miles)
Powerplant: one GAZ-M-1 water-	

AEC armoured cars

The first AEC (Associated Engineering Company Ltd of Southall, London) armoured car was virtually a wheeled tank. The resultant vehicle was large by contemporary standards and equipped with armour nearly as thick as that used on contemporary 'cruiser' tanks. The chassis was based on the Matador artillery tractor. By the time this had been revised for the armoured car role many changes had been introduced, including an engine set at a slight front-to-rear angle to enable the overall height of the vehicle to be lowered.

Initial order
The first example was demonstrated in early 1941

and an order was placed in June of that year. The **Armoured Car, AEC Mk I** mounted a 2-pdr (40-mm) gun and co-axial 0.31-in (7.92-mm) Besa machine-gun in the same turret that was used on the Valentine tank, but only 120 vehicles were produced before calls came for something more powerful for use in North Africa. The result was a revision that introduced a new three-man turret mounting a 6-pdr (57-mm) gun, but this was not powerful enough, and the **Armoured Car, AEC Mk II** was replaced in production by the **Armoured Car, AEC Mk III** with the same turret mounting a British-developed version of the American M3 75-mm

(2.95-in) tank gun. This made the AEC Mk III a very powerful armoured car.

Restricted vision
The AEC armoured vehicles had a full 4x4 drive configuration, but it was possible to alter this to a 4x2 form. The degree of protection for the crew was such that the driver had no direct vision devices, and as a result, had to rely on periscopes. However, with the hatch open, the driver's seat could be raised to allow him to see. The vehicle had a slab-sided appearance, mainly as a result of the large lockers between the front and rear mudguards. Revisions, therefore, had to be made to the front hull on the AEC Mk II to improve obstacle crossing and armour protection.
Production of all the AEC armoured car marks ceased

after 629 had been built. The vehicles were used in North Africa, Tunisia and Italy. Some Mk IIIs were used by regiments in north west Europe until the end of the war.

The AEC vehicles, used to provide fire-support for armoured car regiments until the end of the war, had a conventional layout with the engine located at the rear.

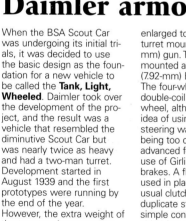

This AEC Mk I, recognisable by the ex-Valentine infantry tank turret and 2-pdr gun, was one of the first to arrive in North Africa.

SPECIFICATION	
Armoured Car, AEC Mk I **Crew:** 3 **Weight:** (in action) 11 tonnes **Dimensions:** length overall 5.18 m (17 ft); width 2.7 m (8 ft 10 ½ in); height 2.55 m (8 ft 4½ in)	**Powerplant:** one AEC 6-cylinder diesel engine developing 78 kW (105 bhp) **Performance:** maximum speed 58 km/h (36 mph); maximum range 402 km (250 miles)

SPECIFICATION	
Armoured Car, AEC Mk II and Mk III **Crew:** 4 **Weight:** (in action) 12.7 tonnes **Dimensions:** length overall (Mk II) 5.18 m (17 ft) or (Mk III) 5.61 m (18 ft 5 in); width 2.7 m (8 ft 10½ in); height 2.69 m (8 ft 10 in)	**Powerplant:** one AEC 6-cylinder diesel engine developing 116 kW (155 bhp) **Performance:** maximum speed 66 km/h (41 mph); maximum range 402 km (250 miles)

Daimler armoured cars

When the BSA Scout Car was undergoing its initial trials, it was decided to use the basic design as the foundation for a new vehicle to be called the **Tank, Light, Wheeled**. Daimler took over the development of the project, and the result was a vehicle that resembled the diminutive Scout Car but was nearly twice as heavy and had a two-man turret. Development started in August 1939 and the first prototypes were running by the end of the year. However, the extra weight of the turret and armour overloaded the transmission. It was some time before these problems were fixed, but in April 1941, the first production examples appeared. By then the vehicle was known as the **Armoured Car, Daimler Mk I**.
The Daimler Armoured Car was basically a Scout Car

enlarged to accommodate a turret mounting a 2-pdr (40-mm) gun. The turret also mounted a co-axial 0.31-in (7.92-mm) Besa machine-gun. The four-wheel drive used double-coil springs on each wheel, although the early idea of using four-wheel steering was discarded as being too complex. One advanced feature was the use of Girling hydraulic disc brakes. A fluid flywheel was used in place of the more usual clutch arrangement. A duplicate steering wheel and simple controls were provided for use by the commander in an emergency to drive to the rear.

New guns
The Daimler underwent surprisingly few changes once in service. An **Armoured Car, Daimler Mk II** version was later introduced with a new gun mounting, a slightly

revised radiator arrangement and an escape hatch through the engine compartment for the driver. There was also an experimental **Armoured Car, Daimler Mk I CS**, which had a 3-in (76.2-mm) howitzer in place of the 2-pdr (40-mm) gun to provide close support fire. Another alteration was a small number of operational Mk Is, which were fitted with the Littlejohn Adaptor, a squeeze-bore muzzle attachment that enabled the 2-pdr gun to fire small projectiles

that could penetrate thicker armour.

Performance
When the first Daimler Armoured Cars arrived in North Africa during 1941-42, they soon gained a reputation for good all-round

The Daimler armoured car was one of the best of all the British armoured cars, and the one that became the standard equipment for many reconnaissance regiments. Armed with a 2-pdr gun, it had limited combat capability but proved to be an excellent and reliable reconnaissance vehicle in all theatres.

performance and reliability. By the end of the war, some were employed as scout or command vehicles with their turrets removed, but turreted vehicles continued to serve for many years after 1945. The total production was 2,694.

SPECIFICATION	
Armoured Car, Daimler Mk I **Crew:** 3 **Weight:** (in action) 7.5 tonnes **Dimensions:** length 3.96 m (13 ft); width 2.44 m (8 ft); height 2.24 m (7 ft 4 in)	**Powerplant:** one Daimler 6-cylinder petrol engine developing 71 kW (95 bhp) **Performance:** maximum speed 80.5 km/h (50 mph); maximum range 330 km (205 miles)

Daimler scout cars

During the late 1930s the British Army was converting to mechanised traction and forming its first armoured divisions. These new formations required a small 4x4 scout car for liaison and reconnaissance duties. BSA Cycles Ltd, Morris Commercial Cars Ltd and Alvis Ltd all produced prototype designs. The BSA submission won. The War Office ordered a total of 172 examples as the **Car, Scout, Mk I** and more orders followed later.

By the time the order was placed the project had been taken over by Daimler, and the designation **Car, Scout, Daimler Mk I** was applied to the vehicle. The War Office also called for more all-round protection, as the original vehicle only provided the two-man crew with frontal armour.

Extra armour
The extra armour and a folding roof added enough weight to require an improved suspension and

These Daimler Scout cars are ready for the Tunis Victory Parade of May 1943. Behind them is a Daimler armoured car and a Humber Mk II; the aircraft is a French Caudron Goeland captured from the Luftwaffe. These vehicles were used on the occasion as escorts for some of the VIPs arriving for the parade.

more powerful engine. Once these changes had been incorporated in the **Daimler Mk IA**, the Daimler Scout Car remained virtually unaltered throughout its long service life. It was a simple design with a full 4x4 drive configuration and front-axle steering from the **Daimler Mk II** onwards. The only armament carried was a single 0.303-in (7.7-mm) Bren Gun firing through a hatch in the front superstructure, although other arrangements such as anti-aircraft mountings were sometimes provided.

The Daimler Scout Car proved itself to be a very tough and reliable vehicle. It had the unusual distinction of being one of the few World War II vehicles in ser-

The Daimler Scout Car was in production as World War II began and was still in production when it ended. Although only lightly armed it was quiet and highly mobile, and proved to be one of the best of all the reconnaissance vehicles in use by any side throughout the war.

vice when the war started and still remaining in production as the war ended. As well as being a reconnaissance platform, it was used by artillery units as a mobile observation post and by the Royal Engineers for locating

mine fields and bridging positions. Many staff officers used them as run-arounds and liaison vehicles, and they were often added to motorised infantry units for reconnaissance and liaison purposes.

SPECIFICATION	
Car, Scout, Daimler Mk I	**Powerplant:** one Daimler
Crew: 2	6-cylinder petrol engine developing
Weight: (in action) 3 tonnes	41 kW (55 bhp)
Dimensions: length 3.23 m (10 ft	**Performance:** maximum speed
5 in); width 1.72 m (5 ft 7½ in);	88.5 km/h (55 mph); maximum
height 1.50 m (4 ft 11 in)	range 322 km (200 miles)

Humber armoured cars

The Humber armoured cars were numerically the most important types produced in the UK and production eventually reached 5,400. The type had its origins in a pre-war Guy armoured car known as the **Tank, Light, Wheeled Mk I**, of which Guy produced 101 examples. By October 1940, it was realised that Guy's production facilities would be fully occupied producing light tanks and production was switched to the Rootes Group and Karrier Motors Ltd of Luton. The Guy design was rejigged for installation on a Karrier KT 4 artillery tractor chassis, Guy continuing to supply the armoured hulls and turrets. Although the new model was virtually identical to the original Guy design it was re-named the **Armoured Car, Humber Mk I**.

The Humber Mk I had a relatively short wheelbase, but it was never manoeu-

vrable and used a welded hull. The turret mounted two Besa machine-guns, a heavy 15-mm (0.59-in) and a lighter 0.31-in (7.92-mm) weapon. The first production batch ran to 500 vehicles before the **Armoured Car, Humber Mk II** introduced some improvements to the front hull, which had a pronounced slope. The **Armoured Car, Humber Mk III** had a larger turret that allowed a crew of four to be carried, while the **Armoured Car, Humber Mk IV** reverted to a crew of three as the turret housed an American 37-mm (1.45-in) gun. An odd feature of this vehicle was that the driver was provided with a lever which raised a hatch in the rear bulkhead for use as rear vision in an emergency.

North Africa
The first Humber armoured cars were used operationally in North Africa from late

1941 onwards, while the Humber Mk IV did not see service until the early stages of the Italian campaign. Thereafter all four marks were used wherever British and Allied troops fought in Europe. A version was produced in Canada with some changes to suit Canadian production methods. This was known as the **Armoured Car, General Motors Mk I, Fox I**. and the main change was that the main armament was a 0.5-in (12.7-mm) Browning heavy machine-gun plus a 0.3-in (7.62-mm) Browning medium machine-gun. There

The Humber Armoured Car Mk II was one of the few armoured vehicles to use the 15-mm (0.59-in) Besa heavy machine-gun as its main armament. Originally known as a wheeled tank, these vehicles gave sterling service in many theatres throughout the war.

was also an extensive conversion of the Humber Mk III as a special radio carrier known as a Rear Link vehicle. This had a fixed turret with a dummy gun. Another radio-carrying version was used as a mobile artillery observation post, and numbers of Canadian Foxes were converted for this role. A later addition to many Humber armoured cars was a special anti-aircraft mount-

ing using Vickers 'K' machine-guns that could be fired from within the turret. A final variant, known as the **Armoured Car, Humber, AA, Mk I**, had four 0.31-in (7.92-mm) Besa machine-guns installed in a special turret. These were introduced in 1943, but they were later withdrawn during 1944 as there was no longer any need for them.

SPECIFICATION	
Humber Mks I to IV	**Powerplant:** one Rootes 6-cylinder
Crew: 3 (4 in Mk III)	water-cooled petrol engine
Weight: (in action) 6.85 tonnes	developing 67 kW (90 bhp)
(Mk I) or 7.1 tonnes (Mks II to IV)	**Performance:** maximum speed
Dimensions: length 4.57 m (15 ft);	72 km/h (45 mph); maximum range
width 2.18 m (7 ft 2 in); height	402 km (250 miles)
2.34 m (7 ft 10 in)	

Light Armored Car M8

Armoured cars have long been a feature of the American armoured fighting vehicle scene, and in 1940 and 1941 the US Army was able to observe operational trends in Europe and so develop a new armoured car with a good performance, a 37-mm (1.46-in) gun, 6x6 drive, a low silhouette and light weight. In typical American fashion, design submissions were requested from four manufacturers. One of the manufacturers, Ford, produced a design known as the **T22**, and this was later judged to be the best of all submissions and was ordered into production as the **Light Armored Car M8**.

Superior performance

The M8 subsequently became the most important of all the American armoured cars and by the time production was terminated in April 1945 no fewer than 11,667 had been produced. It was a superb fighting vehicle with an excellent cross-country performance, and an indication of its sound design can be seen in the fact that many were still in use with several armies until the mid 1970s.

It was a low vehicle with a full 6x6 drive configuration, with the axles arranged as one forward and two to the rear. The wheels were normally well covered by mudguards, but these were sometimes removed in action. The crew of four had ample room inside the vehicle, and the main 37-mm (1.46-in) gun was mounted in a circular open turret. A 0.3-in (7.62-mm) Browning machine-gun was mounted co-axially, and there was a

The American Light Armored Car M8 was considered too light in armour by the British, but was otherwise widely used. The main gun was a 37-mm (1.46-in) gun with a 0.3-in (7.62-mm) machine-gun mounted co-axially. A common addition was a 0.5-in (12.7-mm) Browning machine-gun mounted on the turret.

Right: An M8 armoured car seen during a routine reconnaissance situation during the Normandy fighting of 1944. The crew have stopped to observe some enemy movement or positions, and two men are observing through binoculars to obtain as comprehensive an assessment as possible.

pintle for a 0.5-in (12.7-mm) Browning heavy machine-gun (for anti-aircraft use) on the turret rear.

A close cousin of the M8 was the **Armored Utility Car M20**, in which the turret was removed and the fighting compartment cut away to allow the interior to be used as a personnel or supplies carrier. A machine-gun could be mounted on a ring mount over the open area. In many ways the M20 became as important as the M8 for it proved an invaluable run-about for many purposes, from an observation post to an ammunition carrier for tank units.

Popular vehicle

The US Army employed the M8 and M20 widely from the time the first production examples left the production lines in March 1943. By November of that year over 1,000 had been delivered, and during 1943 the type was issued to British and Commonwealth formations. The British knew the M8 as the **Greyhound** but it proved to be too thinly armoured to suit British thinking, the thin belly armour proving too vulnerable to anti-tank mines. Operationally this shortcoming was overcome by lining the interior floor areas with sandbags. These drawbacks

were more than overcome by the fact that the M8 was available in large numbers and that it was able to cross almost any terrain. The 37-mm main gun was well able to tackle almost any enemy reconnaissance vehicle the M8 was likely to encounter, and the vehicle's crew could defend the M8 against infantry with the two machine-guns. The M8 could be kept going under all circumstances, but its main attribute was that it nearly always seemed to be available when it was wanted.

The M8 can still be found in service in Central and South America, most partially updated with diesel power packs and automatic transmission. A few serve as anti-tank missile carriers.

A typical M3 advances through a wrecked village in early 1945. Judging by the all-opened up state of the vehicle hatches, the crew do not seem to anticipate trouble.

SPECIFICATION	
Light Armored Car M8	82 kW (110 hp)
Crew: 4	**Performance:** maximum road
Weight: (in action) 7.94 tonnes	speed 89 km/h (55 mph); maximum
Dimensions: length 5 m (16 ft	range 563 km (350 miles)
5 in); width 2.54 m (8 ft 4 in);	**Fording:** 0.61 m (2 ft)
height 2.25 m (7 ft 4½ in)	**Gradient:** 60 per cent
Powerplant: one Hercules JXD	**Vertical obstacle:** 0.3 m (1 ft)
6-cylinder petrol engine developing	

Scout Car M3 White

The US Army employed scout cars for reconnaissance and general battlefield liaison duties as far back as 1917. In the 1930s a new 4x4 model was required, with the entrant from the White Motor Company emerging as the final choice.

The main production model was the **Scout Car M3A1** which appeared in 1939 and was manufactured in quantity for the US Army. The M3A1 was lightly armoured (up to a maximum of 12.7 mm/0.50 in) and the top was left open, other than canvas weather protection, to provide a good field of view but this exposed the occupants, up to six in the rear, to overhead fire. Underside protection was

also limited, exposing the occupants to the effects of land mines.

While the 82-kW (110-hp) or 89.5-kW (120-hp) petrol engine provided a good road speed, the cross-country performance was eventually judged as below requirements, even after a front-mounted obstacle crossing roller was added. In addition the original road range (410 km/255 miles) was regarded as too short, although measures were taken to increase this. The M3 half track series, developed from the Scout Car by adding half tracks at the rear and enlarging the rear area, therefore assumed many of the Scout Car's intended tasks in US service.

Varied weapon fits

A total of 20,918 Scout Cars were produced, many handed out as 'Lend-Lease' on a generous scale to Allied armed forces, including the USSR where a post-war copy, the BTR-40, was produced in quantity. The usual armament, if carried, was limited to one or two machine-guns and the crew's personal weapons, although some other weapon fits were proposed. Attempts

The Scout Car M3A1, which first appeared in 1939, was produced for the US Army. It was lightly armoured and had a good road speed performance.

to convert the vehicle into a light tank destroyer with a 37-mm (1.46-in) anti-tank gun came to nothing. Some Scout Cars were employed as light weapon tractors, while others served as light front-line supply carriers, forward area ambulances, or communication and command vehicles.

After 1945 surviving Scout Cars were distributed worldwide where their employment extended to police and other internal security forces. They may still be encountered in Central and South America although many have now been provided with diesel engines.

SPECIFICATION

M3A1 Scout Car
Crew: up to 8
Weight: (in action) 5.92 tonnes
Dimensions: length 5.63 m (18 ft 5 in); width 2.03 m (6 ft 8 in); height 1.99 m (6 ft 5 in)
Powerplant: one 89.5-kW (120-hp)

Hercules JXD petrol engine
Performance: maximum speed 90 km/h (56 mph); maximum range 410 km (255 miles)
Fording: 0.71 m (2 ft 4 in)
Gradient: 60 per cent
Vertical obstacle: 0.31 m (1 ft)

Light Armored Car T17E1 Staghound

A Staghound AA armoured car with twin 0.5-in (12.7-mm) machine-guns intended specifically for the defence of armoured units against low-flying aircraft.

Although the **Staghound** armoured car was an American product, it was not used by the American forces, all output going to the British Army and other Allied and Commonwealth forces. The design had its origins in a US Army requirement for a heavy armoured car, the **T17E1**. The British Tank Mission asked for an initial batch of 300, more orders followed and by the end of 1942 the first examples were coming off the production lines to be issued to British and Commonwealth units as the **Staghound Mk I**.

Sturdy vehicle

It emerged as a large and well-armoured vehicle with a turret mounting a 37-mm (1.46-in) gun and a co-axial 0.3-in (7.62-mm) Browning machine-gun. The type first went into action in Italy in 1943 and was then issued to

Canadian, New Zealand, Indian and Belgian units. The Staghound had several unusual features such as a fully automatic hydraulic

transmission, two engines mounted side-by-side at the rear, and the crew were provided with periscopes. The turret was hydraulically traversed, with additional armament provided by two more 0.3-in (7.62-mm) Browning machine-guns, one pintle-mounted for anti-aircraft use and the other in the hull front.

Once in service several variations appeared. One was the fitting of a 3-in (76.2-mm) close-support

The T17E1 Staghound was a reliable and sturdy vehicle with a 37-mm (1.46-in) main gun and was unusual in being powered by two petrol engines.

howitzer in place of the 37-mm (1.46-in) gun. The **Staghound Mk III** accommodated a Crusader tank turret mounting a 75-mm (2.95-in) gun.

American version

A production variant developed in the US was the **Staghound AA** (**T17E2**) with a power-operated turret mounting two 0.5-in

(12.7-mm) Browning machine guns for anti-aircraft use. There were numerous other conversions and local variations of the Staghound, ranging from mine-clearing experimental models pushing heavy rollers to the **Staghound Command**. The Staghound was a sturdy and well-liked armoured car that gave excellent service.

SPECIFICATION

Staghound Mk I
Crew: 5
Weight: (in action) 13.92 tonnes
Dimensions: length 5.49 m (18 ft); width 2.69 m (8 ft 10 in); height 2.36 m (7 ft 9 in)
Powerplant: two 72-kW (97-hp)

GMC 270 6-cylinder petrol engines
Performance: maximum speed 89 km/h (55 mph); maximum range 724 km (450 miles)
Fording: 0.8 m (2 ft 8 in)
Gradient: 57 per cent
Vertical obstacle: 0.53 m (1 ft 9 in)

T-10 Heavy tank

A T-10 heavy tank showing the 12.7-mm DShKM anti-aircraft machine-gun on the commander's cupola. Developed from 1948, the first prototypes of the T-10 (initially IS-10) appeared in 1955. Although manufacture ended in 1966, the last examples of the T-10 were not retired from the reserve until 1996.

During the later stages of World War II the USSR developed the IS series of excellently protected heavy tanks armed with a very potent 122-mm (4.8-in) gun firing separate-loading ammunition. After the war this basic type saw service in the Middle East with Egypt, and some captured by Israel in the Six-Day War of 1967 were then used for static defence on the Suez Canal against their former operators.

Prototypes

In the immediate post-war period the USSR continued its development of heavy tanks, and prototype vehicles included the IS-5 to **IS-9**. The last was accepted for service as the **T-10**, an improved model being the **T-10A**, with two-axis gun stabilisation. The following **T-10B** version introduced in 1957 had improved sighting and gun stabilisation. It is believed that at least 2,500 tanks of all models were built before production was completed in the late 1950s. The T-10 was never exported. The main role of the T-10 was the provision of long-range fire support for the T-54/55 tanks armed with a 100-mm (3.94-in) gun, and also perhaps to act as the spearhead of any armoured thrust through areas with a high degree of anti-tank defences, where the T-10's heavy armour protection would have proved useful.

The T-10's hull was of rolled steel armour varying in thickness between 20 and 230 mm (0.79 to 9.06 in). The turret was a cast unit varying in thickness between 25 and 250 mm (1 and 9.84 in), the latter figure applying specifically to the mantlet. The

driver was seated at the front of the hull with the other three crewmembers in the turret: the commander and gunner on the left, and the loader on the right. The powerplant was located at the rear of the hull.

Main armament

Comprising a D-25TA 122-mm gun with a double-baffle muzzle brake and a bore evacuator, the main armament fired separate-loading ammunition of the APC-T, HEAT and HE fragmentation types: the APC-T type was the primary anti-tank round, and was capable of penetrating 185 mm (7.28 in) of armour at 1000 m (1,095 yards). Separate-loading ammunition had to be used as otherwise the complete round would have been too heavy and difficult for handling in the cramped confines of the turret, and 30 122-mm rounds were carried. A 12.7-mm (0.5-in) DShKM machine-gun was mounted co-axial with the main armament, and a similar weapon was mounted on the loader's cupola for anti-aircraft defence.

Alterations

The later **T-10M** was characterised by the following recognisable alterations: the 12.7-mm DShKM machine-guns were replaced by weapons of the more powerful 14.5-mm (0.57-in) KPV series also used in a number

of other Soviet AFVs including the BRDM-2 4x4 wheeled reconnaissance vehicle and the BTR-60PB 8x8 wheeled armoured personnel carrier; the new M-62-T2 122-mm gun was fitted with a multi-baffle muzzle brake in place of the double-baffle muzzle brake; the main armament was stabilised in both the horizontal and vertical planes; IR night vision equipment and an overpressure NBC system were installed; and finally a large sheet-metal stowage box was often mounted externally at the turret rear.

The T-10M heavy tank had the original 12.7-mm machine-guns replaced by 14.5-mm KPVs, and had a multi-baffle muzzle brake for the 122-mm gun, infra-red night vision equipment for the commander, gunner and driver, and an overpressure system.

SPECIFICATION	
T-10	
Crew: 4	**DShKM machine-guns**
Weight: 50 tonnes	**Powerplant:** one V-12 diesel developing 522 kW (700 hp)
Dimensions: length (including gun) 9.88 m (32 ft 4¾ in); length (hull) 7.04 m (23 ft 1 in); width 3.57 m (11 ft 8½ in); height 2.25 m (7 ft 4½ in)	**Performance:** maximum road speed 42 km/h (26 mph); maximum road range 250 km (155 miles)
	Gradient: 62 per cent
Armament: one 122-mm (4.8-in) main gun, and two 12.7-mm (0.5-in)	**Vertical obstacle:** 0.9 m (2 ft 11½ in)
	Trench: 3 m (9 ft 10 in)

T-54 Main battle tank

The T-54 tank was developed in the late 1940s and was probably produced in greater numbers than any other Soviet tank in the post-war period. It has seen combat in countless campaigns since World War II, especially in the Middle East, where it has been used by the Arab states against Israel.

A Chinese T-54 with turret traversed to the rear, and the loader manning the 12.7-mm DShKM anti-aircraft machine-gun. The tank can also lay its own smoke screen by injecting diesel fuel into the exhaust outlet.

SPECIFICATION	
T-54	12.7-mm (0.5-in) machine-gun
Crew: 4	**Powerplant:** V-12 diesel
Weight: 36 tonnes	developing 388 kW (520 hp)
Dimensions: length (with gun	**Performance:** maximum road
forward) 9 m (29 ft 6½ in); length	speed 48 km/h (30 mph); maximum
(hull) 6.45 m (21 ft 2 in); width	range 400 km (249 miles)
3.27 m (10 ft 8¾ in); height (turret	**Fording:** 1.4 m (4 ft 7 in)
roof) 2.4 m (7 ft 10½ in)	**Gradient:** 60 per cent
Armament: one 100-mm (3.94-in)	**Vertical obstacle:** 0.8 m (2 ft
D-10 main gun, two 7.62-mm	7½ in)
(0.3-in) machine-guns, and one	**Trench:** 2.7 m (8 ft 10¼ in)

In 1946 prototypes of the new **T-54** design were completed, and this type entered production several years later. The T-54 and its variants were built in larger numbers than any other Soviet and/or Russian tank to appear after World War II, and by the time production of the improved T-55 was completed in 1980-81 it is estimated that production amounted to well over 50,000 vehicles, of which large numbers are still in service. The series was also built in Czechoslovakia and Poland for the home and export markets, while the Chinese produced an almost identical Type 59 version.

The T-54 has an all-welded hull divided into forward driving, central fighting and rear powerplant compartments. The driver is seated at the front of the hull, and an

unusual feature of the T-54 is its 7.62-mm (0.3-in) machine-gun fixed in the centre of the glacis plate to fire forward when the driver presses a button on his right steering lever. The commander and gunner are seated on the left of the turret, with the loader on the right. The turret is a casting with the top welded into position. One of the major weaknesses of the T-54 series has been its engine and transmission, which have proved very unreliable in service.

D-10 main gun

The main armament is a 100-mm (3.94-in) D-10 rifled gun, and a well-trained crew can fire about four rounds per minute: 34 rounds are carried, and the ammunition types are AP-T, APC-T, HE, HE-FRAG, HEAT-FS and

HVAPDS-T. The last was introduced some time after the T-54 entered production and will penetrate well over 200 mm (7.9 in) of armour at 1000 m (1,095 yards). One of the T-54's major drawbacks is that the main gun can be depressed to only -5°, which makes the adoption of a hull-down firing position almost impossible. The secondary armament is a 7.62-mm (0.3-in) SGMT co-axial machine-gun, a similar weapon in the bow, and a 12.7-mm (0.5-in) DShKM anti-aircraft machine-gun on the loader's hatch. The tank does not have smoke dischargers as it can lay its own smoke screen by injecting diesel fuel into the exhaust on the left side of the hull just above the track.

The later **T-54A** added stabilisation of the 100-mm gun

in the vertical plane. The **T-54B** was the first production model to incorporate IR night vision equipment and two-axis stabilisation for the main gun. The **T-54C** was not fitted with the AA machine-gun although such a weapon was later retrofitted. There has been a very large number of T-54 series variants, these including a flamethrower tank, armoured recovery vehicles (including Soviet, Polish and Czechoslovakian versions), bridgelayers (built by Czechoslovakia, East Germany and the USSR), dozer tanks, a combat engineer vehicle fitted with a hydraulic crane and front-mounted dozer blade, and mineclearing vehicles fitted with rollers, ploughs and

rocket-assisted devices, to name but a few. In recent years surviving tanks have been taken in hand for a number of upgrade programmes including the installation of improved fire-control systems, including an externally mounted laser rangefinder.

The T-54 has seen extensive combat in the Middle East, North Africa, Angola and the Far East. On a one-for-one basis Western tanks of the same period, such as the British Centurion and American M48, have proved more than a match for the T-54, especially during the fighting between Israel and its Arab neighbours, Egypt and Syria.

T-55 Main battle tank

Production of the T-55 at the Omsk plant is believed to have continued until 1980-81, long after production of the far more capable T-62 had ceased. With the downsizing of East European armies in the wake of post-Cold War treaties, large numbers of T-55s have been exported in recent years.

The T-54 inevitably underwent a number of improvements including, on later models, an NBC system and provision for a deep-wading snorkel. Later examples introduced what became the standard turret without a bulged rear, and the right-hand cupola had a 12.7-mm (0.5-in) machine-gun. Most of the tanks were later improved to T-54(M) standard with IR driving equipment. The T-54A introduced improved main armament in the form of the D-10TG gun with a bore evacuator, stabilisation in the vertical plane and powered elevation; when retrofitted with IR driving lights it is designated as the T-54A(M). In 1957 the Soviets introduced the T-54B and, apart from being the first model produced with IR night-vision devices as standard, it has the D-10T2S main gun with two-axis stabilisation. Variously described as the

T-54C or T-54X, the next model is identical with the T-54B except that the gunner's cupola is replaced by a plain forward-opening hatch.

Revised T-54

These collective modifications resulted in a basically similar tank with the revised designation **T-55**, which was introduced in the late 1950s with standard features such as no loader's cupola with its 12.7-mm AA machine-gun, no turret dome ventilator, a 432-kW (580-hp) V-55 diesel engine with 960 rather than 812 litres (211 rather than 179 Imp gal) of internal fuel for a range of

500 rather than 400 km (311 rather than 249 miles), and 37 rounds of ammunition for the D-10T2S gun. The 12.7-mm has been reinstalled on some tanks which are then designated **T-55(M)**. Seen for the first time in 1963, the **T-55A** is the final production version, and is similar to the T-55 apart from having a 7.62-mm (0.3-in) PKT co-axial machine-gun in place of the original SGMT, no nose machine-gun to allow an increase in main ammunition stowage to 43 rounds, and a number of detail improvements such as an anti-radiation lining. When

fitted with the AA machine-gun this model is the **T-55A(M)**. The T-55 is still in widespread service in a

number of upgraded forms, and is also the basis of numerous special-purpose variants.

SPECIFICATION	
T-55	developing 432 kW (580 hp)
Crew: 4	**Performance:** maximum road
Weight: 36 tonnes	speed 50 km/h (31 mph); maximum
Dimensions: length (with gun	road range 500 km (311 miles) on
forward) 9 m (29 ft 6 in); length	internal fuel and 600 km
(hull) 6.45 m (21 ft 2 in); width	(373 miles) with external fuel
3.27 m (10 ft 8 in); height (to turret	**Fording:** 1.4 m (4 ft 7 in) without
top) 2.4 m (7 ft 10 in)	preparation and 4.55 m (14 ft 11 in)
Armament: one 100-mm (3.94-in)	with snorkel
D-10T2S main gun, one 7.62-mm	**Gradient:** 58 per cent
(0.3-in) co-axial machine-gun	**Vertical obstacle:** 0.8 m (2 ft 6 in)
Powerplant: one V-55 liquid-	**Trench:** 2.7 m (8 ft 10 in)
cooled V-12 diesel engine	

137

T-62 Main battle tank

The **T-62** is a development of the T-54/55 series with a slightly longer hull to accommodate a turret armed with a 115-mm (4.53-in) smoothbore gun. Production began in 1962 and continued to 1975, ending after the completion of some 20,000 tanks. The type was also made in Czechoslovakia, mainly for the export market, and in North Korea. The T-62 was more expensive to produce than the earlier T-54 and T-55 series, and for this reason the T-55 remained in production for some years after the more modern T-62 had been phased out of production.

The U-5TS main gun is fitted with a bore evacuator and is stabilised in elevation and traverse. An unusual feature of the T-62 is that it has an integral shell case ejection system, which is activated by the recoil of the gun. This system ejects the spent case through a trapdoor in the turret rear, but reduces the rate of fire to about four rounds per minute as the gun has to elevate to +3½° for the ejection cycle to be carried out.

Three rounds

Three main types of ammunition are fired by the U-5TS (otherwise 2A20) gun, namely HE-FRAG-FS (High Explosive Fragmentation Fin-Stabilised) with a muzzle velocity of 750 m (2,460 ft) per second, HEAT-FS (High Explosive Anti-Tank Fin-Stabilised) with a muzzle velocity of 900 m (2,955 ft) per second and capable of penetrating over 430 mm (16.9 in) of armour, and APFSDS (Armour-Piercing Fin-Stabilised Discarding-Sabot) with a muzzle velocity of 1680 m (5,510 ft) per second, a very flat trajectory and the ability to penetrate 330 mm (13 in) of armour at a range of 1000 m (1,095 yards). Some 40 rounds of 115-mm ammunition are carried, of which four are ready rounds in the turret; of the 36 other

rounds, 16 are to the right of the driver and 20 in the rear of the fighting compartment. A 7.62-mm (0.3-in) PKT machine-gun is mounted co-axial with the main armament, and 2,500 rounds are carried for this weapon.

Modern equipment

Standard equipment on all T-62 tanks includes IR night-vision equipment for the commander, gunner and driver; an unditching beam carried at the rear of the hull; a turret ventilation system to remove fumes when the gun is fired; a nuclear collective protection system; and provision for fuel to be injected into the diesel engine's exhaust to provide a smoke screen. The vehicle carries 675 litres (148.5 Imp gal) of fuel internally, with a further 285 litres (63 Imp gal) externally on the running boards, and this gives the T-62 a road range of 450 km (280 miles). A further two 200-litre (44-Imp gal) fuel drums can be fitted on the hull rear, increasing the road range to some 650 km (404 miles). All T-62s can ford rivers to a depth of 5.5 m (18 ft 0.5 in) with the aid of a snorkel erected over the loader's hatch. A centralised fire-extinguisher system is provided for the engine and fighting compartments, and this can be operated automatically or manually by the commander or driver.

Variants

The extent of the T-62's production meant that several variants were produced. Bearing the standard T-62 designation are the **Model 1962** of 1962 with detail enhancements, the **Model 1972** with a 12.7-mm (0.5-in) DShKM AA machine-gun over the loader's position, and the **Model 1975** with a laser rangefinder over the main gun. The **T-72D** has the Drozd anti-tank missile defence system, passive armour protection and the

The upper and lower angled parts of the nose are of well-sloped 102 mm (4 in) armour, while the front of the turret is 242 mm (9.53 in) thick.

V-55U engine, while the **T-72D-1** differs in its V-46-5M engine, while the **T-62M** and **T-62M-1** are equivalent to the T-62D and T-62D-1 but with the Sheksna (AT-10) system that fires a laser beam-riding anti-tank missile from the main gun. The **T-62M1** and **T-62M1-1** are upgrades without the passive armour and Sheksna system, the **T-62M1-2** and **T-62M1-2-1** are upgrades without the Sheksna system and with passive armour protection only for the belly and turret, and the **T-62MV** and **T-62MV-1** are upgrades with the Sheksna system and explosive reactive armour. The only other main variant is the **T-72K** command tank. The series is still in widespread and large-scale service.

Seen above the rear of the hull of this T-62 tank, embarked on a heavy-duty road transporter, are the side-by-side pair of jettisonable drum tanks whose fuel contents can add considerably to the tank's range.

The U-5TS main gun of the T-62 has an elevation arc of 22° (-6° to +16°). The angle to which the gun can be depressed is slightly more than that of the T-54 and T-55 series, offering a slight improvement in the later tank's ability to adopt a hull-down firing position.

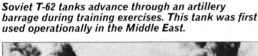

Soviet T-62 tanks advance through an artillery barrage during training exercises. This tank was first used operationally in the Middle East.

SPECIFICATION	
T-62	**Powerplant:** one V-12 diesel developing 433 kW (580 hp)
Crew: 4	
Weight: 40 tonnes	**Performance:** maximum road speed 50 km (31 mph); maximum road range 650 km (404 miles); gradient 60 per cent; vertical obstacle 0.80 m (2 ft 7½ in); trench 2.85 m (9 ft 4¼ in)
Dimensions: length (with gun forward) 9.34 m (30 ft 7½ in); length (hull) 6.63 m (21 ft 9 in); width 3.30 m (10 ft 10 in); height 2.40 m (7 ft 10¼ in)	

T-64 Main battle tank

The T-72 was schemed as a potent MBT with, in its definitive form, a gun able to fire a special anti-tank missile as well as conventional ammunition. The Soviets seem to have bitten off more than they could chew, however, as the T-72 was not a technical success.

In the 1960s the Soviets built prototypes of a new MBT which, in the absence of any information about its real designation, became known in the West as the M-1970. This vehicle had a new suspension consisting of six small dual road wheels with the drive sprocket at the rear, idler at the front and four track-return rollers supporting the inside of the track only. All previous MBTs designed in the USSR since World War II, namely the T-54, T-55 and T-62, had been characterised by larger road wheels with no return rollers. The turret of the M-1970 was similar to that of the T-62 and was armed with the same 115-mm (4.53-in) smooth-bore gun.

Enter the T-64

Further development of the M-1970 resulted in the **T-64** MBT, which was placed in production at one tank plant in the USSR. The first production vehicles were completed with the 115-mm (4.53-in) D-68 (otherwise 2A21) smooth-bore gun with two-axis stabilisation and an automatic loader for 30 rounds, with another 10 rounds carried for partial reloading. So far the T-64 has not been identified as being in service with any country other than the USSR, and of course the nations into which the USSR split during the emergence of the CIS, whereas the later T-72 has been exported on a wide scale, both within the Warsaw Pact and overseas. Some reports have stated that the T-64 was so poor a design and so plagued with mechanical troubles that it was in production only to 1969, although in that time as many as 8,000 were built. Another theory is that the T-64 had advanced armour (including pockets of ceramic) for its time, and was therefore reserved for Soviet units.

The layout of the T-64 is similar to that of the T-72, with the driver's compartment at the front, turret in the centre and powerplant at

the rear. The driver is seated in the centre with a well-shaped glacis plate (probably of laminate armour) to his front. A V-type splashboard on the glacis plate stops water rushing up when the vehicle is fording a deep stream. When driving in the head-out position, the driver can quickly erect a cover over his position to protect himself against rain and snow. The turret is similar in design to that of the T-72, but is thought not to incorporate advanced armour, and carries the gunner and commander on the left and right.

The first definitive variant to reach units, after some 600 examples of the T-64, was the **T-64A**. This differs from its predecessor mainly in its armament, which is centred on the 125-mm (4.92-in) 2A26M2 smooth-bore gun, fitted with a thermal sleeve, and again fully stabilised and supplied with ammunition by a modified automatic loader. Other elements of the armament include a 7.62-mm (0.3-in) PKT co-axial machine-gun with 1,250 rounds, and a 12.7-mm (0.5-in) NSVT anti-

aircraft machine gun on the commander's cupola with 300 rounds, with provision for this weapon to be operated from within the closed-down turret. A more advanced fire-control system was also incorporated, as was a bank of smoke grenade launchers on each side of the turret, and other changes included increased turret protection, a new fire detection and suppression system, a multi-fuel diesel engine, a dozer blade under the nose, and fittings for a mine-clearing system. The T-64 series has an NBC system, a full range of night-vision equipment and, like most other Soviet MBTs, provision for a snorkel to provide deep-wading capability. The only known variant of the T-64A is the T-64AK command vehicle, which carries an additional radio set and, in place of the AA machine-gun, a telescopic mast 10 m (32 ft 10 in) tall. When raised over the turret, this mast is held in position by stays pegged to the ground, a fact that prevents the tank from moving off quickly.

The T-64 has been seen in service only with the USSR and its successors, and by all accounts has been unsuccessful and replaced by the better T-72.

SPECIFICATION	
T-64B	skirts) 4.64 m (15 ft 3 in); height
Crew: 3	2.20 m (7 ft 3 in)
Weight: 39.5 tonnes	**Performance:** maximum road
Powerplant: one 5DTF water-cooled 5-cylinder diesel engine developing 522 kW (700 hp)	speed 75 km/h (47 mph); maximum road range 550 km (342 miles); fording 1.80 m (5 ft 11 in) without
Dimensions: length (with gun forward) 9.90 m (32 ft 6 in); length (hull) 7.40 m (24 ft 3 in); width (with	preparation; gradient 60 per cent; vertical obstacle 0.80 m (2 ft 7 in); trench 2.28 m (7 ft 6 in)

The next T-64 variant to appear was the **T-64B**, created as a major reworking of the T-64A with new hull and turret armour less bulky than the first-generation laminate armour used in the earlier variants. Other changes included provision for the gun to fire the Kobra (NATO AT-8 'Songster') anti-tank missile (a radio command-guided weapon of which six are carried in the automatic loader in addition to 36 conventional rounds of ammunition), a new fire-control system including a laser rangefinder, a napalm-resistant defence system, provision for the attachment of explosive reactive armour to create the **T-64BV** variant, a system to fire smoke grenades, quick-disconnect units for the gun's barrel and breech, side skirts to protect the running

gear against the effects of HEAT warheads, and greater travel in the suspension. Other T-64B variants include the **T-64BK** command tank, **T-64BM** with the 745-kW (999-hp) 6TD six-cylinder diesel engine, **T-64B1** without Kobra missile capability, **T-64B1K** command tank version of the **T-64B1**, **T-64BV1K** command tank with explosive reactive armour, and **T-64R** rebuild of the T-64 to virtual T-64B standard. The Ukraine is planning to upgrade some of its older T-64B and T-64B1 tanks to a virtual T-80UD/T-80 standard under the designation **T-64U**, and CIS armies also operate the BREM-64 armoured recovery version of the T-64 with a front-mounted dozer/anchor blade, winches and a crane on the left-hand side of the hull.

Centurion MBT

The **Centurion** was developed during World War II as a cruiser tank under the designation **A41**, the first prototypes armed with a 17-pounder, (76.2-mm/3-in) gun being completed early in 1945. The A41 was subsequently renamed Centurion and entered production shortly after the end of the war. By the time production was completed in 1962, some 4,423 examples had been completed at the Royal Ordnance Factories at Leeds and Woolwich (early vehicles only), Leyland Motors at Leyland and Vickers at Elswick.

Upgunned Centurions
The **Centurion Mk 1** and **Mk 2** were armed with the wartime 17-pdr gun, while the **Mk 3** carried a new 20-pounder (83.4-mm/ (3.28-in)) weapon. A total of 13 basic marks of Centurion was fielded, some having up to three sub-variants. For example, the **Centurion Mk 10** was a **Mk 8** with more armour and a 105-mm L7 gun, the **Centurion Mk 10/2** was a Mk 10 with a ranging machine-gun.

All through its British army life the Centurion had the standard Rolls-Royce Meteor petrol engine, which was a development of the Merlin aero engine. The Centurion was replaced as a gun tank in the British army by the Chieftain, but the last Centurions, used as observation post vehicles by the Royal Artillery, were not phased out of service until the 1980s.

Exported vehicles
Many countries placed orders for the Centurion, including Denmark, Israel, Jordan, the Netherlands, Somalia, South Africa, Sweden and Switzerland. Many of these countries rebuilt the vehicle to extend its life well into the 1990s. For example, Israel replaced the petrol engine with a Teledyne Continental AVDS-1790-2A diesel coupled to an Allison CD-850-6 automatic transmission, giving the tank a maximum speed of 43 km/h (27 mph) and a cruising range twice that of the **Mk 5** hull on which the conversion was based. The Israeli Centurions, which when rebuilt were redesignated **Upgraded Centurion**, all had the 105-mm gun and carried additional ammunition.

Specialised variants
There have been many specialised versions, including a variety of self-propelled artillery variously carrying the 25-pounder, 5-in (127-mm) and 180-mm guns, and a 120-mm tank destroyer.

The last variants in service with the British army Versions that remain in service included the **Centurion Mk 2 ARV** (Armoured Recovery Vehicle) fitted with large spades at the hull rear and a winch with a capacity of 31 tonnes. The **Centurion/AVRE** (Assault Vehicle Royal Engineers) was fitted with a turret-mounted 165-mm demolition gun for the destruction of battlefield fortifications, and a dozer blade at the front of the hull. It could also carry a fascine (large bundle of wood) which were dropped into anti-tank ditches to enable following vehicles to cross, as well as tow a trailer carrying the ROF Giant Viper mine-clearance equipment.

The **Centurion BARV** (Beach Armoured Recovery Vehicle) served into the 1990s. The BARV was successfully used during the British landings in the Falklands. Other versions include the **Centurion AVLB** (Armoured Vehicle-launched Bridge) and target tanks, while the Israelis fitted a number of vehicles with special dozer blades and roller-type mine-clearing equipment.

The reason why the

Australian Centurions saw extensive combat in Vietnam, fighting a number of epic battles in the defence of firebases. Their 20-pdr main guns were lethal against the unprotected Viet Cong, especially when firing 'Beehive' anti-personnel rounds.

Centurion battle tank has been such a successful design is that it has been able to accept more armour, larger guns, gun-stabilisation systems, advanced fire-control systems and laser rangefinders.

The Centurion, one of the most successful battle tanks in history, saw combat with the British Army in Korea, with the Australian army in Vietnam, with the Indian army against Pakistan and with the armies of Israel, Egypt and Jordan in the Middle East.

SPECIFICATION	
Centurion	3.39 m (11 ft 1½ in); height (without
Crew: 4	AA MG) 3.01 m (9 ft 10½ in)
Weight: 51.82 tonnes	**Performance:** maximum speed on
Engine: one Rolls-Royce Meteor	the road 34.6 km/h (21.5 mph);
Mk II V-12 petrol developing	range 190 km (118 miles)
485 kW (650 bhp)	**Gradient:** 60 per cent
Dimensions: length (with guns	**Vertical obstacle:** 0.91 m (3 ft)
forward) 9.85 m (32 ft 4 in); length	**Trench:** 3.35 m (11 ft)
(hull) 7.82 m (25 ft 8 in); width	

Conqueror Heavy tank

This Conqueror heavy tank clearly shows its 120-mm gun that fired separate loading ammunition, and the commander's cupola, which was fitted with a rangefinder and a 7.62-mm (0.3-in) anti-aircraft machine-gun.

In 1944 authorisation was given to commence the **A45** heavy tank project as the replacement for the A43 Black Prince, which itself was based on the Churchill infantry support tank. The **A45** was intended to work with the A41 Centurion tank and shared a number of common components.

Universal tank family
In 1946 however, it was decided to develop a whole new range of armoured vehicles including the **FV200 Universal Tank** family, and in addition to the **FV201** basic gun tank, a number of specialised vehicles were proposed, including an AVRE, mine-clearing vehicle of the flail type, bridgelayer, ARV, assault personnel carrier, and a number of specialised vehicles for the Royal Artillery. The FV200 series was based on the A45 but had a longer hull, and the first prototype was completed in 1948. It was soon realised that many of the proposed variants were not feasible: the bridgelayer, for example, would be too large for the Royal Navy's standard tank landing craft. A decision was therefore taken to continue development of the Centurion as a gun tank and as the basis for a complete family of specialised vehicles. The Centurion family became the most successful British tank of the post-war period.

There was, however, a requirement for a heavy gun tank, the **FV214**, and the FV201 was used as the basis for this vehicle. To provide some experience with a tank of this size, a chassis was fitted with the complete turret of the Centurion Mk 3 tank and called the **FV221**

Medium Gun Tank Caernarvon.

Just under 200 **FV214 Conqueror** tanks were built between 1955 and 1958, the majority of these being deployed to the British Army of the Rhine, where they were issued to some of the armoured regiments on the basis of a troop of three vehicles per regiment, or one Conqueror per Centurion squadron. The only advantage of the Conqueror over the Centurion with the 20-pounder gun, was the former's much thicker armour protection and the longer range of its main armament.

Its major disadvantages were that it was too large, too heavy and was difficult to maintain. The Conquerors were all withdrawn in the mid-1960s with the arrival of the Centurion with the 105-mm gun, and most ended up on ranges as hard targets, although one or two have been preserved.

In all there were over 30 projected models on the FV200 chassis, but the only model to see service apart from the Conqueror tank was the **FV219 ARV Mk 1**. One of the more interesting projects was the **FV215b** heavy self-propelled anti-tank gun which had the engine moved forward to enable a limited-traverse turret (armed with a 180-mm gun) to be mounted at the rear.

Conventional layout
The layout of the Conqueror was conventional, with the driver at the front on the right and ammunition to his left; turret and fighting compartment in the centre, and engine and transmission at the rear. The commander was provided with his own cupola in the centre of the turret at the rear, with the gunner forward to the right and the loader to the left.

Main armament comprised a 120-mm rifled gun with an elevation of +15° and a depression of -7° in a turret capable of traversing through 360°. A weapon stabilisation system was installed, this being similar to that of the Centurion. A total of 35 rounds of APDS or HESH ammunition was carried, this being of the separate loading type. An unusual feature of the Conqueror was the cartridge case ejection system: this ejected the spent brass cartridge case out through a trap door on the right side of the turret. A 0.3-in (7.62-mm) machine-gun was mounted co-axially with the main armament, and a similar machine-gun was mounted on the commander's cupola for anti-aircraft defence.

<table>
<tr><td colspan="2" align="center">SPECIFICATION</td></tr>
<tr><td>Conqueror</td><td>(810 bhp)</td></tr>
<tr><td>Crew: 4</td><td>Performance: maximum road</td></tr>
<tr><td>Weight: 65 tonnes</td><td>speed 34 km/h (21.3 mph);</td></tr>
<tr><td>Dimensions: length (gun forwards)</td><td>maximum road range 155 km</td></tr>
<tr><td>11.58 m (38 ft); length (hull) 7.72 m</td><td>(95 miles)</td></tr>
<tr><td>(25 ft 4 in); width 3.99 m (13 ft</td><td>Gradient: 60 per cent</td></tr>
<tr><td>1 in); height 3.35 m (11 ft)</td><td>Vertical obstacle: 0.91 m (36 m)</td></tr>
<tr><td>Powerplant: one 12-cylinder</td><td>Trench: 3.35 m (11 ft)</td></tr>
<tr><td>petrol engine developing 604 kW</td><td></td></tr>
</table>

Vickers MBT

Vickers' Elswick facility built many of the 4,423 Centurion MBTs manufactured by 1961, but the company realised that for some operators the Centurion's successor, the Chieftain, would be too heavy and too expensive. At about that time, the Indian army issued a requirement for a new MBT, and in 1961 a Vickers proposal was accepted.

This was based on the company's private venture design which had become known as the **Vickers Main Battle Tank**. This used the proven 105-mm L7 series gun as well as some of the components from the Chieftain MBT, which was then about to enter production at both Royal Ordnance Factory in Leeds and Vickers' Elswick facility. This included the 0.5-in (12.7-mm) ranging machine-gun, Leyland L60 engine, TN12 transmission, brakes and steering.

Indian production
The first two prototypes were completed in 1963 and by the following year a production line had been established at the Avandi Company, Madras, India. Renamed **Vijayanta** (Victorious), the first tank was completed in 1965 from components supplied by Vickers. Over 2,200 Vijayantas were produced. In 1968, Kuwait ordered 70 **Vickers MBT Mk 1** tanks which were delivered between 1970 and 1972. Vickers continued development of the tank with its own funds, the first stage being the replacement of the L60 engine with a Detroit Diesel 537-kW (720-bhp) engine, followed by a new all-cast turret with a welded bustle which could be fitted with different types of fire-control system.

African orders
In 1977 Kenya ordered 38 **Vickers MBT Mk 3** MBTs plus three **Vickers ARV** armoured recovery vehicles; these were delivered by 1980, and a second order was placed in 1978 for a further 38 MBTs plus four ARVs, all these being delivered by late 1982.

In 1981 Nigeria ordered 36 MBTs plus five ARVs and six **Vickers VAB** bridge-layers. In 1990, Vickers received another order from Nigeria; completing deliveries in 1991.These tanks were built at Vickers Defence Systems Armstrong Works, which opened in late 1982. The famous Elswick works, which produced armoured fighting vehicles

This Vickers MBT Mk 3 belongs to the Kenyan army, which took delivery of 76 tanks, plus seven armoured recovery vehicles between 1979 and 1982. The Mk 3 is powered by the Detroit Diesel engine.

and artillery pieces for some 100 years, had since been closed down and demolished.

Mk 3 turret
The Mk 3 is also armed with the 105-mm gun mounted in a turret which can be traversed through 360° and provides the gun with an elevation of +20° and depression of -10°. The gun can fire the full range of ammunition including armour piercing discarding sabot shells, along with traditional high-explosive rounds. A 0.3-in (7.62-mm) machine-gun is mounted co-axially with the main armament and a similar weapon is mounted on the commander's cupola. The latter can be aimed and fired from within the turret and can be elevated to +90°. A bank of six electrically-operated smoke dischargers is mounted on each side of the turret.

The Nigerian tanks are fitted with the Marconi Radar SFCS-600 (Simplified Fire Control System) which gives a high probability of a first-round hit. This system was fitted to some of the Indian MBT Mk 1s. The commander has a Pilkington PE Condor day/night sight enabling him to lay and fire the main armament.

As usual a whole range of optional equipment can be fitted to the Vickers MBT Mk 3 according to requirements. This includes a computerised fire-control system, laser-range finder, Nuclear-Biological-Chemical protection, deep wading/flotation system, fire extinguishing system, and explosive-reactive armour.

The **Vickers Armoured Bridgelaying Vehicle** (**VABV**) is fitted with a bridge 44 ft (13.41 m) long, which is launched hydraulically over the front of the vehicle. The **Vickers Armoured Repair and Recovery Vehicle** (**ARRV**) is provided with a front mounted dozer/ stabilising blade and a winch with a maximum capacity of 25 tonnes, which can be increased to 65 tonnes if required. Some vehicles have a hydraulic crane to enable them to change powerpacks (engine and transmission) in the field.

Artillery version
Vickers Shipbuilding and Engineering Ltd also produced a self-propelled gun variant. The MBT Mk 3 can also be fitted with a with a 155-mm howitzer turret which fires HE rounds to a range of 24000 m (26,250 yards), or 30000 m (32,800 yards) with a rocket-assisted projectile (RAP).

Vickers MBT Mk 1 with its turret traversed to the right and firing its 105-mm L7 rifled gun during a demonstration at the Royal Armoured Corps gunnery range at Lulworth. The Mk 1 is in service with Kuwait and India, the Indian vehicles having been upgraded with the Detroit Diesel engine and new armour.

<table>
<tr><td colspan="2" align="center">SPECIFICATION</td></tr>
<tr><td>Vickers MBT</td><td>3.17 m (10 ft 4¾ in); height (overall)</td></tr>
<tr><td>Crew: 4</td><td>3.10 m (10 ft 2 in)</td></tr>
<tr><td>Weight: 38.7 tonnes</td><td>Performance: maximum road</td></tr>
<tr><td>Engine: 12-cylinder Detroit Diesel</td><td>speed 31 mph (50 km/h); range</td></tr>
<tr><td>diesel developing 537 kW (720 bhp)</td><td>600 km (375 miles)</td></tr>
<tr><td>Dimensions: length (with gun</td><td>Gradient: 60 per cent</td></tr>
<tr><td>forward) 9.79 m (32 ft 1¾ in); length</td><td>Vertical obstacle: 0.91 m (3 ft)</td></tr>
<tr><td>(hull) 7.56 m (24 ft 9¾ in); width</td><td>Trench: 2.44 m (8 ft)</td></tr>
</table>

Sho't

Israel imported more than 1,000 Centurion tanks from the UK in the 1950s and 1960s with the 20-pdr (3.3-in/83.8-mm) gun, but in the 1960s upgunned these with the 105-mm (4.13-in) L7 series of rifled gun. The Israeli army was pleased with the Centurion in all its aspects except its powerplant, for the Rolls-Royce Meteor engine was fuelled by petrol, gave a poor power/weight ratio, suffered from high fuel consumption, and was also prone to problems with its cooling and air filtration systems. The Israeli Ordnance Corps therefore created the Upgraded Centurion or Sho't that re-entered service from 1970 with a diesel engine, automatic transmission, greater fuel capacity, more capable brakes, new electrical system and revised main armament ammunition stowage.

This Sho't served with the Israeli Defence Force (IDF) in Lebanon in 1982. The two white rings on the gun indicate that this is a tank of the second company of the third battalion (indicated by the 'V' on the side) of a tank brigade. The tank is also armed with two 7.62-mm (0.3-in) machine-guns and a 12.7-mm (0.5-in) heavy machine-gun, to provide the maximum of fire in the close-range, anti-personnel role which predominates in city fighting.

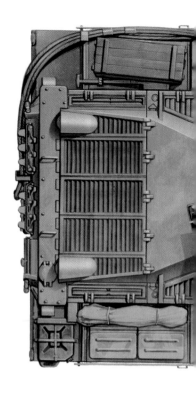

The Sho't has a 7.62-mm (0.3-in) co-axial machine gun to the left of the main gun, and also two further 7.62-mm machine-guns on top of the turret (one on the commander's cupola and the other on the left of the turret) for operation by the loader from his two-part hatch. These local-defence and anti-aircraft weapons are often supplemented by a 12.7-mm (0.5-in) Browning M2HB machine-gun mounted above the main gun for additional firepower in urban situations.

In the Sho't upgrade the original powerplant of the Centurion, the 335.5-kW (450-hp) Meteor Mk IVB liquid-cooled petrol engine driving a Merritt-Brown Z51R manual transmission, is replaced by the 562-kW (750-hp) General Dynamics AVDS-1790-2AC air-cooled diesel engine driving an Allison CD-850-6A1 fully automatic transmission. The rear of the hull has to be enlarged to accommodate the new powerplant, and at the same time the fuel capacity is increased from 1037 to 1090 litres (228 to 240 Imp gal), and in combination with the considerably greater fuel efficiency of the diesel engine this more than doubles the tank's range with fuel that is also safer.

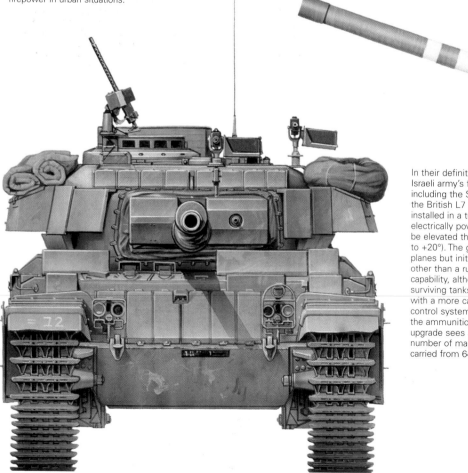

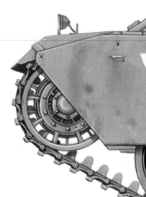

In their definitive forms, all of the Israeli army's first-line Centurion tanks, including the Sho't, were armed with the British L7 series rifled gun. This is installed in a turret with 360° electrically powered traverse, and can be elevated through an arc of 30° (-10 to +20°). The gun is stabilised in two planes but initially lacked anything other than a rudimentary fire-control capability, although from the mid-1980s surviving tanks were further upgraded with a more capable but low-cost fire-control system. The improvement of the ammunition stowage in the Sho't upgrade sees an increase in the number of main-armament rounds carried from 64 to 72 rounds.

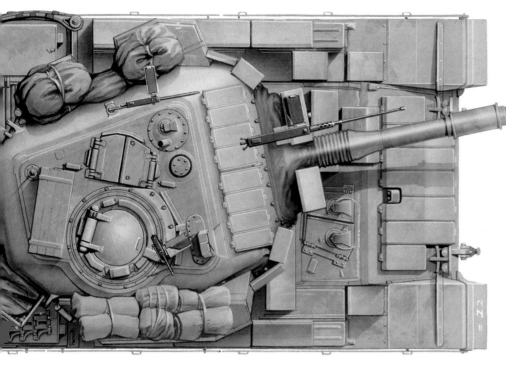

The hull of all Centurion series tanks is a welded unit of rolled steel armour carrying the driver's compartment at the front, the fighting compartment in the centre, and the machinery compartment at the rear. The driver is seated on the right-hand side of the vehicle under a two-piece hatch whose halves (each fitted with a periscope) open to the left and right. To the driver's left is stowage for part of the ammunition supply. The driver controls the tank by means of a triple differential steering arrangement. A notable feature of the upper view of the Sho't are the louvred cooling air outlets above the transmission, and the air filter boxes on the trackguards. Later in its career, the Israeli Centurion was fitted with small plates suspended all over the hull and turret as part of the Blazer explosive reactive armour (ERA). These plates were the answer to the Malyutka (AT-3 'Sagger') and RPG-7, and contain a special explosive detonated by the missile strike, and are intended to 'blast out' the destructive jet of armour-piercing gases formed by the missile's warhead. How successful this addition proved to be on the Centurion is uncertain as few missiles were fired against tanks in the Lebanon, where these up-armoured tanks first saw combat beginning in June 1982.

The turret of the Centurion series is of cast steel armour with the flat roof welded onto it, and carries a crew of three in the form of the commander on the right with the gunner below and ahead of him, and the loader on the left. On the left-hand side of the turret is a small ammunition reloading hatch, on each side there are stowage boxes, and on the rear most vehicles have a wire stowage rack. The commander is seated under a manually operated contra-rotating cupola, and his vision devices include a periscopic day sight (engraved with a ballistic pattern) and seven day periscopes. The gunner has a periscopic day sight with a ballistic pattern graticule, and this is linked to a range drum which ranges between 3,280 and 8,750 m (3000 and 8000 yards). The commander's and gunner's sights are linked by a heat-compensated bar.

The suspension inherited by the Sho't from the baseline Centurion is of the Horstmann type with three units on each side, each carrying two pairs of rubber-tyred road wheels sprung by one set of concentric springs. The first and last road wheel units are fitted with shock absorbers. The length of track on the ground is 5.57 m (18 ft 3 in), the tracks are 0.61 m (24 in) wide, and there are three track return rollers on each side. The drive sprockets and idlers are at the rear and front respectively, and in the Sho't the ground clearance has declined to 0.42 m (16½ in) from the Centurion's figure of 0.51 m (20 in), largely as a result of the Israeli variant's greater weight. The track itself is made up of cast manganese steel links, and the upper part of the track run is protected against the effects of HEAT rounds by removable skirt armour in three large sections on each side.

M47 Medium tank

The M26 Pershing (previously classified as a heavy tank) and the M46 were the standard US medium tanks when the Korean War broke out in 1950. The new T42 medium tank was being developed but was not yet ready for production, so the requirement for an interim medium tank for early production was met by the combination of a modified M26 chassis and the T42's turret, armed with a new 90-mm (3.54-in) gun. This created the **M47** tank, also known as the **Patton 1**, whose manufacture started almost immediately at the Detroit Tank Arsenal and the American Locomotive Company. Even so, the M47 did not see combat in Korea.

The hull and the turret of the M47 were of all-cast construction, with the driver and bow machine gunner in the front of the hull, the commander, gunner and loader in the 360° traverse turret, and the engine and transmission in the rear of the hull. The main armament was a 90-mm rifled gun (elevation +19°/-5°). One 0.3-in (7.62-mm) co-axial machine-gun was mounted to the left of the main gun, and there was a similar weapon in the bow, although this was soon removed to make more volume for additional fuel and main-gun ammunition. A 0.5-in (12.7-mm) M2 heavy machine-gun was carried on the commander's cupola for local defence and protection against aircraft. The torsion-bar suspension comprised six road wheels on each side, with the drive sprocket at the rear and the idler at the front, and there were three track-return rollers on each side.

Variants

The M47 was replaced after only a few years by the M48, so there were few variants of the basic type. The **M102** was an engineer model with the 90-mm gun replaced by a short-barrel 105-mm (4.13-in) howitzer, a dozer blade at the front of the hull and jibs at front and rear. The **T66** flamethrower variant was developed but did not enter service.

The M47 was one of the earlier members of a family of armoured vehicles stretching from the M26 Pershing tank through to the M60. Essentially a modified M26 chassis fitted with the turret developed for the T42 tank, the M47 was too late to see service in Korea. After more than 8,500 examples had been built, the M47 was replaced by the M48.

In the 1950s the M47 was issued to many NATO countries (including Belgium, France, Greece, Italy, Portugal, Spain, Turkey and West Germany) under the Military Assistance Program (MAP), but at the beginning of the 21st century the type remained in service only with Portugal. Other recipients were Austria, Brazil, Iran, Jordan, Pakistan, Saudi Arabia, South Korea, Taiwan and Yugoslavia. Several countries, including Austria, France, Italy and Spain, at various times remanufactured their M47s to more modern standards; in Italy, for example, OTO Melara rebuilt an M47 with a new engine and transmission and replaced the 90-mm gun with the British 105-mm L7 gun, but the type was not adopted. The Spanish army revised some of its M47s with a diesel engine, modified transmission and numerous other incorporated improvements.

SPECIFICATION

Crew: 5
Weight: 46.17 tonnes
Dimensions: length (gun forward) 8.51 m (28 ft 1 in); hull length 6.36 m (20 ft 10 in); width 3.51 m (10 ft 6 in); height 3.35 m (11 ft) including AA machine-gun
Armament: one 90-mm (3.54-in) M36 rifled gun with 71 rounds, one 0.3-in (7.62-mm) M1919A4E1 co-axial machine-gun, one 0.3-in M1919A4E1 bow machine-gun, and one 0.5-in (12.7-mm) M2 machine-gun on the commander's cupola
Powerplant: one Continental AV-1790-5B air-cooled 12-cylinder petrol engine developing 604 kW (810 hp) at 2,800 rpm
Performance: maximum road speed 48 km/h (30 mph); maximum road range 130 km (80 miles);
Gradient: 60 per cent
Vertical obstacle: 0.91 m (3 ft)
Trench: 2.59 m (8 ft 6 in)

M48 Medium tank

Design of a medium tank to supplant the interim M47 began in the early 1950s under the designation **T48**, and this was ordered into production even before the first prototypes had been completed. The first **M48** production vehicles were completed at the Chrysler-run Delaware Tank Plant in July 1952, when the widow of General George Patton christened the type **Patton**. With such a short development period, which was justified by the international situation at that time, there were many problems with the early tanks, including poor reliability and a very short operating range of only

Israel's M48s have 105-mm (3.94-in) guns, diesel engines and low-profile commander's cupolas. Many have been retrofitted with the same explosive reactive armour (ERA) fitted to the IDF's M60 tanks.

113 km (70 miles). The M48 was followed by the **M48A1**, **M48A2** and finally the **M48A3**. The last had many modifications to overcome the earlier vehicles' problems, and was powered by a AVDS-1790-2A diesel which increased the operational range of the tank to some 463 km (288 miles).

Production of the M48 series continued until 1959, by which time over 11,700 had been built. The M48 was succeeded in production by the M60, itself an M48 development. The M48 is still used by many countries including Greece, Iran, Israel, Jordan, Lebanon, Morocco, Pakistan, Portugal, South Korea, Spain, Taiwan (which uses the **M48H** variant with a locally built version of the M68 gun), Thailand, Tunisia, Turkey and Vietnam.

The M48, M48A1, M48A2 and M48A3 are all armed with a 90-mm (4.13-in) M68 gun, with a 0.3-in (7.62-mm) co-axial machine-gun and a 0.5-in (12.7-mm) machine-gun on the commander's cupola. To extend the type's operational life, the **M48A5** was developed in the mid-

An M48 advances during street-fighting in Saigon in May 1968. The M48 was intended for long-range engagements, and in Vietnam a gunner often had to be carried on the rear deck for close-in protection.

1970s. This is an earlier-model M48 rebuilt and fitted with a 105-mm (4.13-in) M68 gun, a 7.62-mm (0.3-in) M60D machine-gun on the turret roof, a new powerpack and many other detailed modifications. From 1975 the Anniston Army Depot converted well over 2,000 older tanks to the M48A5 configuration.

The US also supplied kits to allow other operators to convert their earlier M48s to M48A5 standard. For the West German army the German company Wegmann also upgraded some 650 M48A2 tanks to **M48A2GA2** with the British 105-mm L7A3 gun, new ammunition racks, new commander's cupola, passive night vision equipment, smoke dischargers and modifications to the fire-control system.

The automotive components of the M48 were also used in the M88 ARV and the M53 and M55 self-propelled artillery weapons. Variants of the M48 include the **M67**, **M67A1** and **M67A2** flamethrower tanks (now out of service) and the **M48 AVLB** with a scissors bridge launched over the front of the vehicle. The chassis was also used for the abortive M247 Sgt York Division Air Defense System (DIVADS).

The M48 saw combat in

Left: An M48 leaves a landing craft. With the addition of a deep fording kit and an exhaust extension, the M48 could could ford to a depth of 4.4 m (14 ft 5 in).

Above: The relatively light M48 was suitable for use in the swampy terrain of Vietnam. The M48A3 was the most numerous tank employed by the US in Vietnam.

South Vietnam, with the Pakistani army against India, and with the Israeli army against Jordan, Egypt and Syria. It has now proved to be a reliable tank and, fitted with the 105-mm L7A3 or M68 gun, can destroy most tanks likely to be encountered up to the 1990s, especially when firing modern ammunition such as the APFSDS-T round.

SPECIFICATION

M48A3	M41 rifled gun, one 0.3-in
Crew: 4	(7.62-mm) co-axial machine-gun
Weight: 47.17 tonnes	and one 0.5-in (12.7-mm) AA
Engine: Continental AVDS-1790-2A	machine-gun
12-cylinder diesel developing	**Performance:** maximum road
560 kW (750 bhp)	speed 48.2 km/h (30 mph);
Dimensions: length (with gun	maximum range 463 m (288 miles)
forward) 8.69 m (28 ft 6 in); length	**Fording:** 1.22 m (4 ft)
(hull) 6.88 m (22 ft 7 in); width	**Gradient:** 60 per cent
3.63 m (11 ft 11 in); height 3.12 m	**Vertical obstacle:** 0.92 m (3 ft)
(10 ft 3 in)	**Trench:** 2.59 m (8 ft 6 in)
Armament: one 90-mm (3.54-in)	

M103 Heavy tank

The standard American heavy tank at the end of World War II was the M26 Pershing, which saw action in the closing months of the European campaign; in the post-war period this was reclassified as a medium tank and again saw combat in Korea. Development of heavy tanks continued in the US, a number of prototypes being built including the T29, T30, T34 and T32. With the advent of the Cold War, design work commenced on three new tanks, the T41 light tank which was standardised as the M41, the T42 medium which resulted in the M47, and the **T43**. Trials with prototypes of the last revealed numerous deficiencies, especially in the areas of turret and gun control equipment and in the sighting system, none of which met the specifications of the user. Trials with modified vehicles designated **T43E1** showed that over 100 additional modifications were required, but the vehicle was eventually standardised as the **Tank, Combat, Full Tracked, 120-mm, M103**.

A total of 200 vehicles was built by Chrysler at the Detroit Tank Plant between 1952 and 1954 for deployment with the 7th Army in Europe, where it was found that the tank's weight and small range of action made it difficult to employ.

There were also constant reliability problems, and the M103s were phased out of service with the US Army in the 1960s. A number was supplied to the US Marine Corps, and in the 1960s 153 vehicles were fitted with a type of new engine, which increased operational range from 130 to 480 km (80 to 300 miles); these were designated **M103A2**. They have since been phased out of service with the US Marine Corps, and none was supplied to any foreign countries under the MAP (Military Assistance Program). The role of the M103 was to provide direct assault and long-range anti-tank support to the M47 and later the M48 (a similar role to that of the British Conqueror).

Enlarged M48

In many respects, the M103 tank was virtually a scaled-up M48, with the driver at the front, turret and fighting compartment in the centre, and the engine and transmission at the rear. The commander's cupola, which was provided with an externally mounted 0.5-in (12.7-mm) M2HB machine-gun for anti-aircraft defence, was in the centre of the turret at the rear, while the gunner and one of the loaders were seated forward on the right with the second loader on the left. The torsion-bar suspension con-

A prototype M103A1E1 is seen with its turret traversed to the rear and the gun travel lock open. The size and weight of the M103 made operations difficult.

sisted of seven dual rubber-tyred road wheels (with the drive sprocket at the rear and idler at the front) and six track-return rollers.

Main armament comprised a 120-mm (4.72-in) rifled gun with an elevation of +15° and a depression of -8°, turret traverse being 360°. Ammunition was of the separate-loading type and a total of 38 rounds (38 projectiles and the same number of charges) was carried. The following types of ammunition could be fired: AP-T, HE, HE-T, WP, WP-T and TP-T. A 0.30-in (7.62-mm) machine-gun was mounted co-axial with the main armament, and 5,250 rounds of ammunition were carried for this; stowage was provided for 1,000 rounds of 0.5-in

ammunition. Standard equipment included heaters, deep-fording equipment, infantry telephone and a fire extinguishing system. To support the M103 the **M51 ARV**

was built on the same chassis. This was fitted with a rear spade, winches and a heavy-duty crane for changing major components in the field.

SPECIFICATION

M103	0.5-in (12.7-mm) M2 AA machine-gun
Crew: 5	
Weight: 56.7 tonnes	**Powerplant:** one Continental
Dimensions: length (gun forwards)	AV-1790-5B or 7C V-12 petrol
11.32 m (37ft 1½ in); length (hull)	engine developing 810 hp (604 kW)
6.98 m (22 ft 11 in); width 3.76 m	**Performance:** maximum road
(12 ft 4 in); height 2.88 m (9 ft	speed 34 km/h (21 mph); maximum
5½ in)	road range 130 km (80 miles)
Armament: one 120-mm (4.72-in)	**Gradient:** 60 per cent
rifled gun, one co-axial 0.3-in	**Vertical obstacle:** 0.91 m (36 in)
(7.62-mm) machine-gun and one	**Trench:** 2.29 m (7 ft 6 in)

AMX-30 Main battle tank

When the French army was fully re-formed after the end of World War II, its initial tank fleet comprised American-supplied M4 Sherman tanks and a few examples of the French-designed ARL-44. These were replaced from the mid-1950s by another American type, the M47 battle tank, which was supplied to France in large numbers under the Mutual Defense Aid Program (MDAP). Then in 1956 France, West Germany and Italy drew up a requirement for a new MBT that was to be lighter and more powerfully armed than the M47 currently being used by the armies of all three countries. France and West Germany each built prototypes of MBTs to meet this specification, the French contender being the **AMX-30** and the West German vehicle the Leopard (later the Leopard 1). It was expected that one of these tank types would be adopted by both countries, but in the end each nation adopted its own tank.

The AMX-30 was designed by the Atelier de Construction d'Issy-les-Moulineaux (AMX), creator of most of France's heavier armoured fighting vehicles since the end of World War II. The first prototypes were completed in 1960, the first production tanks were completed by the Atelier de Construction de Roanne in 1966, and production ended in 1993 after the completion of well over 2,000 AMX-30 series vehicles, many of them for export to countries that now include Abu Dhabi (United Arab Emirates), Bosnia, Chile, Croatia, Cyprus, Greece, Iraq,

Above right: A French army AMX-30 showing the 105-mm CH-105-F1 main gun whose primary anti-tank round is the OCC (HEAT) type, which has a muzzle velocity of 1000 m (3,280 ft) per second and will penetrate 400 mm (15¾-in) of armour at an incidence of 0°. At a later date an APFSDS (Obus Fleche) was introduced into French army service but not exported.

The AMX-30 series of main battle tanks has a good power/weight ratio by contemporary standards, and therefore possesses good acceleration and cross-country mobility.

Kuwait, Nigeria, Qatar, Saudi Arabia, Spain (where the type was built under licence) and Venezuela.

The AMX-30 is the lightest of the first-generation NATO tanks, and has a welded hull of rolled steel plate, while the three-man turret is of cast construction. The main armament consists of a 105-mm (4.13-in) rifled gun, and there are a 20-mm co-axial cannon and a 7.62-mm (0.3-in) machine-gun on the commander's cupola. The co-axial weapon is unusual in that it can be elevated independently of the main armament to +40°, enabling it to be used against low-flying aircraft and helicopters.

AMX-30 of the French army showing its cross-country mobility. This is one of the few Western MBTs that is not fitted with a two-axis stabilisation system for the main armament, and cannot therefore fire with any accuracy while on the move.

Ammunition totals are 47 105-mm (19 in the turret and the remaining 28 in the hull), 1,050 20-mm and 2,050 7.62-mm rounds. The types of ammunition fired by the 105-mm gun include HEAT, HE, Smoke and Illuminating, with a modern APFSDS round introduced later in the tank's career. This last has a muzzle velocity of 1525 m (5,005 ft) per second, and will penetrate 150 mm (5.91 in) of armour at an angle of 60° at a range of 5000 m (5,470 yards).

For desert operations there is the **AMX-30S** used

by Qatar and Saudi Arabia, and the definitive production model for the French army is the **AMX-30 B2**, which introduced a number of improvements including an integrated fire-control system incorporating a laser rangefinder and a low-light TV system, and an upgraded automotive system including a new transmission.

The basic AMX-30 chassis has given birth to a family of related vehicles. The **AMX-30D** armoured recovery vehicle has a dozer/stabiliser blade mounted at the front of the hull, two winches and a hydraulic crane on the right side of the hull for changing engines and other components in the field. The AMX-30 bridgelayer has a bridge to fill gaps of up to 20 m (65 ft 7 in). The chassis was also used to carry the launcher for the Pluton surface-to-surface tactical nuclear missile. The **AMX-30 EBG** and **AMX-30 B DT** or, on the chassis of the AMX-

30 B2, **AMX-30 B2 DT** are respectively the combat engineer tractor and mine-clearing tank used by the French army. The chassis is also used for the French version of the Euromissile Roland SAM system and the Shahine SAM system, the latter developed by Thomson-CSF to meet the requirements of the Saudi Arabian army. A twin 30-mm self-propelled anti-aircraft gun system, the **AMX-30-S 401 A**, was developed for Saudi Arabia, this providing close-in protection for Shahine batteries. The **GCT** is essentially a modified AMX-30 chassis with a new turret carrying a 155-mm (6.1-m) howitzer whose automatic loading system enables the GCT's howitzer to fire eight rounds per minute until its ammunition supply is exhausted. The GCT serves with the French army, and in the Middle East was ordered by Iraq, Kuwait and Saudi Arabia.

SPECIFICATION	
AMX 30 B2	2 in); height (overall) 2.86 m (9 ft 4 in)
Crew: 4	
Weight: 36 tonnes	**Performance:** maximum road speed 65 km/h (40 mph); maximum range 600 km (373 miles)
Powerplant: one Hispano-Suiza 12-cylinder diesel developing 537 kW (720 hp)	
Dimensions: length (gun forward) 9.48 m (31 ft 1 in); length (hull) 6.59 m (21 ft 7 in); width 3.1 m (10 ft	**Gradient:** 60 per cent
	Vertical obstacle: 0.93 m (3 ft ½ in)
	Trench: 2.9 m (9 ft 6 in)

AMX-32 Main battle tank

The **AMX-32** was designed by the Atelier de Construction d'Issy-les-Moulineaux as a possible export to countries whose armies required more fire-power and better armour protection than available on the AMX-30. The first proto-type, armed with the same 105-mm (4.13-in) gun as the AMX-30, was revealed in 1979, while the second pro-totype, revealed in 1981, had a new 120-mm (4.72-in) gun as well as improved pro-tection. However, no orders were received.

Layout
In layout the AMX-32 was similar to the AMX-30, with the driver at the front, three men in the central turret, and the engine and trans-mission at the rear. The main armament comprised a 120-mm smooth-bore gun devel-oped by the Etablissement d'Etudes et de Fabrications d'Armement de Bourges with a vertical sliding breech block. The barrel was fitted with a thermal sleeve and fume-extraction system.

Ammunition
The two types of ammuni-tion fired were APFSDS and multi-purpose with muzzle velocities of 1630 and 1050 m (5,350 and 3,445 ft) per second respectively. The gun also fired the range of ammunition developed for the German-designed Leopard 2. A total of 38 rounds of 120-mm ammuni-tion was carried as 17 rounds in the turret, with the other 21 rounds in the hull. Mounted co-axially to the left of the main gun was a 20-mm M693 cannon with

Compared to the AMX-30, the AMX-32 had a redesigned turret and hull front, with improved armour protection. The fire control system included a laser rangefinder and a roof-mounted stabilised sight.

independent elevation to +40°; 480 rounds were car-ried for this weapon. A 7.62-mm (0.3-in) machine-gun was mounted on the commander's cupola, and attached to each side of the forward part of the turret was a bank of three smoke dischargers.

One of the most signifi-cant differences between the AMX-32 and the AMX-30 was the later tank's inte-grated COTAC fire-control system developed from the system fitted to the AMX-10RC 6x6 amphibious reconnaissance vehicle. The COTAC system allowed the AMX-32 to engage moving

as well as stationary targets under day and/or night con-ditions with a 90 per cent first-round hit probability. To the left of the 20-mm can-non was a low-light-level TV camera transmitting its imagery to screens at the commander's and gunner's positions. The commander had a roof-mounted sight with x2 and x8 day magnifi-cation and x1 night magnification, and the sepa-rate gunner's sight had x10 magnification and also incor-porated a laser rangefinder.

The AMX-32 had the same Hispano-Suiza HS 110 engine as the AMX-30, with the option of a supercharged

model developing 597 kW (800 hp). Its greater weight meant that the AMX-32 had an inferior power/weight ratio than the AMX-30, with a slightly adverse effect on mobility. The suspension was a modified version of that fitted to the AMX-30, but side skirts were added to give a measure of protec-tion against attack from HEAT projectiles. The AMX-32 was fitted with an NBC system and a snorkel, the latter allowing the vehi-cle to ford to a depth of 4 m (13 ft 1 in). Optional equip-ment included a different transmission, fire extinguish-ing system, air conditioning system, different tracks and a system to inject diesel fuel into the exhaust to create smoke.

SPECIFICATION	
AMX-32	
Crew: 4	machine-gun
Weight: 40 tonnes	**Powerplant:** Hispano-Suiza 110
Dimensions: length (with 120-mm	12-cylinder multi-fuel engine
gun forward) 9.85 m (32 ft 3¾ in);	developing 720 hp (537 kW)
length (hull) 6.59 m (21 ft 7½ in);	**Performance:** maximum road speed
width 3.24 m (10 ft 7½ in); height	65 km/h (40.4 mph); maximum range
(overall) 2.96 m (9 ft 8½ in)	530 km (329 miles)
Armament: one 120-mm (4.72-in)	**Gradient:** 60 per cent
smoothbore gun, one co-axial 20-mm	**Vertical obstacle:** 0.9 m (2 ft 11½ in)
cannon and one 7.62-mm (0.3-in)	**Trench:** 2.9 m (9 ft 6¼ in)

OF-40 Main battle tank

The standard tank of the Italian army during the 1950s was the American-supplied M47. The country did take part in the formulation of the requirement leading to the production of the French AMX-30 and West German Leopard 1 MBTs, but decided instead to take the American M60A1, of which 300 (including 200 made under licence) were bought. In 1970, Italy ordered 200 Leopard 1 tanks from West Germany, and at the same time OTO Melara (now Otobreda) obtained a licence for Italian production. By 1982 some 720 had been completed for the Italian army and a further 160 of the ARV, AVLB and AEV spe-cialised versions were completed by the mid-1980s.

Export problems
Under the terms of its licence OTO Melara could not export the tank, so the company designed the **OF-40**: the first and second letters in the prefix stand for OTO Melara and Fiat (prime contractor and automotive contractor respectively), and the numerical part indicates an empty weight of 40 tonnes. The first prototype was completed in 1980, and the only production contract was placed by Dubai, which

received its first production vehicles in 1981.

Construction
The hull and turret of the OF-40 are of welded steel construction and divided into a driver's compartment at the front, a fighting compart-ment in the centre, and the engine and transmission at the rear. The main armament is an OTO Melara 105-mm (4.13-in) rifled gun. When the gun recoils the falling-wedge breech block opens automat-ically and ejects the empty cartridge case into a bag under the breech. A total of 61 rounds of ammunition is carried, 42 to the left of the driver and the remainder in the turret. A 7.62-mm (0.3-in) machine-gun is mounted co-axially with the main armament, and a similar weapon is mounted on the turret roof for AA defence. Four smoke/fragmentation grenade launchers are mounted on each side of the turret.

The OF-40 has an OG14LR fire-control system which includes a computer and a laser rangefinder. A fully sta-bilised fire-control system can also be fitted, enabling the OF-40 to engage enemy tanks when moving at speed across country. The com-mander has a roof-mounted

An OF-40 of the Dubai army, which received 36 such vehicles and three OF-40 ARVs. The OF-40 MBT uses automotive components of the Leopard 1 and is armed with a 105-mm gun and two 7.62-mm machine-guns.

stabilised sight, which is used for both surveillance and target acquisition. Standard equipment includes night-vision equipment and an NBC pack mounted to the driver's left.

The **OF-40 Mk 2** intro-duced the more capable OG14L2A fire-control sys-tem, and Dubai ordered 18 of these tanks to supple-ment its 18 OF-40 vehicles upgraded to Mk 2 standard, and the only other in-service variant is the **OF-40 ARV** armoured recovery vehicle, of which Dubai has three.

SPECIFICATION	
OF-40	7.62-mm AA machine-gun
Crew: 4	**Powerplant:** 10-cylinder diesel
Weight: 43 tonnes	developing 830 hp (619 kW)
Dimensions: length (with gun	**Performance:** maximum road speed
forward) 9.22 m (30 ft 3 in); length	60 km/h (37.3 mph); maximum range
(hull) 6.89 m (22 ft 7¼ in); width	(road) 600 km (373 miles)
3.51 m (11 ft 6¼ in); height (turret	**Fording:** 1.2 m (3 ft 11¼ in)
top) 2.45 m (8 ft ½ in)	**Gradient:** 60 per cent
Armament: one 105-mm (4.13-in)	**Vertical obstacle:** 1.15 m (3 ft
rifled gun, one co-axial 7.62-mm	9¼ in)
(0.3-in) machine-gun and one	**Trench:** 3 m (9 ft 10 in)

TAM Medium tank

For many years the M4 Sherman tank was the backbone of Argentine armoured units. By the early 1970s this type was becoming increasingly difficult to maintain and, as most of the tanks available at that time weighed 40 tonnes or more and were therefore too heavy to pass safely over many of Argentina's bridges, it was decided to have a new tank designed specifically to the Argentine army's requirements. The task was contracted to a West German company, Thyssen Henschel (now Rheinmetall Landsysteme), then building the Marder mechanized infantry combat vehicle for the West German army.

The first prototype of the **TAM (Tanque Argentine Mediano)** was completed in 1976, a further two vehicles being completed in the following year. The type was accepted for Argentine service, and a factory was

established near Buenos Aires. By the beginning of the 21st century not all of the 512 vehicles of the family required by the Argentine army had been delivered, and none of the completed vehicles was deployed to the Falklands during the conflict that took place in 1982. To work with the TAM, the **VCTP** infantry fighting vehicle was developed by Thyssen Henschel, and up to 250 of these have been built in Argentina.

Marder derivative

The hull of the TAM is based on that of the Marder MICV. The driver is seated at the front on the left-hand side with the powerpack (engine and transmission) to his right. The glacis plate is well sloped to give the best possible protection within the weight limits of the vehicle. However, the armour does not compare well to that fitted to more advanced and

heavier MBTs. The three-man turret is an electro-hydraulically operated unit of all-welded construction carried over the rear of the vehicle, with the commander and gunner on the right and the loader on the left. The main armament comprises a 105-mm (4.13-in) gun fitted with two-axis stabilisation and an extractor to remove fumes when the gun is fired: the main gun has a total elevation arc of 25° (-7° to +18°). A 7.62-mm (0.3-in) machine-gun is co-axial with the main gun, and a similar weapon can be mounted on the turret roof for anti-aircraft defence. Four dischargers for smoke/fragmentation grenades can be fitted each side of the turret. Totals of 50 rounds of 105-mm and 6,000 rounds of 7.62-mm ammunition are carried, and there is

The TAM tank was designed by the West German company of Thyssen Henschel for the Argentine army, and is based on the chassis of the Marder MICV. Useful numbers of this limited medium tank have been built in Argentina.

an NBC system.

The primary variants of the TAM and VCTP in service with or developed for the Argentine army are the **VCA 155**, **VCRT** and **VCLC**. The in-service VCA 155 is a self-propelled artillery equipment that combines the hull of the TAM with the turret and 155-mm (6.1-in) gun/howitzer developed by Otobreda in Italy for the Palmaria system. The VCRT is an armoured recovery vehicle based on the VCTP with a new superstructure and specialised equipment developed by MaK (now Rheinmetall Landsysteme): the specialised equipment

included a rear-mounted dozer blade, a front-mounted 30-tonne winch, and a 22-tonne crane jib on the right-hand side of the superstructure. The in-service VCLC is a multiple-launch rocket system using the chassis of the TAM with the turret replaced by two 18-round launchers of the Israeli LAR 160 system.

Unbuilt family

Using the chassis of the TAM medium tank, Thyssen Henschel developed a complete family of fighting vehicles, although as yet none of these has been placed in full production.

SPECIFICATION	
TAM	(7 ft 11¼ in)
Crew: 4	**Performance:** maximum road
Weight: 30.5 tonnes (loaded)	speed 75 km/h (46.6 mph);
Powerplant: one MTU 6-cylinder	maximum range 550 km (342 miles);
diesel developing 537 kW (720 hp)	**Fording:** 1.4 m (4 ft 7 in)
Dimensions: length (with gun	**Gradient:** 65 per cent
forward) 8.23 m (27 ft); length (hull)	**Vertical obstacle:** 1 m (3 ft 3¼ in);
6.77 m (22 ft 2½ in); width 3.25 m	**Trench:** 2.5 m (8 ft 2½ in)
(10 ft 8 in); height (turret top) 2.42 m	

Type 59 Main battle tank

Following its victory in the Chinese civil war in 1949, the Communist Chinese army was revised on a more permanent basis, but much of its equipment was obsolete or in urgent need of repair, including a number of American and Japanese tanks of World War II vintage. The USSR supplied large numbers of armoured vehicles including T-34/85 tanks, SU-100 100-mm (3.94-in) tank destroyers, and BTR-40 and BTR-152 armoured personnel carriers. In the early 1950s there followed a quantity of T-54 MBTs, and production of the type was subsequently undertaken in China under the designation **Type 59**.

The first production models were very austere and were not fitted with night-vision equipment or a stabilisation system for the 100-mm Type 59 gun. Later vehicles were fitted with a full range of IR night-vision equipment for the commander, gunner and driver, as well as a stabilisation system. The 7.62-mm (0.3-in) bow-mounted and co-axial machine-guns are designated Type 59T, while the Soviet-designed 12.7-mm (0.5-m) DShKM machine-gun on the

The Chinese-built Type 59 is essentially a Soviet T-54. Later production Type 59s have IR night vision equipment and an externally-mounted (and thus vulnerable) laser rangefinder.

loader's cupola is designated Type 54 by China. MEL, a British company, provided 30 sets of passive night-vision equipment for the Type 59, including the driver's periscope and the commander's and gunner's sights. Later, a number of Type 59 tanks were observed with a laser rangefinder mounted externally above the gun mantlet. This is in a very exposed position, however, and is vulnerable to small arms fire and shell splinters.

Variants are the **Type 59-I** with a simplified fire-control system and laser rangefinder, **Type 59-II** with a 432-kW (580-hp) diesel engine and a 105-mm (4.13-in) rifled gun with two-axis stabilization, and **Type 59 ARV**.

The Type 59 was exported in some numbers, and is known still to be in service with Albania, Bangladesh, Cambodia, Congo, Iran, Iraq, North Korea, Pakistan,

Sudan, Tanzania, Vietnam, Zambia and Zimbabwe.

The Type 59 was replaced in production by the **Type 69-I** main battle tank, which was first seen in public in September 1982. This tank is almost identical in appearance to the Type 59 but has a new 100-mm gun with a fume extractor near its muzzle: early tanks featured both smooth-bore and rifled weapons, but the latter was standardised. Other changes were an improved fire-control with a laser rangefinder, IR night-vision equipment, a complete NBC system, and a semi-automatic fire-extinguishing system. The **Type 69-II** has an improved fire-

control system, smoke grenade launchers on the turret, and an automatic fire-extinguishing system.

In-service variants of the Type 69 include the **Type 69-II MBT Command** (two models), **Type 80** self-propelled anti-aircraft mounting

with two 57-mm (2.24-in) guns, **Type 84 ALVB**, Type 84 armoured mineclearing system, and **Type 653 ARV**. Export sales have been made to Bangladesh, Iran, Iraq, Myanmar, Pakistan and Thailand.

SPECIFICATION	
Type 59	(8 ft 6 in)
Crew: 4	**Performance:** maximum road
Weight: 36 tonnes	speed 50 km/h (31 mph); maximum
Powerplant: one V-12 diesel	range 400 km (249 miles)
developing 388 kW (520 hp)	**Fording:** 1.4 m (4 ft 7 in)
Dimensions: length (with gun	**Gradient:** 60 per cent
forward) 9 m (29 ft 6 in); length	**Vertical obstacle:** 0.79 m (2 ft
(hull) 6.17 m (20 ft 3 in); width	7 in)
3.27 m (10 ft 9 in); height 2.59 m	**Trench:** 2.68 m (8 ft 9½ in)

Merkava Mks 1 and 2 Main battle tanks

The Israeli army's Merkava Mk 1 is armed with the same 105-mm M68 gun as fitted to the M48A5 and M60 series of MBT. The Merkava was first used in combat in the 1982 invasion of the Lebanon, when it engaged and defeated Syrian T-72s. It can carry infantrymen, additional ammunition or a number of stretcher patients in the hull rear.

After the Six-Day War of 1967 Israel became concerned that it might not be able to obtain AFVs from its traditional suppliers (France, the UK and the US), and also that many of the tanks from these sources did not meet Israel's unique requirements. Israel therefore started to develop its own **Merkava** (chariot) tank. This was announced in 1977. The first production vehicles were completed in 1979, and it has been estimated that by 2001 more than 1,000 vehicles had been built. The Merkava was used in action for the first time against Syrian armoured units in southern Lebanon in the summer of 1982.

Unique layout
The layout of the Merkava is unique in that the whole of the front of the vehicle is occupied by the 671-kW (900-hp) AVDS-1790-6A diesel engine, transmission, cooling system and fuel tanks. The driver is seated just forward and to the left of the turret. The turret, of cast and welded construction, is situated well to the rear of the hull with the commander and gunner on the right and the loader on the left. The turret is well sloped to give the greatest possible degree of armour protection, and its small cross section makes it a very difficult target. At the rear of the hull is a compartment able to carry additional ammunition or (supposedly) four litters or 10 infantrymen if the standard ammunition load is reduced. A hatch is provided in the hull rear to allow for the rapid exit of the tank crew or infantrymen. Standard equipment includes a full range of night-vision systems, an NBC system and an automatic fire detection/extinguishing system.

Right: The first production vehicles were delivered to the Israel Defence Force's 7th Brigade in 1979, and the Merkava first saw action during the 1982 invasion of Lebanon.

Below: Although no production figures have been released, it has been estimated that by 2002, total Merkava production had reached over 1,000 vehicles, including the latest Mk 4 version.

Armament
The main armament is the proven 105-mm (4.13-in) rifled tank gun, which can fire a wide range of ammunition (62 rounds). The 105-mm gun has an elevation arc of 28.5° (-8.5° to +20°), turret traverse and gun elevation/depression are electro-hydraulic with manual back-up. A two-axis stabilisation system is fitted, enabling the gun to be aimed accurately and fired while the vehicle is moving across country. The Elbit Matador fire-control system includes a computer and laser rangefinder.

Performance
Compared with other recent MBTs the **Merkava Mk 1** has a very low speed and poor power/weight ratio, but it was designed for a tactical scenario different from that

The Merkava offers a very high level of protection for the crew and vital systems. Potent firepower includes a 60-mm mortar whose availability allows more economical use of the main gun, a very capable fire-control system but only moderate mobility.

prevalent in Central Europe. It should also be remembered that Israel has had more experience than any other country of successful armoured warfare since World War II. In designing the Merkava, the Israelis placed great emphasis on crew survivability: with a national population of around only four million, every trained crew man is a very valuable person who must be given the maximum possible protection.

Further development yielded the **Merkava Mk 2** variant of 1982. This has improved armour on the front and sides of the turret, a revised 60-mm (2.36-in) mortar (which is mounted in the turret roof rather than externally as on the Merkava Mk 1), the more capable Matador Mk 2 fire-control system, spring-attached skirt armour and a more advanced Israeli-developed transmission system. The Merkava Mk 2 increases the range of the tank by 25 per cent compared to the original vehicle, but with only a minor increase in fuel capacity.

SPECIFICATION	
Merkava Mk 1	**Powerplant:** one General
Crew: 4	Dynamics Land Systems
Combat weight: 60 tonnes	AVDS-1790-6A V-12 diesel
Dimensions: length with gun	developing 671 kW (900 hp)
forward 8.63 m (28 ft 3½ in); width	**Performance:** maximum road
3.7 m (12 ft 1½ in); height 2.75 m	speed 46 km/h (28.6 mph); range
(9 ft) to commander's cupola	400 km (248.6 miles)
Armament: one 105-mm (4.13-in)	**Fording:** 2 m (6 ft 7 in) with
rifled gun, one 7.62-mm (0.3-in)	preparation
co-axial machine-gun, two 7.62-mm	**Gradient:** 70 per cent
AA machine-guns and one 60-mm	**Vertical obstacle:** 0.95 m (3 ft 1 in)
(2.36-in) mortar	**Trench:** 3 m (9 ft 10 in)

Type 74 Main battle tank

The **Type 74** main battle tank was designed by Mitsubishi to meet the requirements of the Japanese Ground Self-Defence Force. The first **STB** prototype was completed in 1969, and the first production vehicles followed in 1975. Production continued into the mid-1980s and amounted to 873 tanks.

The main armament is the British 105-mm (4.13-in) L7A1 gun, stabilised in two axes and provided with 55 rounds; there are also a 7.62-mm (0.3-in) co-axial machine-gun (4,500 rounds), a 12.7-mm (0.5-in) machine-gun (660 rounds) on the roof for anti-aircraft defence, and three smoke-dischargers on each side of the turret. The fire-control system includes a ballistic computer and a laser rangefinder to enable the exact range to the target to be determined, so increasing the possibility of a first-round hit. Some models have an IR/white-light searchlight mounted to the left of the main armament, and the driver also has IR night vision equipment.

Unusual suspension

The Type 74's most unusual feature is its hydro-pneumatic suspension, which

The Type 74 MBT entered service in 1976. An unusual feature of the vehicle is its hydro-pneumatic suspension, allowing the driver to adjust the height of the suspension to suit the type of terrain being crossed, and also to improve the gun's elevation arc.

enables the driver quickly to adjust the height of the vehicle to suit the type of ground being crossed or to meet different tactical situations. The ground clearance can be varied from 0.2 to 0.65 m (7.9 to 25.6 in), and the driver can tilt the tank laterally or longitudinally. The 105-mm gun has an elevation arc of 16° (-6.5° to +9.5°), but use of the suspension increases this to +15° and -12.5°. This is a very useful feature when the

tank is firing from behind a crest or from a position on a reverse slope.

Specialised variants

As a result of Japan's ban on weapon exports, only the Japanese army uses the tank. The only variants of the Type 74 are the **Type 78** armoured recovery vehicle and the **Type 87** self-propelled anti-aircraft mounting. The Type 78 has a hydraulically operated dozer/anchor blade at the front of the

hull, a winch, and a hydraulic crane on the right side of the hull. The Type 87 is basically the hull of the Type 74 with a new turret carrying a two-man crew, paired surveillance and

tracking radars, a fire-control system including a laser rangefinder, and the potent armament of two 35-mm Oerlikon Contraves Type KDA cannon. 45 Type 87s had been delivered by 1999.

SPECIFICATION	
Type 74	12.7-mm (0.5-in) machine-gun
Crew: 4	**Powerplant:** one Mitsubishi diesel
Weight: 38 tonnes (loaded)	developing 560 kW (750 hp)
Dimensions: length (with gun forward) 9.41 m (30 ft 10½ in); length (hull) 6.7 m (21 ft 11¾ in); width 3.18 m (10 ft 5¼ in); height (overall) 2.67 m (8 ft 9 in)	**Performance:** maximum road speed 53 km/h (33 mph); maximum range 300 km (186 miles)
	Fording: 1 m (3 ft 3¼ in)
Armament: one 105-mm (4.13-in) L7A1 rifled gun, one 7.62-mm (0.3-in) machine-gun, and one	**Gradient:** 60 per cent
	Vertical obstacle: 1 m (3 ft 3¼ in)
	Trench: 2.7 m (8 ft 10¼ in)

Pz 61 and Pz 68 Main battle tanks

The Federal Construction Works at Thun, which had already designed and built prototypes of the NK I 75-mm (3-in) self-propelled anti-tank gun and the NK II 75-mm assault gun, completed the **KW 30** prototype of a Swiss-designed MBT in 1958 with the armament of one 90-mm (3.54-in) gun; a second prototype was completed in 1959. Between 1960 and 1961 10 pre-production tanks were built under the designation **Pz 58**: these were armed with the British 20-pdr (83.4-mm/ 3.28-in) gun as

Pz 68 MBT of the Swiss army showing the thermal sleeve fitted to the 105-mm L7 gun. Switzerland is now making the German Leopard 2 under licence.

then installed in the Centurion. In 1961 an order was placed for 150 production vehicles armed with another British gun, the 105-mm (4.13-in) L7. These **Pz 61** tanks were delivered to the Swiss army between 1965 and 1966 as a partial replacement for Centurion tanks of British origin.

Enter the Pz 68

The Pz 61 was followed by the **Pz 68**, which featured a 7.5-mm (0.295-in) co-axial machine-gun in place of the 20-mm cannon, a gun-stabilisation system, and wider

tracks with increased ground-contact length. A total of 170 Pz 68 tanks was built between 1971 and 1974, and there followed 50 examples of the **Pz 68 Mk 2** delivered in 1977, 110 of the **Pz 68 Mk 3** delivered in 1978-79 with a larger turret, and finally 60 of the **Pz 68 Mk 4** delivered in 1981-82 to an improved Mk 3 standard.

No radical features

The layout of the Pz 68 is conventional, with the driver at the front, turret in the centre, and engine and transmission at the rear. The turret is of cast steel with the commander and gunner on the right and the

loader on the left; the loader fires the 7.5-mm anti-aircraft machine-gun, allowing the tank commander to carry out his proper command function. The main armament is a 105-mm gun with an elevation arc of 31° (-10° to +21°). There are also three smoke dischargers on each side of the turret, and as a retrofit two Bofors Lyran launchers on the turret roof to provide target illumination at night.

Several other vehicles have been developed on the basis of the Pz 68's chassis. These include the **Entpannungspanzer 68** armoured recovery vehicle, the **Brückenpanzer 68** armoured bridgelayer, and the **Panzerzielfahrzeug** target tank. Prototypes of an anti-aircraft tank (armed

with two 35-mm cannon) and a 155-mm (6.1-in) self-propelled gun were built but neither of these types was placed in production. The ARV is fitted with a dozer/anchor blade at the front of the hull, an A-frame that can lift 15 tonnes, and a hydraulic winch with a capacity of 25 tonnes, which can be increased to 75 tonnes with the aid of snatch blocks.

Service problems

The Pz 61 and Pz 68 have not been among the more successful of post-war designs, and in 1979 a report stated that there were some 50 faults with the Pz 68: some of these were quite serious, including short track life, the gun not staying on the target, and cracking fuel tanks.

SPECIFICATION	
Pz 68	(0.295-in) machine-guns
Crew: 4	**Powerplant:** one MTU 8-cylinder diesel developing 492 kW (660 hp)
Weight: 39.7 tonnes	
Dimensions: length (with gun forward) 9.49 m (31 ft 1½ in); length (hull) 6.98 m (22 ft 11 in); width 3.14 m (10 ft 3½ in); height (including AA MG) 2.88 m (9 ft 5½ in)	**Performance:** maximum road speed 55 km/h (34 mph); maximum road range 350 km (217 miles)
	Fording: 1.1 m (3 ft 7¼ in)
	Gradient: 60 per cent
Armament: one 105-mm (4.13-in) rifled gun, and two 7.5-mm	**Vertical obstacle:** 1 m (3 ft 3¼ in)
	Trench: 2.6 m (8 ft 6¼ in)

Leopard 1 Main battle tank

When the West German army was re-formed in the mid-1950s it was equipped with American M47 and M48 tanks, both armed with a 90-mm (3.54-in) gun. A decision was soon taken that the former would be replaced by a tank armed with a 105-mm (4.13-in) gun, and Gruppen A and B design teams were selected to build prototypes for comparative trials. At the same time France built prototypes of the AMX-30 to replace its American-supplied M47s. It had been expected that one of the West German MBTs or alternatively the French AMX-30 would become the common MBT of both armies, but in the end each country went its own way. Development of the Gruppe A design resulted in its standardisation as the **Leopard 1**. The first production tanks were completed by Krauss-Maffei of Munich in September 1965 and production of the MBT continued until 1979.

Extensive production

Some 2,437 MBTs were built for West Germany in four basic models designated **Leopard 1A1** (with additional armour the **Leopard 1A1A1**), **Leopard 1A2**, **Leopard 1A3** (with a new welded turret) and **Leopard 1A4** (with a new welded turret and new fire-control system). The tank was also adopted by Australia (90 vehicles), Belgium (334), Canada (114), Denmark (120), Italy (920 including 720 built in Italy by OTO Melara), Netherlands (468) and Norway (78). Production was resumed by Krauss Maffei and Krupp MaK in 1982 to meet Greek and Turkish orders (106 and 77 tanks respectively).

Proven British gun

The Leopard 1 is armed with the British L7 series rifled tank gun, which can fire a variety of ammunition including APDS, APFSDS, HEAT,

Above: By the standards of its design period, the Leopard 1 was a capable MBT offering a high level of agility and firepower (the latter through the use of an excellent 105-mm rifled gun) together with modest protection based on welded steel armour.

Right: The impressive capability of the Leopard 1 is attested to by the fact that tanks of this family were delivered to 13 armies around the world, and are still operational in the first years of the 21st century.

Evident in the Leopard 1 are the lessons the Germans learned in World War II. Thus the West German army's first MBT of post-war German design provided an attractive blend of firepower, protection and mobility.

HESH and Smoke, a total of 60 rounds being carried. A 7.62-mm (0.3-in) machine-gun is mounted co-axially with the main armament, a similar weapon is mounted on the turret roof for use in the anti-aircraft role, and four triple smoke dischargers are

mounted on each side of the turret. A gun stabilisation system is fitted, enabling the main armament to be laid and fired while the tank is moving across country. Leopard 1s have an NBC system and a full set of night-vision equipment for the commander, gunner and loader. When originally introduced, the night vision equipment was of the first-generation IR type but this

has been replaced by second-generation passive gear.

Optional equipment

A wide range of optional equipment has also been developed for the Leopard 1, including a snorkel which enables the tank to ford deep rivers and streams to a maximum depth of 4 m (13 ft 1½ in). A hydraulic blade can be mounted at the front of the hull; this is operated by the driver to clear or prepare battlefield obstacles. Most German and Dutch Leopards have appliqué

armour fitted to their turrets to give increased armour protection against missiles and HEAT projectiles.

Family of variants

The basic Leopard 1 chassis has been the basis for a complete family of vehicles which have been designed for full support of the MBT on the battlefield. All of the specialised versions, with the exception of the Gepard, have been designed and built by MaK of Kiel, which also manufactured a few Leopard 1 MBTs.

SPECIFICATION	
Leopard 1	(0.3-in) MG3 machine-guns
Crew: 4	**Powerplant:** one MTU 10-cylinder diesel developing 619 kW (830 hp)
Weight: 40 tonnes	**Performance:** maximum road speed 65 km/h (40.4 mph); maximum range 600 km (373 miles)
Dimensions: length (with gun forward) 9.54 m (31 ft 4 in); length (hull) 7.09 m (23 ft 3 in); width 3.25 m (10 ft 8 in); height (overall) 2.61 m (8 ft 7 in)	**Fording:** 60 per cent
	Vertical obstacle: 1.15 m (3 ft 9¼ in)
Armament: one 105-mm (4.13-in) L7A3 rifled gun, and two 7.62-mm	**Trench:** 3 m (9 ft 10 in)

Leopard 1A4

Like the British Chieftain, the German Leopard 1 MBT was schemed in the second half of the 1950s to meet the possible threat of a Soviet-led armoured offensive across the North German Plain deep into western Europe. Unlike the British, who opted for the predominance of firepower and protection in their heavyweight Chieftain, the Germans preferred firepower and mobility in a lighter MBT. The result was the classic Leopard 1 designed and made by Krauss-Maffei/Krupp MaK (now Krauss-Maffei Wegmann/Rheinmetall Landsysteme), which entered service in 1965. The type was then built in substantial numbers for the home and later the export markets, and also as the basis for a large family of variants. The Leopard 1 was the first MBT designed in Germany since World War II's end, and in several of its features inevitably reflects Germany's armoured experience in that war. The Leopard 1A4 illustrated was the final production model for the West German army with an all-new welded turret with improved armour protection and a stabilised sight for the commander. The rear view shows the tank fitted with a snorkel for deep fording operations, with which the Leopard 1 can ford to a depth of 2.25 m (7ft 4½ in).

Introduced in 1965, the Leopard 1 has proved eminently successful, the total of 2,437 built for West Germany being complemented by export sales to Australia (90), Belgium (334), Canada (114), Denmark (120), Greece (106 vehicles), Italy (200 plus 720 built under licence), the Netherlands (468), Norway (78) and Turkey (77). Second-hand vehicles have also been delivered to several other countries. The Leopard 1 is of conventional layout but with only two compartments: that for the crew of four (driver in the hull, and commander, gunner and loader in the turret) at the front and that for the powerpack at the rear. The manual transmission drives rear sprockets, and the running gear comprises, on each side, seven dual road wheels with independent torsion-bar suspension, a front idler, and four track-return rollers.

When re-created in 1956, the West German army used the American M47 and M48A2 tanks. The West German army realised from its beginning, though, that its tactical concepts, stemming from its experiences in World War II, differed from those of the US. American MBTs turned the scales at about 51 tonnes at that time, but the West German army thought that a figure nearer 30 tonnes should be the norm for Western European operations. In 1957, therefore, the West German army called for a new tank weighing a maximum of 30 tonnes and powered by an air-cooled multi-fuel engine for a minimum power/weight ratio of 22 kW/tonne (30 hp/ton), possessing an overall height of 2.2 m (7 ft 2½ in) or less, and armed with a main gun capable of penetrating 150 mm (5.9 in) of armour at an angle of 60° at optimum range and possessing a maximum effective range of 2250 m (2,460 yards).

Denmark ordered 120 Leopard 1A3s for delivery between 1976-78. These were supplemented by a further 110 Leopard 1A3s from German stocks and all surviving Danish Leopards have since been upgraded to Leopard 1A5 standard with a new fire-control system (FCS). This Danish Leopard 1A5 is seen during service with the UN forces in Bosnia.

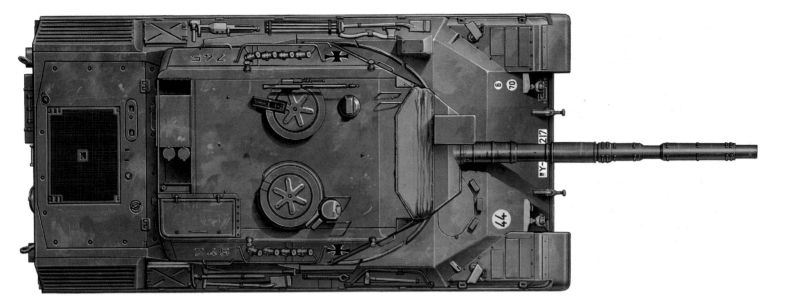

The Leopard 1 has night-vision equipment (IR or image intensification types), provision for a quadruple discharger for smoke grenades on each side of the turret, an NBC system and a British 105-mm (4.13-in) L7A3 main gun firing the standard range of NATO ammunition (13 in the turret and 42 in the hull). There are also two 7.62-mm (0.3-in) MG3A1 machine-guns (one co-axial and the other on the commander's or loader's hatch) with 5,500 rounds. As first delivered the Leopard 1 lacked gun stabilisation or a sophisticated fire-control system, but later improvement added two-axis stabilisation and more advanced fire-control including a laser rangefinder and integral thermal imaging system. The turret can be traversed through 360°, and the main gun can be elevated through an arc of 29° (-9° to +20°).

The MTU diesel, a 10-cylinder Vee rated at 830 hp (619 kW), is well isolated at the rear and water-cooled, which helps to make the Leopard one of the quietest tanks to drive. Changing gear is very effortless because of the hydraulic torque-converter, and as soon as the tank is properly on the move across rough terrain it is obvious that the ride is exceptionally smooth compared with that of some other AFVs.

The Leopard 1's armour varies from 10 mm (0.39 in) on the top of the all-welded hull to 70 mm (2.76 in) on the hull nose and glacis. The first variant was the Leopard 1, and 1,845 were built in the first four production batches; from 1971 these were retrofitted with two-axis stabilisation and a thermal sleeve for the main gun, thereby becoming Leopard 1A1 or, with Blohm und Voss appliqué spaced armour for the turret and mantlet, Leopard 1A1A1 tanks. Next came 232 Leopard 1A2s with the modifications of the Leopard 1A1 and as a cast turret of stronger armour, a better NBC system and passive night-vision devices. The Leopard 1A2 formed the bulk of the fifth production batch, which was completed by 110 examples of the Leopard 1A3 to Leopard 1A2 standard but with a new turret of welded spaced armour with a wedge-shaped mantlet. The final new-build model was the Leopard 1A4, comprising a sixth batch of 250 tanks similar to the Leopard 1A3 apart from their integrated fire-control system. From 1986 some 1,300 Leopard 1s were revised to Leopard 1A5 standard with improvements including the more capable Krupp-Atlas EMES 18 fire-control system, Carl Zeiss thermal imaging system and appliqué armour.

Australia took delivery of 103 Leopard 1s between 1976-78, including 90 AS1 MBTs, eight AS1 medium armoured recovery vehicles (ARV) and five AS1 armoured vehicle-launched bridges (AVLB). These were fitted with a locally-developed air-conditioning system. In order to remain capable into the 21st century, Australia is considering various upgrades for its Leopard 1 fleet. These could include the addition of a new thermal night sight or FCS, or the replacement of the turret with the more advanced unit from the Leopard 1A5.

M60, M60A1 and M60A2 Main battle tanks

In 1956 the US Army decided to develop an improved version of its M48 tank to incorporate a new engine and a larger-calibre main gun. The former was the Continental AVDS-1790-P diesel unit, and the latter the British 105-mm (4.13-in) L7A1 barrel fitted with an American-designed breech. The L7A1 was subsequently licence-made in the US with the designation M68 and fitted to all production examples of the **M60** series of main battle tanks, with the exception of the M60A2. It proved so successful that it was also fitted to the initial variant of the M1 Abrams, the M60's successor and like the earlier type a product of Detroit Arsenal Tank Plant, at that time operated by the Chrysler Corporation but later taken over by the General Dynamics Corporation.

It is worth noting that late-production M48 tanks were rebuilt with the same engine and gun as the M60, making its difficult to tell to two types apart despite the fact that the welded hull of the M60 had less of a 'boat' shape than that of the M48.

The M60 was developed via three **XM60** prototypes, which were converted from M48 standard in 1958, and the tank was standardised for service in March 1959.

A pair of US Army M60A1 tanks participate in a platoon live-fire exercise in Germany in August 1978. Many M60A1s were brought up to M60A3 standard through the addition of thermal night vision equipment.

The M60 baseline model entered service with the US Army in 1960 with basically the same turret as the M48. This turret provided the standard 360° powered traverse, and the gun could be elevated through an arc of 29° between -9° and +20°. Stowage was provided for 57 rounds of 105-mm ammunition, this ultimately being of the APFDS, APDS, HESH, HEAT and Smoke types.

Improved model

The M60 was soon succeeded in production by the **M60A1**, which introduced a number of modifications including a redesigned turret with a more pointed front offering somewhat greater ballistic protection. During the course of M60A1 production, the RISE (Reliability Improved Selected Equipment) package was added to the type, this including a more reliable version of the AVDS-1790 engine, a passive night-vision system, and a smaller searchlight.

Next, during the course of 1964, came the **M60A2** that differed from the M60A1 primarily in its new turret, which was armed with a new and promising weapon system based on a 6-in (152-mm) gun. This could fire the MGM-51 Shillelagh anti-tank missile with semi-automatic command to line-of-sight guidance (which also armed the M551 Sheridan), as well as a range of ammunition types with combustible cartridge cases. A total of 526 M60A2 tanks was built, but there were considerable problems with the weapon

system and the type was introduced to service in 1972, seeing only a short time in first-line use before being withdrawn so that the chassis could become the basis of conversions to the specialised variants listed below.

The two main specialist variants are the **M60 AVLB** and the M728 Combat Engineer Vehicle (CEV). The M60 AVLB has a scissors bridge on top of the hull, and this is launched over the vehicle front to span gaps up to 60 ft (18.29 m) wide. The M728 CEV (discussed in detail elsewhere) has a hull and turret similar to those of the M60A1, but with a 165-mm (6.5-in) low-pressure gun firing a HESH round to demolish battlefield fortifications and pillboxes.

Above: US Army M60 series battle tanks are seen on exercise under typical weather conditions in West Germany. Note the dozer blade of the central example.

The large commander's cupola on top of the turret carries a 0.5-in M85 machine-gun for local and anti-aircraft defence. This weapon is traversed with the cupola, but has independent elevation between -15° and +60°. The weapon is provided with 900 rounds of ammunition.

The M60A2 was intended to be the main production version, but problems with its complex gun/missile armament meant that is was replaced by the M60A3 with a more conventional 105-mm main gun.

M60A1

The M60A1 was a development of the baseline M60, and entered production in 1962 with a number of 'product-improved' enhancements as well as a new turret in place of the turret of the M48 used by the M60. The new turret offered much enhanced ballistic protection, and the revisions also allowed the M60A1 to carry 63 rather than 57 rounds of 105-mm (4.13-in) ammunition for the M68 rifled gun.

The three-man electrohydraulically operated cast turret of the M60A1 is superior to the turret used in the baseline M60. The turret's rear carries a large framed basket that can be used for the carriage of extra gear such as camouflage netting.

The driver is located at the front of the M60A1's hull, and is afforded overhead protection by a single-piece hatch that swings open to the right. The driver has three M27 day periscopes ahead of his position, and an M24 IR periscope can be mounted in the hatch cover.

Surmounted by a one-piece hatch, the commander's cupola can be hand-traversed through 360°, and has eight vision blocks as well as an M28C sight in its forward part. The M28C can be replaced by an M36 IR or M36E1 passive night-vision periscope.

The M68 rifled gun, fitted with a bore evacuator and surmounted by an IR searchlight, is basically the 105-mm (4.13-in) British L7 series tank gun revised with an American breech assembly. Two-axis stabilisation was standard in the M60A3 and then retrofitted in the M60A1.

The M68 gun lacks a muzzle brake or a thermal sleeve to prevent barrel distortion, but uses a useful range of combat and training ammunition types. A well trained crew can fire between six and eight rounds per minute.

The AVDS-1790-2A diesel engine is an air-cooled V-12 unit and is located at the rear of the hull in its own compartment. This is separated from the fighting compartment by a fireproof bulkhead, and is fitted with a fire-extinguishing system.

The one feature that made the M60 series a notable advance over its predecessors was the larger-calibre main gun, a licence-built 105-mm L7A1, the capability of which was then enhanced by the provision of an efficient fire-control system. The M60 series was widely exported, these examples being seen in Italian service.

The M60A2 was produced only in modest numbers with a 6-in (152-mm) main gun capable of firing the MGM-51 Shillelagh anti-tank missile as an alternative to conventional ammunition with a combustible case. The Shillelagh used semi-automatic command to line of sight guidance, and had a large HEAT warhead.

M60A1s on exercise in Norway. The M60 series was mechanically reliable and, despite its use of an air-cooled engine, offered no significant problems for operations in extreme climates. A major improvement in operational capability was provided by the later addition to the series of two-axis stabilisation of the main gun.

Strv 103 (S-tank) Main battle tank

After World War II light tanks formed the bulk of Sweden's armoured strength. To meet the country's immediate requirement for more capable tanks 300 Centurions were purchased from the UK. Development of the KRV heavy tank armed with a 150-mm (5.91-in) smooth bore gun began. At the same time Sven Berge of the Swedish army was developing a new AFV concept in that the gun was fixed to the chassis and not mounted in a turret, traverse being secured by turning the tank on its vertical axis and elevation/depression by lowering or raising the front or rear of the vehicle. Test rigs proved the basic concept, and in 1958 Bofors was awarded a contract for two prototypes, completed in 1961.

So certain was the Swedish army that the concept was sound that it had placed a 1960 order for a further 10 pre-production examples of the **Stridsvagn 103**, or **S-tank**. The first pro-

duction vehicles were completed in 1966 and manufacture continued until 1971, by which time 300 had been built.

Automatic loader

The main armament of the S-tank was the British 105-mm (4.13-in) L7 weapon with an automatic loader supplying ammunition from a 50-round magazine in the hull rear. The ammunition mix depended on the tactical situation, but typically comprised 25 APDS (Armour-Piercing Discarding Sabot), 20 HE and five smoke fired at a maximum 15 rounds per minute. A 7.62-mm (0.3-in) machine-gun was mounted on the commander's cupola, and another two 7.62-mm machine-guns were fixed on the left side of the hull to fire forward; 7.62-mm ammunition amounted to 2,750 rounds. On the roof were two Lyran launchers for illumination of targets.

The engine and transmission were at the front of the

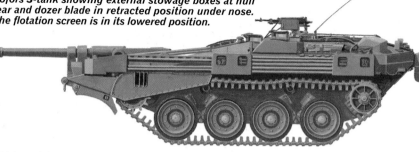

Bofors S-tank showing external stowage boxes at hull rear and dozer blade in retracted position under nose. The flotation screen is in its lowered position.

vehicle, and the powerpack consisted of a 179-kW (240-bhp) Rolls-Royce K60 multi-fuel engine and a 365-kW (490-shp) Boeing 553 gas turbine. In normal use the tank was powered by the diesel, the turbine being engaged when the vehicle was in combat or moving across country demanding a higher power/weight ratio.

The driver was seated on the left of the hull and had a combined periscope and binocular sight with x1, x6, x10 and x18 magnifications, the right eyepiece having a sighting graticule. The radio operator was seated to the rear of the driver and faced the rear. The commander

was on the right, and his optical equipment included a combined periscope and stabilised optical sight almost identical to that of the driver and enabling him to aim and fire the gun. In a typical engagement the commander acquired the target, then used the handlebars on the tiller columns to lay the armament onto the target. The type of ammunition was then selected and loaded, the gun was fired, and the empty cartridge case was ejected through the hull rear.

Suspension system

The suspension was of the hydro-pneumatic type and gave the armament/hull an elevation arc between -10° and +12°. The main drawback of the S-tank was that it could not fire on the move, but Sweden was con-

tent to accept this as its armed forces were optimised for defensive rather than offensive operations.

Mounted under the nose was a dozer blade to prepare defensive positions. Around the top of the hull was a flotation screen (standard on the **Strv 102B** and retrofitted on the initial **Strv 103A**) that could be erected in 20 minutes, and the tank was propelled in the water by its tracks at a speed of 6 km/h (3.7 mph). In the late 1980s the Strv 103 fleet was updated to **Strv 103C** standard with a 216-kW (290-hp) Detroit Diesel 6V-71T diesel in place of the Rolls-Royce unit, an automatic transmission, and a laser rangefinder. The last S-tanks were retired from Swedish service in May 2001.

In order to elevate the S-tank's main gun the front of the hull could be raised. Without a turret the S-tank had a notably low silhouette.

SPECIFICATION	
Stridsvagn 103	**Powerplant:** one diesel engine developing 119 kW (240 hp) and one Boeing 553 gas turbine developing 366 kW (490 shp)
Crew: 3	**Performance:** maximum road speed 50 km/h (31 mph); maximum range 390 km (242 miles)
Weight: 39 tonnes	
Dimensions: length (with gun) 8.99 m (29 ft 6 in); length (hull) 7.04 m (23 ft 1 in); width 3.63 m (10 ft 8¾ in); height (overall) 2.5 m (8 ft 2½ in)	
Armament: one 105-mm (4.13-in) main gun, two co-axial 7.62-mm (0.3-in) machine-guns, and one 7.62-mm AA machine-gun	**Fording:** 1.5 m (4 ft 11 in)
	Gradient: 60 per cent
	Vertical obstacle: 0.9 m (2 ft 11½ in)
	Trench: 2.3 m (7 ft 6½ in)

Chieftain Main battle tank

The **Chieftain** was designed to succeed the Centurion. The first prototype appeared in 1959, and another six followed in 1961-62. The Chieftain was accepted for service in May 1963 and two production lines were laid down. Until the introduction of the Leopard 2 into West German service in 1980, the Chieftain was arguably the best armed and armoured tank in the world. About 900 Chieftain MBTs were built for the British Army, Kuwait ordered 165 **Chieftain Mk 5/2K** vehicles, and Oman took delivery of 12 ex-British tanks in 1981 before adding 15 purpose-built **Qayd al Ardh** tanks. The largest export order was placed by Iran, which ordered about 707 tanks, ARVs and bridge-layers, and later 187

examples of the **Improved Chieftain**. In 1974 Iran ordered 125 **Shir 1** and 1,225 **Shir 2** MBTs, the latter a new design, but this order was cancelled by the new fundamentalist regime that took power in 1979. The Shir 1 became the **Khalid**, of which Jordan took 274. In the 1980s Iraq captured about 100 Iranian tanks, and passed most of these to Jordan.

The Chieftain's layout is conventional, with the driver at the front, turret in the centre (with the commander and gunner on the right and the

A British Chieftain MBT with 120-mm L11A5 rifled tank gun, which has a thermal sleeve to reduce distortion, and is also used by Iran, Iraq, Jordan Kuwait and Oman.

loader on the left), and the engine and transmission at the rear. To reduce overall height, the driver sits in a reclined position, lying almost horizontal when driving with the hatch closed. The turret is of cast steel with a well-sloped front. The commander has a cupola that can be traversed through 360°, and mounted externally on this is a 0.3-in (7.62-mm) machine-gun which can be aimed and fired from within the turret.

Devastating gun

The Chieftain's main armament is the 120-mm (4.72-in) L11A5 rifled gun, which fires separate-loading ammunition with the bagged charges in special water-filled containers below the turret ring to reduce the risk of an explosion. The projectile types include APDS-T (Armour-Piercing Discarding Sabot-Tracer), APFSDS-T (Armour-Piercing Fin-Stabilised Discarding Sabot-Tracer), HESH (HE Squash Head) and smoke. The tanks in British service were retrofitted with the Improved Fire Control System

Until the introduction of the West German Leopard 2 with its 120-mm (4.72-in) gun, the British Chieftain with its 120-mm rifled gun was the most well armoured and powerful tank in NATO's inventory of main battle tanks.

(IFCS) which, used in conjunction with a laser rangefinder, enabled the successful engagement of targets at ranges of well over 2010 m (2,200 yards). Co-axial with the 120-mm gun is a 7.62-mm (0.3-in) machine-gun, and on each side of the turret is a bank of six electrically operated smoke dischargers.

Ammunition totals are 64 120-mm and 6,000 7.62-mm rounds. The NBC pack is mounted on the turret bustle, and a fire detection and extinguishing system is installed in the engine compartment. The night-vision equipment is of the IR type with an IR/white light searchlight mounted on the left of

the turret. This has a range of 1000 m (1,100 yards) in the IR mode and 1500 m (1,640 yards) in the white light mode.

Special variants

The primary operational variants of the Chieftain, now out of British service, were the **Chieftain Mk 2** with a 485-kW (650-bhp) engine, improved **Chieftain Mk 3**, **Chieftain Mk 5** with an uprated engine, **Chieftain Mks 6, 7** and **8** revisions of older marks with an improved engine and ranging machine-gun, and **Chieftain Mks 9, 10, 11 and 12** revisions of intermediate marks with the IFCS and, in the last two, the Stillbrew passive armour

package and the Thermal Observation and Gunnery Sight providing a night and adverse-weather capability. Chieftain variants for other roles are the Chieftain Armoured Vehicle Royal

Engineer (described separately), **Chieftain Armoured Repair and Recovery Vehicle**, **Chieftain Armoured Recovery Vehicle**, and **Chieftain Armoured Vehicle-Launched Bridge**.

SPECIFICATION	
Chieftain Mk 5	**Powerplant:** one Leyland 6-cylinder multi-fuel engine developing 560 kW (750 bhp)
Crew: 4	
Weight: 55 tonnes	
Dimensions: length (with gun forward) 10.795 m (35 ft 5 in); length (hull) 7.518 m (24 ft 8 in); width 3.5 m (11 ft 8½ in); height (overall) 2.895 m (9 ft 6 in)	**Performance:** maximum road speed 48 km/h (30 mph); maximum road range 400 to 500 km (250 to 310 miles)
	Fording: 1.07 m (3 ft 6 in)
Armament: one 120-mm (4.72-in) main gun, one co-axial 0.3-in (7.62-mm) machine-gun, and one cupola-mounted 0.3-in machine-gun	**Gradient:** 60 per cent
	Vertical obstacle: 0.91 m (3 ft)
	Trench: 3.15 m (10 ft 4 in)

Challenger 1 Main battle tank

In 1974 Iran ordered 125 Shir 1 and 1,225 **Shir 2** MBTs from Royal Ordnance Factory, Leeds. The Shir 1 was essentially a late-production Chieftain, already entering service with Iran, while the Shir 2 was a new design with the same powerpack, armament and fire-control system as the Shir 1 in combination with a hull and turret of Chobham armour which would provide a high degree of protection against weapons such as HEAT warheads. It also had hydrogas suspension which gave an excellent ride across rough country as well as being easy to maintain and repair in the field.

The British were to have replaced the Chieftain with a British/West German design,

but this fell by the wayside in March 1977 and the UK went ahead on its own with a new project designated MBT-80. With the fall of the Shah of Iran in 1979, the massive Iranian order was cancelled before deliveries could start, although by that time the Shir 1 was already in production. In 1980 the Ministry of Defence announced that the MBT-80 project had been cancelled as it was becoming too expensive and its in-service date was slipping. Instead an order was placed for 237 (later 319) examples of the **Challenger**, which became the **Challenger 1** after the advent of the Challenger 2. The Challenger is basically the Shir 2 with modifications to suit it for a European

rather than Middle Eastern climate. The first production Challengers were handed over to the British Army in March 1983, and equipped five regiments in Germany.

120-mm main gun

The production vehicles were fitted with the standard 120-mm (4.72-in) L11A5 rifled gun (64 rounds), but plans for its replacement in later vehicles by a new high-technology gun developed by the Royal Armament Research and Development Establishment (RARDE) at Fort Halstead were cancelled. Carried by the Challenger 2, this L30A1 weapon is of electro-slag refined steel with a new split breech design and chromed barrel, firing its projectiles with a very high muzzle velocity to provide increased penetration compared with current projectiles.

Variant family

In most other respects the Challenger 1 is akin to late-variant Chieftain tanks, and the type was operated in four variants as the basic **Challenger Mk 1** without the Thermal Observation and Gunnery Sight, the **Challenger Mk 2** with the TOGS, the **Challenger Mk 3** with a safer interior, and the definitive **Challenger Mk 4** model. Conversions included the **Challenger 1 Control** brigade commander's tank, **Challenger 1 Command** squadron commander's tank, **Challenger Training Tank** with a fixed super-

The first Challengers were accepted by the British Army in March 1983. This retained the Chieftain's 120-mm gun but introduced a new powerpack and advanced Chobham armour for enhanced protection.

structure, and **Challenger Armoured Repair and Recovery Vehicle**.

The last Challenger 1 tanks were retired from first-line British service late in 2000. A refurbishment pro-

gramme is bringing some 288 of the tanks up to 'as new' condition for sale to Jordan, which received its first vehicles in 1999. In Jordan the Challenger 1 is known as the **Al Hussein**.

SPECIFICATION	
Challenger 1	**Powerplant:** one Perkins Condor V-12 diesel developing 895 kW (1,200 bhp)
Crew: 4	
Weight: 58 tonnes	
Dimensions: length (with gun forward) 11.55 m (37 ft 10¾ in); width 3.52 m (11 ft 6½ in); height (overall) 2.975 m (9 ft 9 in)	**Performance:** maximum road speed 56 km/h (35 mph); maximum range about 400 km (250 miles)
	Fording: 1.07 m (3 ft 6 in)
Armament: one 120-mm (4.72-in) main gun, one co-axial 0.3-in (7.62-mm) machine-gun, and one 0.3-in AA machine-gun	**Gradient:** 60 per cent
	Vertical obstacle: 0.91 m (3 ft)
	Trench: 3.15 m (10 ft 4 in)

Packing a powerful punch with its L11A5 rifled gun, the Challenger 1 was able to fire a wide array of ammunition, which proved especially useful during Operation Desert Storm in 1991.

Challenger 1

The Challenger 1 was created by Royal Ordnance Leeds (later Vickers and now Alvis Vickers) in the late 1980s as successor to the Chieftain for British service. The type was derived closely from the Shir 2 designed to meet an Iranian order that was cancelled after the overthrow of the Shah in 1979, and the first of an eventual 420 such tanks was delivered in March 1983 with the Chobham type of laminate armour. The orders for the Challenger were swelled by a Jordanian purchase of 288 vehicles to operate under the local designation Al Hussein after delivery from September 1999. In British service the Challenger 1 was seen as essentially an interim type, and the last tanks of the type were retired in 2000 once the more advanced and capable Challenger 2, with considerably improved protection from its Dorchester armour, had entered service in numbers.

The main armament of the Challenger 1 was the 120-mm (4.72-in) L11A5 rifled gun produced by RO Defence. This was fitted with a thermal sleeve, a fume extractor and a muzzle reference system, was stabilised in both the vertical and horizontal planes, and could be elevated through an arc of 30° (-10° to +20°). The gun as well as the turret were electrically powered with emergency manual back-up, and was controlled by the gunner with an override capability vested in the commander.

The hull of the Challenger 1 was a welded assembly of cast and rolled steel and, like the turret, included Chobham armour over the frontal arc for enhanced battlefield survivability. The hull was divided into three sections: from front to back these were the driver's, fighting, and powerplant compartments. The driver was located on the vehicle's centreline under a hatch that opened horizontally, and in the closed-down mode could see out by means of a wide-angle day periscope that could be replaced for night driving by a Pilkington Badger passive periscope. The driver steered the tank by means of a Commercial Hydraulics STN37 double-differential steering arrangement with hydrostatic control.

British Army Challenger 1
This Challenger 1 of an armoured regiment serving in the British Army of the Rhine (BAOR) is seen in a camouflage scheme suitable for operations in the temperate, wooded regions of northern Europe. In war the outlines of the vehicle and, in particular, its gun would have been broken more comprehensively by the liberal application of netting. Notable features of the vehicle were its low silhouette and the excellent angling of the forward-facing armour, made from flat panels, to increase its effective thickness and thus its resistance to the impacts of anti-tank projectiles striking at the end of a flat high-velocity trajectory.

The turret was electrically powered for traverse through 360°, carried the commander and gunner on the right-hand side (the latter below and ahead of the former) and loader on the left-hand side under a two-piece hatch, and NBC system at the rear.

The Challenger 1 was optimised for firepower and protection rather than mobility measured in terms of speed. Operational service confirmed, however, that the Challenger 1 offered a fair measure of basic mobility and was aided by a ground clearance of 0.5 m (19.7 in) and a ground pressure of 0.97 kg/cm² (13.8 lb/sq in).

Above: The features on the top of the turret are evident in this photograph of this Challenger 1 at speed with its turret traversed partially to the left. The front of the turret was very well angled ballistically, and the radio gear was carried in the rear of the turret's long bustle and was served by prominent aerials.

Right: The Challenger 1 at speed. The basic gun tank was first fielded as the Challenger 1 Mk 1, which was not fitted with the Thermal Observation and Gunnery Sight, the retrofit of which produced the Challenger 1 Mk 2, which in 1987 was further reworked with a Soviet-style quick-release mechanism for the fuel drums at the rear. The Challenger 1 Mk 3 had a safer interior and revised charge stowage, and the Challenger 1 Mk 4 was the final production standard.

The Challenger 1 was the MBT mainstay of the British 1st Armoured Division in the 1991 Gulf War with Iraq. The primary operating units were the 14th/20th King's Hussars of the 4th Armoured Brigade, and the Queen's Royal Irish Hussars, Royal Scots Dragoon Guards and 17th/21st Lancers of the 7th Armoured Brigade. Before the start of the fighting the tanks were upgraded with passive flank armour and ERA on the nose and glacis plate, and a new APFSDS projectile and charge system. The tanks suffered no losses in the fighting, and were credited with the destruction of some 300 Iraqi tanks.

AMX VCI Infantry combat vehicle

To meet a French army requirement for an infantry combat vehicle, Hotchkiss, which is no longer involved in the design, development or production of vehicles, built a number of prototypes in the early 1950s, but these were all rejected. It was then decided to build an IFV based on the chassis of the AMX-13 light tank, which was already in large-scale production for both the French and other armies.

Following trials with proto-type vehicles, the **AMX VCI** (**Véhicule de Combat d'In-fanterie**) was adopted by the French army, first production vehicles being completed at the Atelier de Construction Roanne (ARE) in 1967. Some 3,400 vehicles of the series were built for the domestic and export markets. Once the ARE started to turn out the AMX-30 MBT, production of the AMX-13 light tank

family, including the VCI, was transferred to Creusot-Loire at Chalon-sur-Saône.

Machine-gun turret
In many respects the VCI was an advance on other Western vehicles of its period as not only was it fit-ted with a machine-gun turret for the generation of suppressive fire, but the infantry could also use their rifles from within the vehicle. The drawback of the VCI was its lack of amphibious capa-bility, and when originally deployed it was not fitted with an NBC system or night vision equipment. The VCI is no longer in service with the French army, having been replaced by the amphibious AMX-10P, or with the armies of Belgium and Morocco, but is still operational with the forces of Argentina, Cyprus, Ecuador, Indonesia, Lebanon, Mexico, Qatar,

AMX VCI infantry fighting vehicle of the French army fitted with a cupola-mounted machine-gun. The troop compartment at the rear of the hull is provided with firing ports. In the French army the type has now been replaced by the AMX-10P amphibious MICV.

Sudan, UAE and Venezuela.
The AMX VCI is of all-welded steel construction, with the driver at the front left, engine to his right, com-mander and gunner in the centre and the troop com-partment at the rear. The last has rear doors and hatches in the sides, the latter with four firing ports each. The torsion-bar suspension con-sists of five single road wheels, with the drive sprocket at the front and idler at the rear; there are four track-return rollers.

In addition to the basic VCI, there were also the **VTT/TB** unarmed ambu-lance, **VTT/PC** command

post, **VTT/Cargo** cargo, combat engineer, anti-tank (with ENTAC wire-guided missiles), **VTT/RATAC** ground radar (this system has since been transferred to the 4x4 VAB), **VTT/LT** artillery fire-control, **VTT/PM** mortar carrier (two subvari-ants with an 81- or 120-mm/3.2- or 4.72-in weapon) and **VTT/VCA** sup-port vehicle, the last carrying the remainder of the gun crew and additional ammuni-

tion for the 155-mm (6.1-in) Mk F3 self-propelled gun.
From 1987 the manufac-turer offered the **AMX-13 VTT Version 1987** as a con-version package for the VCI and all other members of the AMX-13 light tank family with a number of automotive improvements, as well as the Detroit Diesel 6V-53T engine developing 208 kW (280 hp) for improved opera-tional range, slightly higher speed and reduced fire risk.

SPECIFICATION

AMX VCI
Crew: 3 + 10
Weight: 15000 kg (33,069 lb)
Dimensions: length 5.7 m (18 ft 8 in); width 2.67 m (8 ft 9 in); height (overall) 2.41 m (7 ft 11 in)
Powerplant: one 186-kW (250-hp) SOFAM liquid-cooled 8-cylinder

petrol engine
Performance: maximum road speed 60 km/h (37 mph); maximum range 350 km (218 miles)
Fording: 1 m (3 ft 3 in)
Gradient: 60 per cent
Vertical obstacle: 0.65 m (2 ft 2 in)
Trench: 1.6 m (5 ft 3 in)

VCC-1 Camillino Armoured IFV

OTO Melara of La Spezia, well known as a manufac-turer of naval weapons and now called Otobreda, has been engaged in the design and production of armoured vehicles since the 1960s, and has built several thousand M113 tracked APCs for the Italian army under licence from FMC of the US.

While the M113 is an excellent vehicle, it suffers

from two major drawbacks, namely its unprotected 12.7-mm (0.5-in) machine-gun mounting and its lack of provision for the infantry to fire their weapons from within the vehicle. The Automotive Technical Service of the Italian army subsequently modified the M113, and after trials this was adopted by the Italian army with the designation

VCC-1, or more commonly the **Camillino**, and well over 1,000 of these were deliv-ered to the Italian army up to 1983. In the same year the manufacturer started delivery to Saudi Arabia of 200 vehicles fitted with the Emerson Improved TOW launcher as fitted to the American-built M901 Improved TOW Vehicle.

The forward part of the

SPECIFICATION

VCC-1 Camillino
Crew: 2 + 7
Weight: 11600 kg (25,573 lb)
Dimensions: length 5.04 m (16 ft 9 in); width 2.69 m (8 ft 10 in); height (to hull top) 1.83 m (6 ft)
Powerplant: one 160-kW (215-hp) GMC Model 6V-53 6-cylinder water-

cooled diesel
Performance: maximum road speed 64.4 km/h (40 mph); maximum road range 550 km (342 miles)
Fording: amphibious
Gradient: 60 per cent
Vertical obstacle: 0.61 m (2 ft)
Trench: 1.68 m (5 ft 6 in)

VCC-1, which has seen active service in Somalia, is identical to that of the M113, with the driver at the front on the left-hand side and the engine to his right. The rest of the vehicle is new, the commander being seated to the rear of the driver and provided with a cupola and periscopes. The 12.7-mm M2HB machine-gun is to the right of the driver in a cupola that can be traversed through 360°, lateral and rear armour protection being provided.

Troop compartment
The troop compartment is at the rear, and in each side of the upper hull, which is angled inward on each side, are two firing ports each sur-mounted by a vision block.

The Otobreda VCC-1 Mk 3 is a development with a 20-mm cannon on the roof. The VCC-1 is a further development of the M113, which has been built under licence by the company.

There is another firing port in the power-operated rear ramp. In the centre of the hull at the rear is a machine-gunner controlling an externally mounted 7.62-mm (0.3-in) machine-gun. To make more room in the troop compartment the fuel tank has been removed and the diesel fuel is now carried in two panniers externally at the hull rear, one on each side of the ramp.

The VCC-1 is amphibious, being propelled in water by its tracks at a speed of 5 km/h (3.1 mph). Before entering water a trim vane is erected at the front of the hull and the two electric bilge pumps are activated.

The basic version is the **VCC-1 Mk 1** described above; the **VCC-1 Mk 2** (not in Italian service) has a remotely controlled 12.7-mm machine-gun, and the **VCC-1 Mk 3** prototype has a 20-mm cannon in a mounting above the roof. The **VCC-2** variant is basically the Italian-built M113 with applique armour on the front and sides.

Type 73 Armoured personnel carrier

The Japanese Type 73 APC and the earlier Type SU 60 APC are the only vehicles of their type with a bow-mounted 7.62-mm (0.3-in) machine-gun.

When the Japanese Ground Self-Defence Force was formed in the 1950s, its first armoured personnel carriers were halftracks supplied by the United States. The first Japanese-designed vehicle to enter service was the **Type SU 60** APC which was produced by Mitsubishi Heavy Industries and the Komatsu Manufacturing Corporation, final deliveries being made in the early 1970s. The Type SU 60 is not amphibious, has a four-man crew and can carry six fully equipped troops. Over 400 of these entered service, and variants include an NBC detection vehicle, 81- and 107-mm (3.19- and 4.2-in) mortar carriers and a dozer.

The **Type 73** then supplemented and largely replaced the Type SU 60, but production was at a very low rate, sometimes as low as six per year, and by the end of the manufacturing programme only 340 such vehicles had apparently been completed.

The Type 73 has a hull of all-welded aluminium armour with the commander, driver and bow machine-gunner at the front. The location of a 7.62-mm (0.3-in) machine-gun in the bow is unique and this weapon can be traversed 30°

left, right, up and down; a similar weapon is installed in the earlier Type SU 60 APC.

The engine is toward the front on the left, with troop compartment at the rear. Entry to the latter is via two doors rather than a power-operated ramp as in the M113 APC and M2 Bradley IFV. One of the nine infantry-men normally mans the roof-mounted 12.7-mm (0.5-in) machine-gun, which is on the right side of the vehicle and can be aimed and fired from within the vehicle. The cupola can be traversed through 360° and the weapon elevated between -10° and +60°. The nine infantrymen are seated on benches down each side of the troop compartment fac-

ing each other; the benches can be folded up to allow stores and other equipment to be carried.

Indifferent equipment

On each side of the troop compartment are two T-type firing ports, although these have a limited value compared with the firing ports/vision blocks fitted to vehicles such as the German Marder. Another unusual feature of the Type 73 is the installation, on the very rear of the hull roof on each side, of a bank of three electrically operated smoke dischargers. In action these would be fired when the vehicle came under attack, allowing the vehicle to pull back to the rear.

The Type 73 has night-vision equipment and an NBC system, but is only amphibious after lengthy preparation. This preparation includes flotation aids along-

side the hull and attached to the road wheels, a trim vane mounted at the front of the hull, and boxes fitted around the air inlet, air outlet and exhaust pipes on the roof of the vehicle. If the last were not fitted, any surge of water over the roof would soon get into the engine.

Unlike many other APCs, there is only one known variant of the Type 73, namely the **Type 75** self-propelled ground-wind measuring unit that is used with the 130-mm (5.12-in) multiple rocket-launcher and uses some automotive components of the Type 73.

The Type 73 is already obsolete as it lacks both armour protection and fire-power, but has not been wholly replaced by the Mitsubishi Type 89 mechanised infantry combat vehicle, armed with a 25-mm chain gun.

SPECIFICATION	
Type 73	Mitsubishi air-cooled diesel
Crew: 3 + 9	**Performance:** maximum road
Weight: 13300 kg (29,321 lb)	speed 70 km/h (45 mph); maximum
Dimensions: length 5.8 m (19 ft	range 300 km (186 miles)
1 in); width 2.8 m (9 ft 1 in); height	**Fording:** amphibious
(with MG) 2.2 m (7 ft 3 in) and (hull)	**Gradient:** 60 per cent
1.7 m (5 ft 7 in)	**Vertical obstacle:** 0.7 m (2 ft 4 in)
Powerplant: one 224-kW (300-hp)	**Trench:** 2 m (6 ft 7 in)

Pbv 302 Armoured personnel carrier

Although the Swedish army deployed tanks well before World War II, it was not until the post-war period that it fielded its first fully tracked armoured personnel carriers. These were called the **Pbv 301** and were essentially the older Strv m/41 light tank stripped down to the basic chassis and rebuilt to armoured personnel carrier standard. The type was armed with a 20-mm cannon and could carry eight fully equipped infantrymen as well as the two-man crew. The conversion work was carried out by Hägglund & Söner in 1962-63.

Even before work had started the Swedish army realised that this would only be a interim solution as the basic chassis was so old. Design work on the new **Pbv 302** armoured personnel carrier started in 1961 and progress was so quick

that the first prototypes were completed in the following year. After the usual trials the company was awarded a full-scale production contract and production was undertaken from 1966 to 1971.

The Pbv 302 was not sold abroad, although it was offered to several countries. The main reason for this lies with the fact that the export of defence equipment is subject to such strict controls that Sweden can deal with only a very few countries.

Advanced concept

In some respects the Pbv 302 is very similar in lay-out to the American M113, although the Swedish vehicle has some noticeable features that, when the vehicle was introduced, put it some way ahead of its competitors. The hull is of all-welded steel armour with

The Pbv 302 APC is only used by the Swedish army, and is fitted with a turret-mounted 20-mm cannon. Before entering water the bilge pumps are switched on and the trim vane erected at the front.

the driver in the centre at the front, the gunner to the left rear and the commander to the right rear. The main armament comprises one 20-mm Hispano cannon mounted in a turret with a traverse of 360° and elevation from -10° to +60°. The cannon can fire either high-explosive (in belts of 135 rounds) or armour-piercing (in 10 round magazines) ammunition. The same turret has also been fitted to a number of other vehicles including the M113s of the Swiss army and EE-11 6x6 vehicles of Gabon.

The troop compartment is at the rear of the hull, with the 10 infantrymen seated

five along each side facing inward. No firing ports are provided, although hatches over the troop compartment allow the troops to fire their weapons from within the vehicle. The infantry enter and leave the vehicle via two doors in the hull rear. The Pbv 302 is fully amphibious, being propelled in the water by its tracks.

The basic vehicle can also be used as an ambulance or a cargo carrier, while more specialised versions include the **Stripbv 3021** armoured

command vehicle, **Epbv 3022** armoured observation post vehicle, and **Bplpbv 3023** fire direction post vehicle. A prototype of the **Pbv 302 Mk 2** APC was built by Hägglund as a private venture. This had a separate cupola at the rear for the squad commander, a Lyran flare system and other minor modifications. The company also proposed that the vehicle be developed as a mechanised infantry fighting vehicle with a turreted 25-mm cannon.

SPECIFICATION	
Pbv 302	diesel developing 209 kW (280 hp)
Crew: 2 + 10	**Performance:** maximum road
Weight: 13500 kg (29,762 lb)	speed maximum road speed
Dimensions: length 5.35 m (17 ft	66 km/h (41 mph); maximum road
7 in); width 2.86 m (9 ft 5 in);	range 300 km (186 miles)
height (turret top) 2.5 m (8 ft 2 in)	**Fording:** amphibious
and (hull top) 1.9 m (6 ft 3 in)	**Gradient:** 60 per cent
Powerplant: one Volvo-Penta	**Vertical obstacle:** 0.61 m (2 ft)
Model THD 100B 6-cylinder inline	**Trench:** 1.8 m (5 ft 11 in)

MOWAG Tornado Mechanised infantry combat vehicle

The MOWAG company has been engaged in the design and development of tracked and wheeled vehicles since just after World War II, and in the early 1960s its was awarded a contract by the then West German government for the construction of prototypes of a mechanised infantry combat vehicle (MICV) that became the Marder.

Private venture

In the 1970s the company developed as a private venture the very similar **Tornado** MICV whose definitive version, called the **Improved Tornado**, was announced in 1980. At this time the Swiss army's standard APC was the American M113, though many of these had been fitted with a Swedish turret carrying one 20-mm cannon. The Swiss decision of 1983 to order the Leopard 2 MBT suggested an obvious need for a complementary MICV, but after great delay Switzerland opted for the CV 9030CH from Sweden.

The hull of the Improved Tornado was of all-welded steel construction and probably offered better protection against armour-piercing projectiles than most vehicles on the market at that time,

The Tornado MICV was developed by MOWAG of Switzerland as a private venture. This Tornado had a 25-mm turret-mounted cannon and two remotely controlled machine-guns at the rear.

as its sides and front were very well sloped for the maximum possible protection. The driver was at the front of the vehicle on the left, with the commander to his rear and the powerpack to his right.

In the centre of the hull could be mounted a wide range of armament installations depending on the mission requirement. One of the most powerful installations was the Swiss power-operated Oerlikon-Bührle Type GDD-AOE two-man turret, which had an externally mounted 35-mm KDE cannon fed from two ready-use magazines each holding 50 rounds. One could hold armour-piercing rounds to engage other vehicles, while the other could hold high-explosive rounds for use against softer target such as trucks. Mounted co-axially with the 35-mm cannon was a 7.62-mm (0.3-in) machine-gun with 500 rounds of

ready-use ammunition to tackle soft targets.

The infantrymen were seated in the troop compartment at the hull rear, and entered and left via a power-operated ramp. On each side of the troop compartment were spherical firing ports that allowed some of the troops to fire their weapons from within the vehicle. If required, two remotely controlled 7.62-mm (0.3-in) machine-guns could be fitted (one on each side) at the rear on the troop compartment roof. These were almost identical to those fitted to the Marder. Each mount

could be traversed through 230° and the guns could be elevated from -15° to +60°.

As with most vehicles of its type, the Improved Tornado was fitted with an NBC system and night-vision equipment. The design of

the chassis was such that it could have been adopted for a wide range of other roles such as command vehicle, missile carrier, recovery vehicle, mortar carrier and so on, but none of these even reached the prototype stage.

SPECIFICATION	
MOWAG Tornado	Detroit Diesel Model 8V-71T diesel
Crew: 3 + 7	**Performance:** maximum road
Weight: 22300 kg (49,162 lb)	speed 66 km/h (41 mph); maximum
Dimensions: length 6.7 m (22 ft);	road range 400 km (249 miles)
width 3.15 m (10 ft 4 in); height (hull	**Fording:** 1.3 m (4 ft 3½ in)
top) 1.75 m (5 ft 8½ in) and (turret	**Gradient:** 60 per cent
top) 2.86 m (9 ft 4¾ in)	**Vertical obstacle:** 0.85 m (2 ft 9½ in)
Powerplant: one 290-kW (390-hp)	**Trench:** 2.2 m (7 ft 2½ in)

M-80 Mechanised infantry combat vehicle

The first armoured personnel carrier designed and built in Yugoslavia to enter service was the M-60P, which was designed to transport men across the battlefield where they would dismount and fight on foot.

Realising the obvious shortcomings of this vehicle, Yugoslavia then started design work on a mechanised infantry combat vehicle which appeared in 1975 as the **M-980**, changed to **M-80** in 1991. The short development period was made possible by the use of a number of

proven components from other sources. For example, the engine came from Renault (formerly Saviem) of France, the road wheels are similar to those of the Soviet PT-76 amphibious light tank, and the 'Sagger' anti-tank missile is fitted to a wide number of Soviet vehicles including MICVs, APCs and tank destroyers.

In many respects the design of the M-80 is very similar to that of the Soviet BMP-1. The driver is seated at the front of the vehicle on the left, with the vehicle

commander to his rear and the engine to his right. The one-man turret is in the centre of the vehicle and armed with a 20-mm cannon with elevation between -5° and +75°; mounted co-axially is a 7.62-mm (0.3-in) machine-gun. The high elevation of these weapons enables them to be used against low-flying aircraft. Mounted externally on the right rear of the turret are two locally-built 'Sagger' wire-guided anti-tank missiles. The compartment for the embarked troops is located at the vehicle's rear, and entry to this compartment is via two doors in the hull rear. Above the troop compartment are roof hatches and firing ports

(with periscopes above) allowing weapons to be fired from within the vehicle.

Fully amphibious

The M-80 is amphibious, being propelled in the water by its tracks; before the vehicle enters the water a trim vane is erected at the front of the hull and the bilge pumps are switched on. The M-80 is also fitted with a fire-extinguishing system, an NBC pack and a smoke laying system.

The **M-80PB** variant is an anti-tank vehicle fitted with two 82-mm (3.23-in) recoilless rifles on a rotating mount on top of the hull. In some respects the M-80 is an improvement over the Soviet BMP-1 as it has two rather than one 'Sagger' missile in the ready-to-launch position, and its 20-mm cannon is probably more suited to the role of the vehicle than the 73-mm (2.87-in) gun of the BMP-1. It is of note that in the BMP-2

the Soviets switched from the 73-mm weapon to a smaller-calibre 30-mm gun, and most Western vehicles of this type are armed with weapons in the 20- to 30-mm range rather than heavy weapons such as the 73-mm gun of the BMP-1.

In 1980 there appeared the improved **BVP M-80A** with weight increased by one tonne due to a more powerful engine being installed; the width and height were also increased. Further BVP development yielded the **M-80AK** IFV with a 30- rather than 20-mm cannon, **M-80A KC** company commander's vehicle, **M-80A KB** battalion commander's vehicle, **M-80A LT** anti-tank vehicle with six 'Saggers', **M-80A Sn** ambulance, and **M-80 VK** command post.

Production completed, the M-80 and M-80A series is now operated by Bosnia, Croatia, Macedonia and Slovenia and Yugoslavia.

M-80 MICVs prior to the break-up of Yugoslavia, showing the twin launchers for AT-3 'Sagger' ATGWs located above the turret roof. The engine is as used in the French AMX-10P armoured infantry carrier.

SPECIFICATION	
M-80	(overall) 2.5 m (8 ft 2 in)
Crew: 2 + 8	**Performance:** maximum road
Weight: 13000 kg (28,660 lb)	speed 60 km/h (37 mph); maximum
Powerplant: one HS 115-2 V-8	range 500 km (310 miles)
diesel developing 194 kW (260 hp)	**Fording:** amphibious
Dimensions: length 6.4 m (21 ft);	**Vertical obstacle:** 0.8 m (2 ft 8 in)
width 2.59 m (8 ft 6 in); height	**Trench:** 2.2 m 7 ft 3 in)

BMD Airborne combat vehicle

From the end of World War II, the Soviet Union placed great emphasis on its airborne forces. For many years it maintained at least seven airborne divisions at full strength. At the start of the Cold War the only armoured vehicles these divisions used were the 57-mm (2.25-in) ASU-57 or the 85-mm (3.35-in) ASU-85 self-propelled anti-tank guns.

To give these units increased firepower and mobility once they were landed behind enemy lines the **BMD** airborne combat vehicle was designed, entering service in 1969. Each Soviet airborne rifle division had 330 of these vehicles in various configurations, although it is unlikely that all seven divisions operated their full complement of vehicles, primarily because the USSR did not have the capability to lift more than one airborne rifle division at any one time.

The BMD was used to spearhead the invasion of Afghanistan in 1979. It has also been used in Chechnya, and has been exported in very small numbers to India and Iraq.

Unusual layout

The layout of the vehicle is unusual, the driver being seated at the front of the hull in the centre with the commander to his left and the bow machine-gunner to his right. The latter operates the two single 7.62-mm (0.3-in) machine-guns mounted internally at the front of the hull, one on each side. The turret, which is identical to that fitted to the BMP-1, is in the centre

of the hull and is armed with a 73-mm (2.87-in) gun, a 7.62-mm co-axial machine-gun and a launcher rail for the 9M14 Malyutka (AT-3 'Sagger') ATGW mounted above the main gun. To the rear of the turret is a small compartment with seats for the gunner, the grenade-launcher and his assistant; the only means of entry to this compartment is via the concertina-type roof hatch.

The independent suspension of the BMD consists of five road wheels, with drive sprocket at the rear and idler at the front; there are four track-return rollers. An unusual feature of this suspension is that a hydraulic system is incorporated that allows the ground clearance of the vehicle to be altered from 100 mm to 450 mm (4 in to 18 in), a factor of

some importance for airborne operations.

The BMD is fitted with an NBC system and a full range of night-vision equipment. It is also fully amphibious, the only preparation required being the erection of the trim vane at the front of the hull and the engagement of the bilge pump.

The command version of the BMD is called the **BMD-U (command)**, and this has a longer chassis with six road wheels on each side and no turret. There is also an 82-mm (3.23-in) mortar version that has seen action in Afghanistan.

The original BMD was replaced in production by the **BMD-2**, in which the original turret has been replaced by a one-man turret mounting a 2A42 30-mm (1.18-in) gun and a 9M113 Konkurs (AT-5

'Spandrel') ATGW. Production started in 1989 and was completed at the end of the 1990s.

Current model

The latest **BMD-3** is in low-rate production at the Volgograd tractor plant. The BMD-3 has the same turret as the previous version, but the chassis is new with much better amphibious capability.

The BMD airborne combat vehicle was used primarily by the Soviet Air Assault Divisions and saw extensive service in Afghanistan. Its turret is similar to that fitted to the BMP-1 MICV, carrying a low-pressure 73-mm gun and a Malyutka or a Konkurs anti-tank guided missile mounted above the gun or on the roof.

SPECIFICATION	
BMD	
Crew: 3 plus 4 troops	230 mm (9 in); ground clearance 0.45 m (17 in)
Weight: 7500 kg (16,530 lb)	**Performance:** maximum road
Powerplant: one 240-hp (179-kW) 5D-20 liquid-cooled V-6 diesel	speed 70 km/h (43 mph); maximum water speed 10 km/h (6.2 mph);
Dimensions: length 5.40 m (17 ft 9 in); width 2.63 m (8 ft 8 in); height 1.62 m to 1.97 m (5 ft 4 in to 6 ft 6 in); track width	maximum range 320 km (200 miles); fording amphibious; gradient 60 per cent; vertical obstacle 0.80 m (2 ft 8 in); trench 1.60 m (5 ft 3 in)

BMP-1 Mechanised infantry fighting vehicle

Finland operates both the original BMP-1 and the improved BMP-2. First used in combat by Arab forces during in 1973, the BMP-1 later saw action with the Soviets in Afghanistan, with Iraq in various Middle East conflicts and with Libyan forces fighting in Chad and Angola.

The **BMP-1** was developed as the replacement for the BTR-50 armoured personnel carrier and caused a major stir throughout Western armies when it rolled through Red Square for the first time in 1967. Previous armoured personnel carriers simply transported the infantry to a point near the scene of action, where it

dismounted to attack the objective on foot. The BMP-1 not only has firing ports that allow all of the embarked troops to fire their weapons from within the vehicle in relative safety, but also a 73-mm (2.87-in) cannon and a wire-guided anti-tank missile.

Fighting vehicles

Since the introduction of the BMP-1 several countries have also developed mechanised infantry combat vehicles: the West German Marder (20 mm cannon), the French AMX-10P (20-mm cannon), the British Warrior (30-mm cannon) and the US M2 Bradley (25-mm cannon) are all good examples. The Marder has been fitted with an externally mounted MILAN ATGW, but although this is more accurate than the 9M14 Malyutka ('Sagger') fitted to the BMP-1 it has a shorter range. The M2 has a twin launcher for the TOW ATGW, which has a longer range than the Malyutka and is much more accurate.

The layout of the BMP-1 is unusual, with the driver at front left, the commander to his rear and the engine on the right. The turret is in the centre of the hull and the infantry compartment at the rear. The eight infantrymen are seated four down each

side, back to back, and enter the vehicle via twin doors in the hull rear. Over the top of the troop compartment are roof hatches. The main drawback of this arrangement is that the troop commander is out of immediate contact with the men he must command in battle.

The 73-mm gun is fed from a magazine that holds 40 rounds of HEAT (high explosive anti-tank) or HE-FRAG (high explosive fragmentation) ammunition, and there is a 7.62-mm (0.3-in) co-axial machine-gun. Turret traverse is electric, with manual controls for emergency use. The main drawbacks of the 73-mm low-pressure gun is its low muzzle velocity and its lack of accuracy in high winds. To fire with any chance of a first-round hit the BMP-1 must first halt.

The Malyutka ATGW is mounted on a launcher rail over the 73-mm gun and controlled (via a joystick) by the gunner. The missile has a maximum range of 3000 m (3,280 yards), but takes 27 seconds to reach this range. The BMP-1 is fitted with a full range of first-generation infra-red night-vision equipment for the commander, gunner and driver, as well as a NBC system. It is fully amphibious with little preparation, being propelled in the water by its tracks.

'Small Fred'
In addition to the basic BMP-1 there were also command versions of the vehicle, a radar carrier fitted with two-man turret armed with a 7.62-mm machine-gun and fitted with a 'Small Fred' mortar/artillery-location radar on turret rear, a reconnaissance vehicle that has a new two-man turret and a mine clearing variant fitted with a mine plough.

SPECIFICATION	
BMP-1	
Crew: 3 plus 8 troops	height (overall) 2.15 m (7 ft 1 in)
Weight: 13500 kg (29,762 lb)	**Performance:** maximum road speed 80 km/h (50 mph); maximum range 500 km (311 miles); fording amphibious; gradient 60 per cent; vertical obstacle 0.80 m (2 ft 8 in); trench 2.20 m (7 ft 3 in)
Powerplant: one 6-cylinder diesel developing 300 hp (224 kW)	
Dimensions: length 6.74 m (22 ft 1 in); width 2.94 m (9 ft 8 in);	

BMP-2 Mechanised infantry combat vehicle

The **BMP-2** mechanised infantry fighting vehicle is a further development of the BMP-1 and was first observed in public during a parade held in Red Square, Moscow late in 1982, although it entered service with the Soviet army several years before that. Since then it has been exported to more than 18 armies around the world, and is in service with most of the former Soviet states.

The basic chassis of the BMP-2 is very similar to that of the original BMP-1, but has a new turret and different crew positions. On the BMP-1 the commander was seated behind the driver and therefore had poor observation to the right side of the vehicle. In the BMP-2 the commander now sits in the much enlarged turret alongside the gunner, and has excellent all-round battlefield observation.

The original BMP-1's 73-mm (2.87-in) weapon suffers from a number of drawbacks and, while powerful, is very inaccurate in high winds. The first-generation 9M14 Malyutka ('Sagger')

missile needed a well-trained gunner to ensure a first-round hit.

Effective armament
These major disadvantages have been overcome in the BMP-2, as the armament now comprises a 30-mm rapid-fire automatic cannon, which can be elevated to +74°, so enabling it to be used against low-flying aircraft and helicopters. The gunner can select either single shots or one of two rates of automatic fire (200/300 or 500 rounds per minute) and 600 rounds of HE-T (High Explosive – Tracer) and AP-T (Armour-Piercing – Tracer) are carried. A 7.62-mm (0.3-in) PKT machine-gun is mounted co-axial with the main armament.

Mounted on the turret roof is a 9M111 Fagot (AT-4 'Spigot') anti-tank guided weapon, which has a maximum range of 2000 m (2,187 yards) and is fitted with a HEAT warhead. Based on plans stolen from Euromissile, the 'Spigot' is much easier to use. All the operator has to do is ensure a hit is to keep the cross-wires of his sight on the target. On the earlier 'Sagger' he had to operate a small joystick.

In addition to being able to inject diesel fuel into the exhaust to lay its own smokescreen, the BMP-2 has three electrically-operated smoke-dischargers mounted on each side of the turret towards the rear. More recent BMP-2s have appliqué armour on their turret sides.

Seven fully equipped infantrymen are carried, compared with eight in the earlier vehicle: one man is seated to the rear of the commander and the other six in the troop compartment at the rear facing outwards, each being provided with a firing port with an observation periscope above.

Like the BMP-1, the BMP-2 is fully amphibious, being propelled in the water

The BMP-2 is an updated version of the BMP mechanised infantry combat vehicle, and substitutes a 30-mm cannon for the 73-mm smooth bore gun of the first model. It also carries 9M111 Fagot (AT-4 'Spigot') ATGMs in place of outdated the 9M14 Malyutka (AT-3 'Sagger').

by its tracks. Before entering the water a trim vane is erected at the front of the vehicle and the bilge pumps are switched on.

Nearly 30,000 BMPs have been built, mainly at the Kurgan Machine Construction plant in the Urals. Production has now been switched to the improved **BMP-3**.

SPECIFICATION	
BMP-2	
Crew: 3 plus 7 troops	width 3.09 m (10 ft 17 in); height 2.06 m (6 ft 9 in)
Weight: loaded 14600 kg (32,187 lb)	**Performance:** maximum road speed 60 km/h (37.3 mph); range 500 km (311 miles); fording amphibious; vertical obstacle 0.7 m (2 ft 3 in); trench 2.0 m (6 ft 7 in); gradient 60 per cent; side slope 30 per cent
Powerplant: believed to be one Type 5D20 turbocharged 6 cylinder water-cooled diesel developing 350 hp (261 kW)	
Dimensions: length 6.71 m (22 ft);	

Like most Soviet AFVs, the BMP-2 was first seen by Western observers at one of the major military parades which took place in Moscow in May and October. At the time of its disclosure in 1982 it had already been in service with the Red Army for several years. Since then the vehicle has been produced under licence in India and in the Czech Republic. The chassis of the BMP-2 is almost identical to the earlier BMP-1, but offers increased armour protection. The driver sits at the front of the vehicle on the left side, and is provided with a hatch and three periscopes. Active/passive night vision equipment can also be fitted.

BTR-50P Armoured personnel carrier

In the mid-1950s the **BTR-50P** was the first fully tracked armoured personnel carrier to enter service with the Soviet army, and is essentially the chassis of the PT-76 amphibious light tank with its turret removed and a superstructure added to the forward part. The commander and driver are seated under armour protection at the front of the vehicle, while the 10 fully equipped infantrymen are seated in the troop compartment on bench seats that run across the width of the vehicle.

The main drawbacks of this model are the lack of an NBC system and overhead armour protection for the infantry carried. The main armament is a 7.62-mm (0.3-in) machine-gun on a pintle mount at the front of the crew compartment. On the rear engine decking ramps are provided so that a 57-mm (2.24-in) or 85-mm (3.35-in) anti-tank gun can be carried and, if required, fired from the vehicle.

The next major model was the **BTR-50PK**, which has a fully enclosed troop compartment and is fitted with an NBC system. The armament comprises a roof-

Soviet BTR-50PK armoured personnel carriers. This model has overhead protection for the troop compartment, whereas the original BTR-50P has an open-top troop compartment, which leaves the 10 seated infantrymen very vulnerable to the effects of shells and mortar bombs bursting overhead.

mounted 7.62-mm machine-gun without protection for the gunner. An improved version of the BTR-50PK was built in Czechoslovakia as the **OT-62**, this being distinguishable from the Soviet vehicle by its lack of chamfer between the side and top of the hull. Whereas most western APCs are propelled in the water by their tracks, the BTR-50P is driven by waterjets at 11 km/h (6.8 mph).

Command versions

There are two command versions, the **BTR-50PU Model 1** and **BTR-50PU Model 2**. Both have a fully enclosed crew compartment, the former having one projecting bay and the latter two. The vehicles have additional communications equipment and can be recognised by their radio aerials, external stowage and a generator. The basic vehicle has been out of production for some time, and in many Soviet units the type was replaced by the BMP-1 MICV. Two later versions are the **MTK** mineclearing vehicle and the **MTP** technical support vehicle. The former is fitted with a rear-deck launcher that fires explosive tubes across the minefield, and the latter has a higher roof with cham-

The BTR-50 armoured personnel carriers are now obsolete, but survive in limited numbers for their ready availability, simplicity, and basic reliability.

fered sides and supports the BMP in the forward battlefield area.

The BTR-50P and its variants are still used by many countries. The type was used in Vietnam by the North Vietnamese army and in the Middle East campaigns by Syria and Egypt, the latter using the BTR-50P in its crossing the Suez Canal during 1973 in the 'Yom Kippur' War.

SPECIFICATION	
BTR-50PK	water-cooled 6-cylinder diesel
Crew: 2+10	developing 179 kW (240 hp)
Weight: 14200 kg (31,305 lb)	**Performance:** maximum road
Dimensions: length 7.08 m (23 ft 0 in); width 3.14 m (10 ft 4 in); height (without armament) 1.97 m (6 ft 6 in)	speed 44 km/h (27 mph); maximum range 400 km (273 miles); fording amphibious; gradient 70 per cent; vertical obstacle 1.10 m (3 ft 7 in);
Powerplant: one Model V-6	trench 2.80 m (9 ft 2 in)

MT-LB Multi-purpose tracked vehicle

In the period immediately after World War II the Soviets introduced the AT-P armoured tracked artillery tractor, which could tow anti-tank guns and howitzers up to 122 mm (4.8 in) in calibre. This was then replaced by the **MT-LB** multi-purpose armoured vehicle, which is used for a wide range of roles in addition to towing anti-tank guns such as the 100-mm (3.94-in) T-12.

Crew compartment

The crew compartment is at the front, with the engine to the rear of this on the left and the troop compartment at the rear. The 11 infantrymen are seated on canvas seats down each side of the troop compartment that can be folded up to allow cargo to be carried. The infantry can quickly leave the vehicle through two large doors in the hull rear, and two hatches are provided over the top of their compart-

ment. Mounted at the front of the hull on the right side is a manually operated turret armed with a 7.62-mm (0.3-in) machine-gun. The road wheels are similar to those of the PT-76 amphibious light tank and the BTR-50 series of armoured personnel carriers. The torsion-bar suspension consists on each side of six road wheels, with the drive

sprocket at the front and idler at the rear. The MT-LB is normally fitted with 350-mm (13.8-in) wide tracks, but when operating on snow-covered ground these can be replaced by the much wider 565-mm (22.25-in) wide tracks, which give a lower ground pressure and therefore better mobility.

Amphibious

The MT-LB is fully amphibious, being propelled in the water by its tracks at a speed of between 5 and 6 km/h (3 to 4 mph), and has IR night vision equipment and an NBC system.

In some areas of the former USSR, where the terrain is swampy or normally covered by snow, the

The MT-LB multi-purpose armoured vehicle is a member of a family of vehicles that all share the same basic automotive components.

MT-LB is used in place of the BMP mechanised infantry combat vehicle.

As usual, the MT-LB chassis has been used for a number of specialised applications including the **MT-LBU** command vehicle, the **MT-SON** with 'Pork Trough' radar mounted on the roof, the MT-LB with 'Big Fred' artillery/mortar locating radar on the roof at the rear, the MT-LB armoured engineer vehicle with a dozer blade, and the **MTL-LB** repair vehicle. The last is used for repair and recovery operations in the forward area and fitted (at

the front) with an A-frame, plus a winch and a full range of tools and other specialised equipment. The chassis is also used as the basis for the SA-13 surface-to-air missile system that has four missiles in the ready-to-launch position. Automotive components of the MT-LB, including the engine and transmission, are also used in the 122-mm (4.8-in) 2S1 self-propelled howitzer, which entered service in the 1970s and is now widely used by the former USSR as well as being exported to many other countries.

SPECIFICATION	
MT-LB	developing 179 kW (240 hp)
Crew: 2+11	**Performance:** maximum road
Weight: 11900 kg (26,235 lb)	speed 61.5 km/h (38 mph);
Dimensions: length 6.454 m (21 ft 2 in); width 2.85 m (9 ft 4 in); height (to turret top) 1.865 m (6 ft 5 in)	maximum range 500 km (311 miles); fording amphibious; gradient 60 per cent; vertical obstacle 0.70 m (2 ft
Powerplant: one V-8 diesel	3 in); trench 2.70 m (8 ft 10 in)

Steyr SPz 4K 7FA Armoured personnel carrier

Between 1961 and 1969 Saurer, which was taken over by Steyr Daimler-Puch in 1970, built 450 fully tracked APCs for the Austrian army, the final production model being the **Schützenpanzer 4K 4FA** with a more powerful engine. In addition to the usual specialised versions, the Austrian army procured two basic models of the 4K 4FA as the **SPz G2** fitted with an Oerlikon-Bührle one-man turret armed with a 20-mm cannon, and the **SPz G1** fitted with a 12.7-mm (0.5-in) M2HB machine-gun.

Improvements

In 1976 Steyr-Daimler-Puch completed the prototype of the **4K 7FA** APC with much improved protection as well as the more powerful engine and transmission of the SK 105 tank destroyer, a type armed with a 105-mm (4.13-in) gun and already in production for the Austrian army and, subsequently, for a number of other countries.

The first production examples of the 4K 7FA were completed in 1977, and orders were secured from countries such as Austria, Bolivia, Cyprus, Greece (where the vehicle was manufactured under licence as the **Leonidas**) and Nigeria.

The all-welded steel hull of the **4K 7FA G127** basic model provides protection against projectiles of up to 20-mm calibre over the frontal arc, and accommodates the driver at the front left with the engine to his right, and the troop compartment at the rear. The gunner is seated to the rear of the driver, and his cupola is provided with a two-part hatch cover that in the vertical position provides protection to his sides, the 12.7-mm machine-gun being fitted with a shield for frontal protection. On the rear of the gunner's cupola are four smoke dischargers.

The eight troops enter and leave the vehicle through twin doors in the hull rear, and sit in two rows of four down the middle of the vehicle facing outward. Over the troop compartment is a two-piece hatch cover that opens to each side, and around the roof can be mounted up to four 7.62-mm (0.3-in) machine-guns; to fire these weapons the troops have to expose their heads and shoulders above the roof. Standard equipment includes heating and ventilating systems, and passive night vision equipment can

be installed.

The chassis is the basis for a family of vehicles. The **4K 7FA-KSPz** MICV has ball mounts for two rifles in each side of the hull. The **4K 7FA FSCV 90** prototype for a fire-support model has a turret with the 90-mm (3.54-in) Cockerill Mk III gun. The **4K 7FA MICV 30/1** prototype has a turret with the 30-mm RARDEN cannon. There are also **4K 7A-Fü** command, **4K 7FA-San** ambulance, **4K 7FA AMC 81** 81-mm (3.2-in) mortar carrier and, not in production, two AA variants.

The Steyr-Daimler-Puch 4K 7FA-KSPz infantry fighting vehicle is a further development of the basic 4K 7FA which is used by Austria, Greece (manufactured under licence) and Nigeria. It shares many components with the SK 105 tank destroyer armed with a 105-mm (4.13-in) gun in a turret.

SPECIFICATION	
SPz 4K 7FA	**Performance:** maximum road speed 63.6 km/h (41 mph); maximum road range 520 km (323 miles)
Crew: 2 + 8	
Weight: 14800 kg (32,628 lb)	
Dimensions: length 5.87 m (19 ft 3 in); width 2.5 m (8 ft 2 in); height (without MG) 1.69 m (5 ft 7 in)	**Fording:** 1 m (3 ft 3 in)
	Gradient: 75 per cent
Powerplant: one 238-kW (320-hp) Steyr liquid-cooled 6-cylinder diesel	**Vertical obstacle:** 0.8 m (2 ft 7 in)
	Trench: 2.1 m (6 ft 11 in)

Chinese APCs YW 531, YW 534 and Type 77 series

Manufactured by a number of Chinese state factories but marketed by NORINCO (China North Industries Corporation) are a number of current tracked APC families. The oldest of these, dating from the late 1960s, is the **YW 531** 12.6-tonne amphibious vehicle with a two-man crew and accommodation for 13 infantry. The organic armament comprises one 12.7-mm (0.5-in) Type 54 machine-gun, and the 238.5-kW (320-hp) diesel provides a maximum road speed of 66 km/h (41 mph). Variants include three upgraded APCs as well as command post, ambulance, two rocket launcher, two mortar carrier, anti-tank and 122-mm (4.8-in) self-propelled howitzer vehicles. The YW 531 series is in large-scale Chinese service and has also been exported to eight other countries.

Also in Chinese service but exported on a smaller scale is the **Type 85**, devel-

oped as the **YW 531 H**, a 13.6-tonne amphibious APC with 2+13 accommodation and an organic armament of one 12.7-mm Type 54 machine-gun. Family variants include the **YW 309** 3+8 ICV which has a 73-mm (2.87-in) low-pressure gun mounted in the turret of a **WZ 501** copy of the Soviet BMP-1; **WZ 702** and Type 85 command posts, **WZ 751** ambulance, **HJ-62C** scout, and Type 85 subvariants for the 120- and 82-mm (4.72-and 3.2-in) mortar carrier, ARV, maintenance engineering, and artillery command post roles. The chassis is also used as the basis for a 122-mm self-propelled howitzer.

APC successor

The **YW 534** APC is used only by China, and is thought to be the successor to the YW 531. It is a 14.3-tonne amphibious type providing 2+13 accommodation, and has the 12.7-mm Type 54

machine-gun as its organic armament. Variants include the **YW 307** IFV with a one-man turret carrying a 25-mm cannon and 7.62-mm (0.3-in) co-axial machine gun, and an anti-tank model with a retractable four-tube launcher for Red Arrow 8 missiles.

The **Type 77** is very similar to the Soviet BTR-50PK, and is thought to be in service only with China. The variants include carriers for the HJ-2J ('Guideline') SAM and HY-2 ('Seersucker') AShM, and recovery vehicle.

The latest models are the 3+8 13.3-tonne **WZ 501** IFV and **YW 535** APC, the latter

The Type 70 is the rocket-launcher variant of the YW 531 APC with a traversing and elevating launcher for 19 130-mm (5.12-in) rockets, and is allocated to armoured and mechanised divisions, with a truck-mounted version allocated to infantry divisions.

serving as the **Type 90**. Both have been developed in several variants for a number of roles, and the organic armament is one 73-mm gun and one 12.7-mm machine-gun respectively.

SPECIFICATION	
Type 90	8-cylinder diesel
Crew: 2 + 13	**Performance:** maximum road speed 67 km/h (41.5 mph); maximum road range 500 km (311 miles)
Weight: 14500 kg (31,966 lb)	
Dimensions: length 6.74 m (22 ft 1½ in); width 3.15 m (10 ft 4 in); height (overall) 2.38 m (7 ft 9½ in)	**Fording:** amphibious
	Gradient: 60 per cent
Powerplant: one 238.5-kW (320-hp) KHD BF8L413F liquid-cooled	**Vertical obstacle:** 0.7 m (2 ft 3½ in)
	Trench: 2.2 m (7 ft 2½ in)

FV432 Armoured personnel carrier

After the end of World War II various prototypes of full-tracked armoured personnel carriers were built in the UK, but it was not until 1962 that one of these, the **FV432**, was accepted by the British army. The FV432 is member of the **FV430** series of vehicles which also includes the **FV433** Abbot 105-mm (4.13-in) self-propelled gun built by Vickers at its Elswick facility in Newcastle between 1964 and 1967.

Production of the FV432 and its many variants was undertaken by GKN Sankey between 1963 and 1971, about 3,000 being built in all. Although offered overseas it was not purchased by any other country as by that time the very similar American M113 APC was already in volume production for the US Army, and this was much cheaper than the FV432. For a short period the FV432 was commonly known as the **Trojan**.

Transportation

The basic role of the FV432 is to transport British infantry across the battlefield to a location close to its objective, where the men dismount and continue the assault on foot. The main difference between the M113 and the FV432 is that the latter has a hull of welded steel construction while the former has a hull of welded aluminium.

The driver is seated at the front on the right, with the commander to his rear and the powerpack to his left. The troop compartment is at the rear of the hull, with entry to this compartment via a large single door in the

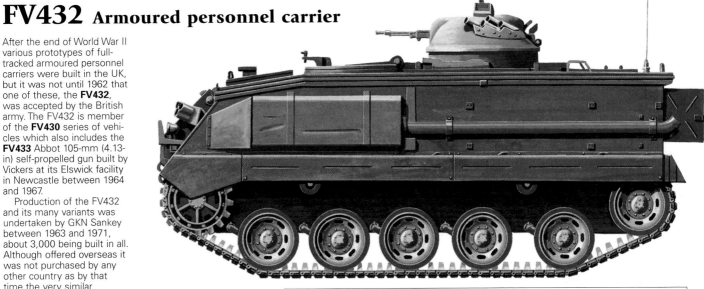

This FV432 is fitted with a Peak Engineering one-man turret armed with a 7.62-mm (0.3-in) machine-gun and four electrically operated smoke dischargers on either side. When fitted with this turret the roof hatches over the troop compartment cannot be used. The FV432 is in service only with the British army.

hull rear. Hatches are provided over the top of the troop compartment, but there is no provision for the infantry to use their weapons from within the vehicle. The 10 embarked infantrymen are seated five on each side of the hull, facing each other on seats that can be quickly folded up to enable cargo to be carried. The vehicle is fitted with night-vision equipment and was also one of the first

vehicles of its type to be fitted with an NBC system, which supplies clean air to the crew and troops.

When introduced to service the FV432 was fitted with a flotation screen attached to the top of the hull; when this had been erected, the vehicle could propel itself across lakes and

An FV432 APC at speed. In many respects this vehicle is similar to the American M113, but it has steel rather than aluminium armour and, as built, was fitted with a multi-fuel engine and a complete NBC system.

rivers with its tracks. These screens were later removed as they were easily damaged and prone to combat damage from small arms fire and shell splinters. The basic vehicle is fitted with a 7.62-mm (0.3-in) machine-gun in an unprotected mount, but many vehicles were then retrofitted with a turret-mounted 7.62-mm machine-gun over the troop compartment.

Versatility

In addition to being used as a troop carrier, the FV432 was or still is employed for a wide range of other roles including ambulance, command with extensive

The FV432's tracked running gear with torsion-bar suspension comprises, on each side, five rubber-tyred dual road wheels, a forward-mounted drive sprocket, a rear-mounted idler and two track-return rollers. In later service many of the vehicles were fitted with a Peak Engineering turret armed with a single machine-gun.

communications equipment installed, 81-mm (3.19-in) mortar carrier, minelayer towing the Bar minelaying system and fitted with the Ranger anti-personnel mine scatterer on the roof, carrier of radar such as the ZB 298 surveillance or Cymbeline mortar/artillery-locating systems, artillery fire-control vehicle with FACE (Field Artillery Computer Equipment), and specialised Royal Signals vehicles.

The maintenance carrier is called the **FV434** and can change tank engines in the field, while the anti-tank member of the family was the **FV438** with Swingfire heavyweight missiles.

SPECIFICATION	
FV432	engine developing 179 kW (240 bhp)
Crew: 2+10	**Performance:** maximum road
Weight: 15280 kg (33,686 lb)	speed 52.2 km/h (32 mph);
Dimensions: length 5.25 m (17 ft	maximum range 483 km (300 miles);
7 in); width 2.80 m (9 ft 2 in); height	fording 1.07 m (3 ft 6 in); gradient
(with machine-gun) 2.29 m (7 ft 6 in)	60%; vertical obstacle 0.61 m (2 ft 0
Powerplant: one Rolls-Royce K60	in); trench 2.05 m (6 ft 9 in)
liquid-cooled 6-cylinder multi-fuel	

M113 Lightweight APC family

The standard US Army APC until the arrival of the M2 Bradley from the early 1980s, the M113 has been the subject of numerous improvement programmes undertaken both in the US and overseas.

By the mid-1950s the US Army was paying increased attention to light vehicles that could easily be transported by transport aircraft to any part of the world. A decision was taken to build prototypes of a new APC whose mechanical components would also be used to form a complete family of vehicles. Prototypes of steel (designated **T117**) and aluminium (designated **T113**) vehicles were built and tested. The latter was standardised for service in 1960 as the **M113**, and was soon in production at San Jose, where it continued until 1992, with production totalling almost 75,000.

Vehicle export

Since then the production line has been periodically reopened in order to fulfil export orders. The vehicle has been constantly improved to meet changing requirements, and has served with 50 countries, current operators including Argentina, Australia, Bahrain, Belgium, Bolivia, Bosnia, Brazil, Cambodia, Canada, Chile, Colombia, DR Congo, Denmark, Ecuador, Egypt, Ethiopia, Guatemala, Germany, Greece, Haiti, Iran, Iraq, Israel, Italy, Jordan, Kuwait, Lebanon, Libya, Macedonia, Morocco, New Zealand, Norway, Pakistan, Peru, Philippines, Portugal, Saudi Arabia, Singapore, Somalia, South Korea, Spain, Sudan, Switzerland, Taiwan, Thailand, Tunisia, Turkey, United States, Uruguay, Vietnam and Yemen. The Italian company Otobreda built almost 4,500 M113s for the Italian army, Chile and Turkey, and further development resulted in the much improved **Infantry Armoured Fighting Vehicle** (**VCC-1**) which is used by the Italian army and by Saudi Arabia in the anti-tank role fitted with the same twin TOW launcher as installed on the M113-derived **M901 Improved TOW Vehicle** (**ITV**). Belgium also maunfactured the **M113A2** version under licence for its army.

The original model to enter service was powered by a Chrysler 75M V-8 petrol engine that developed 156 kW (209 bhp), giving the vehicle a maximum road speed of 64 km/h (40 mph) and a cruising range of 322 km (200 miles). Subsequently, a decision was made to power all future armoured vehicles with diesel rather than petrol engines, both to increase their operating range (diesels being more fuel-efficient than petrol engines) and to reduce the risk of fire. Trials with a diesel-powered model designated **T113E2** were successful and from 1964, the petrol-powered M113 was replaced on the production lines by the diesel-powered **M113A1**. This was powered by the proven General Motors Corporation Detroit Diesel Model 6V-53 six-cylinder diesel which develops 160 kW (215 bhp) to give a cruising range of 483 km (300 miles).

M113A2 production

The next model to enter production (in 1979) was the M113A2, which was

The M125 mortar carrier is armed with an 81-mm (3.19-in) mortar and 114 mortar bombs. The 0.5-in (12.7-mm) machine-gun installation is retained.

SPECIFICATION

M113A2
Crew: 2+11
Weight: 11341 kg (25,002 lb)
Powerplant: one GMC Detroit Diesel Model 6V-53 six-cylinder water-cooled diesel developing 160 kW (215 bhp)
Dimensions: length 2.69 m (8 ft 9 in); width 2.54 m (8 ft 4 in); height (hull top) 1.85 m (6 ft 1 in); height (overall) 2.82 m (8 ft 3 in)
Performance: maximum road speed 67.59 km/h (42 mph); maximum water speed 5.8 km/h (3.6 mph); maximum range 483 km (300 miles)
Fording: amphibious
Gradient: 60 per cent
Vertical obstacle: 0.61 m (2 ft)
Trench: 1.68 m (5 ft 6 in)

This US Army M113 is fitted with a single TOW launcher. The M901 variant carries a pair of TOW tubes, with a further 10 reloads stored internally.

essentially the M113A1 with an improved cooling system and improved suspension. This model retained the same engine as the M113A1 but the increased weight slightly lowered its power-to-weight ratio. At this time the US Army still had over 5,000 of the original petrol-powered M113s in service as well as almost 13,000 of the diesel-powered M113A1s, and a decision was taken to bring all of these vehicles up to the new M113A2 standard, additional vehicles being purchased from FMC as the requirement for M113A2s was almost 20,000 vehicles, including variants. These conversions were carried out both in the US as well as overseas in West Germany and South Korea.

The next version to enter production was the **M113A3**, which was the M113A2 fitted with the more powerful 6V-53T turbocharged diesel engine developing 205 kW (275 bhp), new transmission and new driver's controls. These improvements led to enhanced acceleration, superior cross-country performance, better fuel consumption and generally upgraded reliability.

M113 variants

There are probably more variants of the M113 family than any other vehicle in existence in the world today, and these can be divided into two series. First are those that use the hull of the M113 itself, modified in many applications, and second are those that use the chassis of the unarmoured **M548** tracked load carrier that is also a member of the M113 family and is discussed in a separate entry. In addition, many countries have carried out extensive modifications to meet their own particular requirements.

There are two mortar- carriers, the **M106/M106A1** and the **M125/M125A1**, the A1 models being powered by

Above: A US Army M113 APC prepares to pull an armoured 'Humvee' from the mud in Bosnia during IFOR's Operation Joint Endeavour in May 1996.

Right: An Israeli M113 series APC, one of an estimated 6,000 in IDF service, fitted with an experimental two-man turret armed with a 60-mm hyper-velocity medium support weapon.

the diesel engine. The first of these has a 107-mm (4.2-in) mortar mounted in the rear, the M125 has the 81-mm (3.19-in) mortar mounted on a turntable that can be traversed through 360°. In both cases the mortar can be dismounted and fired away from the vehicle if required.

The anti-aircraft member of the family is the **M163**, which is fitted with a power-operated turret armed with a six-barrelled 20-mm Vulcan cannon. A flamethrower version was developed and deployed to Vietnam, but

this is no longer in use.

The command version is the **M577**, which entered production in 1962. This is easily distinguishable from the basic M113 as it has a much higher roof to allow the command staff to work in an upright position. It also has extensive communications equipment as well as a tent that can be erected at

the rear to increase the work area available.

TOW Vehicle

The M901 Improved TOW Vehicle (or ITV) was developed for the US Army from 1976. This is the basic vehicle fitted on the full roof with an Emerson power-operated launcher that can be elevated from behind cover and carries two Hughes TOW ATGWs in the ready-to-launch position; an additional 10 missiles are carried inside for rapid reloading. A standard ground TOW launcher is also carried so missiles can be launched away from the vehicle if required. Now retired from front-line US Army service on the M113A1/A2, the ITV is used by Egypt, Greece, Jordan, Kuwait, Pakistan (all on the M113A1 chassis), the Netherlands (on **AIFV** chassis), Thailand (M113A1 chassis) and Saudi Arabia (VCC-1 chassis). The latest **M901A1** is capable of firing any of the basic Raytheon

Systems TOW missiles. The **M981 Fire Support Team Vehicle (FISTV)** is similar in appearance to the ITV except that it does not carry missiles in the launcher; these have been replaced by surveillance equipment and a laser. This vehicle is used to locate targets for the artillery and to direct Cannon-Launched Guided Projectiles (CLGPs) onto enemy tanks.

M113 progress

Further development of the M113 by FMC Corporation has resulted in the **Armoured Infantry Fighting Vehicle** (AIFV) operated by Bahrain, Belgium, Egypt, the Netherlands, Philippines and Turkey. The basic chassis has also been selected for a number of private-venture weapons developments including Canada's **M113 ADATS** (Air Defence Anti-Tank System), which has eight Oerlikon missiles in the ready-to-launch position.

The Norwegian army's fleet of upgraded M113A1 vehicles are fitted with a Hägglunds one-man turret armed with a Rheinmetall 20-mm MK Rh 202 cannon.

Transportpanzer 1
Armoured personnel carrier

In the mid-1960s the West German army decided to develop a complete new range of vehicles sharing many common components; the range included 4 x 4, 6 x 6 and 8 x 8 trucks, an 8 x 8 armoured reconnaissance vehicle and 4 x 4 and 6 x 6 APCs. The 8 x 8 armoured reconnaissance vehicle emerged as the Spahpanzer Luchs, of which 408 were built between 1975 and 1978. In the end only the 6 x 6 APC entered production as the **Transportpanzer 1**: it was in 1977 that Rheinstahl (now Rheinmetall Landsysteme) was contracted for an eventual 1,125 vehicles, the first of which was completed in 1979. In 1983 Venezuela ordered 10 Transportpanzer 1 vehicles fitted with a 12.7-mm (0.5-in) and a 7.62-mm (0.3-in) machine-gun, and these were delivered late in 1983.

When used as an APC, the **TPz 1/Standard** can carry 10 troops in addition to the commander and driver. In German service, though, the TPz 1 is normally used for more specialised roles. The **TPz 1A3/ABC** or **Spurpanzer Fuchs** NBC reconnaissance vehicle, of which 140 were built, is fitted with NBC detection equipment, and devices for taking soil samples and for marking the ground. The engineers received 220 vehicles for carrying mines and demolition equipment about the battlefield. The electronic warfare version is the **TPz-1 Eloka**, of which 87 were delivered, has a large number of antennae on the roof and a generator to provide sufficient power to run the equipment. The supply units have 220 vehicles to supply forward units with ammunition and other essential supplies, and this model can also be used as a forward ambulance carrying up to four stretcher patients. The **TPz 1A2/Funk**, of which 265 were delivered, is operated in two subvariants as the **TPz 1A2/FuFu** command and control model with extensive communications equipment and a generator at the rear, and the **TPz 1A2/PARA** radar carrier with RASIT battlefield surveillance radar mounted on a hydraulic arm which is raised above the roof of the vehicle and can be operated up to 30 m (98 ft) from the vehicle by remote control. The German army vehicles are normally armed with a 7.62-mm (0.3-in) machine-gun above the commander's position but other weapons can be fitted on the roof of the troop compartment, including a 20-mm cannon. Mounted on the left side of the hull is a bank of six smoke dischargers.

Internal layout
The commander and driver are seated at the front of the TPz 1 with the engine immediately behind them on the left and the troop compartment at the rear; a small aisle connects the front and rear compartments. The latter has seats on each side, and these seats can be folded to allow cargo to be carried. The compartment

Rheinstahl Wehrtechnik, which became Henschel Wehrtechnik and is now Rheinmetall Landsysteme, built 1,125 Transportpanzer 1 6 x 6 amphibious vehicles for the German army, and these are operated in a wide range of roles including NBC reconnaissance, load carrying and engineer support.

has two doors in the rear, roof hatches and three vision blocks. The TPz 1 is amphibious, being propelled in water by two propellers at 10.5 km/h (6.5 mph). All German vehicles have an NBC system and passive night-vision equipment.

For the export market a wider range of variants is offered, such as anti-tank vehicles with HOT, TOW or MILAN missiles, mortar carriers and a recovery vehicle. The USA bought 110 **M93** vehicles to the Fuch standard for use in the NBC reconnaissance role.

SPECIFICATION	
Transportpanzer 1	armament) 2.30 m (7 ft 6½ in)
Crew: 2+10	**Powerplant:** one Mercedes-Benz
Weight: 17000 kg (37,479 lb)	OM 402A diesel developing
Dimensions: length 6.76 m	239 kW (320 hp)
(22 ft 1 in); width 2.98 m	**Performance:** speed 105 km/h
(9 ft 9¾ in); height (without	(65 mph); range 800 km (497 miles)

UR-416 and Condor Armoured personnel carriers

In the first part of the 1960s Rheinstahl (now Rheinmetall) saw that there was a considerable overseas market for an armoured personnel carrier based on the chassis of the Unimog 4 x 4 truck and the first **UR-416** prototype was completed in 1965. Production got under way four years later, and by the time production ended some 1,030 vehicles had been delivered mainly to countries in Africa, Central and South America, and the Far East.

The all-welded hull provides protection against small arms fire and shell splinters. The commander and driver are seated at the front with eight troops to their rear, three down each side facing outward and two at the rear facing the rear. Firing ports are provided in the hull sides and rear to allow the troops to fire their rifles from inside the vehicle, and if required these standard ports can be replaced by spherical firing ports and an observation block which allows each man to fire his rifle or sub-machine gun from within the vehicle in complete safety. The UR-416 has two roof hatches, the forward one normally being fitted with a 7.62-mm (0.3-in) machine-gun that can also be provided with a shield.

As with most vehicles of this type, the UR-416 can be fitted with a wide range of optional equipment and also a roof-mounted turret.

Condor wheeled APC
Following the success of the UR-416, the manufacturer developed a new vehicle with improved armour protection, greater speed and range, increased load carrying capability, amphibious capability and the ability to mount heavier armament installations. The first prototype of this **Condor** was completed in 1978, and just under 600 are in service.

The Condor has an all-welded steel hull and a three-man crew (driver, gunner and commander) and carries nine infantry who can use their weapons from within the vehicle. The main armament turret is normally in the centre of the hull, and can carry a machine-gun or 20-mm cannon.

The UR-416 is based on the chassis of the Mercedes-Benz Unimog 4 x 4 vehicle, which has exceptional cross-country mobility and is easy to maintain and operate.

This Condor 4 x 4 armoured personnel carrier has a Rheinmetall TUR-1 one-man turret armed with twin 7.62-mm (0.3-in) machine-guns. In 1981 Malaysia ordered a total of 459 Condors, which was by far the largest single order for the type. The vehicle is fully amphibious and can carry several types of turret.

SPECIFICATIONS	
UR-416	**Condor**
Crew: 2+8	**Crew:** 3+9
Weight: 7600 kg (16,755 lb)	**Weight:** 12000 kg (26,455 lb)
Dimensions: length 5.21 m (17 ft 1 in); width 2.30 m (7 ft 6 ½ in); height (without armament) 2.225 m (7 ft 3 in)	**Dimensions:** length 6.05 m (19 ft 10 in); width 2.47 m (8 ft 1 in); height (without armament) 2.10 m (6 ft 10.7 in)
Powerplant: one Daimler-Benz OM 352 6-cylinder diesel developing 89.5 kW (120 hp)	**Powerplant:** one Daimler-Benz OM 352A 6-cylinder diesel developing 125 kW (168 hp)
Performance: maximum road speed 85 km/h (53 mph); maximum range 600 to 700 km (373 to 435 miles); fording 1.40 m (4 ft 7 in); gradient 75 per cent; vertical obstacle 0.55 m (1 ft 9 ½ in); trench not applicable	**Performance:** maximum road speed 100 km/h (62 mph); maximum range 900 km (559 miles); fording amphibious; gradient 60 per cent; vertical obstacle 0.55 m (1 ft 9 in); trench not applicable

TM 170
Armoured personnel carrier

Thyssen Maschinenbau (now Rheinmetall Landsysteme) developed three light wheeled APCs, all based on common commercial components to keep procurement and operating costs to an absolute minimum. The vehicles are the **TM 170, TM 125** and **TM 90**. The largest is the TM 170, which has a two-man crew and can carry 10 fully equipped infantrymen, although more often than not it is used in the internal security role for the rapid and safe transport of riot squads to spots at which they are needed.

Internal security role
Germany's border police and state police selected the TM 170 under the designation **SW4**. At least 250 examples of the SW4 were required, though funding problems meant that the initial order was for only 87 vehicles, the first of these being delivered in 1983.

The TM 170 has a hull of all-welded steel construction with the engine at the very front of the hull and coupled to a manual gearbox with four forward and one reverse gear. For road use the driver normally selects 4

A Thyssen Maschinenbau TM 170 4 x 4 armoured personnel carrier with the hatches over the windscreen in the lowered position. The TM 170 was selected by the West German Border Guard and State Police to replace a miscellany of older vehicles.

x 2 (rear wheels only) drive, while for cross country the front axles are also engaged for 4 x 4 (all-wheel) drive.

The commander and driver have bulletproof windows to their front, and in combat these are covered by armoured shutters, observation then being obtained through roof-mounted periscopes. An entry door is provided in each side of the hull and rear, and firing ports and/or vision blocks enable the troops or police to aim their weapons safely from inside the vehicle. The basic vehicle is amphibious, being propelled in the water by its wheels; before the vehicle enters the water a trim vane is erected at the front of the hull. For increased water speed the TM 170 can be fitted with waterjets, which give a maximum speed of 9 km/h (5.6 mph). A variety

of armament stations can be fitted on the roof including turret- or pintle-mounted 7.62-mm (0.3-in) machine-guns or even 20-mm cannon. Specialised equipment for the riot-control role includes a front-mounted hydraulically operated dozer blade for clearing street barricades and other obstacles out of the way, and a special observation cupola.

The TM 125 is slightly smaller than the TM 170, has a crew of two and can carry 10 men. The TM 90 is an armoured patrol vehicle

rather than an APC and has a crew of four including the driver.

SPECIFICATION	
TM 170	developing 125 kW (168 hp)
Crew: 2+12	**Performance:** maximum road speed
Weight: 9500 kg (20,944 lb)	100 km/h (62 mph); maximum range
Dimensions: length 6.10 m (20 ft	670 km (416 miles); fording
0 in); width 2.45 m (8 ft ½ in); height	amphibious; gradient 80 per cent;
2.22 m (7 ft 3½ in);	vertical obstacle 0.50 m (1 ft 7½ in);
Powerplant: one Daimler-Benz	trench not applicable
OM 352 supercharged diesel	

PSZH-IV Armoured personnel carrier

In the 1960s Hungary developed the FUG 4 x 4 amphibious scout car for service in place of the Soviet BRDM. Development led to the appearance in the mid-1960s of a vehicle that became known in the West as the **FUG-70**. After some time it was discovered that the new vehicle was in reality the **PSZH-IV**, and that it was not a scout car as originally deduced, but an APC.

Orthodox concept
The hull of the PSZH-IV is of all-welded steel construction with a maximum thickness of 14 mm (0.55 in). The commander and driver are seated at the front of the vehicle, forward of each being a windscreen that can be quickly covered by an armoured shutter with an integral periscope. Above their position is a single-piece roof hatch and to each side is a vision block. Mounted in the centre of

When the PSZH-IV was first seen in the early 1960s it was believed to be a scout car, but it was later discovered that the vehicle was in fact an armoured personnel carrier and carried six troops in addition to its three-man crew, the latter consisting of the commander, gunner and driver.

the roof is a one-man Hungarian turret armed with a 14.5-mm (0.57-in) KPVT machine-gun and a 7.62-mm (0.3-in) PKT co-axial

machine-gun. Both weapons have an elevation of +30° and a depression of -5°, turret traverse being 360°. Totals of 500 14.5-mm and 2,000 7.62-mm ammunition are carried.

Full equipment
The troops enter and leave the PSZH-IV through a door in each side of the hull; each door is in two parts, upper and lower, and opens towards the front of the vehicle. The engine is

mounted at the rear of the hull. The PSZH-IV is amphibious, being propelled in the water at a speed of 9 km/h (5.6 mph) by two waterjets. Like most Warsaw Pact vehicles of its period, the PSZH-IV is fitted with a central tyre-pressure regulation system (allowing the driver to adjust the tyre pressure to suit the type of ground being crossed), an NBC system and IR night-vision equipment for the gunner and commander.

There are a number of variants of the PSZH-IV including two command vehicles (one with and the other without the turret), an ambulance model (although loading of stretchers cannot be considered to be an easy occupation), and an NBC reconnaissance vehicle. The last is provided with equipment to detect NBC agents and then drop pennants into the ground to mark a path through these contaminated areas.

SPECIFICATION	
PSZH-IV	diesel developing 74.6 kW (100 hp)
Crew: 3+6	**Performance:** maximum road speed
Weight: 7500 kg (16,535 lb)	80 km/h (50 mph); maximum range
Dimensions: length 5.695 m (18 ft	500 km (311 miles); fording
8½ in); width 2.50 m (8 ft 2½ in);	amphibious; gradient 60 per cent;
height 2.31 m (7 ft 7 in)	vertical obstacle 0.40 m (1 ft 3½ in);
Powerplant: one Csepel D.414.44	trench 0.60 m (1 ft 11½ in)

OT-64 Armoured personnel carrier

Rather than employ the Soviet BTR-60P series of 8 x 8 APCs, Czechoslovakia and Poland decided to develop their own vehicle. This entered service in 1964, and in addition to being used by Czechoslovakia and Poland it was also exported.

Diesel power

The main advantages of the **OT-64** over the Soviet vehicle are that the former is powered by one diesel instead of two petrol engines and that the troop compartment is enclosed.

The hull of the OT-64 is of all-welded steel construction providing protection from small arms fire and shell splinters, the maximum hull armour thickness being 10 mm (0.39 in). The commander and driver are seated at the front of the vehicle with the engine to their immediate rear. At the rear is the troop compartment, which is accessed by two rear doors. Roof hatches are provided over the troop compartment, and firing ports are located in the sides and rear. The OT-64 is amphibious, being driven in the water by two propellers at 9 km/h (5.6 mph). All vehicles have night-vision equipment, a front-mounted winch and an NBC system.

Family variants

The original member of the family, the **OT-64A** (or **SKOT** in Poland) was sometimes fitted with a roof-mounted 7.62-mm (0.3-in) machine-gun. The **OT-64B** (**SKOT-2**) has on the roof behind the engine compartment a plinth carrying a 7.62-mm (0.3-in) or 12.7-mm (0.5-in) machine-gun. The **OT-64C(1)** or **SKOT-2A** has a one-man turret identical to that fitted to the BTR-60PB 8 x 8 APC and BRDM-2 4 x 4 scout car, and carrying a 14.5-mm (0.57-in) and 7.62-mm (0.3-in) machine-gun. The **OT-64C(2)** or **SKOT-2AP** used by Poland has a new turret with a distinctive curved top which has the same armament as the turret of the OT-64C(1) but with an elevation of +89.5° to facilitate the engagement of aerial targets. Other more specialised versions include a recovery vehicle and at least two command vehicles, designated **R-2** and **R-3**.

Czechoslovakia also used the **OT-810** half-track. In World War II the Germans made the SdKfz 251 half-track at the Skoda plant in Pilsen, where production continued after the war. In the 1950s many of these OT-810 vehicles were rebuilt and fitted with a diesel and overhead armour protection for the troop compartment. Most of the OT-810s were fitted with an 82-mm (3.23-in) M59A recoilless gun for the anti-tank role.

SPECIFICATION	
OT-64C(1)	kW (180 hp)
Crew: 2+15	**Performance:** maximum road speed 94.4 km/h (59 mph);
Weight: 14500 kg (31,967 lb)	maximum road range 710 km
Dimensions: length 7.44 m (24 ft 5 in); width 2.55 m (8 ft 4.4 in); height (overall) 2.06 m (6 ft 9 in)	(441 miles); fording amphibious; gradient 60 per cent; vertical obstacle 0.50 m (1 ft 7½ in); trench
Powerplant: one Tatra 928-18 air-cooled V-8 diesel developing 134	2.0 m (6 ft 7 in)

Panhard VCR Armoured personnel carrier

Following the success of its AML and M3 range of 4 x 4 armoured vehicles, Panhard developed the **VCR** 6 x 6 APC. The first VCR (*Véhicule de Combat à Roues*, or wheeled combat vehicle) prototype was shown in 1977, the initial production vehicles being completed just two years later. The VCR was designed specifically for the export market, and known sales have been made to Argentina, Gabon, Iraq, Mexico and the UAE.

The VCR has an all-welded hull which varies in thickness from 8 to 12 mm (0.315 to 0.47 in), the very front of the vehicle being almost identical to that of the Panhard M3 4 x 4 APC. The driver is seated at the front with the engine to his right rear and the commander to his left rear. Both have a single-piece hatch cover and periscopes for observation. The troop compartment is at the rear and has twin doors in the hull rear, with roof hatches and firing/observation ports in the upper part.

Weaponry

The main armament is normally mounted over the forward part of the troop compartment and can consist of a pintle-mounted 7.62- or 12.7-mm (0.3- or 0.5-in) machine-gun, or a turret with similar weapons or a 20-mm cannon.

An unusual feature of the VCR is its wheel arrangement as all six wheels are powered, with power-assisted steering on the front wheels only. When the VCR is travelling on roads, the central pair of road wheels is normally raised off the ground. The VCR is fully amphibious, being propelled in the water by its wheels at 4 km/h (2.48 mph). Optional equipment includes an air-conditioning system, passive night-vision equipment, an NBC system and a front-mounted winch.

The first model to enter production was the four-man **VCR/TH** anti-tank vehicle, of which 106 were supplied to Iraq. This is fitted with the Euromissile UTM 800 turret with four HOT missiles in the ready-to-fire position and a further 10 missiles in the hull. Mounted over the rear part of the troop compartment is a remotely controlled 7.62-mm machine-gun.

Special-role models

The ambulance version is the **VCR/IS** with a higher roof so the medical staff can stand up. This can carry six seated and two stretcher patients or four stretcher patients plus the three-man crew consisting of commander, driver and medical orderly. The command post version is the **VCR/PC**, which has communications equipment and mapboards.

The repair vehicle is the **VCR/AT**, fitted with a block and tackle for lifting engines and other components; it carries a full range of spares and tools, but no winch.

There is also a VCR/TT 4 x 4 model of which 24 were delivered to the Argentine marines. This is propelled in water by two waterjets at 7.2 km/h (4.5 mph).

This Panhard VCR/TT armoured personnel carrier is fitted with a one-man turret armed with a 20-mm cannon. All VCRs are fully amphibious without preparation.

SPECIFICATION	
VCR	(155 hp)
Crew: 3+9	**Performance:** maximum road speed 100 km/h (62 mph);
Weight: 7000 kg (15,432 lb)	maximum range 800 km
Dimensions: length 4.565 m (14 ft 11½ in); width 2.495 m (8 ft 2 in); height (without armament) 2.03 m (6 ft 8 in)	(497 miles); fording amphibious; gradient 60 per cent; vertical obstacle 0.80 m (2 ft 7½ in); trench 1.10 m (3 ft 7½ in)
Powerplant: one Peugeot PRV V-6 petrol engine developing 116 kW	

Panhard M3
Armoured personnel carrier

The **Panhard M3** APC was a private venture, and the first production vehicles were completed in 1971. More than 25 countries purchased the vehicle, some for army use and some for police use. For example, Algeria took delivery of 44 vehicles for its *gendarmerie* fitted with a one-man turret armed with a machine-gun. Algeria also has the VPC, VAT, VLA and VTS variants in service.

Front-mounted engine

The hull of the M3 is of all-welded steel armour construction varying in thickness from 8- to 11-mm (0.315- to 0.43-in). The driver is seated at the front of the hull, with the engine immediately to his rear. The engine is coupled to a manual gearbox with six forward and one reverse gear, and

power is transmitted to the four road wheels by drive shafts that run inside the hull. The troop compartment is at the rear of the hull, a single door being provided in each side of the hull and twin doors in its rear. In the upper part of the hull side, which slopes inward, are three hatches hinged at the top, these enabling troops to use their small arms from within the vehicle. The main armament is normally mounted in the roof to the rear of the engine compartment: this armament ranges from a turret with single or twin 7.62-mm (0.3-in) machine-guns to a power-operated turret with a 20-mm cannon. Over the rear of the troop compartment is a small hatch on which is normally installed a rail mount with a 7.62-mm

machine-gun.

The M3 is fully amphibious, being propelled in the water by its wheels at a speed of 4 km/h (2.48 mph), but it can operate only in lakes and rivers with a slow current. Many vehicles are fitted with channels which can be quickly removed and placed in front of the vehicle to allow it to cross ditches and other battlefield obstacles. If required, the M3 can be fitted with passive night-vision equipment for the driver, an air-conditioning system (essential for Middle Eastern operators) and smoke dischargers. The

This Panhard M3 armoured personnel carrier has the driver's hatch open and is fitted with a Creusot-Loire STB shield with a 7.62-mm (0.3-in) machine-gun. Designed as a private venture, the M3 has been purchased by more than 25 countries, with more than 4,000 vehicles delivered.

basic M3 has also been adopted with particular equipment for a number of more specialised roles.

Role specialisation

The anti-aircraft model is called the **M3 VDA** and is fitted with a power-operated turret armed with twin 20-mm cannon. The **M3 VAT** repair vehicle has a full range of tools and is fitted

with a jib for lifting engines in the field. The **M3 VPC** command vehicle has extensive communications equipment. The ambulance model of the family is called the **M3 VTS** and is unarmed. The engineer vehicle version is the **M3 VLA**, and this is fitted with a hydraulically operated dozer blade at the front of the hull for the clearing of obstacles.

SPECIFICATION	
M3	engine developing 67 kW (90 hp)
Crew: 2+10	**Performance:** maximum road
Weight: 6100 kg (13,448 lb)	speed 90 km/h (56 mph); maximum
Dimensions: length 4.45 m	range 600 km (373 miles); fording
(14 ft 7.2 in); width 2.40 m	amphibious; gradient 60 per cent;
(7 ft 10.5 in); height (without	vertical obstacle 0.3 m (11¾ in);
armament) 2.00 m (6 ft 6.7 in)	trench with one channel 0.80 m
Powerplant: one Panhard Model 4	(2 ft 7.5 in) or with three channels
HD air-cooled 4-cylinder petrol	3.10 m (10 ft 2 in)

ACMAT
Armoured personnel carrier

A builder of cross-country trucks, ACMAT (Ateliers de Construction Mécanique de l'Atlantique) realised that there was a market for an APC on the same basic chassis, and therefore introduced the **ACMAT TPK 4.20 BL**, which is now in service with a number of African countries and also with Saudi Arabia.

Truck-derived design

The layout of the TPK 4.20 BL is similar to that of a truck, with the engine at the front, commander and driver in the centre and the troop compartment at the rear. The commander and driver each have a windscreen to their front which can be quickly covered by an armoured shutter, a side door with a bullet-proof window in its upper part, and a single-piece hatch cover above their position.

The troops are seated on bench seats down each side of the vehicle, and can exit quickly through the two doors in the hull rear. If required, firing ports and/or vision blocks can be provided in the sides and rear of the troop compartment, and a 12.7- or 7.62-mm (0.5- or 0.3-in) machine-gun turret

An ACMAT TPK 420 light APC with all its hatches closed and fitted with a Creusot-Loire one-man turret armed with one machine-gun.

can be mounted on the roof of the vehicle to give covering fire while the infantry dismount from the vehicle. Another model of the vehicle has an open-topped rear troop compartment with sides that can quickly be folded down on the outside.

Mechanical reliability

The well-proven Perkins six-cylinder diesel engine is coupled to a manual gearbox with four forward and one reverse gear and a two-speed transfer case. Steering is of the worm and nut type, and the exceptional operating range of 1600 km (994 miles) results from the large-capacity fuel tank which holds 370 litres (81.4 Imp gal). A spare wheel and tyre are normally carried on the wall to the immediate rear of the commander's and driver's position. Optional equipment includes an air-conditioning system, essential in many parts of the world if the infantry are to arrive at their

objective in any condition to fight, and different radio systems. Other armament options include a Euromissile MILAN anti-tank missile system with additional missiles carried internally in the troop compartment, and an 81-mm (3.2-in) Brandt mortar firing to the rear. In most infantry battalions six or eight mortars are normally issued to provide immediate and close-range support for the infantry. Artillery support is

normally not organic to an infantry battalion, although for some missions (for example a long-range patrol in North Africa by a battalion

of infantry in ACMAT trucks), it would often have a battery of four 105-mm (4.13-in) howitzers towed by similar vehicles.

SPECIFICATION	
TPK 4.20 BL	6.354.4 6-cylinder diesel developing
Crew: 2+8	93 kW (125 hp)
Weight: 7800 kg (17,196 lb)	**Performance:** maximum road speed
Dimensions: length 5.98 m	95 km/h (59 mph); maximum range
(19 ft 7.4 in); width 2.07 m	1600 km (994 miles); fording 0.80 m
(6 ft 9.5 in); height 2.21 m (7 ft 3 in)	(2 ft 7.5 in); gradient 60 per cent;
Powerplant: one Perkins Model	trench not applicable

SIBMAS Armoured personnel carrier

In the mid-1970s the Belgian company B N Constructions Ferroviaires et Métalliques started the development, as a private venture, of a 6 x 6 armoured personnel carrier which would have a number of common and proven commercial components. The first of two **SIBMAS** prototypes was completed in 1976, and one of these was tested by the Royal Malaysian army.

Two choices

Malaysia selected two vehicles, namely the Thyssen Henschel Condor 4 x 4 type from West Germany and the SIBMAS 6 x 6 type. The first SIBMAS vehicles were delivered in 1983, and the order comprised 24 and 162 examples respectively of the **SIBMAS ARV** armoured recovery vehicle and **SIBMAS Armoured Fire Support Vehicle 90**. The latter has a two-man Cockerill turret armed with a 90-mm (3.54-mm) Cockerill Mk III gun, 7.62-mm (0.3-in) co-axial and 7.62-mm anti-aircraft machine-gun, and fitted with an OIP fire-control system.

Steel construction

The hull of the SIBMAS is of all-welded steel construction providing the crew with

complete protection from small arms fire and shell splinters. The driver is seated at the front of the vehicle, with the crew compartment in the centre and the engine at the rear of the vehicle on the left side, an aisle connecting the troop compartment with a door in the hull rear fitted on the right side. Doors are provided in each side of the hull, and there are hatches over the troop compartment. Depending on the model, firing ports and/or vision blocks can be fitted in the

sides and rear of the troop compartment. If required, the vehicle can be fitted with a hydraulically operated winch to assist in self-recovery or the recovery of other vehicles.

The basic model is fully amphibious without preparation, being propelled in the water by its wheels at a speed of 4 km/h (2.4 mph), or optionally two rear-mounted propellers for a maximum water speed of 11 km/h (6.8 mph). Other optional equipment includes night-vision equipment, an

air-conditioning system, a heater and an NBC system.

There were a number of other armament options, most of them based on

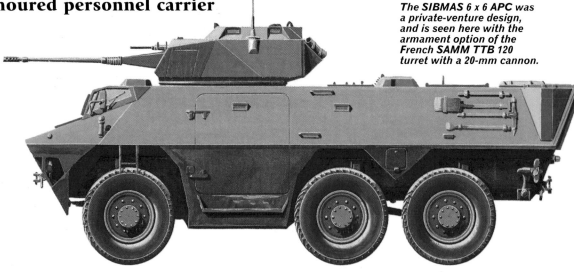

The SIBMAS 6 x 6 APC was a private-venture design, and is seen here with the armament option of the French SAMM TTB 120 turret with a 20-mm cannon.

French turrets and fire-control systems, but none had been ordered before the SIBMAS was taken out of production.

SPECIFICATION	
SIBMAS	liquid-cooled 6-cylinder diesel developing 239 kW (320 hp)
Crew: 3+11	**Performance:** maximum road speed 100 km/h (62 mph); maximum road range 1000 km (621 miles); fording amphibious; gradient 70 per cent; vertical obstacle 0.60 m (1 ft 11½ in); trench 1.50 m (4 ft 11 in)
Weight: 14500 kg to 16500 kg (31,967 to 36,376 lb) depending on role and armament	
Dimensions: length 7.32 m (24 ft 0 in); width 2.50 m (8 ft 2½ in); height (hull) 2.24 m (7 ft 4 in)	
Powerplant: one MAN D 2566 MK	

ENGESA EE-11 Urutu
Armoured personnel carrier

In 1970 ENGESA turned its attention to the development of a range of 6 x 6 wheeled vehicles to meet the needs of the Brazilian armed forces, and it was in 1970 that the **ENGESA EE-11 Urutu** APC appeared, production following from 1974.

The driver is seated at the front on the left side with the engine to his right and the troop compartment to his rear. Sitting on seats down each side of the hull facing each other, the troops enter the vehicle via a door in the side of the hull or through two doors in the hull rear.

Simple armament

Over the top of the troop compartment are four roof hatches, two on each side, which open outward, while

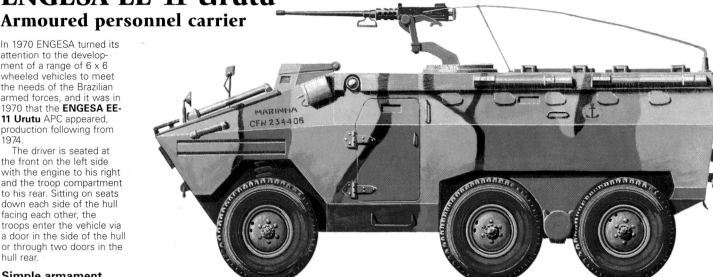

forward of this is the main armament. This can range from a pintle- or ring-

mounted 12.7-mm (0.5-in) M2HB machine-gun, via a turret armed with a 20-mm cannon and 7.62-mm (0.3-in) co-axial machine-gun, to a two-man turret armed with a 90-mm (3.54-in) gun, 7.62-mm co-axial and 7.62-mm anti-aircraft machine-gun. Firing ports and/or vision blocks can be installed in the troop compartment. The EE-11 is amphibious, being propelled in the water at 8 km/h (5 mph) by two propellers at the hull rear.

The ENGESA EE-11 Urutu armoured personnel carrier has a crew of two and can carry up to 12 fully armed infantrymen. The basic armament is one 12.7-mm (0.5-in) M2HB heavy machine-gun.

The EE-11 was produced in seven marks differentiated by their engines and transmissions, and optional equipment includes a winch, night-vision equipment, an NBC system and various radio installations.

A whole range of versions of the basic vehicle has now been designed by

the company, including ambulance, mortar carrier and cargo vehicles. When fitted with the 90-mm (3.54-in) two-man turret the EE-11 is known as the **Urutu Armoured Fire Support Vehicle** (AFSV), and Tunisia operates this variant.

SPECIFICATION	
EE-11 Urutu	diesel developing 158 kW (212 hp)
Crew: 2+12	**Performance:** maximum road speed 90 km/h (56 mph); maximum road range 850 km (528 miles); fording amphibious; gradient 60 per cent; vertical obstacle 0.60 m (1 ft 11½ in); trench not applicable
Weight: 13000 kg (28,660 lb)	
Dimensions: length 6.15 m (20 ft 2 in); width 2.59 m (8 ft 6 in); height (without armament) 2.09 m (6 ft 10 in)	
Powerplant: one Detroit Diesel 6V-53N liquid-cooled 6-cylinder	

BDX and Valkyr Armoured personnel carriers

In the early 1970s Technology Investments of Ireland designed and built the **Timoney** 4 x 4 APC prototype, and after trials with several prototype vehicles the Irish army finally ordered 10 vehicles in two batches of five. In 1976 Beherman

Demoen of Belgium obtained a licence from Technology Investments to manufacture the APC. The Belgian government ordered 123 vehicles under the designation **BDX**, and these were all built between 1978 and 1981. Of the 123, 43

were delivered to the Belgian air force for air-base defence, and the others were supplied to the Gendarmerie. All of the air force vehicles have a 7.62-mm (0.3-in) machine-gun, while the Gendarmerie vehicles comprise 13 fitted

with an 81-mm (3.2-in) mortar, 41 APCs, and 26 with a front-mounted dozer blade.

Limited sales

The BDX was also tested in a number of other countries but the only other operators have been Argentina (five vehicles) and Mexico (95 ex-Belgian vehicles).

Vickers Defence Systems of the UK further developed the BDX as the considerably improved **Valkyr**, whose first two prototypes were completed in 1982 and the third

in 1984. The Valkyr is powered by a General Motors Model 4-53T diesel coupled to an automatic transmission.

Two basic models of the Valkyr were offered as an APC and a weapons platform with a slightly lower profile and options for weapons stations such as a French turret armed with a 90-mm (3.54-in) gun and the Belgian CM-90 Cockerill turret armed with the 90-mm Cockerill Mk III gun, 7.62-mm (0.3-in) coaxial and 7.62-mm (0.3-in) anti-aircraft machine-guns.

As an APC the vehicle normally had a two-man crew and could carry 10 troops, who could leave the vehicle rapidly via twin doors in the hull rear. If required the Valkyr could be fitted with firing ports and/or vision blocks and a wide range of equipment and role-specific options.

The Vickers Valkyr, while based upon the Timoney/BDX design, was of significantly improved capability. The Valkyr could be fitted with a wide range of weapon systems, but it is thought that only two were sold to Kuwait.

SPECIFICATION

BDX
Crew: 2+10
Weight: 10700 kg (23,590 lb)
Dimensions: length 5.05 m (16 ft 7 in); width 2.50 m (8 ft 2½ in); height (hull top) 2.06 m (6 ft 9 in)
Powerplant: one Chrysler V-8 water-cooled petrol engine developing 134 kW (180 hp)

Performance: maximum road speed 100 km/h (62 mph); maximum road range 500 to 900 km (310 to 560 miles); fording amphibious; gradient 60 per cent; vertical obstacle 0.40 m (1 ft 4 in); trench not applicable

Tipo 6614 Armoured personnel carrier

Some years ago Fiat and OTO-Melara designed and built prototypes of the Tipo 6616 4 x 4 armoured car and the **Tipo 6614** 4 x 4 APC with identical automotive components, mostly from standard commercial vehicles, although their layouts were quite different. The Tipo 6616 is used in small numbers by the Italian police, and known export customers included Peru and Somalia.

It is estimated that by 2002 slightly more than 1,000 examples of the Tipo 6614 had been delivered to operators in seven countries, including South Korea, where licensed production has been undertaken by Asia Motors Incorporated, which calls the vehicle the **KM900**.

The hull of the Tipo 6614 is of all-welded steel construction that varies in thickness from 6 mm (0.24 in) to 8 mm (0.315 in), providing protection against

7.62-mm (0.3-in) small arms fire and light artillery splinters. The driver is seated at the very front of the vehicle on the left side with the engine to his right. The troop compartment is toward the rear, and the 10, including the commander, sit on individual bucket seats that can be quickly folded up. The troops enter and leave via a door in each side of the hull, or a power-operated ramp in the hull rear. A total of 10 firing ports is provided. Over the troop compartment is a two-part hatch, while to the front of this is the main armament installation. This is

Seen fording a stream, the Type 6614 APC shares many components with the Type 6616 armoured car. The APC can transport 10 men in addition to the driver, and the usual armament is a 12.7-mm (0.5-in) machine-gun.

normally an M113-type cupola with a single-piece hatch cover that opens to the rear, periscopes for all-round vision and a 12.7-mm (0.5-in) M2HB machine-gun. A turret armed with twin 7.62-mm (0.3-in) machine-guns can also be installed. Variants include a mortar carrier (known to be used by Peru) a command vehicle and an ambulance.

The Tipo 6614 is amphibi-

ous, being propelled in the water by its wheels at 4.5 km/h (2.8 mph), and before the vehicle enters the water four bilge pumps are switched on.

Optional equipment

A range of optional equipment is available apart from the different weapon stations, these including various types of passive night vision equipment, a spare wheel

and holder (often mounted on the roof of the troop compartment), smoke dischargers, an air-conditioning system, a fire extinguishing system, and a front-mounted winch with a capacity of 4500 kg (9,221 lb) and 40 m (131 ft) of cable. This last is designed for use in the recovery of other vehicles or to assist in self-recovery.

SPECIFICATION

Tipo 6614
Crew: 1+10
Weight: 8500 kg (18,739 lb)
Dimensions: length 5.86 m (19 ft 2½ in); width 2.50 m (8 ft 2½ in); height (hull top) 1.78 m (5 ft 10 in)
Powerplant: one Iveco Model 8062.24 liquid-cooled supercharged

diesel developing 119 kW (160 hp)
Performance: maximum road speed 100 km/h (62 mph); maximum range 700 km (435 miles); fording amphibious; gradient 60 per cent; vertical obstacle 0.40 m (1 ft 4 in); trench not applicable

YP-408 Armoured personnel carrier

In 1958 DAF built prototypes of an eight-wheeled APC. With a number of modifications and the replacement of the Hercules JXLD petrol engine by a more powerful DAF diesel, this was accepted for Dutch service as the **YP-408**, the first production vehicles were delivered in 1968. A total of 750 vehicles were built for the Dutch army and five are used by Surinam. The YP-408 has been replaced in Dutch service by the YPR-765, which is the Dutch version of the FMC Armored Infantry Fighting Vehicle.

This YP-408MT is towing a French-built Brandt 120-mm (4.72-in) mortar, and carries the seven-man mortar team as well as up to 50 mortar bombs. The machine-gun is a 12.7-mm (0.5-in) M2HB 12.7-mm (0.5-in) operated by the vehicle commander.

Armoured hull

The hull of the YP-408 is of all-welded steel construction varying in thickness from 8 mm (0.315 in) to 15 mm (0.59 in). The engine is at the front, the commander and driver are to the rear of the engine compartment and the troop compartment is at the rear. The YP-408 has four road wheels on each side, but only six of these are powered, making the YP-408 an 8 x 6 vehicle; it is the second pair of road wheels which is unpowered.

Steering is power-assisted on the front four wheels, and the tyres have reinforced side walls that enable the vehicle to be driven 50 km (31 miles) at a reduced speed after they have been punctured. The driver is seated on the left with the commander/ machine-gunner to his right. The 12.7-mm (0.5-in) M2 machine-gun can be traversed through 360° and elevated from -8° to +70°.

The 10 troops enter and leave through two doors in the hull rear, and are seated five down each side facing each other. Hatches are provided over the troop compartment. Standard equipment includes a heater, but the YP-408 lacks an NBC system and amphibious capability. If required, IR equipment can be fitted for the driver and the machine-gunner.

The basic armoured personnel carrier is called the **PWI-S(GR)**, this standing for **Pantser Wagen Infanterie Standaard (Groep).** The platoon commander's vehicle was the **PWI-S(PC)**, and had a crew of nine and extra communications equipment; and the battalion or company commander's vehicle was the **PWCO** with a crew of six, extra communications equipment and map boards. The **PW-GWT** ambulance was unarmed and can carry two litters and four seated patients plus its crew of a driver and two medical attendants. The **PW-V** cargo carrier could transport 1500 kg (3,307 lb) of freight. The **PW-MT** had a seven-man mortar team and towed a French 120-mm (4.72-in) Brandt mortar and 50 mortar bombs. Later versions were the **PWRDR** fitted with the British Marconi Avionics ZB 298 ground surveillance radar, and the **PWAT** anti-tank vehicle with the TOW missile system.

SPECIFICATION

YP-408
Crew: 2+10
Combat weight: 12000 kg (26,455 lb)
Powerplant: one DAF Model DS 575 6-cylinder diesel developing 165 hp (123 kW)
Dimensions: length 6.23 m (20 ft 5⅛ in); width 2.40 m (7 ft 10½ in);
height (including MG) 2.37 m (7 ft 9⅓ in)
Performance: maximum road speed 80 km/h (50 mph); maximum road range 500 km (311 miles); fording 1.2 m (3 ft 11 in); gradient 60 per cent; vertical obstacle 0.7 m (2 ft 4 in); trench 1.2 m (3 ft 11 in)

Ratel 20 Infantry fighting vehicles

For many years the British-supplied 6 x 6 Alvis Saracen was the South African army's standard APC. When it became apparent that future supplies of armoured vehicles and their all-essential spare parts were in some doubt, the South Africans decided to build a new vehicle to meet their own requirements. Sandock-Austral (now Alvis OMC) was building a modified version of the Panhard AML 4 x 4 armoured car with the name Eland, and received the task of designing and building the new vehicle.

The first production vehicles were completed in 1978. More than 1,350 examples of the Ratel were built for the home market and for export to Morocco. The South African army used the type operationally for the first time in May 1978, and after that Ratels were used on many deep strikes into Angola, where the type's large operating range proved to be very useful. The Moroccans have used their Ratels against Polisario fighters in the Sahara desert.

Internal layout

The basic vehicle is the **Ratel 20** and carries the commander and gunner in the turret, the driver at the front, the anti-aircraft machine-gunner at the rear and seven infantry. The two-man turret is armed with a 20-mm dual-feed cannon and 7.62-mm (0.3-in) co-axial machine-gun, a similar weapon being located on the turret roof for AA defence. Mounted on each side of the turret are two smoke-dischargers, and there is another 7.62-mm AA machine-gun at the right rear of the hull roof.

The **Ratel 60** has a similar crew, but has a two-man turret armed with a 60-mm (2.36-in) breech-loaded mortar and 7.62-mm co-axial and AA machine-guns.

The **Ratel 90** is the fire-support vehicle and has a two-man turret armed with the same 90-mm (3.54-in) gun as fitted to the Eland light armoured car, together with 7.62-mm co-axial and AA machine-guns. Some 69 rounds of 90-mm ammunition are carried (29 in the turret and 40 in the hull). The command member of the family has a nine-man crew consisting of the commander, driver, main gunner and six command staff, and is armed with a turret-mounted 12.7-mm (0.5-in) M2HB machine-gun and two 7.62-mm AA machine-guns. This variant has map boards, a pneumatically operated mast, intercom, internal loudspeakers, public address system and three radios for communication with other vehicles and higher command staff.

Other variants are a repair vehicle, 81- and 120-mm (3.2- and 4.72-in) mortar carriers, a model carrying the ZT-3 Swift anti-tank missile system, and an enhanced artillery observation post. An 8 x 8 logistic support variant was evaluated but not put into production.

SPECIFICATION

Ratel 20
Crew: 11
Weight: 19000 kg (41,888 lb)
Dimensions: length 7.212 m (23 ft 8 in); width 2.516 m (8 ft 3 in); height (overall) 2.915 m (9 ft 6⅔ in)
Powerplant: one Bussing Model D 3256 BTXF 6-cylinder diesel
developing 210 kW (282 hp)
Performance: maximum road speed 105 km/h (65 mph); maximum range 1000 km (621 miles); fording 1.20 m (3 ft 11 in); gradient 60 per cent; vertical obstacle 0.35 m (1 ft 1½ in); trench 1.15 m (3 ft 9⅓ in)

The Ratel series of infantry fighting and special-purpose vehicles was designed to meet the exacting requirements of the South African army, and has proved very successful.

Buffel Personnel carrier

The **Buffel** 4 x 4 vehicle, designed by Armscor on the basis of the Mercedes-Benz Model 416/162 Unimog high-mobility truck, has been the standard mine-protected APC of the South African army since 1978, and estimates suggest that some 2,400 vehicles of the series were completed. In layout the type is fairly conventional, with the engine at the front, and the driver above and to the left of the engine in a fully armoured cab characterised by a bulletproof combination of a windscreen and side windows. The hull's belly is V-shaped to offer the best possible protection against the effect of mines.

Troop compartment

The troop compartment over the rear of the vehicle has an open top and carries 10 infantry seated five down each side in a back-to-back arrangement. The only means of entry and exit is over the compartment's sides, which can be hinged down. Two machine-guns can be pintle-mounted on top of the hull, most generally on the right-hand front and left-hand rear corners of the troop compartment. In recent times the Buffel has been marketed with paired machine-guns with a gunner's shield.

Specialised variants include a mortar carrier, and the **Buffel Mk I** tractor with a fully armoured cab at the front but fitted with a cargo area at the rear with a drop tailgate to carry 2500 kg (5,511 lb). This has also been used as a prime mover towing, for example, a 20-mm light anti-aircraft gun.

During the 1995 International Countermine Conference in Copenhagen, Denmark, a request was made for a cheap MPV (Mine Protected Vehicle). Armscor responded with the combat-proved Buffel, and

The Buffel has the driver's cab and engine at the front of the vehicle on the left and right respectively, and the V-shaped belly helps to divert the blast of any mine detonation outward and upward.

numbers of remanufactured Buffels are now being made available for use in worldwide de-mining operations. Before being delivered for use in this task, each Buffel is completely rebuilt to create what is in effect a new vehicle offering protection against small arms fire, the detonation of one Russian TM57 anti-tank mine (or equivalent) anywhere under the vehicle, and the detonation of two TM57 mines under any wheel.

The **Buffel Mk II** has been developed in two basic sub-variants, namely the **Buffel Mk IIA** and **Buffel Mk IIB** with drum and disc brakes respectively. The Buffel Mk II is a rebuild of an earlier Buffel by No. 61 Base Workshop of the South African National Defence Force with a new and fully enclosed rear troop compartment accessed by a large rear door with steps below it. To the front, sides and rear are bulletproof windows, each of which is provided with one or two circular firing ports.

SPECIFICATION	
Buffel	OM 352 liquid-cooled 6-cylinder diesel developing 93 kW (125 hp)
Crew: 1+10	
Weight: 6140 kg (13,536 lb)	**Performance:** maximum road speed 96 km/h (59.5 mph); maximum road range 1000 km (621 miles)
Dimensions: length 5.10 m (16 ft 8.75 in); width 2.05 m (6 ft 8.75 in); height 2.995 m (9 ft 10 in)	
Powerplant: one Mercedes-Benz	

BMR-600/BLR-600 Armoured fighting vehicle/personnel carrier

In the early 1970s the Spanish army issued a requirement for a 6 x 6 infantry fighting vehicle which was developed by ENASA and the Spanish army under the designation **Pegaso 3.500**, later **BMR-600** (*Blindado Medio de Ruedas*, or wheeled medium armoured vehicle). The type was accepted for service against a requirement for at least 500. The company has now developed a complete family of vehicles using the same basic chassis, namely

the **Pegaso 3560.1** APC, **Pegaso 3560.53E** 81-mm (3.2-in) mortar carrier, **Pegaso 3560.54E** 120-mm (4.7-in) mortar towing vehicle, **Pegaso 3560.5** battalion command vehicle, **Pegaso 3564** fire-support vehicle, which can be fitted with armament such as the French TS-90 two-man turret with a 90-mm (3.54-in) gun, and the **Pegaso 3562.03 VEC** cavalry scout vehicle.

The hull of the BMR-600 is of all-welded aluminium construction. The driver is at the front on the left with the machine-gunner/radio operator to his rear and the engine compartment to their right. The troop compartment at the rear carries 10 troops who enter and leave the vehicle over a power-operated rear ramp. The main armament is normally a 12.7-mm (0.5-in) externally mounted machine-gun. The vehicle is amphibious, and if required can be delivered with waterjets for a maximum water speed of 10 km/h (6.2 mph).

BLR-600 4 x 4

The **BLR-600** (*Blindado Ligero de Ruedas*, or wheeled light armoured vehicle) is a 4 x 4 vehicle designed mainly for internal security operations and used in this role by the Spanish army and civil guard. The BLR's layout is unusual, the commander and driver being seated at the front of the vehicle with excellent observation to the front and sides, and 12 troops to the rear of the commander and driver and along the sides of the hull at the rear with four doors and four roof hatches. The 164-kW (220-hp) engine is in the centre of the hull at the rear. A cupola carries one 7.62-mm machine-gun.

The BMR (Blindado Medio de Ruedas) was designed for a battlefield role, and in addition to its embarked infantry, who can fire their weapons from inside the troop compartment, has a forward-mounted turret armed with a single cannon.

The BLR (Blindado Ligero de Ruedas) was designed by the Empresa Nacional de Autocamiones (which also builds the BMR-600 IFV) for use mainly in the internal security role. It is now used by the Spanish.

SPECIFICATIONS	
BMR-600	**BLR-600**
Crew: 2+10	**Crew:** 3+12
Weight: 14000 kg (30,864 lb)	**Weight:** 12000 kg (26,455 lb)
Dimensions: length 6.15 m (20 ft 2.1 in); width 2.50 m (8 ft 2.4 in); height (to hull top) 2.00 m (6 ft 6.7 in)	**Dimensions:** length 5.65 m (18 ft 6.4 in); width 2.50 m (8 ft 2.4 in); height (without armament) 2.00 m (6 ft 6.75 in)
Powerplant: one Pegaso 9157/8 liquid-cooled 6-cylinder diesel developing 228 kW (306 hp)	**Powerplant:** one Pegaso 9220 liquid-cooled 6-cylinder diesel developing 164 kW (220 hp)
Performance: maximum road speed 100 km/h (62 mph); maximum road range 700 km (435 miles); fording amphibious; gradient 68 per cent; vertical obstacle 0.80 m (2 ft 7.5 in); trench 1.20 m (3 ft 11.2 in)	**Performance:** maximum road speed 86 km/h (53.4 mph); maximum road range 800 km (497 miles); fording 1.10 m (3 ft 7.3 in); gradient 75 per cent; vertical obstacle 0.60 m (1 ft 11.6 in); trench not applicable

Ratel

During the time of its isolation from the international community as a result of its apartheid racial policy, South Africa was concerned to protect itself internally and externally from the threat posed by communist-backed liberation forces. This led to the launch of many fast-moving mobile operations in countries such as South-West Africa and Angola, where the distances to be covered were considerable and the lengths of paved roads minimal. The answer was the wheeled fighting vehicle offering high strategic mobility and good cross-country capability. Fast and reliable, these vehicles were well protected against the effects of mines and light weapons, and carried useful armament in addition to their embarked troops. The classic type was the 6x6 Ratel, seen here as a command vehicle. This version has a raised observation cuploa for the commander and gunner and equipment to support a six-man command post staff. A two-man manually operated machine-gun turret is fitted for defence.

The hull of the Ratel series of vehicles is of all-welded steel construction providing all-round protection against 7.62-mm (0.3-in) small arms fire and shell splinters, while the frontal arc is better protected to offer invulnerability to the effects of armour-piercing rounds up to a calibre of 12.7 mm (0.5 in). The hull was also designed to offer a high level of protection against the effects of mines, which were weapons much favoured by insurgents as they could be laid easily and inconspicuously in uneven dirt roads and tracks. The threat of the mine in the design thinking behind the Ratel is also reflected in the vehicle's ground clearance of 0.34 m (13½ in).

The driver of the Ratel command vehicle is seated, as in all other members of the Ratel series, on the vehicle's centreline in a cab offering good fields of vision through one forward and two lateral bulletproof windows. In a combat area these can be covered by armoured shutters hinged on their lower edges and operated by a single handle, the driver then relying on three periscopes. An overhead hatch opens to the left.

The Ratel command vehicle carries a two-man manually operated turret above the forward part of the hull. The turret provides 360° traverse, and is fitted with two machine-guns in the form of a 12.7-mm (0.5-in) Browning M2HB (designated as the L4 in South African service) and a co-axial 7.62-mm (0.3-in) machine gun. There are also two forward-firing dischargers for 81-mm (3.2-in) smoke grenades on each side of the turret. On top of the turret are a side-by-side pair of cupolas (with rearward-opening hatches) to provide the commander and gunner with good fields of vision.

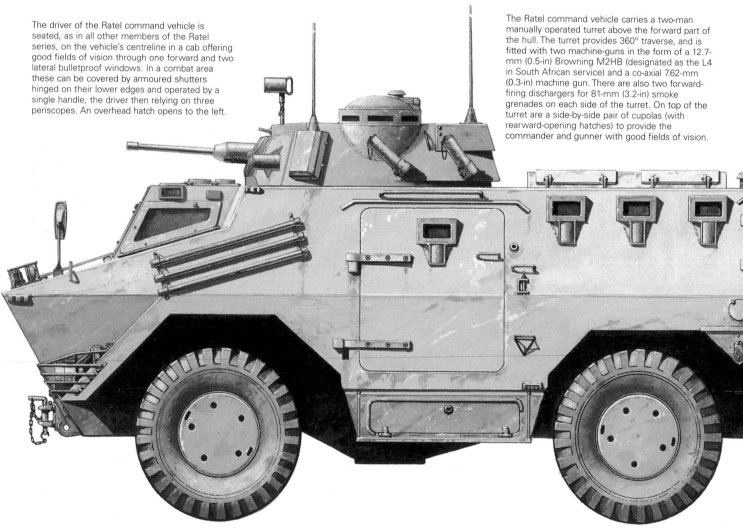

South African infantrymen mount their Ratel 6x6 infantry fighting vehicles. The type was designed by Sandock-Austral to meet very demanding requirements, including excellent cross-country mobility, an operational range of 1000 km (621 miles) and a very high level of mechanical reliability under any and all operational conditions.

All the vehicles of the Ratel family were powered by a Bussing D 3256 BTXF liquid-cooled 6-cylinder turbocharged diesel engine delivering 210 kW (282 hp) at 2,200 rpm. This engine was installed in the rear of the hull on the left-hand side in a compartment with a rear-mounted radiator and access panels in the roof for maintenance. The engine drew its fuel from an internal capacity of 430 litres (94.6 Imp gal), and drove the transmission by means of a Renk HSU 106 automatic gearbox with six forward and two reverse gears.

The hull compartment of the Ratel in its IFV forms carries seven or eight infantrymen, who enter and leave the vehicle by means of two large pneumatically-operated forward-hinged side doors just to the rear of the driver's position and each containing a vision block and firing port, and a door in the rear of the hull to the right of the engine compartment. There are three vision blocks and firing ports on each side of the hull compartment, which has four upward-opening hatches, which can be locked in the vertical position, above it. Above the passage to the rear door are two more hatches and a circular hatch with provision for mounting a 7.62-mm (0.3-in) machine-gun.

In the Ratel command vehicle the hull compartment is laid out for a command staff of six with equipment that includes three radios, a tape recorder with time injection, a combined radio receiver and cassette recorder, an intercom, internal loudspeakers, a public address system, map boards and a pneumatically operated radio mast.

The Ratel's suspension is based on solid axles with single-coil springs and double-acting hydraulic shock absorbers supported by wishbones and longitudinal arms. The front axle was the steering axle with a steering damper, intermediate steering arm and lockable differential, while the two rear axles were non-steering with lockable differentials and lockable differential. The main brakes were hydro-pneumatic on the front two wheels and pneumatic/mechanical on the rear four wheels, while the crawler brakes were pneumatic/ mechanical on the rear four wheels. The six wheels were of steel construction with 14.00 x 20 tyres containing run-flat inserts.

MOWAG Roland
Armoured personnel carrier

The basic Roland was designed from the outset for relatively easy conversion to a number of roles, including, as illustrated, that of the ambulance.

The **MOWAG Roland** 4 x 4 is the smallest vehicle currently produced by MOWAG in Switzerland, and is used mainly for internal security. The first production vehicles were completed in 1964, and known operators have included Argentina, Bolivia, Chile, Ghana, Greece, Iraq, Liberia, Mexico, Peru and Sierra Leone.

Simple concept

The hull is of all-welded steel armour providing the crew with protection from 7.62-mm (0.3-in) small arms fire. The driver is at the front, the crew compartment (with two side doors) in the centre, and the engine at the rear on the left side; there is also an aisle in the right side of the hull leading to a door in the hull rear.

In the centre of the roof is the main armament, normally a simple cupola with an externally mounted 12.7-mm (0.5-in) or 7.62-mm machine-gun. One of the alternative weapon stations is a turret above which is a remotely controlled 7.62-mm machine gun.

The petrol engine is coupled to a manual gearbox with four forward and one reverse gears and a two-speed transfer case, though the Roland was later offered with an automatic gearbox.

Internal security task

For the internal security role the Roland is normally fitted with an obstacle-clearing blade at the front of the hull, a public address system, wire mesh protection for the head lamps and sometimes the vision blocks as well, a siren and flashing lights. Another option is MOWAG bulletproof cross-country wheels. These consist of metal discs on each side of the tyre, the outside ones having ribs which assist the vehicle when crossing through mud.

In the late 1960s the company built another 4 x 4 APC as the **Grenadier**, with provision for nine men including the commander and driver. This model was sold to a number of countries but is no longer offered, having been replaced by the Piranha range of 4 x 4, 6 x 6 and 8 x 8 vehicles. The Grenadier's typical armament included a one-man turret armed with a 20-mm cannon and a turret with twin 80-mm (3.15-in) rocket launchers. The vehicle is amphibious, being propelled in the water by a propeller under the rear of the hull and steered by a pair of rudders moving in conjunction with the forward wheels.

SPECIFICATION	
Roland	developing 151 kW (202 hp)
Crew: 3+3	**Performance:** maximum road
Weight: 4700 kg (10,362 lb)	speed 110 km/h (68 mph); maximum
Dimensions: length 4.44 m (14 ft	road range 550 km (341 miles);
6⅔ in); width 2.01 m (6 ft 7 in);	fording 1.0 m (3 ft 3½ in); gradient
height (with turret) 2.03 m (6 ft 8 in)	60 per cent; vertical obstacle 0.4 m
Powerplant: one V-8 petrol engine	(1 ft 4 in); trench not applicable

BTR-152
Armoured personnel carrier

The USSR did not employ a tracked or wheeled APC in World War II, and Soviet infantry normally went in on foot or were carried on tanks.

Simple yet effective

The **BTR-152** was first seen in public during 1951, but probably entered service several years before this. The vehicle is basically the ZIL-151 truck chassis fitted with an armoured body, though later production vehicles from the **BTR-152V1** were based on the ZIL-157 chassis. From the early 1960s the BTR-152 was replaced in front-line Soviet motorised rifle divisions by the BTR-60 series of 8 x 8 APCs, which offered better cross-country capabilities. The BTR-152 and its variants were widely exported, and even in 2002 remains in service with some 24 countries. The type has seen action in the Middle East (with Syria, Iraq and Egypt), Africa and the Far East.

The first model to enter service was the BTR-152 with an open-topped troop compartment for 17 troops on bench-type seats running across the hull. The second model was the BTR-152V1.

A BTR-152 6 x 6 APC fitted with a central tyre pressure-regulation system, allowing the driver to adjust the pressure to suit the type of ground being crossed.

still with the open-topped troop compartment but fitted with a front-mounted winch and a central tyre pressure-regulation system with external air lines, enabling the driver to adjust the tyre pressure to suit the type of ground being crossed. The **BTR-152V2** was not fitted with a winch, but did have a tyre pressure-regulation system. The **BTR-152V3** had a winch, IR night-vision equipment and a central tyre-pressure regulation system with internal air lines more robust than those of the external system.

The main drawback of these versions was the open-topped troop compartment, which left the infantry vulnerable to overhead shell bursts, and this was rectified in the **BTR-152K** with full overhead protection. In all versions of the BTR-152 firing ports are provided in the sides and rear of the troop compartment, which has two rear doors.

Specialist models

The command version is the **BTR-152U** and has a much higher roof so the command staff can work while standing; it also has an armoured roof. The anti-aircraft model is the **BTR-152A**, which has at its rear a mount with twin 14.5-mm (0.57-in) KPV machine-guns that can be elevated from -5° to +80° with turret traverse through 360°. During the fighting in the Lebanon in 1982, the Israeli army captured a number of BTR-152s from the PLO: these vehicles had the towed ZU-23 twin 23-mm mount in the rear for considerably weightier firepower.

It is worth noting that the first APC deployed by the USSR after World War II was in fact the **BTR-40** 4 x 4 vehicle, which was based on a modified GAZ-63 truck chassis. This could carry eight troops in addition to its two-man crew, and was also used as a reconnaissance vehicle until the introduction of the BRDM-1 in the 1950s. Both the BTR-40 and BTR-152 were normally armed with a pintle-mounted 7.62-mm (0.3-in) machine-gun.

SPECIFICATION	
BTR-152V1	developing 82 kW (110 hp)
Crew: 2+17	**Performance:** maximum road
Weight: 8950 kg (19,731 lb)	speed 75 km/h (47 mph); maximum
Dimensions: length 6.83 m (22 ft	road range 780 km (485 miles);
5 in); width 2.32 m (7 ft 7½ in);	fording 0.80 m (2 ft 7½ in); gradient
height 2.05 m (6 ft 8½ in)	55 per cent; vertical obstacle
Powerplant: one ZIL-123 liquid-	0.60 m (1 ft 11½ in); trench 0.69 m
cooled 6-cylinder petrol engine	(2 ft 3 in)

BTR-60P series Armoured personnel carrier

The BTR-152 6 x 6 armoured personnel carrier introduced into service with the Soviet army during the 1950s had a number of major shortcomings, including poor cross-country mobility, as it was based on a truck chassis, and had a total lack of any amphibious capability.

Enhanced capabilities

In the late 1960s these deficiencies were largely overcome by the introduction of the **BTR-60P**, and this and later variants replaced the BTR-152 force used by the Soviet army: in Soviet service the BTR-60 series was normally used by the motorised rifle divisions, while the tank divisions were allocated the BMP-1 tracked MICVs and its improved variants. The BTR-60 series was exported to some 30 countries, the number of operator countries rising to 42 after the dissolution of the USSR, and Romania has produced a modified version under the designation **TAB-72**. The BTR-60 has seen action in many parts of the world, and the type was even encountered in Grenada during the American operation of 1984, when a few BTR-60PBs were met and quickly

The BTR-60PB 8 x 8 APC has the same turret as that fitted to the BRDM-2 4 x 4 scout car and also on the Czechoslovak OT-64C 8 x 8 vehicle.

destroyed by US forces.

The members of the BTR-60 series are all fully amphibious, being propelled in water by a single waterjet under the rear of the hull at a speed of 10 km/h (6.2 mph), and all based on essentially the same configuration with the commander and driver at the front, troop compartment in the centre and the two petrol engines at the rear. Each of these engines drives one side of the vehicle. Power-assisted steering is provided on the front two axles.

Steady evolution

The first model to enter service was the BTR-60P, and this is characterised by an open-topped troop compartment for 16 infantry seated on bench seats across the hull. Armament normally consisted of one 12.7-mm (0.5-in) and two 7.62-mm (0.3-in) machine-guns. This

The BTR-60PB 8 x 8 armoured personnel carrier is powered by two petrol engines, each of which drives the four wheels on each side of the vehicle. When afloat, the vehicle is propelled in the water by a single waterjet mounted in the hull rear.

The BTR-60 series has good cross-country mobility and can carry a large number of troops, but is hampered tactically by its poor provision for the embarked troops to dismount rapidly and get into action as a cohesive whole.

was soon replaced in production by the **BTR-60PA**, which has a fully enclosed troop compartment and carries a maximum of 16 troops, although its normal complement is 12. This model is generally armed with a pintle-mounted 7.62-mm machine-gun. The **BTR-60PB** is similar to the BTR-60PA but fitted with the same one-man manual turret as installed on the BRDM-2 4 x 4 scout car and the Czechoslovak OT-64C(1) armoured personnel carrier, used by Czechoslovakia and Poland (as the SKOT-2A) in place of the Soviet vehicle. The infantry carried by the BTR-60PA and the BTR-60PB can aim and fire their weapons from within the vehicle, although they normally have to dismount by climbing through the roof hatches. The command version of the vehicle is called the **BTR-60PU**, and this has additional communications equipment. There is also a forward air control vehicle, basically the BTR-60PB with the armament removed, an observation window in the forward part of the turret, and probably different radio equipment.

The BTR-60PB was replaced in first-line Soviet formations by the **BTR-70**, which is very similar in appearance and has the same turret but introduces a slightly more powerful engine and has improved seating and exit arrangements for the infantry. The roof hatches are supplemented by a small door in the lower part of the hull between the second and third road wheels. The BTR-70 has seen action in Afghanistan, where a number were fitted with a 30-mm grenade launcher on the roof.

A BTR-60PB 8 x 8 armoured personnel carrier swims ashore from a landing ship of the Soviet navy during exercises in the Red Banner Caucasian Military District.

SPECIFICATION	
BTR-60PB	each developing 67 kW (90 hp)
Crew: 2+14	**Performance:** maximum road
Weight: 10300 kg (22,708 lb)	speed 80 km/h (50 mph); maximum
Dimensions: length 7.56 m (24 ft	road range 500 km (311 miles);
9½ in); width 2.825 m (9 ft 3 in);	fording amphibious; gradient 60 per
height (to top of turret) 2.31 m (7 ft	cent; vertical obstacle 0.40 m (1 ft
7 in)	3¾ in); trench 2.0 m (6 ft 7 in)
Powerplant: two GAZ-49B liquid-	
cooled 6-cylinder petrol engines	

Humber 'Pig'
Armoured personnel carrier

When World War II was over, the British army drew up its requirements for a complete new generation of wheeled military vehicles including a 1-ton truck which was eventually produced by Humber/Rootes.

Wheeled APC

In the early 1950s the Alvis Saracen 6 x 6 armoured personnel carrier entered service, but as there would clearly be insufficient of these to go around it was decided to build another wheeled APC on the basis of the chassis of **Humber FV1600** series of trucks. This APC was not designed to operate with tanks, but rather to transport the infantry from one part of the battlefield to another, where they would dismount and fight on foot. About 1,700 vehicles were eventually built, the bodies being provided by GKN Sankey and the Royal Ordnance Factory at Woolwich.

By the 1960s the FV432, also designed and built by GKN Sankey, was entering

service in increasing numbers so the **'Pigs'** were phased out of service and placed in reserve or scrapped. The flare-up in Northern Ireland in the late 1960s meant that many of these vehicles were returned to service, remaining operational in Northern Ireland for some years.

Many of the Pigs in Northern Ireland were specially modified for the requirements of the internal security role, being fitted with additional armour protection to stop 7.62-mm (0.3-in) armour-piercing rounds and barricade-removal equipment at the front of the hull.

Related models

The basic armoured personnel carrier model was the **FV1611**, and this was normally outfitted for the carriage of six or eight fully equipped men in the rear, with the commander and

The 'Pig', as it became known, had been withdrawn from service before worsening civil disorder in Northern Ireland required its return to major service in the internal security role.

driver sitting at the front to the rear of the engine. Both the commander and driver were provided with a door in the side of their cab, and there were twin doors in the rear for the embarked infantry. A total of six firing ports/observation blocks are provided in the rear troop compartment (two in each side and one in each of the rear doors). The ambulance member of the family was the **FV1613**, which had a two-man crew and could carry three litter or eight seated patients, and the radio vehicle was the

The FV1609 model of the Humber 1-ton armoured personnel carrier entered service in the early 1950s. With an open top, capacity was two crew and up to eight troops.

FV1612. The anti-tank version was designated as the **FV1620**, otherwise known as the **Hornet/Malkara**, and this model had two Malkara long-range anti-tank guided missiles in the ready-to-launch position. The missile's obsolescence led to the FV1620's retirement.

SPECIFICATION	
FV 1611 'Pig'	Mk 5A liquid-cooled 6-cylinder petrol engine developing 89.5 kW (120 bhp)
Crew: 2+6 (or 2+8)	
Weight: 5790 kg (12,765 lb)	
Dimensions: length 4.926 m (16 ft 2 in); width 2.044 m (6 ft 8½ in); height 2.12 m (6 ft 11½ in)	**Performance:** maximum road speed 64 km/h (40 mph); maximum road range 402 km (250 miles)
Powerplant: one Rolls-Royce B60	

Alvis Saracen
Armoured personnel carrier

After the end of World War II the UK's Fighting Vehicles Research and Development Establishment (FVRDE) designed a complete family of wheeled armoured vehicles known as the **FV600** series which included the FV601 Saladin armoured car and the **FV603 Saracen** APC. The requirement for the latter was much more urgent because of the 'emergency' in Malaya, so the first production vehicles appeared by December 1952.

Production of the FV600 series was undertaken by Alvis at Coventry, and 1,838 vehicles had been completed by the end of production in 1972. Throughout the 1950s the Saracen was the only real APC in British army service, and was used in the Far

First produced in 1952, the FV603 Saracen APC was part of a family of 6x6 vehicles. The turret mounts a 7.62-mm (0.3-in) machine-gun.

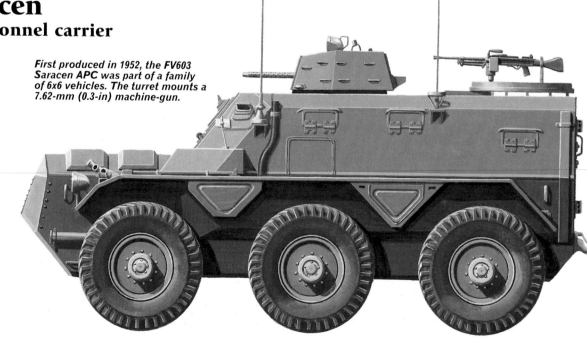

East and Middle East (for example Aden and Libya) as well as in the UK and with the British Army of the Rhine.

Tracked replacement
From the early 1960s the Saracen was replaced in the BAOR by the FV432 fully racked APC, which has better performance across country, improved armour protection and longer operational range. The last Saracens were retired from British service during 1993 in Hong Kong. Sales of the Saracen were also made to Indonesia, Jordan, Kuwait, Lebanon, Libya, Mauritania, Nigeria, Qatar, South Africa, Sri Lanka, Sudan, Thailand, UAE and Uganda, and it is still serving with seven of these.

Although the FV603 Saracen has the same automotive components as the FV601 Saladin armoured car, its layout is quite different, with the engine at the front and troop compartment at the rear. The driver is seated in the centre, with the section commander to his left rear and radio operator to his right rear. To their rear are the eight infantrymen, who are seated on individual seats (four down each side of the hull facing inward). The troops enter and leave via twin doors in the hull rear, and firing ports are provided in the sides and rear. On the forward part of the roof is a manually operated turret with a 7.62-mm (0.3-in) machine-gun, and over the rear part of the troop compartment is a 7.62-mm (0.3-in) light machine gun for air defence.

Steering is hydraulically assisted on the front four wheels, and the vehicle can be driven with one wheel missing from each side. Some vehicles supplied to the Middle East were not fitted with a roof.

Small-scale family
There were not many variants of the Saracen as the FV602 ambulance was cancelled early in the family's programme. The FV604 was a command vehicle, while

Versions of the Saracen included the FV604 command vehicle, seen landing from a Mexefloat while on exercise with the 13th/18th Hussars in Cyprus. Notice the extensive external stowage, the auxiliary generator on the front wing and the lack of the machine-gun turret.

the FV610 was another command vehicle with a much higher roof to allow the command staff to work standing up. The FV611 was an ambulance model and also had a higher roof. The FV610 was also fitted with the Robert surveillance radar but this did not enter service; the same fate befell the 25-pdr self-propelled gun version and a roller-type mineclearing vehicle.

SPECIFICATION

Saracen
Crew: 2+10
Combat weight: 8640 kg (19,048 lb)
Dimensions: length 5.233 m (17 ft 2 in); width 2.539 m (8 ft 4 in); height (overall) 2.463 m (8 ft 1 in)
Powerplant: one Rolls-Royce B80 Mk 6A liquid-cooled 8-cylinder petrol

engine developing 119 kW (160 hp)
Performance: maximum road speed 72 km/h (44.7 mph); maximum road range 400 km (248 miles); fording 1.07 m (3 ft 6 in); gradient 42 per cent; vertical obstacle 0.46 m (1 ft 6 in); trench 1.52 m (5 ft)

GKN Sankey Saxon
Armoured personnel carrier

As a private venture in the early 1970s, GKN Sankey built the **AT100** 4x2 and **AT104** 4x4 vehicles aimed mainly at the internal security role. The former secured no production order, but about 30 AT104s were built for the Dutch state police and Royal Brunei Malay Regiment.

Fresh design
These were followed by the **AT105** which later received the name **Saxon**. This was a completely new design using many automotive components of the Bedford MK 4-tonne 4x4 truck.

Production of the AT105 started by 1976, and by the programme's end 832 vehicles had been delivered to Bahrain, Hong Kong, Malaysia, Nigeria, Oman, UAE and UK. The British army purchased an initial three for evaluation purposes in the 1970s, and in 1983 ordered 50 further vehicles. The first of these were delivered early in 1984 and issued to infantry battalions in the UK which, in time

of war, would have been sent to West Germany to reinforce the British Army of the Rhine. The British army requirement was for up to 1,000 AT105s, but procurement reached just 664.

The AT105 has a hull of all-welded steel construction providing complete protection against small arms fire and shell splinters. Both left-and right-hand drive models were offered, the driver being seated right at the front of the vehicle with the engine to his left or right. The troop compartment is at the rear of the hull, and twin doors are provided in the hull rear and a single door in each side to allow for the rapid exit of troops. British army vehicles do not have the left-hand door as external bins are fitted for the

The AT105P has a commander's cupola with a pintle-mounted 7.62-mm (0.3-in) GPMG. The cupola can be replaced by one of a number of alternative armament installations.

stowage of kit and supplies.

The commander's roof-mounted cupola is fixed and fitted with an observation block in each of the four sides for all-round observation; a 7.62-mm (0.3-in) machine-gun is mounted on a DISA mount for ground and AA fire. A wide range of other armament installations can be fitted, including turret-mounted 12.7- and 7.62-mm (0.5- and 0.3-in) machine-guns or anti-riot weapons. Firing ports and/or vision blocks can be installed in the troop compartment. An unusual feature is that the mudguards are of light sheet steel construction that will blow off in the event of the vehicle hitting a mine so that the blast is not contained under the hull.

Proposed Saxon variants included a command vehicle, mortar carrier, armoured ambulance and various anti-riot versions.

The Saxon is certainly a beast of completely unlovely appearance, but it is a thoroughly utilitarian vehicle, offering good overall capabilities and excellent levels of reliability.

SPECIFICATION

Saxon
Crew: 2+8
Weight: 10670 kg (23,523 lb)
Dimensions: length 5.169 m (16 ft 11½ in); width 2.489 m (8 ft 2 in); height 2.86 m (9 ft 4½ in)
Powerplant: one Bedford 500 liquid-cooled 6-cylinder diesel

developing 122 kW (164 bhp)
Performance: maximum road speed 96 km/h (60 mph); maximum road range 510 km (317 miles); fording 1.12 m (3 ft 8 in); gradient 60 per cent; vertical obstacle 0.41 m (1 ft 4 in); trench not applicable

Verne Dragoon
Armoured personnel carrier

In the late 1970s the US Army Military Police issued a requirement for an air base protection and convoy escort vehicle air-portable in a Lockheed C-130 Hercules transport. The requirement lapsed, but the Verne Corporation (now AV Technology) built two private-venture prototypes of a vehicle which was eventually called the **Verne Dragoon**. In appearance the Dragoon is very similar to the Cadillac Gage V-100 and V-150 range of 4x4 multi-mission vehicles, but shares many common components with the M113A2 tracked APC and M809 6x6.5-ton truck, with obvious logistical advantages.

The hull of the Dragoon is of all-welded steel construction providing protection from 7.62- and 5.56-mm (0.3- and 0.22-in) small arms fire and shell splinters. The driver is seated at the front on the left with another crew member to his right, the main crew compartment is in the centre, the engine is at the rear of the hull on the right-hand side, and an aisle connects the main crew compartment with the door in the hull rear. The troops normally enter and leave the

vehicle via a door in each side of the hull, the lower part of each door folding down to form a step while the upper part hinges to one side. Firing ports with vision blocks above are provided in the sides and rear of the crew compartment. The diesel engine is coupled to an automatic transmission with five forward and one reverse gear and a single-speed transfer case, and steering is hydraulic on the front axle. The Dragoon is amphibious, being propelled in the water by its wheels at a speed of 4.8 km/h (3 mph), with three bilge pumps extracting any water that seeps in through the door and hatch openings.

When being used as a basic armoured personnel carrier the Dragoon is normally fitted with an M 113 type cupola with a pintle-mounted 12.7-mm (0.5-in) or 7.62-mm machine-gun to allow the maximum number of troops to be carried. Other and, indeed, considerably more powerful weapon installations are available, however, these including power-operated two-man turrets armed with a 25-mm cannon or a 90-mm (3.54-in) gun and 7.62-mm co-axial

and anti-aircraft/local defence machine-guns. More specialised versions include command, engineer, anti-tank (with TOW heavyweight missiles), recovery and internal security vehicles.

In 1982 six Dragoons were supplied to the US Army and a smaller number to the US Navy. The former is operated by the 9th Infantry Division High Technology Test Bed in two roles, electronic warfare and video optical surveillance. The first of these has extensive communications equipment and a hydraulically operated mast which can be quickly extended for

improved communications. The US Navy uses its vehicles for the armed patrol of nuclear weapons storage areas in Alaska and the continental USA. Other Dragoon operators are Thailand, Turkey and Venezuela, the last receiving 100 vehicles.

The electronic warfare Dragoon was operated for trials purposes by the US 9th Infantry Division, its roles including the jamming of high-speed communications and advanced battlefield direction finding.

SPECIFICATION	
Dragoon	Model 6V-53T liquid-cooled V-6
Crew: typically 3+6	diesel developing 224 kW (300 hp)
Weight: typically 12700 kg	**Performance:** maximum road
(27,998 lb)	speed 116 km/h (72 mph);
Dimensions: length 5.588 m	maximum road range 1045 km
(18 ft 4 in); width 2.438 m (8 ft);	(650 miles); fording amphibious;
height (hull top) 2.133 m (7 ft) but	gradient 60 per cent; vertical
varies with weapon fit	obstacle 0.99 m (3 ft 3 in); trench
Powerplant: one Detroit Diesel	not applicable

LAV-150 Commando
Armoured personnel carrier

Developed from the V-100 of 1962, the V-150 entered production in 1971. A wide range of armament can be fitted, including a two-man gun turret.

In the early 1960s Cadillac Gage designed a multi-purpose armoured vehicle revealed in 1963 as the **V-100 Commando** with a Chrysler petrol engine. Trials were so successful that the type entered production the following year for the export market. The war in South Vietnam revealed an urgent need for a wheeled vehicle to patrol high-value sites and escort road convoys, so large numbers of vehicles were shipped to Vietnam.

There followed the much larger **V-200** with a more powerful engine, greater weight and increased load-carrying capability. The V-200 was sold only to Singapore. In the 1970s there emerged the **V-150**, which is still the current production model. The V-150 introduced a number of improvements, including a diesel engine providing much greater

range. So far well over 3,000 V-150 vehicles have been

built for 29 countries.

The **LAV-150 S** 'stretched' model secured no US order but has scored limited export sales.

The V-150 is called a multi-mission vehicle as it can be used for a range of roles. In the basic APC model it has a three-man crew (commander, gunner and driver) and can carry nine troops, who enter and

leave the vehicle via doors in the hull sides and rear. A very wide range of armament installations can be fitted, including a one-man turret with various combinations of 12.7- and 7.62-mm (0.5- and 0.3-in) machine-guns; a power-operated two-man turret with 90-mm (3.54-in) or 76-mm (3-in) gun and 7.62-mm co-axial and AA machine-guns; and a turret

with 20-mm cannon and 7.62-mm co-axial and AA machine-guns. There is also an AA vehicle with a 20-mm Vulcan six-barrel cannon, 81-mm (3.2-in) mortar carrier, anti-tank vehicle with TOW missiles, command vehicle with raised roof for greater head room, riot control vehicle with special equipment, and recovery vehicle.

SPECIFICATION	
LAV-150 Commando	developing 151 kW (202 bhp)
Crew: 3+9	**Performance:** maximum road
Weight: 9888 kg (21,800 lb)	speed 88. 5 km/h (55 mph);
Dimensions: length 5.689 m (18 ft	maximum range 643 km (400 miles);
8 in); width 2.26 m (7 ft 5 in); height	fording amphibious; gradient 60 per
(hull top) 1.98 m (6 ft 6 in)	cent; vertical obstacle 0.61 m (2 ft);
Powerplant: one V-504 V-8 diesel	trench not applicable

Cadillac Gage V-300 Commando Armoured personnel carrier

In 1979 Cadillac Gage built two **V-300 Commando** 6x6 prototypes usable for a wide range of roles. In 1982 Panama ordered 12 V-300s all delivered in the following year. Four different models were selected by Panama: a fire-support vehicle with 90-mm (3.54-in) Cockerill gun, a recovery vehicle, and two types fitted with different machine-gun installations. Cadillac Gage also supplied three V-300s for the US Army and US Marine Corps Light Armoured Vehicle (LAV) competition: one was fitted with a two-man turret armed with a 90-mm Cockerill gun, while the other two had a two-man turret carrying the 25-mm Chain Gun.

The driver is seated at the front left with the engine to his right. The troop compartment is at the rear, the troops entering and leaving via the two doors in the hull rear; in addition there are hatches in the roof and firing ports with a vision block in the sides and rear.

The V-300 can be fitted with a wide range of armaments in a turret designed and built by Cadillac Gage. Among the two-man installations is a turret armed with the 90-mm Cockerill Mk III,

The V-300 was developed as a private venture. The heaviest of the wide range of weapons operable is the 90-mm (3.54-in) Cockerill Mk III gun, mounted in a two-man Cadillac Gage turret. A 7.62-mm (0.3-in) machine-gun is pintle-mounted for air defence.

or 76-mm (3-in) ROF gun or 25-mm Chain Gun, or 20-mm cannon; there is also a one-man turret with a 20-mm cannon or a machine-gun. In all of these there is a 7.62-mm (0.3-in) co-axial machine-gun, and a similar weapon can usually be mounted on the roof for AA defence.

Variants of what is now the **LAV-300** include an ambulance with a higher roof, anti-tank vehicle fitted with a TOW missile launcher, and an 81-mm (3.2-in) mortar carrier.

The LAV-300 is fitted with a front-mounted winch and is amphibious, being propelled in the water by its wheels at 5 km/h (3 mph).

SPECIFICATION

V-300 Commando
Crew: 3+9
Weight: 13137 kg (28,962 lb)
Dimensions: length 6.40 m (21 ft); width 2.54 m (8 ft 4 in); height (hull top) 1.981 m (6 ft 6 in) but varies with weapon fit
Powerplant: one VT-504 liquid-cooled V-8 diesel developing 175 kW (235 hp)
Performance: maximum road speed 105 km/h (65 mph); maximum road range 925 km (585 miles); fording amphibious; gradient 60 per cent; vertical obstacle 0.61 m (2 ft); trench not applicable

Cadillac Gage Commando Ranger
Armoured personnel carrier

The US Air Force has hundreds of vast bases spread all over the world, and in recent years these have become possible targets for terrorists and other fringe groups. To protect these assets the USAF issued a requirement for a vehicle which it called a Security Police Armored Response/ Convoy Truck that would, in addition to carrying out patrols on air bases, also escort convoys carrying ordnance to and from bases, or even from the storage dump on the airfield to the aircraft themselves.

After studying a number of proposals, early in 1979 the USAF selected the **Commando Ranger** APC to meet its requirements as the **Peacekeeper**. The first of these vehicles was handed over in the following year, and by 1994 some 708 had been delivered to the

Developed to meet US Air Force base security requirements, the Commando Ranger is also tasked with the escort of ordnance convoys.

USA and allied states.

The Commander Ranger is based on a standard Chrysler truck chassis with a shorter wheelbase. The armoured body provides the crew with protection from small arms fire and shell splinters. The engine is at the front of the vehicle and coupled to an automatic transmission with three forward and one reverse gear and a two-speed transfer case.

The commander and driver are seated to the rear of the engine, each being provided with a bulletproof window to his front and a rearward-opening side door that has a bulletproof vision block and a firing port underneath; in addition there is a firing port between the driver's and commander's windscreens.

The six troops sit three down each side in the rear, and enter via two doors in the hull rear. Each of these doors has a firing port, and the left one also has a vision block. In each side of the troop compartment is a vision block and a firing port.

In the roof is a hatch on which a variety of light armament installations can be fitted, including a shield with a 7.62-mm (0.3-in) machine-gun or a turret with twin 7.62-mm machine-guns.

Standard equipment includes an air-conditioning system and heater, while optional equipment includes 24-volt electrics in place of the normal 12-volt system, and a winch. Specialised versions include a command vehicle and an ambulance.

SPECIFICATION

Commando Ranger
Crew: 2+6
Weight: 4536 kg (10,000 lb)
Dimensions: length 4.70 m (15 ft 5 in); width 2.02 m (6 ft 7½ in); height 1.98 m (6 ft 6 in)
Powerplant: one Dodge 360 CID liquid-cooled V-8 petrol engine developing 134 kW (180 hp)
Performance: maximum road speed 112.5 km/h (70 mph); maximum road range 556 km (345 miles); fording 0.457 m (1 ft 6 in); gradient 60 per cent; vertical obstacle 0.254 m (10 in); trench not applicable

Cadillac Gage M706 Commando

The V-100 Commando was designed specifically to meet the demands of the export market, and was therefore created for the maximum possible reliability and operational flexibility. Reliability was successfully secured through the use of well-proved commercial components, which also made it considerably easier to maintain the vehicle in those parts of the world to which American trucks had been exported. Operational flexibility was provided by the creation of a simple design with a large centrally located compartment for the troops and/or alternative weapons. This central compartment could be of the covered type offering overhead protection and the ability to mount turreted armament, or of the open type for reduced cost but also reduced protection, but also offering the facility for the embarkation of heavy weapons such as an 81-mm (3.2-in) mortar or even an anti-tank missile launcher.

When the US Army found itself without a suitable convoy escort for use in Vietnam and had resorted to withdrawing M113s from front-line troops for these 'in the rear with the gear' duties, the Military Police took small numbers of the V-100 Commando, a private venture light armoured vehicle by Cadillac Gage. These initial XM706 vehicles were used for trials and after the MP recommended a number of small modifications the M706 was taken into service for escort duties in 1967. M706s, popularly called 'Ducks' by the MPs because of their pointed prows, were well received and were soon heavily involved in the fighting along the hazardous convoy routes. The usual armament for the M706 was a one-man turret with twin 0.3-in (7.62-mm) Brownings, but the US Air Force adapted the vehicle for its own use, designated it the M706E2, and replaced the turret with a universal mount on which a variety of guns could be fitted , the most common of which was the Browning M2HB 0.5-in (12.7-mm) machine-gun.

An overhead view of the V-100 reveals the basic layout of the vehicle with a forward section (driver on the left and commander on the right), a central section for the turret and its gunner and/or the embarked troops, and a rear section with the powerplant on the left. The troops entered and left the vehicle via three doors (a two-piece unit in each side and one at the rear to the right of the powerplant), and there was also a roof hatch.

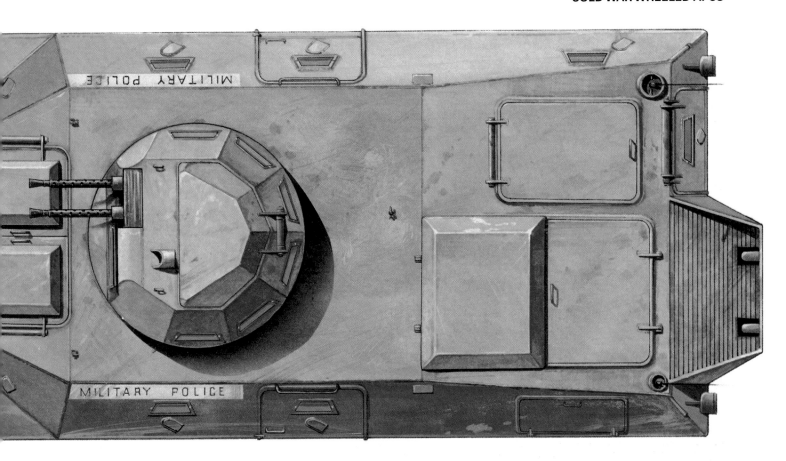

The V-100's large central payload compartment allowed the installation of several types of one-man turrets. That seen here on *Blind Faith*, an M706 of the 16th Military Police Group of the 93rd Military Police Battalion, carries two 0.3-in (7.62-mm) M73 machine-guns of the type developed for employment in tanks and other armoured fighting vehicles. A total of 3,800 rounds of ammunition was carried.

Powered by a Chrysler petrol engine, the V-100 was somewhat vulnerable in the event of damage to the fuel system as the petrol was highly flammable. This was one of the reasons for the option in the later V-150 of a lower-powered Cummins engine running on lower-volatility diesel fuel. Another change in this heavier development was the use of strengthened axles. Early model M706s had no engine protection against Molotov cocktails, but this was soon corrected.

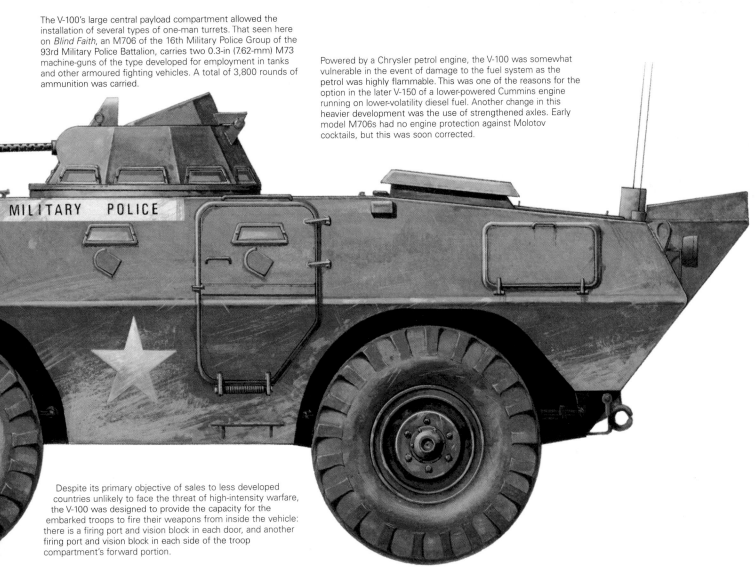

Despite its primary objective of sales to less developed countries unlikely to face the threat of high-intensity warfare, the V-100 was designed to provide the capacity for the embarked troops to fire their weapons from inside the vehicle: there is a firing port and vision block in each door, and another firing port and vision block in each side of the troop compartment's forward portion.

Steyr SK 105 Light tank/tank destroyer

The **Jagdpanzer SK 105** was designed by Steyr in the mid-1960s to an Austrian requirement. The first prototype was completed in 1967, with production beginning during the early 1970s. Some 652 examples were built – 286 for the Austrian army and the remainder for export to Argentina, Bolivia, Botswana, Brazil, Morocco and Tunisia. Over the years some updates, such as a stabilised turret on the **SK 105/A2**, were introduced. Many of the SK 105's automotive components are identical to those of the Saurer 4K 4FA tracked armoured personnel carrier.

Limited protection

Over its frontal arc the vehicle has protection from attack by all weapons up to 20-mm calibre, protection against small aims fire being provided over the remainder of the vehicle. The turret is a modified version of that installed on the AMX-13 light tank. It is of the oscillating type, with the gun fixed to the upper part and pivoting on the lower part. The main armament comprises a 105-mm (4.13-in) gun, and ammunition stowage is provided for 44 main gun rounds as well as 2,000 rounds for the 7.62-mm (0.3-in) co-axial machine-gun. The main gun is fed by two revolver-type magazines in the turret bustle, enabling the gun to fire until the ammunition is exhausted. One of the crew then has to leave the vehicle to reload the magazines. Empty cartridge cases are ejected from the turret through a small trap in the bustle. Fire

An SK 105 climbs an incline, showing the French TCV 29 laser rangefinder on the turret roof at the rear with an IR/white light searchlight above it. The 105-mm main gun is fed by two six-round revolver magazines.

control includes telescopes for the commander and gunner with an IR/white light searchlight above this.

Transmissions

The diesel engine and transmission are at the rear, the latter being a ZF manual box replaced in the **SK 105/A1** by an automatic transmission. The suspension is of the torsion-bar type, consisting on each side of five dual rubber-tyred road wheels with the drive sprocket at the rear, idler at the front and three track-return rollers. The standard equipment includes an NBC system and a heater.

SK 105 variants include the **Greif** armoured recovery vehicle, the **Pionier** combat engineer vehicle, and the **Fahrschulpanzer** driver training vehicle. The Greif is fitted with a 6-tonne hydraulic crane, a dozer/stabiliser blade at the front of the hull, a winch with a pulling capacity of 20 tonne and full provision for spare parts and tools.

SPECIFICATION	
Steyr SK 105	**Powerplant:** one 239-kW (320-hp)
Crew: 3	Steyr liquid-cooled 6-cylinder diesel
Weight: 17.7 tonnes	**Performance:** maximum road speed
Dimensions: length (including gun)	65 km/h (40 mph); maximum road
7.76 m (25 ft 5½ in) and (hull)	range 520 km (325 miles)
5.58 m (18 ft 3½ in); width 2.5 m	**Fording:** 1 m (3 ft 3 in)
(8 ft 2½ in); height 2.53 m (8 ft	**Gradient:** 75 per cent
3½ in)	**Vertical obstacle:** 0.8 m (2 ft
Armament: one 105-mm (4.13-in)	7½ in)
105 G1 main gun, and one 7.62-mm	**Trench:** 2.41 m (7 ft 11 in)
(0.3-in) Steyr MG 74 machine-gun	

ENGESA EE-9 Cascavel Armoured car

During the late 1960s the Sao Paulo company ENGESA, formerly a truck manufacturer, developed two 6x6 armoured vehicles to meet the requirements of the Brazilian army. These were the **EE-9 Cascavel** armoured car and the EE-11 Urutu APC, which shared many automotive components even though their layouts were different. The EE-9 prototype, named after a Brazilian snake, was completed in 1970 and was followed by a batch of pre-production vehicles before the first production examples were completed at what was then the company's new facility at Sao Jose dos Campos during 1974. Large numbers were built, not only for the Brazilian army but also for many other countries, including Bolivia, Burkina Faso,

Chad, Chile, Colombia, Cyprus, Ecuador, Gabon, Ghana, Iraq, Libya, Nigeria, Paraguay, Surinam, Togo, Tunisia, Uruguay and Zimbabwe.

The Cascavel was deployed operationally by Iraq during their war with Iran, which captured a number of vehicles. Although ENGESA is no longer trading, many Cascavels remain in service.

A least six different Cascavel marks were produced, although the layout of all EE-9s remains essentially the same. The driver is seated at the front of the vehicle on the left, with the two-man turret in the centre, and the engine and transmission at the rear. The engine is either a Detroit Diesel or a Mercedes-Benz diesel, coupled to an automatic or

manual transmission. Spare parts for both the engine and transmission are available from commercial sources all over the world. All six wheels are powered, and power-assisted steering is provided on the front two wheels. The armour is of a locally designed type with a hard steel outer shell and a softer inner layer designed to provide the maximum protection within the vehicle's weight limitations.

Armament variations

The **Cascavel Mk II** initial production model had the same 37-mm (1.46-in) gun as the M3 Stuart light tank, then still in service with the Brazilian army, but all of these vehicles were rebuilt with an ENGESA turret armed with a 90-mm

(3.54-in) gun. The **Cascavel Mk III** was only for export, having a French Hispano-Suiza H-90 turret armed with a 90-mm GIAT gun. The other models, the **Cascavel Mks IV, V, VI** and **VII** have a two-man ENGESA ET-90 turret armed with a 90-mm Cockerill Mk III gun made under licence in Brazil by ENGESA as the EC-90, a 7.62-mm (0.3-in) co-axial machine-gun and a 12.7-mm (0.5-in) or 7.62-mm machine-gun on the roof for AA defence.

As in most modern armoured cars, a wide range

of optional equipment could (and still can) be fitted or retrofitted to the Cascavel, including a fire-control system, a laser rangefinder mounted externally over the main armament or operating through the gunner's sight, day/night sights for the commander and gunner, an NBC system and a ventilation system. A characteristic of all the models is a central tyre pressure regulation system to enable the driver to adjust the pressure to suit the nature of the terrain being crossed.

The later production variants of the ENGESA EE-9 Cascavel armoured car carry a laser rangefinder mounted externally over the 90-mm (3.54-in) gun and a 7.62-mm (0.3-in) machine-gun mounted externally at the commander's station. The EE-9 was widely used by the Iraqi army during the 1980s war with Iran.

SPECIFICATION	
ENGESA EE-9 Cascavel	**Powerplant:** one 158-kW (212-hp)
Crew: 3	Detroit Diesel 6V-53 liquid-cooled
Weight: 13.4 tonnes	6-cylinder diesel
Dimensions: length (gun forward)	**Performance:** maximum road
6.22 mm (20 ft 5 in) and (hull)	speed 100 km/h (62 mph);
5.19 m (17 ft ¼ in); width 2.59 m	maximum road range 1000 km
(8 ft 6 in); height 2.29 m (7 ft 6 in)	(620 miles)
Armament: (Mk IV) one 90-mm	**Fording:** 1 m (3 ft 3 in)
(3.54-in) EC-90 gun, one 7.62-mm	**Gradient:** 60 per cent
(0.3-in) co-axial machine-gun, and	**Vertical obstacle:** 0.6 m (1 ft
one 12.7-mm (0.5-in) M2 HB or	11½ in)
7.62-mm AA machine-gun	

Panhard EBR Heavy armoured car

The origins of the Panhard **EBR** (**Engin Blinde de Reconnaissance** or armoured reconnaissance vehicle) can be traced to 1937, when Panhard et Levassor of Paris started design work on a new armoured car that would have superior cross-country mobility to the 4x4 armoured cars then in use by the French army. The first prototype was completed in 1939 with the armament of one 25-mm cannon and one 7.5-mm (0.295-in) co-axial machine-gun. Its most unusual feature was that of its eight road wheels, the four centre ones (two on each side) were fitted with steel rims for improved traction: during road movement, these were raised clear of the ground by a hydro-pneumatic unit operated by the driver, and then lowered again for cross-country travel.

Revived effort

After the end of World War II the French army issued a requirement for a new heavy armoured car and, after a number of proposals from French companies had been studied, Panhard et Levassor was awarded a contract for an 8x8 vehicle while Hotchkiss was awarded a contract for a 6x6 vehicle.

The Panhard EBR 8x8 vehicle was the standard heavy armoured car of the French army from 1950, although its design dated back to before World War II. An unusual feature of the vehicle was that its centre pairs of road wheels, which had steel rims, were normally raised when travelling on roads and lowered only when going across country, so improving ground traction in mud and soft soils.

Each company built prototypes for evaluation by the French army, and the Panhard et Levassor vehicle was subsequently selected for service as the EBR. The first production vehicles were completed in 1950, and in a manufacturing programme that lasted to 1960, some 1,200 vehicles were built. In addition to the French army, the type was also exported to Mauritania, Morocco and Tunisia. An armoured personnel carrier version, the **EBR VTT**, was also developed by Panhard on the same chassis, and a few of these were exported to Portugal, where they were used mainly for internal security duties. The EBR was finally phased out of French Army service in 1987, some 50 years after its design.

The driver was seated at the front, with the commander and gunner in the centre of the vehicle, the engine in the floor and the second driver at the rear. The EBR had an FL-11 oscillating turret armed with a 90-mm (3.54-in) gun, 7.5-mm co-axial machine-gun and two banks of electrically operated smoke dischargers. In an oscillating turret the gun was fixed in the upper part of the turret, which pivoted on the lower part of the turret. The 90-mm gun fired the following types of fixed ammunition: HEAT (muzzle velocity 640 m/2,100 ft per second), HE (muzzle velocity 635 m/2,085 ft per second), smoke (muzzle velocity 750 m/2,460 ft per second) and canister for close defence. Ammunition totals were 43 rounds of 90-mm

and 2,000 of 7.5-mm.

Another unusual feature of the EBR was that the drivers at the front and rear were each provided with a 7.5-mm fixed machine-gun. Some vehicles were fitted with the FL-10 turret of the AMX-13 light tank armed with a 75-mm (2.95-in) gun fed by two revolver-type magazines, each holding six rounds of ammunition. These allowed

12 rounds to be fired very quickly, after which the magazines had to be reloaded manually from outside the vehicle. The main drawback of this combination was that the weight of the vehicle went up to over 15 tonnes, while overall height was also increased, thereby adding to the probability of the vehicle's detection in the field.

SPECIFICATION	
EBR	petrol engine
Crew: 4	**Performance:** maximum road
Weight: 13.5 tonnes	speed 105 km/h (65 mph);
Dimensions: length (gun forward)	maximum road range 650 km
6.15 m (20 ft 2 in); width 2.42 m	(404 miles)
(7 ft 11¼ in); height 2.32 m (7 ft	**Gradient:** 60 per cent
7¼ in)	**Vertical obstacle:** 0.4 m (1 ft
Powerplant: one-149 kW (200-hp)	3¾ in)
Panhard liquid-cooled 12-cylinder	**Trench:** 2 m (6 ft 7 in)

GIAT AMX-13 Light tank

The **AMX-13** light tank was one of three armoured vehicles designed in France immediately after the end of World War II, the other being the Panhard EBR heavy armoured car and the AMX-50 MBT which did not enter service. The AMX-13 was designed by the Atelier de Construction d'Issy-les-Moulineaux, the numeral 13 in the designation being the specified design weight in tonnes.

The first prototype was completed in 1948 and production had begun at the Atelier de Construction Roanne (ARE) by 1952. The AMX-13 continued in production at the ARE until the 1960s, when space was needed for the AMX-30 MBT and AMX-10P IFV families. Production of the whole AMX-13 family, including the light tank, was transferred to Creusot-Loire at Chalon-sur Saône. The AMX-13 finally became a GIAT Industries product before production ceased. Over 7,700 vehicles were built and the type remains in service with several nations, many of them updated in various ways, including a conversion to diesel power. The chassis of the AMX-13 (extensively modified in many cases) was used as the basis for one of the most complete families

An AMX-13 light tank fitted with an FL-10 two-man turret armed with the original 75-mm (2.95-in) gun. Other versions were armed with 90-mm (3.54-in) or 105-mm (4.13-in) guns.

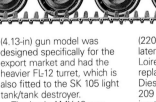

of AFVs ever developed. It included the 105-mm (4.13-in) Mk 61 self-propelled howitzer, 155-mm (6.1-in) Mk F3 self-propelled gun, AMX-13 DCA twin 30-mm self-propelled anti-aircraft gun system, and the AMX VCI infantry fighting vehicle and its countless variants (all discussed elsewhere), the **AMX VCG** engineer vehicle, **AMX-13 ARV** armoured recovery vehicle and the **AMX-13 CPP** armoured bridgelayer. Many further variants were produced exclusively for export.

Light armament

The original model of the AMX-13 was fitted with the FL-10 turret armed with a 75-mm (2.95-in) gun and a 7.62-mm (0.3-in) co-axial machine-gun. This turret is of

the oscillating type and the 75-mm gun is fed by two revolver-type magazines, each of which holds six rounds of ammunition. This model was used in some numbers by Israel during the 1967 Six-Day War, but the gun was found to be ineffective against the frontal armour of the Soviet T-54 and T-55 MBTs operated by Syria and Egypt, so it was phased out of service, most going to Singapore or Nepal.

At a later date all 75-mm models of the French army were fitted with a 90-mm (3.54-in) gun which could fire canister, HE, HEAT and smoke projectiles, later supplemented by an APFSDS projectile capable of penetrating a triple NATO tank target at an incidence of 60 degrees at a range of 2000 m (2,195 yards). The 105-mm

(4.13-in) gun model was designed specifically for the export market and had the heavier FL-12 turret, which is also fitted to the SK 105 light tank/tank destroyer.

The basic AMX-13 was built with a petrol engine offering an operative range of between 350 and 400 km

(220 and 250 miles), but in a later development Creusot-Loire offered a package to replace this with a Detroit Diesel unit developing 209 kW (280 hp) and boosting the operational range to 500 km (311 miles) as well as reducing the risk of fire.

SPECIFICATION	
AMX-13 (90-mm gun)	SOFAM 8Gxb liquid-cooled
Crew: 3	8-cylinder petrol engine
Weight: 15 tonnes	**Performance:** maximum road
Dimensions: length (gun forward)	speed 60 km/h (37 mph); maximum
6.36 m (20 ft 10¼ in) and (hull)	road range 350-400 km
4.88 m (16 ft); width 2.5 m (8 ft	(220-250 miles)
2½ in); height 2.3 m (7 ft 6½ in)	**Fording:** 0.6 m (1 ft 11½ in)
Armament: one 90-mm (3.54-in)	**Gradient:** 60 per cent
main gun, one 7.62-mm (0.3-in)	**Vertical obstacle:** 0.65 m (2 ft
machine-gun, and one optional	1¼ in)
7.62-mm AA machine-gun	**Trench:** 1.6 m (5 ft 3 in)
Powerplant: one 186-kW (250-hp)	

AMX-10RC Reconnaissance vehicle

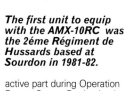

During the 1960s the French army issued a requirement for an amphibious armoured car with a powerful gun, advanced fire-control system and good cross-country mobility. The resulting **AMX-10RC** was placed in production at the Atelier de Construction Roanne for service from 1981.

The AMX-10RC has two major drawbacks: it is more expensive than some MBTs, and is too sophisticated for many potential users. For these reasons the French army trimmed its original requirements to 337 units, and export sales were made only to Morocco (108) and Qatar (12). The type saw action in Chad and played an

The first unit to equip with the AMX-10RC was the 2éme Régiment de Hussards based at Sourdon in 1981-82.

active part during Operation Desert Storm. Production has now ceased and planned update programmes were abandoned, although a battlefield management system and improved thermal cameras have been installed.

Structural details

The hull and turret of the AMX-10RC are of all-welded aluminium construction, with

the driver at the front left, the turret in the centre and the engine and transmission at the rear. The 6x6 suspension is unusual in that the driver can adjust its ground clearance to suit the type of ground being crossed and tilt it from side to side. Many automotive components, including the engine and transmission, are identical with those of the AMX-10P tracked MICV. The vehicle is amphibious, being propelled in the water by two waterjets imparting a maximum speed

The AMX-10RC, seen here in desert operations, is very capable but also very expensive. The type has moderately good armament and advanced fire control.

of 7.2 km/h

The com-
ner are sea-
the turret, v
the left. The
comprises
105-mm (4.
a 7.62-mm
machine-gu
4,000 round
Two electrica.
smoke discharge

SPECIFICATION	
AMX-10RC	8-cylinder diesel
Crew: 4	**Performance:** maximum road speed
Weight: 15.88 tonnes	85 km/h (53 mph); maximum road
Dimensions: length (gun forward)	range 800 km (500 miles)
9.15 m (30 ft ¼ in) and (hull) 6.35 m	**Fording:** amphibious
(20 ft 10 in); width 2.95 m (9 ft 8 in);	**Gradient:** 60 per cent
height 2.68 m (8 ft 9½ in)	**Vertical obstacle:** 0.7 m (2 ft 3¼ in)
Powerplant: one 194-kW (260-hp)	**Trench:** 1.15 m (3 ft 9 in)
Baudouin 6F 11 SRX liquid-cooled	

Panhard AML 90 Light armoured car

The French army used large numbers of British-built Daimler Ferret 4x4 scout cars in North Africa during the 1950s, and then decided to procure a similar vehicle with a wider range of armament installations. After evaluation of prototype vehicles, the design from Panhard was selected. Production began in 1960 under the designation **AML**, (**Auto-Mitrailleuse Légère**, or light armoured car), and since then well over 4,000 vehicles have been built in several variants, with production continuing to this day for export. The type was also built in South Africa by Sandock Austral for the South African army, which calls the type the **Eland**. The AML, which is in service with 40 countries, shares 95 per cent of its automotive components with the Panhard M3 APC, and many countries operate M3 and AML fleets with the obvious financial, logistical and training advantages.

The layout of all variants is similar, with the driver at the front, the two-man turret in the centre (with an entry door in each side of the hull) and the engine and transmission at the rear.

One of the most common models is the **AML 90**. The AML's original H 90 turret

with a 90-mm (3.54-in) gun was replaced by a Lynx 90 two-man turret also designed and built by Hispano-Suiza and armed with a 90-mm GIAT gun, a 7.62-mm (0.3-in) co-axial machine-gun and a 7.62-mm anti-aircraft machine-gun. The 90-mm gun can fire a wide range of fixed ammunition, including HEAT, HE, smoke and canister. The HEAT round will penetrate 320 mm (12.6 in) of armour at an incidence of 0° or 120 mm (4.72 in) of armour at an incidence of 65°. Totals of 21 rounds of 90-mm and 2,000 rounds of 7.62-mm ammunition are carried. Optional equipment for this turret includes passive night-vision equipment, powered controls and a laser rangefinder.

Mortar versions

The **HE 60-7** turret has a 60-mm (2.36-in) breech-loaded mortar and two 7.62-mm machine-guns, the **HE 60-12** turret a similar mortar and a 12.7-mm (0.5-in) machine-gun, and the **HE 60-20** turret has the 60-mm mortar and a 20-mm cannon. The breech-loaded mortar is used both in the indirect and direct fire modes, and is very useful in guerrilla-type operations as it can be fired over

hills and buildings.

One of the more recent turrets is the **HE 60-20 Serval** with a 60-mm long-barrel mortar mounted in its front with a 20-mm cannon and 7.62-mm machine-gun mounted externally at the turret rear. For the export market an AA model of the AML was developed with a two-man **SAMM S 530** turret armed with twin 20-mm cannon, each with 300 rounds of ready-use ammunition. Turret traverse and weapon elevation are powered for enhanced engagement capability.

Lighter armament

More recently, scout car versions of the AML have been developed with various combinations of 7.62-mm and 12.7-mm machine-guns on

The AML 90 has been one of the most successful wheeled AFVs of the period after World War II, with over 4,000 built in France and South Africa. This model has a 90-mm (3.54-in) gun.

pintle mounts or in turrets. These have a lower profile than the 90-mm gun models, are lighter, much cheaper and well suited for light reconnaissance.

As usual a wide range of optional equipment can be

fitted, including passive night vision equipment, an air-conditioning system and a complete NBC system. An amphibious kit was developed, but as far as is known this was not produced in quantity.

SPECIFICATION	
Panhard AML-90	engine developing 67 kW (90 hp)
Crew: 3	**Performance:** maximum road
Weight: 5.5 tonnes	speed 90 km/h (56 mph); maximum
Dimensions: length (including gun)	road range 600 km (375 miles)
5.11 m (16 ft 9¼ in) and (hull) 3.79 m	**Fording:** amphibious
(12 ft 5¼ in); width 1.97 m (6 ft	**Gradient:** 60 per cent
5½ in); height 2.07 m (6 ft 9½ in)	**Vertical obstacle:** 0.3 m (1 ft)
Powerplant: one Panhard 4 HD	**Trench:** 0.8 m (2 ft 7½ in) with one
liquid-cooled 4-cylinder petrol	channel

Panhard ERC Sagaie Armoured car

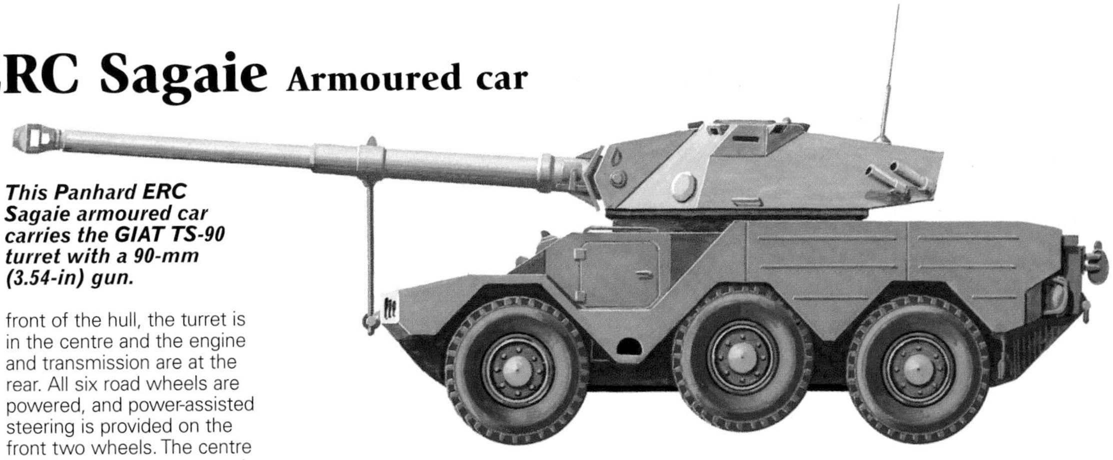

This Panhard ERC Sagaie armoured car carries the GIAT TS-90 turret with a 90-mm (3.54-in) gun.

For many years the backbone of Panhard production of armoured vehicles was the AML 4x4 light armoured car and the M3 4x4 APC with which the AML shares many common components. In 1970 the French army issued a requirement for a VAB (Véhicule de l'Avant Blinde, or front-line armoured vehicle), and Panhard and Renault built prototype vehicles in both 4x4 and 6x6 configurations, all of them amphibious. The competition was won by Renault, and since then large numbers of 4x4 and 6x6 vehicles have been built.

Using the technology gained in this competition Panhard then started design work on a new range of 6x6 vehicles that would include both an armoured car and an APC. The former made its first appearance in 1977 as the **ERC** (**Engin de Reconnaissance Canon**, or cannon-armed reconnaissance machine), while the APC is known as the VCR (Véhicule de Combat à Roues, or wheeled combat vehicle). Production began in 1979, and the ERC was ordered by Argentina, Chad, Gabon, Ivory Coast, Mexico and Niger. The French army also obtained a batch of 192.

The driver is seated at the front of the hull, the turret is in the centre and the engine and transmission are at the rear. All six road wheels are powered, and power-assisted steering is provided on the front two wheels. The centre pair of wheels can be raised off the ground for road travel and lowered again for cross-country travel. The basic vehicle is amphibious, being propelled in the water at 4.5 km/h (2.8 mph) by its wheels, or by two optional waterjets at 9.5 km/h (5.9 mph). Before the vehicle enters the water a trim vane is erected at the front of the hull and two snorkels are erected at the rear.

Turret options

The basic vehicle has been offered with a wide range of turrets including the **GIAT TS-90** and **Hispano-Suiza Lynx 90** units with a 90-mm (3.54-in) gun, the **Hispano Suiza 60-20 Serval** and **EMC** units with a 60 or 81-mm (2.36- or 3.2-in) mortar respectively, and a two-man unit with twin 20- or 25-mm cannon for use in the AA role.

The model selected by the French army, for the use of its rapid intervention force, is fitted with the TS-90 turret and called the **ERC-90 F4 Sagaie**. This turret is armed with a long-barrel 90-mm gun with an elevation of +15 degrees and a depression of -8 degrees. The gun can fire the following types of fixed ammunition: canister, HE, HEAT, smoke and APFSDS. The last has a muzzle velocity of 1350 m (4,430 ft) per second and its projectile will penetrate 120 mm (4.72 in) of armour. A 7.62-mm (0.3-in) machine-gun is mounted co-axial with the main armament, and two electrically operated smoke-dischargers are mounted on each side of the turret. Twenty rounds of 90-mm and 2,000 rounds of 7.62-mm machine-gun ammunition are carried.

Optional equipment includes an air-conditioning system, additional ammunition stowage, a laser rangefinder, passive night vision equipment, an NBC system, an anti-aircraft machine-gun, additional elevation of the 90-mm gun to +35 degrees, various types of fire-control system and a land navigation system. Production is now undertaken only on the receipt of an order.

SPECIFICATION

Panhard ERC Sagaie
Crew: 3
Weight: 8.3 tonnes
Dimensions: length (including gun) 7.7 m (25 ft 2¾ in) and (hull) 5.08 m (16 ft 8 in); width 2.5 m (8 ft 2¼ in); height 2.3 m (7 ft 4¾ in)
Powerplant: one 116-kW (155-hp) Peugeot liquid-cooled V-6 petrol engine
Performance: maximum road speed 100 km/h (62 mph); maximum road range 800 km (500 miles);
Fording: amphibious
Gradient: 60 per cent
Vertical obstacle: 0.8 m (2 ft 7½ in)
Trench: 1.1 m (3 ft 7½ in)

Panhard Sagaie 2 Armoured car

Panhard's private venture range of 6x6 armoured cars has attracted a number of export orders as well as interest from the French army. The Sagaie 2 has a longer, wider hull than the Sagaie 1, and was selected by Gabon with the TTB 190 90-mm gun turret.

In 1977 Panhard unveiled its private venture range of 6x6 armoured vehicles, including families of armoured cars and APCs using identical automotive components in a process providing the operator with obvious training, logistical and cost advantages.

The armoured car family is commonly known as the Engin de Reconnaissance Cannon (ERC) and includes the ERC 90 F4 Sagaie 1, ERC 90 F1 Lynx, ERC 60/20 Serval, ERC 20 Kriss, and ERC 60/12 Mangouste. These were all originally developed specifically for the export market, although the Sagaie 1 was subsequently adopted by the French army.

In 1985 Panhard revealed that it had developed the **Sagaie 2** or **ERC-2** armoured car. It subsequently emerged that Gabon had placed an order for the vehicle, and this nation remains the only customer although extensive marketing has been undertaken elsewhere. The type is no longer in production, and is no longer marketed.

Improved turret

The Sagaie 2 has a slightly longer and wider hull than the Sagaie 1, and instead of the 90-mm GIAT TS-90 turret it is fitted with the **SAMM TTB-190** turret, which has the same gun as the TS-90 turret. The SAMM turret provides much improved armour protection, however, and is offered with a wide range of turret controls, fire control systems and optical devices. Two types of ammunition stowage are available, one having 35 rounds of 90-mm ammunition, 13 of them ready for use, and the other having 32 rounds, with 10 ready for use.

Greater power

The original Panhard Sagaie 1 was powered by a single Peugeot V-6 petrol engine developing 116 kW (155 hp), but the Sagaie 2 is powered by two Peugeot XD 3T turbo-charged diesels developing a total of 146 kW (196 hp). Twin V-6 petrol engines were also offered an an option. The Sagaie 1 and 2 both have full 6x6 drive with powered steering on the front road wheels only. An unusual feature is that when travelling on roads the centre wheels can be raised clear of the ground, reducing resistance and saving wear on the tyres. The wheels are normally lowered for cross- country operations.

A wide range of optional equipment could be installed to meet specific customer requirements, including an NBC system, a heater or air-conditioning system, night vision equipment for the commander, gunner and driver, and a land navigation system.

The Sagaie 2 was unveiled in 1985 and was ordered only by Gabon, which received 10 vehicles – six with the TTB 190 turret (pictured) and the remaining four with the ERC 20 Kriss anti-aircraft turret with two 20-mm cannon.

SPECIFICATION

Panhard Sagaie 2
Crew: 3
Weights: loaded 10000 kg (22,046 lb)
Dimensions: length (overall with gun forward) 7.97 m (26 ft 1¾ in) and hull 5.57 m (19 ft 3⅛ in); width 2.7 m (8 ft 10⅛ in); height 2.3 m (7 ft 6½ in)
Powerplant: two Peugeot XD 3T liquid-cooled 4-cylinder diesels developing a total of 146 kW (196 hp)
Performance: maximum road speed 100 km/h (62 mph); maximum road range 600 km (373 km)
Fording: 1.2 m (3 ft 11 in)
Gradient: 50 per cent
Vertical obstacle: 0.8 m (2 ft 7½ in)
Trench: 0.8 m (2 ft 7½ in)

Panhard VBL Scout car

In 1978 the French army issued a requirement for a light and fast armoured vehicle to carry out two combat roles: anti-tank with an armament of missiles, and reconnaissance/scout. Panhard and Renault were contracted to deliver prototypes for French army trials. Following these trials the **Panhard VBL (Véhicule Blindé Léger)** was accepted for service, and 1,250 such vehicles have been delivered to the French army. Panhard also undertook intensive overseas marketing. Mexico placed an order for 40 VBLs in 1984, and these were followed by significant orders from 13 other nations including Greece, Indonesia, Kuwait, Nigeria and Portugal.

Armoured protection

The VBL's hull provides protection from small arms fire and shell splinters, and to reduce procurement and life cycle costs, proven commercial automotive parts are incorpo-

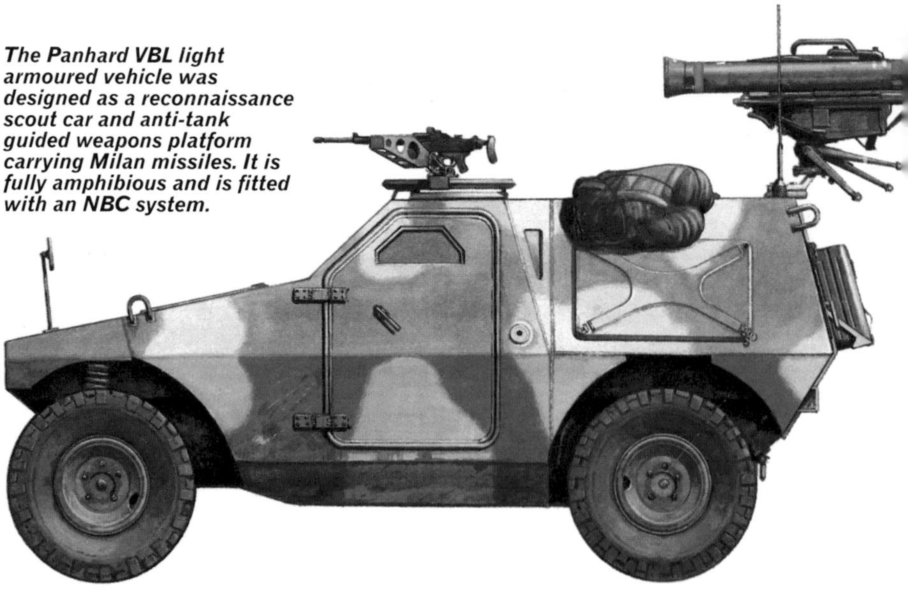

The Panhard VBL light armoured vehicle was designed as a reconnaissance scout car and anti-tank guided weapons platform carrying Milan missiles. It is fully amphibious and is fitted with an NBC system.

In the anti-tank role the VBL carries a three-man crew and, over the rear of the vehicle, a traversing and elevating launcher for anti-tank missiles stowed in the hull. This French VBL is seen in Afghanistan.

rated. The layout is conventional, with the engine and transmission forward, the driver and commander in the centre and space for a third soldier, weapons or other equipment in the rear. Bulletproof windows are provided for all occupants. 'Runflat' tyres allow the VBL to travel 50 km (31 miles) at 30 km/h (19 mph) after being hit.

Anti-tank missiles

The anti-tank model has a crew of three with a Milan anti-tank guided missile launcher, six missiles and a 7.62-mm (0.3-in) machine-gun. The VBL can also mount a

TOW or HOT anti-tank missile launcher. The scout model normally has extra communications equipment, a two-man crew and a 7.62-mm or 12.7-mm (0.5-in) machine-gun.

Panhard offers a wide range of VBL variants including a police/internal security version, a battlefield surveillance model carrying various radars, a version armed with a 20-mm cannon and an AA vehicle carrying Mistral surface-to-air missiles.

SPECIFICATION	
VBL	Peugeot XD 3T liquid-cooled
Crew: 2 or 3	4-cylinder diesel engine
Weight: 3550 kg (7,826 lb)	**Performance:** maximum road speed
Dimensions: length (with additional	95 km/h (59 mph); road range
fuel can) 3.87 m (12 ft 8½ in); width	800 km (497 miles) with extra fuel
2.02 m (6 ft 7½ in); height (hull top)	**Fording:** amphibious
1.7 m (5 ft 7 in)	**Gradient:** 50 per cent
Powerplant: one 78-kW (105-hp)	**Trench:** 0.5 m (1 ft 7¾ in)

Spähpanzer Luchs Reconnaissance vehicle

During the mid-1960s a complete family of 4x4, 6x6 and 8x8 trucks, 4x4 and 6x6 (later to become the Transportpanzer 1, or Fuchs) armoured amphibious load-carriers, and an 8x8 amphibious armoured reconnaissance vehicle were developed specifically for the West German army. These all shared automotive components already in production for civilian applications. Prototypes of the 8x8 amphibious armoured reconnaissance vehicle were designed and built by Daimler-Benz and a consortium of companies known as the Joint Project Office (JPO) in 1968. In 1971 the Daimler-Benz model was selected for production by Thyssen Henschel, and 408 examples of the **Spähpanzer Luchs** (lynx) were built between 1975 and 1978. The Luchs was offered for export, but proved too expensive for all potential customers for this capable type.

Armour protection

Its all-welded steel turret and hull front provides the Luchs with protection against attacks from 20-mm projectiles, and the remainder of the vehicle is proof against small arms fire and shell splinters. The driver is at the

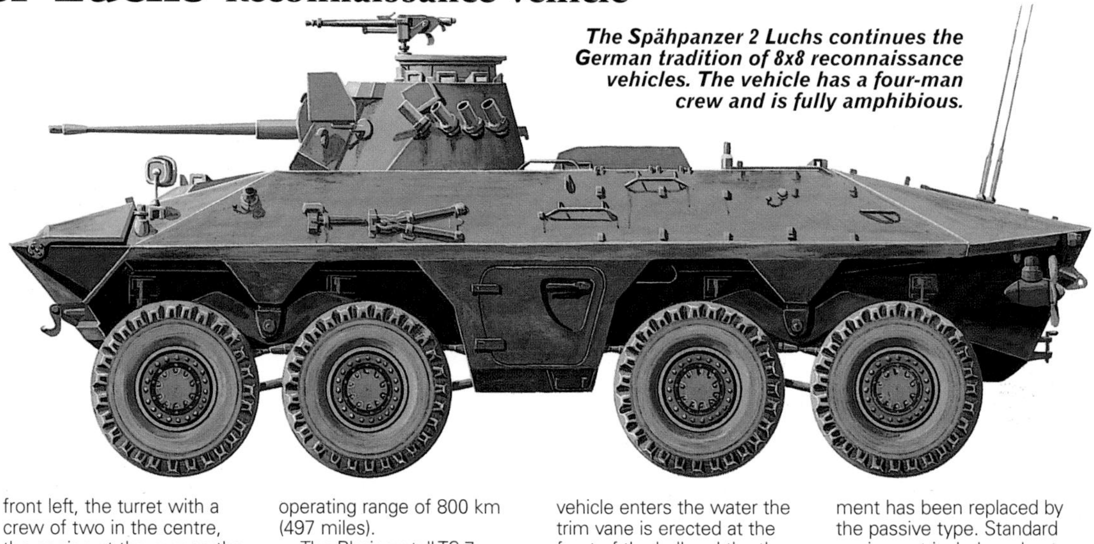

The Spähpanzer 2 Luchs continues the German tradition of 8x8 reconnaissance vehicles. The vehicle has a four-man crew and is fully amphibious.

front left, the turret with a crew of two in the centre, the engine at the rear on the right side and a co-driver is towards the rear on the left side, seated facing the rear. In an emergency the co-driver can take control and drive the vehicle out of trouble. The drivers have powered steering and can select either steering on the front four wheels or on all eight wheels: the latter's turning radius is only 11.5 m (37 ft 8¾ in). The Luchs has the same maximum speed in both directions and also possesses an exceptionally large

operating range of 800 km (497 miles).

The Rheinmetall TS-7 turret is armed with a 20-mm Rheinmetall MK 20 Rh 202 dual-feed cannon with 375 rounds of ammunition, and a 7.62-mm (0.3-in) MG3 machine-gun is also mounted on the turret for anti-aircraft defence. On each side of the turret is a bank of four electrically operated smoke dischargers, all firing forward.

The Luchs is amphibious, being propelled in water at 9 km/h (5.6 mph) by two steerable propellers under the hull rear. Before the

vehicle enters the water the trim vane is erected at the front of the hull and the three bilge pumps are switched on. The Luchs also has an NBC system, and the original range of IR night-vision equip-

ment has been replaced by the passive type. Standard equipment includes a heater for the batteries, engine and transmission oil and cooling liquid, all essential for winter operations in Germany.

SPECIFICATION	
Spähpanzer Luchs	**Performance:** maximum road
Crew: 4	speed 90 km/h (56 mph); maximum
Weight: 20 tonnes	road range 800 km (497 miles)
Dimensions: length 7.74 m (25 ft	**Fording:** amphibious
4¾ in); width 2.98 m (9 ft 9¼ in);	**Gradient:** 60 per cent
height (with MG) 2.9 m (9 ft 6¼ in)	**Vertical obstacle:** 0.6 m (1 ft
Powerplant: one 291-kW (390-hp)	11½ in)
Daimler-Benz OM 403 A	**Trench:** 1.9 m (6 ft 3 in)
liquid-cooled 10-cylinder diesel	

Fennek Multi-purpose carrier

The **Fennek** multi-purpose carrier is an international venture under order by Germany and the Netherlands. It was originally known as the **Multi-Purpose Carrier (MPC)**, an early 1990s Dutch private venture from SP aerospace and vehicle systems, centred around a modular design that allows the vehicle to be con-

figured for numerous battlefield tasks. A total of 612 has been ordered as 410 and 202 for the Dutch and German armies respectively, with production carried out by the ARGE Fennek consortium comprising SP and Krauss Maffei Wegmann of Germany (SP is now part of RDM Technology, also of the

Netherlands). Fennek deliveries are scheduled to take place between 2003 and 2007.

Combat roles vary from battlefield reconnaissance and surveillance, a mobile command and communications centre, an anti-tank missile carrier, front area supply carrier and many other

SPECIFICATION	
Fennek	Deutz BF6M 2013C liquid-cooled
Crew: 3 or according to role	6-cylinder diesel
Weight: 10.2 tonnes	**Performance:** maximum road speed
Dimensions: length 5.58 m (18 ft 3 in); width 2.55 m (8 ft 4 in); height 1.79 m (5 ft 10½ in)	112 km/h (69 mph); maximum road range 1,000 km (621 miles)
Powerplant: one 179-kW (240-hp)	**Fording:** 1 m (3 ft 3 in)
	Gradient: 60 per cent

The Fennek is a versatile light vehicle in which modular design concepts have been fully exploited to multiply the vehicle's suitability for use in any of several roles. Note the sensor pod in the operating position.

tasks such as combat engineer reconnaissance.

The Fennek has an all-welded aluminium armour hull with permanent 4x4 drive powered by a Deutz diesel. Power steering and an automatic transmission are provided to ease the driver's workload. The interior layout can be varied considerably to suit specific roles. For instance, the interior can be all seating for carrying troops, or completely bare apart from handling aids for supply missions, while space and seating can be arranged to suit any electronics carried. The flat roof is designed to allow a small turret to be installed. For some roles a machine-gun or grenade launcher can be carried on an electrically powered and remotely controlled weapon station on the hull roof. For the anti-tank role, missiles can be launched from the roof, via remote weapon stations or manually from hatches, or from dismounted launchers some distance

from the carrier vehicle. The armour protection levels can also be varied to suit the intended role. For most roles the armour is proof against small arms fire and shell splinters, with extra protection, including floor protection against land mines, added by modular armour panels. A fully amphibious version has also been marketed.

Work in the field

The primary role planned for the Fennek is battlefield reconnaissance and surveillance. For this the vehicle carries a sensor pod on a telescopic mast that allows day and night surveillance without exposing the vehicle when suitable cover. The pod contains thermal imaging and day cameras as well as a laser rangefinder. There is also Global Positioning System (GPS) for land navigation. Data from the sensors can be automatically integrated into battle area command and control systems.

FIAT-Otobreda Tipo 6616 Armoured car

During the early 1970s, FIAT and OTO-Melara (now Otobreda) jointly developed the **Tipo 6616** armoured car and the Tipo 6614 APC used by the Italian army and air force. In both cases FIAT was responsible for the powerpack and automotive components, plus final assembly, while OTO-Melara supplied the armoured hull and turret. The first prototype of the Tipo 6616 was ready for tests in 1972, and 40 vehicles were later ordered by the Italian government for the Carabinieri. Sales were also made to Peru (15) and Somalia (30). The Tipo 6616 is no longer in production.

The hull of the Tipo 6616 is of all-welded steel construction with a uniform thickness of 8 mm (0.315 in), somewhat thinner than the figure for other vehicles in its class. The driver is seated at the front of the vehicle on the left, with vision blocks giving good

vision to the front and sides. The two-man turret is in the centre of the vehicle, and the engine and transmission are at the rear.

The Tipo 6616 is amphibious, being propelled in the water by its wheels at 5 km/h (3.1 mph); the only preparation that is required before entering the water is to switch on the bilge pumps and pressurise the submerged mechanical components. Unlike most other comparable vehicles, the Tipo 6616 requires no trim vane at the front of the hull.

Conventional layout

The commander is seated on the left and gunner on the right of the turret, each on an adjustable seat and with observation equipment and a single-piece hatch cover. The communications equipment is mounted in the turret bustle. The main armament comprises a German weapon, the 20-mm Rheinmetall MK 20 Rh 202

The Tipo 6616 armoured car was a collaborative development between FIAT and OTO-Melara (now IVECO and Otobreda), and shares components with the Tipo 6614 APC. It is underarmed, however, and for this reason a model with a two-man turret was developed with a Belgian gun, the 90-mm (3.54-in) Cockerill Mk III weapon used in many other AFVs.

cannon. Turret control is all electric, with traverse at a maximum of 40° per second and weapon elevation at a maximum of 25° per second; 400 rounds of 20-mm ammunition are carried, of which 250 are for ready use and 150 in reserve. Empty cartridge cases are ejected outside the turret automatically, and therefore do not clutter up the crew compartment. A 7.62-mm (0.3-in) MG 42/59 machine-gun is mounted co-axial with the cannon, and 1,000 rounds are carried for this. Mounted on each side of the turret is a bank of three electrically operated forward-firing

smoke dischargers.

One of the main drawbacks of this vehicle on the export market was its small-calibre gun. FIAT (now IVECO Military Vehicles Division) therefore offered the basic Tipo 6616 chassis in upgraded form with a new two-man OTO-Melara turret armed with a 90-mm (3.54-in) Cockerill Mk III gun and a 7.62-mm co-axial

machine-gun. No sales of this version resulted.

Standard equipment includes a front-mounted recovery winch with a capacity of 4500 kg (9,921 lb), while optional equipment includes an NBC protection system, a full range of passive night-vision equipment for the commander, gunner and driver, and a fire-extinguishing system.

SPECIFICATION	
FIAT-Otobreda Tipo 6616	diesel developing 119 kW (160 hp)
Crew: 3	**Performance:** maximum road speed
Weight: 8 tonnes	100 km/h (62 mph); maximum range
Dimensions: length 5.37 m (17 ft 7½ in); width 2.5 m (8 ft 2½ in); height 2.03 m (6 ft 8 in)	700 km (435 miles) **Fording:** amphibious **Gradient:** 60 per cent
Powerplant: one FIAT 8062.24	**Vertical obstacle:** 0.45 m (1 ft 5¾ in)

BRDM-1 Amphibious scout car

In the period immediately after World War II the BA-64 light armoured car (developed in 1942) remained the standard reconnaissance vehicle of its type in the Soviet army. From the late 1950s this was rapidly replaced by the **BRDM-1** 4x4 amphibious scout car, also used by the Warsaw Pact countries and exported to a number of countries in Africa and the Middle East. In most Soviet units the BRDM-1 was later replaced by the much improved BRDM-2 vehicle.

The layout of the BRDM-1 is similar to that of a car, with the engine and transmission at the front, the driver and commander in the centre and a small crew compartment at the rear. The only means of entry are hatches in the roof and rear of the crew compartment. Between the front and rear

wheels on each side of the hull are two belly wheels, which are powered and lowered to the ground by the driver when the vehicle is crossing ditches or rough terrain. A central tyre pressure-regulation system is standard, and this allows the driver to inflate or deflate the tyres according to the conditions: the tyres are deflated for sand crossings, for example, while on roads they are fully inflated.

The BRDM-1 is fully amphibious, being propelled in water at a speed of 9 km/h (5.6 mph) by a single waterjet at the rear of the hull. Before the vehicle enters the water, a trim vane is erected at the front and the bilge pumps are switched on.

The BRDM-1 is normally armed with a single 7.62-mm (0.3-in) SGMB machine-gun mounted on the forward

part of the roof with a total traverse of 90° (45° left and right) elevation being from -6° to +23.5°. A total of 1,070 rounds of ammunition is carried. Some vehicles were observed with a similar weapon at the rear and a 12.7-mm (0.5-in) DShKM machine-gun at the front of the roof.

Specialised models

The **BRDM-U** command vehicle has additional communications equipment, while the **BRDM-1RKhb** radiological/chemical reconnaissance vehicle was designed to mark lines through contaminated areas. Mounted at the rear of the hull are two racks that contain the marking poles and pennants; when required, these racks swing through 90° over the rear of the vehicle, allowing the poles and attached pennants to be planted.

There were three versions of the BRDM-1 fitted with anti-tank missiles. The first model had three 3M6 Shmel

Soviet BRDM-1 4x4 amphibious scout cars, with roof hatches open, ford a stream. The vehicle is propelled in water by a single waterjet at the rear of the hull, which gives it a maximum speed of 9 km/h (5.6 mph). For travel across rough country, belly wheels are lowered between the front and rear axles.

(AT-1 'Snapper') ATGWs with a range of 2500 m (2,735 yards). The missiles on their launcher arms were carried under armour protection and raised above the roof of the vehicle for launching. The second model was similar but had four 3M11 Falanga (AT-2 'Swatter') missiles with a range of 3000 m (3,280 yards); for some reason this mounting was not exported outside the Warsaw Pact nations. The

last model to enter service had six 9M14 Malyutka (AT-3 'Sagger') ATGWs with a maximum range of 3000 m (3,280 yards); additional missiles were carried in the hull. This wire-guided missile, which proved to be highly effective in the 1973 Middle East War, could be launched from within the vehicle or up to 80 m (87.5 yards) away from it with the aid of a separation sight/control unit.

A Soviet BRDM-1 with four Falanga (AT-2 'Swatter') ATGWs in the foreground, and a BRDM-1 with three Shmel (AT-1 'Snapper') in the background. The 'Snapper' has a maximum range of 2500 m (8,200 ft), while that of the 'Swatter' is 3000 m (9,845 ft). Both missiles have a HEAT warhead.

SPECIFICATION	
BRDM-1	**Performance:** maximum road
Crew: 5	speed 80 km/h (50 mph); maximum
Weight: 5.6 tonnes	road range 500 km (311 miles)
Dimensions: length 5.7 m (18 ft	**Fording:** amphibious
8½ in); width 2.25 m (7 ft 4 in);	**Gradient:** 60 per cent
height 1.9 m (6 ft 2¾ in)	**Vertical obstacle:** 0.4 m (1 ft
Powerplant: one 6-cylinder petrol	3¾ in)
engine developing 67 kW (90 hp)	**Trench:** 1.22 m (4 ft)

BRDM-2 Amphibious scout car

The **BRDM-2** 4x4 amphibious scout car was developed as the successor to the earlier BRDM-1, and was first seen in public in 1966, although it entered service some years before that date. The most significant improvements of the BRDM-2 over the earlier vehicle can be summarised as better vision for the commander and driver, a more powerful armament mounted in a fully enclosed turret, a more powerful engine for higher road and water speeds, an NBC protection system and longer operational range.

International service

The BRDM-2 replaced the BRDM-1 in most Soviet units. At one time it was in service with almost 40 countries all over the world,

seeing action in such places as Angola, Egypt, Iraq, Syria and Vietnam. It is still in widespread service.

The all-welded steel hull of the BRDM-2 is only 7 mm (0.275 in) thick, apart from the nose plate which is 14 mm (0.55 in) thick, and

Most BRDM-2 ATGW versions carried six Malyutka (AT-3 'Sagger') missiles in the ready-to-launch position, but some were armed with a quadruple launcher for the earlier 3M11 Falanga (AT-2 'Swatter') or five 9M113 Konkurs (AT-5 'Spandrel' missiles.

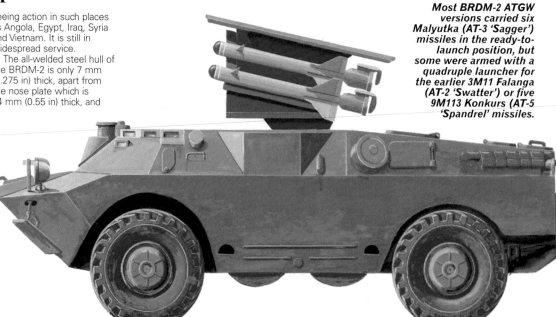

This BRDM-2 ATGW carrier has its launcher for six 'Sagger' ATGWs in the raised position, ready for firing. This model was used with considerable success by the Egyptian army in the 1973 Arab-Israeli war. The missiles can be fired directly, or away, from the vehicle.

the underside of the belly which is only 2 or 3 mm (0.08 or 0.12 in) thick. This leaves the vehicle vulnerable to land mine explosions.

Limited access

The driver and commander are seated at the front of the vehicle. Each has a windscreen covered in combat by an armoured hatch. Over each position is a single-piece hatch cover that opens vertically; these are the only means of entry into the vehicle for the four-man crew. The turret, with no roof hatch, is armed with a highly effective 14.5-mm (0.57-in) KPVT heavy machine-gun, and a 7.62-mm (0.3-in) PKT co-axial machine-gun. Totals of 500 rounds of 14.5-mm and 2,000 rounds of 7.62-mm ammunition are carried.

As with the earlier BRDM-1, the BRDM-2 has two belly wheels that can be lowered to the ground to enable ditches and rough country to be crossed with ease. The vehicle also has a central tyre pressure regulation system, IR night-vision equipment, an NBC system, radios, a navigation system and a winch.

The basic BRDM-2 chassis formed the basis for a family of more specialised vehicles including the **BRDM-2 RKhb** NBC reconnaissance vehicle and the **BRDM-2U** command vehicle without a turret. The first ATGW model carried six 9M14 Malyutka ('Sagger') ATGWs with a range of 3,000 m (3,280 yards). A version with 3M11 Falanga ('Swatter') ATGWs appeared, but the latest model is armed with five 9M113 Konkurs ('Spandrel') ATGWs in the ready-to-launch position on the hull top. These missiles have a range of at least 4000 m (4,375 yards).

The 9M31 Strela-1 (SA-9 'Gaskin') surface-to-air missile system uses the BRDM-2 chassis, with four missiles in the ready-to-launch position.

SPECIFICATION

BRDM-2
Crew: 4
Weight: 7 tonnes
Dimensions: length 5.75 m (18 ft 10½ in); width 2.35 m (7 ft 8½ in); height 2.31 m (7 ft 7 in)
Powerplant: one GAZ-41 petrol engine developing 104 kW (140 hp)
Performance: maximum road speed 100 km/h (62 mph); maximum road range 750 km (465 miles)
Fording: amphibious
Gradient: 60 per cent
Vertical obstacle: 0.4 m (1 ft 3¾ in)
Trench: 1.25 m (4 ft 1 in)

PT-76 Amphibious light tank

The PT-76 light tank was replaced in many Soviet units by special models of the BMP-1 reconnaissance vehicle.

The USSR developed light tanks with an amphibious capability in the 1920s, and these were used with varying degrees of success during World War II. The **PT-76** light amphibious tank was designed in the immediate post-war period by the design team responsible for the IS series of heavy tanks. For many years the PT-76 was the standard reconnaissance vehicle of the Soviet army, and was used alongside the BRDM-1 and BRDM-2 4x4 amphibious scout cars. In Soviet units the type was replaced by MBTs such as the T-72 and variants of the BMP. Although production of the PT-76 was completed many years ago, the tank is still likely to be encountered. It saw action with the Indian army during the conflict with Pakistan, with the Egyptian army during the 1967 Six-Day War, with the North Vietnamese army during the Vietnam War, and with the Angolan army in South-West African operations.

Versatile chassis

The chassis of the PT-76 was subsequently used for a number of other vehicles, including the BTR-50 amphibious APC and the launcher for the FROG (Free Rocket Over Ground) artillery rocket system.

The hull of the PT-76 is of all-welded steel construction, providing the crew with protection only from small arms fire; any additional armour would have increased the type's weight to the point that it would not have been amphibious. The driver is seated at the front in the centre, the two-man turret is in the centre of the vehicle and the engine and transmission are at the rear. The torsion-bar suspension consists on each side of six single road wheels, with the drive sprocket at the rear and the idler at the front; there are no track-return rollers.

Limited penetration

The main armament consists of a 76.2-mm (3-in) D-56T gun. A 7.62-mm (0.3-in) SGMT machine-gun is mounted co-axial with the main armament; many vehicles have a 12.7-mm (0.5-in) DShKM machine-gun on the turret roof. Totals of 40 rounds of 76-mm and 1,000 rounds of 7.62-mm ammunition are carried. Several types of fixed ammunition can be fired, namely APT, API-T, HE-FRAG, HEAT and HVAP-T. The HEAT projectile can penetrate 120 mm (4.72 in) of armour at 0°, while the HVAP-T projectile can punch through 58 mm (2.28 in) of armour at 1000 m (1,095 yards) or 92 mm (3.62 in) at 500 m (545 yards). The lack of armour penetration against more recent tanks must have been one of the reasons why the PT-76 has been phased out of service with many armies.

The most useful feature of the PT-76 is its amphibious capability, which is the reason why the type was also used by Polish and Soviet marines. In water the tank is powered by two waterjets at up to 10 km/h (6.2 mph). The only preparation required before entering the water is the raising of the trim vane at the front of the hull, the activation of the bilge pumps and the engagement of the waterjets. The maximum waterborne range is about 65 km (40 miles). To enable the driver to see forward when afloat, his centre periscope can be raised above the hatch cover, and standard equipment includes IR lights, but no NBC system is installed.

PT-76 Model 2 light amphibious tanks come ashore from landing craft of the Red Banner Northern Fleet. Note the open turret hatch cover and the trim vane at the front in the raised position. The main armament comprises a 76.2-mm (3-in) gun and 7.62-mm (0.3-in) co-axial machine-gun.

SPECIFICATION

PT-76
Crew: 3
Weight: 14.6 tonnes
Dimensions: length (gun forward) 7.63 m (25 ft ¼ in) and (hull) 6.91 m (22 ft 8 in); width 3.14 m (10 ft 3⅝ in); height 2.26 m (7 ft 4¾ in)
Powerplant: one V-6B 6-cylinder diesel developing 179 kW (240 hp)
Performance: maximum road speed 44 km/h (27 mph); maximum road range 260 km (160 miles)
Fording: amphibious
Gradient: 60 per cent
Vertical obstacle: 1.1 m (3 ft 7½ in)
Trench: 2.8 m (9 ft 2 in)

Daimler Ferret Scout car

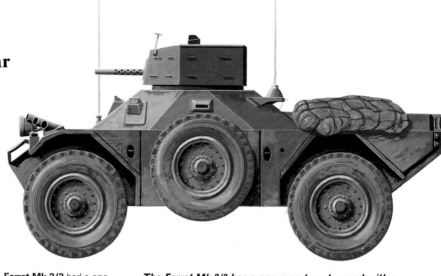

The British War Office issued a requirement for a new scout car in 1946. During 1947 Daimler of Coventry was awarded the development contract, the first prototype was completed in 1949, and after trials the vehicle was accepted for service as the **Ferret** scout car. Production continued at Daimler until 1971, and just over 4,400 vehicles were built. At one time the Ferret was used by some 30 countries as well as the UK.

All Ferrets have the same layout: the driver at the front,

the commander/gunner in the centre and the engine and transmission at the rear. The all-welded steel hull has a maximum thickness of 12 mm (0.47 in), providing the crew with protection from small arms fire and shell splinters.

Ferret variants

The **Ferret Mk 1** had an open top and a pintle-mounted 7.62-mm (0.30-in) machine-gun The **Ferret Mk 1/2** had a crew of three and a low-profile turret with an externally mounted machine-gun. The

The Fox is a Jaguar-powered development of the late production Ferret family. Capable of 104 km/h (64.6 mph) on roads, the Fox is armed with the 30-mm RARDEN cannon.

Ferret Mk 2/3 had a one-man turret armed with a 7.62-mm machine-gun. The Ferret **Mk 2/2** was developed locally in the Far East, being a Ferret Mk 2 with an extension collar between the hull top and turret base to improve all-round observation. The **Ferret Mk 2/6** was the Ferret Mk 2/3 with a Vigilant anti-tank missile on each side of the turret. The wire-guided Vigilant had a maximum range of 1375 m (1,500 yards). The **Ferret Mk 3** and **Ferret Mk 4** were essentially earlier versions rebuilt with stronger suspension units, larger tyres and a flotation screen carried collapsed around the top of the hull. This screen could be quickly erected by the crew

The Ferret Mk 2/3 has a one-man turret armed with a 7.62-mm machine-gun. In addition to being used as a scout car, it is operated in the internal security role.

to make the vehicle fully amphibious. The **Ferret Mk 5** was the final version, a rebuild of earlier marks. It had a turret in each of whose sides were two launcher bins for the Swingfire anti-tank missile with a range of 4000

m (4,380 yards). The Ferret Mk 5 was also armed with a 7.62-mm machine-gun and, like all Ferrets, smoke dischargers. The Ferret is no longer in service with the British army although many remain in service elsewhere.

SPECIFICATION	
Daimler Ferret Mk 2/3	engine developing 96 kW (129 hp)
Crew: 2	**Performance:** maximum road
Weight: 4.4 tonnes	speed 93 km/h (58 mph); maximum
Dimensions: length 3.835 m (12 ft 10 in); width 1.905 m (6 ft 3 in); height 1.879 m (6 ft 2 in)	road range 306 km (190 miles); fording 0.91 m (3 ft 0 in), gradient 46 per cent; vertical obstacle 0.41 m (1 ft 4 in); trench 1.22 m (4 ft 0 in) with
Powerplant: one Rolls-Royce liquid-cooled 6-cylinder petrol	one channel

Fox Light armoured car

During the late 1960s the British army decided to build two new reconnaissance vehicles, one tracked and the other wheeled. These became known as the Combat Vehicle Reconnaissance (Tracked), or Scorpion, and the **Combat Vehicle Reconnaissance (Wheeled)**, or **Fox**. Daimler of Coventry gained the development contract for the Fox, the first prototype appearing in 1967. Following service acceptance as the **FV721**, the Fox entered production in 1972 at Royal Ordnance Leeds. The final deliveries were made during 1979.

In British service the Fox was used for reconnaissance duties. Driver training had to be carefully conducted as the vehicle's centre of gravity was high, resulting in a propensity to turn over when cornering. The Fox was therefore withdrawn from British Army service, never quite replacing the Ferret scout cars it was meant to supplant. Most Fox turrets were removed and transferred to redundant Scorpion reconnaissance vehicle chassis to produce the Sabre, which is still in service. About 13 turrets were mounted on FV432 APC chassis and

issued to the Berlin Brigade, and these have now been withdrawn.

Export sales were made to Nigeria (55) and Malawi (20), but the exact status of these vehicles is now uncertain.

Modernised Ferret

The Fox was basically an updated Ferret with a two-man turret armed with a 30-mm RARDEN L21 cannon. The accuracy of the RARDEN is enhanced by being designed to fire only rapid single shots or short bursts. Ammunition types include armour piercing and high explosive. A 7.62-mm (0.3-in) co-axial machine was the only other weapon carried. A passive night sight was provided for area surveillance or gun aiming. Smoke grenade launchers were provided for rapid concealment of the vehicle when necessary.

Structural details

The Fox had a relatively large all-welded aluminium hull and turret. The driver was seated centrally at the front while the commander and gunner occupied the centrally mounted turret. The militarised Jaguar petrol engine and transmission were at the rear. A full 4 x 4

drive configuration was employed, coupled with a coil spring independent suspension. A flotation collar around the hull periphery was originally a fixture, providing the Fox with full amphibious capability. This was little used so the collar was later removed from British Army Foxes. Without the collar the Fox could wade through water obstacles 1.0 m (3 ft 3 in) deep. The Fox could also be paradropped, the C-130 Hercules transport aeroplane being able to carry two Foxes prepared for para-

dropping or three for normal air transport.

The Fox could carry several reconnaissance aids such as a portable battlefield surveillance radar, navigation devices and an NBC detection suite.

The relationship of the Fox to the Ferret is abundantly clear, although the later vehicle was larger and carried a two-man turret fitted with a 30-mm RARDEN cannon.

SPECIFICATION	
Fox	engine developing 142 kW (190 hp)
Crew: 3	**Performance:** maximum road speed
Weight: 6.12 tonnes	104 km/h (64.6 mph); maximum road
Dimensions: length 5.08 m (16 ft 8 in); width 2.134 m (7 ft); height 1.981 m (6 ft 6 in)	range 434 km (270 miles); fording 1.0 m (3 ft 3 in); gradient 60 per cent; vertical obstacle 0.5 m (1 ft 7.7 in);
Powerplant: one Jaguar XK petrol	trench not applicable

Alvis Saladin Armoured car

Following the success of the AEC Mk III and Daimler Mk II armoured cars during World War II, the British army issued a requirement for a new armoured car with a 2-pdr (40-mm/1.57-in) gun. It was then decided that this gun would be ineffective against future armoured vehicles, and it was replaced by the new 76.2-mm (3-in) L5 gun.

The chassis of the **Saladin (FV601)** is similar to that of the FV603 Saracen APC, also under development by Alvis at the same time. The Saracen was accepted for service with the British army in 1956. Production started two years later at Alvis in Coventry and continued until 1972, by which time 1,177 vehicles (including many for

export) had been completed.

Although it has been replaced in British service by the Alvis Scorpion tracked vehicle, the Saladin remains in military and internal security service (or in reserve) with some 11 countries.

Steel construction

The hull of the Saladin is of all-welded steel armour construction that varies in thickness from 8 mm (0.31 in) to 16 mm (0.63 in); the turret has a maximum thickness of 32 mm (1.25 in) at the front and 16 mm (0.63 in) at the sides and rear. The driver sits at the front of the vehicle with excellent vision to his front and sides. The other two crew members are seated in the turret with the commander/loader on the right and the gunner on

the left. The engine and transmission are at the rear. All six wheels of the Saladin are powered, with steering on the front four wheels. The vehicle can still be driven with one wheel blown off.

Ammunition total

A total of 42 rounds of fixed ammunition was carried for the turret-mounted 76.2-mm

The Saladin is armed with a 76.2-mm (3-in) gun; a lightened version is fitted in the more recent Scorpion, and fires the same range of fixed ammunition. Between 1958 and 1972 Alvis of Coventry built 1,177 Saladin armoured cars.

The Alvis Saladin armoured car shares many common automotive components with the Saracen 6 x 6 APC. The last few Saladins in British service were based in Cyprus.

gun. A 7.62-mm (0.3-in) machine-gun is mounted co-axially, and there is a similar weapon mounted on the turret roof for air defence. Six electrically operated smoke dischargers are mounted each side of the turret.

There were few variants of the Saladin, one being an amphibious model. This had a flotation screen around the top of the hull, and when this had been erected the vehicle could propel itself in water with its wheels.

SPECIFICATION	
Alvis Saladin	8-cylinder petrol engine developing
Crew: 3	127 kW (170 bhp)
Weight: 11.59 tonnes	**Performance:** maximum road
Dimensions: length (including gun)	speed 72 km/h (45 mph); maximum
5.28 m (17 ft 4 in) and (hull) 4.93 m	road range 400 km (250 miles);
(16 ft 2 in); width 2.54 m (8 ft 4 in);	fording 1.07 m (3 ft 6 in); gradient
height 2.93 m (9 ft 7½ in)	46 per cent; vertical obstacle 0.46 m
Powerplant: one Rolls-Royce B80	(1 ft 6 in); trench 1.52 m (5 ft 0 in)

Alvis Scorpion Reconnaissance vehicle

In the late 1960s the British army decided to build two new reconnaissance vehicles, one tracked and the other wheeled. These became known as the **Combat Vehicle Reconnaissance (Tracked)** or **Scorpion** and the Combat Vehicle Reconnaissance (Wheeled), or Fox. In 1967 Alvis was awarded a contract to build prototypes of the Scorpion, the first completed in 1969. Trials were so successful that it was accepted for service the following year. Late in 1970 the Scorpion was also ordered by Belgium and an assembly line was established in that country. The first production Scorpions were delivered to the British army in 1972, but this was only one of a large family of

vehicles based on the same chassis, production of which continues for export sales to many countries.

The Scorpion has an all-welded aluminium hull and turret. The driver is seated at the left front with the engine to his right, and the two-man turret is at the rear. The suspension is of the torsion-bar type, and on each side comprises five road wheels with the drive sprocket at the front and the idler at the rear; there are no track-return rollers.

Indifferent main gun

The basic Scorpion has a 76.2-mm (3-in) gun with 40 rounds of ammunition. A 7.62-mm (0.3-in) machine-gun is mounted co-axially with the main armament to be used as a ranging as well

The original Scorpion light tank was armed with a 76.2-mm (3-in) main gun, but this was withdrawn from British service at a comparatively early date.

as a secondary weapon. Export vehicles may have a diesel engine in place of the standard petrol engine, and some have a 90-mm (3.54-in) gun.

The Scorpion is no longer used by the British Army as the L23 gun was withdrawn from service. Existing Scorpion chassis were then

The original L23 gun of 76.2-mm (3-in) calibre was distinguishable from the 30-mm RARDEN cannon that replaced it by its thicker but shorter barrel. The Scorpion has good cross-country mobility.

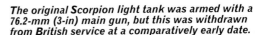

allied with 30-mm RARDEN cannon turrets taken from redundant FV721 Fox reconnaissance vehicles. These hybrids are known as the

Sabre, being similar to the FV107 Scimitar but with the co-axial machine-gun replaced by a 7.62-mm chain gun.

SPECIFICATION	
Alvis Scorpion	142 kW (190 hp)
Crew: 3	**Performance:** maximum road
Weight: 8.073 tonnes	speed 80 km/h (50 mph); maximum
Dimensions: length 4.79 m (15 ft	road range 644 km (400 miles);
8¾ in); width 2.235 m (7 ft 4 in);	fording 1.067 m (3 ft 6 in); gradient
height 2.102 m (6 ft 10¾ in)	60 per cent; vertical obstacle 0. 50
Powerplant: one Jaguar liquid-	m (1 ft 8 in); trench 2.06 m (6 ft 9
cooled petrol engine developing	in)

FV101 Scorpion CVR(T)

Built by Alvis, which by the early years of the 21st century had also acquired GKN Defence and Vickers Defence Systems of the UK as well as Hägglunds Vehicle of Sweden to become the largest British AFV manufacturer, the Scorpion is a capable light tank optimised for the reconnaissance role. The first vehicles, of the type delivered to the British Army from 1972 and now retired from service, were powered by a Jaguar petrol engine and armed with a 3-in (76.2-mm) Royal Ordnance gun, whereas later vehicles have a diesel engine and a 90-mm (3.54-in) Cockerill Mk III gun. Like other such vehicles, the Scorpion has also been the basis for a family of light AFVs for a variety of combat and support tasks. The most important of these is perhaps the FV107 Scimitar reconnaissance vehicle with a 30-mm cannon in a two-man turret, although the FV103 Spartan APC was built in greater numbers than any variant except the Scorpion itself.

A head-on view of the Scorpion reveals the comparatively large size of the two-man turret. This is surmounted by the various vision devices associated with the commander's and gunner's positions, and on each side is a bank of four electrically operated smoke grenade dischargers firing forward and sideways. The front of the turret is occupied, from left to right, by the cover for the passive night sight, the 3-in (76.2-mm) Royal Ordnance L23A1 main gun, and the 0.3-in (7.62-mm) L43A1 co-axial machine gun, the last being used to range for the main gun.

The Scorpion is of typical layout for a light AFV with the driver in the front of the vehicle to the left of the powerplant, and the turret over the rear of the vehicle with the commander on the left and the gunner on the right. All three members of the crew have vision devices, including a rearward-facing periscope for the commander, to ensure that the vehicle can still be operated effectively when fully closed down, and the commander's and gunner's vision equipment incorporate sights. There is main armament ammunition stowage across the rear of the turret, and the standard NBC pack is carried over the left-hand side of this ammunition stowage.

The Scorpion, seen here in the form of a first-generation vehicle as procured by the British Army, still displays the vestiges of the UK's imperial legacy in features such as its compressed width. This feature was dictated by the need to cross narrow bridges and pass between rows of rubber trees and the like.

The Scorpion was designed in the early 1960s as the FV101 to meet a Combat Vehicle Reconnaissance (Tracked) requirement for a successor to the FV701 Ferret, FV601 Saladin and FV603 Saracen. The required vehicle was to be lighter and faster than its predecessors, and the need for it to be air-portable dictated a maximum weight of no more than 8200 kg (18,078 lb), which was about one-third less than equivalent types under development or in service in other countries. This demand for the lowest possible weight, combined with adequate protection for the crew and vital systems against the threats the new vehicle would most likely meet in combat, dictated the use of aluminium rather than steel armour. The thickness of the plates meant that the armour could be used as the new vehicle's primary structural medium, rather than laid over a core of frames and stringers, and the plates were welded together to create the Scorpion's hull and turret.

The need for the Scorpion to operate over rough terrain in many parts of the world demanded not only a light overall weight, but also considerable ground clearance and a low ground pressure. The Scorpion's ground clearance is typically 356 mm (1 ft 2 in), and the ground pressure was kept to a figure as low as 0.345 kg/cm² (4.9 lb/sq in) by ensuring the maximum length of track on the ground. This track is 432 mm (1 ft 5 in) wide.

47 MS 18

The L23A1 gun of the Scorpion is basically a lightened version of the L5A1 installed in the FV601 Saracen armoured car, and uses a falling breech block. The two guns fire basically the same range of ammunition types, of which the most important operational types are L29A3 HESH, L24A4 HE, L32A5 Smoke and L33A1 Canister. The 5.39-kg (11.9-lb) High Explosive Squash Head projectile leaves the muzzle at 533 m (1,750 m) per second and has maximum direct- and indirect-fire ranges of 2200 and 5000 m (2,400 and 5,475 yards) respectively. The 5.36-kg (11.82-lb) High Explosive projectile leaves the muzzle at 514 m (1,685 ft) per second and possess the same range as the HESH projectile. The 8.51-kg (18.76-lb) Smoke projectile leaves the muzzle at 290 m (950 ft) per second and has a range of 3700 m (4,050 yards). The projectile of the 7.76-kg (17.1-lb) Canister round is a thin-walled steel container that breaks up as the round emerges from the muzzle to release a large number of steel balls that spread conically to inflict fearsome casualties on infantry ranges out to 100 m (110 yards). There are also HESH and HE practice rounds.

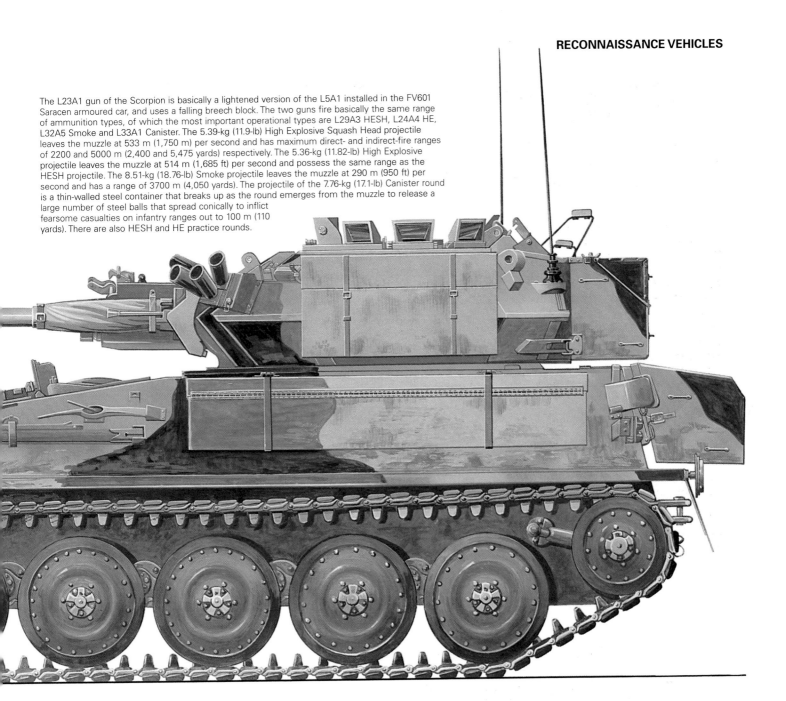

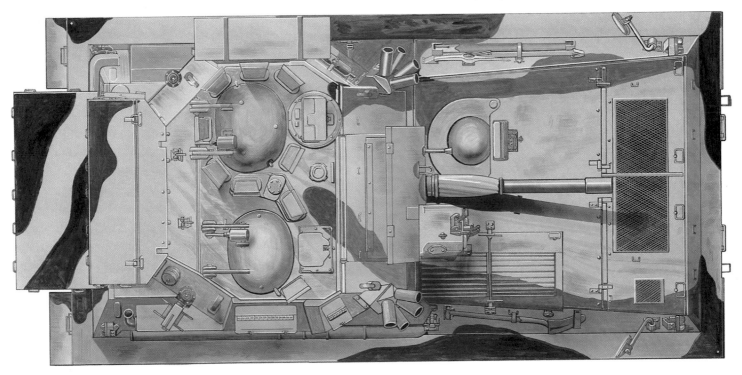

Stingray Light tank

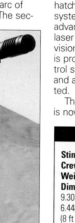

Cadillac Gage Textron (now Textron Marine & Land Systems) produced its **Stingray** light tank for the export market, and to date the only sale has been to Thailand (106 vehicles). The Stingray programme started in 1983, the first prototype was completed in August 1984, and Thailand's order was fulfilled in 1988-90.

Limited protection

The Stingray is too lightly protected for any real battlefield role, and in is effect a reconnaissance tank. The vehicle is of steel construction offering protection against 14.5-mm (0.57-in) and 12.7-mm (0.5-in) armour-piercing rounds over the frontal arc and the rest of the vehicle respectively, and is orthodox in its layout, with

The sides of the Stingray's pointed turret slope inwards with a turret basket at the rear. A bank of four smoke grenade dischargers are carried on each side, with a 12.7-mm gun on the right side of the roof.

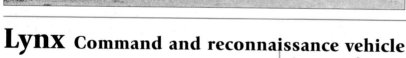

the driver at the front, the three-man turret in the centre, and the powerplant (diesel engine and automatic transmission) at the rear. The suspension is of the torsion-bar type, and the running gear comprises, on each side, six dual rubber-tyred road wheels, drive sprocket at the

rear, idler at the front, and three track-return rollers.

The primary armament is an LRF (Low Recoil Force) version of the British L7 series 105-mm (4.13-in) rifled gun installed in the well angled and electro-hydraulically powered turret with optional stabilisation and eight rounds; another 24 rounds are stowed in the hull. The main armament can be elevated through an arc of 27.5° (-7.5° to +20°). The sec-

The Stingray light tank is the heaviest, largest and most capable of the vehicles offered in Cadillac Gage's series of private-venture AFVs, and is a light or reconnaissance tank providing good firepower and mobility, but only indifferent protection as a result of its thin armour.

ondary armament comprises a 7.62-mm (0.3-in) co-axial machine-gun with 2,400 rounds and a 12.7-mm (0.5-in) AA machine gun with 1,100 rounds on the commander's hatch. The tank's fire-control system is not notably advanced, but includes a laser rangefinder and night-vision equipment, and there is provision for this fire-control system to be upgraded and an NBC system to be fitted.

The company's marketing is now concentrated on the

Stingray II. This has the same armament system as the Stingray, but a more capable digital fire-control system and NBC equipment are standard. The other improvements offered by the Stingray II, which is based on proven automotive elements and in-production turret and armament, lie in its maximised survivability through the use of armour offering protection against rounds up to 23-mm calibre, enhanced mobility, and superior target-engagement capability.

SPECIFICATION	
Stingray	diesel engine developing 399 kW
Crew: 4	(535 hp)
Weight: 21.205 tonnes	**Performance:** maximum road
Dimensions: length (gun forward)	speed 67 km/h (42 mph); maximum
9.30 m (30 ft 6 in); length (hull)	road range 483 km (300 miles);
6.448 m (21 ft 2 in); width 2.71 m	fording 1.07 m (3 ft 6 in); gradient
(8 ft 10 in); height 2.55 m (8 ft 4 in)	60 per cent; vertical obstacle 0.76 m
Powerplant: one Detroit Diesel	(2 ft 6 in); trench 2.13 m (7 ft 0 in)
Model 8V-92TA liquid-cooled V-12	

Lynx Command and reconnaissance vehicle

When the M113 armoured personnel carrier entered production at FMC's facility at San Jose in 1960, it was realised that in addition to being used for a wide range of roles, its automotive component could also be used in other armoured vehicles. At that time the US Army had already selected the M114 vehicle to carry out the role of command and reconnaissance, but the M114 did not

A Lynx Command and Reconnaissance vehicle of the Canadian Armed Forces, armed with a 12.7-mm (0.5-in) M2HB machine-gun forward and a 7.62-mm (0.3-in) machine-gun at the rear. A bank of three electrically operated smoke dischargers is mounted on each side of the hull front.

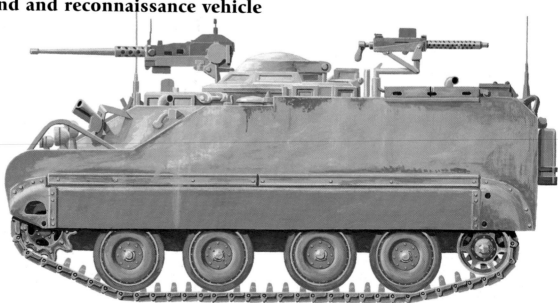

All Dutch vehicles have now been fitted with a Swiss Oerlikon-Contraves one-man turret armed with a 25-mm KBA-B cannon. This is also fitted to the Dutch army's Armoured Infantry Fighting Vehicles, thus facilitating ammunition resupply on the battlefield.

prove a successful design and has long since been phased out of service; moreover, it was never sold overseas. FMC then designed and built a command and reconnaissance vehicle using automotive components of the diesel-powered M113A1, and this was subsequently selected by Canada, which ordered 174 vehicles under the name **Lynx**, and also by the Netherlands, which ordered 250 vehicles; all of these were delivered by 1968. The vehicle is often called the 'M113 and a half'!

In comparison with the M113, the Lynx has a lower-profile hull, the powerpack repositioned to the rear, and one road wheel less on each side. The hull is of all-welded aluminium armour construction that provides the crew with complete protection from small arms fire and shell splinters. The driver is seated at the front of the vehicle, with the commander to his rear and right. The radio operator/observer is seated to the left rear of the commander. The engine compartment is at the rear of the hull on the right side, with access hatches in the roof and hull rear.

Amphibious capability
The suspension is of the torsion-bar type, and consists of four dual rubber-tyred road wheels on each side with the drive sprocket at the front and the idler at the rear; there are no track-return rollers. The Lynx is fully amphibious, being propelled in the water by its tracks at a speed of 5.6 km/h (3.5 mph). Before the vehicle enters the water, a trim vane is erected at the front of the hull, and electric bilge pumps are switched on. Rectangular covers are also erected around the air inlet and exhaust louvres on the hull top to stop water entering the engine compartment, the vehicle having very limited freeboard. Vehicles such as the M113 and the Lynx can cross only calm rivers and lakes; open-sea landings almost inevitably resulting in swamping.

Turret cannon
The commander of the Lynx has an M26 hand-operated turret, with vision blocks for all-round observation and an externally mounted standard 12.7-mm M2HB machine-gun for which 1,155 rounds of ammunition are carried. The radio operator/observer has a pintle-mounted 7.62-mm (0.3-in) machine-gun with 2,000 rounds. A bank of three electrically operated smoke-dischargers is mounted at the front of each side of the hull.

The Dutch vehicles have a slightly different internal lay-out, and as originally supplied were slightly lighter. More recently all of these vehicles have been fitted with a Swiss Oerlikon-Contraves GBD-AOA one-man turret carrying a 25-mm KBA-B cannon. This has three rates of fire: single-shot, 175 rounds per minute and 570 rounds per minute. Some 200 rounds of ready-use ammunition (120 HE and 80 AP) are carried for the cannon. An added advantage for the Dutch is that this Oerlikon cannon (in a different one-man power-operated turret) is also installed in the FMC-designed armoured infantry fighting vehicles of the Dutch army, so providing a very useful element of ammunition commonality.

SPECIFICATION	
Lynx	Type 6V53 6-cylinder diesel developing 160 kW (215 hp)
Crew: 3	**Performance:** maximum road speed 70.8 km/h (44 mph); maximum range 523 km (325 miles); fording amphibious; gradient 60 per cent; vertical obstacle 0.61 m (2 ft 0 in); trench 1.524 m (5 ft 0 in)
Weight: 8.775 tonnes	
Dimensions: length 4.597 m (15 ft 1 in); width 2.413 m (7 ft 11 in); height (including armament) 2.17 m (7 ft 1½ in)	
Powerplant: one Detroit Diesel	

M41 Walker Bulldog Light tank

In 1949 the US Army decided to develop new tanks to replace all its World War II types. The light tank was placed under development as the **Light Tank T41**, based on the T37 whose design as a development model had been launched shortly after World War II. The T37 Phase I prototype with the 76.2-mm (3-in) M32 gun was completed in 1949. Already the T37 was involved in a development programme whose fruits were the T37 Phase II with a redesigned cast/welded turret, a new mantlet, revised ammunition stowage and a fire-control system that integrated a coincidence rangefinder with a Vickers stabiliser for the gun mounting, and the T37 Phase III with an automatic loader for the main armament and an IBM stabiliser for the gun mounting. The T37 Phase II led to the T41, which was standardised in 1950 as the **Light Tank M41 Little Bulldog**, although the name was subsequently changed to **Walker Bulldog** in honour of the US commander killed in Korea during 1951. Production by Cadillac Gage began in 1950, and some 5,500 M41 series vehicles were built before the production line closed.

Classic layout
In design the M41 made full use of US combat experience in World War II but is in many ways similar to the M24 it was designed to replace. The all-welded hull is divided into the standard three compartments, with the driver in the forward compartment, the commander, gunner and loader in the turret/basket assembly over the central compartment, and the powerplant at the rear. The running gear consists on each side of five road wheels with independent torsion-bar suspension, and there are three track-return rollers, a rear sprocket and a front idler. The electro-hydraulically powered turret is mainly of cast construction with a welded roof and bustle, and accommodates the M32 unstabilised gun with an elevation arc of 29° 30' (-9° 45' to +19° 45') but only a primitive optical fire-control system; there are also 7.62-mm (0.3-in) co-axial and 12.7-mm (0.5-in) AA machine guns. Later variants were the **M41A1**, **M41A2** and **M41A3** which differed only in detail, including an increase in main armament stowage from 57 to 65 rounds. The last variants also had a fuel-injected rather than normally aspirated engine. Subsequent variants were to have had a 90-mm (3.54-in) or even 105-mm (4.13-in) main gun, but

The M41 series was widely exported to American allies for whom a readily available and cheap light tank, offering reconnaissance and counter-insurgency capabilities of a high order, was more important than a costlier battle tank offering unwanted capability.

these were not procured. Variants that did appear, however, were the **M42 Duster** with twin 40-mm anti-aircraft guns, the **M44** 155-mm (6.1-in) self-propelled howitzer, the **M52** 105-mm (4.13-in) self-propelled howitzer and the **M75** armoured personnel carrier. The M41 and its derivatives are still in extensive service, update packages centring on the engine and armament, for which a diesel and a 90-mm main gun have been offered.

For its size and weight the M41 offered good capability, but the type was not best suited to operations in any form of high-intensity battlefield, where it might be engaged by battle tanks or large-calibre artillery firing armour-penetrating projectiles.

SPECIFICATION	
M41 Walker Bulldog	895-3 air-cooled 6-cylinder petrol engine developing 373 kW (500 hp)
Crew: 4	**Performance:** maximum road speed 72 km/h (45 mph); maximum road range 161 km (100 miles); fording 1.02 m (3 ft 4 in); gradient 60 per cent; vertical obstacle 0.71 m (2 ft 4 in); trench 1.83 m (6 ft 0 in)
Weight: 23.496 tonnes	
Dimensions: length (gun forward) 8.20 m (26 ft 11 in); length (hull) 5.82 m (19 ft 1 in); width 3.20 m (10 ft 6 in); height (including AA machine-gun) 3.07 m (10 ft 1 in)	
Powerplant: one Continental AOS-	

M41 Walker Bulldog

Until the introduction of the American M60, tanks were divided into light, medium and heavy categories just as they had been during World War II. But as the ability of shells to penetrate armour rapidly improved, the heavy tank became obsolete. Monsters like the British Conqueror and Soviet T-10 vanished and the term 'Main Battle Tank' was coined to describe the new generation of armour. But light tanks soldiered on. In the early 1950s, General Motors manufactured 5,500 M41 light tanks, which equipped US formations until the early 1970s and still serve in many parts of the world. The light tank was designed to fulfil a

number of roles. Its firepower, armour protection and mobility were superior to cannon-armed armoured cars, enabling it to win the battle for reconnaissance information. Its light weight enabled it to fight over ground where a 30-tonne medium tank would bog down. In the early 1960s, the US Army supplied the South Vietnamese forces with M41s rather than any of their larger vehicles for this very reason. Economics also played a part: the M41 was about half the cost of contemporary MBTs, thus making it a popular export. It was supplied to many NATO armies and forces in Latin America.

The M41 missed the Korean War for the simple reason that none of the US tank units equipped with it were deployed there during the conflict. Its chance for action came years later when large numbers were supplied to the South Vietnamese army. South Vietnamese M41s were a familiar sight on the world's TV screens from 1965-75; supplied to the South Vietnamese army, it was one of the ARVN's most effective weapons.

The M41 driver sits in an isolated compartment but has an escape hatch in the hull floor. The driver can operate a ventilator blower system and the fire extinguisher in the engine compartment.

Seperated from the crew compartment by a bulkhead, the Continental six-cylinder air-cooled supercharged petrol engine develops 372.9 kW (500 bhp) at 2,800 rpm. Maximum speed was 72 km/h (44.7 mph) when new, but the range was a pitiful 161 km (100 miles).

The M41 was widely exported to NATO forces during the Cold War. In order to improve the firepower of the M41, the Danish army introduced a new APFSDS (Armour-Piercing Fin-Stabilised Discarding Sabot) round developed by the AA1 Corporation in the US. This significantly improves penetration and is more accurate than the older ammunition.

The barrel length of the 3-in (76-mm) M32 gun – 62 calibres – was necessary to provide the armour-piercing rounds with sufficient muzzle velocity to penetrate. An M41 needed to be uncomfortably close to a T-54/55 to either hit with HEAT or penetrate with HVAP, but South Vietnamese tank crews managed to knock out the heavier enemy armour in the early stages of the 1972 invasion.

The primary post-war use for light tanks in major amries is to arm light formations. However, this M41 Walker Bulldog equipped the US Army's 2nd Medium Tank Battalion, 40th Armor Division, which was based in Korea in the early 1960s.

M551 Sheridan

Although the M551 Sheridan was not a success, it remained in service for more than 20 years as it was the largest and most powerful vehicle that could be air-dropped from a C-130 Hercules transport aeroplane, and thus soldiered on with the 82nd Airborne Division in the absence of any replacement. It was air-dropped by low-altitude extraction. The transport flew low over the drop zone with the tank strapped to a fibreboard platform. A drogue parachute was deployed, pulling the Sheridan out, and the pallet took most of the shock of impact. The crew then parachuted in, unstrapped the tank and drove away. The 82nd Airborne Division is one of the US Army's primary quick-reaction assets, and in addition to seeing action in Desert Storm, the unit's M551s were regularly deployed to the inner German border in the 1980s.

Although the Shillelagh missile was extremely effective when it hit an armoured vehicle, it had two disadvantages: the rate of fire was only two rounds per minute, which was less than half that of a conventional gun, and it could not engage targets within 1000 m (1,095 yards). For this reason, the M60A2 and the Sheridan were provided with a conventional round based on a combustible case. This doubled the rate of fire and was perfectly accurate at short range. This conventional round fired a HEAT projectile capable of penetrating about 500 mm (19.7 in) of armour. A WP (white phosphorus) round was also carried, and was used to lay smoke, to mark targets or for its incendiary effect.

The aluminium-hulled Sheridan's combat weight was 18.37 tonnes. With just 100 mm (3.94 in) of frontal armour, the Sheridan could be penetrated by any MBT's gun and was extremely vulnerable to infantry anti-tank rockets, but the addition of extra armour was impossible since the vehicle had to be capable of being landed by parachute. The Sheridan was already turning the scales at about the maximum for reliable parachute landings. One dropped during the 1989 invasion of Panama broke free during the parachute drop and buried itself up to the turret, prompting a round of jokes that the 82nd Airborne's solution to the Noriega problem was to squash the dictator with a flying tank!

The Shillelagh missile was steered by the gunner, who had to keep the crosshairs of his sight over the target until the missile impacted. He had to concentrate, because once the solid-fuel rocket motor cut in after 1200 m (1,315 yards) of flight, the missile accelerated to 1100 m (3,609 ft) per second! The missile tracker monitored the missile's flight path and compared it with the line of sight, and IR transmitter mounted above the launcher's barrel sending guidance steering commands to a receiver in the missile.

Unlike main battle tanks, the M551 could be dropped by parachute from USAF transport aircraft, making it an important part of the combat power of the 82nd Airborne Division. Here, a C-130E uses the LAPES method to unload a palletised M551.

Powerplant

The Sheridan was powered by a Detroit Diesel water-cooled six-cylinder turbocharged diesel engine developing 224 kW (300 bhp). The engine and transmission were mounted in the rear of the hull, the transmission providing four forward and two reverse gears. The Sheridan was designed to provide the reconnaissance elements of all US Army divisions with their primary vehicle, and was expected to have a very good performance. The maximum road speed was 70 km/h (43.5 mph) and the vehicle's road range was around 600 km (373 miles). The M551 was amphibious after about five minutes of preparation. Driven by its tracks, it could travel at 6 km/h (3.7 mph) while afloat.

An M551 of the 4th/68th Armored Battalion, 82nd Airborne Division, winds its way through the Saudi Arabian desert during a patrol for Operation Desert Storm. The Sheridan had a troubled career since its introduction during the Vietnam War, but was the only light air-portable tank available to US airborne troops at the time of the 1991 Gulf War.

M551 Sheridan Light tank

In the mid-1950s the only mobile weapons with a direct-fire capability in the US airborne divisions were the 76-mm (3-in) M41 light tank and the 90-mm (3.54-in) M56 self-propelled anti-tank gun. In 1959 a requirement was issued for a new airportable vehicle to replace both the M41 and M56, and development of such a vehicle started under the name **Armored Reconnaissance/ Airborne Assault Vehicle (AR/AAV)** and the designation **XM551**. The Allison Division of General Motors was subsequently awarded the development contract, and a total of 12 prototypes was built. In 1965, a four-year production contract was awarded to the company, although at that time the vehicle had not been fully accepted for service.

New vehicles

Production continued until 1970, when a total of 1,700 vehicles had been built. The XM551 was officially classified fit for service in 1966 and called the **M551 General Sheridan**. Although it was evaluated by a number of countries the type was never sold overseas, though it was deployed by the US Army to Europe, South Korea and Vietnam. In the last theatre the M551 earned itself a bad reputation, many faults soon becoming apparent, especially with the 152-mm (6-in) main armament, the power-

Above: An M551 Sheridan, as deployed to Vietnam, showing extensive external turret stowage and additional protection for the commander.

Right: A standard Sheridan during tests at Fort Knox. About 1700 of these vehicles were built between 1966 and 1970, and the last operational battalion, the 82nd Airborne Division, gave up its vehicles in the mid 1990s. Other vehicles have been converted to resemble Soviet vehicles such as the ZSU-23-4 and BMP for use at the National Training Centre, Fort Irwin, California.

pack and the very thin belly armour, which provided little protection from mines, one of the more common Vietcong weapons.

In the late 1970s the M551 was withdrawn from most front-line units, its problematic MGM-51 Shillelagh missiles never having been used in anger, and by early 1983 it remained in service only with the tank battalion attached to the 82nd Airborne Division, though a few remained in service with the Arkansas National Guard into the 1980s. Large numbers are also used by the National Training Center at Fort Irwin, California, where they have been modified to resemble Soviet vehicles such as the ZSU-23-4 23-mm self-propelled anti-aircraft gun, BMP series MICV and the 122-mm (4.8-in) 2S3 self-propelled howitzer.

The hull of the M551 was of welded aluminium construction while the turret was of steel construction. The driver was seated at the front in the centre, the turret was in the centre of the hull, and the engine and transmission were at the rear. Suspension was of the torsion-bar type, and consisted of five dual rubber-tyred road wheels with the drive sprocket at the rear and idler at the front; there were no

track-return rollers. A flotation screen was carried collapsed around the top of the hull and when this was erected the M551 was fully amphibious, being propelled in the water by its tracks at an approximate speed of 5.8 km/h (3.6 mph).

Armament

The main armament consisted of an M81 152-mm (6-in) gun/missile launcher that could fire a Shillelagh missile or one of four types of combustible-case conventional ammunition, namely HEAT-T-MP, WP, TP-T and canister. The last was of some use in Vietnam for beating off massed guerrilla attack at close quarters. The mix of conventional ammunition and missile depended on the mission being undertaken, but was typically 20 conventional rounds and eight missiles. A 0.3-in (7.62-mm) machine-gun was mounted co-axial with the main armament and a 0.5-in (12.7-mm) machine-gun, with a shield, was mounted on top of the commander's cupola for local and anti-aircraft defence. Space was so cramped inside the M551 that much of the machine-gun ammunition was often carried externally on the sides of the turret.

SPECIFICATION	
M551 Sheridan	0.5-in (12.7-mm) M2 machine-gun
Crew: 4	**Powerplant:** one Detroit Diesel 6V-53T 6-cylinder diesel developing 224 kW (300 hp)
Weight: 15.83 tonnes	
Dimensions: length 6.3 m (20 ft 8 in); width 2.82 m (9 ft 3 in); height (overall) 2.95 m (9 ft 8 in)	**Performance:** maximum road speed 70 km/h (43 mph); maximum range 600 km (310 miles)
Armament: 152-mm (6-in) M81 gun/missile launcher with 20 conventional rounds and eight Shillelagh missiles, co-axial 0.3-in (7.62-mm) M240 machine-gun,	**Fording:** amphibious
	Gradient: 60 per cent
	Vertical obstacle: 0 84 m (2 ft 9 in)
	Trench: 2.54 m (8 ft 4 in)

Faults encountered with the Shillelagh anti-tank missile and a poor combat record meant that the Sheridan was only retained by the US Airborne service on account of its air-portability. It did, however, survive in service long enough to see action in Panama in 1989 and in support of Desert Shield.

Rooikat Armoured car

Development of the **Vickers OMC Rooikat** armoured car began in 1976 when three 8x8 vehicles were built to verify platform concepts. This was followed by a further three vehicles which were built and evaluated by the South African Defence Force in the early 1980s.

The main role of the Rooikat is combat reconnaissance during high-mobility operations, using its speed to outmanoeuvre the enemy and strike at his flanks and deep into the rear. Its secondary role is that of hunter/killer against a variety of battlefield targets including AFVs, with its third role being interdiction.

The hull is of all-welded steel armour with the driver seated at the front, three-man power-operated turret in the centre and the power pack at the rear. Over the frontal arc protection is provided against penetration from the 23 mm AP rounds fired from the Russian ZU-23-2 LAAG.

Powerplant

The Rooikat has a V-10 turbocharged water-cooled engine driving through a six-speed fully automatic transmission, drop down gearbox and high/low-range transfer gearbox. This can be field exchanged in 60 minutes. The engine compartment is fitted with an automatic fire detection and suppression system. The driver can select full 8x8 drive or 8x4 drive, depending on the tactical situation. Steering is power assisted on the front four wheels.

The driver, seated on the centreline of the vehicle, enters through the fighting compartment or the single-piece hatch cover that opens to the left. The driver's station (including essential controls) is fully adjustable and when closed down forward observation is via three day periscopes, the centre one of which can be replaced by a passive night periscope. The driver's periscopes can be cleaned by a compressed air cleaning system.

A hull escape hatch is on each side of the hull, between the second and third axles, thus protecting the crew from small arms fire if they evacuate. The commander sits on the right of the turret with the gunner forward and below his position, and the loader on the left. The commander is provided with eight day vision blocks to give observation through 360°. Mounted in the roof, forward of the commander's station, is a x12 day panoramic sight. This enables the commander to observe through a full 360° without moving his head. The sight can also be slaved to the main gun or uncoupled.

Observation

The loader has a single-piece hatch cover that opens to the rear, and is provided with two day periscopes that can be traversed to observe on the left side of the vehicle. The gunner has a roof-mounted periscopic sight that has x8 day and night (image intensification) channels and an integral laser rangefinder. The gunner also has an auxiliary day sight. If required, the commander can override the gunner.

Turret traverse and weapon elevation features solid-state electric controls for both gunner and commander, with manual emergency back up. Traverse is through a full 360° with elevation limits from -10 to +20°. The commander has a single control handle and the gunner twin control handles.

The digital fire-control system receives information from a laser rangefinder and a number of sensors including cant and windspeed. Ammunition type is set manually. The Rooikat can engage and hit targets with a high probability while it is moving across rough terrain.

The fire-control system provides automatic fire control by computing and implementing the ballistic offsets for the ammunition type selection. It takes into account target range, target speed, manually entered environmental data, cross-wind speed, weapon tilt, and gun jump characteristics of the main weapon. A ready to fire indication appears in the gunner's field advising him to fire. Total reaction time from lasing to firing is typically less than two seconds.

GT4 gun

Main armament comprises a 76-mm (3-in) GT4 gun. The 76-mm gun was chosen because of the larger number of rounds that could be carried compared to a 105-mm (4.13-in) gun, the ease of handling ammunition when moving across country and crew comfort when firing. The 76-mm stabilised gun has a vertical sliding semi-automatic breech block, a thermal sleeve and concentric glass fibre fume extractor. The recoil system consists of a concentric hydrospring with an external replenisher with maximum recoil being 370 mm (14.6 in). Two types of fixed 76-mm ammunition have been developed, HE-T and APFSDS-T with a total of 48 rounds of ammunition being carried, nine for ready use stowed vertically below the turret ring on the left side. For safety reasons no main gun ammunition is stowed above the turret ring. Rate of fire is stated to be 6 rds/min, with the APFSDS-T projectile having an effective range of 2,000 to 3,000 m (2,187 to 3,281 yds). It will penetrate the T-54/55 and T-62 from all angles of attack. The HE-T round has a maximum range of 12,000 m (13,123 yds) in the indirect fire role and 3,000 m in the direct fire role.

It is understood that production of the 76-mm Rooikat is now complete with about 240 vehicles being built for the South African Armoured Corps.

Trials have demonstrated that the hull of the Rooikat provides a high degree of protection against anti-tank mines. The Rooikat remains mobile with two same-side wheels blown off by landmine explosion.

The 76-mm Rooikat is shown here during camouflage trials. Smoke-laying equipment includes eight 81-mm (3.19-in) smoke grenade launchers (with two rounds each) as well as an exhaust smoke screen generator.

Configured for the export market, the 105-mm Rooikat has been built in prototype form only. Development was completed in 1997 and the turret has been offered for installation on other tracked and wheeled vehicles.

SPECIFICATION	
76-mm Rooikat	420 kW (563 hp)
Crew: 4	**Performance:** maximum road speed 120 km/h (74.57 mph); cross-country speed 60 km/h (37.28 mph); maximum road range 1000 km (621 miles)
Combat weight: 28 tonnes	
Dimensions: length (including gun) 8.2 m (26 ft 11 in); width 2.9 m (9 ft 6 in); height 2.8 m (9 ft 2½ in)	
Armament: 76-mm (3-in) GT4 rifled gun with 48 rounds, coaxial 7.62-mm (0.3-in) machine-gun, 7.62-mm AA machine-gun	**Gradient:** 70 per cent
	Fording depth: 1.5 m (4 ft 11 in); **Vertical obstacle:** 1 m (3 ft 4 in)
Powerplant: one V-10 water-cooled diesel engine developing	**Trench:** 2 m (6 ft 7 in) at crawl speed; 1 m (3 ft 4 in) at 60 km/h (37.28 mph)

Types 59/69 Main Battle Tanks

Over 6,000 Type 59 and Type 69 tanks have been manufactured for the PLA. This is a Type 69II, a tank which was still in production in the late 1990s. It is equipped with a rifled 105-mm gun.

In the early 1950s China was supplied with a quantity of Soviet T-54 main battle tanks. These were used as a basis for a Chinese-built tank, the **Type 59**, which entered service in the 1950s. The original model is a straight copy of the T-54, armed with a 100-mm (3¾-in) rifled gun as its main armament.

Modernised

Most People's Liberation Army (PLA) equipment is based on Soviet designs of the 1950s, but many of its main weapons have been substantially upgraded, often utilising Western technology. The **Type 59II** is an upgraded version of the original tank, incorporating several Western improvements into the basic vehicle. The main improvement is in fitting a rifled 105-mm (4-in) gun based on the long-serving and highly effective British L7. Stabilised in both

planes, it gives the Type 59 a major increase in striking power.

Iran has developed an upgraded variant of the Type 59 which has a broad range of Western and Soviet upgrades to fire-control, protection and main gun.

First seen in public in 1982, the **Type 69** main battle tank is a modified Type 59, roughly equivalent to the Soviet T-55.

It is a relatively inexpensive and easy to operate tank but it is of an outdated design by modern standards.

The interior is cramped and can be difficult to operate in. The 36-ton Type 69 main battle tank has improved armour, a gun stabiliser, a fire control system including a laser range finder, infra-red searchlights, and a 105-mm smooth-bore gun.

The **Type 69II MBT Command Tank Type B** is fitted with additional radio sets for the command and control function at Regimental level.

At least 6,000 Type 59 and 59II MBTs served in the PLA and many will remain in ser-

vice until China decides on a next-generation tank. A new GEC-Marconi Centaur fire control system is available, and British Barr and Stroud thermal based FCS (fire control system) can also be fitted.

Worldwide use

Type 59 and Type 69 MBTs have seen combat all over the world. Operators include Vietnam, Cambodia, North Korea and Pakistan (more than 1,300). Chinese Type 59s were also sold or given to Albania,

Bangladesh, the Congo, Tanzania, and Zimbabwe. Type 69 tanks saw combat with both sides during the Iran-Iraq war; with the Iraqi Army in the 1991 Gulf War and by the Sri Lankan Army.

A regiment of Type 69 tanks parades at a military review outside Beijing. The Type 69 is an improved Type 59; many have been upgraded with advanced fire control systems and more powerful guns.

SPECIFICATION	
Type 59II **Crew:** 4 **Combat weight:** 36 tons **Dimensions:** chassis length 6.04 m/19.8 ft (9 m/29 ft 6 in with gun forward); height 2.59 m (8 ft 6 in); width 3.27 m (10 ft 9 in) **Armour:** 203 mm maximum thickness on turret front **Armament:** one 105-mm rifled gun, one co-axial 7.62-mm (0.3-in) MG, one 7.62-mm MG in ball	mount on bow, one 12.7-mm (0.5-in) AA MG on turret cupola **Powerplant:** one 380-kW (520 hp) V-12 diesel piston engine **Performance:** max road speed 50 km/h (31 mph); max off road speed 25 km/h (16 mph); range 400 km (240 miles) **Fording:** 5.5 m (18 ft) with snorkel **Vertical obstacle:** 0.79 m (2 ft 7 in)

Types 85/90 Main Battle Tanks

Although the new-generation of Chinese tanks like this Type 85 is based on the mechanical features of the ancient Soviet-era T-54, it is clear that their changed hulls, guns and turrets make them almost entirely new designs.

Although the Type 59 and Type 69 tanks have been the mainstay of Chinese tank forces for more than 40 years, they are very much products of 1940s and 1950s Soviet technology. In spite of modernisation programmes, they would stand little chance in combat against state-of-the-art Western or Russian tanks.

New tanks

In the 1980s, the Chinese began the development of a new, more competitive tank. First revealed outside China in 1987, the Type 80 MBT is a further development of the long-serving Type 59.

However, the chassis has been so extensively modified it is a virtually new design. A new welded turret mounting a new fire-control system and the standard Chinese 105-mm (4-in) gun is used in place of the cast

turret of earlier tanks. The gun can fire APFSDS-T, HEAT-T, HESH, and HE (armour-piercing fin-stabilised discarding sabot-tracer, high-explosive anti-tank-tracer, high-explosive practice-tracer and

high-explosive) rounds.

Production of the Type 80 began in 1988, but in 1991 it was succeeded by the further improved **Type 85**. Variants include the **Type 85IIAP** which can be produced from Type 59s and

Type 69IIs using upgrade kits. The newest model, the **Type 85III** with a 746-kW (1,000-hp) engine, incorporates features also found in the latest Chinese designs. These include a larger 125-mm (4¾-in) smooth bore main gun capable of firing APFSDS, HEAT, and HE-FRAG (HE-fragmentation). A Soviet-style autoloader means that the crew has been reduced to three men. The Type 85III uses modular composite armour, and has been seen fitted with explosive reactive armour. A stabilised image intensification sight allows the tank to engage moving targets while in motion.

Further development has resulted in the **Type 90**, which incorporates significant improvements over the Type 85. Powered by an 895-kW (1,200 hp) eight-cylinder turbo-charged diesel, the Type 90 comes with an autoloading, smooth bore 125-mm gun capable of firing APFSDS, HEAT, and HE-FRAG rounds. The gun is mounted in a stabilised turret with passive thermal imaging. Reactive armour

panels, an improved laser rangefinder, and increased mobility make the Type 90II the most advanced MBT ever built in China.

The PLA ordered 100 Type 90IIs to be delivered in 1999. Completed without fire-control systems, their main purpose was to take part in parades celebrating the 50th anniversary of the People's Republic of China, the vehicle remaining in testing into 2001.

Types 62/63 Light tanks

China is one of the last countries to use large numbers of light and medium tanks in a non-reconnaissance combat role. The diminutive 21-ton **Type 62** is classed as a medium tank. Obviously based on the Type 59, it resembles a scaled-down version of the main battle tank. The cast and welded Type 62 turret is slightly smaller, but it has nearly identical hatches and fittings. Similarly, the wheels and tracks resemble smaller and lighter copies of those used on the Type 59.

The Type 62 mounts an 85-mm (3¼-in) gun that can fire AP, APHE, HE, and HEAT rounds. Its armour protection is limited, offering little resistance to modern anti-tank munitions. North Korea has manufactured a Type 62 variant armed with a 115-mm (4.5-in) main gun.

Amphibian

The **Type 63** light tank was an attempt to get near-MBT firepower onto a light, amphibious chassis. It uses the same turret and 85-mm gun as the Type 62, mounted on a Chinese copy of the Soviet PT-76 light amphibious tank hull. The Chinese version has higher sides, a nearly horizontal front glacis plate and different engine grilles. There are three vertical slot side

The Type 63 is fully amphibious. It is propelled in the water to a maximum of 12 km/h (7.5 mph) by two water jets mounted to the rear.

inlets on the Type 63, in contrast to the single inlet on the PT-76.

Obsolete and vulnerable to advanced anti-tank munitions, the Type 62 tank has largely been relegated to secondary defence and training, though it remains in service with the PLA in large numbers. Type 63 tanks by contrast are very much in the front-line, deployed with PLA Navy Marine units. Both were supplied to regular Chinese customers in Africa and Asia, and both saw combat service with the North Vietnamese at the end of the Vietnam War.

Chinese/Russian hybrid

Although the hull design of the Type 63 is based on that of the Soviet PT-76, its automotive components are adapted from the indigenous Chinese Type 77 armoured personnel carrier.

Above: A Type 63 lays its own smokescreen by injecting diesel fuel into the exhaust.

Light battle tank

In essence a scaled-down Type 59 MBT, the Type 62 light/medium tank was designed for use in rugged terrain not suitable for heavier armour. Although not currently being manufactured, production can be restarted as and when required.

Layout of the Type 62 is identical to the Type 59. The driver is seated front left, the three-man turret is centred (commander and gunner left, loader right) and the engine and transmission are to the rear.

Leclerc
Main battle tank

Above: For many years the French Army had to depend on the ageing AMX-30 main battle tank to provide its armoured punch. The introduction in the 1990s of the Leclerc, with its powerful 120-mm (4.7-in) gun, composite armour and advanced fire control electronics, has provided a quantum leap in the capability of France's spearhead formations.

Named after the Free French liberator of Paris in 1944, it is appropriate that Leclerc main battle tanks should head the parade down the Champs Elysées on Bastille Day. General Leclerc would probably have been proud of the immensely capable machine which bears his name into the 21st century.

The history of tank development is littered with failed multi-national projects which have nevertheless provided the impetus for the production of new fighting vehicles. The current French main battle tank arose out of a failed French/German MBT project of the 1980s. Originally known as the **Engin de Combat Principal**, it was renamed the **Leclerc** in January 1986.

In service with the armies of France since 1992 and of the United Arab Emirates since 1996, the Leclerc is a thoroughly modern weapon system, being well-protected, highly mobile and well armed with a powerful gun.

The 120-mm (4.7-in) smoothbore main armament is longer than the gun on the Leopard 2 and the M1 Abrams, but fires the same combustible cartridge ammunition. It is fully stabilised to allow firing on the move across country, and has an automatic loader which enables the Leclerc to sustain a rate of fire of 12 rounds per minute.

The autoloader can

The United Arab Emirates are the only export customer for the Leclerc. A squadron of the UAE tanks has served in Kosovo, where it reinforced the French Leclerc brigade already on the ground.

quickly switch between APFSDS and HEAT, the two principal types of projectile carried. Normal ammunition load is 22 ready-use rounds in the turret, with a further 18 in the hull. For self-protection the tank has a 12.7-mm (0.5-in) heavy

machine gun mounted co-axially, together with a 7.62-mm (0.3-in) anti-aircraft gun mounted on the turret roof. Nine 80-mm smoke launchers can also deploy infra-red decoys or anti-personnel grenades.

Leclerc is powered by a

SACM V8 high-pressure diesel engine, delivering 1119 kW (1,500 hp) via an automatic hydrostatic transmission. Suspension is hydropneumatic, and cross-country performance is excellent.

As with all of the current generation of MBTs, the Leclerc has an extensive sensor and computerised fire-control fit. The commander's panoramic sight incorporates a laser rangefinder and an image intensifier. The gunner's sight incorporates a thermal imager, while the driver's vision system also has night capability.

Leclerc is fitted with the FINDERS battle management system, which has a coloured map display onto which the positions of allied and opposition forces can be projected. It can be used for route and mission planning.

SPECIFICATION

Leclerc
Type: Main battle tank
Crew: 3
Weight: 54500 kg (120,175 lb)
Dimensions: length (including armament) 9.87 m (32 ft 4½ in); length (hull) 6.88 m (22 ft 6¾ in); width 3.71 m (12 ft 2 in); height 2.53 m (8 ft 3½ in)
Powerplant: one SACM V8X-1500 12-cylinder hyperbar diesel engine

developing 1119 kW (1,500 hp)
Performance: maximum road speed 71 km/h (44 mph); max cross-country c.45 km/h (28 mph); road range 550 km (342 miles) or 650 km (404 miles) with auxiliary tanks; fording depth 1.00 m (3 ft 3 in) without preparation, over 2.00 m with preparation; gradient 60 per cent; vertical obstacle 1.00 m (3 ft 3 in); trench 3.20 m (7 ft 3 in)

Leopard 2
Main battle tank

The Leopard 2's 120-mm (4.7-in) gun ammunition was among the first to have combustible cartridge cases. After the gun is fired, all that remains of the cartridge is the base stub which is ejected into a bag under the breech of the gun.

The **Leopard 2** was a product of the abortive West German/US MBT-70, incorporating the engine, transmission and certain other components developed for the earlier tank. In 1977 the Bundeswehr (German army) placed an order for a total of 1,800 Leopard 2 MBTs, of which Krupp MaK was to build 810 and Krauss-Maffei of Munich the remaining 990. The first production tanks were handed over to the West German army in 1979, with the balance delivered through the 1980s.

In 1979 the Netherlands selected the Leopard 2 to replace its ageing Centurion and AMX-13 tanks, and since then the Leopard 2 has been sold widely to several major European armies. More than 3,000 Leopard 2s have been delivered or are being built.

120-mm gun
The Leopard 2 is armed with a powerful fully-stabilised Rheinmetall 120-mm (4.7-in) smooth-bore gun. A total of 42 rounds of 120-mm ammunition is carried, compared with 60 rounds for the first-generation Leopard 1 with its 105-mm (4.1-in) gun. This is not a great drawback as the 120-mm round has greater penetration and the fire-control system gives a much greater hit probability. A 7.62-mm (0.3-in) machine gun is mounted co-axially with the main armament, and a similar weapon is mounted on the turret roof

Left: Leopard 2 operators include Austria, Denmark, the Netherlands, Sweden, Switzerland and Spain.

The Leopard 2 A6EX has the improved armour of the Bundeswehr's A5, allied to a longer 55-calibre gun. The higher muzzle velocity gives AP rounds even greater penetration.

for anti-aircraft defence.

Advanced armour
From the start, the hull and turret of the Leopard 2 incorporated advanced laminated armour, which gave it a high degree of battlefield survivability, especially against anti-tank weapons with HEAT warheads.

The improved **Leopard 2 A5** currently in service with the Bundeswehr has upgraded armour, heavily reinforced in the turret front and with add-on modules. The next-generation **Leopard 2 A6 EX** is armed with a longer 55-calibre gun; this has a higher muzzle velocity and increased armour penetration.

Both commander and gunner have stabilised roof-mounted sights with thermal imaging: the gun-ner's sight incorporates a laser range-finder linked to the fire-control system. Standard equipment includes passive night-vision equipment, inertial/GPS navigation, an NBC system, a fire extinguishing system and a schnorkel for deep wading.

High mobility
The Leopard 2 is powered by a multi-fuel engine developing 1119 kW (1,500 hp), which gives a power-to-weight ratio of 20 kW (27 hp) per tonne compared with just under 15 kW (20 hp) per tonne for the final production models of the Leopard 1. This gives the tank greater acceleration and improved cross-country mobility, which promote survivability on the battlefield.

SPECIFICATION	
Leopard 2	12-cylinder multi-fuel engine developing 1119 kW (1,500 hp)
Crew: 4	**Performance:** max road speed 72 km/h (45 mph); max range 550 km (342 miles); gradient 60 per cent; fording depth (schnorkel) 4 m (13 ft 1½ in); vertical obstacle 1.10 m (3 ft 7¼ in); trench 3.00 m (9 ft 10 in)
Weight: combat weight 55150 kg (121,725 lb)	
Dimensions: length (with gun forward) 9.67 m (31 ft 8⅜ in); length (hull) 7.77 m (25 ft 6 in); width 3.70 m (12 ft 1⅜ in); height (overall) 2.79 m (9 ft 1¾ in)	
Powerplant: one MTU MB 873	

Ariete Main battle tank

Despite Italy's increasing involvement in peacekeeping and low-intensity operations, the Italian army is still prepared to fight more conventional set-piece land battles. To this end, a second generation MBT, the **Ariete** (ram) has been developed. Delivery of the Ariete began in December 1995. The Italian Army procured 200 of the tanks and final deliveries were completed in 2002.

The Ariete sensor suite includes a stabilised panoramic periscope incorporating an infra-red capability for night operations. Moreover, the tank features a digital fire control system. This computes firing patterns for the main gun based on meteorological data, positioning, ammunition, and targeting information.

The Ariete can engage targets during the day or night with its 120-mm smoothbore gun. The gun contains a fume extraction system, a muzzle reference system and a thermal sleeve. Also, the gun can fire APFDS (Armour-Piercing, Fin-stabilised, Discarding Sabot) and HEAT (High-Explosive Anti-Tank) rounds. The turret accommodates 15 rounds of ammunition, with a further 27 rounds being stored in the hull of the vehicle.

Additional armament includes a 7.62-mm (0.3-in) machine-gun, which is mounted co-axially with the main gun. The tank also features a 7.62-mm air-defence gun mounted on the turret,

which is operated by the commander. The Ariete carries 2,500 rounds of 7.62-mm ammunition.

Ariete is protected by a comprehensive suite of protective measures.

These include electrically operated smoke grenades and a laser-warning receiver. The hull and turret are of all-welded steel construction, and incorporate NBC crew protection.

Above: Mounted on each side of the turret are four forward-firing smoke grenade launchers. These can be automatically launched by a laser warning system.

Below: The Ariete incorporates a layer of additional advanced armour over the frontal arc, offering protection against modern HEAT warheads.

SPECIFICATION

Ariete
Crew: 4
Combat weight: 54 tonnes
Dimensions: length 9.7 m (31 ft 9½ in) including main armament; overall width 3.6 m (11 ft 9½ in); height 2.50 m (8 ft 3 in) to turret roof
Armament: one Otobreda 120-mm smoothbore gun with 42 rounds, 7.62-mm (0.3-in) co-axial machine-gun on left of turret, 7.62-mm AA machine-gun on turret roof

Powerplant: one IVECO V-12 turbocharged 12-cylinder diesel developing 969-kW (1,300-hp)
Performance: maximum cruising speed in excess of 65 km/h (40 mph); maximum cruising range over 550 km (342 miles)
Fording: 1.2 m (3 ft 11 in) unprepared
Gradient: 60 per cent
Vertical obstacle: 1 m (3 ft 3½ in)
Trench: 3 m (9 ft 10 in)

Sabra M60 upgrade

Originally based on the US M60 MBT, Israel Military Industries has up-gunned and upgraded the M60A3 to **Sabra** standard using highly advanced indigenous technology. As well offering an upgrade for Israeli Defence Force M60s, the manufacturer is also expected to upgrade 170 Turkish M60A1s. These upgrades improve on the M60's Cold War technology, whilst extending its operational life and enabling it to destroy

most contemporary MBTs.

The Sabra features a powerful 120-mm smoothbore gun, the same weapon developed for the Merkava Mk 3. The gun is fitted with a fume extraction unit and a thermal sleeve, which reduces barrel wear. This also increases accuracy by reducing the distortion of the barrel. The gun has greater accuracy compared to the 105-mm model originally installed on Israel's M60s. The new gun fires NATO

SPECIFICATION

Sabra
Crew: 4
Combat weight: around 55 tonnes, depending on level of armour protection
Dimensions: length 9.4 m (30 ft 9½ in) gun forward; width 3.63 m (11 ft 11 in) without skirts; height 3.05 m (10 ft) to commander's cupola
Armament: one Israeli Military Industries 120-mm smoothbore gun with 40 rounds, 7.62-mm (0.3-in) co-axial machine-gun, two pintle-mounted 7.62-mm AA

machine-guns on roof operated by commander and gunner, and one 60-mm mortar
Powerplant: one General Dynamics AVDS-1790-5A twin-turbocharged diesel developing 677-kW (908-hp)
Performance: maximum road speed 48 km/h (30 mph); range 450 km (280 miles)
Fording: 1.4 m (4 ft 7 in) unprepared
Gradient: 60 per cent
Vertical obstacle: 0.91 m (3 ft)
Trench: 2.6 m (8 ft 6 in)

standard 120-mm smoothbore ammunition, which can also include APFDS rounds. In common with the Merkava, the Sabra can carry a single 60-mm mortar for infantry suppression.

The crew are protected with a fire and explosion suppression system, and a threat suppression system. The hull is covered with modular passive armour pro-

tection; however, this has been upgraded to an explosive-reactive standard. A smoke grenade launcher also helps to mask the tank.

The Sabra's fire control system manages the dynamics of the turret. It also stabilises the gun, increasing

From a standing start, the Sabra can accelerate from to 32 km/h (20 mph) in 9.6 seconds. Upgraded suspension improves cross country mobility and ride for the crew.

its accuracy and the probability of a 'first hit' against moving and stationary targets. The gun can be slaved to the line of sight; it can also be used in a non-stabilised mode and has an emergency back-up mode for manual operation.

Merkava Mk 3 Main battle tank

Mounted on each side of the Merkava Mk 3's turret is an instantaneous self-screening system for the identification of 'friendly' combat vehicles.

SPECIFICATION	
Merkava Mk 3	**Powerplant:** one General
Crew: 4	Dynamics AVDS-1790-9AR V-12 air-
Combat weight: 65 tonnes	cooled diesel developing 895-kW
Dimensions: length 9.04 m (29 ft	(1,200-hp)
8 in) gun forward; width 3.72 m	**Performance:** maximum road
(12 ft 2½ in); height 2.66 m (8 ft	speed 60 km/h (37 mph); range
9 in) to turret roof	500 km (311 miles)
Armament: one Israeli Military	**Fording:** 1.4 m (4 ft 7 in)
Industries 120-mm smoothbore gun	unprepared
with 48 rounds, 7.62-mm (0.3-in)	**Gradient:** 70 per cent
co-axial machine-gun, two roof-	**Vertical obstacle:** 1.05 m (3 ft
mounted 7.62-mm AA	4¾ in)
machine-guns and one 60-mm	**Trench:** 3.55 m (11 ft 7 in)
mortar fired from within turret	

Design work on the **Merkava Mk 3** began in 1983, and the variant entered Israeli Armour Corps service with the 188th Armoured Brigade in early 1990. Since then earlier Merkava Mk 1 and Mk 2 MBTs have been given certain Mk 3 features during overhaul, although this has not included the 120-mm smoothbore gun, one of the key features of the Mk 3. The Merkava Mk 3 essentially constitutes a new design, with a lengthened hull and increased fuel capacity. The turret is also lengthened and incorporates modular armour, which may be quickly replaced or upgraded.

The 105-mm main armament of the earlier Merkavas has been substituted for a 120-mm thermal-sleeved weapon, similar to that fitted to the M1A1/M1A2 and Leopard 2. The gun has an elevation of +20° and a depression of -7°. The heavily-armoured turret compartment houses some of the 48 rounds for the main gun. A supplementary 60-mm mortar is operated from within the turret and can fire HE or illuminating rounds. Three 7.62-mm (0.3-in) machine-guns are provided with a total of 10,000 rounds of ammunition.

The Merkava Mk 3 has all-electric turret controls and can be operated by the commander or gunner. The Merkava Mk 3 is capable of engaging moving targets while it is on the move, using an advanced fire-control system and an Automatic Target Tracker (ATT). The commander's panoramic sight is relayed to the gunner's stabilised day/night sight. The gunner's sight features a laser rangefinder and an automatic target tracker. The fire-control system offers line of sight stabilisation for the gunner and commander, and is integrated to the turret- and gun-control equipment.

Further Merkava Mk 3 systems improvements include a new threat warning system. The NBC protection system is similar to that of its predecessors, but has a new central filter and air-conditioning.

The 'Hawk'

A increased degree of protection compared to the Merkava Mks 1 and 2 is offered by modular hull and turret armour 'packages'. The **Merkava Mk 3 Baz** (hawk) adds elliptical turret armour providing improved ballistic protection.

In addition, the Baz carries an automatic target tracking system that holds

the sight on target after acquisition by either TV (daytime engagements) or infra-red (night/adverse weather) camera. The system is claimed to be capable of engaging high-speed ground targets and helicopters, irrespective of temporary terrain masking.

Optional equipment for the Merkava Mk 3 includes turret-mounted grenade launchers and a countermeasures system. The latter, mounted either side of the main gun, is similar to the Shtora-1 system fitted to Russian tanks, and is designed to decoy anti-tank guided weapons (ATGWs) prior to impact.

Type 90 Main battle tank

Despite having an advanced self-defence force, Japan is not well known for its defence industry. However, the **Type 90** is considered one of the most advanced MBTs in its class, incorporating composite armour for the hull and turret. The Type 90 project was originally launched in 1977, and the tank was finally accepted for service by the Japanese Self-Defence Force in 1990. In late 1999 some 172 vehicles were in service, with production continuing at around 17 annually.

The Type 90 uses the same smoothbore 120-mm Rheinmetall gun which is fitted to the German Leopard 2 MBT, and in a modified form, the M1A1/M1A2. The main gun can deliver several different types of ammunition, including armour-piercing projectiles, anti-tank howitzer shells and adhesive HE projectiles.

Type 90 details

The Type 90 tank features a highly automated systems suite. This enables operations with a crew of three, due to the installation of an automated ammunition feeder for the main gun. The gun is guided by laser and

With vertical front, sides and rear, the Type 90 turret is similar to that of the Leopard 2, and combines that tank's Rheinmetall 120-mm smoothbore gun with an indigenous recoil system and gun mount.

thermal imaging technology. The commander's targeting periscope affixed to the turret can be independently rotated, increasing visibility. The tank's fire control system has an integrated laser range finder, which uses the infra-red rays of the target to fix the gun. This enables the tank to engage targets in high-precision attacks while on the move;

while allowing the Type 90 to effectively engage mobile targets. An NBC system is fitted as standard, and a mineclearing roller system, recovery crane and winch or dozer blade can be fitted to the front of the hull. A scissor-bridge can also be carried on the vehicle front of the **Type 91 AVLB**, a bridge-laying version of the basic Type 90.

SPECIFICATION	
Type 90	**Powerplant:** one Mitsubishi 10ZG
Crew: 3	10-cylinder diesel developing
Combat weight: 50 tonnes	1119-kW (1,500-hp)
Dimensions: overall length 9.76 m	**Performance:** maximum road
(32 ft); overall width 3.43 m (11 ft	speed 70 km/h (43 mph); maximum
3 in); height 3 m (9 ft 9½ in)	range 400 km (249 miles)
Armament: one Rheinmetall	**Fording:** 2 m (6 ft 7 in)
120-mm smoothbore gun, 7.62-mm	**Gradient:** 60 per cent
(0.3-in) co-axial machine-gun,	**Vertical obstacle:** 1 m (3 ft 3½ in)
12.7-mm (0.5-in) AA machine-gun	**Trench:** 2.7 m (8 ft 10 in)

K1 and K1A1 Main Battle Tanks

For decades, the Republic of Korea has relied on American weaponry to equip its military. However, since the 1970s the country's rapid industrial expansion has fostered the development of a significant indigenous armaments industry. One of the first major products of that industry was the **K1 Main Battle Tank**, originally known as

the **Republic of Korea Indigenous Tank** or **ROKIT**.

The preliminary design was based on the US M1 Abrams tank but the K1 was modified to meet the requirements of the Korean armed forces. The tank has been optimised for maximum manoeuvrability in the muddy off-road conditions of Korea, and is intended to cope with the wide variety

of terrain, including rugged mountains, jungles, paddy fields and swamp.

The K1 is conventional in layout, with its four-man crew of commander, gunner, loader and driver. It is powered by a turbo-charged 895-kW (1200-hp) diesel engine. The main gun is a 105-mm rifled high velocity cannon, with a coaxial 7.62-mm (0.3-in) machine gun. A 12.7-mm (0.50-in) calibre machine gun is mounted on the turret for the commander's station, while the loader also has a 7.62-mm machine gun.

K1 in service

The K1 has been operational with the ROK Army since 1986 and the army plans to keep it in service for the next 30 years. It forms the basis for a family of AFVs, including the **K1 ARV** armoured recovery vehicle, and the **K1 AVLB** armoured

bridge layer.

The **K1A1** is an upgraded version of the K1 MBT, equipped with the 120-mm M256 smoothbore cannon, also used by the M1A2 and the German Leopard 2. The A1 has a new ballistic computer and a Korean-developed fire control system which includes thermal imagers, laser rangefinders and a dual field of view day TV camera. The first two prototypes of the K1A1 successfully completed operational tests in 1997 and the tank has been ordered by the Republic of Korea Army.

Above: Based on the American M1 tank, but with a diesel powerplant, the K1A1 is a thoroughly modern main battle tank. Its firepower, protection and mobility are as good as any fighting vehicle in the world.

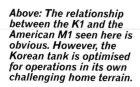

Above: The relationship between the K1 and the American M1 seen here is obvious. However, the Korean tank is optimised for operations in its own challenging home terrain.

Right: The original K1 tank was armed with the American version of the long-serving British L7 105-mm gun. It is more than capable of dealing with any North Korean or Chinese opposition.

SPECIFICATION	
K1A1	**Maximum speed:** road 65 km/h (40 mph)
Type: Main Battle Tank	**Trench:** 2.60 m (8 ft 6 in)
Crew: four	**Fording:** 2.20 m (7 ft 2 in)
Dimensions: length with gun forward 9.71 m (31 ft 10 in); width 3.59 m (11 ft 9 in); height to top of turret 2.25 m (7 ft 5 in)	**Vertical obstacle:** 1.0 m (3 ft 3 in)
Combat weight: 54.5 tonnes	**Armament:** one M256 120-mm (4.7-in) smoothbore rifled main gun with 32 rounds; one co-axial 7.62-mm (0.3-in) M60E1 MG, one M60 7.62-mm, one M2 12.7-mm (0.5-in) MG on turret
Powerplant: MB 871 ka-501 turbo-charged diesel engine delivering 895 kW (1200 hp)	

Challenger 2 Main Battle Tank

The British **Challenger** tank was developed from an upgraded Chieftain design known as the **Shir 2**, ordered by the Shah of Iran in the 1970s. Much faster than its ageing predecessor, thanks to its more powerful diesel engine and greatly improved suspension, its major advance was in protection.

Chobham armour
Challenger was one of the first main battle tanks to be fitted with Chobham laminated armour, a quantum leap in tank protection against both armour-piercing and HEAT rounds.

Its 120-mm (4.7-in) rifled gun was the same as that fitted to the Chieftain, but although it was extremely powerful, the Challenger performed badly in NATO tank gunnery competitions. This was primarily because of serious problems with its modernised fire control system. The British Army actually ceased to enter the annual NATO tank shoot because Challenger kept coming last!

By the time of the Gulf War in 1991, most of the problems had been ironed out, and the Challenger performed creditably in combat – not one vehicle was lost while being credited with destroying over 300 Iraqi tanks and armoured vehicles.

Challenger 2
In the 1980s, Vickers began development of a much improved variant of the Challenger, and in June 1991 the UK government placed an order for 127 **Challenger 2** MBTs, followed by an order for a further 259 in 1994. Production commenced in 1993 and the Challenger 2 was accepted for service with the British Army on 16 May 1994.

Although the Challenger 2 looks very much like the original Challenger, it is in essence a new MBT. Over

Above: Oman is the only export customer for the Challenger 2 to date. The final batch of 38 vehicles ordered were shipped late in 2000, equipping the Royal Oman 1st Main Battle Tank Regiment.

150 improvements were made to the hull alone. The turret, which incorporates second-generation Chobham armour, is also a new design. The L30A1 120-mm rifled gun is chrome-lined, giving longer life and greater accuracy. The gun fires all current 120-mm ammunition, including a new depleted uranium APFSDS round. Normal ammunition stowage is 50 rounds.

Digital fire control
A fully digital system handles fire control, and both commander and gunner are provided with stabilised thermal sights. The driver is equipped with an image-intensifying Passive Driving Periscope (PDP) for night driving.

Under the Strategic Defence Review, the Royal Armoured Corps will have six Challenger 2 MBT regiments, each of which will be equipped with 38 tanks.

So far, the only export customer is Oman, which has ordered 38 tanks in all.

Reliability
Early in 1999, the UK MoD published the results of a demanding series of trials under battlefield conditions, which confirmed that Challenger 2 had exceeded the most rigorous reliability targets ever set. **Challenger 2E**, the latest development model, has been designed for the export market and is capable of operating in harsh environmental and climactic conditions.

Above: The first regiment to be fully equipped with the Challenger 2 was the Royal Scots Dragoon Guards, in June 2000.

Below: The Challenger 2 test squadron fired 2,850 rounds of 120-mm ammunition during 84 simulated battlefield days.

SPECIFICATION	
Challenger 2 **Type:** Main Battle Tank **Crew:** four – commander, gunner, loader, driver **Dimensions:** length (hull) 8.327 m (27 ft 4 in); length with gun forward 11.50 m (37 ft 8 in); width: 3.52 m (11 ft 7 in); height to top of turret 2.49 m (8 ft 2 in) **Weight:** 62500 kg (137,500 lb)	**Powerplant:** 12-cylinder Perkins diesel delivering 895 kW (1200 hp) **Speed:** road 56 km/h (35 mph); cross-country 40 km/h (25 mph) **Range:** 450 km (280 miles); cross-country 250 km (155 miles) **Armament:** one L30 120-mm (4.7-in) rifled main gun with 50 rounds; one co-axial 7.62-mm (0.3-in) chain gun and one L37 7.62-mm anti-aircraft MG

The T-72 has a modest power to weight ratio by comparison with the latest Western tanks and a gun depression angle of only -6° compared to Western tanks' -10°, but it does have a lower silhouette. It has been developed into a number of improved variants, and fires a 7.1-kg (15.65-lb) APFSDS penetrator to pierce 250 mm (9.84 in) of armour at a range of 2000 m (2,185 yards).

Soviet tank development

Cold War MBTs

Soviet tank development between World War II's end in 1945 and the close of the Cold War in the late 1980s was in general an evolutionary process marked by a number of important 'step' improvements. Features that remained standard were a low silhouette with a turret of inverted saucer shape that limited the main gun's depression capability, thick armour, a main gun of steadily increasing calibre, and gradual improvements to the fire-control system. Step improvements included gun-fired missiles, smoothbore rather than rifled guns to fire saboted rounds and, not very successfully, gas turbine propulsion.

The Czech T-72CZ M4 is an upgraded T-72M1 with an Israeli NIMDA powerpack based on a British engine, the 746-kW (1,000-hp) Perkins CV-12 1000 diesel unit. An Italian fire-control system is also fitted: this is the same as that fitted to the Ariete and Centauro.

The T-62 was widely used in the Warsaw Pact and Middle East, although most Soviet front-line divisions replaced it with the T-64, T-72 and T-80 series when these became available. The 1973 Arab-Israeli war revealed some serious weaknesses in the T-62: the 115-mm gun takes too long to reload, the turret traverse rate is slow, and the gun has too limited a depression capability. A late-model T-62 is illustrated, distinguished from the original version by having a second cupola above the loader's position.

This has a shorter range than the NATO 120-mm (4.72-in) gun, but is highly accurate at up to 1500 m (1,640 yards). The flat trajectory of the BR-5 HVAPFDS round means that there is no need for elevation up to this range. The gunner's job is made difficult by the way the loading system prevents the turret rotating. This means that if the first round misses, the target cannot be tracked and kept in the sights. One round every 15 seconds is fair going for a T-62 crew, but dangerously slow.

This is 97 mm (3.8 in) thick and sloped at 58° on the top part, and 99 mm (3.9 in) thick on the lower part. The hull sides are protected by 79 mm (3.1 in) at 0° and the rear is just 49 mm (1.9 in) thick.

By modern standards, the armour-piercing shell from the T-54/55's 100-mm (3.94-in) gun is severely lacking in penetrative power and its more lethal HEAT round is inaccurate. Worse, it takes 15 to 20 seconds to reload, since the gun must be fully elevated to give the loader room to extract the empty case and load a new round. The gunner is seen here manning the 12.7-mm (0.5-in) anti-aircraft machine-gun fitted to many T-54 and T-55 variants.

This sight gives the commander reasonable visibility out to 400 m (440 yards) at night. The gunner's sights function out to a range of about 800 m (875 yards)

The front of the turret is protected by 203 mm (8 in) of armour and the sides by 150 mm (5.9 in). This relatively thick armour combines with a low silhouette to make the T-54 and T-55 well protected for tanks weighing only 36 tonnes.

Like other Soviet-designed tanks, the T-62 can lay its own smokescreen by spraying diesel oil into the exhaust manifold, creating a thick cloud of smoke up to 400 m (440 yards) long. It can do this for 10 minutes before the engine stalls. By remaining stationary and producing smoke, the T-62 can pretend to be knocked out:, a trick some Arab 'tankers' apparently used to lure Israeli tanks to their destruction in 1973. Note also the jettisonable external fuel tanks, each containing 200 litres (44 Imp gal) of fuel, and extending the T-62's range to 650 km (404 miles).

This is a late-production version of the T-55 with a laser rangefinder and radiation covers and 'live' track. T-54/55s have Christie-type torsion bar suspension with five large road wheels (a useful recognition feature is the gap between the first and second wheels). Previous versions had 'dead' (untensioned) track which hung loosely and sometimes caused a tank to shed a track.

Top: The T-64 MBT introduced many advanced features including a crew of three, automatic loading for its 125-mm (4.92-in) gun and advanced armour. However, it also proved expensive and its loader, suspension and transmission are unreliable.

Above: A T-80 series MBT moving across country at speed with long-range fuel tanks fitted to the rear of the hull. While the T-80 retains a similarity to the T-64, it has improved protection and a radically different powerplant in the form of a 746-kW (1,000-hp) gas turbine rather than a 559-kW (750-hp) diesel.

Red Army battle tanks: T-34 to T-80

Production of Soviet light tanks had ceased by 1943 in order to allow concentration of production on medium and heavy tanks and assault guns. The last were usually based on medium or heavy tank chassis and well armed and armoured for their specialised task.

The best Soviet tank of World War II was the T-34. This entered service in 1941 with a 76.2-mm (3-in) gun, and further development led in 1943 to the T-34/85 armed with an 85-mm (3.34-in) gun. The T-34 was followed by the T-44 that entered production in 1945 but was not built in large numbers. The T-44 was essentially a new chassis fitted with the turret of the T-34/85 tank. Further development of the T-44 resulted in the T-54 with a similar chassis but a new cast turret armed with a 100-mm (3.94-in) gun. The first T-54 prototypes were completed in 1946 but development was difficult and production got under way only in 1950.

Further development yielded the T-55, which was produced to the extent of some 27,000 vehicles between 1958 and 1979. The T-55 had many improvements including a new turret with improved 100-mm rifled gun, an NBC system and a more powerful engine. The T-55 was further

Right: The T-62 was armed with a 115-mm (4.53-in) smoothbore gun and first saw action during the 1973 Arab-Israeli War. This example was used for training by the US Army in West Germany in the 1980s.

Lower right: These T-54s are seen in Romanian service; examples were built in China, Czechoslovakia and Poland, whilst some 50,000 were built in the USSR until 1981.

improved in the 1960s and 1970. For example, first-round hit probability was increased by the addition of a laser rangefinder. Later a fully computerised day/night fire-control system was fitted, as was more armour. Some T-55s were even upgraded to fire a laser-guided anti-tank missile from their main guns.

The fielding of the US M60 series tank with a 105-mm (4.13-in) gun came as a shock to the Soviets, although they were already testing a new tank armed with a 115-mm (4.53-in) smoothbore gun. This entered production in 1962 as the T-62 and significant num-

bers were built, including numbers for export. Like the T-55, the T-62 was upgraded over the years with additional armour, a new fire-control system and the ability to fire a laser-guided projectile from its 115-mm smoothbore gun.

The T-64 marked a radical departure for tank design as it was powered by a very compact diesel engine and a

Left: A limitation suffered by nearly all Soviet-designed MBTs is the small depression angle for the main gun. This makes it difficult to adopt a well-concealed hull-down position on a reverse slope.

Below: Soviet doctrine emphasised the value of integrated tank and infantry operations: here T-62s exercise with BMP-1 IFVs.

threeman crew as the main gun was fed by an automatic loader. It also incorporated special armour to provide a higher level of protection against HEAT projectiles.

The T-64 appeared in prototype form in 1960. There were many problems with the type, but large numbers were eventually built for the Soviet army. Early models had a 115-mm gun but the main production run of over 10,000 had a 125-mm (4.92-in) smoothbore gun. Over the years the T-64 was steadily upgraded.

The T-72 entered production in 1972 with advanced armour in its hull and turret, and was constantly improved. As with the T-64, the T-72 was also fitted with ERA to enhance its protection against missiles fitted with a HEAT warhead. Unlike the T-64, the T-72 exported in large numbers and was also made under licence in several countries.

The T-80 began as a T-64 with its diesel engine replaced by a gas turbine. The chassis was fitted with a new turret armed with a 125-mm gun fed by an automatic loader. Accepted for service in 1976, the T-80 has also been produced in the Ukraine as the diesel-engined T-80UD version.

T-72A

This improved model of the T-72 was accepted into service in 1979, was first observed by Western analysts at a parade in Berlin during 1981, and subsequently appeared at the November Parade of the same year in Moscow. Early T-72 tanks had a pronounced hood in front of the right-hand (commander's) cupola; the absence of this cupola on the T-72A (initially known in the West as the Model 1980/1) indicated that optical equipment had been replaced by a laser rangefinder. Soviet T-72 tanks were particularly well protected from nuclear contamination as they carried a skin layer of a lead-based foam; this lining was not fitted on T-72 tanks for the export market.

Early T-72 series tanks, not fitted with the 12.7-mm (0.5-in) roof-mounted NSVT anti-aircraft machine-gun, are seen while moving at speed across country. The design of the T-72 utilised the hull and turret layout of the T-64.

The hull of the T-72 series main battle tank is three sections with the driver's compartment at the front, fighting compartment in the centre, and powerplant compartment at the rear. The driver is seated on the centreline of the forward compartment behind a V-type splashboard, and has overhead protection in the form of a single-piece hatch that opens to the right. When operating the vehicle in the closed-down mode, the driver uses wide-angle TVNE-4E and TVNE-4B day and night observation devices. The driver steers the vehicle by means of a standard clutch and brake arrangement. The T-72 has a ground clearance of 0.49 m (19.3 in), and the length of track on the ground is 4.278 m (14 ft ½ in). The tracks are of the single-pin type with rubber bushes, and their width is 0.58 m (22.835 in).

Six Vietnamese T-54 tanks rest on a barge in the Mekong River in Phnom Penh, awaiting their shipment to Ho Chi Minh City as part of the partial Vietnamese withdrawal from Cambodia in the late 1980s. Unlike the subsequent T-55 series, which was developed by Kartsev and built at Nizhni Tagil, the T-54 was designed by Morozov and built at Kharkov in Ukraine. The Kartsev Bureau later undertook development of the T-62, T-72 and T-90 series MBTs.

The T-72A is powered by the V-46-6 liquid-cooled V-12 diesel engine. Rated at 581.6 kW (780 hp), this is located in the rear of the hull to drive the rear sprockets via a hydraulically assisted synchromesh gearbox with seven forward and one reverse speeds. Fuel is carried in cells extending along each side of the hull at its top, and there is also provision for the carriage of two 200-litre (44-Imp gal) jettisonable drum tanks above the rear of the hull. The suspension is of the torsion-bar type with six road wheels on each side. Only the first, second and sixth wheels have shock absorbers. The idlers are at the front, and on each side there are three track-return rollers supporting only the inner part of the tracks.

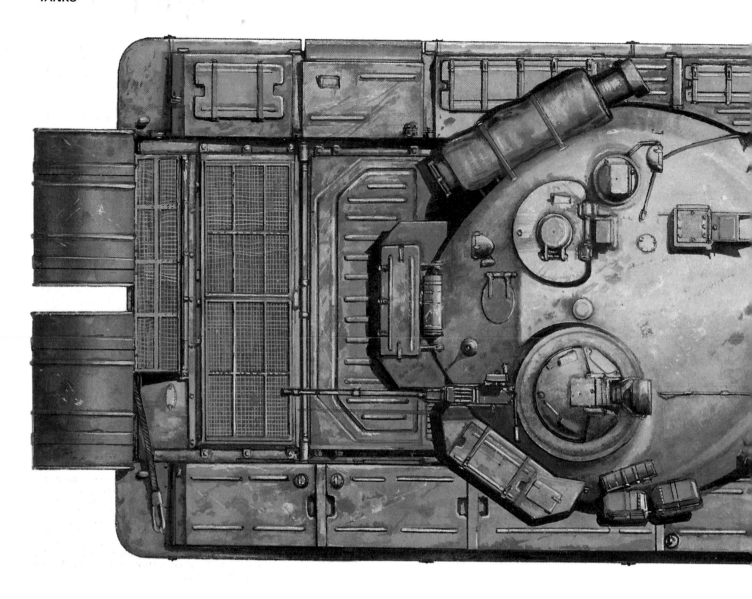

A development of the T-72, the T-72A introduced significantly improved armour protection (especially over the frontal arc of the turret) and the original optical rangefinder was replaced by a TPD-K1 laser rangefinder sight to provide improved first-round hit probability. Further additional equipment included the TPN-3-49 gunner's night sight, TPN-3 searchlight, different plastic side skirts, 125-mm (4.92-in) 2A46M main gun in place of the 2A26M, Type 902B 81-mm (3.2-in) smoke grenade launcher, a napalm protection system, turn signals, TVNE-4B driver night observation system, upgraded suspension for improved cross-country mobility, and V-46-6 diesel engine. The plastic side skirts on the T-72A covered the upper part of the suspension with separate panels protecting the sides of the fuel and stowage panniers.

The T-72 series of MBTs is based on a structure of welded and cast steel armour. The hull is primarily of welded armour, and on its most vulnerable forward face this armour has a thickness of some 80 mm (3.15 in) with additional protection provided by a glacis of laminate armour some 200 mm (7.87 in) thick that, as a result of its angling, provides protection equivalent to a thickness of some 500 and 600 mm (19.69 and 23.62 in). Later examples of the T-72 series also have upgraded turret protection through the incorporation of more advanced armour, thickened armour on the front of the hull, appliqué armour on the front of the turret, and ERA (explosive reactive armour) on the hull and turret. Other defensive features include skirts to protect the upper part of the tracks, one or two seven-barrel dischargers for smoke grenades on the sides of the turret, and an NBC protection package.

T-72A

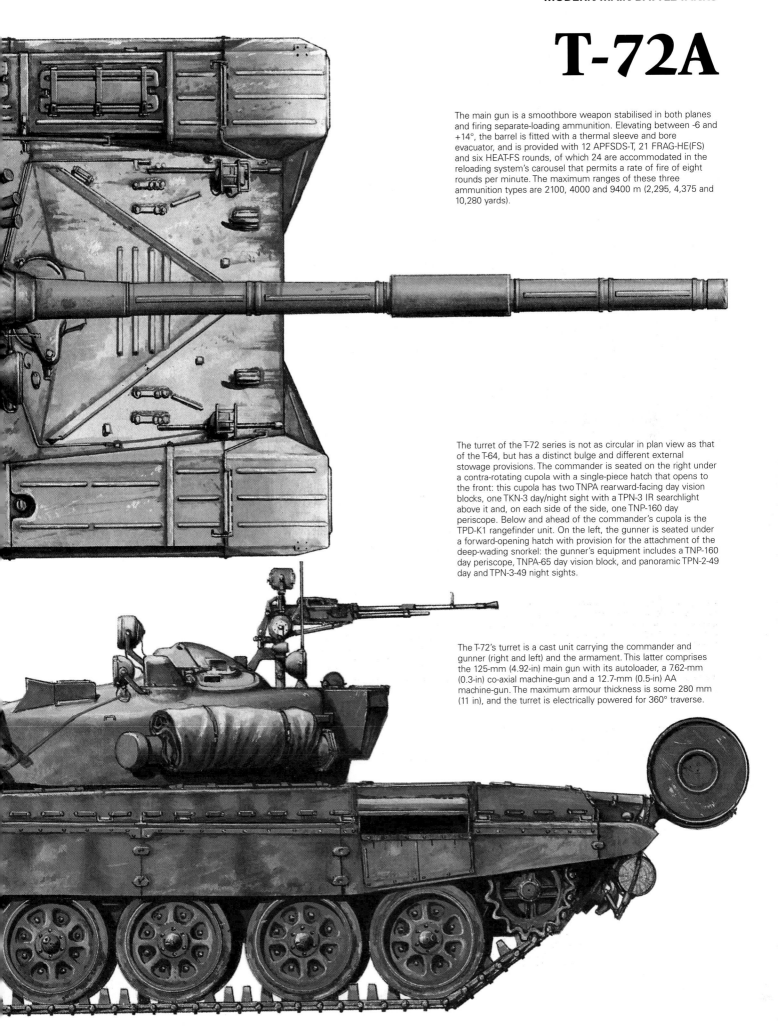

The main gun is a smoothbore weapon stabilised in both planes and firing separate-loading ammunition. Elevating between -6 and +14°, the barrel is fitted with a thermal sleeve and bore evacuator, and is provided with 12 APFSDS-T, 21 FRAG-HE(FS) and six HEAT-FS rounds, of which 24 are accommodated in the reloading system's carousel that permits a rate of fire of eight rounds per minute. The maximum ranges of these three ammunition types are 2100, 4000 and 9400 m (2,295, 4,375 and 10,280 yards).

The turret of the T-72 series is not as circular in plan view as that of the T-64, but has a distinct bulge and different external stowage provisions. The commander is seated on the right under a contra-rotating cupola with a single-piece hatch that opens to the front: this cupola has two TNPA rearward-facing day vision blocks, one TKN-3 day/night sight with a TPN-3 IR searchlight above it and, on each side of the side, one TNP-160 day periscope. Below and ahead of the commander's cupola is the TPD-K1 rangefinder unit. On the left, the gunner is seated under a forward-opening hatch with provision for the attachment of the deep-wading snorkel: the gunner's equipment includes a TNP-160 day periscope, TNPA-65 day vision block, and panoramic TPN-2-49 day and TPN-3-49 night sights.

The T-72's turret is a cast unit carrying the commander and gunner (right and left) and the armament. This latter comprises the 125-mm (4.92-in) main gun with its autoloader, a 7.62-mm (0.3-in) co-axial machine-gun and a 12.7-mm (0.5-in) AA machine-gun. The maximum armour thickness is some 280 mm (11 in), and the turret is electrically powered for 360° traverse.

T-72 Main Battle Tank

Provisional drawings of the T-72, with the commmander's cupola fitted with a 12.7-mm (0.5-in) AAMG traversed rear. Side skirts provide defence against ATGWs with their HEAT warheads.

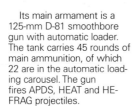

The **T-72** is, by a considerable margin, the most widely used of all modern main battle tanks. Entering production in 1971, it was not seen in public until the late 1970s. Developed in parallel to the more advanced (and considerably more troublesome) T-64, the T-72 was the main Soviet export tank into the 1990s, and is still in production at the Malyshev HMB Plant, Kharkov, Ukraine, and at UKBM Nizhny Tagil in the Russian Federation.

Export tank

While the T-64 was deployed only with front-line Soviet units, the T-72 was exported to non-Soviet Warsaw Pact armies and to other countries. In addition to production in the USSR it has been built under licence in Czechoslovakia, India, Poland and Yugoslavia. At least 50,000 have been built over the last three decades, and T-72s are in service with as many as 30 armies.

The T-72 retains the characteristic low silhouette of earlier Soviet battle tanks. Since 1988, Explosive Reactive Armour (ERA) has been fitted to all variants.

Below: Eyes right! T-72 tanks drive through Moscow streets during a rainy May Day procession. These tanks would provide the vanguard of the Red Army.

Its main armament is a 125-mm D-81 smoothbore gun with automatic loader. The tank carries 45 rounds of main ammunition, of which 22 are in the automatic loading carousel. The gun fires APDS, HEAT and HE-FRAG projectiles.

Later variants can also fire the 9K119 Refleks (NATO codename AT-11 'Sniper') anti-armour missile. This is intended to engage tanks fitted with ERA as well as low-flying air targets. The gun has a range of 100-4000 m (328-13,123 ft) but firing requires the tank to be stationary. The gun's automatic loader will feed both ordnance and missiles.

Variants

Variants of the T-72 include the **T-72A**, which has a laser rangefinder and additional armour. The **T-72B** has thickened frontal turret armour and is commonly known in the USA as the Dolly Parton. The **T-72BK** is a command tank with additional radios.

The current **T-72BM** has second generation Kontakt-5 explosive reactive armour similar to that fitted to the T-90. The **T-72S** is the export variant of the BM. A number of upgrade packages are available for T-72 series tanks. Ukraine is offering the **T-72MP** with SAGEM SAVAN sights. It is also developing a version fitted with a NATO-standard 120-mm smoothbore gun. The Czech Republic is upgrading 140 **T-72M1** tanks to **T-72CZ** standard, which will include Western fire control systems and an Israeli powerpack incorporating a Perkins diesel engine and Allison transmission. Poland has begun an upgrade programme, and India and Croatia are considering modernising their T-72 tanks.

SPECIFICATION	
T-72S	MG on turret
Crew: 3	**Powerplant:** one V-84 12-cylinder liquid-cooled four-stroke multi-fuel diesel engine developing 618 kW (840 hp)
Combat weight: 44.5 tonnes	
Dimensions: length (with gun forward) 9.53 m (31 ft 3 in); length (hull) 6.86 m (22 ft 6 in); width 3.59 m (11 ft 9 in); height (to turret roof) 2.19 m (7 ft 2 in)	**Performance:** maximum road speed 60 km/h (37.25 mph); maximum road range on internal fuel 500 km (310 miles), 900 km (560 miles) with external tanks; gradient 30 per cent; fording depth 1.20 m (3 ft 11 in) unprepared, 5 m (16 ft 5 in) with schnorkel; vertical obstacle 0.85 m (2 ft 9 in); trench 2.90 m (9 ft 6 in)
Armour: laminate plus ERA equivalent to 950 mm plate against HEAT, 520 mm against APFSDS	
Armament: 125-mm 2A46M smoothbore with 45 rounds; coaxial PKT 7.62-mm (0.3-in) MG; NSVT 12.7-mm (0.5-in) heavy AA	

T-80 Main Battle Tank

The most advanced tank in widespread use with the Russian army in 2002, the **T-80** has been in service since the late 1970s. It was originally produced by the Kirov Plant in Leningrad, where the prototype was known as **Obiekt 219**. A modification of the T-64, the T-80 was the first Soviet production tank to be gas-turbine powered. The engine was developed by the Isotov design bureau and built by the Klimov factory, both having had extensive experience with helicopter powerplants.

The GTD-1000T provided more power than contemporary diesels, but with a much higher fuel consumption. The hull had to be redesigned to take twice as much fuel as the T-64. At the same time, a new auto-loader and torsion-bar suspension were fitted since both items had proved unreliable in the T-64.

Build problems

From the start, the manufacturers and the Soviet army encountered problems with the T-80. Manufacturing costs were high, and the engines were unreliable. Nevertheless, the tank went into production in the mid-1970s, and it was accepted for service in 1976 (much earlier than had previously been believed in the West, and four years before production of the M1 Abrams).

Meanwhile, the Kharkhov design bureau in the Ukraine

The gas-turbine-powered T-80 is faster and more agile than other former Soviet tanks, but it is incredibly fuel-thirsty and has a very poor range.

had developed the much improved T-64B, and used its new armour, Kobra guided missile system and improved fire control on the T-80 to produce the **T-80B**. More upgrades were introduced to the T-80B in 1980, including the adoption of the T-64B turret, to reduce logistics problems, and a forced-air version of the GTD-1000 which boosted power to

SPECIFICATION

T-80U
Crew: 3
Combat weight: 46 tonnes
Dimensions: length (gun forward) 9.65 m (31 ft 8 in); length (hull) 7 m (22 ft 11 in); width 3.60 m (11 ft 10 in); height 2.20 m (7 ft 2½ in)
Armour: laminated plus ERA, over 1000 mm armour plate equivalent
Armament: one 125-mm 2A46M smoothbore gun with 45 rounds; co-axial PKT 7.62-mm (0.3-in) MG; NSVT 12.7-mm (0.5-in) heavy AA MG on turret

Powerplant: one GTD-1250T gas turbine developing 932 kW (1,250 hp)
Performance: maximum road speed 70 km/h (43.5 mph); maximum road range on internal fuel 325 km (202 miles), and c.500 km (310 miles) with external tanks; gradient 30 per cent; fording depth 1.80 m (5 ft 11 in) unprepared, 5 m (16 ft 5 in) with schnorkel; vertical obstacle 1 m (3 ft 3¼ in); trench 2.90 m (9 ft 6 in)

The T-80UK is a command tank variant. This example is fitted with the laser detectors, aerosol mortars and reactive armour of the Shtora-1 defensive system.

820 kW (1,100 hp) and doubled service life to 1,000 hours. In 1985, the first-generation Kontakt ERA was fitted.

In the mid-1980s, the Shipunov design bureau at Tula developed a new generation of laser-beam-riding missile. The 9K112 (NATO designation AT-8 'Songster') has a range of 5 km (3 miles) and can penetrate 700 mm (27.6 in) of armour. It can

also engage helicopters. The system was fitted into the **T-80U**, which was the first model of the T-80 to be appreciably more capable than the T-64 from which it was descended.

Reactive armour
The T-80U is fitted with new-generation Kontakt-5 reactive armour. It has an advanced fire control system incorporating an optical sight and

laser rangefinder paired with a stabilised image intensifier and active infra-red sight.

Production of the T-80 in Leningrad ceased in 1990. Low-rate production continues at Omsk and at Kharkhov in the Ukraine.

The 2002 production version is the **T-80UM-1 Bars (Snow Leopard)**. This can be fitted with advanced Shtora and Arena defences. Arena's turret-mounted radar detects incoming anti-tank missiles at 50 m (164 ft) or more, and detonates one of a number of outward-facing

fragmentation charge launchers arranged in a semicircle around the turret front. Future versions of Shtora will include radar and electronic jammers.

By Russian standards (though not Western) the T-80 is expensive to produce. Orders from the Russian military have therefore been cut and T-80s have recently been touted in export markets.

T-80 in combat
T-80s were used extensively in the Chechen war, where their fuel consumption was

unacceptably high, and they proved vulnerable to RPG strikes from above. Former Defence Minister Pavel Grachev therefore ordered the redesign of ammunition storage in all Russian MBTs. The first result of his order is the Black Eagle, a mock-up of which was shown by the Omsk plant in 1997. This mounts a completely new turret with highly sloped front and a bustle-mounted autoloader which permits a likely rate of fire of 10-12 rounds per minute, on a standard T-80U hull.

T-90 Main Battle Tank

Curiously, for a nation that finds itself in a perpetual state of financial crisis, Russia maintains two main battle tank programmes. In addition to the expensive turbine-powered T-80, the Russian army also operates the **T-90** – initially a simpler and cheaper diesel-powered machine, but which has been upgraded with new weapons systems and has nominally replaced the T-80 as the standard army tank.

The original T-90 was a modestly upgraded T-72. In 1988 the Uralvagon plant in Nizhni-Nagil, builder of the T-72, developed the T-72BM or **Obiekt 187**. This was fitted with Kontakt-5 third-generation ERA, giving similar protection to the T-80. Although the T-72 carried a less sophisticated fire-control system than the T-64 or the T-80, the design bureau planned to fit more advanced electronics to make its design more competitive. The **T-72BU**, which appeared in

the early 1990s, carried a full T-80 fire-control system.

Marketing ploy
In 1992, after the fall of the USSR, it was decided to redesignate the tank T-90. This was partly to indicate its increased fighting power, and partly a marketing measure. The poor showing of Iraqi T-72s in the Gulf War reflected badly on Russian attempts to export the type, so the designation change was approved personally by President Boris Yeltsin.

The T-90 entered low-rate production in 1994. The first unit to be fully re-equipped was the tank regiment of the 21st Motor Rifle Division in Siberia in 1995.

In 1996, following T-80 losses in Chechnya, the T-90 was selected as the Russian army's new standard battle tank. The T-90 had not been used in the Chechen war, so it avoided the bad reputation the turbine-engined tank gained. In many respects this

was an illusion – large numbers of virtually identical T-72s were lost in the conflict, and there is nothing to say that the T-90 would have fared any better.

Army objection
There was considerable opposition to the move in the Russian army, since the T-80 is faster and more agile. But as a stopgap, until more advanced tanks can be developed (and until economic conditions in the bankrupt former Soviet Union allow), the T-90 has one great advantage. Each tank costs about $1.6 million against the T-80's $2.2 million. But both continue in production – probably to prevent economic hardship in areas of tank production.

The current **T-90S** has similar offensive and defensive power to the T-80. It has the same stabilised 125-mm smoothbore gun which can fire the 9M119 Refleks missile. Missiles weigh 23.40 kg (51.59 lb) each, and are treated like any other round of ammunition by the automatic loader.

The T-90 tank is protected

Although the T-90 is being marketed as a new tank, it is in fact an upgrade of the T-72. This example is fitted with Kontakt-5 reactive armour on the turret.

by both conventional armour and explosive reactive armour (ERA). These provide a substantial increase in protection over the T-72, especially against HEAT and kinetic energy projectiles. T-90 can be equipped with the the Arena active countermeasures system and with the with the TShU-1 Shtora-1 defensive aids suite. Shtora-1 is intended to provide protection against command and semi-active laser-guided anti-tank and air-to-ground missiles, and against guided artillery projectiles.

Active defence
The two main components are the Electro-Optical Countermeasures Station (EOCS), and the Quick-Forming Aerosol Screening System. The EOCS includes two IR emitters, two modulators and a control panel. It is designed to disrupt the guidance of enemy anti-tank guided missiles with flare feedback, by confusing

the guidance system's co-ordinator.

The aerosol screening system detects laser illumination, determines its direction and type and generates warning signals. In two to three seconds the launchers can lay a quick-forming aerosol cloud up to 80 m (262 ft) from the tank, to disrupts hostile guidance lasers.

The T-90S is in service with the Russian Army. In February 2001, the Indian Army signed a contract for 310 T-90S tanks.

A new Russian MBT reportedly started State acceptance trials at the Kubinka Proving Ground in 1998. Very little is known about this vehicle, apart from the fact that it was designed at Nizhniy Tagil.

Any future Russian tank is likely to weigh around 50 tonnes, and be armed with a large-calibre fully automatic weapon externally mounted, while the crew will be housed in the hull.

SPECIFICATION

T-90S
Crew: 3
Combat weight: 50 tonnes
Dimensions: length (with gun forward) 9.53 m (31 ft 3 in); length (hull) 6.86 m (22 ft 6 in); width 3.37 m (11 ft 1 in); height (overall) 2.23 m (7 ft 4 in)
Armour: 520 mm on turret plus Kontakt ERA offering a total of 1220 mm equivalent against HEAT and 810 mm equivalent against APFSDS
Armament: 125-mm 2A46M smoothbore with 43 rounds; coaxial

PKT 7.62-mm (0.3-in) MG; NSVT 12.7-mm (0.5-in) heavy AA MG on turret
Powerplant: one V-84MS multi-fuel diesel engine developing 618 kW (840 hp)
Performance: maximum road speed 60 km/h (37.28 mph); maximum range on internal fuel 500 km (310 miles), 650 km (404 miles) with external tanks; gradient 30 per cent; fording depth (schnorkel) 5 m (16 ft 5 in); vertical obstacle 0.85 m (2 ft 9 in); trench 2.90 m (9 ft 6 in)

M60A3 Upgraded Main Battle Tank

A further development of the M48 series, just over 15,000 examples of the **M60** MBT family had been built for the home and export market when manufacture was completed in 1987. As the final production variant for the US Army, the **M60A3** featured a computerised day/thermal sighting system incorporating a laser rangefinder and passive night vision equipment for improved 'first round' hit probability under most weather conditions.

Enhanced features

A number of features of the M60A3 were originally introduced to the **M60A1**, including add-on stabilisation systems, RISE (Reliability Improved Selected Equipment) engine and smoke grenade launchers. In addition, many M60A1s were effectively brought up to M60A3 standard after the addition of thermal night vision equipment. Out of a total of 5,400 M60A3 tanks delivered to the US Army from 1978, 3,600 were converted from earlier models in Germany and the US, while 144 were improved M60A1 tanks retrofitted to **M60A3 TTS** (Tank Thermal Sight) standard. The remaining tanks were new-build M60A3s.

The principal advantage of the M60A3 over its predecessors lies in its fire

Above: the M60A3 MBT was fitted with a thermal sleeve for the 105-mm gun, designed to increase the number of shots able to be fired before needing a barrel change.

control system, incorporating a Raytheon laser rangefinder with a range of 5000 m (16,000 ft) in place of the original optical device. This is coupled to an M21 ballistic computer, which replaced the earlier mechanical computer. This system receives range data, as well as information on wind speed, air temperature and density, altitude, target tracking rate and ammunition ballistics, providing firing commands for the gunner and commander.

The gunner or commander are responsible for selecting one of up to six different types of ammunition for the 105-mm M68 gun, which on the M60A3 variant is fitted with a thermal sleeve. In addition, the coaxial 0.50-in (12.7-mm) machine-gun mounted to the left of the main gun on the original M60 was replaced by a 0.3-in (7.62-mm) M240 weapon. The AN/VGS-2 TTS was included from 1980, improving all-weather capability and allowing the tank to 'see' through smoke and ground cover. Several years later, an new air filtra-

Above: the M60 is one of the world's most successful Main Battle Tanks, having served with more than 20 armies since its introduction in 1960.

tion system was fitted to the fleet.

Reserves

No longer in service with the US armed forces, large numbers are retained in reserve, although many of

these are now being passed on to other operators. A total of 100 M60A3 tanks were ordered by Saudi Arabia in 1983, followed by a further 150 conversion kits (with TTS) for existing M60A1 models

– these saw service during Desert Storm. M60A3 production was scheduled to end in 1985, however, a further 94 orders from Egypt meant that production continued for another two years.

M60s served in large numbers during the Gulf War, primarily with the USMC and with Saudi forces.

SPECIFICATION	
M60A3	width 3.63 m (12 ft); height 3.27 m
Crew: 4	(10 ft 8 in)
Weight: 52617 kg (116,000 lb)	**Performance:** max road speed
Powerplant: one 12-cylinder	48 km/h (30 mph); road range
Continental air-cooled diesel	480 km (298 miles)
developing 559 kW (750 hp)	**Fording:** 1.22 m (4 ft)
coupled to a fully automatic	**Gradient:** 60 per cent
transmission	**Vertical obstacle:** 0.914 m (3 ft)
Dimensions: length 9.44 m (31 ft);	**Trench:** 2.59 m (8 ft 6 in)

M1 Abrams series Main Battle Tank

The original M1 Abrams MBT was armed with the M68 rifled gun, based on the long-serving and highly effective British L7 weapon. Later models use a more powerful German 120-mm smoothbore.

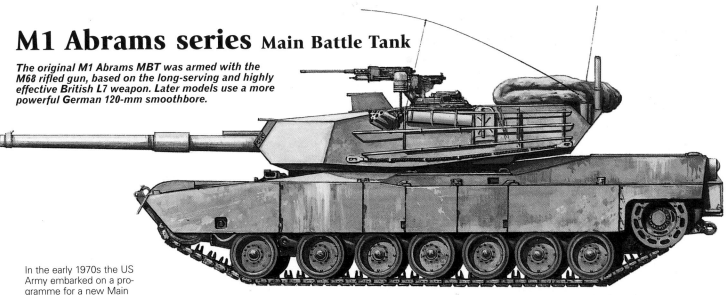

In the early 1970s the US Army embarked on a programme for a new Main Battle Tank to replace the 105-mm M60 series, as by that time it had reached the end of its development potential. In mid-1973, the then Chrysler Corporation (which was subsequently taken over by General Dynamics) and General Motors were each awarded a contract to design and build prototypes of a new MBT designated **XM1**, and armed with the 105-mm M68 series gun as fitted to the M60 series. Following trials, the Chrysler design was selected and a production contract placed. Production was undertaken at the Detroit Tank Plant and the Lima Army Tank Plant but eventually production was concentrated at the latter facility.

Improved M1

The first production **M1 Abrams** was armed with the 105-mm M68 rifled gun, and this was followed by the **Improved M1** with a higher level of armour protection. The next model was the **M1A1** which had many improvements including a 120-mm smooth bore gun which was a further development of the weapon installed in the German Leopard 2 MBT. All versions of the M1 series have a 0.3-in (7.62-mm) co-axial machine-gun with a similar

weapon at the loader's station, while the tank commander has a 0.5-in (12.7-mm) machine-gun.

Final model

The final model of the M1A1 incorporated depleted uranium armour in its hull and turret. The current production model is the **M1A2** which has many improvements. There is currently a programme to upgrade older M1 to the latest M1A2 standard, and in a further development 240 tanks are to be upgraded to **M1A2 SEP** (Sytem Enhancement Package) standard. In the future the AGT 1500 gas turbine is expected to be replaced by a more fuel efficient unit, and there have also been significant improvements in 120-mm tank ammunition in recent years. The standard equipment on the Abrams includes a NBC system and a fire detection and suppression system.

Export

So far there have been three export customers for the M1 series, Egypt (M1A1 assembled under licence at the Egyptian Tank Plant near Cairo), Kuwait (M1A2) and Saudi Arabia (M1A2). One of the more recent developments is the General

Dynamics **120S** which is an upgraded M60 chassis with the complete combat-proven M1A2 turret. An M1A2 has also been tested with a German 1119-kW (1,500-hp) MTU EuroPowerPack.

The M1 chassis is also used as the basis of a series of engineer vehicles, including the **Heavy Assault Bridge (HAB)** that is now in service with the US Army. The private venture **Abrams Recovery Vehicle** remains at the prototype stage, while the **Grizzly** Counter Obstacle Vehicle (COV), fitted with a mine clearance blade, has been cancelled.

Above: From its earliest days, the M1 has been equipped with sophisticated fire control systems, incorporating day/night sights and laser rangefinders.

Above: All Abrams since the M1A1 have been equipped with the Rheinmetall 120-mm smoothbore, one of the most powerful tank guns in the world.

Left: The M1A2 version of the Abrams has upgraded sights and fire control systems, greatly increasing the chances of hitting the target with a single round.

SPECIFICATION	
M1A2	height 2.89 m (9 ft 6 in)
Crew: 4	**Performance:** max road speed 68 km/h (42 mph); max range 426 km (265 miles)
Weight: 63036 kg (138,968 lb)	
Powerpack: gas turbine developing 1119 kW (1,500 hp) coupled to a fully automatic transmission	**Fording:** 1.22 m (4 ft)
	Gradient: 60 per cent
	Vertical obstacle: 1.067 m (3 ft 6 in)
Dimensions: length 9.83 m (32 ft 3 in); width 3.66 m (12 ft);	**Trench:** 2.743 m (9 ft)

Inside the M1 ABRAMS

The US Army's Abrams incorporates a wealth of sophisticated electronics and systems, but is very much a 'traditional' tank, a lineal descendant of the World War II era Sherman with its tracked chassis and high-velocity gun in a rotating turret. But the sheer fighting power of the Abrams would have been beyond the wildest dreams of a World War II tanker. It can make first round kills at unbelievable ranges – even while moving across broken gouns at full speed.

This is a development of the FN MAG general purpose machine gun, one of the finest weapons of its kind to have appeared in the last half century. It is used to engage soft targets such as unarmoured vehicles or attacking infantry, where using the main armament would be inappropriate.

Below: Three of the Abrams' four crew members are housed in the turret. The commander sits to the left, while the gunner sits to the right of the breech with the loader immediately behind him. The gunner's seat is special, being designed to lock him into position at his sight, so that his eyes remain firmly fixed on the target no matter how much the vehicle is being thrown about by the terrain.

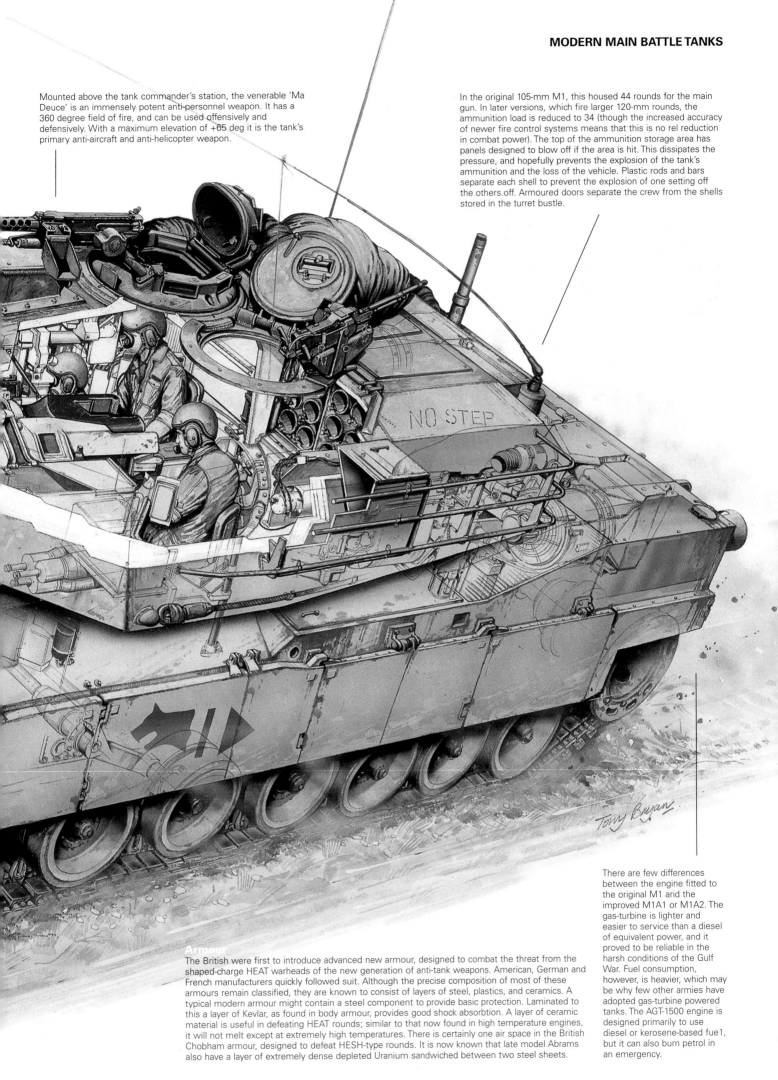

Mounted above the tank commander's station, the venerable 'Ma Deuce' is an immensely potent anti-personnel weapon. It has a 360 degree field of fire, and can be used offensively and defensively. With a maximum elevation of +65 deg it is the tank's primary anti-aircraft and anti-helicopter weapon.

In the original 105-mm M1, this housed 44 rounds for the main gun. In later versions, which fire larger 120-mm rounds, the ammunition load is reduced to 34 (though the increased accuracy of newer fire control systems means that this is no rel reduction in combat power). The top of the ammunition storage area has panels designed to blow off if the area is hit. This dissipates the pressure, and hopefully prevents the explosion of the tank's ammunition and the loss of the vehicle. Plastic rods and bars separate each shell to prevent the explosion of one setting off the others.off. Armoured doors separate the crew from the shells stored in the turret bustle.

NO STEP

There are few differences between the engine fitted to the original M1 arid the improved M1A1 or M1A2. The gas-turbine is lighter and easier to service than a diesel of equivalent power, and it proved to be reliable in the harsh conditions of the Gulf War. Fuel consumption, however, is heavier, which may be why few other armies have adopted gas-turbine powered tanks. The AGT-1500 engine is designed primarily to use diesel or kerosene-based fue1, but it can also burn petrol in an emergency.

Armour

The British were first to introduce advanced new armour, designed to combat the threat from the shaped-charge HEAT warheads of the new generation of anti-tank weapons. American, German and French manufacturers quickly followed suit. Although the precise composition of most of these armours remain classified, they are known to consist of layers of steel, plastics, and ceramics. A typical modern armour might contain a steel component to provide basic protection. Laminated to this a layer of Kevlar, as found in body armour, provides good shock absorbtion. A layer of ceramic material is useful in defeating HEAT rounds; similar to that now found in high temperature engines, it will not melt except at extremely high temperatures. There is certainly one air space in the British Chobham armour, designed to defeat HESH-type rounds. It is now known that late model Abrams also have a layer of extremely dense depleted Uranium sandwiched between two steel sheets.

AMX-10P Mechanised infantry combat vehicle

The **AMX-10P** was created as the replacement for the AMX-VCI, and was designed by the Atelier de Construction d'Issy-les Moulineaux in the mid-1960s, production being undertaken from 1972 at the Atelier de Construction Roanne (ARE), where production of the AMX-30 MBT was undertaken together with that of the AMX-10RC 6 x 6 reconnaissance vehicle which is automotively related to the AMX-10P despite the fact that it is a wheeled vehicle. The first production vehicles were completed in 1973, and up to the end of manufacture in 1994 more than 1,800 vehicles were completed for the French army and for export to countries such as Greece, Indonesia, Iraq, Qatar, Saudi Arabia, Singapore and the United Arab Emirates.

Aluminium hull

The AMX-10P has a hull of all-welded aluminium, with the driver at the front left, engine to his right, two-man turret in the centre and troop compartment at the rear. The eight troops enter and leave the vehicle via a power-operated ramp in the hull rear; there is a two-part roof hatch above the troop compartment. Apart from the roof hatches and two firing ports in the ramp, there is no provision for the troops to use their rifles from within the vehicle. The power-operated turret is armed with a 20-mm dual-feed (HE and AP) cannon with a 7.62-mm (0.3-in) co-axial machine-gun; mounted on each side of the turret are two smoke dischargers. The weapons can be elevated between -8° and

The AMX-10P has a two-man power-operated turret armed with a 7.62-mm (0.3-in) machine-gun and a dual-feed 20-mm cannon. It is possible that the latter will be replaced by a 25-mm weapon, which offers improved penetration characteristics against more recent vehicles, to create the AMX-10P 25.

+50°, and the turret traverse is 360°. Ammunition totals are 800 20-mm and 2,000 7.62-mm rounds respectively.

The AMX-10P is fully amphibious, being propelled in the water by waterjets at the rear of the hull, and is also fitted with an NBC system and night-vision equipment for the commander, gunner and driver.

Variants of the AMX-10P include an ambulance, a driver training vehicle, **AMX-10**

ECH repair vehicle with a crane for lifting engines, **AMX-10 HOT** anti-tank vehicle with four HOT missiles in the ready-to-fire position, **AMX-10 PC** command vehicle, a RATAC radar vehicle, **AMX-10 SAO** and **VAO** artillery observation vehicles, **AMX-10 SAT** artillery survey vehicle, **AMX-10 SAF** artillery fire-control

The AMX-10P is a useful infantry combat vehicle of a fairly early generation, but is still effective and could be made more so by the retrofit of a one-man turret armed with a 25-mm cannon offering longer stand-off range and the ability to penetrate harder targets.

French infantry dismount from the rear of their AMX-10P MICV which forms the basis of a complete family of vehicles including command post, HOT anti-tank, mortar tractor, fire control, artillery observation, repair, ambulance, radar and fire-support variants.

vehicle, **AMX-10 TM** mortar tractor towing the 120-mm (4.72-in) Brandt mortar and carrying 60 mortar bombs, **AMX-10P Marines** vehicle for marines, and **AMX-10 PAC 90** fire-support vehicle. The last has been adopted by the Indonesian marines and has a GIAT TS-90 two-man turret armed with a 90-mm (3.54-in) gun, for which 20 rounds of ammunition are carried, and a 7.62-mm co-axial machine-gun. As with most turrets today, a wide range of options is offered including an AA machine-gun and various types of fire-control

equipment. In addition to its three-man crew of commander, gunner and driver, the AMX-10 PAC 90 carries four infantrymen in the rear. The vehicles delivered to Indonesia have improved amphibious characteristics and they are meant to leave landing craft offshore rather than just cross rivers and streams, as is the basic vehicle. Indonesia also took delivery of a number of AMX-10P Marines with the original two-man turret replaced by a new one-man turret at the rear armed with a 12.7-mm (0.5-in) M2HB machine-gun.

SPECIFICATION	
AMX-10P	HS 115 water-cooled V-8 diesel developing 209 kW (280 hp)
Crew: 3+8	**Performance:** maximum road speed 65 km/h (40 mph); maximum range 600 km (373 miles); fording amphibious; gradient 60 per cent; vertical obstacle 0.70 m (2 ft 4 in); trench 1.60 m (5 ft 3 in)
Weight: 14200 kg (31,305 lb)	
Dimensions: length 5.78 m (18 ft 11 in); width 2.78 m (9 ft 1 in); height (hull top) 1.92 m (6 ft 4 in) and (overall) 2.57 m (8 ft 5 in)	
Powerplant: one Hispano-Suiza	

Marder Mechanised infantry combat vehicle

When the West German army was re-formed in the 1950s, its first mechanised infantry combat vehicle was the **Schützenpanzer 12-3**, based on a Swiss chassis, and subsequently manufactured both in the UK and West Germany. A decision was taken at an early stage that a complete family of vehicles would be developed on the same basic chassis. The first members of this family to enter service were the **Jagdpanzer Kanone** with a 90-mm (3.54-in) gun and the **Jagdpanzer Rakete** armed with SS.12 anti-tank missiles that were later replaced by HOT missiles. After many different prototypes had been built and subjected to extensive tests, one of these was finally adopted by West Germany as the **Marder Schützenpanzer Neu M-1966**, and Rheinstahl was selected as prime contractor with MaK of Kiel as the second source: both companies are now part of Rheinmetall Landsysteme. The first production vehicles were delivered late in 1970 and production continued until 1975, by which time 2,136 had been built. The Marder was not exported.

Speedy vehicle

At the time of its introduction the Marder was the most advanced MICV in the West, and today is still an effective type whose primary failings are the cost and difficulty of its maintenance. The Marder has good armour protection and a high cross-country speed to enable it to operate with the Leopard 1 and Leopard 2 MBTs within the context of the German army's combined arms team.

The driver is seated at the front left with one infantry-man to his rear and the

The Marder was the first MICV to enter service in the West, and is fitted with a power-operated two-man turret armed with a 20-mm cannon and a 7.62-mm (0.3-in) machine-gun. No export orders were received.

engine to his right. The power-operated turret (commander and gunner) is in the centre of the vehicle, and the troop compartment is at the rear. The infantry enter and leave via a power-operated ramp in the hull rear,

and on each side of the troop compartment are two spherical firing ports, each surmounted by a roof-mounted periscope to enable infantrymen to aim and fire their rifles from within the vehicle.

The turret is armed with a 20-mm MK20 Rh 202 dual-feed cannon and a 7.62-mm (0.3-in) MG3 co-axial machine-gun. These can be

elevated from -17° to +65°, turret traverse being 360°. From the later part of the 20th century there was considerable discussion of the idea of upgrading the Marder in a number of ways, including the replacement of the MK20 Rh 202 cannon with a larger and more modern cannon, but in the event Germany has opted for the development of a new infantry fighting vehicle. Most Marders were retrofitted a Euromissile MILAN anti-tank missile launcher on the turret to enable them to engage MBTs out to a range of 2000 m (2,190 yards). Mounted above the rear troop compartment is a remotely controlled 7.62-mm machine-gun.

Variants of the Marder in service with the German

army include the Roland SAM system with two missiles in the ready-to-fire position and a further eight in reserve, and a model with a surveillance radar on a hydraulically operated arm that can be raised above the top of the vehicle for increased radar coverage.

Variants

The Marder was produced for Germany as the **Marder 1A1**, and upgrades include the **Marder 1A2** with thermal imaging sight equipment and the **Marder 1A3** with upgraded protection. There are also a number of intermediate upgrade standards, differentiated mostly by their radio equipment, and the **Marder 1A5** is the Marder 1A3 with better mine protection.

Above: Many Marders have been fitted with new passive night vision equipment and a Euromissile MILAN ATGW system. The retrofit of a larger-calibre cannon was planned to enable the vehicle to defeat the latest light combat vehicles such as the Russian BMP-2.

The Marder is still a powerful mechanised infantry fighting vehicle, but is now showing the age of its design and manufacture. Faced with rising maintenance costs and lower operational requirements, Germany has ordered the creation of a lighter and cheaper replacement.

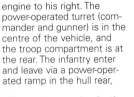

SPECIFICATION	
Marder	kW (600 hp)
Crew: 4+6	**Performance:** maximum road
Weight: 28200 kg (62,169 lb)	speed 75 km/h (46.6 mph);
Dimensions: length 6.79 m (22 ft 3 in); width 3.24 m (10 ft 8 in); height (overall) 2.95 m (9 ft 8 in)	maximum range 520 km (323 miles); fording 1.50 m (4 ft 11 in); gradient 60 per cent; vertical obstacle 1.0 m (3 ft 3 in); trench 2.50 m (8 ft 2 in)
Powerplant: one MTU MB 833 6-cylinder diesel developing 447	

Dardo Armoured infantry fighting vehicle

In 1992 the Italian army awarded Otobreda and IVECO a contract for the construction of three prototypes of an advanced armoured infantry fighting vehicle capable of operating successfully on the modern high-intensity battlefield. These were completed by 1988 for official evaluation with the designation **VCC-80**. The type was fitted with a two-man turret carrying a 25-mm cannon and a 7.62-mm (0.3-in) co-axial machine gun, controlled by means of a fire-control system similar to that of the Ariete MBT and Centauro 8x8 tank destroyer.

New model

It was then decided to use the VCC-80's chassis as the basis of a harder-hitting AIFV with a turret in which the cannon and machine-gun were supplemented by launchers for the TOW heavy-weight anti-tank missile. This led in the later stages of 1988 to a production order being placed with the Consorzio Iveco Oto for 200 **Dardo** AIFVs, including the standard version (with a two-man turret carrying the 25-mm cannon and 7.62-mm co-axial machine gun) as well as four specialised models. These latter were anti-tank, 120-mm (4.72-in) mortar, command post and ambulance variants. The anti-tank model has a one-tube launcher for the TOW missile on each side of the turret, and provision for the Galileo Avionica (originally Officine

Galileo) HITFIST integrated fire-control system as an alternative to the Kollsman Day/Night Range Sight specified for Italian army variants. All Dardo turrets are fitted to accept the TOW launchers and guidance system, and the variant with the Italian rather than American fire-control system is known as the **Dardo HITFIST**.

Armour and turret

The Dardo's hull and turret are of all-welded aluminium armour construction, with an additional layer of ballistic steel armour bolted to the hull and turret for enhanced protection. The driver sits at the front of the vehicle on the left-hand side. The engine compartment is to the driver's right and is occupied by the IVECO diesel engine developing 388 kW (520 hp). This is the same engine that powers the Centauro.

Main armament

The electrically operated Otobreda TC 25 turret is in the centre of the vehicle with the commander on the left and the gunner on the right, but can be operated by just one man. The main armament comprises one 25-mm Oerlikon Contraves Type KBA dual-feed cannon, and there is a 7.62-mm MG 42/59 machine-gun co-axial with this. These weapons have 200 and 700 ready-use rounds respectively, and the cannon also has two-axis stabilisation. The cannon can

The Dardo AIFV can be operated with or without a pair of single-tube launchers for the TOW heavyweight anti-tank missile on the sides of its turret, the use of these missiles providing the ability to destroy a tank out to 3430 m (3,750 yards).

be elevated through an arc of 70° (-10° to +60°). Mounted on each side of the turret is a one-tube launcher for the TOW anti-tank missile, which can be elevated through an arc of 37.5° (-7.5° to +30°), and also a bank of four 80-mm (3.15-in) forward-firing smoke grenade launchers.

The six infantrymen sit at the rear of the vehicle, enter-

ing and leaving by means of a power-operated rear ramp with an inset door: two are seated on each side facing the front, and the other two in the centre as one facing left and one facing the rear. The troop compartment has five firing ports each with an associated vision block allowing five of the infantrymen to fire their weapons from inside the vehicle. Above the troop compartment is a single rearward-opening roof hatch that is also employed when TOW missiles are being loaded into the launcher units.

The torsion-bar suspension on each side comprises dual road wheels, a front-mounted drive sprocket and a rear-mounted idler; there are three track-return rollers. The upper part of the sus-

pension is covered by skirts. The standard equipment includes passive night-vision equipment, air-conditioning system, NBC system, automatic fire-extinguishing system for the crew and engine compartments, and equipment permitting the vehicle to ford to a depth of 1.5 m (4 ft 11 in).

Potential

At present there are no other in-production variants of the Dardo, although the chassis could be the basis for a complete family of vehicles including air defence, engineer, command post and specialised liaison vehicles. Among the other turret options are the Otobreda T 60/70A two-man all-welded unit carrying a 60-mm (2.36-in) High-Velocity Gun System and, as an alternative to the 25-mm version, the Otobreda HITFIST turret carrying the 30-mm Bushmaster II cannon.

The embarked infantry can enter and exit the Dardo's rear troop compartment via a large power-operated ramp, which has an inset manually operated door for emergency use in the event that the ramp mechanism is disabled.

SPECIFICATION	
Dardo Hitfist	**Performance:** maximum road speed 70 km/h (43.5 mph); maximum road range 500 km (311 miles)
Crew: 2 + 7	
Weight: 23 tonnes rising to 26 tonnes with maximum armour	
Dimensions: length 6.71 m (22 ft); width 3 m (9 ft 10 in); height (overall) 2.64 m (8 ft 8 in)	**Fording:** 1.5 m (4 ft 11 in) without preparation
	Gradient: 60 per cent
Powerplant: one IVECO 8260 liquid-cooled V-6 diesel developing 388 kW (520 hp)	**Vertical obstacle:** 0.85 m (2 ft 9½ in)
	Trench: 2.5 m (8 ft 2 in)

The construction of the Dardo from aluminium armour helps to keep basic weight down to a minimum, but also opens the spectre of vulnerability. Thus, the Dardo has provision for the attachment of steel armour over several of its most vulnerable areas.

ASCOD Armoured infantry fighting vehicle

The **ASCOD** armoured infantry fighting vehicle, which first ran in prototype form in 1990, is a collaborative Austrian and Spanish programme by the Austrian Spanish Co-Operative Development undertaking created by Steyr-Daimler-Puch and Santa Barbara.

The first customer was the Spanish army with a contract for 144 **Pizarro** vehicles to be manufactured by a Santa Barbara subsidiary, and comprising 123 AIFVs and 21 command posts. The Spanish army's total requirement is for 463 vehicles including variants such as armoured command post, ambulance, communications, 81- and 120-mm (3.2- and 4.72-in) mortar carriers, anti-tank guided missile, armoured engineer, armoured recovery, artillery forward observation post and tank-destroyer vehicles, the last with a 105-mm (4.13-in) gun in a new turret.

Austrian contract

In May 1999, the Austrian defence ministry contracted with Steyr-Daimler-Puch for 112 **Ulan** AIFVs for delivery in 2002-04 as partial successor to the 4K 4FA family of tracked APCs. The Ulan contract does not currently include any variants of the baseline model, and the Austrians will operate the tracked type alongside the Pandur 6x6 wheeled APC. Late in 1999, the Thai marine corps selected the ASCOD, of which 17 are to be delivered as 15 **ASCOD 105** light tanks and single command post and recovery vehicles.

The ASCOD's hull and turret are of all-welded steel construction providing protection against 7.62-mm (0.3-in) armour-piercing projectiles everywhere except

Above: The ASCOD vehicle is offered with the choice of two engines and several armament fits. The standard arrangement is a turret offset to the right and providing 360° traverse for guns that can be elevated between -10° and +50°.

Right: The ASCOD's baseline weapon is the 30-mm Mauser Model F cannon, which is fitted with two-axis stabilisation and controlled via a Kollsman Direct Night Range Sight with optical and thermal sights, a digital computer and a laser rangefinder.

the frontal arc, where protection is offered against 14.5-mm (0.57-in) rounds. The ASCOD can also be fitted with additional steel armour on the front and sides of the turret, glacis plate and hull sides.

The driver is seated at the front of the hull on the left with the powerpack to his right. This powerpack is based on the German MTU 8V-183 TE22 V90 liquid-cooled diesel developing 447 kW (600 hp). The Ulan is powered by an MTU 8V 199 diesel developing 529 kW (710 hp). The complete powerpack can be removed in approximately 15 minutes.

Offset to the right in the centre of the hull is the electrically operated SP-30 two-man turret. The main armament comprises a 30-mm Mauser Model F dual-feed cannon with 200

The ASCOD at speed. This is the standard armoured infantry fighting vehicle version with a 30-mm cannon as its main armament, but there is also a considerably more potent light tank variant armed with a 105-mm (4.13-in) main gun in a different turret.

rounds of ready-use ammunition together with 202 reserve rounds. On the cannon's left is a 7.62-mm MG3 co-axial machine-gun, and this has 700 rounds of ready-use ammunition together with 2,200 reserve rounds.

Troop compartment

The troop compartment is at the rear with eight men seated on individual fold-up seats (five and three along the left- and right-hand sides respectively). The troops enter and leave their compartment by means of a large power-operated rear door. Above the left-hand

side of the troop compartment's roof is a cupola with day periscopes and a rearward-opening hatch.

The suspension is of the torsion-bar type with seven dual road wheels on each side, the drive sprocket at the front and the idler at the rear; there are three track-return rollers. Standard equipment includes a fire detection/suppression system for the engine compartment, a centralised environmental suite based on an NBC/ventilation system with optional air conditioning and water heating system, and a driver's passive night-vision device.

SPECIFICATION	
Pizarro	speed 70 km/h (43.5 mph);
Crew: 3 + 8	maximum road range 600 km
Weight: 27.5 tonnes	(373 miles)
Dimensions: length 6.99 m (22 ft 11 in); width 3.15 m (10 ft 4 in); height (overall) 2.65 m (8 ft 8½ in)	**Fording:** 1.2 m (3 ft 11 ¼ in) without preparation and 1.5 m (4 ft 11 in) with preparation
Powerplant: one MTU 8V 153 TE22 8 V-90 liquid-cooled V-8 diesel developing 447 kW (600 hp)	**Gradient:** 75 per cent **Vertical obstacle:** 0.95 m (3 ft 1½ in)
Performance: maximum road	**Trench:** 2.5 m (8 ft 2 in)

CV 90 Infantry combat vehicle family

For many years the standard armoured personnel carrier (APC) of the Swedish army was the then Hägglund & Söner Pbv 302 which was fitted with a manually operated one-man turret armed with a 20-mm cannon.

To supplement the Pbv 302 the Swedish army issued a requirement for a new ICV (Infantry Combat Vehicle) and awarded the development contract to a very small company called HB Utveckling.

This company in turn awarded contracts to what was then Hägglunds Vehicle for development of the chassis and to Bofors for development of the turret and its associated weapon system. Final vehicle integration, for example the mating of the hull and turret, was carried out by what is now Bofors Defence.

Early production

Following extensive trials with prototype vehicles, a production contract was placed and the first production vehicle was handed over to the Swedish army in November 1993 with final deliveries following in September 2002. By this time, total production for the Swedish army amounted to almost 700 vehicles including related variants.

The basic **CV 9040** is fitted with a power-operated two-man turret armed with a Bofors Defence 40-mm 40/70B cannon characterised by ammunition feed from the bottom and empty cartridge case ejection out of the roof.

The 40/70B is a further development of the famous 40-mm L/70 anti-aircraft gun and fires a variety of ammunition types, these including APFSDS-T (Armour-Piercing Fin-Stabilised Discarding Sabot – Tracer), the advanced 3P which is programmed as it leaves the muzzle, preformed high explosive and a multi-purpose tracer.

An M/39 7.62-mm (0.3-in) machine-gun is mounted co-

Above: The CV 9040 of the Swedish army is typical of current ICV thinking in all but its primary armament, which is of larger calibre than that of most other ICVs. This 40-mm Bofors turreted weapon can be elevated between -8 and +35 degrees. The gun is supplied with 238 rounds of ammunition, and the 7.62-mm (0.3-in) co-axial machine-gun has 3,000 rounds.

Infantrymen disembark from the troop compartment of the CV 9030 during trials. This is accessed by a large rear door that opens to the right.

axial with the main gun, and a computerised day/night fire-control system is fitted as standard. The French Galix grenade launching system is fitted. This can fire several types of grenade including smoke and screening.

The crew consists of the driver, commander and gunner, and eight fully equipped infantrymen can be carried in the rear compartment, where they are seated four down each side facing inward. The troops can enter and leave the vehicle rapidly by means of a power-operated ramp in the rear of the hull.

In addition to the CV 9040, the Swedish army operates several specialised variants including a **CV 90 FCV** forward command vehicle, **CV 90 FOV** forward observation

vehicle and **CV 90 ARV** armoured recovery vehicle. Finally there is the **TriAD** air-defence vehicle with a turret similar to that of the CV 9040 but carrying to its rear a large dome over the Thales air-defence radar.

Upgrade programme

An upgrade programme has been under way for some time to upgrade early production vehicles to the enhanced **CV 9040A** and **CV 9040B** configurations. The latest CV 9040 upgrade includes additional hull and turret armour for increased battlefield protection. A number of improvements have also been undertaken to enhance the lower part of the hull against the effects of anti-tank mines, which have

proved to be a particular problem in Balkan peacekeeping operations.

In the future the Swedish army will procure another version of the CV 90 fitted with the twin 120-mm (4.72-in) Advanced MOrtar System (AMOS) turret, which has already been successfully demonstrated on a number of other chassis, tracked and wheeled.

Using its own funding, Hägglunds Vehicle, which late in 2002 became Alvis Hägglunds, developed the **CV 9030** ICV. This has a hull similar to that of the Swedish army's CV 9040 but carrying a Hägglunds Vehicle turret

armed with an American ATK Gun Systems Company 30-mm Chain Gun. The first customer for this was Norway, which took delivery of 104 vehicles.

A further development of the CV 9030 fitted with the Boeing 30-mm/40-mm MK 44 cannon has been adopted by Finland (first order for 57 **CV 9030FIN** units) and Switzerland (first order for 186 **CV 9030CH** units).

Alvis Hägglunds has also developed the **CV 90120-T** light tank for the export market. This is essentially an upgraded CV 90 chassis fitted with a new three-man turret armed with a Swiss RUAG Land Systems 120-mm (4.72-in) smoothbore gun fitted with a muzzle brake. This is coupled to a computerised fire control system that enables targets to be engaged and hit while the CV 90120-T is stationary or moving. The 120-mm gun fires the various standard types of NATO 120-mm tank gun ammunition.

The two-man turret of the CV 9030 can be electrically traversed though 360 degrees. There is a moderately advanced Celsius Tech Electronics Universal Tank and Anti-Aircraft System fire-control system, but no stabilisation of the gun.

SPECIFICATION	
CV 9040	X-300-5N automatic transmission
Crew: 3 + 8	**Performance:** maximum road speed
Weight: 22800 kg (50,265 lb)	70 km/h (43.5 mph); maximum range
Dimensions: length 6.47 m (21 ft	600 km (373 miles)
2¾ in); width 3.19 m (10 ft 5¾ in);	**Fording:** 1.4 m (4 ft 7 in)
height 2.5 m (8 ft 2½ in)	**Gradient:** 60 per cent
Powerplant: one 410-kW (550-hp)	**Vertical obstacle:** 1 m (3 ft 3½ in);
Scania diesel coupled to a Perkins	**Trench:** 2.4 m (7 ft 10½ in)

BMP-3 Infantry combat vehicle

The **BMP-3** infantry combat vehicle (ICV) was developed by the Kurgan Machine Construction Plant, which was also responsible for the earlier BMP-1 and BMP-2. Production of the BMP-3 began in 1989, and the type was first shown in public during 2000. It is estimated that since then about 1,000 have been built. The Russian army had hoped to replace the older BMP-2 with the BMP-3 on a one-for-one basis, but funding problems mean that production for the Russian army is estimated to have reached only 200 to 300 vehicles.

Export successes
The BMP-3 has also been offered on the export market and in recent years it has been one of the best-selling Russian ICVs with almost 600 examples sold to Cyprus, Kuwait, South Korea and the UAE.

The BMP-3 is the best armed ICV in the world as it has a power-operated two-man turret fitted with a 100-mm (3.94-in) gun, a 30-mm co-axial cannon and a 7.62-mm (0.3-in) co-axial machine-gun, all coupled to a computerised day/night fire-control system so that targets can be engaged with a high first-round hit probability, regardless of whether the vehicle is stationary or moving. In addition to HE-FRAG projectiles, the rifled main gun can also fire laser-guided 9M117 (AT-10 'Stabber') projectiles to a range of 5000 m (5,470 yards) or more. Early examples of this missile car-

ried a HEAT warhead with a claimed capability to penetrate more than 650 mm (25.6 in) of conventional steel armour. More recently a new missile with a tandem HEAT warhead has been developed to counter tanks fitted with Explosive Reactive Armour (ERA).

The driver is seated at the front of the vehicle with an additional crew member on each side, and mounted on each side of the hull front is a 7.62-mm machine-gun to provide suppressive fire.

The remaining five troops are seated to the rear of the turret under very cramped conditions as the engine compartment is at the rear of the hull. The troops can enter or leave by two rear doors or roof hatches. Firing ports and associated vision devices allow the infantry to fire their weapons from within the vehicle.

The BMP-3 is amphibious, being propelled in the water by two hydrojets. Before

entering the water a trim vane is erected at the front of the vehicle and the electrically operated bilge pumps are activated. A special marinised version of the BMP-3, the **BMP-3F**, has been developed for service with marine forces.

Standard equipment includes an NBC system and night-vision equipment for the commander, gunner and driver. To enhance the fighting capabilities of the BMP-3 still further, thermal vision equipment can be fitted.

Battlefield survivability can be enhanced by the installation of ERA, which defeats HEAT warheads, and this has already been adopted by one export customer. The Arena active defence system can also be installed on the BMP-3.

Family of variants
A complete family of vehicles has been developed on the chassis of the BMP-3, although most of these have so far only reached the pro-

totype stage as a result of Russia's funding problems.

The armoured recovery vehicle is the **BREM-L,** and it is known that this has been built in small numbers. Anti-tank missile platforms include the **BMP-3 Kornet-E** and **BMP-3 Krizantema**, neither of which has entered quantity production. There is also the **2S31 Vena** 120-mm (4.72-in) self-propelled mortar system, but this too is still only a prototype.

The dedicated reconnaissance vehicle is the **BRM-3** or **Rys** (lynx) with a specialised optronic suite for day/night reconnaissance under all weather conditions. The **BMP-3K** is a command vehicle with radio equipment. There is also a driver training vehicle with the turret removed. The baseline BMP-3 chassis has been offered with Western turrets such as the German Wildcat air-defence system which can be armed with a system of 30-mm cannon and/or guided missiles.

*The **BMP-3** is notably well armed, its turret alone carrying a 100-mm (3.94-in) gun, 30-mm cannon and 7.62-mm (0.3-in) machine-gun. The main gun has 40 rounds including 22 within an automatic loader, as well as eight laser-guided anti-tank projectiles, and the cannon has 500 rounds. The machine-gun armament, including the two fixed weapons, has 6,000 rounds.*

*The **BMP-3** chassis has been used as the basis of an extensive AFV family including that seen here, the **BREM-L** recovery vehicle with a dozer blade, winch, crane with a telescopic jib, cargo bed, and a mass of specialised equipment.*

SPECIFICATION	
BMP-3	forward and two reverse gears
Crew: 3 + 7	**Performance:** maximum road speed
Weight: 18700 kg (41,226 lb)	70 km/h (43.5 mph); maximum water
Dimensions: length 7.14 m (23 ft 5 in); width 3.23 m (10 ft 6¾ in); height 2.65 m (8 ft 8½ in)	speed 10 km/h (6.25 mph); maximum range 600 km (373 miles)
Powerplant: one UTD-29M diesel developing 373 kW (500 hp) and coupled to a transmission with four	**Fording:** amphibious **Gradient:** 60 per cent **Vertical obstacle:** 0.8 m (2 ft 7½ in) **Trench:** 2.5 m (8 ft 2½ in)

Warrior The 'battle taxi'

In the late 1960s and early 1970s the British Army carried out a number of studies to field a more capable vehicle to replace the FV432 armoured personnel carrier (APC) and, in the late 1970s, GKN Sankey (now Alvis Vehicles) was selected to develop a new vehicle which was referred to as **MCV-80 (Mechanised Combat Vehicle 80)**.

Following extensive trials with prototypes, a production order was placed and eventually a total of 789 was built for the British Army with final deliveries made in 1995.

The basic Warrior is designated **FV510** and is fitted with a two-person Vickers Defence Systems turret, armed with a 30-mm RARDEN cannon and 0.3-in (7.62-mm) co-axial machine-gun. It has a crew of three consisting of commander, gunner and driver, and carries seven fully-equipped troops that can rapidly dismount via the rear door. The interior is also fully insulated against nuclear, biological and chemical (NBC) attack.

Warrior variants

Variants of the Warrior used by the British Army include the **FV511** command vehicle, **FV512** repair vehicle, **FV513** recovery vehicle, **FV514** artillery observation vehicle, **FV515** artillery battery command vehicle and **FV516** anti-tank vehicle.

Despite many overseas trials, so far there has been only one export customer. In 1993 Kuwait placed an order for a total of 254 **'Desert Warriors'**. These vehicles were completed to a much higher standard than the Warriors delivered to the British Army and featured a US Delco Defense two-person turret armed with an ATK Gun Systems Company 25-mm M242 cannon with a 0.3-in (7.62-mm) co-axial machine gun. Mounted either side of the turret is a TOW launcher, which is used in conjunction with a day/thermal fire control system.

More recently, Alvis has developed an advanced **Warrior 2000** for the export market, which features a new two-person turret armed with a 30-mm cannon with three different rates of fire.

The Warrior 2000 was developed for the Swiss Army, which ultimately ordered the rival Hägglunds CV 9030CH. The two-crew turret is armed with a 30-mm Bushmaster cannon.

SPECIFICATION

British Army Warrior
Crew: 3 + 7
Weight: 28000 kg (61,730 lb)
Powerpack: diesel developing 410 kW (550 hp) coupled to fully automatic transmission
Dimensions: length 6.34 m (21 ft); width 3.03 m (10 ft); height 2.74 m (9 ft)

Performance: maximum road speed 75 km/h (47 mph); maximum range 660 km (410 miles)
Fording: 1.13 m (3 ft 8½ in)
Gradient: 60 per cent
Vertical obstacle: 0.75 m (2 ft 6 in)
Trench: 2.5 m (8 ft 2½ in)

Stormer Multi-role armoured personnel carrier

The origins of the **Alvis Vehicles Stormer** armoured personnel carrier can be traced back to the late 1970s, when the Fighting Vehicle Research and Development Establishment (FVRDE) developed a prototype vehicle designated **FV4333**. This used some automotive components from the Alvis Scorpion Combat Vehicle Reconnaissance (Tracked) series of vehicles. However, the FV4333 was longer and wider, and therefore had greater internal volume and could undertake more battlefield roles.

The design and marketing

SPECIFICATION

Stormer APC
Crew: 3 + 8
Weight: 12700 kg (28,000 lb)
Powerpack: diesel developing 186 kW (250 hp) coupled to semi-automatic transmission
Dimensions: length 5.27 m (17 ft 3½ in); width 2.76 m (9 ft); height 2.49 m (8 ft 2 in)

Performance: Maximum road speed 80 km/h (50 mph); maximum range 664 km (412 miles)
Fording: 1.10 m (3 ft 7 in)
Gradient: 60 per cent
Vertical obstacle: 0.60 m (1 ft 11 in)
Trench: 1.75 m (5 ft 8 in)

Using a single chassis design, the Stormer can be configured for several different duties, such as this mobile command/control vehicle for Indonesia.

rights for the FV4333 were subsequently purchased by what is now Alvis Vehicles, and the concept was developed into a family of light tracked vehicles ranging from an APC to a light tank.

The largest customer to date is the British Army, which currently uses it in a number of specialised versions. These include a flatbed carrier fitted with the US ATK Volcano anti-tank mine scattering system, a troop reconnaissance vehicle for use with Starstreak High Velocity Missile (HVM) units and the actual Stormer-based HVM launcher.

The first export customer for the Stormer was Mayalsia, which has two APC versions, one fitted with a one-person turret armed with a 20-mm cannon and the other with machine-

guns. Oman has a command post version for use by its Challenger 2 tank regiments.

The most recent export customer for the Stormer is Indonesia, which has taken delivery of a large number of variants including APC, logistics carrier, command post vehicle, ambulance, recovery and bridgelayer versions, the latter fitted with a scissors bridge system.

A new minelaying Stormer variant, to be known as **Shielder**, is being developed in cooperation with Alliant Technosystems Volcano.

Stormer can be tailored to specific customer requirements. The ambulance version, fitted with a higher roof, has been bought by Indonesia.

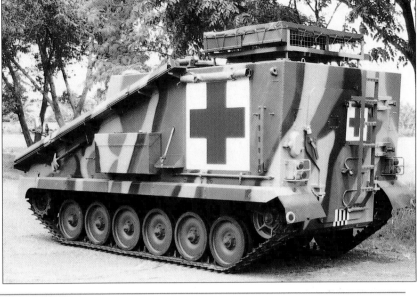

M2 Bradley Infantry fighting vehicle

Following a competition, the company which became United Defense Ground Systems Division was awarded a contract in the spring of 1972 to develop a new Mechanised Infantry Fighting Vehicle (MICV) to meet the requirements of the US Army as a successor to the M113 series APC. The requirement was for a vehicle with with greater armour and mobility, and improved firepower.

Variants

After a protracted development period, two vehicles were finally type classified: the **M2 Bradley Infantry Fighting Vehicle (IFV)** and the **M3 Bradley Cavalry Fighting Vehicle (CFV)**. The former carries seven fully equipped troops, while the latter has a smaller crew and is used principally in the reconnaissance/scout role. The M2 and M3 are both air, land and sea portable. This enables them to undertake rapid deployment.

The M2 and M3 are very similar and both are fitted with an advanced two-person turret armed with an ATK Gun Systems Company

The M6 Bradley Linebacker is intended to replace the M163 Vulcan air defence system, equipped with a four-round Stinger SAM launcher with six reloads. The main armament is retained, with a reduced ammunition capacity.

stabilised 25-mm M242 cannon, 0.3-in (7.62-mm) co-axial machine-gun and have a twin launcher on the left side of the turret for a Raytheon Systems Company TOW anti-tank guided weapon (ATGW). An advanced day/night fire control system

has also been installed.

First production Bradley vehicles were completed in 1981 and production continued through to 1995 with just under 6,800 units being built, including 400 for Saudi Arabia, which is the only export customer.

Over the years the Bradley has been continuously enhanced through the **A1**, **A2** and **A3** standards, with the latest models being fitted with explosive reactive armour, a Commanders Independent Thermal Viewer (CITV) and enhanced engine and transmission.

Automotive components of the Bradley are used in the widely deployed Multiple

Launch Rocket System (MLRS), while more specialised versions of the Bradley include the **M7 FIST (Fire Support Team)** vehicle and **M6 Bradley Linebacker**, which has the twin TOW launcher replaced by a pod with four Stinger fire-and-forget surface-to-air missiles in the ready to launch position.

SPECIFICATION	
M2A3 Bradley IFV	**Performance:** maximum road
Crew: 3 + 7	speed 61 km/h (38 mph); maximum
Weight: 30391 kg (67,000 lb)	range 400 km (249 miles)
Powerpack: 447-kW (600-hp)	**Fording:** amphibious
diesel coupled to automatic	**Gradient:** 60 per cent
transmission	**Vertical obstacle:** 0.91 m
Dimensions: length 6.55 m	(2 ft 11 in)
(21 ft 6 in); width 2.97 m (9 ft 8 in);	**Trench:** 2.54 m (8 ft 4 in)
height 3.38 m (11 ft 1 in)	

The M2A3 Bradley Modernisation Plan was initiated following Operation Desert Storm. This view of the M2A3 shows the applique armour, and Commander's Independent Viewer mounted on the right rear.

Fahd
Armoured personnel carrier

Designed and built in proto-type form in Germany by Thyssen Henschel (now Rheinmetall Landsysteme) as the **TH 390**, this 4x4 APC was created to meet a requirement of the Egyptian army. The type was then placed in production during 1985 by the Kader Factory for Developed Industries (part of the Arab Organisation for Industrialisation) as the **Fahd** and entered service in the following year with the Egyptian army as successor to obsolescent types such as the Soviet BTR-40 and indigenous Walid wheeled APCs. It was estimated that by a time early in 2001 more than 1,000 examples of the family had been completed for Egypt and export customers such as Algeria, Democratic Republic of Congo, Kuwait, Oman and Sudan.

The AFV Fahd 240/30, used only by Egypt and then just in small numbers, has boosted firepower in the form of the BMP-2's two-man turret with a 30-mm cannon and 7.62-mm (0.3-in) co-axial machine-gun.

The Fahd is based on the chassis and automotive system of the Mercedes-Benz LAP 1117/32 4x4 truck, on which an armoured body is installed.

This body is of all-welded steel construction offering protection against shell splinters as well as small arms fire up to 7.62-mm (0.3-in) calibre. The driver (on the left) and commander are seated side-by-side in the front of the body and behind bullet-proof windscreen halves that can be covered by top-hinged armoured shutters. There is a door, with a bullet-proof window and shutter, in each side, and above the commander is a hatch.

Embarked infantry

The hull's rear is occupied by the troop compartment. This is laid out for the carriage of up to 10 infantry, who sit on

two longitudinal rows of outward-facing seats along the centreline of the compartment. These troops enter and leave their compartment by means of a two-part rear door: the upper part hinges up and to the rear, and the lower part down to form a step. Above the troop compartment are two rectangular hatches hinged along the centreline. The troops can fire their weapons from inside the Fahd, for their compartment has 10 pairs of firing ports and superimposed vision blocks (four along each side and one on each side of the rear door). There is also provision for the installation of three machine-guns on the Fahd's roof.

The engine is mounted toward the front of the vehicle, and the tyres (of the run-flat type) are improved in all-terrain capability by the incorporation of a central tyre pressure-regulation system. Optional equipment includes a front-mounted winch, an NBC and ventila-

The Fahd is a thoroughly unexceptional APC of the 4x4 wheeled type, but has the advantage of being based on a well-proved commercial chassis, which facilitates logistic support for the type.

tion system, passive night vision equipment, and a bank of four smoke dischargers on each side of the troop compartment, at either the front or rear.

There is provision over the hull for a one-man turret carrying one 12.7-mm (0.5-in) or alternatively one or two 7.62-mm (0.3-in) machine-guns, or one 20-mm cannon. Kader has also proposed the Fahd as the basis of a complete family of derivatives in the

whole gamut of battlefield and internal security roles.

The only two developments to have entered production are the **Fahd 240** and its **AFV Fahd 240/30** derivative. Announced in 1996, the former is similar to the basic Fahd except for being mounted on the chassis of the Mercedes-Benz LAP 1424/32 truck, while the latter carries the complete turret of the Russian BMP-2 IFV complete with its 30-mm cannon.

SPECIFICATION	
Fahd	turbocharged diesel engine delivering 125 kW (168 hp)
Crew: 2+10	**Performance:** maximum road speed 90 km/h (56 mph); maximum road range 800 km (497 miles); fording 0.7 m (2 ft 3.5 in); gradient 70 per cent; vertical obstacle 0.5 m (1 ft 7.75 in); trench 0.9 m (2 ft 11.5 in)
Weight: 10.9 tonnes	
Dimensions: length 6 m (19 ft 8.25 in); width 2.45 m (8 ft 0.5 in); height to the top of the hull 2.1 m (6 ft 10.67 in)	
Powerplant: one Mercedes-Benz OM 352A liquid-cooled 6-cylinder	

Centauro Tank destroyer

Designed by FIAT and OTO Melara (now IVECO and Otobreda respectively), the **Centauro** 8x8 tank destroyer is a member of the AFV generation that the Italian army requested in the 1980s, the other three types being the Ariete MBT, Dardo IFV and Puma 4x4 and 6x6 light vehicles. FIAT was responsible for the hull and automotive system, and OTO Melara for the armament system.

The Italian army's 1984 requirement demanded a highly capable tank destroyer armed with a 105-mm (4.13-in) rifled gun firing the standard range of NATO ammunition and employing an advanced fire-control system and possessing a high road speed, long range and good cross-country mobility.

First run in prototype form during 1987, the Centauro was delivered from 1991, and by 1996 some 400 vehicles had been completed for the Italian army, which is the sole operator of the type.

Steel protection

The Centauro is built of all-welded steel armour providing protection against 20-mm projectiles over the frontal arc and 12.7-mm (0.5-in) projectiles elsewhere. The front of the vehicle is occupied by the powerpack (on the right)

A Centauro is pictured during main armament firing trials. Evident in this photograph are the overall layout and the low-silhouette turret with a large bustle.

The Centauro's turret has 360° electrohydraulic traverse, and the main armament can be elevated between -6° and +15°. The sights and fire-control system are both comprehensive.

with the driver to its left under a hatch that can be fitted with night vision devices. This forward compartment is separated from the rest of the vehicle by a fireproof bulkhead. Located over the rear of the hull is the fighting compartment with its low-silhouette turret. The turret carries the commander on the left and the gunner (with his own dedicated sight unit including a day optics, a thermal imaging device and a laser rangefinder) and loader on the right. The commander has his own roof hatch, four day periscopes and a stabilised sight, while the other two members of the turret crew have a single hatch above the loader's position.

The turret armament comprises an Otobreda 105-mm gun with 40 rounds (14 of them in the turret for ready use), 7.62-mm (0.3-in) co-axial and 7.62-mm AA

machine-guns with 1,400 rounds, and smoke dischargers on each side of the turret. The TURMS fire-control system is the same as that of the Ariete MBT.

Well equipped
Standard features include an NBC system, central tyre pressure-regulation system, front-mounted winch, fire and explosion detection and suppression systems, and provision for passive armour.

Several variants have been proposed, and those to have reached hardware form are a close-defence vehicle with provision for four infantry using the door in the rear of the hull, a longer and wider model with the 60-mm (2.36-in) Otobreda gun, a 155-mm (6.1-in) self-propelled howitzer testbed and a Centauro VBC armoured personnel carrier with a turreted 25-mm cannon.

SPECIFICATION

Centauro
Crew: 4
Weight: 25 tonnes
Dimensions: length (with gun forward) 8.555 m (28 ft 0.8 in) and (hull) 7.85 m (25 ft 9 in); width 3.05 m (10 ft 0 in); height (overall) 2.735 m (8 ft 11.67 in)
Powerplant: one IVECO VTCA liquid-cooled V-6 turbocharged

diesel engine delivering 388 kW (520 hp)
Performance: maximum road speed 105 km/h (65 mph); maximum road range 800 km (497 miles); fording 1.5 m (4 ft 11 in); gradient 60 per cent; vertical obstacle not available; trench not available

Puma APC

The smallest of the new generation of vehicles requested by the Italian army in the mid-1980s (the others being the Ariete MBT, Dardo IFV and Centauro tank destroyer), the **Puma** was developed by FIAT and OTO Melara (now IVECO and Otobreda respectively) as an APC to operate with the Centauro. The origins of the type can in fact be traced back to the early 1980s, when FIAT built its 4x4 Armoured Vehicle Light as the starting point of a proposed 4x4 and 6x6 series of wheeled AFVs.

The Italian army wanted something larger than the AVL, and the result was the Puma that initially ran, in the form of the first of five prototypes, in 1988. The Italian army also asked for the creation of six specialised models as three four-crew weapons carriers (TOW and MILAN anti-tank missiles

and Mistral SAM), a four-crew 81-mm (3.2-in) mortar carrier, a two-crew ambulance with provision for two litters and a five/six-man light armoured command post.

Development of the Puma series of 4x4 and 6x6 vehicles was completed in 1999, and the Consorzio Iveco Oto received orders for 580 vehicles in the form of 330 4x4 and 250 6x6 APCs to be delivered from the first half of 2001 to 2004. The 4x4 vehicles are used by five reconnaissance regiments to work in concert with the Centauro tank destroyer, and the 6x6 vehicles are distributed among light infantry, mountain, paratroop and light amphibious regiments. The 4x4 vehicles carry six persons, allowing them to deploy a pair of two-man scout teams, and the 6x6 vehicles carry seven persons in the form of a driver and a six-man combat team.

Conventional layout
The Puma is of all-welded steel armour construction providing protection against small arms fire and shell splinters. From front to rear, the vehicle comprises the

The Puma has a very well sloped upper nose, and an unusual feature is the use of a single side plate rather than two plates welded together along the angle.

engine compartment, the position for the driver on the left-hand side under a domed hatch and with three day periscopes of which the central unit can be replaced by a passive night periscope, and the troop compartment. This last is accessed by a single inward-opening door in each side of the one-piece hull side, and by an outward-opening door in the rear of the hull. There is a firing port and, above it, a vision block in each of the three doors. Above the troop compartment is the commander's cupola with a circular hatch, five day periscopes and provision for one 12.7- or 7.62-mm (0.5- or 0.3-in) machine-gun. On each side of the rear hull, aligned to fire forward, is a bank of three smoke dischargers.

Standard equipment includes an NBC system, a

fire detection and suppression system, an integrated air-conditioning system and a rear-mounted winch. The vehicle has run-flat tyres, and while the early vehicles have the IVECO 8141.47 diesel engine delivering 93 kW (125 hp) via a manual transmission system, later machines have a more powerful engine with an automatic transmission.

Larger variant
It was in 1990 that the first prototype of the Puma's 6x6 version first ran, and among

the variants that have been proposed for this model are a carrier for the 81-mm mortar and a command post vehicle. The prototype was completed with an externally mounted 12.7-mm machine-gun and a bank of three forward-firing smoke dischargers on each side of the commander's turret, although a possibility for later production vehicles is an Otobreda powered turret with a 12.7-mm machine-gun that can be operated from under the armour.

The Puma 4x4 vehicle is sized for air transport inside machines such as the Boeing CH-47 Chinook twin-rotor helicopter, with obvious mobility advantages.

SPECIFICATIONS

Puma (4x4)	Puma (6 x 6)
Crew: 1+6	**Crew:** 1+8
Weight: 5.7 tonnes	**Weight:** 7.5 tonnes
Dimensions: length 5.108 m (16 ft 9 in); width 2.09 m (6 ft 10.25 in); height (hull top) 1.678 m (5 ft 6 in)	**Dimensions:** length 5.526 m (18 ft 1.5 in); width 2.284 m (7 ft 6 in); height (hull top) 1.678 m (5 ft 6 in)
Powerplant: one IVECO 8042.45 liquid-cooled 4-cylinder diesel delivering 134 kW (180 hp)	**Powerplant:** one IVECO 8042.45 liquid-cooled 4-cylinder diesel delivering 134 kW (180 hp)
Performance: maximum road speed 105 km/h (65 mph); range 800 km (497 miles); fording 1 m (3 ft 3 in); gradient 60 per cent; vertical obstacle/trench not available	**Performance:** maximum road speed 100 km/h (62 mph); range 700 km (435 miles); fording 1 m (3 ft 3 in); gradient 60 per cent; vertical obstacle/trench not available

BTR-80 Armoured personnel carrier

For many years the Soviet and now Russian army has employed a mix of tracked and wheeled infantry fighting vehicles (IFVs) and armoured personnel carriers (APCs). Each offers several significant advantages: wheeled vehicles have greater strategic mobility, while the tracked vehicles generally have better cross-country mobility and can be fitted with a more powerful weapon system.

Early service

The first 8x8 APC to enter service with the Soviet army was the BTR-60, and this was followed by the BTR-70 and more recently the **BTR-80**. All of these were designed and built by GAZ (Gorky Automobile Plant) which today is known as the Arzamas Construction Plant. Development of the BTR-80 began in the late 1970s, and the first production vehicles were completed and deployed in the early 1980s.

The layouts of all the BTR series vehicles are very similar, with the commander and driver at the very front and the weapon station on the roof to their immediate rear. The troop compartment is in the middle of the hull with the powerpack at the very rear. When compared to Western vehicles such as the Swiss-designed MOWAG Piranha 8x8 APC, the overall design of the BTR-80 has significant limitations as a result of the powerpack's location at the rear of the hull.

The infantry have to dismount via the roof hatches or via the door in the side of the hull between the second and third road wheels. The lower part of the door folds down to form a step, while the upper part forms a door that opens to the front.

The manually operated one-person turret is armed with a 14.5-mm (0.57-in) KPVT machine-gun and a 7.62-mm (0.3-in) PKVT co-axial machine-gun.

Small arms

A bank of six electrically operated 81-mm (3.2-in) smoke grenade launchers, firing forward over the front of the vehicle, is mounted on the rear of the turret. The crew can also fire their small arms from within the vehicle with a high level of safety as firing ports and associated vision devices are provided in the sides of the hull.

Like the BTR-60 and -70, the BTR-80 is amphibious, being propelled in the water by a water jet at the rear of the hull. Before the vehicle enters the water, a trim vane is erected at the front and the electrically operated bilge pumps are activated.

The BTR-80's standard equipment includes night vision gear for the commander, driver and gunner, and steering is powered on the front four road wheels. A central tyre inflation system allows the driver to adjust the tyre pressure to suit the terrain, and an NBC system is standard. A winch is mounted internally at the front of the hull, and this can be used for self-recovery or the recovery of other vehicles on the battlefield.

Some BTR-80 vehicles have been fitted with explosive reactive armour to provide the occupants with some protection from attack by anti-tank weapons with a HEAT (high explosive anti-tank) warhead.

Variants

As usual with Russian vehicles, a whole family of variants has been developed on the same basic chassis. These include **BTR-80K** series of armoured command posts, **BMM** series of armoured battlefield ambulances, the **BTR-80 SPR-2** electronic warfare vehicle, and the **BREM-K** armoured recovery vehicle.

The chassis of the BTR-80 is also used as the basis for the **BTR-80 2S23** 120-mm

The BTR-80A variant displays its rough-terrain capabilities. The tyre pressure of these vehicles can be centrally altered to suit terrain requirements.

Right: The BTR-80A is armed with the same 30-mm 2A72 gun as the BMP-3. This weapon has a range of 4000 m (4,374 ft) firing HE incendiary projectiles.

Below: The BREM-K armoured recovery vehicle is based on the BTR-80 armoured personnel carrier. The vehicle is fitted with an 'A' frame jib and towbars.

SPECIFICATION	
BTR-80	1 in) ; width 2.9 m (9 ft 5 in); height 2.46 m (8 ft 1 in)
Crew: 3 + 7	
Weight: 13600 kg (29,982 lb)	**Performance:** maximum road speed 90 km/h (56 mph); maximum water speed 5.1 kts (9.5 km/h; 5.9 mph); maximum road range 600 km (373 miles)
Powerplant: one V-8 turbocharged diesel developing 179 or 194 kW (240 or 260 hp)	
Armament: one 14.5-mm (0.57-in) KPVT machine-gun and one 7.62-mm (0.3-in) coaxial PKVT machine-gun	**Fording:** amphibious
	Gradient: 60 per cent
Dimensions: length 7.65 m (25 ft	**Vertical obstacle:** 0.5 m (1 ft 8 in)
	Trench: 2 m (6 ft 7 in)

(4.72-in) self-propelled gun/mortar system The BTR-80 chassis has also been marketed for a number of civilian applications, these including a fire-fighting conversion of the vehicle. On this version, the turret is removed and the top of the vehicle is instead fitted with 22 launchers which are designed to launch fire suppressant cartridges.

Further development of the BTR-80 has resulted in the **BTR-80A**, which is based on the same hull as the earlier vehicle but in this application fitted with a new one-person turret. This is a power-operated unit armed with an externally mounted 30-mm 2A72 cannon and a 7.62-mm co-axial machine-gun.

Weapon stations

The BTR-80 has also been marketed with a number of other weapon stations, including the Russian Kliver turret armed with four Kornet laser-guided anti-tank missiles and a 30-mm cannon. This turret is also offered for installation on Western vehicles, as well as on the Russian BMP-1 and BMP-2 IFVs. A version of the vehicle fitted with a Western diesel engine, of Cummins manufacture, is also available.

The standard BTR-80 APC is operated in the largest numbers by Hungary, Kazakhstan, Russia, Turkey, Turkmenistan, Ukraine and Uzbekistan.

ARTEC MRAV Multi-Role Armoured Vehicle

As with many European armoured fighting vehicle (AFV) programmes, the **ARTEC Multi-Role Armoured Vehicle** (**MRAV**) has had a very chequered development history. The MRAV was originally conceived in an effort to meet the operational requirements of France, Germany and the United Kingdom. In the end, France pulled out and went its own way with the development of the Satory Military Vehicles Véhicule Blindé de Combat d'Infanterie (VBCI) infantry combat vehicle (ICV). This is slated to replace the AMX-10P tracked ICV, currently in service with the French army, later in the first decade of the 21st century.

Germany and the United Kingdom were not looking for an IFV, but wanted a vehicle that could be used for a variety of roles including armoured personnel carrier (APC) and as a command post vehicle (CPV). While the British army calls the vehicle the MRAV, the German army designates it as the **GTK** (**Gepanzertes Transport Kraftfahrzeug**).

Development

Late in 1999, Germany and the UK went ahead and awarded a development contract for the MRAV to a new industrial consortium based in Munich called ARTEC (ARmoured TEChnology). This company comprises Krauss-Maffei Wegmann and Rheinmetall Landsysteme of Germany and what is now Alvis Vickers of the UK. Under the terms of this contract a total of eight prototypes was to be built, four for each country.

Subsequently, the Netherlands joined the programme and the number of prototypes to be built has increased to 12, with each country now having four prototype vehicles. It is expected that the first production contract will be for 600 vehicles to provide each country with 200 units. As with any programme of this type, there have been delays and the first prototype was not completed until early 2002, with the second fol-

lowing in late 2002.

There are some who believe that MRAV is now too heavy and large for many future potential operational requirements and that greater emphasis should be placed on a type for rapid-deployment forces. There is now an emphasis on equipment that can be rapidly transported by air in tactical transport aircraft such as the Lockheed Martin C-130 Hercules.

When the MRAV enters production, it is expected that there will be production lines in Germany, the Netherlands and the UK, with each country feeding subsystems to each other. Some parts, such as communications and weapon stations, will be unique to each country.

Unusual design

The design of the MRAV is unusual in that the vehicle consists of two key parts; the chassis complete with the powerpack and driver's station, and a dedicated mission module at the rear which can be detached from the vehicle if required.

MRAV features a high level of protection against not only small arms fire but also shell splinters, anti-tank mines and top attack munitions; the vehicle is also fitted with an NBC system. Stealth characteristics are also incorporated into the design. The vehicle's protection is enhanced through the reduction of both its thermal and acoustic signatures.

To reduce overall life cycle costs, the MRAV uses proven and off-the-shelf components wherever possible – including the engine, transmission and drive line. The basic vehicle has a crew of three, consisting of commander, driver and gunner, and will typically carry eight fully equipped infantry plus supplies for 24 or 48 hours. The infantry will be able to rapidly dismount via the power-operated ramp at the rear of the vehicle.

Armament

It is expected that the armament of the vehicle will be a 40-mm (1.57-in) automatic grenade launcher, and a 12.7-mm (0.5-in) or 7.62-mm (0.3-in) machine-gun in a turret or remotely controlled from within the vehicle.

If the latter were fitted, it would not only reduce the height and overall weight of

An artist's impression of the MRAV. The vehicle is designed to be air-portable and also retains low-observable characteristics. Deliveries are expected to take place between June 2006 and March 2009.

the vehicle but also make more space available within the hull for additional troops or supplies.

Standard equipment on the MRAV will include a full range of passive night vision equipment, a central tyre inflation system, powered steering and an anti-skid braking system.

Several specialised mission modules are already under development. The UK and the Netherlands, for example, have a requirement for an **Armoured Treatment and Evaluation Vehicle**, which will be able to stabilise injured troops in the forward area and then transport them to the rear. This model will have a module with a higher roof line to provide greater volume for litters and medical personnel. Other variants include communications and cargo vehicles.

Other MRAV variants are also projected, including command and control, electronic warfare, 81-mm (3.2-in) or 120-mm (4.72-in) mortar carrier, battle damage repair, pioneer and anti-tank guided missile vehicles.

SPECIFICATION	
MRAV	**Dimensions:** length 7.88 m (25 ft 10 in); width 2.99 m (9 ft 10 in); height 2.38 m (7 ft 10 in)
Crew: 3 + 8	
Weight: 33000 kg (72,751 lb)	
Powerplant: one MTU diesel developing 530 kW (711 hp) and coupled to Allison fully automatic transmission	**Performance:** maximum road speed 103 km/h (64 mph); maximum range 1000 km (621 miles)
	Fording: 1.5 m (4 ft 11 in)
Armament: one 40-mm (1.57-in) grenade launcher and one 12.7-mm (0.5-in) or 7.62-mm (0.3-in) machine-gun	**Gradient:** 60 per cent
	Vertical obstacle: 0.8 m (2 ft 7½ in)
	Trench: 2 m (6 ft 7 in)

Pandur Armoured personnel carrier

Dating in concept from 1979, when the Austrian company Steyr-Daimler-Puch Spezialfahrzeug AG began work on this private-venture type using commercial and 'off-the-shelf' components wherever possible, the **Pandur** is a 6x6 APC that was first revealed in 1985 after the company had started trials with two 2+8-seat prototypes, which were followed in the period to December 1986 by six pre-production vehicles.

The Pandur vehicle family is manufactured by the parent company and also by AV Technology International (a General Dynamics company) in the US. The Pandur has been operational with the Austrian army since 1996 (68 vehicles) and is also used by Kuwait (70 vehicles), Belgium (60 vehicles) and Slovenia (70 vehicles). The US Army has awarded a contract for up to 50 Pandur vehicles with new applique armour to form a possible basis for the Armored

Ground Mobility System.

All variants are based on the same chassis but configured in two basic forms, namely the 'A' and 'B' models with an extended centre and flat roofs respectively, and the variants include APCs with cupolas and turrets (including the AV-30 and US Marine Corps' upgunned Weapon Station) carrying machine-gun armament, an MICV with a more powerfully armed turret, a reconnaissance vehicle with the Multi-Gun Turreted System mounting a 25-, 30- or 35-mm cannon, combat support vehicles mounting a 90-mm (3.54-in) anti-tank gun or any of several mortar types, and service support vehicles including ambulance, engineer, logistics and command/control variants.

Upgraded model

Steyr-Daimler-Puch has also developed the **Pandur II**, trialled from September 2001. This has a longer wheel base and a modified hull, is

offered in 6x6 and 8x8 versions, and is powered by a higher-rated engine, the 265-kW (355-hp) Cummins ISC 350 diesel. The first 8x8 prototype is an IFV armed with a 30-mm cannon, and the type's standard equipment includes a central tyre pressure-regulation system.

For the reconnaissance and fire support role the vehicle is equipped with a Cockerill LCTS turret with a 90-mm Mk 8 gun and two 7.62-mm (0.3-in) machine-guns, one mounted co-axially and the other on the overhead cupola. Four smoke grenade dischargers are fitted on each side of the turret.

The turret is electro-mechanically powered with manual back-up. The 90-mm gun can be elevated from -9 to +20 degrees, and the turret can be traversed through 360 degrees. The gunner's station has a combined day and thermal imaging sight with a stabilised head mirror and an integrated laser

The Pandur can be fitted with a large number of sensor and weapon fits, this illustration of a 6x6 vehicle carrying a machine-gun and two HOT anti-tank missile launchers as well as an elevating sensor head. The Pandur's hull was designed with the aid of a computer for the smallest possible radar cross section.

rangefinder. The commander has a panoramic day sight featuring a gyro-stabilised line of sight, and a monitor displays the gunner's thermal channel.

The APC is armed with one 0.5-in (12.7-mm) M2HB machine-gun mounted with a shield on a ring providing 360-degree traverse, and one 7.62-mm (0.3-in) MG3 general-purpose machine-gun. For vision in the closed-down state the driver has three episcopes, and the commander's observa-

tion cupola has five episcopes. Six smoke grenade dischargers are fitted on each side of the turret. The amphibious version of the Pandur has a lengthened exhaust and is driven in the water by two waterjets. Protection against 12.7-mm projectiles over the frontal 60-degree arc, and the rest of the vehicle is proof against the effects of 7.62-mm rounds. Other defensive features include engine and exhaust silencing, and IR absorbent paint.

A 6x6 amphibious Pandur emerges from a river crossing with its right-hand waterjet evident under the hull. The embarked infantry leave the vehicle by means of two outward-opening rear doors as well as three roof hatches.

SPECIFICATION	
Steyr-Daimler-Puch Pandur (6 x 6 amphibious model)	engine delivering 212.5 kW (285 hp)
Crew: 2+10	**Performance:** maximum road speed 100 km/h (62 mph); maximum road range 700+ km (435+ miles); fording amphibious; vertical obstacle 0.5 m (1 ft 8 in); trench 1.1 m (3 ft 8.25 in)
Weight: 14000 kg (30,864 lb)	
Dimensions: length 6.297 m (20 ft 8 in); width 2.6 m (8 ft 6.33 in); height 1.82 (6 ft) to top of hull	
Powerplant: one Steyr WD 612.35 liquid-cooled 6-cylinder diesel	

XA-200 Armoured personnel carrier

The **XA-200** 6x6 wheeled vehicle is the latest version of the XA series, of which over 700 vehicles have been produced by Patria Vehicles of Finland, formerly Sisu Vehicles. The Finnish army has contracted for 100 XA-200 APCs for delivery by 2004, the Swedish army has ordered 104 **XA-202** vehicles (86 **XA-203S** basic and 18 **XA-202S** command vehicles) for delivery by 2003, and in May 2002 ordered an additional 63 vehicles for delivery in 2003-04. The Norwegian army has ordered 32 APCs.

The variants of the family include, in addition to the baseline APC developed from the XA-185, command and communication, anti-aircraft missile, anti-tank missile, ambulance, folding-mast radar carrier, mine scatterer, mortar carrier, recovery and repair, and NBC reconnaissance vehicles. The APC has a crew of three and provision for up to eight infantrymen, whose means of access and egress are two rear-mounted doors and two roof hatches.

The vehicle's chassis is

welded from high-hardness steel armour, and the modular construction of the hull's armour helps to provide protection against small arms ammunition up to 14.5-mm (0.57-in) calibre, shell fragments and mines. The engine is a turbocharged diesel unit driving the wheels via an Allison MD 3560PR electronically controlled automatic gearbox.

A number of different turrets can be added above the basic hull according to customer requirements, and these turrets offer the

The XA-200 is a multi-role APC of Finnish design and manufacture, and can be fitted with a number of different role-specialised turrets.

The hydraulically operated telescopic mast of the command variant of the XA-200 has hydraulic support legs and an automatic guy rope system with hydraulic tightening, and can be erected by two persons in 10 minutes.

choice of armament between a 7.62-mm (0.3-in) machine-gun and a 30-mm cannon. Other options include launchers for surface-to-air and anti-tank missiles, night sights, an air-conditioning system and an NBC package.

The XA-202 command vehicle is based on the XA-200 but with its hull divided into four sections (operator, driver/commander, engine and auxiliary power unit compartments). The 10-kW (13.4-hp) diesel APU is required for the electrical power demanded by the equipment in the operator compartment. There is an optional ring mount for a 0.5-in (12.7-mm) machinegun above the commander's position, add-on armour provides protection against 0.5-in armour-piercing projectiles, and there are four points at which VHF antennae can be added. The command vehicle can also be fitted with a 24-m (78.75-ft) hydraulically operated extending mast.

Trialled on an XA-200 by the Finnish army, the AMOS (Advanced Mortar System) turret is a development by Patria Hägglunds, formed by Patria and Alvis Hägglunds AB of Sweden, and carrying two 120-mm (4.72-in) breech-loaded mortars. The system has 360-degree tra-

Armoured shutters with vision slots can be closed over the windscreen and side windows of the driving compartment of the XA-200 in high-threat conditions.

verse, a direct-fire capability and a digital fire-control system for the accurate delivery of a variety of bombs including the Saab Bofors Strix 'smart' weapon. Possessing a maximum range of 5000 m (5,470 yards, this top-attack bomb has an imaging IR seeker for terminal guidance against targets such as armoured vehicles.

SPECIFICATION

Patria Vehicles XA-200	(271 hp)
Crew: 3+8	**Performance:** maximum road speed 95 km/h (59 mph); maximum road range 600 km (373 miles); fording amphibious if required but otherwise 1.5 m (4 ft 11 in); vertical obstacle not available; trench not available
Weight: 22000 kg (48,501 lb)	
Dimensions: length 7.45 m (24 ft 5.33 in); width 2.95 m (9 ft 8 in); height 2.6 m (8 ft 6.33 in)l	
Powerplant: one Valmet 612WIBIC liquid-cooled 6-cylinder diesel engine delivering 202 kW	

VBCI Armoured personnel carrier

After it had pulled out of the Multi-Role Armoured Vehicle programme with Germany and the UK, France undertook its own programme to find a successor to the AMX-10P tracked APC of its army's current generations of wheeled and tracked APCs. The programme envisaged a production total of at least 700 and ultimately more than 1,000 vehicles in the form of an initial 550 AIFVs and 150 command post vehicles.

In 2000, after a design competition, the Délégation Générale pour l'Armement issued a contract to Satory Military Vehicles (formed by GIAT Industries and Renault Véhicules Industriels) for the design, development, manufacture and complete logistic support of what had by now been designated as the **VBCI** (Véhicule Blindé de Combat d'Infanterie, or infantry combat armoured vehicle). The programme envisaged the construction and evaluation of four prototypes leading to the delivery of the first production vehicles in 2005 and the completion of sufficient vehicles for the equipment of an initial battalion in 2006.

The overall concept of the VBCI reflects the modern concern for modest initial procurement cost combined with low life-cycle cost, and is one of the reasons that the type was schemed as a wheeled rather than tracked vehicle, and another aspect of the programme is the use wherever possible of commercial and 'off-the-shelf' components.

Unexceptional design

The VBCI is based on a 8x8 configuration with steering on the front four wheels and, as standard, a central tyre pressure-regulation system. In its layout the vehicle is orthodox, with the driver in a compartment at the front left of the vehicle with the powerpack to his right and the commander to his rear, the power-operated turret in the centre, and the eight infantrymen in a compartment at the rear with a rear-set ramp/door arrangement as their primary means of entering and exiting the vehicle. There are vision blocks and firing ports in the sides as well as the rear of the vehicle to allow the embarked infantrymen to use their personal weapons from inside the troop compartment.

The turret selected for the AIFV version of the VBCI is the GIAT Dragar unit, which is a one-man turret armed with a 25-mm cannon and a 7.62-mm (0.3-in) co-axial

The VBCI is being developed as an 8x8 wheeled APC in AIFV and command post forms as a low-cost and durable successor to the obsolescent AMX-10P.

machine-gun with possibly some 620 and 1,400 rounds of ammunition respectively. Variants with the Eryx and MILAN anti-tank missiles are also proposed.

The command post variant will weigh some 23300 kg (51,367 lb), carry a crew of two in addition to the command staff of five, and be provided with a local defence capability by the installation of an off-the-shelf remotely controlled weapon station armed with a 0.5-in (12.7-mm) machine-gun.

SPECIFICATION

Satory Military Vehicles VBCI	cooled 6-cylinder diesel engine delivering 410 kW (550 hp)
Crew: 3+8	**Performance:** maximum road speed 100 km/h (62 mph); maximum road range 750 km (466 miles); fording not available; vertical obstacle not available; trench not available
Weight: 25600 kg (56,437 lb)	
Dimensions: length 7.6 m (24 ft 11.25 in); width 2.98 m (9 ft 9.33 in); height 2.2 m (7 ft 2.5 in) to the top of the hull and 3.06 m (10 ft 0.5 in) to the top of the turret	
Powerplant: one Renault liquid-	

Renault VAB Armoured Personnel Carrier

To meet a French army requirement for a wheeled APC (Armoured Personnel Carrier) for its infantry units, prototypes of the **VAB** (**Véhicle de l'Avant Blindé**, or front-line armoured vehicle) were built by Panhard and Saviem/Renault in both 4x4 and 6x6 configurations. In May 1974 the Renault design was selected, and the first production vehicles were delivered to the French army in 1976. The total French army requirement was for some 4,000 vehicles, and production quickly rose as high as 50 vehicles per month. Large numbers of VABs were used during Desert Storm, and the vehicle has been deployed on peacekeeping missions in Bosnia, Cambodia, Croatia, Lebanon, Rwanda and Somalia.

World sales

The VAB was a major export success, over 1,000 having been sold to the armies of at least 15 countries, including Argentina, Brunei, Central African Republic, Cyprus, France, Indonesia, Ivory Coast, Kuwait, Lebanon, Mauritius, Morocco, Norway, Oman, Qatar and the United Arab Emirates. Of these, Morocco is the largest operator, having purchased over 400 vehicles; a number were lost in the fighting in the Sahara against the Polisario guerrillas.

The VAB has a hull of all-welded steel armour construction, with the driver and commander at the front. The latter also operated the roof-mounted 7.62-mm (0.3-in) machine-gun. The engine compartment is behind them, with the troop compartment at the rear of

The VAB is a conventional wheeled APC, offering greater road mobility than tracked vehicles. It is protected against small arms fire and shell splinters.

the hull; an aisle connects the front of the vehicle with the troop compartment. The infantry enter and leave via two doors in the hull rear, and the troops are seated five down each side facing the centre. The VAB is fully amphibious, being propelled in the water by its wheels or, as an option, by two waterjets at the rear of the hull. Standard equipment on French army vehicles includes an NBC system and passive night-vision gear.

The basic vehicle has also been adapted to a wide range of other roles and, since 1976, more than 30 different versions of the VAB have been produced. These include a forward ambulance, internal security vehicle, command vehicle, repair vehicle, 81-mm (3.2-in) mortar carrier, 120-mm (4.7-in) mortar tractor, NBC reconnaissance vehicle, anti-aircraft vehicle (with twin 20-mm rapid-fire cannon or short range SAMs) and anti-tank vehicle. The latter includes VABs fit-

ted with UTM 800 or Mephisto turrets, equipped with HOT ATGWs (Anti-Tank Guided Weapons). Standard French army VABs are fitted with a cupola-mounted 7.62-mm machine-gun, but a wide range of other armament options is available, including turret-mounted 12.7-mm (0.5-in) machine-guns and stabilised 20- or 25-mm cannon.

Improved VAB

Combat and operational experience over three decades in places as far afield as Chad, Djibouti, Iraq and French Guiana has seen the Armée de Terre carrying out numerous VAB enhancement programmes. More than 1,100 improvements have been implemented in the design of the **VAB New Generation** (VAB NG), developed by Renault and Mecanique Creusot Loire. The development of the new programme has been completed, and VAB NG is now ready for production.

Above: A VAB of the 1st Regiment Etrangere Cavalrie (Foreign Legion Cavalry Regiment) crests a sand dune in Djibouti. This vehicle is equipped with the Mephisto turret, carrying four HOT heavy anti-tank missiles. Eight reloads are carried inside the VAB.

Left: A six-wheeled VAB carrying an experimental winter/urban camouflage scheme. It is possible to convert 4x4 VABs to this configuration, the hulls of the two vehicles being of the same size.

SPECIFICATION	
VAB **Type:** Wheeled armoured personnel carrier **Crew:** 2+10 troops **Combat weight:** 4x4 version 13600 kg (29,980 lb); 6x6 version 14800 kg (32,630 lb) **Powerplant:** Renault MIDR 062045 intercooled Turbo-Diesel delivering 219 kW (300 hp) **Dimensions:** length 5.98 m (19 ft	7½ in); width 2.49 m (8 ft 2 in); height without armament 2.06 m (6 ft 9 in) **Performance:** maximum road speed 110 km/h (68.4 mph); maximum road range 1000 km (621 miles); fording unlimited – vehicle is amphibious; maximum water speed 8.50 km/h (5 mph); gradient 60 per cent; vertical obstacle 0.60 m (2 ft); trench (6x6) 1.50 m (4 ft 11 in)

MOWAG Piranha Armoured Personnel Carrier

The **Piranha** range of 4x4, 6x6 and 8x8 APCs was designed by the Swiss firm of MOWAG (now owned by General Dynamics Land Systems) in the late 1960s, the first prototype being completed in 1972.

The hull of the Piranha is of welded steel, providing protection from small arms fire. All members of the Piranha family are fully amphibious, being propelled in the water by two propellers. Optional equipment includes night vision sights, an NBC system, and an air-conditioning system.

Canada

In 1977 Canada decided to adopt the 6x6 version and production was undertaken by the Diesel Division of General Motors Canada, 491 being built for the Canadian Armed Forces between 1979 and 1982. Canada initially built three versions of the 6x6 Piranha. The Cougar Fire Support Vehicle has a 76-mm (3.0-in) gun, while the Grizzly APC is armed with 12.7-mm (0.5-in) and 7.62-mm (0.3-in) MGs. The Husky is a Wheeled Maintenance and Recovery Vehicle.

After evaluating a number of different vehicles, both tracked and wheeled, the USA selected the 8x8 version of the Piranha to meet its requirement for a **Light Armored Vehicle (LAV)**. The first of these was completed for the US Marine Corps in late 1983.

Piranha armament depends on the role, but can range from a single machine-gun turret up to a power-operated turret armed with a 105-mm low-recoil gun.

The basic **LAV-25** has a two-man power-operated turret armed with a 25-mm cannon and a co-axial 7.62-mm machine-gun. Other Marine variants include logistics support vehicles, command vehicles, repair vehicles, mortar carriers, anti-tank and anti-aircraft platforms and electronic warfare vehicles.

Marine combat

LAVs played an important part in the Gulf War, and were the first American armoured vehicles flown into Afghanistan when the Marines established their forward base near Kandahar.

In 1983 the 6x6 model was evaluated by the Swiss army as an anti-tank vehicle fitted with the TOW anti-tank system, entering service in the late 1980s.

Piranha III

The current **Piranha III** features a new lightweight hull, higher payloads, improved hydropneumatic suspension, and quick-change power-trains. Available in 6x6, 8x8, and 10x10 versions, the Piranha III incorporates lessons learned in peacekeeping operations all over the world, and is well protected against mines.

The US Army withdrew from the original LAV programme early in 1984, but recent operational experience of rapid reaction and peacekeeping missions has shown the value of air mobility and cost-efficiency. The US Army's future combat system (FCS) was launched in 1999 as a result of the experience of the Kosovo conflict when it took several weeks for Task Force Hawk to deploy to Albania. Since the FCS is not due to enter service until after 2010, there is a need to field seven interim brigade combat teams equipped with off-the-shelf wheeled vehicles.

In November 2000, the US Army ordered 2,131 Piranha IIIs, with the first interim brigade to be equipped by the end of 2001. Several different versions are being acquired, including a mobile gun with a 105-mm cannon, infantry carrier, reconnaissance, anti-tank guided missile platform,

The latest Piranha IV has thicker armour, an upgraded MTU powerplant delivering 406 kW (544 hp), hydropneumatic suspension, ABS and a traction control system.

ambulance, mortar carrier, engineer, command post, fire support co-ordination and NBC reconnaissance.

Piranha IV

The latest vehicle in the Piranha family is the 8x8 **Piranha IV**. With increased armour and mine protection, and an upgraded MTU powerplant delivering 406 kW (544 hp), the Piranha IV is fitted with hydropneumatic suspension, ABS and a traction control system. Combat weight is up to 24 tonnes with a 10 tonne payload and the vehicle is air transportable in Lockheed C-130 Hercules aircraft. Also known as the **LAV III**, it is expected to supplement and replace earlier models in Canadian service.

In addition to Canada, the USA and Switzerland, the Piranha range of vehicles is used or has been ordered by Australia, Chile (licence production), Denmark, Ghana, Ireland, Liberia, New Zealand, Nigeria, Oman, Saudi Arabia, Sierra Leone and Sweden. Canada is the main licence manufacturer, but production licences are also held in the UK by Vickers Defence Systems and Alvis Vehicles.

SPECIFICATION	
Piranha III 8x8	Caterpillar 3126
Crew: 2+14	**Dimensions:** length 6.93 m (22 ft 8 in); width 2.66 m (8 ft 9 in); height 1.98 m (6 ft 6 in)
Combat weight: 16500 kg (36,380 lb); payload 6000 kg (13,230 lb)	
Powerplant: will accept numerous diesel engines in the range of 260-331 kW (350-450 hp), including Scania DSJ9-48A, Detroit Diesel 6V53TA, MTU 6V183 TE 22, Cummins 6CTAA 8.3-T350 or	**Performance:** maximum road speed 100 km/h (62 mph); maximum range 800 km (497 miles); fording amphibious; maximum water speed 10 km/h (6.2 mph); gradient 60 per cent; vertical obstacle 0.60 m (1 ft 11 in); trench 2 m (6 ft 7 in)

Since its entry into service in the 1980s, the LAV used by the US Marine Corps has seen action all over the world, most recently in Afghanistan.

Internal security vehicles

The use of APCs on urban streets leads invariably to 'tanks quell riot' headlines in the media, and thus a spate of public unease. Moreover, both tracked and wheeled APCs are very expensive to maintain and are not optimised for internal security (IS) operations. It was this and other reasons that persuaded the British Army to retain obsolete wheeled APCs for use in Northern Ireland, and wheeled APC manufacturers also offer specialised IS variants of battlefield vehicles.

Tracked APCs such as the American M113 are not suited to the IS role for a variety of reasons, including the high cost of procuring, maintaining and operating a tracked vehicle, their size and lack of manoeuvrability in confined spaces, lack of doors for rapid entry and exit, poor observation for the driver and commander, and the political consequences of bringing 'tanks' on to the streets.

The Alvis Saxon 4x4 APC is typical of wheeled vehicles for the IS role. This vehicle has a mast-mounted TV camera and a turret armed with a machine-gun and grenade launchers.

Design planning

Ever since the requirement for specialised IS vehicles emerged, many companies have devoted considerable effort to the design and development of wheeled vehicles for use in IS operations. The hull of such vehicles must provide protection against attack with 7.62-mm (0.3-in) rifle projectiles. In some countries the terrorist's most commonly employed weapon is the mine, often laid in culverts under roads in remoter areas and intended for detonation when a vehicle runs over it. More often than not, such mines are exploded by remote control so that the

terrorist can hit just a military or paramilitary vehicle, leaving civilian traffic to pass in safety.

If the mine is a standard anti-personnel mine or small anti-tank mine, the vehicle designer can help to minimise the amount of damage inflicted on the vehicle by careful design of the hull armour so that the blast is deflected sideways and upward, and thus not contained under the hull of the vehicle, which would lead to the vehicle being lifted and turned over, or alternatively to having its lower surface penetrated by the blast. For example, the British Saxon vehicle has an

integral hull with the areas above the wheels manufactured of sheet steel so that they blow should a mine detonate under the vehicle. The South African Rhino and Bulldog APCs have a V-shaped lower hull raised well above the wheels so that if the vehicle runs over a mine, it is the wheels and suspension that take the blast, and not the hull.

Preference for diesel

The designers and users of IS vehicles prefer diesel engines to petrol engines because diesel fuel is of lower volatility than petrol and therefore does not catch fire as easily. The

position of the fuel tank is also critical in any IS vehicle, whether it is petrol- or diesel-engined.

The commander, driver and troops must have excellent all-round fields of vision through windows that must provide the same degree of protection as the rest of the hull. The commander's and driver's windows must have wipers and a reservoir of special cleaning liquids to ensure that paint thrown by demonstrators is removed speedily and efficiently.

Entry and exit points

The means of entry and exit must be as numerous and large as possible. If the main door is at the rear and the vehicle is ambushed from the rear, for example, the occupants cannot leave the vehicle in safety unless they also have access to side doors. Moreover, the doors and handles must be designed so that unauthorised entry is not possible, and there should be no external fittings that rioters could use to help them climb on to the vehicle.

The tyres must be of the run-flat type to enable the vehicle to be driven some distance after the tyres have been damaged by bullets. The vehicle should also have a fire detection and suppression system, especially around the wheel arches as rioters often throw petrol bombs at IS vehicles' rubber tyres, which catch fire easily.

The roof of the IS vehicle must be sloped so that grenades that land on the roof can roll off before exploding. The openings

around the doors and the engine compartment must be carefully designed so that any flaming liquid from petrol bombs runs down to the ground and not into the vehicle.

As the troops or police may have to stay inside the vehicle for considerable periods, the interior must be insulated and provided with a heating/cooling system. The seats must have belts because if the vehicle does run over a mine many of the casualties could result from occupants being thrown around the vehicle's interior. Adequate stowage space must be provided for riot shields, weapons and other essential equipment.

Some IS vehicles are fitted with turret-mounted 12.7- or 7.62-mm machine-guns, while others have a simple armoured observation cupola for the commander. Specialised equipment such as a barricade remover at the front of the vehicle is standard on some vehicles, while others have provision to be outfitted as specialised command post vehicles or as ambulances. The type can also be used to carry EOD (explosive ordnance disposal) teams and their equipment, such as remote-control devices fitted with TV cameras and other appliances, and it is common for IS vehicles to be fitted with water cannon or launchers for tear gas grenades.

Some countries use standard military wheeled APCs for the IS role while others, perhaps faced with financial problems and/or a more persistent need for IS capa-

Operational utility and ease of manufacture take a considerably higher position in the APC designer's order of priorities than beauty, and in this capacity the Alvis Saxon is an excellent example.

Right: The Cadillac-Gage V-150 Commando series of APCs have been produced in a number of variants; the police and riot-control versions carry much lighter armament than combat vehicles.

Below: To reduce costs, internal security vehicles like the Hotspur Hussar are based on commercial chassis – in this case the Land Rover One-Ten. It has a crew of two and can carry 13 passengers, and can be fitted with a weapons turret.

Below: Developed for the British Army, the Alvis Saxon entered service in the late 1970s, and has been bought by police and military units in six countries, including the United Arab Emirates. This example is fitted with fold-out riot screens.

bility, prefer to operate cheaper vehicles based on standard light truck chassis such as those from Mercedes Benz and Land Rover.

APCs for the IS role
Some wheeled APCs are used in an internal security role. These include the MOWAG Roland, MR 8 and Piranha ranges of 4x4, 6x6 and 8x8 vehicles, AV Technology Dragoon, Cadillac Gage Commando family and Commando Ranger, Humber 'Pig', Alvis Saracen, GKN Sankey AT 105 Saxon, ENGESA EE-11 Urutu, SIBMAS, Vickers Defence Systems/BDX Valkyr, Fiat Tipo 6614, Renault VAB, Berliet VXB-170, Panhard VCR and MS, ACMAT, BMR-600 and BLR-600, Ratel, Transportpanzer, Condor, UR-416, TM 170 and Soviet BTR series.

IS vehicles based on a Mercedes Benz chassis from Germany include the UR-416 delivered from 1969, and also the more recent TM 170 and TM 125. Since 1965 Shorts of Northern Ireland has built very substantial numbers of its Shorland armoured patrol car, and 1974 introduced the Shorland SB 401 APC. Hotspur of Wales has also developed APCs in 4x4 and 6x6 configurations based on the Land Rover chassis.

The Fiat 11A7 A Campagnola 4x4 light vehi-

cle is used by many countries, so the Advanced Security Agency SpA of Milan developed the Guardian range of 4x4 IS and now offers such vehicles not only on the original Fiat chassis, but also on the Land Rover One Ten and Mercedes Benz 280 GE chassis.

In addition to making the Piranha range of 4x4 and 6x6 vehicles under licence, Chile also builds the VTP 2 which is similar in some respects to the German Thyssen IS vehicle, and the Multi 163 APC that is also used to patrol airports and other high-risk areas. The Bravia company of Portugal has built the Chaimite range of 4x4 APCs in variants almost identical to the V-100 family by Cadillac Gage, which has built for the US Army National Guard the Commando Mk III APC that is similar in basic concept to the Shorland vehicles, although somewhat larger.

Warsaw Pact IS
While Western countries have, over the years, developed many types of vehicle suitable for use in IS operations, up to the time of its collapse the Warsaw Pact countries in general and the USSR in particular did not develop vehicles specifically for this role.

Events in Afghanistan, where for the first time during the 1980s the USSR was faced with the type of IS problem it had not previously encountered, revealed that the BTR-60 and BTR-70 series of 8x8 APCs suffered from a number of drawbacks in the IS role. Some of the vehicles were fitted with additional armour protection and more firepower, including an AGS 17 grenade launcher.

Some time ago the former East Germany built two types of vehicles for IS operations in the form of the SK-1 armoured car and the SK-2 armoured water cannon. The SK-1 was armed with a turret-mounted machine-gun. The SK-2 armoured water cannon was built on the chassis of the G5 6x6 truck, and on its roof to the rear of the cab was a high-pressure water cannon.

Given the political situation, it is likely that development will continue.

SPECIFICATION	
Alvis OMC Casspir Mk III	speed 90 km/h (56 mph); maximum road range 850 km (528 miles); maximum cross-country range 564 km (350 miles); fording 1.0 m (3 ft 3.75 in); gradient 65 per cent; vertical obstacle 0.50 m (1 ft 7.5 in); trench 1.06 m (3 ft 5.75 in)
Crew: 2+10	
Weight: 12.58 tonnes	
Dimensions: length 6.87 m (22 ft 6.5 in); width 2.45 m (8 ft 0.5 in); height 3.125 m (10 ft 3 in)	
Powerplant: one ADE-352T liquid-cooled 6-cylinder diesel developing 127 kW (170 hp)	**Armament:** between one and three 7.62-mm (0.3-in) machine-guns
Performance: maximum road	

M728 Combat Engineer Vehicle

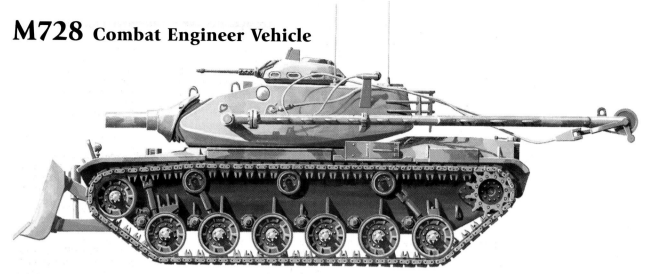

In the 1950s the standard MBT of the US Army was the M48, which was to have been replaced by a new vehicle called the T95. Using the same chassis, a combat engineer vehicle was developed under the designation T118. In the end the whole T95 project was cancelled along with the T118, and further development of the M48 took place. The result was the M60, which entered production in 1960. A decision was then taken to develop a combat engineer vehicle on this chassis under the designation **T118E1**. After trials with prototype vehicles, this type was finally accepted in 1963 for service as the **M728 Combat Engineer Vehicle**. Some 300 M728s were built at the Detroit Tank Plant, which was

then operated for the US Army by General Dynamics Land Systems. In addition to being used by the US Army the M728 was also sold to the armies of Oman, Saudi Arabia and Singapore.

Squash-head round
The M728 is essentially an M60A1 MBT with its 105-mm (4.13-in) M68 gun replaced by a short-barrel 165-mm (6.5-in) demolition gun for destroying battlefield fortifications; 30 rounds of high explosive squash-head (HESH) ammunition are carried for this gun. A 0.3-in (7.62-mm) machine-gun is mounted co-axial with the main armament, and the commander has a cupola-mounted 0.5-in (12.7-mm) machine-gun.

Pivoted at the front of the hull is an A-frame which can lift a maximum load of 15876 kg (35,000 lb). When the vehicle is travelling the A-frame is normally swung through about 120° to lie back on the rear engine decking. The winch to operate with the A-frame is mounted at the rear of the turret and controlled by the vehicle commander. Mounted at the front of the hull is a hydraulically operated dozer blade which can be used for filling-in holes, clearing obstacles and preparing fire positions. Standard equipment on all vehicles includes night-vision equipment (including a searchlight mounted above the main armament), an NBC system and provision for deep-fording apparatus.

Above: The standard combat engineer vehicle of the US Army was the M728, which was the M60A1 tank with its 105-mm gun replaced by a 165-mm demolition gun, an A-frame for lifting at the front of the hull and a hydraulically operated dozer blade for obstacle clearing. It has also been used by Singapore and Saudi Arabia.

Above: The M728 Combat Engineer Vehicle was designed for use by engineers in forward areas to clear and prepare battlefield obstacles. In addition to its 165-mm demolition gun it also had a 0.3-in (7.62-mm) co-axial machine-gun and a cupola-mounted 0.5-in (12.7-mm) machine-gun.

Left: This M728 Combat Engineer Vehicle (CEV) has its A-frame lowered over the rear engine decking for travel. When required for use, the A-frame was swung forward through about 120° and could be used to lift a maximum load of 15876 kg (35,000 lb).

SPECIFICATION	
M728 CEV	(travelling) 3.2 m (10 ft 6 in)
Crew: 4	**Performance:** maximum road
Weight: 53200 kg (117,285 lb)	speed 48.3 km/h (30 mph);
Powerplant: one Continental	maximum range 451 km (280 miles)
AVDS-1790-2A V-12 diesel	**Fording:** 1.22 m (4 ft 10 in)
delivering 559 kW (750 hp)	**Gradient:** 60 per cent
Dimensions: length (travelling)	**Vertical obstacle:** 0.76 m (2 ft
8.92 m (29 ft 3 in); width (overall)	6 in)
3.71 m (12 ft 2 in); height	**Trench:** 2.51 m (8 ft 3 in)

Grizzly Combat Mobility Vehicle

For many years the standard Combat Engineer Vehicle (CEV) of the US Army was the M728 which was based on a much modified M60 series tank. To replace the M728 CEV a new vehicle was developed under the leadership of the now United Defense LP, Ground Systems

Division which eventually merged as the **Combat Mobility Vehicle (CMV)**, or **Grizzly** as it is also known.
This is based on automotive components of the General Dynamics Land Systems M1 series of main battle tanks, and thus has similar cross-country mobility

The Grizzly CMV with its mine-clearing blade in V-configuration and telescopic arm (complete with earth-moving bucket) on the right-hand side of the hull traversed partially toward the vehicle's rear.

SPECIFICATION	
Grizzly CMV **Crew:** 2 **Weight:** 64005 kg (141,100 lb) **Powerplant:** one AGT 1500 gas turbine delivering 1118 kW (1,500 hp) and coupled to an Allison fully automatic transmission with four forward and two reverse gears	**Dimensions:** length 10.62 m (38 ft 10 in); width (hull) 3.66 m (12 ft); height 3.6 m (11 ft 10 in) **Performance:** road speed 66 km/h (41 mph); range 402 km (250 miles) **Fording:** 1.22 m (4 ft) **Gradient:** 60 per cent **Trench:** 2.28 m (7 ft 6 in)

This view of the Grizzly CMV reveals the mine-clearing blade being used in its V-configuration, and the vehicle's telescopic arm in its stowed position aligned rearward along the right-hand side of the hull.

and a very high level of armour protection as it is required to operate in the forward battle area. It is also fitted with smoke grenade launchers and a remotely controlled 0.5-in (12.7-mm) machine-gun.

The vehicle is operated by a crew of two (commander and driver), either of whom can control all functions of the vehicle. The Grizzly is based on a new all-welded steel armour hull, and mounted at the front of the hull on the right-hand side is a telescopic arm which is tra-versed to the rear when not required. This is fitted with a bucket and used to dig holes and trenches. The bucket can be removed, allowing the arm to be fitted with other attachments.

Mounted at the front of the vehicle is a full-width mine-clearing blade with extendible side elements. This advanced blade can clear a path 4.2 m (13 ft 9 in) wide and 305 mm (12 in) deep, and is fitted with replaceable tines.

Two prototypes of the Grizzly Combat Mobility Vehicle were built and tested, but in the end the whole programme was can-celled in order to release funding for the the US Army's Future Combat System (FCS).

The M728 CEV was sub-sequently retired without the adoption of a wholly compat-ible replacement, and as a result the US Army today lacks a dedicated combat engineer vehicle type for its heavy forces.

M9 Armored Combat Earthmover

The **M9 Armored Combat Earthmover** (**ACE**) is used by the US Army engineers in the forward combat area for a variety of missions, such as preparing fire positions and river crossings, filling in trenches and clearing roads and battlefield obstacles.

The vehicle began life as the **Universal Engineer Tractor** (**UET**) in the late 1950s, but development was slow as at that time the US Army had higher priorities. Prototypes were built by a number of contractors, and final development was undertaken by Pacific Car and Foundry. The UET was later redesignated as the **M9 Tractor, Full Tracked, High Speed, Armored Dozer-Scraper Combination** before finally becoming the ACE.

Into production

As usual in the US, produc-tion was put out to competitive tender and the BMY Corporation (now part of United Defense) was awarded the M9 ACE pro-duction contract in 1986, with the first production vehicles delivered several years later. The M9 is air-transportable in many of the US Air Force's logistic trans-port aircraft, and can also be carried by heavy-lift heli-copters.

Almost 600 M9s were built for the US Army and US Marine Corps, and addi-tional vehicles were manufactured for a number of export customers.

Foreign service

The South Korean army has more than 200 examples of the M9 in service, and these were produced under a co-production programme between Samsung and United Defense. The M9 saw extensive use with the American armed forces in Middle Eastern operations during the 1991 and 2003 Gulf War campaigns against Iraq.

The M9 is of all-welded aluminium armour that pro-vides the driver/operator (seated under a cupola with eight vision blocks for all-round fields of vision) with protection against small arms fire and shell splinters, and is fitted as standard with an NBC protection system.

When operating the vehicle with the cupola hatch open, the driver/operator is pro-vided with a rectangular windscreen characterised by round-off corners.

The M9 is unarmed but normally fitted with smoke grenade launchers. With preparation the M9 is fully amphibious, being propelled in the water by its tracks at 4.8 km/h (3 mph), but this capability is no longer sup-ported in US Army vehicles. The standard equipment includes a power-operated winch, bilge pump and periscopes for the driver and operator.

The front part of the vehi-cle is occupied by the scraper bowl, which has a capacity of more than 6 m³ (212 cu ft), and the driver is seated to the rear on the left side with the powerpack to his right. The dozer blade is mounted at the front, and scraping and dozing are per-formed by using the hydro-pneumatic suspension to raise or lower the vehicle.

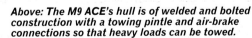

Above: The M9 ACE's hull is of welded and bolted construction with a towing pintle and air-brake connections so that heavy loads can be towed.

Left: Two M9 ACE vehicles in the Middle East show off the raised position of the hydro-pneumatic suspension, this being used for normal travel and the lowered position for scraping or dozing.

SPECIFICATION	
M9 ACE **Crew:** 1 **Weight:** 16400 kg (36,155 lb) **Powerplant:** one Cummins water-cooled 8-cylinder diesel delivering 220 kW (295 hp) and coupled to a Clark transmission with six forward and two reverse gears	**Dimensions:** length 6.248 m (20 ft 6 in); width 3.2 m (10 ft 6 in); height 3 m (9 ft 10 in) **Performance:** maximum road speed 48 km/h (30 mph); maximum range 322 km (200 miles) **Fording:** 1.83 m (6 ft) **Gradient:** 60 per cent

BARV Beach Armoured Recovery Vehicle

In the UK the Royal Marines have always placed great emphasis on their ability to undertake amphibious operations, in which men and equipment are transported from ships lying offshore onto the beach by various types of landing craft. The landing craft are run onto the beach and their bow ramps are lowered to allow the men and vehicles to disembark rapidly onto the beach.

Beached craft

Very often the landing craft can become stuck on the beach, especially in rough water. A specialised vehicle called the **Beach Armoured Recovery Vehicle** (BARV) is then used to push the landing craft into deeper water. For many years the Royal Marines' standard BARV has been based on a much modified Centurion tank chassis. This was developed in the late 1950s and entered service in the early 1960s.

The BARV has two main roles, first to push landing craft into deeper water and second to recover onto land any vehicles that have been stuck or disabled while trying to come ashore.

The **Centurion BARV** can ford to a depth of 2.97 m (9 ft 9 in), is fitted with a large push bar on the front of its hull, and is also equipped with tow cables that can be attached to the disabled vehicle by a diver.

Toward the future

The Centurion BARV is the last member of the Centurion tank to serve with the UK armed forces, and in 2000 the Norwegian company Alvis Moelv was awarded a contract to design and build a **Future Beach Recovery Vehicle (FBRV)** based on the much modified chassis of the Leopard 1 tank.

The modifications have been extensive, and include the complete removal of the turret and the installation of a new superstructure to enable the vehicle to ford to a depth of 2.9 m (9 ft 6 in). The suspension and hull have also been optimised for use in a salt water environment.

A total of four FBRVs was ordered, the first vehicle being delivered for trials purposes in 2001 and the remaining three following by 2003, after which the elderly Centurion BARV will finally be phased out of service.

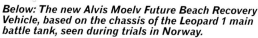

Above: A Centurion Beach Armoured Recovery Vehicle (BARV) comes ashore during amphibious operations.

Below: A Centurion Beach Armoured Recovery Vehicle of the Royal Marines prepares to assist a beached landing craft pushed broadside to the waves.

Below: The new Alvis Moelv Future Beach Recovery Vehicle, based on the chassis of the Leopard 1 main battle tank, seen during trials in Norway.

SPECIFICATION	
Centurion BARV	
Crew: 4	**Powerplant:** one Rolls-Royce Meteor water-cooled V-12 petrol engine delivering 484.5 kW (650 hp)
Weight: 40597 kg (89,500 lb)	
Dimensions: length 8.076 m (26 ft 6 in); width 3.402 m (11 ft 2 in); height 3.453 m (11 ft 4 in)	**Performance:** maximum speed 34 km/h (21 mph)

Husky Wheeled Maintenance and Recovery Vehicle

In the late 1970s, following an international competition, the Canadian Armed Forces selected a version of the Swiss MOWAG Piranha series of 6x6 light armoured vehicles to meet their future operational requirements.

In the end a total of 491 vehicles were manufactured in Canada by the now General Dynamics Land Systems – Canada (at the

The hydraulically operated crane installed on the Husky Wheeled Maintenance and Recovery Vehicle is used to lift complete powerpacks. The vehicle also carries a kit of specialised equipment.

The Husky Wheeled Maintenance and Recovery Vehicle is armed with a 7.62-mm (0.3-in) machine-gun. The crane has a capacity of 4536 kg (10,000 lb).

SPECIFICATION	
Husky WMRV	**Powerplant:** one Detroit Diesel
Crew: 4	diesel delivering 160 kW (215 hp)
Weight: 10500 kg (23,148 lb)	**Performance:** max road speed
Dimensions: length 5.97 m (19 ft	100 km/h (62 mph); max road range
10 in); width 2.5 m (8 ft 2½ in);	600 km (373 miles)
height 1.85 m (6 ft 1 in) excluding	
crane	

time called the Diesel Division, General Motors Canada). Three versions were supplied, all of them sharing the same basic hull and drive train. These were the 76-mm (3-in) Cougar Wheeled Fire Support Vehicle (WFSV), Grizzly Wheeled Armoured Personnel Carrier (WAPC) and the **Husky Wheeled Maintenance and Recovery Vehicle** (**WMRV**).

Some 27 examples of the WMRV were built to support the other members of the family, and the type is oper-ated by a crew of four. The hull is similar to that of the Cougar and Grizzly except that the roof line of the rear section is raised to provide additional volume for the car-riage of the specialised equipment required for the Husky's task.

Mounted in the centre of the hull roof on a turntable is a HIAB Model 650 hydraulic crane with a telescopic jib, and this is capable of lifting a complete powerpack. When the crane is used, a hydrauli-cally operated stabiliser is normally lowered to the ground on either side of the vehicle between the first and second road wheel stations.

The Husky is fully amphibi-ous, and is propelled in the water by two propellers mounted one at each side of the rear. Before entering the water a trim vane is erected at the front of the vehicle, and the electric bilge pumps are activated.

The vehicle is armed with a 7.62-mm (0.3-in) machine-gun and carries two banks of electrically operated smoke grenade launchers. Standard equipment includes powered steering and automatic trans-mission.

With the introduction into service of Piranha 8x8 vehi-cles, some of the 6x6 vehicles are being retasked, the remaining 23 WMRVs being re-designated as the Mobile Repair Team. The vehicles' amphibious capabil-ity is being removed, and some versions, including the 76-mm Cougar, are being wholly phased out of Canadian service.

LAV-E Light Armored Vehicle – Engineer

Following extensive trials of a number of tracked and wheeled armoured vehicles, the US Army selected a ver-sion of what is now General Dynamics Land Systems – Canada Light Armoured Vehicle III (LAV-III) for its new Interim Brigade Combat Teams (IBGT).

A total of six of these IBCTs are being formed to give the US Army an interim rapid deployment capability before the introduction of the Future Combat System.

For the US Army applica-tion the LAV-III has been modified in a number of areas and is called the Stryker. The first version to enter service was the Infantry Carrier Vehicle (ICV) in the spring of 2002, other versions then following. These others are the engi-neer squad, medical evacu-ation, anti-tank guided mis-sile, fire-support, mortar carrier, commander's, NBC reconnaissance, reconnais-sance, and 105-mm (4.13-in) mobile gun system vehicles.

All of these have the same powerpack and sus-pension, and most also have the same all-welded steel hull that provides the occu-pants with protection from small arms fire and shell splinters.

The engineer squad vehi-cle, otherwise the **LAV-E**, provides the squad with a highly mobile protected transport to decisive loca-tions on the battlefield to provide the required mobility and limited counter-mobility support to the IBCT. Current obstacle neutralisation, lane

The Engineer Squad Vehicle, or LAV-E, is based on the Infantry Carrier Vehicle (ICV) version of the Stryker, and can be fitted with a variety of specialised attachments, suiting the vehicle to specific tasks.

marking and mine detection systems are integrated into the LAV-E. The relevant obstacle neutralisation equipment is provided by Pearson Engineering of the UK, and includes a surface mine plough and a roller sys-tem. Either of these can be rapidly attached to the vehi-cle depending on the threat.

Weapon station
Mounted on the roof of the vehicle is a remotely con-trolled weapon station that can be armed with a 0.5-in (12.7-mm) M2 machine-gun or a Mk 19 automatic grenade launcher. Standard equipment on all members of the Stryker family includes powered steering, hydro-pneumatic suspen-sion, a power-operated braking system and a central tyre pressure-regulation sys-tem that allows the driver to adjust the vehicle's tyre pressure to suit the terrain being crossed.

The vehicle is also fitted with an NBC system and a complete climate-control system. The Stryker is not amphibious, however, as the US Army had no require-ment for this.

SPECIFICATION	
LAV	**Powerplant:** one Detroit Diesel
Crew: 2 + 8	6V-53T diesel delivering 205 kW
Weight: 17400 kg (38,360 lb)	(275 hp)
Dimensions: length 6.98 m (22 ft	**Performance:** maximum road
11 in); width 2.717 m (8 ft 11 in);	speed 97 km/h (60 mph); maximum
height 2.64 m (8 ft 8 in)	road range 540 km (335 miles)

Index